ITRAVELBOOKS
EUROPE

Elissa Altman,
Contributing Editor

ibooks
new york
www.ibooks.net

A Publication of ibooks, inc.

© 2002 Tembo LLC

Original Material © 2002 Tembo LLC
New Material © 2002 ibooks, inc.

ibooks, inc.
24 West 25th Street
New York, NY 10010

The ibooks World Wide Web Site Address is:
http://www.ibooks.net

ISBN 0-7434-4519-8
First ibooks, inc. printing December 2002
10 9 8 7 6 5 4 3 2 1

Cover photo copyright © 2001 Philippe Colombi
Cover design by Mike Rivilis

Welcome to ITRAVELBOOKS

Congratulations! By choosing an *ITRAVELBOOK*, you have just selected the savviest, most reliable, up-to-date guidebook available today. In a world filled with travel guides of every shape and kind, why pick us?

The answer is simple: *ITRAVELBOOKS* does what no other guidebook does. It is dedicated to providing you with the most affordable, authoritative, up-to-the-minute information available. If you're planning a trip, why spend your vacation dollars on expensive guides that you'll only use once before the information becomes obsolete?

ITRAVELBOOKS gathers all the critical knowledge you'll need for an enjoyable, fun vacation at every price level, and packs it into an inexpensive, user-friendly paperback format that you can take anywhere. Need a quick tip on what to eat in a Parisian cafe? Check our *ITRAVELBOOK TIPS* for fast, at-your-fingertips information. Want to know the fabulous things you can do for free in Paris, Madrid or Dublin? Go straight to *ITRAVELBOOK FREEBIES.* Or, simply download the entire guidebook for free – or any parts of it you wish – from our website, and take it with you on your laptop or your PDA. Our electronic version will contain the most current, up-to-the-minute travel advice and information, including real-time rate changes; great new restaurants for you to try at every price range; exciting new sights to see; location-finder maps; and much more.

The first truly interactive print/electronic guidebook, *ITRAVELBOOKS* values the traveler's opinion over all others and puts you in the travel writer's seat; we want to hear about your experiences — what you liked, what you didn't like, new discoveries and finds you might have stumbled upon on your adventure, and we'll use your information in our next edition. Please join us at **http://travel.ibooks.net** to become a part of the *ITRAVELBOOKS* team.

HOW TO USE YOUR ITRAVELBOOK

Our goal at *ITRAVELBOOKS* is to provide you with the most user-friendly companion for your trip available. Underline us; circle us; highlight us; write on us; download us; upload us. Load us into your PDA or your laptop. We're meant to be used.

Your *ITRAVELBOOK* is designed to put information at your fingertips: each country chapter opens up with basic information on everything from the currency used to customs regulations and more. The main section of each chapter is devoted to the locales themselves.

Here, you'll find some brief historical information, followed by important details about hotels, restaurants, museums, hikes, activities for every age group, and our recommended attractions and sights. In addition, you will find *ITRAVELBOOK TIPS* sprinkled throughout the book: these are quick and easy suggestions on everything from what to wear, to what kind of bicycle to rent, and will help make your travel to paradise all the more wonderful.

A Special Note on European Currency

All but three members of the European Union have switched currencies, and now use the Euro exclusively. While a few nations continue to grumble about losing the right to use their own national currency (Italians reportedly were less than pleased to lose the Lire), the Euro actually makes things much easier for the traveler. Instead of having to run to the "Cambio" to change your dollars into Deutschmarks, Lire, or Francs every time you arrive in a new country, you can just continue to use the Euro. And to make matters even easier, the Euro and the American dollar are nearly identical in value (although not exactly even).

As of this writing, the following countries use the Euro:

Austria, Belgium, Germany, Greece, Spain, France, Ireland, Italy, Luxembourg, The Netherlands, Portugal, Finland.

Currently, the following countries have not yet adopted the Euro:

Denmark, Britain, Sweden.

Rating the Accommodations and Restaurants in this Guide

ITRAVELBOOKS include accommodations, activities, and dining experiences of every type, and in all price ranges and levels of quality, which are subjective and therefore may not always be equal.

Airport Information

Mainland travelers flying to European airports from the United States should familiarize themselves with the following before embarking on their trip:

- Check with your airline on how early you should arrive. Usually it is 3 hours ahead of the departure time.

- When you arrive at the airport, go directly to the agriculture inspection station. All luggage must be checked and tagged before you go to the airline check in.

- Some airlines have worked out an agreement with the FAA for curbside check in. Ask your airline if they provide this service. If so, the porter will take your bag through agriculture inspection and you can proceed to the ticket counter or gate to check in. Some airlines will only permit persons with electronic tickets to use curbside check in. Ask in advance about this service.

- You will be asked for a passport when you check in your bags, get your boarding pass, go through security, and before you can board your plane. Keep your passport handy.

- Check in as much of your luggage as possible. It will reduce the time you spend having your carry ons searched at security check points, and will speed up boarding of the plane.

- Check with your airline about how many carry-on items you are allowed. Most airlines limit carry ons to a personal item (purse, briefcase) and one other item, such as a backpack, computer, bag, etc.

- Say your goodbyes at home. Only ticketed passengers are permitted beyond the security check point. If you need assistance, let your airline know and they will arrange for whatever help you need.

- Unaccompanied minors may be escorted to a gate. Make arrangements with your airline.

- Check your pockets, key chains and carry ons for any sharp objects, including knives, letter openers, scissors, nail clippers, knitting needles, etc. These items are not permitted aboard the plane, but may be placed in check in luggage. These items will be confiscated at security checkpoints.

EUROPE

TABLE OF CONTENTS

INTRODUCTION

Europe in the Millenium

It's the Old World in modern dress, a drama which never ceases to fascinate the fresh-faced first-time visitor or veteran travelers who return to Europe with joyous regularity. For many, in fact, it is becoming a second home. As the globe shrinks more and more, North Americans are finding it just as easy to have a cottage in the Cotswolds as it is to trek each summer to Martha's Vineyard. Even in expensive Sweden, it is cheaper to rent a magnificent retreat in the Stockholm Archipelago—surrounded by gleaming seas, gull-white sailing ships, and 24,000 islands, skerries and rock dots—than it is to take a prolonged car trip to the travel attractions of our nation. Tuscan villas can be rented for as little as a thousand dollars a week (I know, I did it). New World adventurers are finding that it is more fun to learn French in a Provençal village than in a classroom back home. And then there are the nations which were once out-of-bounds: Budapest is one of the most alluring targets on the tourist map. Prague is a wonderland of architecture; it still bears the time-honored title as the *Golden City* of Europe. St. Petersburg used to take weeks to get into because of lengthy visa applications, but now you can hop on a morning flight from Helsinki's *White City*, visit the Winter Palace of the Hermitage, the resplendent redoubts of the czars, and be back in the Finnish capital for dinner.

As if you didn't already know, Europe has been enjoying a festival of red-tape cutting. From the Arctic to the Aegean, it is beginning to behave almost as one nation and you will scarcely sense that there are borders between France, Germany, Spain, Portugal, and the Benelux nations. Someone might look at your passport as you enter the UK, possibly down in Greece, maybe in Ireland or Northern Ireland where security checks are not unknown, but generally almost no formalities exist nowadays. On a recent car trip from Paris to Barcelona, the frontier crossing which used to be chaotic with non-stop bureaucracy, visa stamping, passport checking, customs inspections and endless delays was almost like a ghost town. There was not even an official in sight, either at the French kiosks or at the Spanish station. Still, with all this buoyant fashion for togetherness, each country in Europe remains staunchly unique. If anything, the efforts by ministries in Brussels toward official homogenization have created stronger motivations for preserving local color and distinctive regional personality.

Trends

- Inner city pollution is being attacked in a major assault by the European Commission. It's called the *Eurocity Scheme*. Already travelers report improved air in central *Athens* (severe car traffic ban), *Amsterdam* and *Brussels*.

- **Boutique hotels** are the rage in Paris. Usually they contain about 15 rooms, often no restaurants and they are overloaded with decorative zeal. They are usually expensive. The *Montalembert* and the *Pavillon de la Reine* elicit praise from Parisian visitors.

- Train trips have mushroomed since the spectacular success of the fabled Orient Express. Add to your choo-choo list the awesome alpine *Jungfraujoch* which begins in the picturebook Swiss city of Interlaken and ends in Heaven, the *Ventimiglia* links between Italy (Turin) and the French Riviera, or the almost unknown *Transcantabrico* across the northern Iberian brim.

- The **Champs-Elysées** looks better than in many-a-year after its face-lifting. Service lanes are gone and walkways are wider; more plain trees have been planted; underground parking has expanded; more traditional street lamps have been illuminated.

Transportation Trends

The main topic, of course, remains the Channel Tunnel (**http://www.raileurope.com/us/rail/eurostar/channel_tun-nel.htm**). Since its opening in 1994, it has had a slight image problem and a few financial glitches, but overall it is a wonder of engineering and a marvel of convenience.

The 31-mile submarine tunnel link has, of course, roiled the seas above for surface carriers. Upon opening, a price war immediately ensued with ferry operators; now it is imperative that you do some comparative shopping if cost alone is a major consideration. There are two techniques for crossing. One is by passenger train (no autos) which operate between Waterloo Station in central London and Paris or Burssels. These circuits are aboard the 200-m.p.h. *Eurostar*, a sleek speedster where you can have a meal brought to you at your seat. Business travelers also can use these facilities as work stations. Travel time is a little over three hours. The second option is with the drive-on-off *Le Shuttle* which only operates between Folkestone (UK) and Calais (France); Chunnel time equals 35 minutes. Incidentally, major car rental agencies on either side will swap left-or-right-hand-drive vehicles for no extra charge to make your motoring safer. You can find out the latest tunnel prices—and they do fluctuate—by phoning ☎ *800-94-CHUNNEL* or obtain general information from ☎ *800-4-EURAIL*. When the Chunnel first opened a roundtrip fare with any number of passengers was 160-pounds, rising in stages to 260-pounds in high season. For normal ferry changes, also request the latest postings from your travel agent. If you think you are going to be in a hurry, be sure to inquire about the zippy *CitySprint Hovercraft* or *Hoverspeed's* ultra-swift *Seacat* (between Boulogne and Folkestone) and motorway service which swiftly transports you from London to Paris, Brussels and Amsterdam. Tariffs are very reasonable compared to the earlier Chunnel chomps—they may come down radically—but by taking the tunnel you will be adding a new feature to your travel inventory. In the actual matter of saving time, coast-to-coast by sea, ferries such as P & O and Sealink do the job very nicely (meal service included if you wish) in about 100 minutes.

ITRAVELBOOK TIP: DESPITE PRICE FLUCTUATIONS, A ONE-WAY RIDE THROUGH THE CHUNNEL CAN COST AS LITTLE AS $60 US. CHECK THE WEBSITE ABOVE FOR MORE INFORMATION.

Pennywise and Other Currencies

Saving Euros can be an important factor in your travel budget when it comes to something as basic as transportation. When you arrive at most international gateways you are stuck far out at a strange airport, so you often fall for the easiest solution for getting into town—the taxi. Sadly, that is one of the best ways to become a first-class spendthrift. Moreover, riding in this style will not necessarily guarantee that you will arrive in mid-city any faster than by other more economical methods. Paris, Munich, Frankfurt, Zurich, Geneva, Barcelona and many other hubs now help the tourist with rail connections to and from the air terminals. As a guideline, here are some of the more noteworthy airport rail services sprinkled around Europe, with the distances and times from the cities.

Airport	Distance to Town	Frequency
Amsterdam	15 km	every 7 mins
Berlin Schonefled	18 km	every 20 mins
Berlin Tempelhof	5 km	regular subway
Brussels	12 km	every 20 mins
Düsseldorf	8 km	every 20 mins
Florence-Pisa	84 km	hourly
Frankfurt	10 km every	10 mins
Geneva	4 km every	10 mins
Munich	37 km	every 20 mins
Paris CDG	26 km	every 15 mins
Paris Orly	16 km	every 15 mins
Rome	32 km	every 30 mins
Stuttgart	20 km	every 15 mins
Zurich	12 km	every 12 mins

In all of the above stations there has always been a baggage cart or some other mechanical means to lug luggage to the rails or an easy way to obtain a porter when needed. The savings can be dramatic, too—both in time and money.

What's Fare in the Air

The events of September 11th, 2001 resulted in, among many other things, a severe drop in travel abroad; the impending price wars promised those willing to fly sharp reductions in already-reduced fares. While prices have nearly returned to normal, it is still absolutely possible to find astoundingly good fares... if you do your homework. Check the internet, newspapers, and travel agencies for the most up-to-date, discounted fares available.

Internationally, low-season cut-rate passage between London and New York can sometimes be picked up for as little as $165 one way or $250 between Great Britain and Los Angeles. Certainly, travel agencies still exist, but if you do the homework yourself and make your own bookings, your savings will be significant.

> ITRAVELBOOK TIP: DO YOUR HOMEWORK BEFORE YOU HAND OVER YOUR CREDIT CARD. CHECK COMPETING RATES ON http://www.expedia.com, http://www.travel.com, http://www.orbitz.com, http://www.cheaptickets.com.

Charters

Here, too, the skies are rumbling with innovations. In fact, today it is becoming more and more difficult to distinguish between a charter and a standard fare. Airlines—regular scheduled ones too—may now sell individual charter tickets directly to the public rather than through middlemen; hence, a whole new marketing approach has been developed.

Discounts are appearing for every imaginable category: preferential dates of departure, children, families, one-way travel, where you sit in the airplane, the color of your eyes, or the flatness of your feet. There are still charters that incorporate your hotel, a car rental or other goodies. These, of course, will vary with the quality and character of the holiday you desire.

Jet-Lag Miseries

Contrary to popular belief, some people are just more susceptible to jet-lag than others. And since a bad case of jet-lag can leave you dragging for weeks, do everything you can to avoid it. Here are some sage bits of advice:

The Day Before: Drink at least 3 liters of bottled water. Be calm. Get all details out of the way. No matter what time you fly tomorrow, try to avoid crises, conflicts, or agitation on flight day or the day before. Eat a full balanced dinner high in carbohydrates, like pasta. Go VERY light on wine, liquor, and caffeine. Go to bed at the normal time and plan to get up as you normally would.

Flight Day: Again, drink as much water as you can possibly consume, before, during and after the flight, and avoid all caffinated beverages, liquor, and wine. As soon as the plane is airborne, re-set your watch to your destination's time zone, and try to think in that time zone. Sleep if you can, watch the movie (if there is one), get up and stretch your legs periodically to avoid cramping.

Arrival Day: As soon as the cabin lights come on, go to the restroom; wash up as much as you can. Change your shirt, your socks, your underwear. When you return to your seat, continue to drink as much water as you possibly can.

ITRAVELBOOK TIP: IF IT ALL POSSIBLE, AVOID -- AT ALL COSTS -- OVER THE COUNTER SLEEP MEDICATION. YOU WILL ARRIVE AT YOUR DESTINATION WEARY, CRANKY, SLIGHTLY STONED, AND JET-LAG WILL INVARIABLY SET IN.

Baggage

IATA, the governing body of civil aviation, allows passengers on flights of U.S. origin two free bags plus a carry-on, but the length, width, and height of each bag must total no more than 62 inches and the heaviest should not weigh more than 70 lbs. From some airports you may carry aboard as many pieces of hand luggage as you like as long as their combined lengths, widths, and heights do not exceed 45 inches. (Tighter security restrictions today, however, often limit this allowance to only one onboard item per person.) For additional items, you are charged by the piece, according to a scale of flat amounts determined by the distance you are flying. Some bulky sports equipment (skis, golf clubs, etc.) is also hauled free when the gear is considered the largest piece.

ITRAVELBOOK TIP: SINCE SEPTEMBER 11TH, 2001, BOTH CHECKED AND CARRY-ON BAGGAGE HAS BEEN SHARPLY MONITORED, AND EACH CARRIER MAY CHANGE THEIR BAGGAGE ALLOWANCES WITHOUT NOTICE...LEAVING YOU AT CHECK-IN WITH ONE-TOO-MANY BAGS. TO MAKE ABSOLUTELY SURE THAT YOU HAVE UP-TO-THE-MINUTE INFORMATION, CONTACT YOUR CARRIER DIRECTLY THE NIGHT BEFORE YOU FLY.

Lost Baggage

About one percent of the world's personal cargo (15 million pieces) will be misplaced this year. Approximately 90 percent of that luggage is recovered by the owner within 24 hours of loss. While airlines permit seven days for notification, you should report your misfortune while you are still at the airport. If you are with a tour, then collar your group leader as soon as you are aware that your bundle has not followed you to your hotel. Some airlines, when they know they cannot retrieve the pieces quickly, provide emergency overnight kits to defrocked travelers; others hand out modest sums of money for basic necessities.

A "property irregularity" form must be filled in describing all the particulars of your loss. If you put some identification inside your suitcase, it will help tremendously should the outside tag have been ripped off. You are required nowadays to have your own personal luggage card on every piece. (All airlines, incidentally, have keys to every sort of luggage.) If it finds your baggage, the carrier will deliver it to you promptly.

After a week has passed and your caboodle still hasn't been located, you should then begin the process of extracting a settlement. Experience reveals that you won't get anything near the value of your carryall or wardrobe (not to mention valuables such as cameras or jewelry—which should have been among hand luggage anyway). The best protection, in other words, is your own insurance policy.

Bumping or Bouncing

Artistically labeled "involuntary boarding denial" by the airlines, this is yet another name of a widespread game played by airlines which use you as the ball. It goes like this: the 747 that's supposed to wing you to, say, Paris has 352 seats. Because Carrier X knows from experience that a number of people with reservations will be "no-shows," it covers itself when its loads reach capacity by overselling perhaps 20 extra passages. (Usually airline officials figure that 15 percent of the registrants on the computer won't arrive at the airport.) Sure enough, 19 inconsiderate individuals fail to appear—but what if you are customer number 353? "Sorry," says the clerk, "no more room." You have been bumped. What to do?

Know your "fly rights" and use them.

Provided you hold a confirmed reservation plus a properly validated ticket on a regularly scheduled flight and have shown up on time, the airline must deliver you to your overseas destination by other means within four hours of your planned arrival time. If unable to do so, it is required to give you at least partial compensation, depending upon the distance, of not less than $37.50 (or the one-way fare) or more than $200, plus free passage on the next available flight. If they don't get you to your destination within two hours of the scheduled time, their apology must be doubled, to a maximum of $400 plus overnight expenses. This is in addition to the price of your original ticket, which you can turn in for a 100 percent refund. Moreover, you must be paid this "denied boarding compensation" (DBC) within 24 hours; if you aren't, you have 90 days in which to file a claim. So if you get the bounce, insist that you be given the printed regulation on the subject as well as the necessary forms you must fill out to collect this penalty. This applies, of course, only within the U.S., before or after international flights. European carriers within the community are following the U.S. example and a lost ride might cost the carrier from $100 to $700 (if the departure is from an EC terminus). Community law provides $180 DBC for short flights and $352 for hauls over 3500 kms. This can be halved if your delay is no more than two or four hours respectively. SAS employs a voucher system with a spread of $100 to $300 depending upon the delay or inconvenience. European airlines on their own home territory vary dramatically on how they handle such delicate matters. SAS, BA and KLM are as thoughtful as U.S. airlines in crisis situations. You might have to demand your DBC from Iberia or Alitalia, and outside of Europe you might not receive any compensation whatsoever. If you display defiance plus a knowledge of the intimidations at your disposal, it's probable that any wise airline official will break into a righteous sweat and come to your aid.

In-Flight Gadgets

Some you can use and others you shouldn't. The entire subject is still a little mysterious. Don't turn any of them on until the "Fasten Seat-Belt" sign is switched off. Today many carriers have their own cabin telephone systems which can operate on a charge or credit card. If you need to phone down to the planet beneath you, use this facility and never a mobile phone. Beepers and person locators as well as walkie-talkies may upset the aircraft's communications or navigation systems. Technicians also frown on transistors and radio-operated toys. Under favorable conditions you may utilize lap-top PCs (not printers), CD players, tape recorders, or video walkman or camera video units. If you have any doubts just ask the airline personnel.

Passports

For a couple of years now U.S. citizens have been issued green passports instead of blue. Also they incorporate a sneak-proof optical device similar to a hologram, special inks, and they are valid for 10 years for persons 18 years or older and cost $65; for those under 18, it's $40 and valid for five years. In addition, there's a $7 fee for applicants who are required to apply in person. However, in a few special conditions that sum is waived. If you meet the requirements, you are eligible to apply by mail and should obtain Form DSP-82, "Application for Passport by Mail," which may be sent to one of the passport agencies mentioned below.

Have two identical photos (2" x 2" and snapped within the last six months) ready to adorn the document. These must have a plain white or off-white background. For your first passport, you must present in person a completed Form DSP-11, "Passport Application," at one of the agencies located in Boston, Chicago, Honolulu, Houston, Los Angeles, Miami, New Orleans, New York, Philadelphia, San Francisco, Seattle, Stamford, and Washington, D.C., or at one of the several thousand federal or state courts or U.S. post offices that accept passport applications. Be sure you have proof you are a U.S. citizen (birth or naturalization certificate) as well as proof of identity (driver's license). Forms are available from any of those offices.

For those abroad, petitions for new passports may be made by mail in numerous countries; otherwise, you'll have to appear in person at the nearest American Embassy or Consulate. Your old, dog-eared, canceled friend will be returned as a souvenir when the new one is issued.

As a precaution against loss or theft, have two photocopies made of your passport identification page. Leave one at home and carry the other with you, but separate from your passport.

Medical Advice

Immunization isn't required for European travelers. Europe has good public health officials, fine doctors and the latest drugs; many of the last appear on pharmacy shelves years before they are put up for sale in North America—even when they may be produced by U.S. manufacturers. (Europeans often test the new products quicker than the FDA.)

Though shots are not required in Europe, information on foreign immunization laws for countries farther afield can be obtained from the U.S. Public Health Service. Check your phone book under U.S. Government, Department of Health, Education and Welfare. Also helpful is an organization called **International Association for Medical Assistance to Travellers.** IAMAT *(736 Center St., Lewiston, NY 14092,* **http://www.iamat.org/***)* can provide the names of English-speaking doctors in many foreign nations. If you are moving on to hotter lands than Europe, be sure to read IAMAT's information on malaria prevention, still a major health problem in some areas.

Here are some tips on staying in shape. Naturally, everyone is cautious about the drinking water in questionable places; this should include the water for brushing your teeth and ice cubes. Raw vegetables and fruits also require attention if your stay is to be a short one. If you are making a longer visit, it might be better, according to some medical opinion, to go ahead and live as the locals do unless the area suffers from extreme pollution. If the area is warm, avoid mayonnaise, which might have been left in the sun. Factory-bottled dressings (made with preservatives) are usually safer than fresh ones, which may invite bacteria if they are not properly protected. More people are staying away from slightly cooked meat, poultry, fish and eggs (also dressings made of raw egg). Beer is drinkable almost everywhere, but wines are more suspect.

Turista

"Turista" is likely to lurk anywhere, so nonprescription Polymagma or Pepto-Bismol are useful health aids in liquid or tablet form. We are also hearing good reports about Hoffmann-La Roche's Bactrim tablet. Diarrhea can cause loss of salts and fluids, so take lots of sugar in hot tea; it apparently enhances the absorption of salt. Imodium (also in liquid or capsule forms) is useful, fast-acting, and seems to be effective in keeping people on the tourist trails and worry-free.

Motion Sickness

Motion sickness has many combatants in tablet form, some of which produce drowsiness, so it may be a trade-off as to whether you would prefer to be alert or queasy. Meclizine (generic), Antivert, Dramamine and Bonine taken anywhere from a half to one hour before the motion begins are often effective. At the onset of nausea, lozenges, suppositories, or injections of Phenergan, Compazine, or Tigan are indicated. CIBA's Transderm-V (scopolamine) is a novel approach to relief. It's a dime-size adhesive patch that can be worn behind the ear or elsewhere on the body; the skin absorbs protective chemicals for up to three days—an easy way to wear instead of swallow your medication. However at press time the patch was being studied for side effects and its use has been restricted, so check with your doctor about its availability.

Handicapped

For the **handicapped** traveler, the **American Automobile Association** (AAA) distributes a guide (<u>http://www.aaa.com/ scripts/WebObjects.dll/ZipCode</u>). Another organization, **Society for the Advancement of Travel for the Handicapped**, offers further aid; it is located at *26 Court St., Brooklyn, NY 11242* (<u>http://www.sath.org/</u>).

Ambulance Service

Ambulance service? Three companies specialize in airlifting disabled travelers back to stateside medical centers. Since their programs are tailored to specific needs, write to them for details. NEAR, SOS and Travel Assistance Int'l. Here's how you reach them: **NEAR**, *450 Prairie Ave., Suite #101, Calumet City, IL 60409*, ☎ *(708) 868-6700 or* ☎ *(800) 654-6700*; **SOS Assistance**, *P.O. Box 11568, Philadelphia, PA 19116*, ☎ *(215) 244-1500 or* ☎ *(800) 523-8930*; **Travel Assistance Int'l**, *1133 15th St, N.W., Suite #400, Washington DC 20005*, ☎ *(202) 331-1609 or* ☎ *(800) 821-2828*. If your normal insurance does not include this expensive phase of assistance (and most will pay only for land ambulances), it is worth considering separate coverage.

Special Diet

A friendly Iowa reader who could eat only certain foods prepared in special ways had instructions written in detail for the language areas she was to visit; these were shown to waiters along her travel path and she never heard even the slightest growl from a stomach which traveled more than 5000 miles of foreign terrain.

Medic Alert

Medic Alert Foundation renders an invaluable nonprofit service to travelers who suffer from any hidden medical problem. It furnishes lifesaving emblems of 10-karat gold-filled, sterling silver, or stainless steel to be worn around the neck or wrist. Should the patient be unable to talk, medical personnel or law-enforcement officials are instantly informed of dangers inherent in standard treatment. The tag carries such warnings as "DIABETIC," "ALLERGIC TO PENICILLIN," "TAKING ANTICOAGULANTS," "WEARING CONTACT LENSES," "NECK BREATHER," or whatever difficulty. It also bears the telephone number of the Medic Alert headquarters in California to which anyone may call "collect" from anywhere in the world at any hour of day or night for additional file material about the individual case. The organization also features an electric unit worn around the neck or wrist that alerts a telephonic standby facility if the wearer suffers a medical crisis. For more information about this splendid organization (donations are tax deductible), write to **Medic Alert Foundation International**, *Turlock, CA 95380-1009* (http://www.medicalert.org/).

ITRAVELBOOK CURRENCY TIP

For ease of use and uniformity, we have rated hotels, restaurants, and cultural activities (museums, etc.) on the following scale, <u>which is meant to correspond to the American dollar:</u>

Hotels

Very Expensive: @$300+ per night, double occupancy

Expensive: @$200+ per night, double occupancy

Moderate: @$125-$200 per night, double occupancy

Budget: @$50-$125 per night, double occupancy

Restaurants and Other Dining Establishments

Very Expensive: $150+, dinner for two not including wine or dessert

Expensive: $100+, dinner for two not including wine or dessert

Moderate: $50-$75, dinner for two not including wine or dessert

Inexpensive: $25-$50, dinner for two not including wine or dessert

The ratings speak for themselves; the stars, however, rate the subjective experience. (For example, a very expensive accommodation may be experientially only "good" and therefore receive only two stars.)

Refer to the following quality chart when making your selection:

**** Extraordinary

*** Very good

** Good

* Very basic, good value

Customs Officials

When you travel in Europe you will probably not be processed if you are moving from one Community nation to another. Sometimes there are separate lines for E.C. nationals. The attitude is very relaxed everywhere nowadays. If you're lucky, you could sail through your entire tour through the "Nothing to Declare" gates without one bag being checked. The speed of your clearance usually depends upon the inspector's state of digestion. Here are some helpful hints:

Be affable and cooperative, but don't be overly conversational. Their sole interest is to get rid of you; if you keep your mouth shut, things will move twice as fast.

Hold your passport casually in hand—don't flaunt it!—so that the inspector can identify you. (This might sound absurd, but sometimes it's surprisingly helpful.) And speak English solely, *not* a foreign language.

Liquor in your luggage: Break the seals before you get to Customs. In some lands (British Isles excepted) this may get around the import duty. Some countries forbid more than one. If you have an extra, stick it in the pocket of the topcoat or raincoat that hangs "carelessly" over your arm.

The Common Market nations permit 300 cigarettes, 1-1/2 liters of hard liquor (2 "fifth" bottles should pass), 3 liters (3/4-gallon) of wine, 1-1/3 lbs. of coffee, and 1/4 lb. of tea.

Shopping Abroad

Today's duty-free allowance is $400 in retail value. (The next $1000 in value is taxable at only 10 percent.) These goods must accompany you personally on your return. Your free importation of wines or booze is one quart per person 21 years or over—a monument to the enormous power of the U.S. liquor lobby in Washington. Most states admit more than a quart if a modest duty is paid on the overage; others, such as California, are tougher.

Regarding other regulations, here are some key facts and suggestions: (1) Go easy on Coronas and champagne because 100 cigars and one quart per person are all you may import without fee (*foreign-made cigarettes* are limited to one carton). With certain limitations, booze may be "shipped to follow." (2) Foreign fruits, meats, plants, and vegetables might carry pests that could destroy millions of dollars in livestock, food, forests, or ornamentals; virtually all are confiscated. Most foreign-made eatables are banned unless all ingredients are printed on the label. (3) Your exemptions may include alterations or repairs on anything you originally took abroad; if your car throws a piston or your watch gets a dunking en route, charge off the cost of making them tick again. (4) Antiques 100 years old (exceptions: rugs and carpets made after 1700) are unrestricted. They include furniture, hardware, brass, bronze, marble, terra cotta, porcelain, chinaware, and "any object considered to have artistic value." Be sure to bring certificates of verification, if available. (5) Original works of art (not copies)—paintings, drawings, and sculptures of any age—and stamps are duty-free. So are books, prints, lithographs, and maps over 20 years old. (6) Gifts costing less than $50 may be mailed from abroad on a duty-free basis, with no effect on your exemptions. Alcohol, tobacco, and perfume are ineligible. No one person may receive more than one gift in one day; plainly mark the package "Gift—Value Under $50." (7) If you sell some articles within three years after importation on a duty-free basis, you'll be fined double the normal quotation. But you are permitted to sell anything that was initially purchased for your personal or household use. Original intent is the key factor. (8) Everything in your baggage must be for your personal use or the use of your immediate family, or for gifts; samples and other merchandise could be taxed. (9) Finally, egret feathers, ammunition, narcotics, and various other commodities are contraband.

Value Added Tax (VAT) by Country

This chart lists the percentage of the purchase price that is VAT and required minimum purchase per store. The chart gives an indication of the tax saving potential for the tourist. The tax refund operator's handling fee will be deducted from the VAT amount.

Country	VAT	Maximum Purchases
Austria	16.7	$95
Belgium	17	$230
Denmark	20	$50
Finland	18	$25
France	17.1	$235
Germany	13	$35
Greece	11.5–15.3	$170

Italy	13–16	$185 + VAT
Luxembourg	13	$100
Netherlands	14.9	$180
Norway	18.7	$50
Portugal	14.5	$65 + VAT
Spain	13.8	$120 per item
Sweden	20	$15
Switzerland	6.1	$405
Source: Europe Tax-free Shopping		

For more information, contact: **http://www.eurunion.org/ legis-lat/VATweb.htm**

Be especially careful of items made from the skins of certain types of crocodile, spotted cat, or other endangered species. The list of God's creatures that are rapidly vanishing from our planet is too lengthy (and stretching day by day) to include here for purposes of up-to-the-minute accuracy. If you're considering this type of purchase, ask U.S. Customs before departure for a summary of those species; critters dispatched in a brutal fashion are also under protection and thus these pelts too can be seized by officials. Arrests for violations are not unknown; moreover, ignorance of the law is, as usual, no excuse.

On the European side, cigarettes are usually what officials look for first—if they look at all. Above the prescribed number, there's a fat duty to be paid. In some cases the excess will be confiscated, or (in England) the levy must be paid on the entire supply. Most wink at a reasonable excess. They *never* wink, however, at drugs, so these should never be transported across any frontier. Punishment for drug possession or use can be far in excess of U.S. norms.

If you have three or four parcels, your inquisitor has been trained to inspect the one wrapped with the greatest care. Likewise, if there is a choice between a bag and an independent package or case, he will usually examine the latter.

If the duty is too high, or if you're carrying a taxable item to a second or third country, Customs will hold it in escrow at the border for your return, without charge—and it's usually safe. One or two lands won't do this.

U.S. Consular Services Abroad

If you should encounter serious trouble on your trip—anything from a lost passport to an arrest, to death of a companion, to a spectrum of other deep crises—communicate immediately with the nearest American consular office. They are, however, proscribed from extending loans to travelers in financial distress. Although they will give restricted aid in a dispute that could lead to legal or police action, furnish a list of reputable local lawyers, and try to prevent discrimination under foreign law, regulations prohibit them from participating on the direct level. If a citizen is arrested, they will visit him or her in detention, notify relatives and friends, provide a roster of attorneys, and attempt to obtain relief if conditions are inhumane or unhealthy. Here are some of their other duties: (1) Assistance in finding appropriate medical services, including English-speaking physicians. (2) Guidance on how to inform the local police about stolen funds or on how to inform the issuing authorities about missing traveler's checks. (3) The full extension of notary facilities. (4) Help in locating missing Americans. (5) Protection of U.S. voyagers and residents during civil unrest or in natural disasters.

It may be useful to leave behind at home the following direct Washington telephone number of the Office of Special Consular Services *(202) 647-5225*. The automated system will direct your call for the following services.

• To find missing wanderers about whom there is special concern or to transmit emergency messages.

• To transmit funds to foreign soil when commercial banking facilities are unavailable or to arrange medical evacuation.

• For questions about members of your clan who have been arrested and how to get money to them.

• For help when an American dies abroad.

• For civil judicial inquiries and assistance.

• Night and weekend emergency number for all of the above.

The Overseas Citizens Services is a general helpmate for troubled travelers.

Don't ask these officials to do the work of travel agencies, information bureaus, or banks; search for missing luggage; settle disputes with hotel managers or shopkeepers; help get work permits; or find jobs.

Trains and Passes

Eurailpass ("Your-rail-pass") and **Eurail Youthpass** are two of the most rewarding bargains on the continent today. Any *resident* of North, Central, or South America may roam wherever and whenever desired on any continental train (not British; they have a separate **Brit Rail Plan**) without further payment except for routine sleeper or *couchette* supplements. This more luxurious plan than its alternate for young people offers 15 days of unlimited first class travel for a low set fee, plus plans for 21 days, a full month and even for two and three months are available. Children under 12 are charged half-fare; those under four ride free. Including Trans-Europ Expresses (TEE) and all other extra-fare runs, it is valid on the national railways and many private trains, steamers, and ferry crossings in the following 17 nations: Austria, Belgium, Denmark, Finland, France, Germany, Greece, Holland, Hungary, Ireland, Italy, Luxembourg, Norway, Portugal, Spain, Sweden and Switzerland, as well as on sea crossings that link Ireland into the continental system. (BritRail includes English Channel crossings.) You may choose its continuous usage period during six months following its purchase. Anyone under 26 (the limitation to students has been dropped) may opt for the **Eurail Youthpass,** which opens one month of unlimited roving in all of the same carriers in *second class* for a lower flat sum, plus the option of bumping it up to two months of railroading. Among its other alluring financial benefits are substantial savings on hotel bills by dozing sitting up, spending these nights in an inexpensive *couchette,* or, for slightly more, taking a tourist sleeper. Neither of these arrangements includes reservation fees (strongly urged always and compulsory for berths), meals, refreshments, nor with the latter, fees and supplements required to board certain trains. Both cards are personal and nontransferable, with the penalty of confiscation if another bearer is caught showing them. Your passport must always be produced when requested by conductors, gatemen, and other authorized personnel. Neither is refundable if lost or stolen. If you are traveling off season (Oct. 1–March 31), ask about the **Saverpass**, which knocks off about 25 percent of the 15-day rate and applies only to couples or larger groups. There's also a **Flexipass**, for any five-day use over a 15-day span, another scheme for any nine-day use over a 21-day span, and yet another for any 14-day use over a 30-day span. The **Youth Flexipass** is a great money saver for any 15-day use over a two-month span.

Your Eurailpass, incidentally, is becoming increasingly valuable for

airport-to-downtown rail connections. Barcelona, Brussels, Dusseldorf, Frankfurt, Paris, Vienna, Amsterdam, Rome, and Zurich are now on rails. If you have this card, why pay $35-or-so extra for taxi fare?

Note

You must buy these passes before heading for Europe, because they are not sold abroad. To secure confirmed reservations booked through U.S. agencies is tricky unless application is made long in advance. For further inquiries, see your travel agent or write to **Eurailpass**, *P.O. Box 325, Old Greenwich, CT 06870-03255.*

Intercity and **EuroCity** trains are the top-grade sizzlers all over Europe. In most nations, second class is being upgraded; both first and second are being equalized in terms of air conditioning, modern styling, and other basics. (The main difference today is in the size and comfort of the seats.) If your destination is within 250 miles, your door-to-door travel time will probably be less than if you bid for airline travel—and at nearly 1/4 the cost! Moreover, in winter or foggy periods, rail is far more reliable; punctuality is assured. Average running speed is about 80 m.p.h.; as examples of their high-stepping gait, Paris-Brussels is only two hours, 22 minutes (3–1/2 hours by air *et al.* from midtown-to-midtown), and Paris-Zurich is only six hours. Dining facilities are always on hand; frontier formalities have been streamlined to a minimum.

On all other trains abroad make sure *first* that there's a diner. Also check the times and reserve your place for the seating you prefer (see below). Advance knowledge can also give you time to improvise your own picnic—much better than the station platform vendors' snacks.

When you leave your seat for a meal, put some bulky possession on the cushion. Otherwise, the first incoming passenger is liable to take over, leaving you the worst place and lousiest view.

Dining Cars

Here's the procedure: Usually there are two (sometimes three) separate servings spanning more than two hours overall. First the steward will come to your compartment, learn your time preference, and give you a table-booking slip that must be returned when he greets you in his own domain. The closer your car is to the diner, the bet-

ter your chance for getting the sitting that you wish. Although a few
meager à la carte items are available (some trains offer cheese or
coldcuts platters), probably 98 percent of the customers consume
the standard, fixed meal at the standard, fixed price (usually $9 to
$13 with some of the gourmet attractions in France topping out at
more than $65). Course after course is served on a one-shot, uni-
versal basis; everybody eats the soup, the veal, the salad, and the fruit
from the same service trays. When the whole car has finished, the
cashier presents the check. Almost nobody tips. On the *Eurostar*
train, which slides under the English Channel en route between
London and Paris or Brussels, a tray is brought to you at your seat.
The 35-minute *Le Shuttle* auto-carrying train offers no food except
snacks in the terminals at either end.

Sleeping Cars

The European railways offer three first-class and two second-class
categories. First class consists of regular one-berth or two-berth
accommodations, plus "Specials" for shorter runs (20 small single
compartments per car). Second class offers the T-2 berthing with 18
double-decked twin compartments per car; these are gradually sup-
plementing the older three-bunk units. Finally, there's the second-
class *couchette*—a minimum-price six-seat (or six-berth) compartment in which passengers may lie down without undressing. These
are for the hardy.

Check the date of expiration of your round-trip ticket. On short
rides in some countries they expire within 24 hours.

The Orient Express

This is one of the greatest steps backward in recent generations—a
delight in every way to recapture on wheels the nostalgia of the
1920s. The lifestyle recreated on the journey between Venice and
London or Vienna and London (you can join or exit at other termini) is a moment shared with the Emperor of Austria, King Edward
the VII, Menalik II, and other luminaries of that graceful era of elegance. With professional attention to cuisine, wines, presentation
and service, it is probable that today's reincarnation excels that of
the original. Exquisite devotion to restoration and comfort is evidenced in every polished surface. To plan the exact adventure that
appeals to you, check the myriad details with your travel agent or be
in touch directly with **Orient-Express**, ☎ *(800) 524-2420*. This has

to be one of the most beguiling and sybaritic anachronisms of today's Europe.

There are more fine trains on line each year—many of them described in the national chapters to come. But while you are considering your travels, you might like to think of zipping along on the *French TGV* which can link **Paris** to **Brussels** or **Geneva** in only two hours. Maybe you'll rise to the top of Europe on Switzerland's *Jungfraujoch Bahn or enjoy* stunning views aboard *El Cantabrico* across **northern Spain**.

Motoring

With minor exceptions, road signs are standard. There are three basic categories: (1) triangular, to indicate danger (intersection, railway crossing, slippery road, etc.), (2) circular, to lay down prohibitions (road closed, one-way street, no passing, etc.), (3) rectangular, to provide information (garage ahead, telephone ahead, first-aid station ahead, etc.).

Gasoline rings up at twice or triple the U.S. price—and, thank goodness, you can usually purchase it with major credit cards along important national routes. Most modern rental cars use only unleaded fuel. Generally the pumps and hoses are green. If in doubt, ask in the station because the leaded gas can immobilize your vehicle. In most countries a top speed limit of 110 to 130 kilometers per hour (kph) is imposed for freeway traffic with 90 kph set for secondary highway runs, and 50 to 60 kph pegged for suburban cruising. Since the speed limits are not uniform, be sure to watch carefully or to ask at each frontier concerning that nation's rules.

In most European countries those in the front seats are required to buckle their safety harnesses; in many, this means only for highway driving, but a few sticklers (Switzerland, for example) enforce the edict full-time and on Sundays—front seats *and* back!

Other Lifestyles

Not everyone plunks his or her suitcase down in a hotel while abroad. In our various national chapters, programs are described that will expand your economy while broadening your experience. Excellent *parador* and *pousada* systems comprise networks of inns in Spain and Portugal. France has its **Federation Nationale des Agents Immobiliers**, where you can find accommodation in a *chalet* or a *villa*, and also the **Gite de France**, which turns on hospitality in *farmhouses*. Germany has its **Gast im Schloss** assemblage for those who prefer to hobnob in *castles*. There is the superb **Relais et Chateaux** organization spotlighting intimate deluxe havens all over Europe and the U.K. Greece is guaranteeing that you can vacation in a "traditional settlement" that has not been spoiled by rampant tourism.

Metric Measurement

The metric system used in every European country is still confusing.

Here are a few translations. Conquer these four and you'll get along fine:

• A kilometer (pronounced kill-OM-eter by the "mile"-minded British and Irish and KILL-o-meter by the continentals) is roughly 6/10 of a mile. Multiply by 6, knock off one decimal point, and you've got it in miles.

• A kilo or kilogram (potatoes and onions) is 2.2 pounds.

• A meter (dress material) and a liter (gasoline, beer) are both roughly 11/10ths—one of a yard, the other of a quart. There are about 2–1/2 centimeters to 1 inch.

• A gram (airmail letters) is very tiny. There are about 28 to the ounce.

Below are some conversions that might come in handy. Since sizes are not standardized, this is a fairly rough yardstick. Try on the items whenever possible.

APPROXIMATE CLOTHING SIZE					
(American-Continental)					
WOMEN'S CLOTHING (SIZES)					
American	6	8	10	12	14	16
Continental:					
France	36	38	40	42	44	46
Italy	38	40	42	44	46	48
Rest of Europe	34	36	38	40	42	44
WOMEN'S SHOES					
American	4	5	6	7	8	9
Continental	35	36	37	38	39	40
MEN'S SWEATERS					
American	S	M	L	XL	
Continental	48	50	52	54	
MEN'S SHOES					
American	8	8 1/2	9 1/2	10 1/2	11 1/2
Continental	41	42	43	44	45

Last, here's a refresher on how to change Centigrade temperatures into Fahrenheit. The classic method is to take 9/5ths of the Centigrade temperature (the reading on European thermometers) and add 32. A much easier way is to double the Centigrade reading, deduct 10 percent, and add the same 32. Example: Let's imagine that the mercury says 15°. Twice 15 is 30, and 10 percent of 30 is 3. Taking 3 from 30 leaves 27. Add 32 to 27, and you'll have the Yankee version of 59°. In print it looks complicated—but in practice it's so simple that almost any traveler can do it in his head. Try it and see!

AUSTRIA

Austria has it all—sophistication, rustic simplicity, antiquities, riches, excellent restaurants, music festivals, towering mountains, green valleys, flowers during the summer and world-famous snow during the long winter season.

Geographically, three-quarters of the country is covered with mountains. The Alps cut a curved swathe across Austria's face, sparing only sections in the south and eastern regions. Lush valleys flank the river courses, the most famous being the River Danube, Europe's longest. Austria's other rivers—the Inn, the Ill, the Drau—as well as its many lakes also are extremely scenic.

Austria is bordered to the north by Germany, to the west by Switzerland and Liechtenstein, to the south by Italy, Slovenia (formerly part of Yugoslavia) and Hungary, and to the east by the Czech Republic. Austria itself is divided into nine regions or states: Voralberg, Tyrol, Salzburg Land, Upper Austria, Lower Austria, Vienna, Burgenland, Styria and Carinthia.

Snow begins in late November and continues through May in the higher regions. Summer (which means from Easter to mid-October) brings warmer temperatures, with periodic rains.

High season depends on your itinerary. For skiers, peak times run from December through April. Many ski resorts and hotels close down during some or most of the warmer months. For city touring, any time is fine, but beware that in July and August Salzburg is inundated with music lovers who come each year to its famous festival. During all the major holidays (Christmas, New Year's, Easter weekend), throngs invade the cities and popular ski spots.

Off the beaten track, the smaller towns provide all the charm without the crush of people. Away from the major hubs, daily life retains its rustic rhythms, preserving old- world customs.

Outdoor Activities

Skiing, both downhill and cross-country, is synonymous with Austria. During winter, you also have your choice of ice-skating, curling and tobogganing, not to mention the romance of a horse-drawn sleigh ride. In the summer, visitors and residents alike hike, stroll, or ride on horseback or mountain bikes. Schools and instructors teach beginning and advanced techniques in almost any sport.

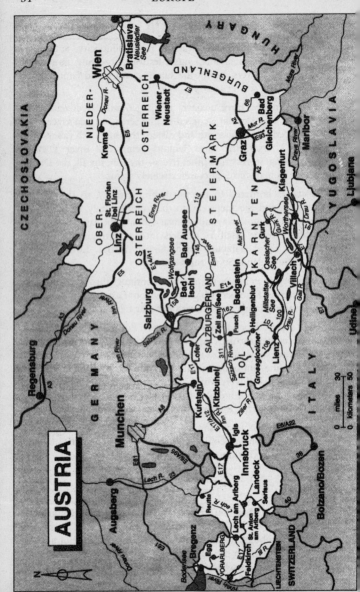

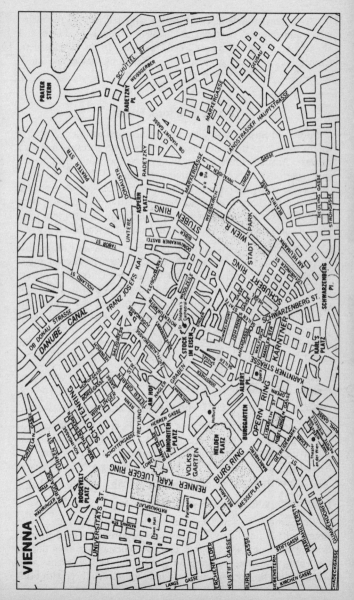

VIENNA

Challenging mountaineering treks are offered near all the major peaks, and almost every town and hamlet provides guided hikes and alpine tours. Golf and tennis are also popular. In the lake districts, trout fishing and water sports, such as swimming, sailing and wind-surfing, prevail.

Arts and Cultural Events

Music and Austria have been intertwined for centuries. Vienna is the birthplace of the waltz, and Salzburg is the ancestral home of Mozart. Austria's musical contributions to the world include the vast repertoires of Schubert, Strauss, Haydn and Wagner, to name only a few. Today the country is filled with musical festivals, from the renowned Salzburg Festival to countless music weekends held in small villages at the height of summer. Visiting Austria without sampling its music is like leaving without enjoying an apple strudel.

The Salzburg Festival runs from late July to the end of August, and celebrates Mozart, Strauss, Verdi and others. The Festival brings together a splendid array of concerts, instrumental recitals, Mozart matinees, serenades, ballet and sacred music. Virtuosi, duets and chamber music groups perform in the numerous halls and salons nearby, often with several events happening at once. But you won't get into the top concerts or operas without confirmed reservations made well in advance. Tickets for headline events sell out a year ahead. Plan ahead, too, to attend the Easter or Whitsun festivals.

For comprehensive information on the Festival, write directly to the box office, **Salzburg Festival**, *P.O. Box 140, A-5010, Salzburg, Austria,* ☎ *(0662) 8045 (*http://www.salzburgfestival.com/index2.html*).* Don't forget that, during Festival time, lodging in Salzburg is at a premium—if you can't get hotel reservations, you might find room in the surrounding suburbs. Or try writing the Salzburg tourist information office *(Mozartplatz 5, Salzburg, Austria,* ☎ *(0662) 846568,* http://www.salzburginfo.at/desk/framehome_e.htm*)* to find accommodations with a local family.

Vienna hosts its own Festival from mid-May to June, while Bregenz has a July Festival that features performances on a gigantic floating stage on Lake Constance. Graz comes into its own during the Styrian autumn, featuring an arts festival with an avant-garde accent, while the area around Feldkirch honors Schubert with both spring and autumn festivals that draw famous performers from all across Europe. For information on these activities, consult the **Austrian National Tourist Office**, *P.O. Box 1142, New York, NY 10108-1142, (212) 944-6880* (**http://www.austria-tourism.at/**).

Transportation

Airlines

With change sweeping away old borders throughout Europe, Austria has become an important airport hub. Since 1989, Austrian Airlines (toll-free ☎ (800) 843-3002 **http:// www.aua.com/**) has offered nonstop service from New York or Chicago to Vienna. Although flight schedules vary, many U.S. carriers require passengers to change planes in London or Frankfurt. International carriers, such as Lufthansa and British Airways, also feature extensive Austrian service. Inside Austria, its national airline provides service throughout the country, Europe and points beyond. Austrian Air Services (a subsidiary of Austrian Airlines) and Tyrolean Airways (jointly owned by the national carrier) link Austria's cities.

Trains

Comprehensive service, efficient schedules and competitive fares make train travel the hands-down choice for thousands of Austrians and visitors alike. If you don't want to drive, the trains will carry you almost anywhere in Austria, plus the schedules are designed to mesh with bus lines, cable cars, and even boat tours. Eurail Passes (**http:// www.eurail.com/**)are valid in Austria, and senior citizens (women over 60, men over 65) can ride at 50 percent reduction in first- or second-class. Cars and bicycles can be rented through rail agents, and returned when you're finished at a dozen Austrian stations.

Bus

Bus lines maintain service over 19,000 miles of roads, linking rail stations with outlying villages. Buses ferry passengers (plus their luggage and ski equipment) from the valley floor to the loftier ski resorts and alpine hamlets. Discounts for children are substantial.

For information, ☎ (0222) 71101, but be aware that if you're placed on "hold" the wait might be long.

Taxis

In the cities, taxis are designated by official seals on the taxi meters. Surcharges are to be posted in the vehicle, and supplements are charged for luggage stowed in the trunk. Set charges are the rule in many resort areas.

Driving and Roads

Austria is easily accessible by car. Main roads are hard-surfaced, and four-lane autobahns link Salzburg and Vienna, while a six-lane autobahn links Vienna with Ediltz. Mountain driving is the main challenge, with steep gradients (6 to 16 percent, or even more). Although the impressive Arlberg tunnel (nearly 9 miles long) makes it easier to reach ski destinations, even if you are an experienced alpine driver, you may want to take the train or bus to reach points at higher elevations.

Car Rental

To rent a car, present a valid driver's license, your passport—and for convenience—a major credit card. BUT YOU SHOULD KNOW THAT CAR RENTALS ARE SUBJECT TO A WHOPPING TAX, AS HIGH AS 21.2 PERCENT. In addition, you must figure in airport surcharges (6 percent for any car rented at a municipal airport). When shopping for rates, make sure you know whether the price includes all applicable taxes. **Budget-Rent-A-Car**, **Avis**, and **Hertz** all offer vehicles in Austria. For about $21 a day (added to the rental costs), you can purchase a "loss-damage-waiver" that allows you to waive all financial responsibility for eventual damage to your car, even if you are at fault. Drivers who pass up this coverage may be liable for up to the full value of the car in the event of an accident. Some credit cards offer loss-damage-waivers as a benefit, which could create a savings for you. The best advice is to plan your car-rental strategy well in advance.

Boats

Touring Austria by boat is a splendid way to take in the scenery. Cruising the Danube can be accomplished by luxury craft, steamship, or ferry. Enjoy a seven-day tour, a riverboat shuttle or an evening dinner cruise. Other possibilities include trips on the Rhine, the Drau, or on one of Austria's lakes. For luxury cruises on the Danube, contact **Europamerica Cruises**, toll-free ☎ (800) 221-4770 (**http://www.deilmann-cruises.com**/). For excursions on **Lake Constance**, ☎ (05574) 42868. **Lake Wolfgang** and its sights are linked by the Austrian Federal Railway boat system; ☎ (06138) 2231.

Bicycles

Bicycle touring through the cities on miles of designated paths is a great way to see the country. From the beginning of April until November, you can rent bikes and procure passes to take your bike on most trains (the bikes ride in a special car). The cost is under $10 a day, with substantial reductions if you're taking the train to your destination. Rented bikes can be returned to almost any train station, simplifying the logistics.

Hotels

The listings include samplings of hotels in a variety of price ranges, with an emphasis on the unique or special. A night's stay at a renovated castle, cloister or former brewery will make your trip especially memorable. Throughout Austria, most prices include breakfast. During the winter, ski resorts and snow-destination hotels often include "half-board" rates in their prices. Some resort hotels require half-board when you book three days or more. Guests are provided with breakfast and either lunch or dinner in the hotel's dining rooms. This practice is reflected in serving times at nearby non-hotel restaurants—many are not open for lunch.

Food and Drink

Each region has its specialty, with influences coming from Italy, Slovenia and Germany. Much of traditional Austrian food relies on simplicity—*meat schnitzels* (cutlets) are served with salads and potatoes, sometimes with soups beforehand. *Tafelspitz*, or boiled beef, is the most well known national specialty, although, if you are after something more unusual, you could try the Styrian specialty, blood-and-liver sausages. Game and fish are often prepared using old aristocratic recipes. The more famous Austrian chefs have taken these old dishes and interpreted them in new exciting ways. From the most exclusive elegant dining room to the smallest stube or gasthof, there's much to enjoy.

> **ITRAVELBOOK TIP:** IF YOU FIND YOURSELF TRAVELING THROUGH THE BUCOLIC AUSTRIAN COUNTRYSIDE (OR OUTSIDE THE CITY IN ANY COUNTRY, FOR THAT MATTER), LET THE LOCALS BE YOUR CULINARY GUIDE. VERY OFTEN, THEY WILL INTRODUCE YOU TO LOCAL DELICACIES AND DISHES THAT YOU WOULD NEVER HAVE THE OPPORTUNITY TO TRY IN THE CITY.

And don't forget dessert—Austria is noted for its pastries, chocolates and cakes. Each afternoon, most citizens take a break, stopping at cafes or small sweet shops for a pastry served with coffee. *Sachertorte* is a staggeringly delicious, dense chocolate covered cake and is not to be missed (especially if you can get it at the Cafe Sacher in Vienna). The apple strudel is an absolute must, as is the *Salzburger Nockerln* (a soufflé heaped to resemble the three mountains surrounding Salzburg). Coffee is served in any conceivable concoction; espresso lovers will believe they are in paradise.

Vineyards and breweries keep Austrians well supplied with an array of wines and beers. *Klosterneuburger* is perhaps the best white wine. Other choices include the popular *Gumpoldskirchern* and *Welschriesling*. Red wines include *Bluer*, *Protugieser* and *Zweigelt*.

In Vienna and Lower Austria, take time to visit a *heuriger*, or "new wine" garden. Found principally in Grinzing and other regions near the Vienna Woods, these establishments sell "new wines" made from the grapes of the current year. These full-bodied, potent wines were beloved by Joseph II. A trip to one of these family-owned taverns is a must for anyone who appreciates wines.

Of the beers, *Gosser Brau* is a rich brew made in Styria. It's full-bodied and fine, available in light or dark. *Schwechater* is tops in Vienna. Imported liquors are often exorbitantly priced, but local schnapps and fruited brandies can be found at prices that won't hit your wallet too hard. On the ski slopes, schnapps (often flavored with fruit juices or spices) warms up chilled bones. Finally, popular—especially in Vienna—*bowle* is a delicious summer punch made of cognac, white wine, champagne or curacao and fresh fruits, served from a bowl.

CURRENCY: Euros.

Tipping

Here is a rough guide to the gratuities you'll be expected to give: the waiter (the person who serves you, not the headwaiter), 5 percent extra above your total; bartender, 10 percent of the drink cost; hotel housekeeper, $5 per night; washroom attendant, $2; taxi driver, 10 percent of fare; doorman, $1; porter and bellhop, $2-$5. For more information, see the **ALL ABOUT EUROS** section in the introduction.

Telephone

The international access code for both the United States and Canada is 001, followed by the area code and seven-digit local number. To telephone Austria, dial 43; time difference (Eastern Daylight) plus 6 hours.

For More Information

Austrian National Tourist Office, *P.O. Box 1142, New York, NY 10108-1142,* ☎ *(212) 944- 6880* (**http://www.austria-tourism. at/**)

Carinthia
Klagenfurt

This is the provincial capital of Carinthia, the region that borders Italy and Slovenia. Carinthia's sunny weather and numerous lakes make it a summer tourist center, though it seems to be visited little by North Americans. Known for its rings of streets along its former city walls (the walls were destroyed in 1809 during Napoleonic invasions), Klagenfurt lies near Lake Worther, a popular place for watersports.

Where to Stay

Hotels and Resorts

Romantik-Hotel Musil

Expensive

Oktober Strasse 14. Town center, near Neuer Platz.

☎ *(04) 63-51-16-60.*

Credit Cards: *V, MC, DC, A.*

Balcony or patio, in-room minibars.

Pricey but intimate (some say a bit dusty), this small hotel has earned its reputation, and rooms are booked months in advance. Located in the heart of town, the building features an oval courtyard with inward-facing balconies. The 16 rooms are unique, the eclectic decor includes Baroque, Biedermeier and rustic furnishings. Each has bath and TV with hookup to BBC news.

Schloss Hotel Worthersee

Inexpensive to Moderate
Villacher Strasse 338. Head west from the center for 2 miles toward Villach.

☎ *(04) 63-21158.*

Credit Cards: *V, MC, DC, A.*

Beach location, water sports, balcony or patio.

Built as a private villa in 1845, this hotel features a tunnel that leads to a private beach and shoreline promenade on the eastern banks of Lake Worther. The yellow mansion is trimmed with ornate wood-work and has jutting towers and balconies. Inside, the 29 rooms and five suites are modern and well-furnished; the best views, of course, are from those overlooking the lake. The hotel has its own dinner restaurant, a bar and a cafe. Closed Jan.

Where to Eat

Bistro Musil

Moderate

Oktober Strasse 14, ☎ *(04) 63-51-16-60.*

Credit Cards: *V, MC, DC, A.*

Dine by candlelight in this locally popular hotel where Klagenfurters come to celebrate. Owner Bernhard Musil has been named the top pastry chef in central Europe, so be sure to try out the luscious desserts and sweets. Regional favorites, such as calves' brains and venison medallions, are served along with fresh fish.

Cafe Moser Verdino

Inexpensive

Domgasse 2. North of Domkirch. Located at Moser Verdino.

☎ *(04) 62-57878.*

Specialties: *Pastries, light meals, snacks, coffee, wine, beer.*
Cafestop, own baking, reservations not accepted.

Not the oldest, but certainly a favorite with residents, who stop by for espresso and dazzling pastries. This unpretentious cafe is decorated with framed lithos and filled with marble, brass accents and lots of plush, upholstered furnishings.

Strohschein's Heuriger

Moderate

Villacher Strasse 338. ☞ *Head west toward Villach. Located at Schloss Worthersee.*

☎ *(04) 63-21158.*

Specialties: *Lamb, fish, beef.*
Credit Cards: *V, MC, DC, A.*

Closed: *Sun.*

Reservations recommended, jacket required.

This formal restaurant's kitchens are supervised by the hotel's family owner, and the menu features regional dishes served with elegance and flair. The six-course fixed-price dinner is a superb way to tour the tastes of Carinthia. Desserts are extravagant and well worth the splurge.

What to Do

Historical Sites

Magdalensberg   ★★★★★

http://www.landesmuseum-ktn.at/ magdalensberg.htm

Inexpensive

Outside St. Viet an der Glan South of St. Viet, north of Klagenfurt on Route 83. *(04) 224- 2555.*

Special Hours: *Open from May through Oct.*

Long before the Hapsburg Empire rose to power, Austria was a part of the vast Roman Empire. Magdalensburg is considered the oldest Roman settlement north of the Alps. Romans occupied this site the last century before Christ, and today excavations have revealed a Roman villa (complete with central heating), public baths, temples and a forum. Admission.

Neuer Platz   ★★★★★

Free

Neuer Platz. Near the Town Hall, New Town. *(04) 63-53-72-23.*

Don't miss seeing the Lindwurm, or Dragon Fountain, that dominates the square. Carved by Ulrich Vogelsang in about 1590 from a single block of grey schist, this snarling beast is the heraldic emblem of the city. The tale goes that Klagenfurt was built on a swamp favored by the dragon, and safety was finally ensured once the creature was slain.

Villach

This bustling town serves as a railway junction linking Carinthia to Italy and Slovenia. Straddling the River Drau, Villach is within easy driving distance of Lake Ossiach, Spittal and Velden. In July and August, Villach hosts the Carinthian Summer Festival. Nearby Warmbad offers radon-laced thermal baths for those seeking "the cure." Situated in serene gardens in the center of Warmbad, the Warmbaderhof is the largest of the hotels in the area and exudes an air of quiet comfort.

Where to Stay

Romantik Hotel Post ★★★★★

http://www.romantik-hotel.com/

Moderate

Hauptplatz 26. In the Pedestrian zone, old town.

☎ *(04) 242-26101.*

Credit Cards: *MC, DC, A.*

Secluded garden atmosphere, sauna, balcony or patio, in-room mini-bars, fitness center.

Once the town palace of one of the richest families in Carinthia, this hotel still retains its regal air, with vaulted ceilings, an arcaded court-yard and a baronial fireplace. The exterior is extravagantly decorated with stone columns, carvings and wrought iron. Built in 1500, the manor has played host to kings and archdukes as well as an empress. There are 76 rooms and one suite; all have elegant decor plus sitting area, satellite TV, tile or marble bath (half without tub).

Warmbaderhof ★★★★★

http://www.warmbad.at/englisch/ index.htm

Expensive

Kadischenallee. *Two and one-half miles south of Villach.*

☎ *(04) 242-30010.*

Credit Cards: *V, MC, DC, A.*

Taking "the cure" draws many to the Warmbad-Villach area, and this 100-year-old hotel provides a comfortable retreat. Set in flowering gardens, south of Villach, the hotel has its own indoor swimming pool, housed in a large vaulted building, plus covered passageways that lead to the warm springs. Accommodations include 116 rooms and 12 suites, most in the hotel's modern wing; all are pleasantly furnished and have satellite TV, combination bath, robes. The hotel offers walking tours of the town and evening dances on its outdoors terrace. Closed one week in Dec.

Where to Eat

Bleibergerhof ★★★★★

Moderate

Bleibergerhof. South of Villach on Route 86, Untere Fellach.

☎ *(04) 244-2205-0.*

Specialties: *Game, beef, veal, freshwater fish.*

Reservations required. Jacket at lunch, jacket and tie at dinner.

Reached by car or bus from Villach, this restaurant is a hidden delight that is considered one of the top establishments in Austria. Known for its impeccable service amid tasteful surroundings, it serves both international and Carinthian specialties. The ever-changing menu contains soups, light first courses, and a variety of meat and game dishes. The wine list offers vintages from around the world.

Postillion ★★★★★

Moderate to Expensive

Hauptplatz 26. In the pedestrian zone. ☎ *(04) 242-26101.*

Specialties: *Venison pates, stews and soups, boiled beef, schnitzels.*

Credit Cards: *V, MC, DC, A.*

Outside dining, own baking, reservations required.

With recipes adapted from cuisine served to aristocracy in the 1800s, this hotel restaurant transports guests to another era. Famous in the region for its venison, it prepares an array of specialties dressed with cheeses, butter and cream. Those more health-conscious should consider the selections of lighter fare. In July and August, guests can be seated on the flower-filled courtyard, where piano music and candlelight create a special atmosphere.

What to Do

Special Tours

Villach Alpine Highway

10-mile road southwest of Villach, ☎ *(04) 242- 24-44.*

This modern mountain road traverses wooded areas and contours across the rugged face of the Dobstrach massif. Marked turnouts offer breathtaking views of the Gail Valley and Julian Alps to the south. Turnout numbers 2, 5 and 6 offer particularly beautiful vistas. Near Turnout 6 is an Alpine botanical garden, open mid-June through Aug. daily from 9 a.m. to 6 p.m. At the roadway's end, a chair lift carries hikers from 5682 ft. (1731 m)to a spot near the summit 7107 ft. (2166 m). From the lift, continue on foot, but be prepared for a high-altitude, two-hour walk. Your reward at the hike's end is a stunning panorama that includes the jewellike Carinthian lakes.

Land Salzburg
Badgastein

Situated on the slopes of the rugged Tauren, Badgastein is known for its radon thermal springs and its winter sports. Channeled by a mossy gorge, the river Gasteiner Ache flows through the heart of town. Filled with elegant resort hotels, and surrounded by the slopes of the high Alps, Badgastein has drawn such visitors as the philosopher Schopenhauer and the composer Johann Strauss. Hiking, skiing, fishing, sauna treatments.

Where to Stay

Hotel Elisabethpark

Moderate

Franz-Josef-Strasse 5. Located 62 miles south of Salzburg; by car, A-10 south to 311 west to 167 south.

☎ *(06) 434-25-5-10.*

Credit Cards: *V, MC, DC, A.*

Pool, sauna.

This large, reasonably-priced but lavish hotel offers the best of resort amenities. Comprised of several interconnected buildings, the hotel has decor from Moorish geometrics to Austrian rustic, with elegant French touches. Accommodations include 115 rooms and nine suites, all uniquely decorated, with double-glazed windows, TV, bath, hair dryer, robes.

Hotel Gruner Baum

<u>http://www.lodgingaustria.com/ Bad Gastein/GrunerBaum/</u>

Moderate

Kotschachtalstrasse 25. Located 62 miles south of Salzburg; by car, A-10 south to 311 west to 167 south.

☎ *(06) 434-2516-0.*

Credit Cards: *V, MC, DC, A.*

Mountain location, pool, tennis, skiing, balcony or patio.

A chalet-style ski and mountain resort on the outskirts of Badgastein in the Kotschach Valley. This is the PERFECT HEADQUARTERS FOR CROSS-COUNTRY SKIING IN WINTER AND FOR HIKING AND HUNTING IN SUMMER—WHEN THE RATES ARE MUCH LOWER. The 90 cozy rooms have warm wood paneling, and recessed sleeping alcoves are featured in some singles; 30 suites. All have TV, bath, robes. The hotel rents skis, and operates a beginner's slope nearby with a T-bar.

Budget Lodging

Hotel Mozart

Inexpensive

Kaiser-Franz-Joseph-Strasse 25. Located 62 miles west of Salzburg; by car, A-10 south to 311 west to 167 south.

☎ *(06) 434-2037.*

Credit Cards: *MC, DC.*

With comfortable rooms offered at a reasonable price for a resort area, this 19th- century hotel sports a gabled mansard roof and a long ground-floor veranda. Thermal baths are located on each floor, but each of the 70 rooms includes a private bath. Warm and inviting, this hotel is full of luxurious old-world details, such as lots of Oriental rugs and crystal chandeliers.

Where to Eat

Villa Hiss

Moderate

Erzherzog-Johann-Promenade 1, ☎ *(06) 434- 3928.*

Specialties: *Rack of lamb, wild trout, game dishes.*

Credit Cards: *V, MC, DC, A.*

Closed: *Mon.*

Reservations required.

Chef-owner Jorg Worther oversees all the details at this acclaimed restaurant. Using classic ingredients served in fresh combinations, Worther has earned the praise of critics throughout Austria. The fixed-price menu varies according to the season.

What to Do

Brockstein

Sports and Recreation

Natural Saunas

☎ *0643/42-53-10.*

Located two miles south of Badgastein, near the tiny village of Brockstein, this abandoned gold mine with tunnels carved into Radhausburg mountain now serves as a unique place to take "the cure." Those seeking the radon-laced mineral waters (believed to cure arthritis and other ills) travel into the mine tunnels on a small electric train. In the heart of the mountain is what has been called the "world's only natural giant sauna." Also at Brockstein, take time to see the parish church, where the domed ceiling is painted with frescoes of hard rock miners. Hikers can reach Brockstein by following a one-hour footpath from Badgastein.

Salzburg

The birthplace of Mozart, the site of *The Sound of Music*, Salzburg *is* a city of music—with the vibrant tones of church bells that peal throughout the day, the strains of symphonies that fill the concert halls, the organ pipes and choirs at Sunday mass, the hearty folk tunes and drinking songs, and even the bird songs heard in the gardens along the River Salzach. Rimmed by the Eastern Alps with their snowy crags and glistening ice caves, the city of Salzburg itself is filled with treasures, from Baroque cathedrals and thickly walled fortresses to heavenly public gardens. Austria's most famous music festival is held here each year. Whether you have a day or a week, take time to savor Salzburg.

Where to Stay

Hotels and Resorts

Goldener Hirsch

http://www.goldenerhirsch.com/ index1-e.htm

Expensive

Getreidegasse 37. In Old Town, at Getreidegasse and Herbert-von-Karajan Platz, just blocks from Mozartplatz.

☎ *(06) 62-84-85-11.*

Credit Cards: *V, MC, DC, A (free Fridays for Amex holders)*

Air conditioning in rooms, in-room minibars.

Situated a few blocks from Mozart's birthplace in the heart of Old Town, the "Golden Stag" pampers guests in luxurious, uniquely appointed medieval town houses that date back to 1407. Accommodations include 70 rooms and five suites, all beautifully furnished and maintained, with satellite TV, trouser press, marble or tile bath, hair dryer, robes. Immensely popular with music lovers during the annual music festival, this hotel combines historic surroundings with high-quality service. To make your Salzburg visit a first-class experience, Johannes von Walderdorff, general manager, and his staff can provide anything from extra pillows to opening-night theater tickets. Formal and casual dining are available, along with 24-hour room service, baby-sitting, and laundry.

Hotel Bristol

http://www.bristol-salzburg.at/

Moderate to Expensive

Makartplatz 4. At Makartsteg Road, south of Dreifaltigskeitsgasse.

☎ *(06) 62-87-35-57.*

Credit Cards: *V, MC, DC, A.*

Centrally located and filled with an eclectic mix of antiques, crystal chandeliers and newer pine furnishings, this hotel combines traditional quality with elegance. The refined Old-World public areas feature upholstered armchairs and large paintings, some of museum-quality. There are 70 rooms and 10 suites, with decor ranging from expensive through functional to lavishly Baroque. All have satellite TV, tiled bath, hair dryer, robes, toiletries; some have air conditioning. Close to Mirabell Gardens and the theater.

Hotel Elefant

http://www.elefant.at/english/ index.html

Moderate

Sigmund-Haffner-Gasse 4. Near City Hall in Old Town.

☎ *(06) 62-84-33-97.*

Credit Cards: *V, MC, DC, A.*

A special delight for history buffs and those who enjoy the ambience
of the 700-year-old building. With the pink-and-white marble flooring in the lobby, the extensive antique furnishings and the many
high-ceilinged rooms, this family-run hotel provides a quiet retreat
at a good price. The 36 comfortably furnished rooms have TV, bath,
hair dryer.

Hotel Kobenzl

http://www.kobenzl.at/ Pages English/First.html

Moderate to Very Expensive

*Gaisberg 11. Seven miles east of Salzburg; drive toward Ganz, follow
signs to hotel.*

☎ *(06) 62-64-15-10, FAX 528-1234.*

Credit Cards: *V, MC, DC, A.*

Pool, sauna, in-room safes, fitness center.

Perched atop Gaisberg mountain, this glamourous hotel invites
guests to relax in a serene alpine setting above Salzburg. A favorite
retreat for royalty, government figures and celebrities, it offers
world-class amenities. The 22 rooms and 16 suites are filled with
antiques and have bath of marble or tile, hair dryer, robes, TV; many
have separate sitting rooms. Children age 12 and under stay free in
their parents' room, plus there is a playground complete with tricy-
cles.

Hotel Schloss Monchstein

[http://www.monchstein.at/ frame1_en.htm](http://www.monchstein.at/frame1_en.htm)

Very Expensive

Monchsberg 26. Monchsberg tram from Gstattengasse at the Casino, or by car from Left Bank.

☎ *(06) 62-84-85-55.*

Credit Cards: *V, MC, DC, A.*

Mountain location, secluded garden atmosphere, tennis, in-room safes, in-room minibars.

A member of the exclusive Relais & Chateaux group of small hotels, this delightful establishment was constructed as a fortified tower in 1350. Adorned with gables, watchtowers and large bay windows, the house is surrounded by elegant gardens as well as a dining terrace overlooking a statue of Apollo. Also on the grounds is a wedding chapel: a favorite with couples who desire fairy-tale nuptials. Accommodations include 11 rooms and six suites, many with walk-in closets, tile or marble bath, hair dryer, robes. Elegant salons, extremely formal dining and the intimate setting all give a royal touch to this romantic mountain retreat.

Hotel Weisse Taube

[http://www.weissetaube.at/ e_einstieg.htm](http://www.weissetaube.at/e_einstieg.htm)

Inexpensive to Moderate

Kaigasse 9. In the pedestrian area, Old Town.

☎ *84-24-04.*

Credit Cards: *V, MC, DC, A.*

Run by the Hauber family since 1904, the "White Dove" is situated in a stone- trimmed building with massive interior ceiling beams, some which date back to the hotel's origins in 1365. Most of the 33 rooms have been renovated and have bath, TV. Friendly service and thoughtful touches, such as a nonsmoking breakfast room, make this medium-priced hotel a favorite among seasoned travelers.

Osterreichischs

Moderate

Schwartzstrasse 5-7. On Right Bank, at Schwartzstrasse and Elisabethkai. ☎ *(06) 62- 889-77, FAX 223-5652.*

Credit Cards: V, MC, DC, A.

Air conditioning in rooms, in-room minibars.

Built in 1866 on the Right Bank, this popular hotel has survived even the ravages of WWII. Renovated most recently in 1988, the OH, as it's often called, is decorated with Victorian antiques, wrought-iron detailing, lush potted plants and Oriental rugs. Big windows afford breathtaking vistas of the River Salzach. All 120 rooms have distinctive furnishings, but the riverfront rooms obviously are the best choice. There are six restaurants, ranging from formal to casual. Guests also can enjoy a hearty buffet in the historic and rustic wine cellar.

Villa Pace

Moderate to Expensive

Sonnleitenweg 9. "Nord" exit north of Salzburg to bottom of Gaisberg mountain, follow green signs.

☎ *(06) 62-641501.*

Credit Cards: V, MC, DC, A.

Secluded garden atmosphere, pool, sauna, balcony or patio, in-room safes, in-room minibars. Minutes from central Old Town, this luxurious alpine chalet was originally built more than 400 years ago and is now completely and carefully restored. There are 12 rooms and two suites; all have satellite TV, combination bath, hair dryer, robes, toiletries; many have baronial beds and other classic details. Evening dining is by candlelight, with a full wine list and exquisitely prepared Austrian dishes. The villa is where international society guests retreat to catch their breath, especially during the annual music festival.

Inns

Dr. Wuher's Haus Gastein ★★★

Inexpensive to Moderate

Ignaz-Rieder-Kai 25.

Public Transportation: *Bus 49.*

☎ *(06) 62-25-65.*

Credit Cards: *V, MC.*

Secluded garden atmosphere, balcony or patio, in-room minibars.

Off the beaten path on the bank of the Salzach River, this Teutonic-style villa (once a private home) features an authentic Salzburg atmosphere within relaxing surroundings. The flower garden is the perfect place for conversation and afternoon tea with Austrian pastries. The 13 rooms and three suites are spacious and decorated with furnishings crafted by local artisans. All have TV, radio; many have balcony. During festival time, the villa fills with musicians. It has an upper-class feel without the hustle-bustle of a resort hotel.

Budget Lodging

Pension Goldene Krone ★★

Inexpensive

Linzer Gasse 48. On Linzergasse near St. Sebastian's Church

Public Transportation: *Bus 1 or 2.* ☎ *(06) 62- 872-300.*

Credit Cards: *Not Accepted.*

This family-run guesthouse is somewhat spartan but is appreciated for its central location and good value. After a day of strolling through the nearby forested hill of Kapuzinerberg, the ivy-covered sun terrace is a wonderful place to relax with a cup of coffee. A light breakfast is included, but the pension offers fewer amenities than a hotel. The rooms in the front (more expensive) have charming street views.

Where to Eat

Austinerbrau

Inexpensive

Austinergasse 4. ☎ *(06) 62-43-12-46.*

Specialties: *German-style beer garden.*
Busy bar scene, outside dining.

A trip to Austria isn't complete without a stop at a traditional beer garden, such as this sprawling hall and gardens where patrons sit elbow-to-elbow to heft their steins of Mullner Kloster beer. Feast on picnic items you bring yourself (recommended by seasoned revelers), or purchase reasonably priced sausages, breads and other fare inside the hall. This is no place for quiet conversation, but rather an opportunity to make toasts and enjoy a frothy brew in a legendary setting.

Cafe Furst ★★★

Brodgasse 13. ☎ *(06) 62-84-37-59. Near Alter markt*

Specialties: *Coffee, Austrian pastries and sweets.*
Reservations not accepted.

Austrians love pastries and sweets, so specialty cafes such as this one offer a vast array of pastries, strudels, tortes, cakes, chocolates and other candies. Try the signature sweet of Salzburg—Mozartkugelin, or "Mozart Balls" (no joke). Another local specialty is the extravagant *Salzburger Nockerln*, a souffle of eggs, sugar and raspberry filling that is baked and served in three mounds, meant to represent the three hills of Salzburg. An apple strudel with a steaming cup of strong coffee is a great way to begin or end the day.

Goldener Hirsch

Expensive

Getreidegasse 37. ☎ *84-85-11.*

Specialties: *Game dishes (in season), such as venison, roast hare, also filet of lamb, smoked trout.*

Credit Cards: *V, MC, DC, A.*

Reservations required.

Authentic Austrian cuisine beautifully prepared and served is the hallmark of this renovated 15th-century inn adjoining the Hotel Goldener Hirsch. Respected by Salzburgers and visitors who care about fine food, the restaurant offers a wide range of traditional dishes in an elegant European setting. Expensive, but worthwhile for a true Salzburg experience.

Krimpelstatter

Inexpensive to Moderate

Mullner Hauptstrasse 31, ☎ *0622/43-22-74.*

Specialties: *Homemade sausages, game dishes.*

Closed: *Mon., Sun.*

Busy bar scene, outside dining, own baking, reservations recommended.

This is where Salzburgers go for good food—whether a quick snack with a stein of beer in the rose-trellised beer garden, or for a full dinner in one of three intimate dining rooms hidden at the top of a narrow flight of stone steps. The historic building has a long culinary history; since 1548 it has served as an inn, and the dining rooms are tucked under vaulted ceilings beamed with thick timbers. Embellished stone columns add to the ambience. Salzburg's regional dishes are the house specialties, including *Wiener schnitzel* and other sausage-based main courses.

Wilder Mann

Inexpensive

Getreidegasse 20/ Griesgasse 17. In the passageway near Griesgasse 17. ☎ *0622/84-17- 87.*

Specialties: *Wiener schnitzels, boiled beef, potato dishes.*

Busy bar scene, outside dining, cafestop, reservations recommended.

Off-the-beaten track, this local bistro has indoor dining as well as a bustling outside courtyard during the summer. Lavish portions, good prices and mugs of popular Steigl beer make this cafe a hit with "the wild man" (or woman) who wants to tame a hearty appetite. It's sometimes smoky and always crowded inside, but the rough timber beams, stag antlers and other woodsy touches give the place an earthy, honest feel. WORTH FINDING AND EASY ON THE WALLET.

Zum Eulenspiegel   ★★★★

http://restaurant-austria.net/ salzburg/eulenspiegel/

Moderate

Hagenauerplatz 2. Opposite Mozart Gerburtshaus. *84-31-80.*

Specialties: *Salmon, boiled beef, sausage and pork dishes, and Salzburger nockerln.*

Credit Cards: *V, MC, A.*

Closed: *Sun.*

Reservations required.

This narrow Old Town establishment, painted white and peach on the outside, is situated on the side of a quiet cobblestone square. Inside, intimate nooks and crannies for romantic dining can be found by following a winding staircase. With a sophisticated, ever-changing menu and an elegantly rustic setting overseen by owners Walter and Gabi Ritzberger-Wimmer, this restaurant combines city style with friendly service.

Zum Fidelen Affen   ★★★

Inexpensive

Priesterhausgasse 8. *East of the River Salzach, by the Staatsbrucke.*

Specialties: *Goulashes and dumplings, pastries.*

Closed: *Sun.*

Happening bar, reservations not accepted.

For great, inexpensive food and lots of atmosphere, the "Jolly

Monkey" is the place to go. Close by the river, the restaurant is
housed in one of Salzburg's oldest buildings (the structure once
served as the post office). Today the interior is decorated with painted, carved and sculpted monkeys—an interesting contrast to the
traditional dishes on the menu. Always crowded, the huge circular
bar caters to those who want a drink as well as diners who are waiting for tables. Once seated, choose from simple, inexpensive but
delicious regional favorites. The dumplings are flavored with meats,
cheeses and herbs, and casseroles feature seasonal mushrooms.

Zum Mohren

Inexpensive to Moderate

Judengasse 9/Rudolfskai 20. Near Mozartplatz. ☎ *84-23-87.*

Specialties: *Fish dishes, veal, game (in season).*

Closed: *Sun.*

Reservations recommended.

Hidden away in the basement of a 15th-century house that was once
a riverfront tavern, this restaurant is a favorite for locals, and worth
finding for the visitor. Although the intimate interior can be smoky,
the arched ceilings make you feel like you've stepped back in time.
The food is an excellent value, and the service is friendly. Dress is
casual, but city-neat.

s'Herzl

Inexpensive

Sigmundplatz 7, ☎ *8485-178-89.*

Specialties: *Game stews (in season), boiled beef, grilled sausages, sauerkraut.*

Credit Cards: *V, DC, A, A.*

Reservations recommended.

The food comes from the Goldener Hirsch kitchens, but the final
tab is easier on the wallet, making s'Herzl a hit with Salzburgers and
visitors alike. Servers in dirndls and loden cater to guests, offering a

wide selection of Austrian dishes. A more intimate, less formal setting than the Goldener Hirsch.

St. Gilbert

Timbale   ★★★

Moderate

Salzburger Strasse 2, ☎ *(06) 227-7587.*

Specialties: *Changing menu, also beef, fish, game (in season).*

Closed: *Thur.*

Reservations recommended.

For a break from the usual rustic restaurants you see so much in this region, try this tiny spot, where the specials generally aren't on the menu—you have to ask about them. Dress is fairly formal; expect to see locals.

> ITRAVELBOOK TIP: EVEN IF YOU FIND YOURSELF IN SALZBURG FOR JUST 24 HOURS, AVAIL YOURSELF OF A SALZBURG CARD, WHICH, FOR A SMALL SUM, WILL ALLOW YOU FREE ENTRY TO THE CITY'S PUBLIC TRANSIT SYSTEM, A VARIETY OF ATTRACTIONS, HISTORICAL SITES, AND MUCH MORE. FOR INFORMATION, CONTACT: HTTP://WWW.SALZBURGINFO.OR.AT/CARD/CARD_E.HTM

What to Do

Excursions

Krimml Falls   ★★★★★

Krimml Valley, Gerlospass Road near Krimml. In Hohe Tauren National Park near Gerlos Pass. ☎ *(06) 542-239.*

Situated in a vast national park, Krimml Falls are Europe's largest at 1300 ft. (396 m). Not quite as dramatic as Niagara Falls, but still spectacular, the falls are surrounded by the rugged Hohe Tauern Alps. The tiny town of Krimml can be reached by train or bus from Zell am See, or by car. The best time to see the falls is during the summer. The hike to the Lower Falls takes one hour each way. For the hardy, strenuous trails lead to other viewpoints. Bring a raincoat and protect your camera: the ever- present mist drenches visitors. Experienced hikers can scale the Krimmler Tauernhaus nearby, a tough, four-hour climb. Admission: Free.

The Sound of Music Tour

http://www.panoramatours.at/en/ city-country.htm

Salzburg Panorama Tours, Mirabellplatz, ☎ *(06) 62-87-40-29.*

Special Hours: *Tours depart at 9:30 a.m. and 2 p.m.*

Salzburg and environs were the location for the 1964 Julie Andrews classic *The Sound of Music,* and today you can see these sights yourself on guided bus tours. Panorama Tours offers daily excursions, with complementary hotel shuttle services. Along with stops in the Lake Region outside Salzburg, the tour pauses at Nonnberg Abbey (near the Festung) and the Aldstalt, where several scenes were filmed. See the opera house where the family sang in the final performance, and the church in Mondsee where the Hollywood version of the Von Trapp marriage was filmed (in reality, the couple wed at Nonnberg Abbey). Everything but the Nazis. Admission: expensive.

Historical Sites

Hohensalzburg Fortress

Monchsberg 34. Funicular from Festungsgasse, by car.

☎ *(06) 62-80-42-21-23.*

Metro Stop: *Festungsgasse.*

Special Hours: *Oct. through May open only until 6:00 p.m.*

Looming above the southern end of the Old Town, this is the largest completely preserved castle in all of central Europe. Work began on this princely stronghold in 1077 and continued until 1681, resulting in a mix of architectural styles. The castle affords sweeping views of the Alps as well as the copper-green domes and square towers of Salzburg. The Burg museum features medieval art, while the Ranier museum's exhibits of armor and weapons are especially popular with children. Admission: Inexpensive, or free with Salzburg Card (see information above).

Residenz

Residenzplatz 1. In pedestrian area near Domplatz.

☎ *(06) 62-80042-22-70*

Public Transportation: Bus 5 or 6.

Special Hours: *Oct.-Jan., 10-5 Thurs.-Tues., closed Feb.-Mar.*

When the Salzburg prince-archbishops moved from the Hohensalzburg Fortress, they ensconced themselves in this opulent palace in the heart of Salzburg. Dating from 1120, the palace was extensively modified from the late 1500s to about 1782. Today the second floor houses a 15-room art gallery. Music lovers will like to know that young Mozart often played in the Conference Room. More than 12 rooms decorated in rich Old-World style are open to the public. Across from the Residenz is the Glockenspiel at Mozart-platz, with 35 bells that play classical tunes three times a day. Admission: *nominal fee, or Free with Salzburg Card.*

Salzburg Cathedral

South side of Residenzplatz, ☎ *(06) 22-84-52- 95.*

Public Transportation: Bus 1.

Special Hours: *Closed mid-Oct. through Easter.*

Salzburg is a city filled with churches, and the finest is the grand cathedral at Domplatz. The original cathedral's foundations date to A.D. 744, and visitors can tour (fee required) the excavations. A Romanesque cathedral was built between 1181 to 1200, but it was destroyed by fire in 1598. The structure that greets visitors today was begun in 1598 and was consecrated in 1628. Damaged in WWII, the cathedral has been rebuilt. Today its twin symmetrical towers and magnificent bronze doors make it a Salzburg landmark. Inside, visitors can view the world-famous 4000-pipe organ and the Romanesque font where Mozart was baptized. Each year during the music festival, the allegorical morality play *Everyman* is performed near the cathedral in the Domplatz. Admission: nominal.

Music

Mozart Gerburtshaus

Getreidegasse 9. ☞ *West of Town Hall.* ☎ *84- 43-13.*

Special Hours: *Sept. through June, 9 a.m. to 6 p.m.*

For music lovers, no trip to Salzburg is complete without paying homage to Wolfgang Amadeus Mozart, and the best place to begin is at Mozart's birthplace, now converted to a small museum. Mozart was born on the third floor of this typical burgher's house on January 27, 1756. Today the museum displays Mozart's small violin and his fortepiano spinet. Walking along the narrow street, the visitor can sense what it was like for the young Mozart, who composed his early works here. Admission: nominal. Free with Salzburg Card.

Parks and Gardens

Mirabell Gardens ★★★★★

Off Makartplatz.

Laid out partly by Fischer von Erlach in 1606 for the mistress of Wolf Dietrich, the public gardens today are a photographer's dream. Flower beds, hedges and reflecting pools cover several acres, but the gardens are most famous for the statuary, urns and marble balustrades that are set against the greenery. From the gardens is a splendid view of the Hohensalzburg Fortress, but don't miss the bastion devoted to baroque marble statues of dwarfs and other figures. Also take time to find the Pegasus Fountain near Schloss Mirabell, the palace situated on the northwest side of the gardens. The palace now houses the City Hall, but inside is the Angel Staircase, embellished with drowsy cupids and baroque details. Both the gardens and palace are free, but wear comfortable walking shoes and bring plenty of film. Admission: nominal, free with Salzburg Card.

Shopping

In Salzburg you'll find traditional Austrian clothing such as lederhosen, loden and dirndls. Also worth looking at is the selection of jewelry, crystal and glassware; wood crafts; dolls in handmade outfits; Christmas ornaments and decorations, and confections such as Mozart Kugeln. An extensive range of sportsgear also is offered. Salzburg carries good selections of Alt Wien and Augarten porcelain as well.

Shops are located along the Getreidgasse, Judengasse, and in Residenzplatz. Across the river (and less packed with tourists), try the stores at Linzer Gasse, especially for clothing and other staples. Steingasse's old town houses contain jewelry and antique shops, which are perfect for browsing.

Hellbrunn

Schloss Hellbrunn

Morgerstrasse. Five miles south of Salzburg. ☎ *(06) 62-820-372.*

Public Transportation: *Bus 55.*

Special Hours: *Oct. through Nov. open to 4:30 p.m.*

Schloss Hellbrunn is worth half a day, especially for families. Built as a hunting lodge and summer residence for Prince-Archbishop Markus Sittikus, the 17th-century lemon-yellow palace features trompe-l'oeil paintings and a domed octagonal music room. The palace also houses a folk museum. The gardens are a special treat, with statuary and "trick" fountains designed to squirt visitors when they least expect it—a sure hit with kids. Also on the grounds is a gorge that has served as a natural outdoor theater since 1617. The Zoo (separate admission) is situated on the estate's deer park and features exhibits of alpine animals in large, natural habitats. Admission: *moderate, free with Salzburg Card*

St. Gilgen

South of Salzburg, on the shore of Lake Wolfgang, this beach resort offers myriad opportunities for outdoor recreation. St. Gilgen is especially popular with Austrian and German tourists, who flood home during the summer to swim, boat, windsurf, sunbathe, hike and stroll. During the Salzburg Music Festival (from late July to the end of August), the town fills up with "overflow" guests. For lake views, the Parkhotel Billroth can't be beat. Nearby Mount Zwolferhorn provides panoramic vistas, and, in winter, skiers use the four lifts to reach its slopes.

Where to Stay

Hotels and Resorts

Parkhotel Billroth

Medium

Billrothstrasse-2. One mile from town. ☎ *(06) 227-217.*

Credit Cards: *Not Accepted.*

Beach location, tennis, skiing, water sports, balcony or patio.

This medium-priced resort hotel offers lakeside views and a private beach. The original structure of the chalet-style hotel was built in the 1890s, but many additions were made in the 1960s. There are 44 comfortable, modern rooms, with bath. Guests can sunbathe on the hotel's floating "raft" or stroll along the shore. Ski lifts are nearby. Closed Oct. 10 to May 1.

Inns

Zur Post

Inexpensive to Medium

Mozartplatz 8. In center of town.

☎ *(06) 227-239.*

Credit Cards: *MC, A.*

Skiing, water sports, sauna.

Dating back to 1415, this small, attractive hotel features a solarium. There are 15 simply furnished, comfortable rooms, most with private bath. The hotel's restaurant serves up regional favorites such as hearty soups and boiled beef. Closed from early Nov. through early Dec.

Where to Eat

Cafe Nannerl ★★★★

Inexpensive

Kirchenplatz-2. *Upstairs, second floor.* ☎ *(06) 227-368.*

Home-baked cakes and coffee are served in an intimate, homey set-ting in this Viennese-style cafe tucked away on the second story of an old house. Relax in the living room, which is decorated with upholstered sofas and antique armchairs. Newspapers and conversation make this a place to discover the local heartbeat.

What to Do

Sports & Recreation

Lake Wolfgang ★★★★

☎ *(06) 227-348.*

The Wolfgangsee is a summer playground for German and Austrian tourists who gather here to swim, boat, windsurf, sunbathe, hike and stroll. From St. Gilgen, you can rent boating equipment, or take a ferry ride. With myriad opportunities for physical recreation, St. Gilgen serves as a base for those attending the Salzburg Music Festival. Nearby Mount Zwolferhorn provides panoramic views, and in winter, skiers use the four lifts to reach its slopes.

Lower Austria

Baden< bei Wien

The thermal springs here were frequented by ancient Romans, but Baden reached its height in the 18th century when members of the Hapsburg court flocked to its sulfur-laced waters. Today both Austrians and visitors relax in the town's posh hotels or bathe in the public pools. Near the Vienna Woods, Baden also boasts a casino and several small museums.

Where to Stay

Hotels and Resorts

Grand Hotel Sauerhof

http://www.sauerhof.at/english/ index.html

Expensive

Weilburgstrasse 11-13. Located 15 miles southwest of Vienna; by car take Autobahn A-2 south to Junction 305, go west to Bad.

Metro Stop: *Josefplatz.*

☎ *(02) 252-41251.*

Credit Cards: *V, MC, DC, A.*

Pool, golf, tennis, in-room minibars, fitness center, country location.

If price is no object, try this historic hotel that dates back to 1583, where Beethoven once stayed (hence the Beethoven Suite, which can be had for $1000 a night.). Although the estate gained its fame when sulfur springs were discovered here in 1757, the three-story neoclassical building, with its steeply sloped slate roofs, served as a sanatorium during both world wars. In 1978, renovations were complete and the hotel opened with 81 rooms and seven suites. All have bath (some without tub), hair dryer, robes, toiletries, satellite TV; some are for nonsmokers. Spend time in the spa's sulfur baths, or stroll the green lawns before tea. After a game of tennis, relax in the covered courtyard, which has a Roman-style vaulted ceiling. Russian icons and medieval halberds decorate the walls of the hotel's farm-style restaurant. Also worth seeing is the historic wine cellar.

Hotel Gutenbrunn

Medium

Pelzgasse 22. Located 15 miles south of Vienna; by car take Autobahn A-2 to Junction 305, turn west, near town square

☎ *(02) 252-43171.*

Credit Cards: *DC, A.*

Gutenbrunn appropriately means "healthful waters," as this historic building sits next to the public spa that taps the sulfur springs. With its original foundations dating back to 1480, the hotel was known throughout the Austrian Empire by 1890. Today the pink-and-white structure with its slate roof also sports a Baroque steeple and a hexagonal tower. Inside, skylights brighten the lobby area, while an interior passageway connects the building to the town spa. Accommodations include 78 rooms and two suites, all well appointed, with bath, TV. The hotel also has private gardens, indoor and outdoor pools, plus other modern features.

Where to Eat

Badner Stuberl ★★★

Inexpensive to Medium

Guttenbrunnstrasse 19. In the older section of Baden.

☎ *(02) 252-41232.*

Specialties: *Stroganoff, pork and beef steak dishes.*

Closed: *Tues.*

Reservations recommended.

After a day of exploring the nearby Vienna Woods, expect to see locals and in-the- know Viennese at this coffeehouse and restaurant. Feast on stroganoff, or enjoy a lighter dish of green salad and grilled chicken.

What to Do

Kurmittelhaus ★★★

Brustattipl 4. *In Baden, near Gruner Markt.* ☎ *(02) 24-41251.*

This curative spa complex is also surrounded by other thermal complexes worth exploring. At the indoor pool, visitors can treat themselves to underwater massage therapy, sulfur mud baths and massages at prices far less than would be found at Baden's hotel spas. Nearby are free outdoor hot and cold pools, and a large pool (fee required) fronted by an artificial beach. Viennese come here for the day to "take the waters." Admission: moderate.

Vienna

The heart and soul of Austria lies here, in this sprawling metropolis that covers 160 square miles. Filled with palaces, churches, theaters, museums, shops and parks, Vienna has a long history dating back to around A.D. 100, when it was founded as a Roman military encampment. It was once one of the major capitals of Europe and the base for the Hapsburg rulers of the Austro-Hungarian Empire. The 1814 Congress of Vienna redesigned the map of Europe, and today Vienna continues to create itself daily, with an endless repertoire of cultural events. A multifaceted, multicultural city, Vienna offers something for every taste. For the most up- to-date information on this magnificent city, go to **http://www.vienna.at/pubs/ redaktion/New-English/**.

Where to Stay

Hotel Am Parkring ★★★

http://www.schick-hotels.com/Park/ parke.htm

Medium

Parkring 12,. On the 11th through 13th floors of an office building near Stadparkt.

☎ *(01) 51-48-00.*

Credit Cards: *V, MC, DC, A.*

Air conditioning in rooms, in-room minibars.

OK, we admit it: a hotel in an office building is a little odd. But it works here. The building isn't historic (circa 1960), but the hotel's upper floors afford rewarding city views. Situated near the Stadparkt gardens, the hotel is popular with both business and pleasure travelers. Semiprivate elevators carry guests to the hotel's floors, so they needn't fear getting caught in a rush of office workers. The 56 rooms and seven suites have comfortable furnishings, fabulous views, combination bath, hair dryer, toiletries, satellite TV.

Hotel Ambassador ★★★★★

http://www.abnet.at/hotel/vienna/ ambassad/

Expensive

Karntnerstrasse 22. At Karntnerstrasse near Johannesgasse.

☎ *(01) 514-66.*

Credit Cards: *V, MC, DC, A.*

Air conditioning in rooms, in-room minibars.

Mark Twain and Theodore Roosevelt once stayed here, and even today it isn't unheard of for the management to roll out a real red carpet as a welcome for a royal guest. All the romance of Old Vienna comes to life at this venerable establishment. Located right on the square facing the Donner Fountain, the hotel enjoys a prime position between the State Opera and St. Stephen's Cathedral. Inside, the plush turn-of-the-century decor vibrates with red, from the silk wall coverings to the upholstered furnishings to the bedspreads in the rooms. There are 106 rooms and one suite, all with period furnishings, tile or marble bath, hair dryer, toiletries; satellite TV furnished on request; the quieter rooms face Neuer Markt. Lehar restaurant serves Austrian and international cuisine; stunning bar. Renovated in 1990, the hotel is one of the most sumptuous in Vienna.

Hotel Bristol

http://www.abnet.at/hotel/vienna/ bristol/

Expensive to Very Expensive

Karntner Ring 1. Next to the State Opera.

☎ *(01) 515-16, FAX 223/5652.*

Credit Cards: *V, MC, DC, A.*

Air conditioning in rooms, sauna, balcony or patio, in-room minibars.

Now owned by the Westin conglomerate, the hotel served as the U.S. military headquarters during the 1944-'45 Occupation. Today the interior is fitted with modern luxuries, such as huge fireplaces made of carved black marble and black-tiled bathrooms. The furnishings are exquisite, with Biedermeier antiques, statues and paintings. There are 137 rooms and nine suites, some with open fireplace, private sauna, separate living-room area, balcony with view of the

Ringstrasse; all are lavishly decorated, with bath, TV.

Hotel Im Palais

Schwarzenberg

http://www.palais-schwarzenberg.com/

Expensive to Very Expensive

Schwarzenbergplatz 9. On the southeast side, outside the Kartner Ring near Rennweg.

☎ *(01) 798-45-15.*

Credit Cards: *V, MC, DC, A.*

Away from the city bustle in the middle of classically landscaped gardens, this 300-year old palace serves as the address for guests who cherish their comfort. The palace was gutted by Nazi troops during World War II, but today it is restored to splendor, with striated marble and glittering chandeliers, and gilt touches everywhere. The 38 rooms and four suites are filled with art and precious antiques; all have TV, VCR, marble or tile bath, hair dryer, robes. Miles of private paths; lawns for croquet.

Hotel Imperial

Very Expensive

Karntner Ring 16. Two blocks from State Opera, central Vienna.

☎ *(01) 50-110-0, FAX 221-2340.*

Credit Cards: *V, MC, DC, A.*

Air conditioning in rooms, in-room minibars.

Undeniably, the Imperial reigns as the grandest hotel in Vienna, with its carved pediment reliefs on the outer facade and its lavish salons, palatial royal suites and famous dining areas. Built in 1869, this Viennese landmark was originally the private residence of the Duke of Wuttemberg. Restored to its glory after a forced servitude as the Nazi headquarters during WWII, the hotel now attracts heads of state and headline musicians who come to perform at the nearby

Staatsoper (Opera House). Inside, the lobby is bordered on the right with a formal marble staircase, leading to public salons ornamented with statuary, royal portraits, chandeliers and rainbow hues of polished marble. The 128 rooms and 32 suites are richly decorated and have large marble bath, hair dryer, robes, satellite TV with English-language programming. Sophisticated Viennese and visitors alike linger at the Imperial Cafe, featuring live music.

Hotel Konig Von Ungarn

Medium

Schulerstrasse 10. Northeast of Stephansplatz.

☎ *(01) 515-84-0.*

Credit Cards: *V, MC, DC, A.*

Designated as the oldest continuously operated hotel in Vienna, this grand dame was built in the 16th century, when it played host to Hungarian nobility. Mozart is said to have stayed here in 1791, living for a while in an upstairs apartment, which today is a Mozart museum. Completely renovated, the hotel preserves its historic air while offering all the modern conveniences. The solarium is designed with a glass-roofed atrium and has a full-grown live tree as its centerpiece. Antiques and more green plants fill the public areas. The 32 pine-paneled rooms have rustic furnishings, radio, TV, small tiled bath, hair dryer. Book in advance and ask for written confirmation.

Hotel Sacher

http://wien.sacher.com/index_en.asp

Expensive

Philharmonikerstrasse 4. Near the State Opera House off Karntner Strasse.

☎ *(01) 514-56.*

Credit Cards: *V, MC, DC, A.*

Air conditioning in rooms, in-room mini-bars.

Famous as a "location" for films and novels (not to mention the birthplace of Sachertorte), this is the hotel where the Emperor Franz Josef frequently stayed during the height of the Austrian Empire. Built in 1876, the structure has neoclassical details in the front that befit its royal heritage, and, in an international tribute, the flags of seven nations fly from the front of its second story. Inside, brocade curtains, red velvet, glittering chandeliers and antique furniture all testify to the glory of Old Vienna. If need be, the hotel concierge can even obtain tickets to "sold-out" events.

Budget Lodging

Hotel Austria

Inexpensive

Am Fleischmarkt 20. In the cul-de-sac lane at Fleischmarkt 20.

Public Transportation: *Tram 1 or 2.*

☎ *(01) 515-568.*

Credit Cards: *V, MC, DC, A.*

Air conditioning in rooms, in-room mini- bars.

Save your Euros for a night at the opera by staying at this comfortable, family-run hotel tucked away on a quiet street. Close to all the sights, this hotel offers triples, and some rooms without baths. The breakfast room is fitted with chandeliers and the bedrooms are homey, with pine paneled walls and Oriental carpets. If you have any questions, the staff will gladly assist you in personalizing your Viennese itinerary.

Pension Zipser

Inexpensive

Lange Gasse 49. Five minutes walk from the Rathaus.

Public Transportation: *Bus 13A, Streetcar J.*

☎ *(01) 404-54-0.*

Credit Cards: *V, MC, DC, A.*

Located near jazz clubs, small cafes and shops for diversion, this pension has modern rooms and family-run management. Outside, the facade sports a repeating seashell motif, and inside all bedrooms contain large private baths. Some rooms have balconies overlooking a tree-filled residential neighborhood. The friendly staff will help you get the most out of your stay.

Where to Eat

> **ITRAVELBOOK TIP:** VIENNA IS PACKED WITH RESTAURANTS THAT SERVE MEAT, NOODLES, MEAT, NOODLES, MORE MEAT, AND STRUDEL. VEGETARIANS NEED NOT WORRY: NEARLY EVERY RESTAURANT OFFERS A GOOD VARIETY OF VEGETARIAN DISHES. EVEN IF YOU DON'T SEE THEM ON THE MENU, BE SURE TO ASK YOUR WAITER. GENERALLY, THEY'LL BE MORE THAN HAPPY TO OBLIGE.

Cafe Demel   ★★★★★

Medium

Kohlmarkt 14. Between Michaelerplatz and Graben.

☎ *(02) 22-533-55-16.*

Specialties: *Demel-Coffee, cakes, tortes, tea sandwiches.*

Cafestop, own baking, reservations not accepted.

Evoking the glory of Imperial Vienna, this cafe has displays of sugar-spun figures in the windows and, inside, rococo mirrors and chandeliers with milk-glass globes. Guests are ushered formally to one of the small round marble-top tables by servers who address their female patrons as *gnadige Frau*, or "gracious lady." Imagine you are a member of the Emperor's court as you sip a Demel Coffee and enjoy exquisite tea sandwiches or an artfully prepared Maximilian Torte.

Cuadro   ★★★★★

Moderate

5, Margaretenstraaße, ☎ *(77) 5447550*

Credit Cards: *V*

Closed: *Sat., Sun.*

Futuristic and retro, all at the same time (if that's possible), this new diner features a menu packed with delicious sandwiches, burgers, even the ubiquitous strudel, and they all have one thing in common: they're all square. Try the curry burger for a change. Even vegetarians will have something to entice them at this new hot spot.

Im KunstHaus ★★★

Inexpensive

3 Wiessgerberlande, *(02) 7185152*

Credit Cards: *V, MC, A, DC*

Reasonably new to the Viennese restaurant scene, this oddly decorated eatery is part of the Kunsthaus Gallery, which houses a permanent exhibition on Austrian modernist, Friendensreich Hundertwasser. Bedecked with flowers, the restaurant operates independently of the gallery (so you can eat without seeing the exhibit). The menu is heavy on seasonal soups and salads, and dining al fresco in the summertime is a must.

Korso bei Der Oper ★★★★★

Medium to Expensive

Mahlerstrasse 2, ☎ *(02) 22-515-16-546.*

Specialties: *Veal, boiled beef, seafood, game.*

Credit Cards: *V, MC, A.*

Closed: *Sat.*

Reservations required.

In the heart of the extremely elegant Bristol Hotel, this restaurant has its own entrance facing the State Opera, making it a magnet for opera stars and celebrities. The dining room has a baronial fireplace, Baroque columns, dark paneled walls and, of course, glittering chandeliers. The cuisine is presented with style, and guests can enjoy caviar or fresh oyster appetizers before the main courses. Entrees may be accompanied by freshly made, flavored noodles and delicate sauces. For those who relish superb cuisine, a night here is highlight of any Vienna visit.

Motto

Moderate

5, *Schönbrunner Straße 30 (entrance Rüdigergasse)*

Credit Cards: *Not accepted*

Larger than life, over-the-top, outrageous, campy-to-die for, Motto has been serving members of Vienna's thriving gay community for years. Heteros have finally caught on, and are enjoying the great eats including the restaurant's famed flambe dishes. Vegetarians won't be left out in the cold. The place closes at 4 am, so if you fancy steak in cream sauce with truffles in the middle of the night (or a great cocktail), this would be the place to go.

Rotisserie Sirk

Moderate

Karntnerstrasse 53. Near the State Opera. Located at Hotel Bristol.
☎ *(02) 22-515-16- 552.*

Specialties: *Three-course dinners, including duck, meat platters, game.*

Cafestop.

With a reputation for delicious food at prices that don't empty your pockets, especially considering its glitzy address, this restaurant features a fixed-price three- course "opera supper." A triple-filet sampler of beef, pork and veal, or venison medallions will set the stage for a memorable evening. After the opera, head to the lower level, where pastries are served in an Art Nouveau cafe bedecked with beveled glass. At noon, businesspeople fill the upstairs tables to enjoy the view of the State Opera.

Steirereck

Expensive

Rasumofskygasse 2. *Near Danube Canal between Central Station and the Prater.* ☎ *(02) 22-713-31-68.*

Specialties: *Game dishes, "new Austrian" cuisine.*

Credit Cards: *V, A.*

Closed: *Sat., Sun.*

Reservations required.

The name translates as "corner of Styria," and this restaurant recreates the romance of the region by incorporating beams and archways from a Styrian castle into its decor. Classically prepared Viennese dishes and innovative Styrian cuisine are the trademark of this pricey but acclaimed establishment. Rack of wild boar, pike, filet of beef or saddle of lamb may be on the ever-changing fixed-price menu. The wine cellar boasts 35,000 bottles.

Trzesniewki ★★★★

Inexpensive

Dorotheergasse 1. Three blocks down the Graben from the Stephansdom.

Specialties: *Tea sandwiches and spreads.*

Cafestop, reservations not accepted.

For about 80 years, this venerable mainly stand-up restaurant has served a variety of petite open-faced sandwiches. Nosh on sandwiches that Franz Kafka (who used to live next door) might have enjoyed when taking a break. Eighteen varieties of spreads, including vegetarian choices, make these tasty treats perfect for energizing snacks. Counters plus a few cramped tables.

Zu den Drei Husaren ★★★★★

Moderate to Expensive

Weihburggasse 4. Near Stephenplatz. ☎ *(02) 22-512-10-92.*

Specialties: *Appetizers, roast beef, game, desserts.*

Credit Cards: *V, MC, DC, A.*

Reservations required.

Residents, business leaders, socialites and visitors come here to savor the history, atmosphere and most especially the cuisine. The chefs prepare more than 35 tempting appetizers, showcased to guests on rolling carts. But be aware that these tidbits are charged by the piece, sampling them will send your billing soaring. Carefully prepared entrees include guinea fowl, fish and lobster, plus veal and boiled beef. Near the front, a display includes life-size replicas of the three Hungarian officers who founded the restaurant just after WWI. The dining room is decorated with tapestries and antiques; there's live piano music during the evening hours.

What to Do

ITRAVELBOOK TIP: Be sure to visit http://www.vienna.at/pubs/redaktion/New-English/ for the most up-to-date information on all happenings Viennese.

Historical Sites

Dompfarre St. Stephan   ★★★★★

Stephansplatz 1, ☎ *(02) 22-515-52.*

Metro Stop: *U-Bahn Stephansplatz.*

Special Hours: *Tours 11:00 a.m.–7:00 p.m.*

Built on the site of a Romanesque sanctuary, this cathedral is the most enduring Viennese landmark. With its 450-foot steeple rising toward the heavens, St. Stephen's stands as the greatest Gothic structure in Europe. Historically, the cathedral is famous as the site of Mozart's "pauper's funeral" in 1791 and as the place where Napoleon posted his farewell edict in 1805. Designed with a roof that is exactly twice the height of its walls, the structure is rich in symbolic measurements and veiled meanings. The south tower, called "Old Steve," contains 344-steps, while the north tower has an elevator. Views from the towers extend across Vienna. For various fees, visitors can tour the catacombs, the north and south towers or the cathedral itself. Admission: moderate.

Hofburg Palace

Michaelerplatz 1. Head up Kohlmarkt to Michaelerplatz 1.

☎ *(02) 22-587-55-54.*

Special Hours: *Hours and cost at attractions vary.*

The winter palace of the Hapsburgs, this self-contained complex of palaces, apartments, stables and churches reflects 700 years of Austrian imperial history. The first structures were built in 1279, with the final additions erected when the Hapsburg Empire finally crumbled at the dawn of the 20th century. Architecturally eclectic, due to changing tastes and the desire of each monarch to leave an individual mark, the Hofburg is Vienna's premier attraction. Housing the Imperial Apartments, two Imperial treasuries, the National Library and the Winter Riding School, the entire Hofburg complex demands a full day for exploration. Highlights of the complex are treated in individual descriptions.

Schonbrunn Palace

Schonbrunner Schlosstrasse, ☎ *(02) 22-81- 113.*

Public Transportation: *Green Line. Metro Stop: U-Bahn: Schonbrunn.*

Special Hours: *Wagenburg, Apr.-Oct. Tues.- Sun. 10 a.m.–6 p.m.*

Vienna's answer to Versailles, the Schonbrunn Palace was originally constructed in 1696 but extensively modified a century later. Designed by the masters of the baroque, the Von Erlachs, the 1441-room palace was the summer residence of the Hapsburgs. During the reign of Empress Maria Theresa, the buildings were finished, complete with rococo detailing. During the 40-year reign of the Empress, Schonbrunn was the site of lavish balls and huge banquets. The palace came to its greatest glory during the Congress of Vienna. Schonbrunn has come to represent Austria as much as the Hofburg or St. Stephan's Cathedral. Franz Josef was born here, and six-year-old Mozart performed in the Hall of Mirrors. Today you can stroll through the gardens and visit the **State Apartments**, which are furnished with antiques and ornamented with 23 1/2-karat gold. In the same complex, visit the Schlosstheater, where performances are still given. Admission: nominal.

Museums and Exhibits

Kaiserappartements

Hofburg, Schweizerhof, ☎ *(02) 22-587-55-54.*

Metro Stop: *U-Bahn: Michaelerplatz.*

Special Hours: *Sunday open only to 1:00 p.m.*

Discover how the Hapsburgs truly lived by exploring the opulent Imperial Apartments. Occupying parts of the Chancellery Wing and the Amalientrakt, these lavish rooms are filled with tapestries and luxurious furniture. The extravagance is especially evident in the dining room, where the empty chairs face a formal table laid out for 20 guests of the court. Emperor Franz Josef and his wife, Elizabeth of Bavaria, spent much time here. Elizabeth, perhaps ahead of her time, kept a wooden gymnasium in her quarters. Although only German-language guided tours are offered, English-speaking independent tour guides are usually stationed around the entrance. Admission: moderate.

ZOOM Kindermuseum

http://www.kindermusem.at

MuseumsQuartier Museumsplatz ☎ *(02) 524- 79-08*

Public Transportation: *U3/Volkstheater or U2/ Museumsquartier*

Austria's only children's musem, ZOOM Kindermuseum is an absolute must for anyone traveling to Vienna with small children. The ZOOM Kindermuseum's goal is to engage the senses in a fun and educational manner. The staff, all of whom speak English, are ready to help you plan your visit to the museum. Pre-schoolers will enjoy ZOOM Ocean, in which they will move among sea creatures such as sea anemones; older children can paint, sculpt, build, and play to their heart's content. An exciting, barrier-breaking establishment that every adult should visit (with our without the kids). The website is spectacular. Admission: moderate.

Schatzkammer

Hofburg, Schweizerhof, ☎ *(02) 22-533-79-31.*

Metro Stop: *U-Bahn: Michaelerplatz.*

Special Hours: *Closed Tues.*

At the top of a staircase from the Swiss Court lies the Imperial Treasury, the repository for the priceless treasures belonging to the Hapsburgs. Divided into "Profane" and "Sacerdotal" collections, the Treasury contains 1000 years of crowns, scepters, jewels, robes, oil paintings and other riches. Outstanding exhibits include the huge imperial crown, dating from 962. Encrusted with diamonds, emeralds, sapphires and rubies, this crown was taken to Nuremburg by Hitler, but returned to its rightful home after the war. Another highlight is the Holy Lance, believed in medieval times to have pierced Christ on the cross. According to legend, whoever held the Holy Lance would be invincible. Admission: moderate.

Sigmund Freud Museum

http://freud.t0.or.at/freud/index- e.htm

Berggasse 19. Near the Votivkirche. ☎ *(02) 22- 319-15-96.*

Public Transportation: *Tram D. Metro Stop: U- Bahn: Schotentor.*

Founder of psychoanalysis and the theory of the unconscious, Freud changed the way we think of the human psyche. This was the doctor's residence and office from 1891 to 1938. Among the antiques, on display are some of Freud's belongings, including his velour hat, ivory-handled walking stick and other mementoes. Attached is a small gift shop where you can buy postcards or a volume of Freud's writings, something deep to read at your next cafe stop. Admission: nominal.

Uhrenmuseum de Stat Wien

Schulhof 2. ☞ *Near Judenplatz.* ☎ *(02) 22- 533-22-65.*

Special Hours: *Closed Mon.*

Throughout the day, but especially at noon, this museum explodes into a cacophony as 3000 clocks and timepieces chime, peal, boom, warble, chirp and cuckoo all at once. Housing an outstanding collection, ranging from primitive 15th-century timepieces to modern electronic ones, this museum sets time in perspective. See an exhibit of the wheel works of St. Stephen's Cathedral, an array of cuckoo clocks, and an 18th-century astronomical clock by Rutschmann. Admission: nominal.

Parks and Gardens

The Prater   ★★★★

Hauptallee. Reached from the Ring by U- Bahn, Tram 1, or by car. *(02) 22-512-83-14.*

Metro Stop: *U-Bahn: Praterstern.*

Special Hours: *Mar., Oct. 10:00 a.m.-10:00 p.m., closed Nov.-Feb.*

Emperor Joseph II opened this park in the northeast portion of Vienna in 1766. Located between the Danube River and the Danube Canal, this one-time hunting preserve has become an entertainment center. Historically, the Prater is considered the home of the waltz, but today the carnival amusements, including the Riesenrad, the giant Ferris wheel, and other rides, draw Viennese and visitors alike. A 2.6-mile Lilliputian railroad is another favorite diversion, especially for children, and more than 150 booths offer drinks, food and souvenirs. For adults, there is gambling, a sports center, plus riding schools and race courses. Sunday afternoon, the Prater is packed, so savvy visitors plan a weekday excursion. BE WARNED THAT, AFTER DARK, THE PRATER TAKES ON A DANGEROUS EDGE. Entrance is free, but rides and attractions charge individual fees.

Wienerwald   ★★★★★

From Vienna, by car or bus 43, Tram D, J. *(02) 22-211-14-54.*

Public Transportation: *Tram 1 to Bus 38A.*

Made famous by Strauss, the Vienna Woods lay just beyond Vienna, providing refreshing vistas and quaint *heurigen* (wine taverns). By car, you can travel a round-trip of about 50 miles in less than four hours. Public transportation (strongly recommended if you plan to sample wines in the Grinzing *heurigens*) is also available and easy to use. At Grinzing, you can rent a bicycle and pedal on gentle paths through the leafy woods. While at the Wienerwald, take the bus or climb up on foot to the summit of Kahlenberg, a hill on the northeastern spur of the Alps. From the terrace of the church on the summit, you can look all the way into Hungary.

Shopping

Shopping Hours

Weekday shopping hours are generally from 8 or 9 a.m. to 6 or 6:30 p.m. (or sometimes 8 p.m. on Thurs.); usually no noon closing in midtown; shuttered Sat. at noon or 1 p.m.; shopping until 5 p.m. every first Sat. of each month. Other cities have same openings; closing hours vary.

Best Areas

The pedestrian areas around the **Kartner Strasse**, **Graben** and **Kohlmarkt** are filled with chic shops and stores. Expect high prices but also quality and selection. There are numerous shops on the side streets as well, and many small boutiques offer goods in the Sonnhof passage between Landstrasser Haupstrasse and Ungargasse.

Vienna abounds in specialty shops featuring petit-point, wrought-iron or leather items; Wiener Augarten porcelain; gold and silver jewelry and placeware; handmade dolls; various ceramics; crystal, and glass.

The Dorotheum, held at *Dorotheergasse 17*, is a state-sponsored auction that dates back to 1707. Set up by Emperor Josef I, the auction now handles furs, furniture and antiques. Auctions are generally held daily, and information on bidding procedures is available in English. In addition, the Dorotheum area is home to several fine antique shops. Other antique shops are in the Josefstadt area, where prices are generally a bit lower.

Naschmarkt (between Linke and Rechte, beginning at Getreidemarkt) is a sprawling complex of food and produce markets. The stalls are worth a visit if only to soak up the local color, especially on Saturdays when the farmers bring their produce into town.

Also every Saturday, except holidays, the **Flohmarkt** sets up its stalls from 7:30 a.m. to 4:30 p.m. at the back of Naschmarkt. This famous flea market is a browser's paradise of real antiques and genuine junk. Expect to haggle over prices.

Another outdoor shopping area is the **Art and Antiques Market**, held Saturday and Sunday along the Danube Canal, from the Schwedenbrucke past the Salztorbrucke. The selection here is generally better than what you'll find at Flohlmarkt, and you can bargain for the best price.

Theater

Staatsoper

Opernring 2, ☎ *(02) 22-51444-26-55.* Metro Stop: *U-Bahn; Karlsplatz.*

The legendary State Opera stands as one of the three most important opera houses in the world. If you don't have tickets for a production, you can still see inside. Tour times are posted daily. The grand staircase, sparkling chandeliers, three stages (including a rotating stage) and tiers of box seats will impress even the most jaded traveler. The building was constructed in the French Renaissance style and has arcades and carved columns. The front facade was all that remained of the original structure (built in the 1860s) after the devastation of World War II. But State Opera was such an important symbol to the people that Austria began to restore it, in the original style, as soon as the war was over. Today the Vienna Philharmonic Orchestra occupies the pit and leading stars headline performances. Daily performances are given from the first of Sept. to the end of June. Ticket prices range from $10 to $200, not counting surcharges and gratuities for those who use ticket brokers. Admission: nominal to very expensive.

Styria
Graz

Straddling the River Mur in southeastern Austria, this city is the provincial capital of Styria. With the brooding Schlossberg, garden parks, a university and many museums, Graz has cosmopolitan appeal, yet it is relatively unknown to many non-Austrian tourists. Nearby are the stud farm where Lippizaner horses are bred and trained, an open-air museum that will take you back in time, and opportunities for hunting and trout fishing.

Where to Stay

Hotels and Resorts

Grand Hotel Wiesler Graz

http://www.abnet.at/hotel/styria/ gwiesler/

Medium to Expensive

Grieskai4-8. On left bank of River Mur, southwest quarter.

☎ *(03) 16-90660.*

Credit Cards: *V, MC, DC, A.*

Sauna, in-room safes, in-room minibars.

Situated on the River Mur, this recently renovated establishment dates back to 1603. With neoclassical architecture and an expansive marble-floored lobby, it takes pride in gracious hospitality. There are 78 rooms and 20 suites, with double-glazed windows, cable TV, marble combination bath, robes, hair dryer, toiletries; many offer tantalizing views of the Schlossberg and medieval buildings that surround the mountain. The restaurant is decorated with crystal chandeliers and copious paneling. The coffeehouse-style cafe and piano bar are popular with local residents.

Schlossberg Hotel

Medium

Kaiser-Franz-Josef-Kai 30. Near the Schlossberg mountain, on right bank of River Mur.

☎ *(03) 16-80700.*

Credit Cards: *V, MC, DC, A.*

Pool, sauna, in-room minibars, fitness center.

Rebuilt in 1982, this Baroque inn has served patrons since the 15th century. It overlooks the Mur, at the foot of the massive Schlossberg, in the heart of Graz. Its historic beginnings remain visible in its thick original walls. Today guests can stroll in the courtyard by a lion's head fountain or linger on the terrace with a drink. Biedermeier antiques, provincial furnishings and Baroque sculptures abound. Accommodations include 51 rooms and five suites. Each is individually decorated and has bath, TV.

Inns

Hotel Pfeifer

http://www.graz.net/kirchenwirt/ e_default.htm

Medium to Expensive

Kirchplatz 9. Three and one-half miles northeast of Old Town Graz.

☎ *(03) 16-391112-0.*

Credit Cards: *V, MC, A.*

Secluded garden atmosphere, sauna.

For those who want to unwind in a natural setting, this family-run Austrian inn lies just beyond the bustle of the city in a wooded area. A sauna and solarium provide quiet retreats, the restaurant serves local dishes, and the comfortable 45 rooms all come with private bath. Access to city sights is made easy by streetcar. The inn is closed in Jan., but nearby is a 40-room hotel managed by the same family that is open year-round.

Where to Eat

Cafe Glockenspiel

Inexpensive

Glockenspielplatz 4. Ground floor by Glockenspiel. ☎ *(03) 16-830291.*

Specialties: *Coffees, light snacks, pastries.*

Closed: *Sun.*

Cafestop, reservations not accepted.

Take time out on your Graz tour for an espresso and a fresh pastry at this trendy cafe situated in the heart of the neoclassical square. At 11 a.m. or 3 p.m., you can hear the melodious chimes of the nearby clock tower, the cafe's namesake. Eat at sidewalk tables in fair weather, or sit inside at serpentine banquettes. The decor is classical, with many paintings and lithographs.

Kepler-Keller ★★★★★

Medium

Stempfergasse 6. Bottom floor of building between the Landeszeughaus and the Glockenspielplatz in pedestrian area. *(03) 16-822449.*

Credit Cards: *V, MC, DC, A.*

Closed: *Sun.*

Named after the Renaissance astronomer Johannes Kepler (who purportedly lived in the building), this popular dinner restaurant serves up local wines in open carafes along with its main courses. The house wine is a Styrian rose called Schilcher, made from grapes grown only south of Graz. The Styrian beer Gosser is a favorite choice for beer lovers. Besides libations and food, this restaurant has other charms. You can dine inside in rustic wood-panelled rooms, or, during the warm months, spend a late evening in an outside courtyard surrounded by a three-story arched facade. The courtyard has live music at night.

Landhaus-Keller ★★★★★

Medium

Schmiedgasse 9. Entrance at rear of Landhaus, proceed to center of building, near the casino. ☎ *(03) 16-830276.*

Specialties: *Seafood, fish, veal, beef, pork and chicken dishes, all based on old Styrian recipes.*

Credit Cards: *V, DC, A.*

Closed: *Mon., Sun.*

Reservations recommended.

Situated inside the Landhaus, the provincial armory that was built during the Turkish wars from 1642 to 1645, this restaurant has several intimate dining areas, including the Hunter's Room, Knights' Room, and a small courtyard. With winding hallways and rustic Teutonic decor, it provides hearty casual dining for both residents and visitors. The menu features traditional Styrian fare such as *tafelspitz* (boiled beef) and cheese dumplings. Local wines are available to complement each dish.

Stainzerbauer ★★★★★

Medium to Expensive

Burgergasse 4, ☎ *(03) 16-821106.* *One block south of the Graz Cathedral.*

Specialties: *Bread-and-meat dumplings, pork dishes, salads.*

Closed: *Sun.*

Outside dining, reservations recommended, jacket and tie advised.

A hands-down favorite with local residents, this restaurant serves generous portions of traditional Styrian dishes, including ready-made platters and salads for the lunch crowd. Diners can eat inside or, during the warm months, outside in a comfortable courtyard.

What to Do
Historical Sites

Schlossberg ★★★★

Cog railway from Kaiser-Franz-Josef-Kai 38. ☎ *(03) 16-872-4902.*

Public Transportation: *Zahnradbahn.*

Special Hours: *Closed from Nov. through Apr.*

This large, wooded dolomite hill rises high above the city, providing glorious views of Graz and the River Mur. Once fortifications against the Turks, the Schlossberg's walls and castle bastions were dismantled by the victorious Napoleon. Today, you can visit the remains of the citadel, a large park, and the Styrian landmark Uhrturm ("the clock tower"). Rebuilt in the mid- 16th century, the square clock tower has a circular wooden gallery and four huge clock faces. A cafe by the funicular offers garden seating. Admission: *nominal*.

Museums and Exhibits

Osterreichisches Freilichtmuseum

Stubing bei Graz. Train from Graz to Bruck an der Mur

☎ *(03) 16-53-700.*

Metro Stop: *Stubing.*

Special Hours: *Closed from Nov. through Apr.—and Mon.*

Ten miles north of Graz, this museum features more than 70 authentic buildings from all over Austria, preserved on 100 acres of hilly, wooded farmland. Here history comes alive in a collection that includes farmhouses, barns, Alpine huts, forges, belfries, and even working water mills. "Living" exhibits, with working artisans dressed in costume, and period landscaping such as hayricks and country gardens make visitors feel like time travelers to another era. The examples of architecture range from the 16th through the early 20th centuries. Many structures are open to walk through and are decorated with original furnishings. Admission: *nominal*.

Tirol

Innsbruck

Once favored by Emperor Maximilian I, and today filled with skiers from mid-December to March, Innsbruck, the capital of Tyrol, is a charming Baroque town with unforgettable Alpine views. During the warm season, visitors can hike or tour glaciers or linger in the Renaissance palaces. With more than 150 lifts and cable chairs in its surrounding mountains, Innsbruck hosted the Winter Olympic Games in 1964 and 1976, earning it top ranking as a winter-sports center. Perhaps its leading tourist attraction is Goldenes Dachl. Commissioned by Maximilian I, it now houses the Olympic Museum.

Where to Stay

Hotels and Resorts

Gasthof-Hotel Weisses Kreuz   ★★★★

Medium

Herzog-Friedrich-Strasse 31.

☎ *(05) 12-59479.*

Credit Cards: *V, MC, A.*

Built in 1465 as an inn, the "White Cross" played host to 13-year-old Wolfgang Mozart and his father in 1769 and today attracts many German actors and actresses as guests. The hotel's ground floor has stone arches and huge windows, and its upper story is stuccoed white and stenciled with regional patterns. The symbol of the hotel, a white cross, adorns the wrought- iron sidewalk gate. A special area on the ground floor is designated to hold guests' skis and equipment. Accommodations include 39 cozy rooms, 28 of which have private bath; those without are offered at a lesser rate. Some have TV. With the exception of the elevator, this historic inn has changed very little.

Hotel Central   ★★★

http://www.central.co.at/english/ home.htm

Medium

Gilmstrasse 5.

Public Transportation: *Tram 1 or 3.*

☎ *(05) 12-5920.*

Credit Cards: *V, MC, DC, A.*

Sauna, in-room minibars, fitness center.

Although constructed in 1860, this hotel isn't filled with Tyrolean antiques, as you might expect. Instead, the mood is modern yet intriguing, with textured concrete accents, long, narrow windows and hand-set tiles in abstract, pastel-colored patterns. Dozens of illuminated glass balls, each anchored by a glistening strand of gold wire, hang from the ceiling. The hotel's ground floor houses a Viennese cafe, complete with chandeliers and soaring marble columns. In striking contrast, the 87 rooms are comfortably but quite simply furnished; all have bath, TV. On the fourth floor, guests can work out in the fitness center or take a steam bath.

Hotel Europa Tyrol

http://www.europatyrol.com/

Medium to Expensive

Sudtirolerplatz 2. Opposite the railway station.

☎ *(05) 12-5931, FAX 223-5652.*

Credit Cards: *V, MC, DC, A.*

Skiing, sauna, in-room minibars.

One of the crown hotels of Innsbruck, this establishment was built in 1869. Having been bombed during World War II, it has been rebuilt and has since hosted notables from Queen Elizabeth II to the crew of Apollo 14. The public rooms are decorated with chandeliers, red velvet, and green marble accents. The formal lobby is paneled with rich woods and sports an English-style bar. Of historical interest are the ballroom, commissioned by King Ludwig, and the Barock Saal salon, used by the Tyrolean government for official functions. The 110 rooms and 12 suites are fitted with period furnishings. All have combination bath, TV; some have marble bath, mountain views, private steam bath. The inner-courtyard rooms are prized as quiet retreats. Bear in mind, it's across from the rail station, which some guests might find noisy.

Hotel Goldener Alder

Medium

Herzog-Friedrich-Strasse 6. In the Old City, directly across from Goldenes Dachl.

☎ *(05) 12-48-63-34.*

Credit Cards: *V, MC, DC, A.*

In-room safes, in-room minibars.

Goethe once stayed at this 600-year-old hotel, as did the violinist Paganini. Look for the names of other famous guests on plaques by the doors of the second-floor rooms. Decorated with Tyrolean antiques, travertine tiles, leaded windows with stained glass and chandeliers with human figures intricately carved from rams' horns, this family-run hotel has stone walls, winding staircases and lots of intimate nooks that add to the allure. There are 35 rooms and two suites, varying in terms of size and appointments. All have bath, TV. Nearby is the Goldenes Dachl, the celebrated gold-roofed edifice built by Emperor Maximilian I.

Inns

Villa Blanka

Inexpensive to Medium

Weiherburggasse 8. Near Alpenzoo on left bank, opposite Old Town Innsbruck.

☎ *(05) 12-29-22-11.*

Credit Cards: *V, MC, DC, A.*

Country location.

Nestled in a forested nature reserve just west of the historic town center, this quiet, small, relatively modern hotel is only a 20-minute walk from the main square. From the ample sun terrace on the second floor, guests can view the landscaped grounds and Innsbruck across the river. Inside, the lobby and reception areas are inviting with leather chairs and paintings on the walls. The 19 rooms are simple, but well-furnished; all have bath, TV.

Low Cost Lodging

Pension Alpina

Inexpensive

Hungerburgweg 4. From Muhlauerbrucke (north end of town), or by car

Public Transportation: *Hungerburgbahn. Metro Stop: Muhlauerbrucke.*

☎ *(05) 12-29-33-40.*

Credit Cards: *V, MC, DC, A.*

Secluded garden atmosphere, balcony or patio, country location.

Operated by the Mair family, in the summer this pension has balconies decorated with colorful flower boxes, and grassy lawns where guests can relax under sunshades. Inside is a small restaurant with a large ceramic oven surrounded by a banquette. The owners bake their own pastries, fresh daily, so no matter what the season, this is a special place to recharge after a day exploring the town or skiing the slopes.

Where to Eat

Cafe Munding ★★

Inexpensive

Kiebachgasse 16. In Old Town between Silergasse and Scholossergasse.
☎ *(05) 12-58-41-18*

Specialties: *Coffee, pastries, Tyrolean cuisines.*

Cafestop, reservations not accepted.

If you need a break after walking through Old Town, this 1720 house shelters a cafe behind its Baroque facade and heavily carved bay windows. Inside, diners are seated in the inner rooms for traditional Tyrolean fare, but many patrons visit the chocolate and pastry shop, or pause for a steaming cup of coffee. Wine is sold by the glass, and the menu also features pizza and other light snacks.

Europastuberl ★★★★★

Medium to Expensive

Brixnerstrasse 6. Opposite the railway station. Located at Hotel Europa Tyrol. ☎ *(05) 12- 95931*

Specialties: *Fresh Tyrolean trout, venison, boiled beef, Tyrolean apple strudel.*

Reservations required.

This celebrated restaurant provides both hotel guests and the general public with memorable cuisine. Diners are seated in paneled rooms at formal tables that befit this elegant restaurant. Both hot and cold appetizers are available, as well as fixed-price offerings. The menu features continental classics and Tyrolean favorites served with creative flair. The extensive wine list includes both Austrian and international vintages. Some dishes, such as the pike-perch and guinea hen, are prepared to serve two people.

Restaurant Goldener Adler   ★★★★★

Expensive

Herzog-Friedrich-Strasse 6, ☎ *(05) 12-58-63- 34.*

Specialties: *Boiled beef (recommended), veal, trout, game in season.*

Credit Cards: *V, MC, DC, A.*

Reservations required.

Housed in a 600-year-old hotel, this restaurant has earned a high reputation among German-speaking travelers. With four dining areas, two on the ground floor and two on the second floor, patrons can pick the spot that best fits their mood. The menus are the same in all rooms, but the Goethe Stube on the street level features zither music in the evenings. The upstairs restaurant is more formal. Dishes are traditionally and superbly prepared. The house prides itself on its Salzburger nockerln, a fluffy souffle inspired by the mountains outside the city of Salzburg. Ask about the Tyrolean specials of the day, or if you can't decide, consider the daily platter, which comes at fixed prices.

Tiroler Stuben   ★★★★

Medium to Expensive

Innrain 13, ☎ *(05) 12-57-79-31.*

Specialties: *Classic Tyrolean dishes, large salads, seafood (fresh), venison platter (served year-round).*

Credit Cards: *V, MC, DC, A*.

Closed: *Sun*.

Reservations recommended.

In spite of serving many groups and lots of local businesspeople, the Tiroler Stuben has semiprivate booths and out-of-the-way corners for intimate dining. Elegantly decorated with Tyrolean antiques, this fairly formal restaurant offers a menu that is divided into Tyrolean and Austrian specialties. A popular choice is the venison platter of sausages and medallions, served year-round. Specialties include a wide range of fresh seafood as well as dishes prepared with local freshwater fish such as wallerfillet (a Tyrolean whitefish).

Weisses Rossl ★★★★

Mediun

Kiebachgasse 8. Near Seilergasse at Kiebachgasse. ☎ *(05) 12-583057*

Specialties: *Tyrolean grustl (a beef hash), veal, schnitzels, game in season*.

Credit Cards: *V, A*.

Closed: *Sun*.

Outside dining, reservations recommended.

An old crucifix marks the door to this establishment, which began serving platters back in 1590. The owners offer a variety of seasonal dishes using combinations of fresh and wild ingredients. The local favorite is Tyrolean *grustl*, a hash of beef strips, onions, herbs and potatoes sauteed and served in a frying pan. In midwinter, try fresh blood-and-liver sausages with sauerkraut, a distinctly regional dish. Summer months, dine outdoors on the terrace. Special dishes for seniors and children are available.

What to Do

Historical Sites

Goldenes Dachl

Herzog-Friedrich-Strasse 15. ☞ *Site of Olympic Museum, Old*

Town. ☎ *(05) 12-53-60-575*

Public Transportation: *Tram 1 or 3.*

The "Golden Roof" that adorns this large white-walled 1420 building is actually a three-story balcony set with 2657 gold- plated tiles commissioned by Emperor Maximilian I. Designed as a "royal viewing box," the balcony was added on to the existing building, allowing the Emperor and his entourage to watch events performed in the square below. Dedicated in honor of Maximilian's second marriage, the balcony is decorated with elaborate carvings and coats of arms, along with the gilded copper tiles on the roof. Admission also covers entrance into the nearby Stadtturm (City Tower), a former prison cell built in the 1400s that stands near the Rathaus. Admission: *nominal.*

Sports & Recreation

ITRAVELBOOKS FREEBIE

Bergisel

Bergisel mountain. South of Innsbruck. ☎ *(05) 12-59850.*

During winter, this is the center for skiing, with jumps built for the 1964 and 1976 Winter Olympics, but, even in warm months, Bergisel is perfect for strolling and enjoying panoramic views. In 1809, Tyrolean peasants led by Andres Hofer fought against French and Bavarian forces, and today this "field of remembrance" bears memorials to recall the fight. Admission: *free.*

Kitzbuhel

Just 81 miles from Munich, Germany, and 62 miles from Innsbruck, Kitzbuhel attracts the chic and well-heeled, plus skiers of every skill level, who come to enjoy the soaring Kitzbuhel Alps that ring this small walled city. More than 1000 years old, Kitzbuhel offers postcard-perfect vistas of church spires and sharply defined roofs. A vast network of cable cars makes the Kitzbuheler Horn to the east (6553 ft./ 1997 m) and the Hahnenkamm to the west (5428 ft./1654 m) easily accessible, and ski lifts cover the mountain slopes. The town boasts a casino, several trendy night clubs and some of the best dining in Austria.

Where to Stay

Hotels and Resorts

Hotel Goldener Greif

http://members.tirol.com/ hotel.ggreif/engl.htm

Medium to Expensive

Hinterstadt 24. Next to Spiel Casino, near the Hahnenkamm cable-car station. ☎ *(05) 356- 3511.*

Credit Cards: *V, MC, DC, A.*

Pool, skiing, sauna, balcony or patio, in-room safes.

Just steps from the Casino, this well- known hotel makes a great in-town headquarters. In a building that dates from 1271, the hotel clearly has a Tyrolean atmosphere, with its balconies, vaulted lobby, large fireplaces and many antiques. There are 54 rooms; some have canopy beds, whirlpool tub, steam bath; all have cable TV; most have working fireplace, standard tile bath. The two deluxe suites feature a Jacuzzi, hunting-lodge decor and fireplaces. As with most Kitzbuhel hotels, summer rates are lower. Closed Apr. to May, Oct. to Dec.

Hotel Schloss Lebenberg ★★★★

Medium to Expensive

Lebenbergastrasse 17. One mile west on outskirts of town.

☎ *(05) 356-4301-0.*

Credit Cards: *V, MC, DC, A.*

Pool, skiing, balcony or patio, country location.

Open year-round, this hotel combines the historic foundations of a medieval castle with modern additions. Little of the original castle remains, the walls and turrets are covered with stucco, but the location provides princely views of Kitzbuhel's church spires and Tyrolean town houses. Accommodations include 68 rooms and 42 suites; all are richly furnished; the baths are small, and 10 have showers only. A full range of health-related and social activities are available.

Hotel Weisses Rossl

http://www.lodgingaustria.com/Innsbruck/WeissesRossl/

Medium to Expensive

Bilchlstrasse 3-5. A 2-minute walk from ski lifts.

☎ *(05) 356-2541.*

Credit Cards: *V, MC, DC, A.*

Secluded garden atmosphere, skiing, in-room minibars.

Popular with skiers, this establishment was originally a 19th-century inn on a coach route. Recently renovated, the hotel features homey public rooms with lots of hidden nooks and a 4th-floor terrace with superb mountain views. The 34 pine-trimmed rooms have comfortable furnishings, radio, VCR; 15 suites. Many guests choose half-board in order to dine in town, but the hotel serves well-prepared cuisine at its a la carte restaurant. Closed Oct. to Dec.

Where to Eat

Cafe Praxmair

Medium

Vorderstadt 17. In center of town.

Specialties: *Coffee, pastries, especially florentines.*

Happening bar, cafestop, own baking, reservations not accepted.

Famous throughout Austria for its florentine pastries, this crowded cafe is where the apres-ski folk gather for hot chocolate topped with frothy whipped cream. After the coffee-and-cake types move on, the Praxmair Keller springs to life as a dark- till-dawn cellar bar. It's a good spot, day or night, if only to watch the chic passersby. Open year-round.

Florianistube

Medium

Goensbachgasse 12, ☎ *(05) 356-2437.*

Specialties: *Tyrolean dishes, plus spaghetti, fondue.*

Credit Cards: *DC, A.*

Outside dining, reservations recommended.

Tucked in the Gasthof Eggerwirt Hotel, this restaurant is named in honor of St. Florian, the patron saint of the hearth. After a day hiking or on the slopes, you'll enjoy the cozy atmosphere here. Summer months, buffet-style meals are sometimes served outside in a tree-shaded back garden. Low-key, not ostentatious.

What to Do

Parks and Gardens

Alpenblumengarten

Kitzbuheler Horn, ☎ *(05) 356-2155-0.*

Public Transportation: *cable car.* Metro Stop: *Kitzbuheler Horn.*

Special Hours: *Open from mid-Oct. through Apr., 8:30 a.m.–5:30*

Take a strenuous three-hour hike or ride the cable car up to the Kitzbuheler Horn (6553 ft./1997 m), and visit the Alpine Flower Garden, where you can stroll over several acres of natural alpine terrain. Native flowers, bushes, trees and grasses grow in a variety of habitats. More than 120 types of flowers bloom in the spring. For other hiking paths, mountain bike riding, and guided treks for all fitness levels, contact the tourist office for its mountain-hiking program at ☎ (05356) 21-55-0. Admission: free.

Sports and Recreation

Kitzbuhel Ski Circus

Outside Kitzbuhel. Contact tourist office for directions, lift prices

Everyone flocks to Kitzbuhel for its "Ski Circus," a network of lifts and cables on the Hahnenkamm. Skiing as a sport began here in 1892, with the first cable car installed in 1928. Today, skiers can whisk downhill for more than 50 miles on every conceivable type of run. Site of the prestigious annual Hahnenkamm Ski Competition, Kitzbuhel attracts championship pros and royal skiers, who turn this small town into a seven-day nonstop party each January. In addition to skiing, other winter sports are offered such as curling, skibobbing, jumping, ice skating, winter hiking and even hang gliding.

St. Anton am Arlberg

The Arlberg Alps are beloved by skiers, and St. Anton is the center for the sport on the eastern slopes. Host of World Cup Skiing each December, St. Anton attracts other sports enthusiasts as well, including hard-core mountain bikers in August, when racers compete for the Arlberg Mountain Bike Trophy. The area also is popular with strollers, who come to witness the flowers that carpet the mountain meadows and slopes during the brief warm season.

Where to Stay

Arlberg Hospiz

http://www.stantonaustria.com/ antadv/arlberg_hospiz/

Medium to Expensive

A-6580 St. Christoph. From St. Anton by cableway, or Arlsberg Pass Road. ☎ *(05) 446- 2611.*

Credit Cards: *MC, DC, A.*

Mountain location, pool, skiing, sauna.

High in the Arlberg Pass just above St. Anton, this famous hotel in St. Christoph stands on the site of the legendary hospice that once sheltered weary pilgrims. An annex is connected to the main hotel by an underground passageway. The 31 rooms and 68 suites have plush furnishings, TV, good-sized bath, hair dryer, robes. Guests can dine in the "farmhouse"-style restaurant and enjoy entertainment in the hotel's "party room."

Hotel Schwarzer Adler

http://www.sudtirol.com/schwarzer- adler/

Expensive

A-6580 St. Anton am Arlberg. In center of town.

☎ *(05) 446-22440, FAX 528-1234.*

Credit Cards: *V, MC, DC, A.*

Sauna, fitness center.

Originally constructed as an inn to shelter weary pilgrims crossing the Arlberg Pass, this venerable establishment was given official approval by Empress Maria Theresa. Owned and operated by the Tschol family since 1885, the hotel surrounds its guests in history. The frescoes on the exterior are carefully restored to match original designs that date back 400 years. Antiques include baroque armoires and an unusual country-baroque sundial. There are a total of 56 rooms; all have bath (singles do not have tub). The original inn's rooms are lushly appointed, and guests can also stay in the comfortable (and more reasonably priced) rooms in the hotel's annex across the street. Closed May, and Oct. through Nov.

Hotelkertess

http://www.kertess.com/englisch/ html/start_e.htm

Medium

A-6580 St. Anton am Arlberg. In suburb of Oberdorf, by shuttle or car from center of town.

☎ *(05) 446-2005.*

Credit Cards: *V, MC, DC, A.*

Mountain location, pool, sauna, balcony or patio, in-room safes.

Renovated in 1993, this family-run hotel is situated outside the town on a steep hillside. A large fireplace in its lobby welcomes winter guests. The 40 cozy wood-paneled rooms have comfortable furnishings, bath, TV, some with view of Rendl ski slope. Guests can linger in the hotel bar, and take meals in the stylish restaurant. A hotel shuttle carries skiers down the hill to the ski lifts. Closed two weeks in April (specific dates vary) and from mid- Oct. to mid-Nov.

Sporthotel St. Anton

Medium to Expensive

A-6580 St. Anton am Arlberg. Near main pedestrian thoroughfare.

☎ *(05) 446-3111.*

Credit Cards: *V, MC, DC, A.*

Pool, sauna, balcony or patio.

This modern chalet-style hotel is situated only a three-minute walk from the ski lifts. In the lobby, a full-time organist fills the air with music, setting the tone for this popular resort. The 53 rooms have comfortable furnishings, bath, TV. After a workout on the slopes, guests can refresh themselves in the heated indoor pool, which features a waterfall and mineral- laced waters. There are also two discos in the basement. Closed May, and Oct. through Nov.

Where to Eat

Cafe Aquila

Inexpensive

St. Anton am Arlberg, ☎ *(05) 446-2245.*

Specialties: *Pastries, coffee, light meals and snacks, beer, wine.*

Cafestop, reservations not accepted.

Formerly known as the Cafe Tschol, the Aquila serves the ski crowd coffee, pastries and simple but delicious meals. Wines and beer are also available. You can order pasta or goulash dishes, or serve yourself at the appetizer buffet.

Fuhrmannstube   ★★★★★

Inexpensive

St. Anton am Arlberg. *Near the church on the main street.*

☎ *(05) 446-2921.*

Specialties: *Teutonic dishes, schnitzels, spatzl, game in season.*

This bustling stube combines both a cafe and a restaurant under one roof. It's kind to your pocketbook, with such filling specialties as hearty spatzl noodles and goulashes.

Hotel Kertess Restaurant ★★★★

Medium to Expensive

St. Anton am Arlberg. Outside town, by shuttle or car to Oberdorf. Located at Hotelkertess. ☎ *(05) 446-2005.*

Specialties: *Venison, fish, regional desserts, including apple fritters.*

Credit Cards: *V, MC, DC, A.*

Reservations required.

This hotel restaurant has three dining rooms, each appointed with Oriental carpets and equipped with ceramic-tiled stoves to warm the air. Looking out on snow-covered ski slopes, diners can feast on what many consider some of the best food in the area. The hotel's bar is a perfect spot for apres-ski drinks and conversation. In summer, hot meals are served only at dinner.

What to Do

Museums and Exhibits

Ski un Heimat Museum ★★★

Arlberg-Kandahar House. In center of Holiday Park, St. Anton. ☎ *(05) 446-2475.*

Special Hours: *Closed Sat.*

Although St. Anton is known as the home of skier Hannes Schneider (who pioneered the "Arlberg ski method"), during Roman times tribes migrated through the nearby pass. You can learn more about both skiing and Roman history by visiting this museum. With exhibits that trace the history of skiing in the Arlberg Alps, it also houses displays outlining the cultural and archeological history of the region. Admission: *moderate*.

Nightlife

Krazy Kanguruh

Moos 113. Phone ahead for driving conditions or ski routes.

☎ *(05) 446-2633.*

Special Hours: *Closed Apr. 15 through Dec. 15.*

For daytime fun, the adventurous head to this one-time stable now converted into a restaurant-disco. Located at the top of a steep hill outside town, it can be reached on cross-country skis, on foot (if you're in great shape) or by car (if you don't mind hairpin curves). After a lunch of a hamburger or schnitzel, revelers fill the basement disco, fueling their energy with espresso or drinks. If you favor liqueurs, ask for the pear- and plum-favored schnapps.

Vorarlberg
Feldkirch

Called "The Gateway to Austria," this small town is certainly worth a visit, with its medieval buildings and cobbled squares nestled between rugged hills. Located only a short distance from bordering Switzerland and Liechtenstein, Feldkirch is close to popular Bregenz, but is not inundated with the crowds of Swiss and German tourists. The Hotel Alpenrose, in the old district, is a great spot to base explorations to Schattenburg Castle or retire after a day at the annual Schubert Festival, held each spring and autumn.

Where to Stay
Hotels and Resorts

Hotel Alpenrose
Medium
Rosengasse 4-6. In Old Town, close to pedestrian precincts.

☎ *(05) 522-22-17-50, FAX 528-1235.*

Credit Cards: *V, MC, DC, A.*

This venerable hotel has been run by the Gutwinksi family for the most recent 100 years of its five-century history. The 24 intimate rooms are furnished in the Biedermeier style; all have bath, TV. Public lounge; elevator. The hotel has a traditional feel not found in chain establishments.

Where to Eat

Gasthof Lingg ★★★★

Am Markplatz. *Near main square, Markplatz.*

☎ *(05) 522-72-6-62.*

Specialties: *Meat, fish, game, especially roast goose.*

Credit Cards: *V, MC, DC, A.*

Closed: *Mon.*

Reservations recommended.

Housed on the second floor of a historic building, with views of the medieval square, this restaurant serves carefully prepared Austrian specialties. Established in 1878, and highly praised by locals, the restaurant features an array of fruit and fish salads, soups and hearty game entrees. Attached is a guesthouse, run under the same name, offering one single and three double rooms, each with shower and toilet.

What to Do

Historical Sites

Schattenburg Castle ★★★★

Neustadt. By foot, up Schlossteig, by car, Burgasse. ☎ *(05) 522-73467.*

Built as the seat of the Counts of Monfort from the 1200s to 1390, the castle has a courtyard and traditional medieval banquet room and affords great views of the old city. In 1825, the town of Feldkirch purchased the castle and its grounds to save it from demolition. Today a restaurant operates from the Rittersaal ("Knights Room"), and the museum houses an interesting collection of weapons, locks, medallions and paintings. Admission: nominal.

Lech

This alpine-village resort is perched at 4730 feet on the north-western flank of the Arlberg massif. Linked by cable car to its satel-lite resort Oberlech, this ski mecca features 34 lifts that can be trav-eled on one ski pass. Snow is "guaranteed from the end of November to April." In the summer, strollers head to the less trav-eled but beautiful Upper Lech Valley.

Where to Stay

Hotel Arlberg

Expensive

A-6764 Lech. By train to Langen am Arlberg, then bus.

☎ *(05) 583-2134.*

Credit Cards: *Not Accepted.*

Pool, tennis, sauna, balcony or patio, fitness center.

This chalet was built in 1965, but it is filled with Austrian antiques, embellished paneling and a baronial fireplace that give it an old-world feel. There are 54 rooms and 10 suites, many with large bal-conies and picture windows, all with satellite TV, new beds, tile or marble bath, robes, hair dryer. Elegant meals are available in the hotel dining room. Closed Apr. 20 to June 25 and Sept. 25 to Nov.

Hotel Kristiania

Expensive

A-6764 Lech. Above the center of the resort, near the pickup spot for cross-country ski school students.

☎ *(05) 583-2561-0.*

Credit Cards: *DC, A.*

Mountain location, sauna, in-room safes, in- room minibars.

Popular with hard-core skiers, this intimate winter-only hotel is situated just above the resort town. There are 22 rooms and 10 suites; those that face the south have balconies and mountain views, while those that face the north overlook the resort and valley of Lech. All have satellite TV, tiled bath (half with tub), attractive decor in pastel tones. The hotel features many special services for skiers. One restaurant on-site serves half-board guests, while another is designed for a la carte dining. Closed Apr. 18 to Dec.16.

Hotel Montana

Medium

A-6764 Oberlech. From Lech, cable car only, daily 7:00 a.m.–1:00 a.m.
☎ *(05) 583-2460.*

Credit Cards: *Not Accepted.*

Pool, tennis, fitness center.

The only way to reach this hotel is to take a short cable-car ride from Lech (free for those with lift passes). The Montana provides a large sun terrace, but the hotel is best known for its Vinothek or "wine library," where selected wines are sold by the glass or bottle. Brightly colored walls contrast with warm wood paneling. The 43 rooms and 17 suites are furnished in an alpine style; some contain antiques; all have bath, TV. The owner is French, which is evident in the hotel's restaurant. Closed May to Nov.

Where to Eat

Alrberg Brunnerhof

Expensive

A-6764 Lech. North of the center of town. Located at Hotel Arlberg.
☎ *(05) 583-2134.*

Specialties: *Perch and other fish dishes, beef, game.*

Happening bar, reservations required, jacket recommended.

Formal, elegant dining is the hallmark of this respected establishment. Classical European decor; expensive linens. Guests sample a broad range of innovative European and Austrian dishes. The wine list contains selections from around the world. The intimate, softly illuminated bar is an apres-ski magnet. During summer, meals are often served on a terrace brightened by colorful flowers. Make reservations early: although pricey, the restaurant is always busy.

The Red Umbrella

Medium

By cable car from Lech. Located at Petersboden. ☎ *(05) 583-3232.*

Specialties: *Liqueurs, coffees, pastries, Austrian dishes.*

Happening bar, outside dining, cafestop, reservations not accepted.

This establishment is named for its huge, bright red umbrella, which is raised and opened by hydraulics (weather permitting) each morning at 11:00 a.m. Under the 36-foot umbrella's protection, skiers and nonskiers alike sit at the circular bar on a large wooden deck, sipping flavored schnapps, rum and vodka. Meals and espresso are also served. If the weather's too nasty, guests retire inside to drink and dine in the comfort of a roaring log fire.

Oberlech

Zur Kanne

Medium to Expensive

Oberlech. By cable car from Lech. Located at Hotel Montana.

☎ *(05) 583-2460.*

Specialties: *Fish, lobster, beef, game, all served with a French accent.*

Reservations required.

Run by hotel owner, Guy Ortlieb, this distinguished restaurant is well-known throughout Austria. The menu reflects Ortlieb's French heritage, and the sophisticated offerings range from fish, lobster and frog legs Provencal to filet of beef. The fixed-priced dinner selections provide an excellent way to experience the chef's talents.

What to Do

Sports and Recreation

Upper Lech Valley

North of Lech, by car. ☎ *(05) 533-21-61-0.*

When the snow melts, the Arlberg massif is cloaked in greenery and Alpine flowers. The ski lifts carry summer visitors to the peaks, and local associations oversee a network of trails and hiking huts. Check before you visit between May and Nov., because many of Lech's resorts are closed. Seldom seen by the average tourist, the 38-mile road north of Lech leads from Warth to Reutte, making it a perfect choice for a summer drive.

Western Arlberg Skiing

☎ *(05) 583-21-61-0.*

World-renowned for its skiing, the Arlberg range is studded with winter resorts. Lech and Zurs attract both the well-heeled and the fanatical skiers, but even beginners can find miles of runs. Lech is centered in a region linked by 88 lifts, cable cars and T-bars. Schools abound, teaching all levels of cross-country and downhill skiing techniques. When dusk falls, apres-ski action gears up. Unwind in an intimate bar, waltz at a tea dance or enjoy live music that ranges from rock and roll to regional folk tunes.

Schruns

Ernest Hemingway spent his winters here by the banks of the River Ill, writing his novel *The Sun Also Rises.* Today Schruns attracts skiers and hikers of every stripe. The region boasts 73 lifts that carry visitors up to 7550 feet. Trails and guided hikes abound. On the left bank of the river is Tschagguns (three minutes by shuttle bus), site of World Cup Ski Races. In Tschagguns, you'll find the Hotel Montafoner Hof, a resort with an authentic alpine atmosphere yet modernized rooms—and panoramic mountain vistas.

Where to Stay

Hotel Montafoner Hof ★★★★★

Medium to Expensive

Dorfstrasse 852. Outside Schruns in Tschagguns, left bank.

☎ *(05) 556-7100-0.*

Credit Cards: *Not Accepted.*

Pool, skiing, sauna, balcony or patio, in- room minibars, fitness center.

This peach-colored building is positioned to provide panoramic mountain views. Inside, warm pine paneling and rustic furnishings impart a country air, yet in other respects the hotel is quite modern. There are 49 rooms and one suite; all units have bath, TV, radio, lounge. Two restaurants, indoor and outdoor pools, a whirlpool and steam bath are available to pamper guests. They offer special packages during the summer; call ahead. Closed Easter through May and Nov. to Dec. 20.

Lowen Hotel Schruns

Expensive

Silvrettastrasse 8. In the center of town. ☎ *(05) 556-7141.*

Mountain location, pool, skiing, balcony or patio, in-room minibars.

The main building of this lavish hotel is a large, imposing chalet, encircled by an elegantly landscaped lawn. Beneath the lawn, which serves as a roof, a modern steel-and-glass structure houses restaurants and an Olympic-size pool. Dark wood paneling and rustic furnishings fill the public areas. The 81 creatively designed, spacious rooms have bath, satellite TV. Undoubtedly the most luxurious hotel in Schruns.

Inns

Hotel Krone ★★★

Medium

Austerlitz 2.

☎ *(05) 556-72255.*

Secluded garden atmosphere.

Leaded-glass windows, carved and lacquered paneling and baroque architecture are the defining points of this small, hip-roofed, shuttered inn. Owned by the Mayer family since 1847, the hotel has a shaded beer garden, an in-house restaurant, and public rooms filled with rustic antiques. The snug rooms are pleasantly furnished. Closed Easter to late May and Oct. through Dec. 20.

Where to Eat

Feuerstein   ★★★★

Inexpensive

Dofstrasse. *Center of town.*

Specialties: *Pastries, coffee.*

Cafestop, reservations not accepted.

Beautifully prepared pastries that look almost too good to eat are the order of the day at this popular cafe. Located in a historic building right in the center of town, the cafe offers coffee and an array of cakes, pastries and ice cream that will satisfy even the most discriminating sweet tooth. The upstairs rooms are filled with splendid antiques. Closed Easter to June.

Restaurant Francais   ★★★★★

Expensive

Silvrettastrasse 8, ☎ *05556/7141.*

Specialties: *French cuisine, trout, venison, beef.*

Reservations required, jacket recommended.

Candlelight dining and elegant cuisine make this upscale restaurant the choice for a special evening. The formal table settings create a luxurious atmosphere for dining on regional dishes with a French flair. The ever-changing menu emphasizes freshness and may include venison or stuffed hare, fish or beef.

What to Do

Museums and Exhibits

Montafoner Heimat Museum/ Pfarrkirche

Schruns, A-6780. Center of town. ☎ *(05) 556- 721 66.*

Special Hours: *Closed holidays and Oct. 26- Dec. 26.*

After a morning of hiking or skiing, take time to tour this four-floor museum. Exhibits include wooden skis with leather and metal bindings, plus an extensive display of antique tools that were used in daily life. Nearby, the ornate Pfarrkirche dominates the Kirchplatz, its domed yellow tower rising against a backdrop of mountains. An intricate mosaic depicting St. George slaying the dragon adorns the outer church wall. Inside, the stained-glass windows are jewellike, and the altarpieces are heavily carved and covered with gold leaf. The church is open daily from 8 a.m. to 6 p.m. Admission: inexpensive.

Special Tours

Silvretta High Alpine Road

From Bludenz to Landeck. ☞ *The 59-mile road between Montafon and Trisanna val*

Special Hours: *Closed due to snow from Nov. to May.*

More than 30 spine-tingling hairpin turns challenge drivers on this high-altitude scenic road that links the Ill (Montafon) Valley with the Trisanna Valley. Along this twisting route, you'll see spectacular views of alpine passes, best at dawn or dusk, silver lakes, and ski resorts dotting the countryside. As you head from Bludenz south to Schruns, you'll pass through the deep Montafon Valley, where cattle graze and towns are filled with timbered buildings with arched doorways. Silvretta Lake, southeast of Schruns, is man-made, but a stop by its shores (elevation 6680 ft./ 2036 m) is well worth the drive.

BELGIUM

Within your first hour on Belgian soil, you'll confirm that its skies are punctuated by more spires and castle turrets than any other nation you've ever visited. The size of the state of Maryland, Belgium is one of the most densely populated countries in Europe. The extent of its beauty, culture and elegance is not seen in thousands of miles of travel elsewhere.

The Flemings are the Northerners, the Walloons the Southerners. Belgium is a nation divided into two major linguistic areas: Flanders, where Flemish is spoken by about 5.6 million, and the Walloon section, where French is the official tongue of a minority of 3.2 million. The capital, a city of a million convivial souls, is bilingual. Yet another idiom exists—German is spoken by about 60,000 Belgians near the eastern frontier in a region called Ostkantone (or Eastern County).

As Belgium is so small, you'll very likely see most of it in a brief time span—and much of it will be in bloom if the season is right. Don't think that Holland has a monopoly on blossoms, bulbs and botany in the Lowlands. The Royal Palace at Laeken is a worthy target.

Antwerp, **Ghent** and **Bruges**, less than an hour from Brussels on the superhighway, draw the most attention outside the capital. To cover a lot of territory fast (which is not recommended, as the greater rewards come from lingering), here's an itinerary that can be comfortably done in one highly active day: Start from Brussels at 8:30 a.m. Take the expressway straight to Bruges, ignoring Ghent, which you'll be seeing later. Enjoy a 35-minute boat ride on a canal, sightsee where you will and then amble down either the expressway or Route N-10 (distances are about even) to Ostend, with its salty scenery and modern Kursaal Casino. If there's time, you might wish to run out to **Knokke**, Belgium's most chichi seaside resort, a few miles along the coast to the north. If not, perhaps you'd be happier heading straight for lunch in **Bruges**. Then climb back on the expressway to **Ghent** for a view of Van Eyck's *Holy Lamb* at the **Cathedral**. Follow this with tea at the Cour St.-Georges, the oldest hotel in the north; the rooms are poor but the dining facilities passable. Those with extra fortitude may want to run out to the **Castle of Laarne** for a peek at its multimillion-dollar silver collection, tapestries and furniture. You should be back in Brussels by dinnertime—dog-tired but well pleased with your comprehensive excursion.

The **Ardennes**, a sizable area that stretches south and southwest, to the French and Luxembourg borders, unfolds the most beautiful vistas in the nation, along with the most heartwrenching: it is the site of the Battle of the Ardennes Forest. With its rolling hills, lazily gliding waters, dense forests, tidy farms and classic villages, it is now a kaleidoscope of bucolic charm. A special attraction is the **Grottos of Han**, about two hours from the capital. The underground streams are interesting, the colors are exquisite and the rooms are so huge that musical events sometimes are presented in them.

Sound and Light *(Son et Lumiere)* spectacles glow from May 1 through September 30 in the courtyards of medieval castles at **Bouillon, La Roche, Ghent** and **Bruges**, and there's a stunning eyepopper several nights each week in the **Grand' place** of the capital.The **Carnival de Binche** (pronounced Bahn-ssh), inaugurated by Maximilian more than four centuries ago, is worth a 500-mile detour from any set itinerary if you happen to be in Europe just before Lent. The pseudo-Peruvian costumes are fantastically colorful—with ostrich-feather headdresses four feet high. On the climax day, 500 people are known to participate in the grand parade. *Wear your oldest clothes if you go to this*—blue jeans, if possible—because the crowd will kiss you, hit you painlessly with air-filled skin bags and throw oranges at you, all simultaneously. Odd, but everyone seems to enjoy it.

Transportation

Airline

Your first glance of Belgium will probably be via Brussels Airport, one of Europe's best, cleanest and most thoughtfully constructed. It even provides quick rail service to town (at less than a tenth of the taxi fare). **Sabena** is fine on intra-European flights. In North America it calls on Montreal, Toronto, New York, Atlanta, Boston and Chicago. Globally, you can carry on with Sabena to Africa (where it covers 21 cities) and the Far East.

Taxis

Belgian taxi fares are among the highest in the world. Tips are included, so don't bother with any further doles, even though drivers may grumble, whine or even withhold change.

Metro

Belgium's metro is possibly the most civilized in the world. With one $10 card, the subway can be used for 10 trips. Buses, metros and trams stop running at midnight.

Trains

The trains are very good. The five-day-minimum Tourist Card (*abonnement*) is perfect for excursioners. (Five days should be sufficient to cover this little land, but versions of this T-Travel Card now are issued for 16 days, too.) There is also the wider-ranging Benelux Tourrail plan, which covers three nations for 10 days of limitless conveyance.

Ferry Connections

There's a Jetfoil between Ostend and Dover or Folkestone. The 250-passenger P & O vessel skims along at close to 50 m.p.h. A larger conventional ferry also plies these routes, but the travel time is longer, of course. Trains meet the ships for swift passage to the capitals.

Food

It's easy to gain weight in Belgium. In its top establishments, gustatory standards are so high they challenge or rank even better than the leaders in France. The approach to cuisine, too, is similar. Local traditions include a delectable fish or chicken stew, called Waterzooi. Also, look for beer soup, eels in green sauce and mussels in many disguises.

ITRAVELBOOK TIP: THE NATIONAL DISH OF BELGIUM SHOULD BE, BY RIGHTS, FRITES (FRENCH FRIES). SOLD BY STREET VENDORS, RESTAURANTS, BARS, CAFES, AND NEARLY EVERY KIND OF EATING ESTABLISHMENT, THEY WILL BE THE MOST SPLENDID FRIES YOU'LL EVER TASTE. AVAIL YOURSELF WHENEVER YOU FIND THEM.

The citizenry takes justified pride in the sweep and the scope of its cheeses. There's a bewildering assortment, from strong, classic, Muenster to local goat-milk preparations, to those from such abbeys as **Westmalle**, **Trappist**, **Folies de Beguine**, **La Pave de Bastogne**, **Fromage de Brussels** and perhaps four or five dozen others.

Drinks

Trappist beer is unique and cheap. There are two main types: "Double" (the normal variety) and "Triple" (hard to find). Both are different from anything brewed anywhere else—with vague Coca-Cola overtones, a curiosity. The Rochefort monks produce a third kind from oranges. Other national quaffs (Artois, Haecht, Gueuze-Lambic, Duke, Ginder Ale and the like) produce many international prizes for Belgian brew-masters. A good one-third of the nation's 189 breweries are based in Brabant. The native brew of Brussels is Le Lambic. Sipped naturally, it will make you pucker, so many locals add sugar; we suggest you do the same. The locals also down Kriek-Lambic, a cherry beverage found only in the oldest taverns. Speaking of pubs, don't fail to visit an *estaminet*, a purely Belgian invention that is the ultimate in coziness. They are usually very old, dark and chummy and serve light bites as well as drinks. **Image de Notre Dame**, up a narrow lane off rue Marche aux Herbes, is possibly the most authentic one in Brussels, but many others exist.

Telephone

Access code to USA: 00.

To telephone Belgium: 32; time difference (Eastern Daylight) plus 6 hours.

CURRENCY: Euros.

For More Information

Belgian National Tourist Office, *745 Fifth Ave., New York, NY 10151*, (<u>http://www.visitbelgium.com/</u> ☎ (212) 758-8130).

Brussels, for Tourist Information for the capital: Town Hall (right wing) at the Grand' place, (☎ *(02) 513-8940*).

Central
Brussels

Home to about a million, Brussels is the center of government, industry, business and culture. For some time it had been enjoying the wildest construction boom of any capital in Europe—a low country that swiftly became an ultra high-riser. It has polished its glorious architecture and recently freshened up a splendid heritage that had begun to wilt from earlier neglect. The results are stunning, making it one of the most glittering capitals in captivity. It also has become headquarters for virtually every multinational firm of importance needing a base on the Continent. Art Nouveau has deep-set roots in this city, and today's Belgians are wisely focusing appreciative attention on the designs of Victor Horta and his disciples. It boasts an excellent airport, six railroad stations, a luxurious music-fed subway, plenty of excellent hotels, gourmet restaurants, movies and shops. Its art—the city itself is a living museum—is shown in some of the finest museums on the Continent.

Where to Stay

Hotels and Resorts

Belson Hotel ★★★

Medium to Expensive

Chaussee de Louvain 805.

☎ *448-8355, (2)* ☎ *735-0000,* FAX: *(2) 735-6043.*

Credit Cards: *V, MC, DC, A.*

Complimentary airport pickup service.

This attractive hotel is convenient for motorists with its location between the city and the airport, allowing for a more remote atmosphere. Within this six-story brick structure are 140 contemporary rooms. While just 50 are air-conditioned, all come with TV, telephone, radio, fax and computer hookup, minibar and combination bath with blow-dryer.

Carrefour De L'Europe Hotel

Expensive
rue du Marche aux Herbes 110.

☎ *(2) 504-9400*, FAX: *(2) 504-9500*.

Credit Cards: *V, MC, DC, A.*

With a definite European flair, this modern hotel is sleekly styled. The 63 large guest rooms feature climate control, cable TV, telephone, radio, minibar, safe and bath with blow-dryer.

Conrad Brussels

Medium to Expensive
Avenue Louise 71.

☎ *445-8667*, (2) ☎ *542-4242*, FAX: *(2) 542-4200*.

Credit Cards: *All Major.*

Behind a 19th-century facade lies a stately display of elegance. The marble reception area has chandeliers, tasteful art, stylish furniture and an attractive lounge. Adjoining this entryway is an eclectic array of fashionable shops. Dining options are plentiful, with a formal French restaurant, summer terrace, cafe and 24-hour room service.

Hotel Amigo

http://www.hotelamigo.com/
Medium to Expensive
1-3, rue de l'Amigo.

☎ *(2) 547-4747*, FAX: *(2) 513-5277*.

Credit Cards: *All Major.*

One step out of its slate-floored lobby lies one of the most breathtaking assemblages of medieval architecture in existence—the Grand Place. Within the hotel's five stories are displays of art and antiques, a traditional restaurant, attractive bar and 186 rooms done in period decor and equipped with cable TV, telephone, radio, minibar, pants press and bath with blow-dryer and bidet.

Hotel Astoria ★★★★

Expensive

rue Royale 103.

☎ *221-4542, (2)* ☎ *217-6290,* FAX: *(2) 217-1150.*

Credit Cards: *All Major.*

A belle-epoque hotel dating to 1909, this gracious hotel distinguishes itself with six stories of Old World charm. Its address is convenient to the Grand Place, government offices, museums and shopping. With 125 guest rooms decorated in period style, all have cable TV, telephone, minibar, twin beds and spacious bath with blow-dryer and bidet. The most peaceful rooms face the courtyard.

Hotel Manos Stephanie ★★★★

http://www.manoshotel.com/ stephanie/index.html

Medium to Expensive

Chaussee de Charleroi 28.

☎ *(2) 539-0250,* FAX: *(2) 537-5729.*

Credit Cards: *All Major.*

This elegant yet unpretentious hotel opened in 1992 and has quickly earned a loyal following of repeat clients. Decorated in traditional style with a Louis XV influence, the 55-art adorned guest rooms have cable TV, telephone, minibar, comfortable queen beds and private bath with a blow-dryer.

Le Dome ★★★★

Expensive

Boulevard du Jardin Botanique 12-13.

☎ *(2) 218-0680*, FAX: *(2) 218-4112*.

Credit Cards: *All Major*.

This art nouveau hotel opened in 1989, though the building dates back to 1902. Full of vibrant character, the turn-of-the-century building is accented with modern furnishings. The 78 guest rooms come with telephone, cable TV, minibar, pants press and private combination bath with blow-dryer and toiletries.

Where to Eat

Bruneau   ★★★★

Expensive

73-75 Avenue Broustin. ☎ *(02) 427.69.78.*

Specialties: *Angus beef with truffles, lasagna with langoustines.*

Credit Cards: *All Major*.

Outside dining, own baking, reservations required.

Gracious Mme. Bruneau coddles guests at this modern restaurant decorated in a rather spare, yet elegant style. Some might prefer the garden room, with a terrace protected from fickle weather. But wherever you sit, you'll enjoy her husband's ever-changing cuisine. He continually invents superb new wonders. A small folder lists from five to 12 different seasonal specialties.

Chez Leon

Moderate

rue des Bouchers 18. ☎ *(02) 511.14.15.*

Metro Stop: *Central Station*.

Specialties: *Mussels, Eels in Green Sauce, waterzooi.*

Credit Cards: *All Major*.

Outside dining, reservations required.

This restaurant might be viewed as the quintessential, popular national restaurant —crowded, noisy, but efficient and rewarding at a moderate price. It's probably the best place in the city to savor the Belgians' favorite dish: mussels served any one of eight ways, but always with a mountain of *frites* (french fries).

Claude Dupont

Expensive

Avenue Vital Riethuisen 46. ☎ *(02) 426.00.00.*

Specialties: *Grilled langoustines, Bouillabaisse, Pigeon de Bresse.*

Credit Cards: *All Major.* Closed: *Mon., Tues.*

Own baking, reservations required.

Claude Dupont stands tall, even in the highest ranks of haute cuisine across Europe. His restaurant fare is a celebration for the hedonistic senses. Master Chef Claude Dupont inclines his extraordinary talents toward modern cuisine. The freshly poached duck liver on a bed of three salads and topped with shaved truffles was super. So was the langouste vinaigrette. The steamed turbot in a light sauce perfumed with leeks is a delight.

Comme Chez Soi

Expensive

place Rouppe 23. ☎ *(02) 512.29.21.*

Specialties: *Sole with a Reisling mousseline and grilled prawns.*

Credit Cards: *DC, A.* Closed: *Mon., Sun.*

Own baking, reservations required.

Unquestionably, this eatery offers some of the finest food in the nation. Quarters may feel cramped, especially if you are seated on an aisle, where waiters bump into your chair or lean over you to serve diners seated against the wall. In-season mousses of ham, salmon, wood-pigeon, snipe, woodcock and others are superb. Book weeks in advance.

De Bijgaarden

Expensive

Van Beverenstraat 20, 1702 Groot Bijgaarden. ☎ *(02) 466.44.85.*

Specialties: *Pressed duck.*

Credit Cards: *All Major.* Closed: *Sun.*

Outside dining, own baking, reservations required.

This four-star establishment, along with **Le Trefle a Quatre**, *(Avenue du Lac 87, 1332 Genval* ☎ (02) 654.07.98), are both top performers in the gastronomic world, but they are on the outskirts of the city. If you take your eating seriously, you must go to both, but take lots of cash (or plastic) and find transportation. Le Trefle features classic, high-quality French and Belgian specialties, including *loup de mer en croute de sel, sauce choron,* and *tournedos of beef with morels and Bordeaux wine sauce.*

Falstaff   ★★

Inexpensive to Moderate

rue Henri Maus 23-25. ☎ *(02) 511.98.77.*

Metro Stop: *Bourse.*

Specialties: *Belgian.*

Credit Cards: *All Major.*

Happening bar, outside dining, cafestop

Bustling and busy, it's a must for a first- time visit. Budget travelers will dine well enough on sandwiches or a lunch plat du jour for 350 BF. Other worthwhile cafes are the **De Ultieme Hallucinatie** *(The Ultimate Hallucination, 316 rue Royale* ☎ (02) 217.06.14), but the only hallucination comes from the gorgeous art nouveau decor or the huge selection of beers and wine. Dining is in a garden area, and dancing is downstairs. **Cirio**, *(rue de la Bourse 18;* ☎ (02) 512.13.95), is where you go to read the newspaper. Artist Max Ernst preferred to doodle at **Fleur en Papier Dore**, *(rue des Alexiens*

55, ☎ *(02) 511.16.59),* which is one of the oldest cafes in town. Don't forget to try Gueuze, possibly Brussels' best-tasting beer; it goes great with bread and cheese.

La Maison du Cygne

Expensive

rue Charles Buls 2. ☎ *(02) 511.82.44.*

Metro Stop: *Bourse.*

Specialties: *Turbot braise a l'armoricaine.*

Credit Cards: *All Major.* Closed: *Sun.*

Reservations required.

La Maison du Cygne is as good as ever—and just as beautiful. Head for the elevator and ride upstairs, where you'll dine grandly amid paneled walls and sumptuous banquettes. Richard Hahn's cuisine adds classic French to Belgian specialties.

Rugbyman No. Two ★★★

Moderate

Quai aux Briques 12. ☎ *(02) 512.37.60.*

Specialties: *Lobster.*

Credit Cards: *All Major.*

Outside dining, reservations recommended.

This restaurant at the municipal Fish Market serves some of the best lobster in town—its other name is "La Maison du Homard." Another plus—it never closes. Other specialties include oysters, *soupe de poissons*, shrimp croquettes and foie gras.

Scheltema

Inexpensive to Moderate

rue des Dominicains 7. ☎ *(02) 512.20.84.*

Specialties: *Seafood platter, Sole with lobster ragout.*

Credit Cards: *All Major.* Closed: *Sun.*

à Outside dining, reservations required.

This busy Grand Place bistro is a long, narrow room furnished simply. It's inexpensive, and makes a good after-theater spot. Good value for the money.

T'Kelderke ★

Inexpensive

Grand' Place 15. ☎ *(02) 513.7344.*

Specialties: *Belgian, mussels.*

Credit Cards: *All Major.*

Cafestop, reservations recommended.

A real cellar that's also a hit with budget-minded eaters. The large menu features Belgian specialties, including mussels and hearty stews.

Trente Rue de la Paille ★★

Moderate

rue de la Paille. ☎ *(02) 512.07.15.*

Specialties: *Gazpacho.*

Credit Cards: *All Major.* Closed: *Sat., Sun.*

Reservations recommended.

Situated in an old house, this is a very good bistro with a slightly clubby atmosphere, fireplace and bar. The house specialty is smoked fish—they make it fresh. The decor and young waiters are cheery; the menu appears on a blackboard.

Villa Lorraine ★★★★★

Very Expensive

Avenue du Vivier d'Oie. *(02) 374.31.63.*

Specialties: *Oysters with champagne, lobster salad with truffles.*

Credit Cards: *All Major.* Closed: *Sun.*

Outside dining, own baking, reservations recommended.

The Villa Lorraine remains a gem for diners with no shortage of money. This is one of the world's finest restaurants, and certainly Belgium's most famous. It has a glorious park location bordering the Bois de la Cambre, about 20 minutes from downtown. In winter there's a crackling hearth, in summer a garden patio captivates, glass- lined for dining with nature on inclement days. The BIG prices match the rewards in every way.

What to Do

Amusement Parks

Atomium ★★★★

20 Blvd. du Centennaire, Bruparck.

Metro Stop: *Heysel.*

Looking like a gigantic silver space creature, the Atomium, built during the Belgian International Exposition in 1958, is a model of an enlarged atom; within is a health and science museum. You can ride to the top in a matter of seconds via a special elevator. But wait, there's more: the Bruparck Complex, where the Atomium is located, is the pride of the Belgian Tourist Board: acres of family fun await in the Mini-Europe model park, the Oceade, and an IMAX theater, the Kinepolis. Kids and families can try the toboggan rides (mini and giant size) in the Oceade tropical aquatic park; afterward, a movie on one of the Kinepolis' 24 regular screens or the giant IMAX theater might appeal. Admission: varies.

Historical Sites

Grand'Place

Grand'Place.

Metro Stop: *Central Station.*

Much of the history of Brussels is traced to this square; one of the most spellbinding in Europe. A thriving marketplace in the Middle Ages, it now is home to baroque guild houses with golden facades, the King's House (Maison du Roi), where no monarch has ever actually lived, and the Town Hall. If you see it first by daylight, be sure to return at nightfall and vice-versa. Surrounding the Grand'Place are narrow cobbled streets that welcome visitors daily to the square's bird and flower markets (except winter).

Hotel de Ville

Grand'Place.

Metro Stop: *Bourse.*

A premier example of 15th-century architecture and the loveliest building in Brussels, the Town Hall is purely Gothic. Topping the spire is a statue of St. Michael, patron saint of the city. A rare collection of tapestries hangs inside. The Brussels city council meets here. Admission: *free.*

St. Michael's Cathedral ★★★

Parvis Ste.Gudule.

7 a.m.–7 p.m.

Special Hours: *Winter to 6 p.m.*

Begun in the 13th century, the national cathedral celebrates Belgian Gothic architecture. In the beautiful mausoleums (visited by appointment only) lie Charles of Lorraine and the Archduke Albert and his wife. The facade and other areas have now been fully restored; excavations of its Romanesque foundations are fascinating; the choir can be visited. Admission: *free.*

Museums and Exhibits

Belgian Centre for Comic Strip Art

20 rue des Sables.

10 a.m.–6 p.m.

Possibly the only one of its kind in the world (at least the only one ensconced in an art nouveau masterpiece by Victor Horta), the museum pays tribute to talented Belgian cartoonists. Special attention is paid to Tintin creator Herge (hugely popular in Europe, a cult fave in the U.S.), and of course the lovable blue thingies, the SMURFS (created by Peyo). Admission: varies.

Maison Horta

rue Americaine 23.

2–5;30 p.m.

Architecture and interior design buffs (especially aficionados of art nouveau) will discover the magic of Horta, one of the premier modernists. Admission: varies.

Museum of Ancient Art and Modern Art

3 rue de la Regence.

Metro Stop: *Central Station or Parc.*

10 a.m.–5 p.m.

Special Hours: *Closed for lunch*

These two compatriots (they are situated next door to each other) certainly form one of the world's finest showcases for intelligent viewing of graphic and plastic arts. Semicircular light fixtures impart soft, reliable natural illumination to the cunningly situated galleries. The sculpture collection, especially, is revealed in all its purity. Though many international titans are represented, artists are predominantly from the French and Belgian schools. Admission: *free.*

Museums at the Palais Mondial

Palais Mondial, 11 Parc du Cinquantenaire.

10 a.m.–6 p.m.

Special Hours: *Winter until 5 p.m.*

Vintage cars glitter by the score—actually 950—some famous, some cute (like a 1903 Olds), some massive. Films and refreshments are offered. Hitler, Roosevelt, Kennedy, and several monarchs were back-seat drivers in some of these venerable classics. Also in the park is the **Royal Army Museum** ☎ (02) 733.44.93, at No. 3, featuring a collection of some twelve centuries of arms, armor, over 130 airplanes and armored vehicles; admission free. Open daily, 9 a.m.– 4:45 p.m. (closed for lunch). At No. 10, are the **Royal Museums of Art and History** ☎ *(02) 741.72.11*, chock full of ancient artifacts from Egypt, Mesopotamia, Greece, Rome, Pre-Columbian America, Asia, Polynesia and Micronesia. There's also an impressive array of European decorative arts from the 10th to the 20th centuries. Open 9:30 a.m–4:45 p.m., Tuesday–Friday. Saturday–Sunday, holidays, from 10 a.m.

Music

Palais de Beaux Arts

rue Ravenstein 23.

Built in 1928 and designed by Victor Horta, the famous art nouveau architect (his buildings are all over town), this structure is the center of the city's cultural life. Home to the National Orchestra of Belgium, with a 3000-seat concert hall, it also has several smaller theaters, a movie house, a king-size exhibition hall, a restaurant and the headquarters of many artistic associations.

Nightlife

Brussels Jazz Club

Grand'Place 13.

One of the world's most breathtaking nightscapes; big names in jazz stop here frequently. Other venues for dancing and music include: **Griffin's** at the Royal Windsor Hotel, *rue Duquesnoy 5* (02) 505.55.55; very respectable, chic; closed Sundays and **Le Garage**, *16 rue Duquesnoy,* ☎ (02) 512.66.22, near the Grand'Place, is loud, dark and typical of outsize discos. Open Wednesday-Sunday from 11 a.m.–6 p.m. Admission: varies.

Shopping

Art et Selection ★★

83 rue Marche aux Herbes.

At the edge of the Grand Place. All the greats are in stock: Val St. Lambert, Rosenthal, Christofle, Lladro and many more, with savings running up to 40 percent of stateside prices. Shipping available. Elegant.

Dandoy ★★★★

rue au Berre 31.

Tempting Belgian pastry shop ships molded *speculoos* (crisp, rich, spice cookies) worldwide; large individual ones available to eat on the spot for a song. Also ice cream and Belgian waffles. Other location, *rue Charles Buls 14-18* ☎ (02) 512.65.88 is close by. World-famous **Wittamer**, at *place du Grand Sablon 12-13* (02) 512.37.42, is tops for its patisserie and chocolates. Possibly the best chocolate in town is at **Mary's**, *73 rue Royale,* ☎ (02) 217.45.00; purveyor of handmade temptations commissioned by the Royal Family. The ubiquitous Godiva shops are now Japanese-owned, and you can find numerous shops all over the U.S.

Delvaux ★★

Galerie de la Reine 31.

European nobility has patronized this establishment for almost two centuries, but the name hasn't traveled afar like Loewe, Gucci, Hermes or others in this specialty. Other location: *22-24 Adolphe Max* ☎ (02) 217.42.34.

F. Rubbrecht

23 Grand'Place.

Sited in a charming 16th century building known as the "House of the Angel," F. Rubbrecht is famous for quality, fair prices and reliability. It offers a tempting variety of rectangular, round, oval, and bridge tablecloths; place mats with napkins, guest towels, christening gowns and more. Antique lace, unique pieces from private collections, is also on display. Friendly welcome from owners and staff. Tops in the nation.

Flea Market

Place du Jeu de Balle.

7 a.m.–2 p.m.

The Flea Market or Vieux Marche, can provide plenty of laughs if you're a bargain hunter. Always wrangle until your face is purple. The Antique Market teems next to Sablon Church Saturday from 9 a.m. until 6 p.m., Sundays from 9 a.m. to 2 p.m. The tents in which it is held are in the official colors of Brussels; green and red. The merchandise runs from modest to very expensive doohickies, including silver, porcelain, and furniture.

Galleries St. Hubert

rue du Marche aux Herbes.

10 a.m.–6 p.m.

Covered galleries that shelter the walker from inclement weather abound. The oldest, built in 1846, is the Galeries Saint- Hubert, near the Grand'Place. The Rue Nueve has been closed off as a pedestrian browsing street. **Innovation** (or Inno), at *No. 11,* ☎ (02) 211.21.11, is the No. 1 department store. The huge

American-style mall, **City 2** is nearby, at *No 235,* *(02) 34.97.30)* with a cinema (eight theatres) and numerous eateries. Perhaps Brussels' toniest shopping area is around the Avenue Louise, where you'll find City Gardens, a complex that takes pride in its surrounding flora. **Les Jardins du Sablons**, at *36 Place du Sablon,* houses many antique shops, plus three restaurants and a tearoom.

W.H. Smith and Son

Blvd. Adolphe Max 71-75.

Stocks a large selection of hardcover titles and more than 2000 paperbacks. **Librairie des Galeries**, *Galerie du Roi 2,* has a large and versatile selection of art volumes.

Theatre

Toone Theatre ★★★★

21 Impasse Schuddeveld.

12 p.m.–12 a.m.

This theatre has a fine museum (open every day) which is free to all during intermissions. Traditional marionnette shows are performed daily (except Sunday and Monday) at 8:30 p.m., each about 2.5 hours in duration. There's a pub on the premises for another great tradition: beer. Guided tours on request; you can even arrange for private showings--great birthday ideas for a lucky kid. Admission: nominal.

East

Liege

Close to the German border, **Liege** is embraced by the Meuse basin, which long ago inspired the masters of Mosan art; today it has become a student center and a springboard to the Ardennes. The panorama from the **Cointe** is particularly worth enjoying. The **Batte Sunday Market** is formidable for hagglers and adventurers; go before noon.

Where to Stay

Forte Posthouse

Moderate

rue Hurbise.

☎ *255-5843,* ☎ *(41) 646-400,* FAX: *(41) 480-690.*

Credit Cards: *All Major.*

Wheelchair-access rooms, pool, nonsmoking rooms.

This deluxe hotel is in a wooded area offering wonderful views of the Meuse Valley. The epitome of comfort, these 96 rooms are tastefully decorated and include some with cable TV, telephone, radio, coffee maker and spacious bath. There is an outdoor pool and a garden on the premises, with tennis, squash, horseback riding and ice skating nearby. This popular hotel treats guests to a pleasant and relaxing stay.

Hotel de la Couronne ★

Moderate

Place des Guillemins 11.

☎ *(41) 522-168,* FAX: *(41) 541-669.*

Credit Cards: *All Major.*

Wheelchair-access rooms.

This plain but comfortable hotel has been around since 1958. Last renovated in 1991, the 77 rooms are quite comfortable. Though plain, this hotel provides comfortable, clean quarters.

Namur

Chateau de Namur

Moderate to Expensive

Avenue de l'Ermitage 1.

☎ *(81) 742-630*, FAX: *(81) 742-392*.

Credit Cards: *All Major.*

Tennis, balcony or patio.

Housed in a distinctive, charming 19th-century chateau dating to 1930, this hotel is a real gem. The hotel has 29 guest rooms, each attractively decorated in traditional style. The rooms, some with balconies, are air-conditioned and equipped with TV, radio, telephone, minibar and spacious bath. Room views of the Meuse River are splendid.

Where to Eat

Au Vieux Liege ★★★★

Moderate to Expensive

quai de la Goffe 41. ☎ *(041) 23.77.48.*

Credit Cards: *All Major.* Closed: *Sun.*

Own baking, reservations required.

Sometimes called Maison Havart, this strikingly handsome, four-story mansion dating back to the 16th century sits on the banks of the Meuse River. Declared a national monument, it is constructed of brick and crosshatched wood. The experience is one of extreme pampering, with tuxedoed waiters hovering discreetly, serving complimentary appetizers, and multicourse meals. A good value for the money, especially at lunch.

Brasserie as Ouhes ★★★

Moderate

place du Marche 21. ☎ *(041) 23.32.25.*

Specialties: *Lotte, Lobster.*

Credit Cards: *V, MC, A.* Closed: *Sun.*

Cafestop

This is a luxury bistro serving local specialties plus some robust

French dishes, including Alsatian *choucroute garnie*. It's possible to eat well here for less than 1200 BF, including wine and dessert.

What to Do

City Events

La Batte Market   ★★★

quai de la Batte.

9 a.m.–2 p.m.

Special Hours: *Sunday only*

The granddaddy of street markets is this mile-long bazaar (food stalls too,) held Sunday mornings only, in this square on the left bank of the Meuse between place Cockerill and Maghin Bridge. Old books, furniture, plants, antiques galore, all things wacky and wonderful, junky and fine, exist side by side.

Museums and Exhibits

Arms Museum   ★★★

quai de Maastricht 8.

Liege is home to several prominent arms manufacturers, including the FN Browning plant; the Liege hunting gun is a work of art, often magnificently engraved. This museum maintains an awe-inspiring collection of weaponry, (more than 8000 items) from a medieval bow and arrow to a 14-barrel rifle. Admission: varies.

Northern
Antwerp

Antwerp is one of the greatest ports on the European Continent—yet it's 54 miles from the sea. The Scheldt River is the answer: As many as 45,000 barges and 17,000 oceangoing ships tie up to the 60 miles of docks every year. In warm weather, you can see much of the waterfront by boat. The six-lane, 2000-foot-long John F. Kennedy Tunnel eases train and car traffic under the river. This city remains the world center for the diamond trade, much of it concerned with cutting and industrial applications. Its heartbeat is Pelikaanstraat, but if you want to observe the entire process from mining exhibits to cutting to setting to, yes, even selling the highly finished product, go to fabulous **Diamond Land** at *Appelmansstraat 33-A* in the same district or visit the Provincial Diamond Museum at *Lange Herentalsestraat 31-33.* Flemish is the regional language. The **Rubens mansion** is a sightseeing must, along with the **Royal Art Gallery.** The **Mayer van den Bergh Museum** is in a house that creates a perfect showcase for some of the nation's finest artworks. Also in midcity is the 12th-century **Steen Castle,** housing the **National Maritime Museum**; so is the magnificent statue in the Grand' place of the Roman centurion who saved the town, thus providing the legend from which the metropolis took its name. On a religious note, **Our Lady's Cathedral** is a marvelous example of the 30 Christian churches; there are also 22 synagogues, 16 mosques and three Buddhist temples in town. If you have more time, the **Butchers' Hall** and **Brewers' House** museums are lesser known but contain fascinating collections of art, musical instruments, archaeological finds and furniture, none of which is related to their guild or trade names. The **Museum of Regional Ethnology** is a lively, folkloric trip into the past, even with puppets to spice it up for kids; the **Museum of Ethnography** is more studious. The **Zoo** includes an aquarium in the gardens, a dolphinarium, a unique aviary and a nocturama. About five minutes by car from the center, stroll through the fabulous open-air **Middelheim Park,** a year-round sculpture garden; there's dining at the palace among moats, swans, Rodins and Moores. On a more solemn note, about halfway between Antwerp and the capital is a former Nazi concentration camp. It has been preserved intact as a national museum.

Where to Stay

Alfa de Keyser Hotel   ★★★★

http://www.alfahotels.com/ ALFA GB DEKEYSER.htm

Moderate to Expensive

De Keyserlei 66.

☎ *(3) 234-0135,* FAX: *(3) 232-3970.*

Credit Cards: *All Major.*

Pool, sauna, nonsmoking rooms.

This midcity hotel evokes a clean, modern air enhanced by quality features. Its sleek European look is maintained by a top-notch staff. The 123 rooms are done in modern style, with textured walls, colorful fabrics, indirect lighting and radio, cable TV, telephone, minibar, climate control and private bath with blow-dryer. Helpful concierges and a good staff maintain the standards of this fine establishment.

Hotel De Rosier

Expensive

Rosier 21-23.

☎ *(3) 225-0140,* FAX: *(3) 231-4111.*

Credit Cards: *All Major.*

Pool, sauna.

The De Rosier is head and shoulders above the competition as the finest and most exclusive lodging in the area. Housed in a 17th-century mansion, the lap of luxury is an intimate one with just 12 guest rooms. Without a grand facade, the hotel instead relies on its stately garden courtyard and tastefully decorated interior. Each room is individually decorated and includes cable TV, telephone, radio, tile and marble baths with blow-dryers, robes and luxury toiletries. Bar. An absolutely exquisite experience.

Plaza Hotel

Moderate to Expensive

Charlottalei 43-49.

☎ *(3) 218-9240,* FAX: *(3) 218-8823.*

Credit Cards: *All Major.*

Nonsmoking rooms.

On a shady street in the center of the city, this traditional hotel sits near a park. There are 86 spacious rooms adorned with antique

English furnishings. Each unit is equipped with a cable TV, telephone, radio, safe and bath with blow-dryer. Those with a balcony overlooking the rear garden are the most peaceful and scenic.

Eurotel Antwerp Hotel

Moderate to Expensive

Copernicuslaan 2.

☎ *(3) 231-6780,* FAX: *(3) 233-0290.*

Credit Cards: *All Major.*

Pool, tennis, Jacuzzi, sauna.

This giant 11-story structure opened in 1974 and holds the title of the largest hotel in the city. It has 330 contemporary guest rooms, handsomely done in light wood, modern furnishings, tasteful fabrics and plush carpeting. Each comes with a telephone, cable TV, radio, minibar, refrigerator, balcony and luxurious bath with blow-dryer. The staff prides itself on courtesy and efficiency.

Where to Eat

Cafe Kulminator

Inexpensive to Moderate

32 Vleminckveld. ☎ *(03) 232.45.38.*

Credit Cards: *All Major.* Closed: *Sun.*

Happening bar, outside dining, cafestop

Here you'll find 550 varieties of beer, all of which are served in special glasses at proper temperatures. This establishment, with a garden in back, is named for a Berlin beer that is served extremely cold in a mug that is smaller than a cognac glass. Snacks are served. Other bars include **De Groote Witte Arend** *(Reyndersstraat 18,* open 11 a.m.–1:30 a.m.), formerly an old convent. There's a myriad of rooms, benches and an open courtyard for sunny day sipping. Classical music wafts through the air. Selected beers (particularly Trappist types) are available here, as are cheese or pate plates and cakes. **Den Engel** *(3 Grote Markt,* open 24 hours), is a famous old haunt often packed with local devotees. Though plain, the tone in this bar is lively. Patrons play a game called De Ton (Barrel), in which brass cylinders are tossed at the 12 holes in a board. Special De Koninck (The King) beer, is dark and delicious. Less expensive, but bigger than the other bars is **Bierland** *(28 Korte Nieustraat,* open Sun.–Thurs., 8 a.m. until closing, Fri. and Sat. from 12 p.m.), which boasts some 1000 varieties of beer.

Het Vermoeide Model ★★★

Moderate

2 Lijnwaadmarkt. ☎ *(03) 233.52.61.*

Credit Cards: *V, MC.* Closed: *Sat., Sun.*

Reservations recommended.

It's unclear what the name (The Bored Model) has to do with its interesting location (it's actually part of the Cathedral), but the excellent seafood served here will certainly keep you awake.

L'Elephant Bleu ★★★

Moderate

1120 Chaussee de Waterloo. ☎ *(02) 374.49.62.*

Specialties: *Emerald chicken, grey mullet with vegetables.*

Credit Cards: *All Major.*

Reservations recommended.

Exotic and extraordinary, this Thai restaurant serves some of the priciest ethnic food in town. Part of a European chain, L'Elephant Bleu has branches in London, Paris and other major cities. The menu descriptions are endearingly comical; sauces are described as "sweet as a first kiss," or "fiery as a volcano." The vegetarian menu is fairly extensive.

La Perouse ★★★

Moderate to Expensive

Ponton Steen. ☎ *(03) 231.73.58.*

Specialties: *Waterzooi de poussin.*

Credit Cards: *All Major.* Closed: *Mon., Sun. Outside dining, own baking, reservations required.*

A novel location, La Perouse is the dining area of a Flandria sight-seeing boat, which is moored September 15 to May 15 at the Flandria Co. dock on the Schelck River. (In summer, the boat makes daily shuttles between Antwerp and Flushing.) The restaurant has a refitted wooden deck and piano music at night. The ambience is enjoyable in sunlight or starlight. Try a definitive version of *water-zooi de poussin*, a seafood stew with vegetables and a butter and cream sauce. Ordering is strictly a la carte.

Les Baguettes Imperiales ★★

Moderate

70 Avenue Jean Sobieski. ☎ *(02) 479.67.32.*

Specialties: *Vietnamese-Belgian cuisine.*

Credit Cards: *A.* Closed: *Tues.*

Outside dining, own baking, reservations required.

This unique restaurant serves Vietnamese and Belgian cuisine, an inspiring combination. Proprietors Huu Duy and Tam Ma provide truly elegant surroundings for you to savor such delicacies as *pigeon-neau farci aux nids d'hirondelles* or Barbary duck for four.

Sir Anthony Van Dyck ★★★

Expensive

Oude Koornmarkt 16. ☎ *(03) 233.19.25.*

Credit Cards: *All Major.* Closed: *Sat., Sun.*

Own baking, reservations required.

To enter you must stroll through an old grain market, which is a courtyard complex of restored 16th-century buildings called the

Vlaaikensgang. Decor is sophisticated and lighting is soft, provided mostly by a candle at each table. Dine on delicacies like baked goose foie gras, while piped classical music plays in the background. This is possibly one of Antwerp's (and Belgium's) most renowned restaurants.

What to Do

Historical Sites

Cathedral of Our Lady   ★★★★

Hansschoenmarkt.

10 a.m.–5 p.m.

Special Hours: *Saturday 1 p.m.-4 p.m., Sunday, 1 - 9 p.m.*

Built between the 14th and 16th centuries, this Gothic cathedral is one of the largest houses of worship in Europe; certainly it is the largest in either Holland or Belgium, boasting seven naves and 125 pillars. Don't miss (it's hard not to) two masterpieces by Rubens; "Descent from the Cross," a triptych painted in 1612, and "The Assumption." An exhaustive, 28-year restoration was completed in the summer of 1994. Admission: nominal.

Museums and Exhibits

Diamondland   ★★★

Appelmansstraat 33A.

9 a.m.–6 p.m.

Diamonds are forever. In an elegant, subdued setting, you can see some 12,000 cutters magically coaxing dowdy rocks into glittering beauties. Tours are given, and you can purchase a bauble or two as well. Not far away, at *Lange Herentalsestraat 31-33* (in the heart of the Diamond District), you can visit the **Provincial Diamond Museum** (03/202.48.90), where this thriving industry comes to life by means of photos, models, and a fascinating treasury with exhibits of antique and modern diamond jewelry. Admission: nominal.

Museum Mayer van den Bergh

Lange Gasthuisstraat 19.

10 a.m.–5 p.m.

This museum in the former home of art maven Fritz Mayer van den Bergh was actually built in the early 20th century, although it is a faithful enough reproduction of a 16th century dwelling. There are some distinguished paintings by Flemish artists and some lovely examples of Flemish decorative art, tapestries and lace, but the piece de resistance is the visually arresting "Mad Meg" by Brueghel the Elder, a frightening commentary on the horrors of war. Admission: varies.

Royal Museum of Fine Arts

Leopold de Waelplaats.

10 a.m.–5 p.m.

More of Rubens' largesse is seen here in this beautiful museum with a Greek/Roman facade. Two naturally-lit upstairs rooms are set aside for a breathtaking collection of the Baroque master's sketches, oils and larger-than-life canvases. All told, there are over 2500 major Flemish (and a smaller collection of foreign) paintings from the 14th to the 20th centuries. Admission: $3.00 and up.

Rubens' House

Wapper 9-11.

10 a.m.–5 p.m.

Lucky Peter Paul Rubens, the great painter, never languished in obscurity, his works selling for millions after his death. Only in his early 30s, already wealthy and renowned, he was able to build this grand dwelling, where he subsequently lived and worked. Situated in Main Street Antwerp (the Meir), it contains a collection of his tasteful furnishings and objets d'art. Admission: nominal.

Parks and Gardens

Antwerp Zoo

Koningen Astridplein 26.

9 a.m.–6:30 p.m.

Special Hours: *Winter until 5 p.m.*

This is one city where you don't have to drive for miles to get to the zoo; it's located just behind the Central Station. The 25-acre park is fascinating as well as environmentally sensitive; uncaged birds fly about freely in the aviary, and there are frequent exhibitions dealing with endangered species, including a recent tropical rain-forest insect show. Worth the pricey admission, if you have the time to spare. Admission: varies.

Middelheim Open-Air Museum of Sculpture

Middelheimlaan 61.

10 a.m.–7 p.m.

Always free and eternally open to the skies, this conglomeration of important sculptures features 200 pieces by Rodin, Henry Moore, Aristide Maillol and others.

Mechelen
Special Tours

Mechelen Tours ★★★★

Town Hall, Grote Markt.

A worthwhile excursion from either Antwerp or Brussels is Mechelen, home of the most renowned Carillon school in the world. Mini-concerts are heard daily at noon from St. Rombold's Cathedral. Groups meet every weekend (and public holidays) from Easter until September at the Tourist office at 2 p.m. for a historic walk through the city. Highlights include a visit to St. Rombold's bell tower at 2:15 p.m. (also Mon. at 7 p.m. from July 1– Sept. 15). You can also inquire about the boat trips to **Planckendael Wild Animal Park** nearby in Muizen-Mechelen. Over 1000 animals (including rare tigers) can be seen roaming in recreated natural habitats. Open daily, 9 a.m.–6:30 p.m. in summer and until 5 p.m. in winter; admission 350 BF, Children (3–11) and seniors; 215 BF. Also fun for kids is the **Toy Museum**, *Nekkerspoel 21,* (015) 55.70.75, open 10 a.m.–5 p.m., closed Mondays; admission is nominal. There are over 30 departments of antique toys, some of them very intricate indeed.

Northwest
Bruges

Bruges is often labeled the "Venice of the North." Back when it was world-renowned for its immensely prosperous wool and cloth trade and equally as a trading center and port, it boasted a population of nearly 40,000—as big as London or Cologne. Over the past decade it has been restored with cobblestones, and hundreds of old houses have been reconstituted, facades cleaned and trees planted in squares. Large areas have been closed to traffic. With the reverberations from the belfries instead of the roar of traffic, here is a convivial transport to the sights and sounds of the Late Middle Ages. Now, save for Brussels, it is the greatest attraction to visitors in Belgium.

Where to Stay
Bed and Breakfast

Hotel Adornes

Medium

Saint Annarei 26.

☎ *(50) 341-336,* FAX: *(50) 342-085.*

Credit Cards: *V, A, A.*

Hotel Adornes gets high ratings for the ambience that can only be found in a small bed and breakfast. This picturesque hotel lies beside a canal bridge and is managed by the owner's daughter. There are three adjacent 17th-century houses with polished wood floors and exposed beams. The cozy rooms, although small, are inviting and comfortable; some offer canal views. The cheerful staff serves a wonderful breakfast in a warmly decorated breakfast room with fireplace.

Guests have use of free bicycles to tour this lovely town and surrounding countryside. It's a memorable lodging experience.

Hotels and Resorts

Hotel Die Swaene

http://www.dieswaene-hotel.com/

Expensive

Steenhouwersdijk 1.

☎ *525-4800,* ☎ *(50) 342-798,* FAX: *(50) 336-674.*

Credit Cards: *All Major.*

Pool, sauna.

A true gem in every detail, this hotel exudes romance and elegance. This three- story hotel opened in 1981 in a restored 16th-century patrician residence on a picturesque canal with boats and carriages passing by day and a lulling silence by night. With just 23 guest rooms, the size allows for the kind of personal attention this hotel is known for. Each individually decorated room comes with cable TV, telephone, radio, minibar, bath with blow-dryer and some have canopy beds and fireplace. Caring management provides concierge service and baby-sitting.

Hotel Portinari

Moderate

't Zand 15.

☎ *(50) 341-034,* FAX: *(50) 344-180.*

Credit Cards: *V, DC, A, E.*

Outside of the old town yet still within walking distance to the Markt, this charming hotel is situated on a large square. The attitude is relaxed and friendly and the 40 guest rooms are well maintained. The rooms are comfortable, tastefully decorated in contemporary. Each comes with TV, radio, telephone, minibar and bath with blow-dryer; some are wheelchair accessible.

Oud Huis Amsterdam

Moderate to Expensive

Spiegelrei 3.

☎ *(50) 341-810,* FAX: *(50) 338-891.*

A beautifully restored 17th-century mansion, this old house is graced with period furniture that accents its stately facade. It has 20 rooms and two suites, all with lovely decor and polished furniture. Some of the rooms offer canal views. A favorite spot is the lovely sitting room, which offers pure comfort.

Inns

Alfa Dante Hotel

Coupure 29.

☎ *(50) 340-194,* FAX: *(50) 343-539.*

Credit Cards: *All Major.*

This cheerful hotel resides on a small canal outside of the old town center. It houses 22 spacious guest rooms with views of the canal. Each unit features cable TV, telephone, minibar, safe and private bath with blow-dryer. A health-oriented restaurant serves good food and there's a bar adjacent to the lobby.

De Snippe

Moderate to Expensive

Nieuwe Gentweg 53.

☎ *(50) 337-070,* FAX: *(50) 337-662.*

Credit Cards: *All Major.*

This 18th-century house is tucked away on a peaceful street close to the town center. Only four suites and five double rooms comprise this attractive, distinctive abode. The rooms are brightly lit and pleasantly decorated.

Europe Hotel

Inexpensive to Moderate

Augustijnenrei 18.

☎ *(50) 337-975*, FAX: *(50) 345-266*.

Credit Cards: *All Major.*

Situated alongside a canal in the center of town, this quiet hotel first opened in 1968 in a building that dates back to 1789. The hotel offers modern comfort while maintaining a distinctive character. Each of the rooms has a TV, radio, telephone and shower or bath; the latter are modest, with just rudimentary showers in most.

Hotel Prinsenhof

Moderate to Expensive

Ontvangersstraat 9.

☎ *(50) 342-690*, FAX: *(50) 342-321*.

Credit Cards: *All Major.*

With all of the warmth expected of a family-run hotel, the Prinsenhof has been welcoming guests since 1986. The 16-room hotel features wood decor, TV, telephone, minibar, radio and bath with blow-dryer. Housekeeping is of the highest standards. Breakfast is served in the breakfast room, and 24-hour room service is available.

Where to Eat

'T Bourgoensche Cruyce

Expensive

Wollestraat 41. ☎ *(050) 33.79.26.*

Credit Cards: *V, A, E.* Closed: *Wed.*

Outside dining, reservations required.

Directly facing the Duc de Burgogne from across the canal, this old stone building with an outdoor terrace enjoys an equally captivating view. The cooking is refined, beautifully served, expensive and somewhat regional. It's small, so be sure to reserve ahead.

(de) Witte Poorte

Moderate

Jan van Eyckplein 6. ☎ *(050) 33.08.83.*

Specialties: *Waterzooi with Langoustines, Turbot.*

Credit Cards: *All Major.* Closed: *Sun.*

Outside dining, reservations required.

Located in one of the city's most historic quarters, this restaurant is Old World in mood, but modern in gastronomy. The garden is blissful. There's a set menu with a choice of five wines.

Breydel - de Coninck

Inexpensive to M oderate

Breidelstraat 24. ☎ *(050) 33.97.46.*

Specialties: *Mussels in a bucket, Eels, Lobster.*

Credit Cards: *V, A, E.* Closed: *Tues., Wed.*

Reservations required.

This lively, cheery, centrally located cafe is popular for its endless buckets o' mussels. Other specialties include lobster and eels.

De Bretoen-Creperie ★★

Inexpensive

4 Ezelstraat. ☎ *(050) 34.54.25.*

Specialties: *Crepes.*

Credit Cards: *All Major.* Closed: *Tues.*

Outside dining, cafestop, own baking, reservations recommended.

This pancake-creperie house offers a wide variety of Breton-style crepes, regional snacks and omelettes.

De Snippe

Moderate to Expensive

Nieuwe Gentweg 53. ☎ *(050) 33.70.70.*

Specialties: *Wild duck, Caviar, Langoustines.*

Credit Cards: *All Major.*

â Own baking, reservations required.

This upscale restaurant features a snug and cozy dining room housed in an 18th-century townhouse with comfortable black-leather chairs. The ample menu features fish, crustaceans and game, with wild duck a specialty. The wine cellar is fabulous.

Restaurant Belfort ★★

Inexpensive

32 Markt.

Specialties: *Belgian.*

Credit Cards: *All Major.*

Outside dining, cafestop

This is a simple, working man's cafe in the heart of the Grote Markt that serves high- quality, reasonably priced daily specials. The four-course feasts include fresh vegetable soup, smoked fish, an entree featuring chicken or beef and dessert.

What to Do

If you're headed toward this land for Ascension Day, Bruges' globally famous **Procession of the Holy Blood** shouldn't be missed. The ancient architecture now glows. Its intimate, fine museums are superb; be sure to see Memling's work at the **Hospital of St. John**, the **Town Hall** and the **Belfry Tower**. Noteworthy churches are Notre Dame and the 10th-century St. Saviour.

Handmade lace and the wonderful little local pastries are the industries of greatest interest. Two pint-size but outstandingly pleasant excursions: Take up a seat in one of the small motorboats and laze at random along the canals, which are among the most romantic settings on this planet. The duration is about 30 minutes. Or glide along the canal **Damme** for about the same time. Because some trips ply the year-round while others are limited to High Season, you might wish to inquire at the Bruges Tourist Office for schedules. It's a delightful town, through which a tour is highly recommended.

City Celebrations

Procession of the Holy Blood

Various locations.

Even if you are not particularly religious, this major traditional event should probably be seen by everyone at least once. A relic of the blood of Christ, brought back from the Second Crusade by Thierry d'Alsace in 1150, is promenaded through the city streets, while citizens re-enact, in pantomime, stories from the Bible. Held every year, on Ascension Day, around the 25th of May.

Excursions

Straffe Hendrik Brewery

Walplein 26.

10 a.m.–5 p.m.

Special Hours: *Oct.–Mar., 11 a.m. and 3 p.m.*

Everything you ever wanted to know about medieval beer (produced here since 1546) you'll learn at this brewery with a pub attached. The pride and joy of the place is "Straffe Hendrik," a maltarama that'll put hair (or inches) on your chest. Admission: nominal.

Historical Sites

Belfry and Halles

Markt 7.

Special Hours: *Closed 12:30 p.m.–1:30 p.m.*

The medieval tower is the city's centerpiece, looming benevolently over everything at 275 feet high. You can (huff! puff! 366 steps!) climb your way to the top for excellent views. Bruges' mighty carillon, all 27 tons of it, and boasting 47 bells, is world-famous (at least among carillonites); concerts are given Wednesdays and weekends from 2:15 p.m.–3 p.m., and in summer Monday, Wednesday and Saturday from 9 p.m.–10 p.m. and Sundays from 2:15 p.m.–3 p.m.

Town Hall   ★★★

The Burg.

9:30 a.m.–6 p.m.

Special Hours: *Closed noon–2 p.m.*

A masterpiece of Gothic design (1376-1420), Bruges' town hall is one of the oldest in Europe. Even if you don't have time to look inside, take a moment to study the exterior of the building, which is resplendent with statuary. There's more Gothic within, especially on the first floor, where murals visually explain how Bruges came to be. Admission: $5.00 and up.

Museums and Exhibits

Groeningemuseum   ★★★

http://www.brugge.be/Musea/en/ mgroee.htm

Dijver 12.

Special Hours: *Winter closed from 12:30–2 p.m.*

A major museum, noted for its impressive collection of Old Flemish and Flemish Impressionist paintings (15th-20th century). Van Dyck, Hans Memling, Roger van der Weyden, and Hieronymus Bosch are well represented. Admission: varies.

Shopping

Kantcentrum Brugge (Lace Center)   ★★★

Peperstraat 3.

🕐 *10 a.m.–6 p.m.*

Special Hours: *Closed from 12 p.m.–2 p.m.*

Located next to the Jerusalem Church, the Lace Center is ensconced in an 15th century almshouse. Demonstrations of one of Bruges' most famous art forms are given in the afternoons. Hobbyists can buy lace to turn into their own masterpieces in the museum-shop on the premises. Admission: $5.00 and up.

Special Tours

Brugge by Boat

Various locations.

10 a.m.–6 p.m.

Special Hours: *Winter: weekends and holidays only*

Seeing the city's sights couldn't be much better (or easier) than on this reasonably-priced, leisurely boat trip via Bruges' interlocking system of canals. Boats leave every half-hour from several points around the city, with several stops near the Burg (center square). Consult your city map; wherever you see anchor icons, a boat won't be far away. Night tours available on request. Admission: varies.

Windmill Tours ★★★

Koning Leopold III- laan 41.

Flanders is windmill country; once upon a time there were over 800 dotting the landscape. The two big wars decimated most of them, but there are still some 60 left (with sails). Concerned windmill preservation groups (including the Environment Dept. of the Provincial Administration of West Flanders, see below) conduct tours to some 25 windmills open to the public, and you can even observe the sails turn.

Sports and Recreation

The Back Road Bike Co.

The Burg (in front of the tourist office).

The name says it all: bike the back roads of Brugge with an English-speaking guide, on top-quality mountain bikes. Leisurely tours, exploring the Flemish countryside, usually last from 2-4 hours, and you'll see little wonders often bypassed by the everyday tourist. Bikes, packs, bottled water, rain gear and insurance included. Tours leave from the Burg square, in front of the Tourist Office. Reservations recommended. Admission: varies.

Ghent

Culture, beauty and charm abound, and most of the finest edifices are now freshly steam-cleaned. Once second only to Paris in terms of continental influence, the city at the confluence of the Lys and the Scheldt is full of memories. After you've been awed by Van Eyck's splendid *Adoration of the Lamb* at St. Bavon Cathedral there are more than a dozen museums to visit, as well as a fine botanical exhibit and merchant- and guildhouses that recall medieval prosperity. The hotel situation has improved dramatically in recent times.

Where to Stay

Hotels and Resorts

Alfa Flanders Hotel　　　　　　　　　　　　

http://www.alfahotels.com/ ALFA GB FLANDERS.htm

Expensive

Koning Albertlaan 121.

☎ *(9) 222-6065,* FAX: *(9) 220-1605.*

Credit Cards: *All Major.*

Nonsmoking rooms.

Oriented to business travelers, this hotel proves a quality choice for any traveler. The hotel has 24-hour room service and concierge service. The 49 guest rooms are handsomely decorated and come with a cable TV, radio, telephone, pants press, safe, minibar and combination bath with a blow-dryer and toiletries. Personal attention and flawless service are provided by the hard-working staff.

Flor Hotel

Moderate

Grote Huidevettershoek 10.

☎ *(9) 223-8919*, FAX: *(9) 223-3378*.

On a canal in the middle of town, this hotel opened in 1992. The main attraction here for most is the hip restaurant that serves creative French and Belgian food in an artsy atmosphere. Accommodations are limited to the two guest rooms designed for the open-minded traveler seeking an unpretentious stay. The rooms have an eclectic character—parquet floors and tile walls, draped four-poster beds and windows that are shaded by Venetian blinds. Amenities are limited, with a radio and telephone only. Bathrooms are highlighted by marble sinks, blow-dryers and plenty of toiletries.

St. Jorishof Hotel

Moderate

Botermarkt 2.

☎ *(9) 224-2424*, FAX: *(9) 224-2640*.

Credit Cards: *All Major.*

A hotel since 1228, many consider St. Jorishof Europe's oldest hotel. Mary of Burgundy was forced to sign Ghent's Great Privilege here in 1477; Charles V and Napoleon have been on the guest list in past centuries. The original structure now houses the restaurant and lobby. Across the way are the 28 guest rooms in a more modern 18th-century buildings. Each was renovated in 1992 and is equipped with central heating, TV, telephone, bath and some with minibar.

Inns

Hotel Gravensteen

http://www.gravensteen.be/

Moderate to Expensive

Jan Breydelstraat 35.

☎ *(9) 225-1150,* FAX: *(9) 225-1850.*

Credit Cards: *All Major.*

This intimate hotel occupies a restored 19th-century mansion close to the Castle of Counts. This small, modest hotel houses just 17 guest rooms. Each antique-decorated room comes with a TV, telephone, minibar, twin bed and combination bath with a telephone, blow-dryer and robes. Tennis courts, squash courts and a small beach are nearby. This hotel is a delightful choice with character, charm and friendly service.

Where to Eat

Apicius   ★★★★

Expensive

8 Maurice Maeterlinckstraat. ☎ *(09) 22.46.00.*

Specialties: *Belgian.*

Credit Cards: *All Major.* Closed: *Sun.*

Own baking, reservations required.

This imposing *palais* features important cuisine— it's rated as one of the top ten destinations in the country. David Hicks designed the interior, creative owner/chef Willy Slawinski serves up French-Belgian cuisine, and his wife, Nicole, greets guests.

De Dulle Griet   ★★

Inexpensive

Vrijdagmarkt 50. ☎ *(09) 224.24.55.*

Specialties: *Belgian, 250 varieties of beer.*

Credit Cards: *All Major.*

Cafestop, reservations recommended.

Regional meals are served on the second level of this beer bar in a 15th-century setting. Below, the bar offers specialty brews produced in Trappist monasteries and abbeys on tables made from old beer kegs. Other atmospheric old taverns that are open late include **Oud Middelhuis** *(Graslei 6)*, a 17th-century building featuring 300 varieties of beer; and **Het Waterhuis** in the *Groentenmarkt (No. 9)*, which offer a canal-side setting.

Jan Breydel ★★★

Moderate

Jan Breydelstraat 10. ☎ *(09) 225.62.87.*

Credit Cards: *V. MC.* Closed: *Sun.*

Own baking, reservations recommended.

Someone in this family-run restaurant has the magic touch with all things green: There's a profusion of blooming wonders all around the dining room. Although decor is California-style, you won't forget you're in Flanders. Cuisine is decidedly regional, with fresh seafood the specialty.

Raadskelaar ★★

Moderate

Sint Baafsplein. ☎ *(09) 225.43.34.*

Specialties: *Belgian.*

Credit Cards: *All Major.*

Reservations recommended.

The city's cloth and wool merchants once met in this restaurant situated under the Lakenhal, or Cloth Hall, adjoining the Belfry. Dating back to the 15th-century, it has plenty of atmosphere and also is obviously a favorite of tour groups. But don't let that deter you, as you'll get a lot of fuel for your Euros. Seating is on church pews, and the four-course tourist menu, which includes dessert, is satisfying regional specialties, waterzooi is often featured); a la carte offerings are less of a value, but portions are large enough to share.

Waterzooi ★★

Moderate

Sint Veerleplein 2. ☎ *(09) 225.05.63.*

Specialties: *Waterzooi.*

Credit Cards: *All Major.* Closed: *Wed.*

Reservations recommended.

Centrally located, this eatery is famous for waterzooi with fish or chicken (a stew with a rich brew of cream and vegetables, Ghent's foremost regional specialty). Generous portions are served here.

What to Do

City Celebrations

The Festival of Flanders ★★★

http://www.festival-van-vlaanderen.be/index_english.html

Various locations.

Chamber orchestras, choirs and symphonies of world renown perform yearly in September and October in Ghent's Town Hall, various medieval abbeys and in St. Bavo's Cathedral. For information, contact the **Festival Secretariaat**, *Kasteel Borluut, Kleine Gentstraat 46, 9051 Ghent - St. Denijs Westrem.* Ticket Information: *Graaf van Vlaanderenplein 40, 9000 Ghent;* ☎ (09) 225.77.80; Fax (09) 224.11.80. Other festivals of renown include the Flanders International Film Festival in October, various locations. Some 140 films by independent and not so independent filmmakers are shown citywide, drawing the requisite glitterati and hangers-on. There are also free workshops and symposiums. For information, call ☎ (09) 221.89.46; Fax; (09) 221.90.74. In mid-July, a people's fair, the Ghent Festivities, are held all over town, lasting about ten days. Springing from a small, local folkloric celebration, it's now a full-blown touristic event, with music, entertainment, comedy and impromptu "happenings" on street corners throughout the city.

Historical Sites

Graslei

Graslei.

The guild houses facing the Graslei (quay) are a remarkable melding of 12th to 17th century architectural styles. Each individual structure was built to reflect the taste and lifestyles of what were once powerful, enterprising commercial unions; they are particularly impressive when illuminated. You can see this phenomenon nightly from May through October from sunset until midnight. Other months, they are lit up on Friday and Saturday evenings.

St. Bavo's Cathedral

Sint Baafsplein.

Special Hours: *Sun 1–6 p.m., closed 12 p.m.– 2 p.m.*

A juxtaposition of styles, Romanesque, Gothic and baroque, St. Bavo's Cathedral houses the magnificent polyptych *The Adoration of the Mystic Lamb* by Jan and Hubert van Eyck, which should not be missed. Dating from around 1432, the painting is composed of 24 vividly colored and impressively detailed panels (front and back). Over 300 faces and more than 200 species of flowers, trees and shrubs are represented. Other art treasures include Rubens' *The Entry of St. Bavo into the Monastery* (1623). Admission: *free.*

The Castle of the Counts/Het Gravensteen

Sint-Veerleplein.

9 a.m.–6 p.m.

Special Hours: *Winter until 4 p.m.*

Seen on every postcard and guidebook to the city, the moated, turreted 12th-century fortification is both beautiful and forbidding. The castle was built by Phillip of Alsace in 1180, count of Flanders, partially as a defense against his own rebellious citizens. Abandoned by the court in the 14th century, it was later used for various other purposes, including a prison. Inside, the Museum for Court Paraphernalia contains a guillotine and other instruments of torture.

Admission: $5.00 and up.

Museums and Exhibits

Museum of Fine Arts   ★★

Nicolaas de Liemaeckereplein 3.

9:30 a.m.–5:30 p.m.

Special Hours: *Closed 12:30 p.m.–1:30 p.m.*

Paintings from the Flemish Primitive school dominate this impressive museum, especially Jeroen Bosch's "The Bearing of the Cross," showing a beleaguered Christ taunted by a teeming crowd of vulgar louts. Works by European masters Rubens (The Stigmata of St. Francis of Assisi), Pieter Brueghel the Younger and others are also represented, as well as a collection of contemporary art works by the Flemish School of St. Martens in Latem, which is a suburb of Ghent. Admission: $5.00 and up.

Special Tours

Canal Boat Rides   ★★★

Graslei.

10 a.m.–6 p.m.

Leisurely boat trips (both covered and uncovered) on Ghent's canals (the Leie and the Lieve) can be taken every day from the Graslei, leaving every 30 minutes. Each trip is about 40 minutes in duration. Independent travelers can charter a mini-yacht to explore the canals on their own, available from the **Minerva Company**, *Kareelstraat 6*, (090) 221.84.51. The vessels can be rented by the hour or by the day. Larger, skippered yachts can also be rented, for as long as you want, dependent on the depths of your pocket. Boats leave from the Minerva Harbor, corner of Coupure/Lindelei near the center of Ghent, about three miles from St-Pieters station. Reservations recommended. Another company, the **Benelux Rederij**, *Recollettenlei 10*, ☎ (09) 224.33.33, takes groups on the Leie; summer cruises include visits to Ooidonk Castle, a 14th century fortification about 20 miles from Ghent. The boats also travel to Bruges, and include a tour to the Straffe Hendrik Brewery. Admission: varies.

Tours of Ghent

 Town Hall, Botermarkt and Hoogpoort.

The medieval jewel that is Ghent (it was the second largest city in Northern Europe in the Middle Ages) may seem overwhelming at first; perhaps a city tour conducted by the Association of the Guides of Ghent and East Flanders might help. Tour highlights include a visit to St. Bavo's Cathedral, with its collection of priceless paintings, including the Van Eyck brothers' "The Adoration of the Mystical Lamb," (1426-1432) and Rubens' "The Vocation of St. Bavo." Tours leave daily at 2:30 p.m., (from January 1 - October 31) from the inquiry desk in the crypt of the Town Hall. Tours last about two hours, and no reservation is required. Admission: varies.

South
Ardennes

Here is a glorious area, which is a one- to three-hour drive south and southwest of **Brussels** and which incorporates the lion's share of the provinces of Namur, Liege and Luxembourg (not to be confused with the neighboring Grand Duchy). Here you will enjoy the bucolic serenity of rolling hills, dotted with woods and heaths, precipitous narrow valleys and sleepy rivers, from the Meuse to smaller serpentine streams, and picture-postcard tidy farms.

Liege, its largest city, is industrial. **Charleroi**, **Namur** and **Arlon**, next down the scale in size, beckon with only mild interest. **Dinant**, about 60 minutes from the national capital, is a very popular resort hub. The Meuse is particularly lovely here; cruise boats are available for short runs. Its preeminent specialties are *Cookee Dinant*—a type of gingerbread that is normally pressed in ancient molds—and copper items, ham and sausages.

Bastogne is way down in the Ardennes Forest. On a nearby hill stands the magnificent **Mardasson Monument**, a mammoth five-pointed star that is dedicated to the American fighting men who were lost in the Battle of the Bulge. The **War Museum** and the

Bastogne Historical Center also provide something to see in this otherwise somnolent settlement. If you're lingering or merely hungry, the centuries-old, pink-faced **Lebrun** is just about the only show in town.

Le Borges could be your alternative choice, located smack on place McAuliffe. All the rest of the centers in this vast area are small towns or villages, some of them charming and some less so. Don't miss a drive to **Orval's Abbey** nearby and the Basilica in the French town of **Avioth**.

Where to Stay

Arlon

Hotels and Resorts

Hotel Arlux ★★★

Moderate

rue de Lorraine.

☎ *528-1234, (63) 232-211,* FAX: *(63) 232- 248.*

Credit Cards: *All Major.*

Nonsmoking rooms.

Peacefully situated in a wooded area on the outskirts of town, this contemporary hotel first greeted guests in 1991. This hotel provides 78 rooms, well-styled with sleek lines and soft colors. Each comes with cable TV, telephone, minibar, safe and well-maintained bath.

Bastogne

Inns

La Ferme au Pont

Moderate

La Ferme au Pont, on the N834.

☎ *(84) 433-161.*

Credit Cards: *V, MC, DC, A.*

On a country road between Bastogne and La Roche, this delightful farmhouse has just seven guest rooms. Surrounded by forests with the flowing Ourthe River nearby, peace and serenity soothe the weary traveler. The rooms are cozy and modestly furnished, with only four sporting a private bath. Good country meals are served in the dining room with views of the lush greenery outside.

Charleroi
Hotels and Resorts

Socatel Hotel ★

Moderate

Boulevard Tirou 96.

☎ *(71) 319-811,* FAX: *(71) 319-811.*

Credit Cards: *All Major.*

Jacuzzi, nonsmoking rooms.

This low-rise hotel is oriented towards business travelers more concerned with practicality than ambience. It opened in 1940 and was renovated in 1993. The 65 well-kept rooms feature cable TV, telephone, radio, minibar and bath with blow-dryer. There are seven suites, nonsmoking rooms and executive suites with sitting areas, pants press and Jacuzzi.

Where to Eat
Durbuy

Les Sanglier des Ardennes

Moderate to Expensive

Grand Rue 99. ☎ *(086) 21.32.62.*

Specialties: Wild Boar, Ardennes Ham.

Credit Cards: *All Major.* Closed: *Thurs.*

Outside dining, own baking, reservations recommended.

Sandwiched between the town's main street and the Ourthe River in

Durbuy, an enchanting spot on the map that bills itself as "the smallest town in the world," this inn is spotlessly clean. It has a very well-used family-type atmosphere with a rather cluttered decor, except for the second dining room, which is a terrace overlooking the stream. The cuisine, though, is delectable. Specialties include fresh homemade foie gras, trout pate, wild duck, wild boar, Ardennes ham, grilled trout fillet on a salad bed and local cheeses. The wine cellar is extraordinary.

Noirefontaine

L'Auberge du Moulin Hideux ★★★★★

Expensive

route de Dohan. *2.5 miles from Bouillon. Located at Auberge du Moulin Hideaux.* ☎ *(061) 46.70.15.*

Credit Cards: *All Major.*
Reservations required.

Located five miles from the frontier on the highway to Sedan (France), this pleasant, 13-room hotel has a captivating restaurant, one of Belgium's finest. It's also one of the first inns in the country to become a member of the prestigious Relais et Chateaux organization. The rose-colored house is nestled in a sleepy hollow, offering homey comforts, crackling fires in cold weather and river views through cottage windows. Menu specialties include fresh fish and lobster.

What to Do

Arlon

Museums and Exhibits

Victory Memorial Museum ★★★★

Highway E25/E411. Located five miles south east of Arlon.
8 a.m.–7 p.m.
Special Hours: *Winter 10 a.m.–5 p.m.*

Spread out over 25 acres, this important military museum is dedicated to all the Allied forces that fought for freedom in World War II. Its modern facade is capped by a large, white dove of peace, flying above the flags of participating nations. There are some 200 military vehicles, 300 uniforms, weapons, and equipment on display. The museum also shows a full-length film made from assembled footage of serials shot during the War, spotlighting the liberation of North Africa and Western Europe. Cafeteria, bookshop. Admission: $8.00 and up. Lower for seniors, students, and children.

Bastogne

Bastogne Historical Center

and American Memorial ★★★★★

Colline du Mardasson. One mile outside of Bastogne.

9:30 a.m.–5:30 p.m.

Special Hours: *Winter 10 a.m.–4 p.m., open from February 15*

It's only fitting that this memorial and museum is shaped like a five-pointed star—it was near here where the Battle of the Bulge was heroically played out in the winter of 1944—marking a decisive, but very hard-won, Allied victory against German troops. On the grounds you'll find an amphitheater, where a multivision account of the Battle of Bastogne is shown on a continual basis; a cinema, featuring a film of the account made for the 50th anniversary of the Battle, and a museum with authentic uniforms, weapons and other gripping mementos. Admission: $8.00 and up.

Dinant

The Citadel ★★★

Le Prieure 25.

10 a.m.–6 p.m.

Special Hours: *Winter to 4 p.m., closed Fridays*

Although this impressive fortification above the town of Dinant can be reached by a 400-step stairway, the fun in getting here is via cable car. The view from the top of the 16th-century fortress is breathtaking; below you'll see the entire Meuse valley on a clear day. There's a museum of arms, dioramas, and ruins of a shelter. Meals can be taken from the terraced cafeteria. Sometimes gets inundated with tour groups. Admission (includes cable car): $5.00.

Han-Sur-Lesse

Kid's Stuff

The Grottoes of Han

Highway E411.

9:30 a.m.–6 p.m.

Special Hours: *Winter, 10 a.m.–4 p.m.*

Awarded three stars by *Guide Michelin*, this three-mile long series of underground caves are a major family attraction in the Ardennes area. Formed by the waters of the river Lesse just 100 years ago, the entrance to the caverns can be reached by train from the village center. Visitors proceed on foot through some interesting underground galleries; highlights include a "Mystery" room, with brightly colored formations, followed by a sound and light show.visual show highlighting the glories of the grottoes, plus a children's mini- farm. Contact: **Domain of the Grottoes of Han**, *rue J. Lamotte 2, 5580 Han-sur- Lesse,* ☎ (084) 37.72.13.

Seraing

Museums and Exhibits

Val Saint-Lambert

rue du Val 245.

9 a.m.–5 p.m.

Some of the finest crystal in the world comes from this region of Belgium, and you can watch the whole process at this museum/demonstration/exhibition hall, in Seraing, a suburb of Liege. First you'll watch the glassware being blown, decorated and engraved. Afterwards, peruse a mouth-watering collection of recently created vases, bowls, plates and other pieces. Some of the displays are available for purchase. Admission: $5.00 and up.

FRANCE

For more than 13 centuries the Gallic influence has been manifest throughout the civilized world, and all those occurrences are revealed in some beautiful, historic, or interesting way in today's France.

You can live in abbeys where the vaults date back a thousand years, dine where Benedictine monks maintained our cultural heritage through the Dark Ages, dance in cellars reminiscent of the Renaissance. The country is so ancient, the history so rich and the sights so resplendent that every corner beckons tourists to follow their special interests or whims. Naturally, Paris is the heartbeat, but very nearby are the playgrounds of France's royalty—the Loire Valley with scores of splendid châteaux to be visited, and even closer are the elegant palaces of Versailles, Fontainebleau and Saint Germain, plus the gracious estates that border the Marne and St-Cloud. The haunting forests of Barbizon also lie within a short drive of the capital.

Farther afield, but still within easy reach of the "City of Light," are the tranquil shores of Brittany and the snug half-timbered clusters of houses in Normandy. Mont St-Michel towers above the lonely sands, while not far away, at Giverny, Monet's willows and lily ponds create a mood of pastoral springtime.

The great wine districts of Bordeaux, Champagne, Burgundy, Alsace and the Rhone Valley have plenty of sites and scenery, plus some of the finest cuisine in the world. In the Alps, where you can ski on Olympic runs, or along the Pyrenees and down to the sunburnished flowered hills of Provence, there are marvelous vacation spots. The highest peak in Europe is Mont Blanc. The bluest sea is at the doorstep of the French Riviera. You have 13 centuries to cover, so get going.

Transportation
Airline

Air France (http://www.airfrance.com/) not only covers the home territory, but it spans the globe, bringing French refinement and finesse to scores of destinations. U.S. gateways (including New York, Boston, Newark, Washington, Chicago, Houston, Miami, Los Angeles, San Francisco and Anchorage) lead to Charles de Gaulle Airport Terminal II. Out of New York you can fly directly to Lyon year-round, and there's a nonstop Riviera run between New York

and Nice. From Newark, you can fly to Orly. Rail and bus get you to central Paris in 40 minutes or to Orly in under an hour. (If you are connecting with a flight from the other airport, ask for the free bus transport voucher due you.) If you plan to fly within the nation, ask your travel agent or Air France stateside about the Air-Inter discounts for domestic travel. The savings are truly impressive.

Taxis

At night, when it rains, during meal hours and at the peak of the rush-hour Paris' 14,500 taxis are as elusive as ever. Until just a few years ago, cabbies just plain quit as soon as the clock struck the lunch or dinner hour. But now, legally at least, they're supposed to take you where you want to go, instead of only in the direction of their garage, mistress or home. Unfortunately, the brutes usually won't, and few additional vehicles seem to be available during these key periods.

Fares are based on tiers. The meter should read "libre" until the flag is lowered. In midcity on weekdays and Saturday (except at night) the "A" designation should be visible; "B" (more expensive) is for suburban hauls, such as to the airport (around $33 compared to approximately $6.50 by bus); "C" is the most costly holiday and night rate. The driver is supposed to change the meter to a new level as you pass into the suburban zone, usually the *peripherique*, or ring road.

ITRAVELBOOK TIP: STAY AWAY FROM LARGE, LUXURIOUS TAXIS WITHOUT METERS THAT ROAM THE GIN-MILL AREAS AT NIGHT. DRIVERS PURPOSELY AVOID QUOTING A PRICE OR INDICATING A FEE, BUT WHEN YOU ARRIVE AT YOUR DESTINATION, YOU'LL KNOW YOU'VE BEEN TAKEN FOR A RIDE. COSTS ARE OUTRAGEOUS. DON'T BE STARTLED BY THE SHAGGY COMPANION RIDING BESIDE YOUR DRIVER. MANY CABBIES, ESPECIALLY WOMEN, ENJOY THE FELLOWSHIP AND PROTECTION OF DOGS TO DISCOURAGE WHEELBORNE CRIMINALITY.

Trains

The French National Railroads (SNCF) are among the best and the fastest in the world. Don't forget to have your ticket *composté* on the quay; if not, you might get fined. Regular routings include 125-m.p.h. cannonballing along numerous strips of trackage. TGV, for *Train à Grande Vitesse*, was the pioneer of swift rail travel, and now a new generation has come into being with the TGV *Atlantique,* which offers a commercial speed of 186 m.p.h. (Brittany, Loire Valley and Bordeaux); it hit 320 m.p.h. on a test run not long ago! So who needs Concorde?

If you plan much train travel, take advantage of the Eurailpass. SNCF also offers a very innovative and flexible **Rail-and-Drive** combo plus the well-established and money- stretching **France Railpass** scheme, so be sure to check with your travel agent. The savings don't stop with the transport alone, but extend to the attractions you'll want to visit en route.

Food

It's the *dernier-cri,* of course. Within the nation there are regional styles as well as the latest food fashions. Nouvelle cuisine is being supplanted by *libre, moderne, instantane, marché, personnalisée, actuelle, courante* and other terms suggesting yet another twist in the historic French gastronomic trail. Nevertheless, around almost every bend, you will find delectable pleasures. You may also discover today a return to older conventions in cooking. And to dump carloads of cholesterol back into your blood vessels, many a chef is specializing in tasty *abats,* the richest visceral innards of the animal kingdom.

If you are touring, country hotels usually charge extra for breakfast; a simple coffee and bread will add $8 to $15 to your bill (per person!). If this rapacity galls you, take your first meal in a village café, and be sure that the hotelier does not automatically tag breakfast onto your overnight bill.

Tipping

Every human being who serves you will proffer a hand with stunning rapidity. At the movies, if you don't tip, the usherette will probably flash her light into your eyes until you do.

Hotels add up to 30 percent in service charges and taxes, depending on class and location. "*Restaurants de Tourisme*"—most of the better-known places fall into this official category—automatically take a 15 percent service bite; you are expected to add another 5 to 7 percent for the waiter. Give the checkroom attendant one franc, the washroom attendant one franc and the wine steward (if you use him) five francs. Taxi drivers get 10 to 15 percent; hotel doormen (when calling a taxi) get about the same ordinarily but more if they go out in the rain to capture your vehicle.

Telephone

Access code to USA: 19 (dial tone). USA Direct: 19 (dial tone) 0011 (a special AT&T service). To phone France: 33; time difference (Eastern Daylight) plus 6 hours.

CURRENCY: The EURO. As of this writing, the French Franc is obsolete.

For More Information

French Government Tourist Office,
http://www.francetourism.com/

610 Fifth Ave., New York, NY 10020, ☎ *(212) 757-1125;*

645 N. Michigan Ave., Chicago, IL, ☎ *(312) 337-6301;*

2305 Cedar Springs Rd., Dallas, TX 75201, ☎ *(214) 720-4010;*

9454 Wilshire Blvd., Beverly Hills, CA 90212, ☎ *(310) 271-2358;*

30 St. Patrick St., Suite 700, Toronto M5T 3A3, ☎ *(416) 593-4723;*

1981 McGill College Ave., Suite 490, Montreal H3A 2W9,

☎ *(514) 288-4264.*

(1) The **City of Paris** has its own Information Bureau, (http://www.paris-touristoffice.com/index_va.html*) 127 ave. Champs-Elysées*, linked to similar centers in other French hubs. At your service are an exchange office, accredited representatives of touring agencies and hotel reservations facilities.

(2) Additional locations for aid in Paris are at the Palais de Congres, Invalides, Gare du Nord, Gare de l'Est and Gare de Lyon.

Alsace-Lorraine

Strasbourg

Perhaps best known for its International Music Festival held every year in June, Strasbourg is a thriving city with an amazing cathedral, several museums, a major university and an important port. The capital of Alsace, it is also the seat of the Council of Europe as well as the European Parliament. Its eastern border lies along the Rhine, and two branches of the Ill River and numerous canals cross it. Aside from scenic river cruises, there is much in Strasbourg for sightseers to enjoy, including the ancient covered bridges, the towers of its former fortifications and architecture dating back to the 15th century.

Where to Stay

Hotels and Resorts

Hotel Regent Contades
http://www.regent-hotels.com/contades/

Moderate to Expensive

8 avenue de la Liberté. About 1 km from the train station; near the river and the cathedral.

(88)36-26-26.

Credit Cards: *All Major.*

Although opened in 1987, this hotel has quickly become a leading symbol of luxury in Strasbourg. There are 44 rooms decorated with soothing color schemes, coordinated furnishings and subdued lighting. Modern amenities include TV, radio, telephone, minibar, safe and tiled bath with hair dryer and robes. Breakfast is the only meal served in the dining room, with 24-hour room service and nearby restaurants making up for the lack of dining options in the hotel.

Hotel des Rohan
http://www.hotel-rohan.com/

Budget to Moderate

17-19 rue du Maroquin. Located about 50 meters from the cathedral in the pedestrian precinct.

☎ *(88)32-85-11.*

Credit Cards: *All Major.*

A well-appointed hotel in a choice location near the cathedral. The structure is a restored four-story building with origins from the 17th-century. Within are 36 smallish, elegant rooms decorated either in Louis XV style or with pine paneling in a more rustic decor. All are well-equipped with cable TV, telephone, radio, minibar and private bath with hair dryer.

Monopole-Metropole
http://www.bw-monopole.com/eng/

Budget to Moderate

16 rue Kahn. Located at rue Kageneck; near train station (Gare Centrale).

☎ *(88)14-39-14.*

Credit Cards: *All Major.*

Residing on a quiet side street, this is a very traditional Alsatian hotel, is now part of the Best Western chain. The 94 rooms are decorated in modern or traditional style and come with satellite TV, telephone, radio, minibar and private bath or shower. Breakfast is served in the high-ceilinged dining room for an additional charge.

Where to Eat

Le Crocodile
Moderate to Expensive

10 rue d l'Oure. ☎ *(88)32-13-02.*

Credit Cards: *All Major.* Closed: *Mon., Sun.*

The number one spot in town, Le Crocodile is all aglow with burnished woods, tasteful flower arrangements and natural light.The food reflects the rich bounty of the Alsace region, with plenty of pork dishes, including pig's trotters and black truffles stuffed in a caul "crepe," as well as typically French classics like pressed duck, artichokes and mushrooms. Le Crocodile is also noted for its wine cellar, which can push your bill into the stratosphere.

Maison Kammerzell
Inexpensive to Moderate

16 place de la Cathedrale. ☎ *(88)32-42-14.*

Credit Cards: *All Major.*

This brasserie would be more appropriately named the "House of Choucroute," as it serves several different versions of this local standby, a stew of cabbage cooked in white wine, usually served with a slew of pork parts, sausages and potato. Other dishes are served as well, of course, including chicken with noodles or fresh fish, but it's really not for vegetarians.

Winstub Strissel ★
Inexpensive

5 place de la Grande Boucherie. ☎ *(88)32-14-73.*

Closed: *Mon., Sun.*

Informal and inexpensive, this winstub serves wines by the glass along with typical Alsatian dishes. The king of the winstubs is **S'Burjerstuewel** (also called "Yvonne's Place"), *10 rue du Sanglier* (88-32-84-15); it's good for a splurge and the local specialties that go with wine, including Alsatian white cheese (*bibbeleskas*), stuffed pig's stomach, and cheesecake. Also, try **Au Pont Saint Martin**, *15 rue des Moulins* (88-32-45-13), for a taste of great choucroute or equally good baekoffe (no cabbage, several kinds of meats).

What to Do

Cathedrale de Notre-Dame ★★★★
place de la Cathedrale. ☎ *88.32.37.92.*

🕐 *10 a.m.–6 p.m.*

Special Hours: *Closed noon-2 p.m.*

Strasbourg's Gothic-Romanesque cathedral is a stunner. Besides a plethora of lacy stone carvings, statues and a vividly-colored rose window, it's memorable for the Astronomical Clock that strikes daily at 12:30 p.m., releasing a mechanical tableaux retelling the denial of Christ by St. Peter. Admission: varies.

Bordeaux/Atlantic Coast

Bordeaux

The port city of Bordeaux, on the Garonne River, is surrounded by 260,000 acres of some of the finest and most famous vineyards in the world. Dating back to the 18th century, Bordeaux has several elegant hotels in buildings still standing from that era and a number of fabulous restaurants with, naturally, unforgettable wine lists. **Le Chapon Fin** is one of the city's most well known gastronomic temples, with specialties changing depending on the supply of fresh ingredients and wines selected from the most respected and expensive vintages of France. Tours of the vineyards are organized by the **maison du vin**, the Tourist Office and International Wine Tours, or point your cursor to **http://www.french- wines.com/Bordeaux %20trail.htm.**

Where to Stay

Chateau Chartrons ★★

Expensive

81 cours St-Louis. Located between rue Prunier and rue Barreyre; near place Tourny.

☎ *(56)43-15-00.*

Credit Cards: *All Major.*

Composed of several converted 19th-century wine warehouses, the Chateau Chartrons has a Victorian facade that belies its ultramodern, extremely luxurious interior. The 143 rooms and seven suites are equipped with every imaginable amenity, including high-tech bathrooms and soundproofing. A health club close by also avails its facilities to any guest of the hotel who wants to use them. There's also a bistro featuring simple regional dishes at moderate prices. Regularly scheduled tastings of fine Bordeaux are held in the hotel's own wine cellars. The desk will also book bus tours or arrange a car for touring the nearby chateaux.

Grand Hotel Francais ★★
http://www.grand-hotel-francais.com/

12 rue du Temple. Located at Cours de l'Intendance; between rue Vital Charles and rue Grassi.

☎ *(56)48-10-35.*

Credit Cards: *All Major.*

Wheelchair-access rooms, air conditioning in rooms, balcony or patio, in-room minibars.

This renovated 18th-century five-story mansion with wrought-iron balconies has been upgraded and bought by the Best Western chain, and it's now one of the best moderately priced hotels in Bordeaux. Accommodations include 35 soundproofed, spacious rooms with private bath, contemporary decor and amenities. Just breakfast is served. It is within walking distance of all of the city's major sights and shopping areas.

Where to Eat

Jean Ramet ★★★★
Moderate to Expensive

7-8 place J.-Jaures.

Credit Cards: *V, MC, A, E.* Closed: *Sun.*

Jean Ramet's superb but unpretentious Bordelaise cuisine is made with only the best seasonal ingredients available. The fresh fish, pigeon and lamb dishes are especially notable. The no-frills cuisine is matched by the dramatic yet clean-lined decor. Attentive service.

L'Alhambra
Moderate

111 bis, rue Judaique. ☎ *(56)96-06-91.*

Credit Cards: *V, MC, A.* Closed: *Sun.*

Chef Michel Demazeu's acclaimed, light, spa-type cuisine is surprisingly affordable for a restaurant with a Michelin rating. Just ignore the a la carte menu and concentrate on the reasonable fixed-price lunch menu, which includes dessert. You won't be eating leftovers, and your entree may be fresh seafood.

La Chamade
Expensive

20 rue des Piliers-de-Tutelle. ☎ *(56)48-13-74.*

Credit Cards: *V, MC, A, E.*

Situated in a vaulted 18th-century cellar, La Chamade offers masterful cooking and an impressive collection of Bordeaux. Regional yet modern and light, the specialties include a marinated and grilled monkfish salad served with artichokes and poached duck with baby vegetables; simply prepared fish dishes are also featured.

La Tupina
Moderate to Expensive

6 rue de la Porte-de-la-Monnaie. ☎ *(56)91-56- 37.*

Credit Cards: *All Major.* Closed: *Sun.*

Operated by one of Bordeaux's most talented chefs, La Tupina features regional cuisine with Southwestern origins, including plenty of duck—chef Xiradaki's specialty. The restaurant is in an 18th-century building with two cozy fireplaces, and many meals are cooked in them.

Le Chapon Fin
Expensive to Outrageous

5 rue Montesquieu. ☎ *(56)79-10-10.*

Credit Cards: *All Major.* Closed: *Mon., Sun.*

The leading restaurant in Bordeaux, Le Chapon Fin upholds its reputation with its Catalonian-inspired cooking and stellar wine cellar. Famous guests through the years have been Winston Churchill, Aristide Briand, Sarah Bernhardt and Toulouse Lautrec.

Le Vieux Bordeaux ★★★
Moderate to Expensive

27 rue Buhan. ☎ *(56)52-94-36.*

Credit Cards: *V, MC, DC, A, E.* Closed: *Sun.*

Reliable and steady, "Old Bordeaux" is practically a neighborhood institution. Recent renovations, however, include a sunny new dining room looking out on a pool, where guests can enjoy such specialties as red peppers stuffed with fresh cod, au gratin of lobster with noodles, or turbot with buttery truffle sauce. Also featured are rich desserts laced with wine and vintage claret from the cellar.

What to Do
Historical Sites

Grande Theatre ★★★
place de la Comedie. ☎ *57.81.90.81.*

The spectacular facade of this 18th-century building protects a jewelbox interior. Architect Victor Louis' creation inspired Charles Garnier to build the Paris Opera in a similar style in 1862. Tours of the auditorium conducted by the tourist office July- September, at 10:30 a.m., 3 p.m. and 4:30 p.m., daily, except Monday, Saturday and Sunday. Other months, Saturday only, at 3 p.m. and 4 p.m.

Special Tours

Maison du Vin ★★★
1 cours du 30 Juliet. *56.22.66.*

🕒 *8:30 a.m.–6 p.m.*

Special Hours: *May-October only*

A wonderful wine resource, the Maison du Vin offers free tastings, maps, and detailed information on wine tours of the surrounding regions, including the hard-to-get into Chateau Mouton-Rothschild in Pauillac. Neophytes will also learn the dos and don'ts of tasting etiquette, so you won't look like a rube. Ask for the English-version of the handy booklet, "Petit Guide des Vins." Also open Saturday, 9 a.m.–5 p.m. Another good resource is the tourist office, *12 cours du 30 Juillet* ☎ (56.44.28.41), or **International Wine Tours**, *12 place de la Bourse* ☎ (56.90.91.28).

Brittany

Brittany

Blue predominates here. Never mind that the northern littoral with its craggy cliff-bound ports is called the *Emerald Coast*, where the scenic ramparts of St-Malo and Dinard reside. Never mind that the great thumb of France that shoves into the Atlantic is called the *Granite Rose Coast*, which runs to the extremity of Brest. And never mind that the interior, with its early Christian Calvaries and its druid megaliths is today devoted to whatever agriculture can be scratched from the gray stony soil. The tone of the air itself is derived from the azure of the sky and the sea that surrounds this distinctive peninsula.

To see it properly, you will need at least a week and a car. A bicycle is another possibility, if your resolve is strong—and so are your legs. If you are planning to incorporate the neighboring province of Normandy into your itinerary, it would be better to concentrate on southern Brittany. The roadways are improving, but the distances are deceptively long and time-consuming during the summer months. In winter the pikes are empty, except for trucks bearing the maritime cargo. However, it is a harsh and inhospitable land when the chill winds blow.

The once sovereign realm of Brittany is designed for leisure and for rambling. To enjoy it best will take time, so stay at one of the retreats and strike out on your own each day for new discoveries at the pace you select.

Where to Stay

Chateau de Locgunol
Expensive to Very Expensive

Route de Port-Louis. Located 10 km east of Lorient on N165, at

Lorient, exit Port-Louis on D781 for 4 km.

☎ *(97)76-29-04.*

Credit Cards: *All Major.*

This 900-acre hilltop estate overlooking the tree-covered Blavet River Valley has been owned by the same family for more than 500 years. The 20 rooms, all with private bath, vary widely in size and furnishings. The second floor has great old bedrooms, but the upper-floor accommodations, the converted maids' rooms, also are charming. Some of the rooms are in a converted Breton cottage.

Manoir du Stang   ★★★
http://www.manoirdustang.activehotels.com/MIL
Moderate to Expensive

La Forêt-Fouesnant. Located 2.5 km north of city, sign posted from the N783; access is by private road.

☎ *(98)56-97-37.*

Credit Cards: *Not Accepted.*

To get to the courtyard that leads to the entrance of this ivy-covered manor house, travel down a long, tree-lined avenue and under a stone tower gate. On the right is a formal garden, and raised stone terraces lead to 25 acres of rolling woodland and a lake. Guest are lodged either in the main building or in the older annex; the latter has a circular stone staircase. The 26 guest rooms (all with private bathrooms) are furnished with silks and fine antiques.

Belle-Ile-En-Mer

Castel Clara Hotel   ★★★★
Expensive

Port Goulphar.

☎ *(97)31-84-21,* FAX: *(97)31-51-69.*

Credit Cards: *V, MC, E, A.*

A country style inn of four stories, this hotel is a member of Relais and Chateaux, a symbol of tranquil lodging. After dining at the superb in-house restaurant of the same name, guests retire to one of the 43 bed chambers in comfort. Each water view room comes with cable TV, telephone and spacious bath.

Manoir de Goulphar
Moderate to Expensive

Bangor.

☎ *(97)31-80-10*, FAX: *(97)31-80-05*.

Credit Cards: *V, MC.*

This first rate hotel, built in the 1970s, is perched on the Goulphar Harbor. There are 65 guest rooms, many with balconies overlooking the ocean and the harbor, equipped with comfortable amenities such as TV, telephone and private bath.

Brest
Hotels and Resorts

Mercure Hotel Continental
Budget to Moderate

24 rue de Lyon.

☎ *(98)80-50-40*, FAX: *(98)43-17-47*.

Credit Cards: *All Major.*

This five story hotel offers good, basic accommodations. The 75 rooms are quiet and come with TV, telephone, minibar and private bath or shower. There is an average restaurant serving big meals and a bar in the hotel. Its convenience to the train station for tourists without an auto is one of its best aspects.

Carnac

Hotel Les Alignements
http://www.carnac-hotel.com/

Moderate

45 rue St-Cornely.

☎ *(97)52-06-30*, FAX: *(97)52-76-56*.

Credit Cards: *V, MC.*

Set on the edge of town, this hotel's location is most convenient for touring the prehistoric Field of Megaliths. Constructed in the early 1970s, this four-story building is home to 27 guest rooms. Last improved in 1991, the rooms are comfortable and come with TV, telephone and private bath. The choice rooms are those on the upper floors with balconies facing the garden in back. Those facing the street are equipped with double-paned windows to buffer the noise from below. An ideal base for visiting the historic stones.

Lann-Roz
Budget to Moderate

36 avenue de la Poste.

☎ *(97)52-10-48*, FAX: *(97)52-03-69*.

Credit Cards: *V, MC, DC, A.*

The pleasant demeanor of the family owners who manage this hotel makes each guest feel as though they are an old friend. There are 14 rooms, modestly yet comfortably attired and including TV, telephone and bath or shower. One of the biggest delights of staying here is relishing a sumptuous meal in the living room facing the grounds. Meals are a fantastic value.

Concarneau

Hotel des Sables Blancs
Budget

plage des Sables-Blancs.

☎ *(98)97-01-39*, FAX: *(98)50-65-88*.

Credit Cards: *V, MC, DC.*

The kind owners of this hotel and restaurant warmly welcome all of the guests. While perhaps better known for the dining facilities, the 48 guest rooms are also quite pleasant. All of the cozy rooms are well kept and comfortable, and most come with private bath. Always a reliable seaside lodging option.

Grand Hotel
Budget

1 avenue Pierre Gueguen.

☎ *(98)97-00-28.*

Credit Cards: *V, MC.*

Very basic accommodations in a central location to the marketplace. There are 33 rooms, with the better half having private baths. Even with the most simple of amenities, the chambers are definitely comfortable.

Dinan
Bed and Breakfasts

La Tarais ★★
Budget

Calorguen.

☎ *(96)83-50-59.*

Credit Cards: *Not Accepted.*

A lovely stone and brick country house on a village farm, La Tarais is charming in its simplicity. The product of a friendly Anglo-Dutch husband-wife duo, there are four rooms with bath kept in immaculate condition. While basic in furnishings, the understated effect works well here. The complementary breakfast is taken outdoors when it's warm or in the dining room at separate tables when the winter chill has arrived; other meals are available in the summer months. The multilingual owners make every guest feel at home.

Hotels and Resorts
Dinard

Le Grand Hotel
Expensive

46 avenue George-V.

☎ *(99)88-26-26,* FAX: *(99)88-26-27.*

Credit Cards: *V, MC, DC, A.*

The premier hotel of Dinard, this hotel represents the grandeur of the 19th century and its architectural styles. Built in 1859, the five-story brick building is dotted with balconies off of the 63 guest rooms. Spaciously arranged, the rooms are furnished with period furniture and come with TV, telephone, minibar and beautiful, private bath.

Bed and Breakfasts

Manoir de la Duchee
Budget

La Duchee, Saint-Briac-sur-Mer.

☎ *(99)88-00-02.*

A short drive through the countryside leads to this relaxing B&B outside of Dinard. A duplex with a capacity for four persons is also available. The breakfast room, with exposed beams and attractive stonework, sets the scene for the complementary breakfast. The service is friendly, and the accommodations are fit for any traveler who appreciates getting away from the city.

Hotels and Resorts

Reine Hortense   ★★★
http://www.carnac-hotel.com/

Moderate to Expensive

19 rue de la Malouine.

☎ *(99)46-54-31,* FAX: *(99)88-15-88.*

Credit Cards: *V, MC, DC.*

The luxurious surroundings here originally pampered one of the Russian courtiers of the mother of Napoleon III. With only eight rooms, the atmosphere is intimate, and service is wonderful. Rooms are equipped with a TV, telephone and private bath (one room has the silver-plated bathtub of Napoleon's mother). Splendid.

Inns

Hotel de la Plage   ★★★
http://www.hoteldelaplage.com/

Moderate to Expensive

Ste-Anne-la-Pallud.

☎ *(98)92-50-12,* FAX: *(98)92-56-54.*

Credit Cards: *V, MC, DC, A.*

Just a few feet from the shore, this seaside inn is worth the short drive from town. There are 26 comfortable guest rooms dressed in traditional decor and standard with central heating, TV, telephone, minibar and private bath. The choice rooms afford a view of the sea or the countryside and are filled quickly. Incredibly talented kitchen staff.

Plonevez-Porzay

Manoir de Moellien ★★★
Budget to Moderate

☎ *(98)92-50-40*, FAX: *(98)92-55-21.*

Credit Cards: *V, MC, DC, A.*

The lodging side of this inn, a stone manor house with a fine restaurant (see "Where to eat"), flows with charm and comfort. There are just 10 guest rooms, many residing in the 19th-century barn and all modestly furnished and equipped with central heating, telephone and private bath. Each has a viewful terrace and unique decor. Be sure to sample the fare in the Old World restaurant while enjoying a quiet stay here.

Pont-Aven

Pen Ker Dagorn ★★★
Budget

Chemin des Vieux-Fours.

☎ *(98)06-85-01.*

Credit Cards: *Not Accepted.*

A B&B deserving of its three stars for its charm and personal attention. Stay for the two day minimum at this lovely house in the country, shaded by well developed shrubbery and trees. There are just three rooms, each with its own bath or shower. All are spaciously comfortable, individually decorated and bright and airy. A classic countryside getaway.

Quimper
Chateau

Chateau du Guilguiffin ★★★
Moderate to Expensive

Landudec.

☎ *(98)91-52-11.*

Credit Cards: *Not Accepted.*

An absolutely enrapturing chateau fronted by a grand facade of 18th century architecture. Each of the four rooms presents itself in proud

style and comfort with very attractive bathrooms. The public drawing rooms and the lounge are evidence to the careful attention paid
to tradition in design. Breakfast is included, and dinners are available
in the dining room.

Hotels and Resorts
Rennes

Central Hotel   ★★★
Budget

6 rue Lanjuinais.

☎ *(99)79-12-36*, FAX: *(99)79-65-76.*

Credit Cards: *V, MC, DC, A.*

An air of elegance surrounds this hotel with origins from the late
1800s. Snuggled in a back street location, the noise is kept to a minimum. There are 44 tidy guest rooms, most of which have a private
bath. Views from the windows are of the street or the courtyard. Car
travelers will enjoy the off street parking in this town center situation. The helpful staff is very accommodating and speaks functional
English.

St-Malo
Bed and Breakfasts

La Korrigane   ★★★
http://www.st-malo-hotel-korrigane.com/

Moderate

39 rue le Pomellec.

☎ *(99)81-65-85*, FAX: *(99)82-23-89.*

Credit Cards: *V, MC, DC, A.*

A splendid turn of the century mansion, La Korrigane is guaranteed
to enchant its guests with its classic charm. Each room is tastefully
decorated with antiques and equipped with central heating, TV, telephone and a private bath or shower. Guests enjoy breakfast in the
cozy garden and linger in the sitting rooms in the evenings.

Hotels and Resorts

Hotel Elisabeth
Moderate

2 rue des Cordiers.

☎ *(99)56-24-98*, FAX: *(99)56-39-24.*

Credit Cards: *V, MC, DC, A.*

Quite a comfortable arrangement in the Elisabeth. Behind the 16th century facade lie 17 guest chambers of contemporary comfort and convenience. Each comes with a TV, telephone and private bath, and many afford fine views of the harbor. A complementary breakfast is included with the stay.

La Digue
Budget to Moderate

49 chaussee du Sillon.

☎ *(99)56-09-26*, FAX: *(99)56-41-65.*

Credit Cards: *V, A.*

Soak in the views offered by the many rooms overlooking the town beaches. There are 53 guest rooms of outstanding comfort and cool, bright designs. Rooms vary greatly in size and luxury, so it's wise to see the room prior to checking in. One of the greatest delights here is enjoying breakfast on the terrace facing the sea— don't miss it.

Vannes

Image Ste-Anne
Budget to Moderate

8 place de la Liberation.

☎ *(97)63-27-36*, FAX: *(97)40-97-02.*

Credit Cards: *V, MC.*

A leisurely walk through historic Vannes leads to this old country charmer. The old structure housing the 38 rooms shows its age in a somehow romantic, rustic manner. Each of the cozy, comfortable rooms comes with modest furnishings and private shower or bath.

Where to Eat
Belle-Isle-en-Mer

Castel Clara
Expensive

Port-Goulphar. ☎ *(97)31-84-21.*

Credit Cards: *V, MC, E.*

The best view in town is from the tiny dining room of this well-known restaurant in a Relais & Chateau rated hotel. Yves Perou creates simply prepared seafood dishes using prime ingredients. His desserts are lovely. Along the Cote Sauvage, in the town of Sauzon, you'll find the **Roz-Avel**, *rue du Lt-Riou* ☎ (97-31-61-48), featuring large, steaming portions of shellfish and fresh fish. The meat dishes are excellent too. There's a garden for warm weather dining.

La Chaloupe
Inexpensive

8 avenue Carnot. ☎ *(97)31-88-27.*

Credit Cards: *All Major.*

For simple meals, including Breton crepes, this informal and friendly place is the best in town. Similar fare can be found at **Traou-Mod**, *9 rue Willaumez* ☎ (97-31-84- 84), also in Le Palais; the crepes are sweet and savory. Open daily from 11:30 a.m.– 12 p.m. Market: place de la Republique, 8 a.m.–1 p.m. Tue., Fri., Sat.

Brest

Le Nouveau Rossini
Moderate

22 rue du Commandant-Drogou. ☎ *(98)47-90- 00.*

Credit Cards: *V, MC, A, E.* Closed: *Mon.*

One of Brest's prettiest restaurants, Le Nouveau Rossini is in a newer section of the city, where chef Maurice Mevel can provide more space and patio dining for guests. Modern seafood cuisine, with an emphasis on natural juices and vegetables, is featured. Good wine cellar with vintages available by the glass. Fixed-price lunch menu weekdays and Sat. Brest also has some good creperies and places for light meals. **La Chaumine**, *16 rue J. Bart* ☎ (98- 45-10-

70), open until 10:30 p.m; **Creperie St-Martin**, *3 rue Graveran* ☎ (98-44-42-04), near the old quarter;. Late-night pizzas (open to midnight) at **La Scala**, *30 rue d'Algesiras* ☎ (98-43-11-43) All inexpensive to moderate.

Concarneau

La Coquille ★
Moderate

1 rue du Moros. ☎ *(98)97-08-52.*

Credit Cards: *All Major.*

For harbor dining, this charming restaurant with high-beamed ceilings is a winner. It has great views of all the nautical action, especially from its rather snug patio. The fixed-price lunch menu is an excellent deal. Also worthwhile is the restaurant at the **Hotel des Sables-Blancs**, not far from the center of town, right on Sables-Blancs beach ☎ (98-97-01-39). Good for simply prepared seafood, especially clams and lobster. Closed Nov.-Mar.; open until 9:30 p.m.; terrace dining. Even less expensive is **L'Escale**, *19 quai Carnot* ☎ (98-97-03- 31), seafood and meat dishes. Market: pl. Jean Jaures, open daily 7 a.m.–1 p.m.

Le Galion ★★
Moderate

15 rue St-Guenole. ☎ *(98)97-30-16.*

Credit Cards: *All Major.* Closed: *Mon.*

Concarneau's best restaurant. With granite walls and sturdy wooden beams, and it is also one of the most atmospheric. Located in the old hamlet, the sea laps at it from all sides. In cold weather, with the fireplace roaring, it's a cozy place to dine. Owned and run by Henri and Marie Louise Goanac'h, it is an unpretentious establishment, and the seafood dishes are utterly fresh.

Pont-Aven

Moulin de Rosmadec ★★★
Expensive

Pont-Aven. ☎ *(98)06-00-22.*

Credit Cards: *V, MC, E.* Closed: *Wed.*

Owners Monsieur and Madame Sebilleau converted a 15th-century mill into this engaging hotel-restaurant. Excellent seafood from the southern coast is featured, as well as choice duck and chicken dishes. Inventive desserts, cheeses; highly recommended. Critics are buzzing about **La Taupiniere**, *route de Concarneau* ☎ (98-06-03-12), 4 km from the center on D783. Guy Guilloux presents seafood in a modern vein; unusual desserts include warm strawberries with pistachio ice cream. Open kitchen, pretty decor.

Quimper

L'Ambroisie   ★★
Moderate

49 rue E.-Freron. ☎ *(98)95-00-02.*

Credit Cards: *V, MC, A, E.*

Not far from the cathedral but hidden slightly away, L'Ambroisie is an attractive restaurant decorated with art and fresh flowers. Chef Gilbert Guyon prepares wonderful crepes with seafood. Some say **Les Acacias**, *88 bd. Creach'h-Guen* ☎ (98- 52-15-20), is even better, at least more adventurous, and there's also a patio for dining. Seafood, great desserts, well-chosen wine list. A fixed-price lunch is offered. No lunch Sat., or dinner Sun. Closed: August 1–15.

Rennes

L'Escale   ★
Inexpensive

178 rue St.-Malo. ☎ *(99)59-19-55.*

Credit Cards: *V, MC, E.* Closed: *Mon., Tues.*

L'Escale is a nice local hangout that's open late; it's a good spot for filling meals and sweet and savory crepes. Also notable is **La Chope**, *3 rue de la Chalotais* ☎ (99-79- 34-54), also open until the witching hour, brasserie food; **Le Serment de Vin**, *bd. de La Tour-d'Auvergne* ☎ (99-30-99-30), wines and regional dishes, open until 11 p.m.

Le Corsaire   ★★★
Moderate to Expensive

52 rue d'Antrain. ☎ *(99)36-33-69.*

Credit Cards: *V, MC, DC, A, E.* Closed: *Mon.*

Located in an impressive townhouse in old Rennes, Le Corsaire is one of the city's top restaurants. Some of chef Luce's specialties include pan-fried langoustines with duck foie gras, and coq au vin with baby onions and *lardons* (bacon).

St-Malo

A la Duchesse Anne ★★
Moderate to Expensive

5 place Guy La-Chambre. ☎ *(99)40-85-33.*

Credit Cards: *V, MC.* Closed: *Wed.*

Outside dining, own baking, reservations required.

Guests dine in an elegant, old-fashioned setting at A la Duchesse Anne—possibly St-Malo's best restaurant. There are a few meat dishes available, but no-frills, classically prepared seafood is what this house does best. Prices are reasonable for what you get. A makeshift patio is set up for dining in the warmer months.

Le Chalut ★★
Inexpensive to Moderate

8 rue de la Corne-du-Cerf. ☎ *(99)56-71-58.*

Credit Cards: *V, MC, A, E.* Closed: *Mon.*

Le Chalet is a homey, unpretentious restaurant within the old city walls. Chef Jean-Philippe Foucat specializes in seafood dishes, and his sauces are interesting and savory.

Vannes

Regis Mahe ★★
Moderate to Expensive

place de la Gare. ☎ *(97)42-61-41.*

Credit Cards: *V, MC, A, E.* Closed: *Mon.*

Regis Mahe's acclaimed cuisine combines traditional, regional seafood dishes with contemporary Provencal touches. He has brought the sunny south to the Breton coast with a menu full of fresh produce, fragrant herbs and fine olive oils.

What to Do
Brest
Museums and Exhibits

Oceanopolis   ★★★
Port de Plaisance. ☎ *98.34.40.40.*

🕐 *9:30 a.m.–5 p.m.*

Special Hours: *Monday, from 2 p.m.*

The kids can play Captain Nemo while manipulating the various navigation exhibits, and ogle the sea creatures in the 132,000-gallon aquarium at this sizable marine research center. There's also an area set aside for frolicking seals. Admission: inexpensive.

Carnac
Historical Sites

Prehistoric Monuments/Menhirs   ★★★★
rue des Alignements.

Carnac's prehistoric (4000-6000 BC) monuments stand out for their sheer size and diversity. Some of them are over 12 feet high and weigh over 300 tons. Although barriers have been erected around them, (for good reason), all the important formations are placed within a few miles of each other. If you can spare at least three hours, you can visit as many of them as you can stomach. The more common stones are the stand-alone, upright menhirs, which are believed to have been erected to protect burial sites (from evil spirits?) Unique to the area are menhirs set in parallel lines, ending in a semi-circle, called cromlechs. These may be remnants of ancient temples devoted to sun or moon deities. Close to the Musee de Prehistoire is the St-Michel Tumulus, a 38-ft. mound of earth and rocks which housed two burial chambers. Admission: inexpensive, varies.

Museums and Exhibits
Concarneau

Musee de la Peche   ★★★
rue Vauban. ☎ *98.97.10.20.*

🕐 *9:30 a.m.–7 p.m.*

Special Hours: *Winter, to 6 p.m., closed 12:30- 2 p.m.*

Informative placards, old photographs, and three-dimensional reconstructions painstakingly explain why Concarneau is France's third largest shipping port. There are exotic boats and ship models, and a 40-tank aquarium. Your child will leave knowing how much work goes into making a tuna sandwich. Admission: varies.

Paimpont
Excursions

Forest of Paimpont ★★★
45 km from Rennes. ☎ *99.07.84.23.*

The legend goes that Merlin the Magician and his amour, the fairy Viviane (The Lady of the Lake) lived within this forest together after the sorcerer retired from the spell-casting business. Just to be sure, Viviane kept him in a magic circle so he couldn't stray. It was also here where Joseph of Arimathea, original owner of the Holy Grail, lived, until he and the relic disappeared. You can cycle or walk to some of the more interesting sites, including Merlin's "tomb," and the Valley of No Return, where Fata Morgana would ensnare young men. There are real people who live here, however, in the town of Paimpont, which has been around since the Revolution. The tourist office can provide guides, brochures and information on how to get to the sites.

Pont-Aven
Museums and Exhibits

Musee de L'Ecole de Pont-Aven ★★★
pl. de Hotel de Ville. ☎ *98.06.14.43.*

🕐 *10 a.m.–6:30 p.m.*

Special Hours: *Summer to 7:30 p.m.*

This splendid museum devoted to the style of painting developed by Paul Gauguin and his acolytes in the 1880s, does a quick change act about every three months. Admission: inexpensive.

Quimper
City Celebrations

Festival de Cornouaille   ★★
http://www.festival-cornouaille.com/ popup_cornouaille.html

Various locations. ☎ *98.53.04.05.*

A lively traditional music, dance and film festival, named after the medieval Duchy of Brittany; Quimper was once its capital. It draws mobs from all over the country a week before the fourth Sunday in July. Call for more information.

Museums and Exhibits

Musee Departemental Breton   ★★
1 rue de Roi-Gradlon. ☎ *98.95.21.60.*

🕘 *9 a.m.–6 p.m.*

Special Hours: *October–May, to 5 p.m.,except Sunday–Monday*

Hundreds of years worth of regional life and lore is tastefully displayed, gallery style, in the 16th-century bishop's palace. Exhibits include the inevitable Quimper ware, statuary, furniture, and costumes. Admission: inexpensive.

Musee des Beaux Arts   ★★★
40 pl. St-Corentin. ☎ *98.95.45.20.*

🕘 *10 a.m.–6 p.m.*

Special Hours: *Closed noon-2 p.m.*

Holding their own among a decent collection of Old Masters (including Rubens' Martrydom of Saint Lucia) are a representative bloc of paintings from the 19th century Pont-Aven school: Haan, Serusier, Bernard and others. Contributions from the school's founder, Paul Gauguin, are noticeably missing. Admission: inexpensive.

Shopping

Faiences de Quimper HB Herriot   ★★★
rue Haute. ☎ *98.90.09.36.*

🕘 *9:30 a.m.–4:30 p.m.*

Special Hours: *Friday to 5 p.m., closed 11:30 a.m.-1:30 p.m.*

Vividly hand-painted pottery cast from Breton clay has been a proud local art form since the late 17th-century, when the first workshop was established in Quimper. This venerable factory conducts guided tours in English and French during the week from March-October. Admission: inexpensive.

Rennes
City Celebrations

Nightfall Festival ★★★
Various locations. ☎ *99.79.01.98.*

Also called the Festival des Tombees de la Nuit, this bash is an eight-day welcome to summer, with poetry readings, storytelling, dancing, music, and yummy Breton galletes, crepes, seafood and more. Event tickets cost 35F-150F. Contact the **Office de Tourisme**, at *8 place du Marechal June, 35000 Rennes*; FAX: *99.30.13.45.*

Museums and Exhibits

Musee de Bretagne ★★
20 quai Emile Zola. ☎ *99.28.55.84.*
🕐 *10 a.m.–6 p.m.*

Special Hours: *Closed between noon-2 p.m.*

Several galleries showcase Breton costumes, jewelry and furniture; others focus on megalithic monuments from Carnac and Locmariaquer. Right next door is the Musee des Beaux-Arts, with paintings from the 14th-20th centuries, including a few from the Pont-Aven school. Also Quimper porcelain and Egyptian, Greek and Etruscan artifacts. Hours are the same as the Museum of Brittany. Admission.

Parks and Gardens

Thabor Garden ★★★
rue Victor Hugo, near Notre-Dame-en-St- Melanie.
🕐 *7:15 a.m.–9:30 p.m.*

A beautiful oasis, this 27-acre jardin is a tribute to the art of French landscape design. Located in what was once the garden of the Benedictine Abbey of Notre-Dame-en-St-Melanie alongside it, there's a section devoted to roses, as well as a traditional formal garden.

St-Malo
Historical Sites

Fort National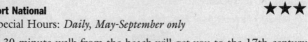
Special Hours: *Daily, May-September only*

A 30-minute walk from the beach will get you to the 17th-century fort built by Vauban. Its imposing look warned would- be intruders to think twice before attacking the city; nowadays shutterbugs are daunted by the myriad photo opportunities from atop the walls. Must be attempted at low tide only, or you WILL be left stranded. Leaving St-Malo from the Champs-Vauvers Gate, cross the beach to the Grand Be, the burial island of the poet Chateaubriand; views from here are stupendous. Low tide only.

Ville Close (Walled City)   ★★★★
Entrance through St-Vincent's Gate.

As a result of unceasing bombing attacks for two weeks in August, 1944, the majority of the old walled city of St-Malo was rendered supine. Through local effort, historic buildings were gingerly taken apart and put back together again; a herculean effort. Now the number one activity is to walk the fortified walls (which escaped destruction) from one end to the other, marked by towers and bastions. From the Bidouane Tower, you can see the National Fort, built by Vauban, which disappears at high tide. The old city is separated from the suburbs and modern sprawl by an estuary. Entrance is at the St-Vincent's Gate, near Esplanade St-Vincent.

Museums and Exhibits

Chateau de St-Malo   ★★★
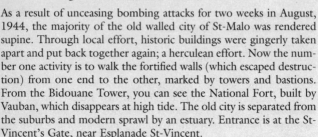
between St-Vincent and St-Thomas Gates. ☎ *99.40.71.57.*
🕐 *10 a.m.–6 p.m.*

Special Hours: *Closed between noon-2 p.m.*

Two museums of Malouin life and history are within the medieval Chateau, built between the 14th and 17th centuries. The great keep (the oldest part of the castle) houses the St-Malo museum. Here you can read documents relating to the founding of the city, and take in exhibits encompassing ships and fishing. The highlight of the visit, though, is the great view from its towers. Admission: inexpensive.

Vannes
Excursions

Belle-Ile ★★★★
45 minutes by ferry from Port Maria in Quiberon. ☎ *97.31.81.93.*

Although often used as an excursion point from Quiberon, Belle-Isle is one of Brittany's largest islands, with hotels, a youth hostel, campgrounds and restaurants. Its shores and valleys have sheltered lots of harried folk, including French Canadian families shipped here by the English in the 18th century, and later on, famous artists and actors (most notably, Sarah Bernhardt). The island was once owned by Nicolas Fouquet, Louis XIV's finance minister, who beefed up the already forbidding Vauban Citadel with cannons; unfortunately, he was arrested in Nantes on corruption charges before he could hole up there. The Citadel, with a museum and views from its ramparts, can be visited daily from 9:30 a.m.–7 p.m. daily. If you have time, you'll probably want to leave Le Palais, Belle-Ile's tourist center, for a driving, walking or cycling tour of the Cote Sauvage. Highlights include Sarah Bernhardt's old estate in Poulains Point (a half-hour walk from the port of Sauzon, northwest of Le Palais on D30). **Port-Donnant**, the island's most beautiful (and least crowded) beach, is on this route, (take D25) but it's unsafe for swimming.

Historical Sites

Old Town ★★★
Promenade de la Garenne.

The cobblestoned old quarter, closed off to car traffic, sits serenely, protected from modern-day Vannes by its sturdy walls. The ducal palace of Vannes no longer exists, but from the promenade de la Garenne, a public park which used to serve as its gardens, you can view the fortified walls of the old city from the Constable's Tower. Entering through the Porte St-Vincent gate, you can visit the market square at place des Lices; some of the medieval buildings house elegant shops. Still in use today, it's the scene of a food and crafts market on Wednesday and Saturday mornings. Occupying the most prominent space is **St-Peter's Cathedral**, with an unusual Italian-Renaissance style chapel, not common to this part of the world. Two museums, the **Beaux Arts** and the **Musee du Golfe et de la Mer**, are housed in La Cohue, *(9-15 pl. St-Pierre)* both a marketplace and court of law in the 14th century.

Burgundy

Autun

One of the oldest towns in France, Autun was founded by Augustus in 15 B.C., so many of its charms are Roman. The archaeology, the Christian relics and the modern comforts conspire to provide great appeal. **Ursulines**, with 38 rooms and an adequate restaurant, is probably your best bet for a pause in this heartland of Burgundy. The highlight of the town is the ancient **Cathedrale**, dating back to the 12th century.

Where to Stay

Ursulines
Moderate to Expensive

14 rue Rivault. Located between bd. Mac- Mahon and rue Dufraigne; also between the cathedral and Tour des Ursulines.

☎ *(86)52-68-00.*

Credit Cards: *All Major.*

A former convent, this quiet hotel has views of the countryside and the mountains of the Morvan. Accommodations include 38 rooms, all with lively decor and thoughtfully equipped.

Where to Eat

Le Chalet Bleu ★
Inexpensive to Moderate

3 rue Jeannin. ☎ *(85)86-27-30.*

Credit Cards: *V, A, E, A.* Closed: *Tues.*

à Reservations recommended.

At this restaurant, with pleasant eclectic decor Middle-Eastern specialties are served along with French cuisine. It's reasonably priced and the service is friendly.

Le Petit Rolin ★
Inexpensive to Moderate

12 pl Saint-Louis. ☎ *(85)86-15-55.*

Credit Cards: *V, MC, E.*

This is a pleasant and friendly regional restaurant, especially good for crepes and salads. Near the tourist office, on pl. Champ du Mars, is a lively market for provisions, open 8 a.m.–1 p.m. Wed. and Fri.

What to Do
Historical Sites

Cathedrale St-Lazare ★★★
place du Cathedral.

🕘 *9 a.m.–5 p.m.*

Built high above the city, the Cathedrale St-Lazare impresses for its collection of 12th-century stone carvings by Gislebertus. Above the central doorway is his Romanesque "Last Judgment," which has an interesting story behind it. Covered over by plaster by someone with foresight in the 18th century, it escaped being desecrated by revolutionaries. Until a few years ago, one could climb the 15th-century towers, but today, they may be off limits to visitors for safety reasons. More of Gislebertus' work can be seen at the **Musee Rolin**, *5 rue des Bancs,* ☎ *(85.52.09.76)* including the bas relief "The Temptation of Eve," plus other worthwhile medieval, and Gallo-Roman art treasures. Admission: inexpensive, varies.

Theatre Antique ★★
Near ave. du Dragons, off place de Charmasse.

Surrounded by tall poplars, Autun's circular Roman amphitheatre is mostly in ruins now, but you can see the remains of the 12,000 seats that once filled the structure. In August, residents shake out their old Roman gladiator costumes, and oil the spokes of their chariots for a three-week sound-and-light spectacle. Call the tourist office at ☎ 86.86.30.00 for information and tickets.

Champagne
Reims

About an hour and a half drive from Paris, Reims (pronounced Rans) is (with nearby Epernay) one of the main champagne production centers in the country. In addition to the surrounding vineyards and the champagne cellars, the ancient town is known for its **Cathedral**—one of the most famous in the world. In an estate setting, the **Boyer-Les-Crayeres**—with 16 rooms, 18th century appointments and sublime gastronomy overseen by Gerard Boyer—is almost a destination in itself.

Where to Stay

Boyer-Les-Crayeres ★★★★★
http://www.gerardboyer.com/uk/ indexsommaire.htm

Expensive to Very Expensive

64 boulevard Henry-Vasnier. Located at av. Gal. Giraud; near St-Remi and Parc de Expositions/Parc Pommery.

☎ *(26)82-80-80.*

Credit Cards: *All Major.*

This elegant Belle Èpoque hotel is housed in one of the finest chateaux in eastern France. The public areas have 18-foot ceilings, enormous windows, burnished paneling and marble columns. The 16 rooms all have completely equipped bathrooms, satellite TV and other amenities. Each room is uniquely decorated and has a terrace view of the park; two rooms have a large balcony. Superb cuisine is served in the wood-paneled and candlelit dining room; reservations are required. Professional, courteous English-speaking staff.

L'Assiette Champenoise ★★
http://www.assiettechampenoise.com/

Moderate

40 avenue Paul-Vallent-Couturier. Located about 6 km from Reims' center; take autoroute A4 west bound, exit at Tinqueux.

☎ *(26)04-15-56.*

Credit Cards: *All Major.*

In a chateau just outside Reims, this acclaimed hotel is set among century-old trees. It is a former private Norman estate, and some of the present structure dates from 1896, although much of it was constructed in the 1980s. Its 60 rooms have private bath and are luxuriously furnished. The hotel restaurant is locally renowned and features both classical and innovative French cooking.

Paix
Budget to Moderate

9 rue Buirette. Located between the train station and the cathedral; at place Drouet d'Erlon.

☎ *(26)40-04-08.*

Credit Cards: *All Major.*

A contemporary hotel in a perfect setting near the imposing Sube fountain. All of its 105 rooms have private bathrooms and comfortable beds. The hotel has a brasserie/tavern, which serves excellent dishes, including grills, oysters and seafood.

Where to Eat

Boyer ★★★★
Expensive

64 boulevard Henry Vasnier. ☎ *(26)82-80-80.*

Credit Cards: *All Major.* Closed: *Mon.*

A very French, and very rich, clientele patronize the Boyer family's acclaimed establishment, isolated within a private estate and chateau in the heart of the city. Gerard Boyer breezily combines humble dishes like pig's feet with a noble stuffing of foie gras and cepes. The desserts are inventive, softly textured and dizzyingly sweet, especially the ice creams. What's to drink? Champagne, of course! Reserve as far ahead as a month for weekend dining. Le famille Boyer also owns a bistro, **Au Petit Comptoir**, *17 rue de Mars* ☎ (26-40- 58-58), helmed by a Boyer acolyte, Fabrice Maillot. He prepares hearty cuisine at people prices, and the crowds love it. Seating is on comfy booths, or on a patio; the champagne is reasonably priced. Open until 10:30 p.m., no lunch Sat., closed Sun. and Aug. 8-23.

Le Chardonnay ★★
Moderate

184 avenue d'Epernay. ☎ *(26)06-08-60.*

Credit Cards: *V, MC, DC, A, E.*

This former Boyer cottage is now owned **and run** by Jen-Jacques Lange, who offers a scaled down version of **Gerard Boyer's** exceptional cuisine. Prices are also much lower, as **are** the wines. Dishes include quail stuffed with mushrooms and a **feuillete** of frogs' legs and leeks. Gracious service and atmosphere.

What to Do
Historical Sites

Cathedrale Notre Dame   ★★★★
place du Cardinal Lucon.
🕐 *7:30 a.m.–7 p.m.*

The Cathedral (1211–1294) is a marvel of the Gothic style. It has abundant sculpture and statuary (The Smiling Angel) and six stained glass windows by Chagall that replaced a few of the many that were destroyed in World War II. At sunset, view the Rose Window atop the center doorway of the West facade; you can see in greater detail the sculpted forms of the Virgin, the 12 apostles and a band of angels. Next door is the Palais du Tau, the archbishop's palace, with a Gothic chapel, and the Salle, a banquet hall where just-crowned monarchs would hold sumptuous banquets. Today it houses a tapestry-rich Treasury, including the baptismal tapestry belonging to Clovis, King of the Franks, and Charlemagne's talisman, a relic reportedly from Christ's cross. Admission: inexpensive.

ITRAVELBOOK FREEBIE
Special Tours

Mumm Champagne Caves   ★★★
34 rue du Champ-de-Mars. ☎ *26.49.59.70.*
🕐 *9 a.m.–5 p.m.*

Special Hours: *Closed weekends November– April*

Free samples of bubbly are given after a video and tour of the champagne cellars; it's also closest to the town center. **Pommery's tour,** *5 place General-Gouraud* ☎ (26.61.62.55) is the most popular among travelers; very atmospheric, with eerie underground tunnels built well below ground. Slide shows in English. Free admission, open 9 a.m.–5 p.m. daily, winter, closed weekends. Even better champagne adventures await in Epernay, some 16 miles south of Reims, home of Moet et Chandon, which owns the Dom Perignon label. Moet's free tours are given daily in English from 9:30 a.m.–5 p.m.; you'll have the rare sight of seeing the art of champagne bottle turning (required to get the sediment in the champagne into the neck). Free tastings afterwards.

French Riviera

For years tourists have been led to believe that this glorious stretch of beach is a shallow, sybaritic enclave and a cultural wasteland. Nothing could be further from the current truth. Apart from a rich history involving the entire Mediterranean population and dating back through antiquity, the Côte d'Azur today is a dazzling showcase for graphic and plastic arts. Running from A-to-V, **Antibes** offers the Château Grimaldi, containing one of the best Picasso collections in the nation. **Cagnes-sur-Mer** is not only the preserve and former domain of Renoir, but it's also host to the Museum of Modern Mediterranean Art. **St-Jean-Cap-Ferrat** is bristling with Impressionist work in its Ile-de-France Museum; the Renoirs, Monets and Sisleys are outstanding. **Nice** is jammed with treasures by Chagall, Matisse, Degas, Signac, Rodin and a cavalcade of other titans. **St-Paul-de- Vence** presents a stupefying indoor-outdoor collection at the Maeght Foundation. **St-Tropez**, long a rendezvous of painters, has collected works by its finest within the l'Annonciade Museum. At **Vallauris**, Picasso's "War and Peace" adorns a chapel, and a special museum for Alberto Magnelli also resides in this town. **Vence** has warm links with Matisse—demonstrated at the famous Chapelle du Rosaire. Another chapel—St-Pierre at **Villefranche**—evokes the clear light and coastal disposition of Cocteau. This is only a sampler because the entire list of masters and masterworks is too vast to include here.

Information Centers

Try either the **Services du Tourisme de la ville de Cannes**, at the Palais des Festivals (on the Croisette), or the **Welcome Information Service** branches in Nice and Cannes. The first offers an Information Desk, an English-speaking staff, a greeting service (at the Maritime Station, the rail terminals and on the autoroute), a cruise ship and other aids. It's open every day until midnight during the rush season. The second provides the same type of aid, plus a helping hand to locate immediate hotel accommodations for stranded travelers. Both have absolutely nothing to sell; their only aim is to assist you so that you'll get the best possible impression of the Côte d'Azur.

Antibes

The port town of Antibes on the main Nice-Cannes line has an unassuming charm, unusual for the Riviera. Fishing boats and luxury yachts rest gently in its small harbor. Among its attractions is an amusement center, **La Siesta**, with a casino. Also diverting are its **Marineland** and **Automobile Museum**, displaying such dazzlers as Bugatti, Ferrari, Rolls and a glamorous 1925 Hispano Swiza.

Along with Menton, nearby Beaulieu has the mildest weather along the Azure Coast, making it a popular resort also in winter. Many expensive yachts are docked at its extensive marina. The **Metropole** offers about the most luxurious accommodations you'll find in the region.

Where to Stay
Hotels and Resorts

Hotel du Cap-Eden Roc   ★★★★★
http://www.edenroc-hotel.fr/

Very Expensive

boulevard J.F. Kennedy. From Antibes: south on bd du Cap, continue south on bd. F. Meilland, and west on bd. Kennedy.

☎ *(93)61-39-01.*

Credit Cards: *Not Accepted.*

Mind-bogglingly rich. The 121 rooms and nine suites are exquisite, with luxurious period furnishings, and all of the rooms have private bath. The staff-guest ratio is an almost unheard of 3-to-1. There are exceptional views of both the gardens and the wide coastline from the hotel. Throughout the years, many celebrities have been seen, and can still be found, lounging by the swimming pool. The world-famous **Pavilion Eden Roc**, with its stylish restaurant overlooking the sea, snackbar, pool and cabanas, is near a rock garden apart from the hotel. Lunch is served on an outer terrace, under umbrellas and an arbor. Dinner specialties include bouillabaisse, lobster Thermidor and sea bass with fennel.

Royal   ★★
Moderate to Expensive

boulevard du Marcechal-Leclerc. Three blocks south of bd. Albert.

☎ *(93)34-03-09.*

Credit Cards: *All Major.*

The Royal has 37 rooms, all with private bath. It has its own beach with watersports, a cafe terrace in front with an extensive view and two restaurants and an English bar just off the lobby. **Le Dauphin** restaurant, open for lunch and dinner, specializes in seafood.

Where to Eat

Auberge Provencale ★★
Inexpensive

61 place Nationale. ☎ *(93)34-13-24.*

Credit Cards: *V, MC, A, E.*

One of the few budget offerings in town, the Auberge is an old favorite. Tasty, uncomplicated seafood and meat dishes.

Les Vieux Murs ★★★
Expensive

avenue de l'Amiral-de-Grasse. ☎ *(93)34.-66- 73.*

Credit Cards: *V, MC, A, E.*

All the elements are here for an intimate evening of pure romance: a table for two on a protected terrace facing the sea, under an arched ceiling in a 300-year-old building. You want more? How about a bottle of regional wine from the excellent cellars, and fragrant plates of fresh seafood cooked in unpretentious sauces.

Restaurant de Bacon ★★★★
Moderate to Expensive

boulevard de Bacon. ☎ *(93)61-50-02.*

Credit Cards: *All Major.* Closed: *Mon.*

The best bouillabaise in France—some say the world—is served daily at this atmospheric restaurant on a promontory facing the Nice coastline. There's a wide variety of unusual fish and shellfish dishes as well.

What to Do
Museums and Exhibits

Musee Picasso ★★★★

Chateau Grimaldi, place Marijol. ☎ *92.90.54.20.*

🕐 *10 a.m.–6 p.m.*

Special Hours: *July-August, until 7 p.m.*

Picasso was offered refuge here to paint and create for about six months in 1946. His sojourn resulted in over 100 art works, including ceramics, sculptures, lithographs and more, all of which were donated to the museum. It's located along the sea front in the former palace of the Grimaldi family.

Cannes

Located about 25 minutes from Nice via the *autoroute*, Cannes is so popular in High Season that it can be uncomfortably overcrowded. There's a magnificent second yacht harbor, called Port Canto, at the eastern extremity of the bay, with a 450-car parking lot adjoining; it's connected to a second car park west of these piers by a free bus shuttle service. This auxiliary port has a clubhouse, heated pool, exhibition hall, card rooms and bowling facilities— the works. Take a stroll along the Croisette, the main boulevard that separates the beach from the more lush hotels. Overlooking the city and illuminated at night is the 10th-century Castrum Canois, housing the **Museum of Mediterranean Civilization**. Smack in the center of town is the original yacht basin, crowded by the Maritime Station; big ships must be reached by lighter ones, however, because of the harbor's relatively narrow and shallow conformation. Boats run frequently to the Lerins, where the 5th-century **Monastery of the Cistercians** was St. Patrick's starting point for evangelizing Europe. At the **Royal Fort** on Ile Ste-Marguerite, you might want to visit the cell that has inspired stories, plays and movies by the score— once occupied, they say, by "the man in the iron mask." The beaches surrounding Cannes (summer bathing only) are the best east of St-Tropez now that the tankers have been rerouted to avoid oil spills. (Helicopters resolutely police the coast to beckon the ships away.) As the country's premier gambling town, Caanes boasts a number of glittery casinos. The town also maintains a $100-million hub for meetings, receptions, theater and congresses. In addition, you'll find a Sports Palace, an active polo green, three golf courses, an annual Film Festival, a spate of luxurious hotels, a collection of villas unequaled in France, a continuous parade of suntanned celebrities and a gala almost every night.

ITRAVELBOOK TIP: CANNES AND NICE HAVE RECENTLY BOTH EXPERIENCED A SURGE IN STREET CRIME; WHILE PARADISE IS BEAUTIFUL, IT MAY NOT ALWAYS BE SAFE. TRAVEL WITH YOUR WITS ABOUT YOU.

Where to Stay

Carlton Intercontinental ★★★
http://cannes.interconti.com/

Very Expensive

58 boulevard de la Croisette. Located between rue du Canada and rue Einesy.

☎ *(93)06-40-06.*

Credit Cards: *All Major.*

Built in 1912, this luxurious hotel is immediately recognized by the twin gray domes at both ends of its facade and the Art Deco grand gate. Its 326 rooms and 28 suites, all with private bath, are predictably lavish and comfortable. The hotel also has a 13-room penthouse, probably the most regal on the Riviera. There is a well equipped health club, with many spa facilities, as well as a private beach, where guests can check in directly from their yachts. Many guests at the Carlton are celebrities, especially during the annual film festival. Also offered is the Carlton Casino Club, on the 8th floor, which opened in 1989. **La Cote** restaurant (listed separately with the Carlton's other noted restaurant, **La Belle Otero**) is considered one of the most distinguished along the Riviera.

Fouquet's ★★
http://www.le-fouquets.com/

Moderate

2 rond-point Duboys-d'Angers. Located between rue d'Antibes and bd. de la Croisette.

☎ *(93)38-75-81.*

Credit Cards: *All Major.*

For a moderately priced hotel, Foquet's is a good choice. It's situated on a circular street with a number of other hotels several blocks from the beach. Each of its 10 comfortable rooms is decorated in bold colors and has private bath, hair dryer, dressing room and loggia. Very courteous service.

Juana
Moderate to Expensive

*La Pinede, avenue G.-Gallice. Located next to the casino gardens/
park, south of Palais des Congres.*

☎ *(93)61-08-70.*

Credit Cards: *Not Accepted.*

A 1930s Art Deco hotel facing the pine grove and the sea.
Accommodations include 45 guest rooms with spacious baths in
Italian tile and marble, featuring hair dryer, robes and deluxe toi-
letries. Most rooms have a balcony that overlooks the beautiful casi-
no garden. Also featured are a solarium and a private beach nearby.
La Terrasse, its first-class gourmet restaurant, specializes in
Mediterranean style dishes.

Moliere
http://www.hotel-moliere.com/ accueil_e.html

Budget to Moderate

*5 rue Moliere. Located between bd. de la Republique and rd. pt.
d'Angers, just south of rue d'Antibes.*

☎ *(93)38-16-16.*

Credit Cards: *All Major.*

In a 19th-century town house, this budget- priced hotel is conveniently located near the center of Cannes and just a five-minute walk
to the sea. It has 45 bright and comfortable rooms, only some with
private bathrooms with bath or shower. Most of the rooms are narrow, but they are all spotless.

Victoria
Moderate to Expensive

*rond-point Duboys-d'Angers. Located between rue Amouretti and rue
d'Oran.*

☎ *(93)99-36-36. 0.*

Credit Cards: *All Major.*

This small, stylish, modern hotel is nestled among the fancy boutiques on the main shopping street in the heart of Cannes. Guests are greeted in an English-style lobby, and there's a pleasant English bar. Nearly half the 25 rooms have a balcony overlooking a garden and pool.

Where to Eat

Au Bec Fin ★★
Moderate

12 rue 24-Aout. ☎ *(93)38-35-86.*

Credit Cards: *All Major.* Closed: *Sun.*

This rather plain family restaurant near the beach offers tasty southern-style seafood, salads and soups. Nearby, at No. 15, and a bit cheaper still, is **le Monaco**, a popular spot that resembles the jeweled principality only in name. It's clean, and serves big portions of starchy dishes like couscous and paella. Open daily, except Sun. for lunch (until 2 p.m.) and dinner (until 10 p.m.). No credit cards, and reservations are required.

Cannes Beach ★
Inexpensive

La Croisette. ☎ *93.38.14.59.*

Credit Cards: *V, MC, A, E.*

Yes, you can be on a budget and have lunch on this precious beach. This one is very pleasant, not as flashy as others on the strip; mostly fish dishes.

Carlton Intercontinental ★★★★
Moderate to Expensive

58 La Croisette. ☎ *(93)39-69-69.*

Credit Cards: *All Major.*

The posh Carlton Intercontinental has two excellent restaurants that play off each other. When you want light, inventive southern French cuisine, repair to **La Belle Otero**. **La Cote** ☎ (93-68-91-68) stays on the safe side by comparison, featuring well-loved classics like the original Provencal pizza, pissaladiere with anchovies, olives and onions. The elegant dining room beautifully blends Belle Epoque and Art Deco decor. Closed Tuesdays and Wednesdays, and Apr.-Nov.

La Palme d'Or ★★★★
Modersate to Expensive

73 La Croisette. *(92)98-74-14.*

Credit Cards: *All Major.* Closed: *Mon., Tues.*

The recently renovated Martinez is all the more impressive with the addition of this highly praised and elegant Provencal restaurant. The dining room and terrace face the hotel's eight-sided pool. Lobster, fresh fish from local waters (rouget, monkfish), plump olives and faultless produce play a substantial role in chef Christian Willer's La Croisette daily extravaganzas.

Cagnes-sur-Mer

Le Cagnard ★★★
Moderate

rue Pontis-Long. ☎ *(93)20-73-22.*

Within a remarkable medieval dwelling is this terrific hotel restaurant with a terrace where you can see the surrounding coastline; its retractable roof slides open to let the sunshine in. Inventive cuisine from Jean-Yves Johany with an emphasis on natural flavors, fresh fruit and vegetables. If you can't get into Le Cagnard, try **Restaurant des Peintres**, *71 montee Bourgade au Haut-de-Cagnes* ☎ (93-20-83-08), for Alain Llorca's memorable, slightly Asian- flavored cuisine that changes with the seasons; specialties include *bonito carpaccio* and roast suckling pig. Closed Wednesdays.

Eze

Chateau Eza ★★★
Moderate

Eze Village. ☎ *(93)41-12-24.*

Credit Cards: *All Major.*

For those who are interested in this sort of thing, the lilting sounds of the chef minuet have been heard here recently, with Maximintrained Bruno Cirino out and Andre Signoret in. He has adapted nicely, introducing his own innovations to the menu of Southern specialties (fresh fish, shellfish, and lamb) and utilizing the finest produce. The setting, an ancient village complex above the sea, remains as enchanting as ever. Accommodations here include six rooms and two suites, with luxurious decor and priceless antiques, most with a private entrance.

Chateau de la Chevre d'Or ★★★
Moderate to Expensive

rue de Barri. ☎ *(93)41-12-12.*

You'll probably have a hard time keeping your cool around the celebrity guests, unless, of course, you are one yourself. Chef Elie Mazot has the best credentials, having worked with the Troisgrois brothers in Roanne. His pan-roasted langoustines in coconut milk and raspberry souffle are decadent, which they must be, in order to draw guests away from their cocktails on a terrace with such a heavenly. A Relais and Chateaux rated establishment, it also offers 15 well-appointed rooms, some with a private terrace.

What to Do
City Events

Cannes Film Festival ★★★★
http://www.festival-cannes.com/ index.php?langue=6002

Palais des Festivals, 1 blvd de la Croisette. 93.39.24.53.

Unless you have connections, or are there to hawk your own piece of celluloid, you won't be allowed to attend any screenings. That's the bad news. The good news is that no one will stop you from gawking all you want. Held the second and third week of May, every year since 1946.

Nightlife

Casino Municipale ★★
1 jetee Albert-Edouard. ☎ *93.38.55.26.*

🕐 *5 p.m.–5 a.m.*

Cannes' largest casino, the Municipale shares Croisette space with the ultra-posh **Palm Beach Casino** ☎ (93.43.91.12) and the more intime **Casino du Carlton** (in the Carlton International Hotel, *58 blvd. de la Croisette,* ☎ (93.68.9.68). Slots, roulette, blackjack and more; Jimmy's nightclub on premises (Wednesday-Sunday, 11 p.m.–6 a.m.). All three casinos require a passport; dressy attire required, no shorts or bathing gear. Admission: expensive.

Cagnes-sur-Mer

Maison le Colettes   ★★
av. des Colettes. ☎ *93.20.61.07.*

🕐 *2–6 p.m.*

Special Hours: *Mid-Nov–May to 5 p.m.*

This poignant museum is where Auguste Renoir spent his last years (1907-19). Sadly crippled by arthritis, he could only paint by having his brushes tied to his fingers. You can see the wheelchair he was confined to, his coat and cravat, left as they were when he died. Along with memorabilia, letters and photos are 10 canvases attributed to the artist. In the garden sits one of his bronzes, entitled "Venus."

Eze
Parks and Gardens

Jardin Exotique   ★★★
rue du Chateau. ☎ *93.41.10.30.*

🕐 *9 a.m.–8 p.m.*

Special Hours: *Winter until 6 p.m.*

At the very summit of this hilltop village, you'll find the Jardin Exotique, part of an unoccupied old villa; flora is deemed exotic for the region—cactus and other succulents abound. The prime appeal is the view; price menu for FR125. There are outdoor tables in summer. Also serving Italian dishes is **Piccolo Mondo,** *10 rue Trenca* (93-57-53-11), featuring batter-fried zucchini flowers, pasta and a variety of meat dishes, and decent wines. The fixed-price menu is FR80. No dinner Mon.-Tues., open until 9:30 p.m. Nearby is the municipal market, with everything you'll need for your picnic basket, including game; open everyday from 5 a.m.–1 p.m.

Nice

It's the biggest city on the Côte d'Azur, but you'll probably stay along the shoreline, where most of the tourist activity occurs. It also is convenient to reach as Air France now provides nonstop flights between Nice and New York. The city offers a race track, an opera house, the nearby **Matisse Museum**, the **Museum of Modern and Contemporary Art**, plus 14 other museums, nightclubs, tennis, speedboating, water-skiing and scores of hotels and restaurants. The **Promenade des Anglais**, extending for miles along the sparkling waterfront, is wonderful for strollers, as is the **Flower Market** (1–5 p.m.) on a handsome pedestrian mall. The beaches are basically sand over pebbles and not too wide; they're jammed in summer and empty all winter.

Where to Stay

Beau Rivage ★★★★
http://www.nicebeaurivage.com/

Expensive

24 rue St-Francois-de-Paule. Located just east of Le Jardin Albert-Ier, along promenade des Anglais.

☎ *(93)80-80-70.*

Credit Cards: *All Major.*

Located near the opera, this Belle Epoque hotel had both Matisse and Chekhov as past guests. The five-story building on the beach-front walk was restored in the early 1980s, and the hotel now has a modern decor. Its 118 rooms have elegant Art Deco furnishings, marble bath, TV and soundproof windows. There's a restaurant on a deck looking out on the beach offering salads and light meals from May to September. The street-level Bistrot du Rivage is more formal, with excellent Mediterranean-style cuisine prepared year-round. Also offered is a private beach with bathing facilities. The service is excellent in every respect.

Chateau de la Chevre d'Or ★★★★★
Expensive

rue du Barri. Located off the Moyenne Corniche, exit the Autoroute A8 at La Turbie; west of Jardin Exotique.

☎ *(93)41-12-12.*

Credit Cards: *All Major.*

All 23 rooms have private bathrooms and views of the coastline, plus some have private terraces. There is an incredible view from the lounge, which has French doors that open onto a terraced swimming pool. Classic French cuisine is served at the **Chateau de la Chevre d'Or** restaurant, which has a formal dining room and a terrace—both have breathtaking views. **Cafe du Jardin** serves simple meals like fresh salads and fruit cocktails over the Mediterranean. The hotel is closed December through February. The main restaurant is closed on Wednesdays as well as December through February. Cafe du Jardin is closed on Tuesdays as well as mid-October through mid-April.

Elysee Palace   ★★★★
Moderate to Expensive

59 promenade des Anglais. Located on the promenade at rue Honore-Sauvan.

☎ *(93)86-06-06.*

Credit Cards: *All Major.*

There are 121 deluxe rooms plus 22 suites, all in contemporary decor with private marble bath. Most rooms offer a sweeping vista of the sea. The hotel has a gourmet restaurant, a dining terrace and a piano bar. Also featured are a rooftop pool with a city view, a hairdresser, a conference room and other facilities for business travelers. All guests are admitted to a private beach through the Beau Rivage, which is under the same Franco-American management.

Meridien   ★★★★
Moderate to Expensive

1 promenade des Anglais. Angled at the promenade and the flowering park, Le Jardin Albert-Ier.

☎ *(93)82-25-25.*

Credit Cards: *All Major.*

In a 10-story building in a great location, Le Meridien is a modern commercial hotel. All of its 314 rooms have a sea view and are comfortable and well furnished. TV, trouser press, telephone, modern bath with hair dryer and thick towels are standard features.

Petit Palais
Moderate

10 avenue Emile-Bieckert. *Located at av. de Picardie in Carabacel. residential district—west of Palais des Congres.*

☎ *(93)62-19-11.*

This turn-of-the-century hotel, now operated by the Best Western chain, is a 10- minute drive from the city center in the Carabacel residential district. There are 25 spacious rooms, with fine paintings, comfortable armchairs and excellent bathrooms. The management is friendly and helpful. Only breakfast is served.

West-End
http://www.hotel-westend.com/

Moderate to Expensive

31 promenade des Anglais. Located at the promenade and rue Rivoli.

☎ *(93)88-79-91.*

Credit Cards: *All Major.*

In a prime location with outstanding sea views, the West-End is a traditional hotel that's been completely renovated. There are 126 modern rooms with bath, hair dryer and many with sea view. Also featured are a solarium and a private beach with water sports. L'Orangerie serves outstanding meals; for drinks, there's Le Shaker Bar with a terrace.

Windsor
Moderate

11 rue Dalpozzo. A short walk from the promenade des Anglais, in the heart of Nice.

☎ *(93)88-59-35.*

Credit Cards: *All Major.*

This moderately priced, family-run hotel is a charmer. In fact, it looks more like a villa than a hotel. The 60 beautifully maintained rooms have bath or shower and French windows—many of which open onto a tropical garden and palm-fringed pool. Its fitness center offers a sauna, a Turkish bath and shiatsu massages.

Where to Eat

Chantecler
Very Expensive

37 promenade des Anglais. ☎ *(93)88-39-51.*

Credit Cards: *All Major.*

Although the appointments are glamorous, the Chantecler is more of a showcase for its outstanding chef. Terrific regional wine list; generous fixed-price menu for FR200 at lunch, including wine. Terrace dining in good weather. This is one of the finest hotel kitchens in France.

L'Ane Rouge
Expensive to Very Expensive

7 quai Deux-Emmanuel. ☎ *(93)89-49-63.*

Credit Cards: *All Major.* Closed: *Sat., Sun.*

So traditional is this restaurant that it has not moved with the times and provided a fixed-price menu. However, the largely seafood preparations are ultra-fresh and classically prepared. Guests are seated in the flamboyantly decorated salon or on the terrace, with colorful views of the port.

La Merenda
Inexpensive to Moderate

4 rue de la Terrasse. none.

Closed: *Mon., Sat., Sun.*

There is no phone, it's open only four days a week, it's closed in February and August, and it makes no concessions to creature comforts. But the food is a wonderful collection of local favorites, some of them made at your miniscule table (there are only eight of them). You'll probably have to wait in line to get in.

What to Do
City Celebrations

Carnavale
Various locations. ☎ *93.87.16.28.*

Just before the somber days of Lent, the city lets out a long, collective whoop of abandon during the two-week Carnaval. It's a typically uninhibited bang-up flurry of parades, fireworks, yacht parades, balls, etc. It all ends with the burning (in effigy) of the King of Carnival.

Museums and Exhibits

Musee Chagall ★★★
Avenue du Docteur Menard. ☎ *93.81.75.75.*
🕐 *10 a.m.–7 p.m.*

Special Hours: *October-June 10 a.m.-5:30 p.m.*

This light-filled, modern museum houses over 500 major works in several different mediums by the Russian-born artist, who lived the good life in Nice with his wife. On permanent exhibition are 17 startling canvases that make up the "Biblical Message" series. Admission: moderate, varies.

Musee Matisse ★★★
164 av des Arenes de Cimiez. ☎ *93.81.08.08.*
🕐 *11 a.m.–7 p.m.*

Special Hours: *October-March, 10 a.m.-5 p.m.*

The artist loved Nice so much he spent more than 40 years here, painting and sketching. His donated work, including children's book illustrations, bronzes, and fabric designs, fills several rooms of one of Nice's oldest villas. His final work, "Flowers and Fruits," is displayed here. Admission: varies, moderate.

Musee d'Art Moderne et d'Art Contemporain
http://www.mamac-nice.org/

Promenade des Arts. ☎ *93.62.61.62.*
🕐 *11 a.m.–6 p.m.*

Special Hours: *Friday to 10 p.m.*

Hundreds of Pop-Art, Neo-Realistic and Avant-garde pieces are given an appropriate home in this towering marble and glass museum, which is Nice's newest kid on the art block. There's a fairly large representation of American and Nicoise artists, (and self-propagandists) including Warhol, Liechtenstein, Yves Klein, and Cesar. Free admission October-June.

St-Jean-Cap-Ferrat

St-Jean is a rare pearl on a gem-studded coastline, and famous for its secluded villas. It is the only village on Cap-Ferrat, a rugged promontory jutting into the sea six miles east of Nice.

Where to Stay

Clair Logis   ★★★
Moderate

12 avenue Centrale. Located at the center of the peninsula, just south of av.de Verdun.

☎ *(93)76-04-57.*

Credit Cards: *All Major.*

A small, turn-of-the-century villa set in two acres of lush semitropical gardens. All of the 18 rooms have a private bath, and four have a large balcony. The most romantic accommodations are located in the main building; the rooms in the outlying annex are the most modern.

Hotel Bel Air du Cap-Ferrat   ★★★
Expensive to Very Expensive

boulevard du General-de-Gaulle. Located at southern tip of peninsula.

☎ *(93)76-50-50.*

Credit Cards: *All Major.*

A leading feature of this Belle Epoque palace is its location- it's hidden away in a 12-acre garden of semitropical trees and manicured lawns at the tip of Cap-Ferrat. The 59 luxurious rooms, each with a different decorative theme, are soundproof and have marble bath. Ten suites and a gorgeous honeymoon suite are also available.

La Voile d'Or
Expensive

31 avenue Jean-Mermoz. *Located at the south end of Port de Plaisance, near Capitaine Cook restaurant. Rated Restaurant: La Voile d'Or.*

☎ *(93)01-13-13.*

Credit Cards: *Not Accepted.*

On the edge of a little fishing port and yacht harbor, "The Golden Sail" affords panoramic views of the coast. The lounges, rooms and restaurant all open onto terraces, making this luxury hotel a romantic haven. There are 50 rooms and five suites; all are soundproofed and individually decorated with hand-painted reproductions of antiques, antique clocks and paintings.

Where to Eat

Le Provencal ★★★
Moderate

avenue D. Semeria. ☎ *(93)76-03-97.*

Credit Cards: *V, MC, E.* Closed: *Mon.*

This elegant, muraled restaurant, ablaze with flowers, is a laboratory for Jean-Jacques Jouteux's experimental cooking. One of his recent specialties was roasted St-Pierre fish wrapped in a puff-pastry shell with figs.

What to Do
Museums and Exhibits

Fondation Ephrussi de Rothschild ★★★
Chemin du Musee. ☎ *93.01.33.09.*

🕐 *10 a.m.–7 p.m.*

Special Hours: *September-June, to 6 p.m., closed November*

The estate of the Baroness de Rothschild has opened the doors of her old digs to the public. Named after her yacht (not the Baroness), the pastel-painted manse has furnishings fit for a queen (some of the antiques were Marie Antoinette's), including a recently unveiled Louis XV room. Admission: inexpensive to moderate.

St-Paul-de-Vence

This ancient hill town has 16th-century houses flanking its narrow streets, a 13th-century Gothic church and a plethora of upscale restaurants, hotels and art galleries—but its main attraction undeniably is its **Museum of Modern Art**; it alone is worth a transatlantic journey. High on a hill above the village, the **Maeght Foundation** features exhibits by such 20th-century masters as Matisse, Chagall, Braque and Kandinsky, and outside there's an equally impressive sculpture garden. If you are anywhere on this coast, make an effort to experience this celebration of the senses.

Where to Stay

Colombe d'Or   ★★★
Expensive

1 place du General-de-Gaulle. Located just south (a short walk) from the Foundation Maeght.

☎ *(93)32-80-02.*

Credit Cards: *All Major.*

This legendary hotel has almost as much modern art as an art museum. There are a Leger mural on the terrace, a Braque dove by the pool, a Picasso and a Matisse in the dining room, and works by Chagall, Rouault, Dufy, and Miro in the other public areas. The hotel's 16th-century ramparts which surround the hotel, gardens, terrace and pool, offer views over a landscape of cypress trees, red-roofed villas, palm trees and swimming pools. There are 15 rooms and 11 suites; all are full of antiques and have private bathrooms. Dining is available at **Colombe d'Or** on the garden patio or inside. Guests can also enjoy an after-dinner drink in front of the fireplace in the lower "pit lounge." Reservations are recommended for accommodations as well as for meals.

Le Hameau
http://www.le-hameau.com/

Moderate

528 route de la Colle. Located on hilltop at Hauts-de-St-Paul.

☎ *(93)32-80-24.*

Credit Cards: *All Major.*

On the outskirts of St-Paul-de-Vence, this romantic Mediterranean villa is on a hilltop and has lovely views of the surrounding hills and valleys. Accommodations include 16 rooms and three suites, all with bath or shower. Most of the comfortable, whitewashed rooms have a small terrace or balcony that overlooks a vineyard.

Where to Eat
Saint-Raphael

L'Arbousier   ★★
Moderate to Expensive

6 avenue de Valescure. ☎ *(94)95-25-00.*

Credit Cards: *V, MC, A, E.* Closed: *Wed.*

Featuring cuisine prepared in the modern Provencal style, this is probably the most innovative restaurant in town. Chef Phillipe Troncy does seafood best, in tandem with exceptional, seasonal produce (potato cakes with lobster, chicken breast and pickled lemon).

What to Do

Fondation Maeght   ★★★★
http://www.fondation-maeght.com/*chemin des Gardettes.*
☎ *93.32.81.63.*

🕐 *10 a.m.–7 p.m.*

Special Hours: *October–June to 6 p.m.*

Jose-Luis Sert's fantastic confection of a building contrasts sharply with the medieval village of St-Paul-de-Vence just below it. The Fondation showcases the (strictly) 20th-century art treasures accumulated by dealers Aime and Marguerite Maeght. Even more spectacular than the exhibitions inside is the magical sculpture garden set amidst pine trees, pools and meandering terraces. Mobiles, mosaics and water sculptures by Calder, Arp, Miro, Zadkine, and Pol Bury are around every corner. Admission: moderate.

St-Tropez

In season St-Tropez crawls—especially on weekends. But why not, as it boasts what are probably the finest beaches of the province? Topless sunning is legally indulged in, especially on the Tahiti or Salins beaches, but an anything-goes (off) attitude exists nearly everywhere, despite a recent effort by police to levy fines on bottomless basking. Moorea is a beckoning strip (of sand and more) and so is Voile Rouge, while "55" is a bit more straitlaced as beaches go. Down on this coast, nightlife becomes formal when the customers wear shoes. With consistently great live music, **Les Caves du Roy** is one of the best discos along the Riviera. The **Café de Paris**, below the Hôtel Sube, is a summer meeting spot of the famous. On the same road, you'll find **Les Collettes**, where Auguste Renoir did his painting from 1908 until his death in 1919. It is now a museum. Another museum you shouldn't miss is the **Musée de l'Annonciade**, housed in a former chapel. Containing one of the finest collections of modern art on the coast, the museum has several pieces depicting the St-Tropez port.

Where to Stay

Byblos ★★★★
Expensive

avenue Paul-Signac. Located at base of Citadelle, on Place de Lices, near Montee G. Ringrave.

☎ *(94)97-00-04.*

Credit Cards: *All Major.*

This deluxe complex is situated on a hill above the harbor just a few minutes from all the beaches. There are 60 rooms and 47 suites, each uniquely decorated with paisley brocades, rich mosaics and hammered brass. Some rooms have a balcony overlooking an inner courtyard; others open onto a flowered terrace. Standard features are double-glazed windows, telephone, TV and tile or marble bathroom with robes and sunken tub. Accommodations also include 10 duplex apartments built around a small courtyard with an outdoor spa. The hotel provides such services as a beauty salon, 24-hour room service, same-day laundry and valet. Its restaurant, **Les Arcades**, is only open for dinner. Also featured are a Moorish-style bar, a nightclub and a disco.

Domaine/Villa de Belieu ★★★★★
Very Expensive

Gassin on Route de St-Tropez. Located 2 km north on rte. de St-Tropez, near intersection of Gassin and Ramatuelle.

☎ *(94)56-40-56.*

Credit Cards: *All Major.*

A short drive from the center of St-Tropez, this opulent hotel was converted from a Mediterranean-style villa on the grounds of the Domaine de Bertaud-Belieu. This estate has been producing grapes for wines for more than 2000 years. All of the 12 rooms and five suites are uniquely decorated in styles ranging from rococo to art deco; many have antiques and trompe l'oeil murals. All of the units are spacious and have private bath and every modern convenience. Guests are invited to visit the wine cellar and the nearby golf course. The romantic **Restaurant Belieu** offers dining outside under the stars as well as dining inside. In the wood-beamed restaurant, tables are graced with French porcelain and antique silverware. The Provencal cuisine focuses on seafood, and the wines are the estate's best. Both lunch and dinner are served daily, but reservations are required.

Ermitage ★
http://www.nova.fr/ermitage/ index_f.htm

Moderate to Expensive

avenue Paul-Signac. Located at base of Citadelle, on Place de Lices, near Montee G. Ringrave.

☎ *(94)97-52-33.*

Credit Cards: *All Major.*

Originally built as a private villa, this three-story hotel is a plush yet comfortable hideaway. It is next door to the Byblos, but has a more relaxed atmosphere than its neighbor, and it is one of the few hotels with a sweeping view of old St-Tropez. The 29 rooms have been renovated and now have private bath and tastefully refurbished decor. Breakfast is the only meal served.

Residence de la Pinede ★★★★
http://www.residencepinede.com/

Expensive to Very Expensive

plage de la Bouillabaisse. Located about 1 km south on D98 via la plage de la Bouillabaisse.

☎ *(94)97-04-21.*

Credit Cards: *All Major.*

Built in 1952, this chic resort hotel is tucked away in a grove of pine trees above its private beach. There are 42 spacious and comfortable rooms, which were recently remodeled and redecorated in pastel colors. They all have small tile and marble bathrooms with hair dryer and thick towels. Other standard features are satellite TV, video, telephone and terrace overlooking the bay. The restaurant has excellent food, which is served in the dining room or on the terrace under the pine trees.

Where to Eat

Bistrot des Lices ★★★
Moderate

3 place des Lices. ☎ *(94)97-29-00.*

Credit Cards: *V, MC.*

Deceptively simple-looking, this establishment is actually a highly regarded local favorite, with a chic crowd (probably a celebrity or two), and a changing menu of Provencal favorites. There are several dining areas, a main room, a terrace facing the square, and a garden in the back.

Chateau de la Messardiere ★★★
Expensive

avenue Roussel on the rte de Tahiti. ☎ *(94)56- 76-00.*

Credit Cards: *V, MC, DC, A, E.*

Fresh seafood and Asian spices are the hallmarks on the menu here. This restaurant, in a restored, and now very expensive, chateau, was once managed by the current St-Tropez restaurant king Christopher Leroy. Lunch is served by the pool, dinner indoors in the country-French dining room. Leroy is now well established at **La Table du Marche**, an art-deco style bistro, with somewhat lower prices, *38 rue Clemenceau* ☎ (94-97-85-20), open noon to 12:30 p.m. daily; specialties include roast Bresse chicken, steak and macaroni gratin and cheese souffles. Upstairs, a maximum of 20 people squeeze into **La Salle a Manger** (dinner only), giving it a dinner-party atmosphere. There's an a la carte menu, but most patrons leave it up to Christopher, who serves a set menu, which he changes nightly.

What to Do

Musee de L'Annonciade/Citadel ★★★
place Grammont. ☎ *94.97.04.01.*

🕐 *10 a.m.–8 p.m.*

Special Hours: *Winter until 6 p.m., closed November*

Not surprisingly, most of France's 20th-century masters have passed through here at one time or another, often staying for long periods. This harborside museum contains an enviable collection of modern pieces by Paul Signac, Utrillo, Maillol, and many more. Admission: moderate.

Nightlife

Cafe de Paris ★★★
Quai Suffren. ☎ *94.97.56.*

🕐 *8 a.m.–3 a.m.*

Special Hours: *Winter to 7 p.m.*

Varied entertainment is offered in this velvety boudoir in the heart of the port area. You can shoot pool, have a coffee (reasonably priced) or a stiff drink (stratospheric) in a makeshift turn-of-the-century bordello atmosphere. Always crowded.

Les Caves du Roi ★★★
avenue Paul-Signac, in the Hotel Byblos. ☎ *94.97.04.*

🕐 *11 p.m.–5 a.m.*

Special Hours: *June–September only*

Like something out of *1,001 Nights,* Les Caves du Roy's decor apes a Middle-Eastern pleasure palace, with mirrors and columns in abundance. The clientele is a mixture of wannabes and the seriously moneyed. Drinks are expensive. Live music, no cover.

Parks and Gardens

Tahiti Beach ★★★
Route de Tahiti, Pampelonne. ☎ *33.94.97.18.02.*

Admission: *FR80.*

St. Tropez's public beaches, including the popular Plage des Graniers, are often intensely crowded and pebble-pocked. For the real ST experience, you can lounge on a slender striped cushion for a few Euros a day at one of the private beach clubs on the tony Pampelonne strip (about three miles southwest of the port of St-Tropez). Tahiti is one of the most fashionable, and your fee includes a chance to shell out more Euros for lunch, a massage, and shower facilities.

> **ITRAVELBOOK TIP:** THE MONTHS THAT PARIS IS MOST CROWDED ARE MARCH AND OCTOBER. A HOTEL RESERVATION IN ADVANCE IS WELL ADVISED AS TRADE SHOWS OCCUPY SO MUCH OF THE SPACE EVEN YEARS BEFORE THE ANNUAL FAIRS.

Ile de France

Paris

One of the most beautiful and romantic cities in the world, Paris, the capital of France, lies on both banks of the Seine. The river divides the "City of Light" into the Right Bank and the Left Bank, and it's made up of 20 municipal districts, or *arrondissements*, each with its own town hall and distinctive style and character. Paris has it all—wide tree-lined boulevards, sidewalk cafés, magnificent monuments, Gothic cathedrals, world-famous art museums, chic shops, impeccable cuisine, cabarets, the Sorbonne, the Seine. And like everywhere else in France, it is expensive.

Where to Stay

The **City of Paris Tourist Information Bureau (http://www. paris-touristoffice.com/index va.html)** at *127 avenue Champs-Elysées*, will spring to your rescue in emergencies by finding you a room within a 60-mile radius of Cannes, Nice, Marseille, Reims, Lourdes, Strasbourg, Tours, Rouen, Lyon, Vichy, Dijon, Aix- les-Baines, or (of course) the capital. Reservations are guaranteed for one night only (this avoids competition with travel agencies). Passengers arriving at Charles de Gaulle Airport without a room reservation can waltz right over to a push-button computer that indicates the availability of space in more than 300 Paris hotels. Look for it in Aerogare #1 near the Aeroport de Paris Information Counter.

Hostels

Three Ducks Hostel
http://www.3ducks.fr/

Budget

6 place Etienne Pernet.

Public Transportation: *Eight.* Metro Stop: *Commerce.*

☎ *(1)48-42-04-05.*

Definitely one of the cheapest places to stay in Paris, the Three Ducks Hostel is the scene for traveling youths and backpackers. While not exactly ideal for a peaceful night with the spouse, this place definitely exudes a bohemian, raucous attitude. There is a TV room, patio, kitchen and bar in the building with laundry facilities next door. Summer time translates to reservations needed, barbecues and many young Americans drinking cheap beer. There is a 1 a.m. curfew, a lockout period from 11 a.m. to 5 p.m. and only cash is accepted for the 90 francs per bed price. This is also the embarkation point for the guided mountain bike tours of Paris offered in four languages and lasting six hours. It's a wonderful way to see the city and have some fun for about 24 Euros, including a bike and insurance.

Hotels and Resorts

Bretonnerie
Moderate to Expensive

22 rue Sainte Croix de la Bretonnerie.

Public Transportation: *One, Eleven.* Metro Stop: *Hotel de Ville.*

☎ *(1)48-87-77-63,* FAX: *(1)42-77-26-78.*

Credit Cards: *All Major.*

There are 31 guest rooms, all of which are generously sized and attractively furnished. Each comes with a minibar and a safe. Breakfast is served in the medieval-times basement displaying wood tables and high backed chairs under a vaulted ceiling. A good choice for lesbian and gay travelers. Take note that this popular choice is closed for part of August.

Duc de Saint Simon
Expensive

14 rue de St. Simon.

Public Transportation: *Twelve.* Metro Stop: *rue du Bac.*

☎ *(1)45-48-35-66*, FAX: *(1)45-48-68-25.*

Enjoying a location among the gardens, one of this hotel's most appealing aspects is its quiet atmosphere. It offers 34 rooms, each individually decorated with period furnishings and immaculately kept. Garden view balconies are available with some rooms. Although there are no dining facilities, there is a small bar. Reservations are a must.

Four Seasons George V
http://www.fourseasons.com/paris/

Expensive to Staggering

31 avenue George V.

Public Transportation: *One.* Metro Stop: *George V.*

☎ *225-5843*, ☎ *(1)47-23-54-00*, FAX: *(1)47-20- 40-00.*

Credit Cards: *All Major.*

This fabulously cosmopolitan hotel first lavished its guests with superior service in luxurious surroundings in 1928. Now operated by the superlative Four Seasons Group, the hotel continues its commitment to consistently high standards of maintenance. Guests delight in the dining options which include a gastronomic dream called **Les Princes**, a brasserie, a bar and a quaint tea room. The 260 plush accommodations are air-conditioned and include cable TV, radio, telephone, minibar, bath with bidet, hair dryer and robes and some rooms with a balcony. A grand choice under skillful management.

Hotel Eber
Moderate

18 rue Leon Jost.

Public Transportation: *Two.* Metro Stop: *Courcelles.*

☎ *(1)46-22-60-70*, FAX: *(1)47-63-01-01.*

Credit Cards: *V, MC, DC, A.*

This hotel's focus lies on a peaceful stay for its guests. Its membership in the Relais du Silence, a group of 275 individual hotel owners who focus on providing a calm atmosphere for guests, proves exemplary in its dedication to serenity. There are just 18 guest rooms in this renovated, former bordello. Families particularly enjoy the spacious two level suite with private balcony on the top floor.

Hotel Lido ★★★
Budget to Moderate

4 passage de la Madeleine.

Public Transportation: *Eight, Twelve.* Metro Stop: *Madeleine.*

☎ *528-1234,* ☎ *(1)42-66-27-37,* FAX: *(1)42-66- 61-23.*

Credit Cards: *V, MC, DC, A.*

A definite charmer, the Lido revels in its right bank location within close walking distance to many of the major sights and the Champs-Elysees. The 32 guest rooms come with a telephone, TV, minibar and private bath or shower with a hair dryer. About half of the rooms are air-conditioned.

Hotel de Crillon ★★★★★
http://www.crillon.com/fr/indexsommaire.htm

Expensive to Very Expensive

10 place de la Concorde.

Public Transportation: *One, Eight, Twelve.* Metro Stop: *Concorde.*

☎ *(1)44-71-15-00,* FAX: *(1)44-71-15-02.*

Credit Cards: *All Major.*

Originally constructed in the 18th century under orders of Louis XV, this classic palace rates as one of the grandest hotel in Paris. Guests are invited to utilize the 24-hour room service, 24-hour concierge service and available babysitting. Each of the 163 guest rooms is air-conditioned and equipped with a TV, telephone, radio, minibar, marble bath with hair dryer and some with a terrace and marble fireplace. Exquisite in every way.

L'Abbaye Saint Germain
http://www.hotel-abbaye.com/

Moderate to Expensive

10 rue Cassette.

Public Transportation: *Four.* Metro Stop: *St. Sulpice.*

☎ *(1)45-44-38-11,* FAX: *(1)45-48-07-86.*

Abeautiful conversion of a convent from the 1600s, a classic meld of the charm of an earlier day with the function of today. There are 46 guest rooms, four of which are suites. While a bit cozy in size, the chambers demonstrate taste in decorations and elegance in furnishings. Some room layouts include alcoves and other unique architectural nuances. Rooms on the first floor are the most desirable, opening onto the garden.

L'Hotel Guy Louis Duboucheron
Expensive

13 rue des Beaux Arts.

Public Transportation: *Four.* Metro Stop: *St. Germain des Pres.*

☎ *(1)43-25-27-22,* FAX: *(1)43-25-64-81.*

This exquisite hotel, adorned with antiques and lavish decorations with an emphasis on velvet, has been operating since 1900. There are just 27 cozy guest rooms here, each individually decorated in such styles as the Cardinale room with an abundance of purple and the art deco room with furniture from Mistinguett. Perhaps room #16 is of interest, considering Oscar Wilde died there. In addition to 24-hour room service, guests enjoy sumptuous cuisine in **Le Belier**, breakfast in the vaulted cellar and relaxing social evenings in the piano bar.

Le Britannique   ★★
Budget to Moderate

20 avenue Victoria.

Public Transportation: *One, Four, Eleven.* Metro Stop: *Chatelet.*

☎ *(1)42-33-74-59,* FAX: *(1)42-33-82-65.*

Credit Cards: *V, MC, DC, A, E.*

This former Quaker mission from World War I boasts a fine city center address. Tastefully decorated, each of the 40 rooms comes with comfortable furniture, a minibar, cable TV and private bath with hairdryer. Although the staff doesn't speak much English, the genuine welcome and personal attention are easily understood.

Le Raphael ★★★★
http://www.raphael-hotel.com/

Expensive to Very Expensive

17 avenue Kleber.

Public Transportation: *Six.* Metro Stop: *Kleber.*

☎ *447-7462,* ☎ *(1)44-28-00-28,* FAX: *(1)45-01- 21-50.*

Credit Cards: *V, DC, A, E.*

Situated close to the Place Etoile and the Arc de Triomphe, this statement of refinement and quiet elegance was constructed in 1925. There are just 87 rooms, each with air conditioning, TV, telephone, radio, minibar, safe and bath with hair dryer and robes. Forty of the rooms are suites, and nonsmoking rooms are available. There is a quiet restaurant and an English style bar. An ideal hotel for the discriminating guest prefering tasteful elgance and personal attention over glitz and glamour.

Les Marronniers ★★★
Moderate to Expensive

21 rue Jacob.

Public Transportation: *Four.* Metro Stop: *St. Germain des Pres.*

☎ *(1)43-25-30-60,* FAX: *(1)40-46-83-56.*

A true gem, this hotel is situated in the heart of St. Germain. The garden atmosphere accents the hotel's location set back from the street, setting the scene for a peaceful stay. There are 37 guest rooms available, all comfortable and quiet. Lesbian and gay friendly.

Pavillon de la Reine ★★★
http://www.pavillon-de-la-reine.com/version_anglaise/
framegene/F_gene_accueil.htm

Expensive

28 place des Vosges.

Public Transportation: *One, Five, Eight.* Metro Stop: *Bastille.*

☎ *(1)42-77-96-40,* FAX: *(1)42-77-63-06.*

Credit Cards: *All Major.*

With origins to the 1600s, this hotel overflows with character and charm. The 53 accommodations are tastefully decorated in Louis XIV style with antiques and attractive furnishings. Each is air-conditioned and comes with cable TV, telephone, minibar and a beautiful marble bath.

Plaza Athenee   ★★★★★
http://www.plaza-athenee-paris.com/

Expensive to Astronomical

25 avenue Montaigne.

Public Transportation: *One, Nine.* Metro Stop: *Franklin D. Roosevelt.*

☎ *225-5843, (1)47-23-78-33,* FAX: *(1)47-20- 20-70.*

Credit Cards: *All Major.*

Glamor found in every detail, this elegant hotel attracts a large share of celebrities and those involved in the fashion world. A professional and discrete staff of 400 lavishes guests with service unmatched by any other hotel. Its 211 guest rooms are commodious and feature climate control, cable TV, radio, telephone, minibar and bath with bidet, hair dryer, robes and telephone. Some standard rooms come with a Jacuzzi and a balcony, and the suites exude Old World charm with period style furnishings. Guests enjoy casual drinks in the two celebrity frequented bars, one of which was where Mata Hari was arrested, and later dine in one of the two gourmet restaurants, **Le Regence** and **Le Relais Plaza**.

Regina
http://www.regina-hotel.com/

Expensive

2 place des Pyramides.

Public Transportation: *One, Seven.* Metro Stop: *Palais Royal.*

☎ *(1)42-60-31-10*, FAX: *(1)40-15-95-16*.

Credit Cards: *All Major*.

An ideal address for visiting the Louvre or a stroll through the Tuileries gardens, the Regina continues to be a classic symbol of luxury. Operating since 1904, it now offers 130 large accommodations with beautiful furnishings, cable TV, minibar, telephone, safe, fax and computer hookup, bath with bidet and hair dryer and some with air conditioning, balcony and kitchenette. A first class hotel all the way.

Relais Christine   ★★★★
http://www.relais-christine.com/

Moderate to Expensive

3 rue Christine.

Public Transportation: *Four, Ten*. Metro Stop: *Odeon*.

☎ *(1)43-26-71-80*, FAX: *(1)43-26-89-38*.

Credit Cards: *All Major*.

Occupying a former monastery from the 16th century, the Relais Christine's old world charm lives on within the 50 guest rooms and the lovely public rooms. Each of the rooms displays fine period furnishings and antiques, standard with air conditioning, radio, telephone, cable TV, minibar and marble bath. Always courteous, the personable staff is sure to please.

Ritz   ★★★★★
http://www.ritzparis.com/default.asp

Very Expensive

15 place Vendome.

Public Transportation: *Eight, Twelve*. Metro Stop: *Madeleine*.

☎ *(1)43-16-30-30*, FAX: *(1)43-16-31-78*.

Credit Cards: *All Major*.

The definition of elegance, this hotel is decidedly one of the most famous hotels in the world. Founded by Caesar Ritz in 1898, it is unrivaled by any other hotel in luxury and service. Such public figures as Coco Chanel, Ernest Hemingway and the Duke of Windsor have resided here. With an emphasis on exclusiveness, the hotel has bulletproof windows in some of the rooms, and there is no lobby so as to avoid paparazzi gatherings. The 187 guest rooms have retained their original charm with modern appurtenances. Each is adorned with lovely antique furniture, brass beds, cable TV, telephone, radio, air conditioning, minibar, safe, marble bath (Caesar Ritz was the first to include private baths in guest rooms) and some with Jacuzzi. L'Espadon is the hallmark restaurant, and there is a garden terrace restaurant, several bars and 24-hour room service. A courteous, intelligent, multilingual staff wrote the book on service, making the entire experience here unforgettable.

Universite   ★ ★ ★
Budget to Moderate

22 rue de l'Universite.

Public Transportation: *Twelve*. Metro Stop: *rue du Bac*.

☎ *(1)42-61-09-39*, FAX: *(1)42-60-40-84*.

A former 17th-century private residence now houses this friendly hotel. Abundant with antiques and tapestries, the hotel beautifully shows its beamed ceilings and period furnishings. Each of the 27 guest rooms is attractively, individually decorated in comfortable style and comes with a TV and a telephone. Uniquely designed, some come with balconies while others enjoy a spacious feeling with high ceilings.

Grand Hotel Jeanne d'Arc
Budget

3 rue de Jarente.

Public Transportation: *One*. Metro Stop: *St. Paul*.

☎ *(1)48-87-62-11*, FAX: *(1)48-87-37-31*.

Credit Cards: *V, MC, DC, E*.

A standard hotel which proves to be one of the better value choices in the area. The 36 guest rooms are slightly worn and eclectically decorated, with a telephone, cable TV and tidy bath. Return visitors appreciate the location near the many shops, the place des Vosges and the Picasso Museum.

Hotel du College de France ★★
http://www.hotel-collegedefrance.com/

Budget

7 rue Thenard.

Public Transportation: *Ten.* Metro Stop: *Maubert Mutualite.*

☎ *(1)43-26-78-36*, FAX: *(1)46-34-58-29.*

Credit Cards: *A.*

Situated on a quiet street in the heart of the Latin Quarter, this little hotel offers comfortable Left Bank lodging. There are 29 bed chambers, all of which are modestly decorated in similar, subtle colors. Each is well kept and equipped with a telephone, TV and modern bath with a hair dryer. Those rooms on the top floors are the most desirable, with vistas of the towers of Notre Dame and exposed wood beams.

Chartres
Bed and Breakfasts

Chateau de Blanville
Saint-Luperce.

☎ *(37)26-77-36*, FAX: *(37)26-78-02.*

As impressive as the facade, the interior houses the six charming guest rooms, each tastefully furnished and including a bath or shower. The young owners invite their guests to wander the house and linger in the sitting rooms, salons and library. All of the public areas are accented with 17th-century furnishings and beautiful antiques that add to the already wonderful charm. A truly enjoyable experience from the moment one arrives to the almost sad moment one leaves.

Ferme du Chateau
Leveville.

☎ *(37)22-97-02.*

Credit Cards: *Not Accepted.*

Capturing great views of the spire of the Chartres Cathedral from all around the property, this lovely farm house sits beside a beautiful chateau. Describing this house as quaint is an understatement, as there are just two guests rooms. Handsomely decorated with attractive color schemes, the rooms are quite comfortable and include a bath or shower. Join the owners for a complementary breakfast, and enjoy dinner and wine at the communal table for a tiny sum. Day tours might include the nearby cathedral, museums, Old Town or golf. No matter what activities the day brings, starting it off and winding it down at this small B&B makes it all that much more enjoyable.

Hotels and Resorts

Chateau d'Esclimont   ★★★
http://www.esclimont.com/esclimont.htm

Expensive

Saint-Symphorien-le-Chateau.

☎ *(37)31-15-15*, FAX: *(37)31-57-91.*

Credit Cards: *V.*

The 53 rooms at this delightful chateau are elegantly done in period style with modern amenities including TV, telephone and private bath. In addition to the helipad, facilities include an outdoor pool, two tennis courts and a beautifully kept garden. Dining options are plentiful with four restaurants from which to choose.

Inns

Hostellerie du Royal-Lieu   ★★★
http://www.hostellerie-du-royal- lieu.com/accueil.htm

Budget

9 rue de Senlis.

☎ *(44)20-10-24*, FAX: *(44)86-82-27.*

Credit Cards: *V, MC, DC, A.*

Offering views over the sylvan park on the outskirts of town, this small hotel is the result of the time and effort spent by the friendly husband-wife owners. The 20 guest rooms and three suites, most with views over the lush garden, are lovingly decorated and looked after. Each room, whether decorated in such unique style or in period style, comes with TV, telephone and private bath.

Fontainebleau
Hotels and Resorts

Grand Hotel de l'Aigle Noir
Moderate to Expensive

27 place Napoleon Bonaparte.

☎ *(1)64-22-32-65*, FAX: *(1)64-22-17-33.*

Credit Cards: *All Major.*

Albeit the most expensive hotel in town, its luxury is worth every franc. With a distinguished attitude and glamourous appearance, this former private mansion was converted into a hotel in the early 1700s. The 57 guests rooms are delicately furnished with 18th-century reproduction furniture and blessed with climate control, cable TV, telephone, radio, minibar and private bath with hair dryer and robe. The most lavish rooms come with a balcony or Jacuzzi. Be sure to sample the fixed-price menu in the hotel's restaurant, **Le Beauharnais**, and relax in the piano bar for a casual drink. A well-rounded hotel with fabulous service, well maintained facilities and luxury in every detail.

Hotel de Londres
Moderate

1 place du General-de-Gaulle.

☎ *(1)64-22-20-21*, FAX: *(1)60-72-39-16.*

Credit Cards: *V, MC, DC, A.*

Occupying a choice location next to the Palace of Fontainebleau, this hotel exudes the warm welcome of a home. There are 22 balconied rooms decorated in Louis XV style and modestly equipped with TV, telephone and bath. Across from the Cour des Adieux, where Napoleon gave his farewell speech to his troops, this peaceful hotel creates an inviting ambience.

Napoleon
http://www.hotelnapoleon-fontainebleau.com/
Moderate to Expensive

9 rue Grande.

☎ *(1)64-22-2—39*, FAX: *(1)64-22-20-87.*

Credit Cards: *V, MC, DC, A*.

A long ways from its days as a coaching inn in the 1800s, the Napoleon remains one of the most charming hotels in Fontainebleau. The 57 guest rooms are attractively decorated in pastel colors and equipped with TV, minibar, telephone and private bath or shower; request a room facing the courtyard, as they are quieter and more spacious. The restaurant, **La Table des Marechaux**, is known for some of the best dishes in town with great fixed-price meals.

Giverny

Normandy
http://giverny.org/hotels/normandy/

Budget

1 avenue Mendes-France.

☎ *(32)51-97-97*, FAX: *(32)21-01-66*.

Credit Cards: *V, MC, A*.

With so few choices for decent lodging near Giverny, this hotel's opening in 1990 was a welcomed event. Situated in the center of Vernon, this simple hotel has 45 guest rooms, all comfortable and well equipped. Request a room facing the back, as those are the quietest. The fine staff has already earned a reputation as being courteous, and the restaurant has become known for its hearty breakfasts. A well-rounded lodging choice making visits to Giverny much more relaxing.

Inns

Hostellerie St-Pierre   ★★
Budget to Moderate

Chemin des Amoureux.

☎ *(32)59-93-29*, FAX: *(32)59-41-93*.

Credit Cards: *V*.

On the banks of the Seine sits this small hotel in all of its design wonder. Triangular in layout, this half-timbered modern building in white resembles a classic Norman house, with a turret on one end. The 14 comfortable rooms are modestly decorated and equipped with central heating, TV, minibar, private bath and most with a balcony overlooking the river. While enjoying lovely views of the river, sit down to a delicious seafood dinner chosen from the fantastic specialty menu.

Versailles
Hotels and Resorts

Bellevue Hotel
Moderate

12 avenue de Sceaux.

☎ *(1)39-50-13-41,* FAX: *(1)39-02-05-67.*

Credit Cards: *V, MC, DC, A.*

A quaint little hotel with a convenient address on a lovely street for walking to the chateau. Constructed in 1850 and recently improved, the decor of the public rooms is modern and functional. Louis XV designs are prevalent in the 24 guest rooms, each equipped with TV, telephone, minibar and bath or shower.

Trianon Palace ★★★★
Expensive

1 boulevard de la Reine.

☎ *772-3041,* ☎ *(1)30-84-38-00,* FAX: *(1)39-49- 00-77.*

Credit Cards: *All Major.*

The Trianon Palace is worth the indulgence even for travelers who plan on spending most of their time in Paris. This distinguished hotel first opened in 1910 and served as the headquarters for the Versailles Peace Conference in 1919. Now operated by the Westin chain, the hotel is set in its own beautiful seven-acre park on the border of the chateau park, this palace defines luxury. There are 94 distinctive rooms, divided between the palace and the new building. No matter how one spends the day, be sure to wind up at least one evening dining in the gourmet restaurant, **Les Trois Marches**, and relaxing in the cozy piano bar. An unforgettable experience in pampering and luxury found in few hotels.

Where to Eat

A. Beauvilliers ★★★★
Moderate to Expensive

52 rue Lamarck. ☎ *(42)54-54-42.*

Metro Stop: *Lamarck-Caulaincourt.*

Credit Cards: *V, MC, A, E.* Closed: *Sun.*

An enchanting, terraced Montmarte restaurant with a flower and bibelot-filled dining room. There's a mood of luxury, but the cuisine is not complicated, with such offerings as grilled turbot, leg of lamb with herbs and cassoulets.

Au Grain de Folie ★
Inexpensive to Moderate

24 rue de Lavieuville. ☎ *(42)58-15-57.*

Metro Stop: *Abbesses.*

One of Paris' handful of strictly vegetarian restaurants (albeit clouded with cigarette smoke), located in Montmarte. The mixed-veggie platter is served in good-sized portions; try the organic wine. Outdoor tables.

Au Pied de Cochon ★★
Moderate to Expensive

6 rue Coquilliere. ☎ *(42)36-11-75.*

Metro Stop: *Chatelet les Halles.*

Credit Cards: *All Major.*

A must for the first-timer. Beautiful turn-of-the-century decor, huge portions of (you guessed it) pig's feet and piles of shellfish served by bustling waiters to crowds of diners.

Au Trou Gascon
Moderate to Expensive

40 rue Taine. ☎ *(43)44-34-26.*

Metro Stop: *Daumesnil.*

Credit Cards: *All Major.* Closed: *Sat., Sun.*

This bistro, helmed by the talented Andre Dutournier, may be somewhat past its prime. But Dutournier can still perform the same tricks with several other dishes, including a belt-busting cassoulets, and robust Chalosse ham. Splendid!

Baracane
Moderate

38 rue des Tournelles. ☎ *(42)71-43-33.*

Credit Cards: *V, MC, E.* Closed: *Sun.*

One must get here early to get a good seat, as it's small and popular, especially at lunch, with its fixed-price menu. The cuisine is from southernwestern France, which means a hearty, delicious, and fattening cassoulets, made here with confit of duck. Whatever the restaurant lacks in space, the chefs more than make up for it with the sizable portions on your plate.

Chez Elle
Moderate

7 rue des Prouvaires. ☎ *(45)08-04-10.*

Metro Stop: *Chatelet–Les Halles.*

Credit Cards: *V, MC, A.* Closed: *Sun.*

This unpretentious bistro, decorated with risque photographs, doesn't take many chances with the menu, and that makes regulars happy. A salad of warm lentils with bacon starts off many a meal. The desserts are the deceptively light kind, including creme brulee and creme caramel.

Guy Savoy
Expensive

18 rue Troyon. ☎ *(43)80-40-61.*

Metro Stop: *Etoile.*

Credit Cards: *V, A, E, A.* Closed: *Sun.*

What remains more or less constant (besides the high quality of the cuisine, the presentation and the service) is the wild game offered in season, usually winter. Reserve weeks in advance.

Jacques Cagna   ★★★
Moderate to Expensive

14 rue des Grands-Augustins. ☎ *(43)26-49-39.*

Metro Stop: *St.-Michel/Odeon.*

Credit Cards: *All Major.* Closed: *Sun.*

A longtime favorite with well-heeled locals and in-the-know expatriates, Jacques Cagna occupies one of the oldest buildings in Paris. The turbot farci and the John Dory with artichokes were splendid examples of melding delicious light flavors with color choices. Less costly than the big-name houses, and very pleasing gastronomically. Small, attentive staff.

Joel Robuchon
Expensive to Very Expensive

59 avenue Raymond-Poincaire. ☎ *(47)27-12- 27.*

Credit Cards: *V, MC, E.* Closed: *Sat., Sun.*

You'll probably have to call the restaurant months before your arrival to eat here; there's a mile-long waiting list, as the amiable chef-proprietor Joel Robuchon occupies the highest place in the French culinary firmament. Only a limited number is let in daily through the portals of the two-story, turn-of-the century house where he holds court. Interestingly, instead of a bar, there's a basement "smoking salon," where patrons can sit around puffing cigars and sipping cocktails, later returning for after-dinner drinks. His cuisine involves ingredients you've encountered before, but in his hands, white beans are spun into creamed nectar, potatoes scale new heights, lamb sings and langoustines trill.

L'Etoile Verte
Moderate

13 rue Brey. ☎ *(43)80-69-34.*

Metro Stop: *Charles-de-Gaulle/Etoile.*

Credit Cards: *All Major.*

A simple eatery near a stellar neighborhood, the "Green Star" is always open, while others take their endless summer break. The rather plain dining room is often ablaze with creative flower arrangements. A vast a la carte menu with many choices is offered. Also daily specials and a three-course set meal, with beverage, dessert or cheese. Expect a long wait to get in.

L'Incroyable ★

Inexpensive to Moderate

26 rue de Richelieu and 23 rue de Montpensier. ☎ *(46)96-24-64.*

Metro Stop: *Palais-Royal.*

Closed: *Sun.*

It's incredible, but this restaurant near the arcade in the Palais Royale (it has two addresses) once charged the French equivalent of 65 cents for a three-course meal! That was back in the 1950s; today you can still get the same deal for $25. The presentation is attractive, and the quality is surprisingly high for the price.

La Cagouille ★★★★

Moderate to Expensive

12 place Constantin-Brancusi.

Metro Stop: *Gaite.*

Credit Cards: *All Major.*

Located in the Place Brancusi, an offbeat neighborhood not known for quality restaurants, La Cagouille serves the freshest, and possibly the best, seafood in Paris, direct from ports all over France. Selections change daily, depending on what turns up, with a minimum of fuss; pure flavors are allowed to shine through.

La Tour d'Argent ★★★★

Expensive to Staggeringly Expensive

15 quai Tournelle. ☎ *(43)54-23-31.*

Metro Stop: *Sully-Morland*.

Credit Cards: *All Major*. Closed: *Mon*.

La Tour d'Argent remains a landmark, attracting North Americans
and other outlanders, who comprise so much of its clientele. The
spectacular penthouse views of the Seine and Notre Dame (illuminated at night) are the chief reasons for going; the food, in my opinion, is secondary (though the duck specialties are first rate!). Opposite the entrance is Comptoirs de la Tour, a smart boutique where
you can purchase the restaurant's wares for sky-high prices. La Tour
d'Argent is a Parisian fixture, and a costly one, especially after dark.
You'll need a "tower of money" to dine here.

Le Bar a Huitres
Inexpensive to Moderate

112 boulevard du Montparnasse. ☎ *(43)20-71- 01.*

Metro Stop: *Vavin*.

Credit Cards: *All Major*.

You can sit here until 2 a.m. and eat your fill of oysters and shellfish,
or from a seafood platter for two, which you can design to your taste
from the varied menu. There are fresh fish dishes as well, including
grilled sole meuniere, but most patrons prefer the other.

Le Monde des Chimeres ★★
Inexpensive to Moderate

69 rue St-Louis-en-l'Ile. ☎ *(43)54-45-77.*

Credit Cards: *V, MC*. Closed: *Mon., Sun.*

Expertly cooked, very authentic French family-style food is served
here, in a house that's more than 200 years old. The highest-quali-
ty ingredients are used, and the menu runs the gamut from potted
game meats to homemade desserts.

Le Petit Plat
Moderate

3 rue des Grand-Degres. ☎ *(40)46-85-34.*

Credit Cards: *V*. Closed: *Mon., Sun.*

This bistro is highly touted, and with good reason—the food is wonderful. Excellent pastas and terrines, stews, and roast chicken. You'll probably eat elbow-to- elbow with a stylish clientele.

Michel Rostang   ★★★★★
Expensive

20 rue Rennequin. ☎ *(47)63-82-75.*

Metro Stop: *Ternes.*

Credit Cards: *All Major.* Closed: *Sun.*

Possibly the brightest light in Michel Rostang's mini-culinary empire, this is also one of the more intimate havens in the city. The dining salon has a view of the chef and his busy kitchen, which is diverting and a little gimmicky. Lace curtains adorn the arched windows of the dining room, and textiled walls lend further softness; quiet music ripples the air. The Bresse chicken is his signature dish. Reserve a week in advance.

Miravile   ★★★
Inexpensive to Moderate

72 quai de l'Hotel -de-Ville. ☎ *(42)74-72-22.*

Closed: *Sun.*

You'll pay only one price to eat here, which will get you a delectable southwestern-style feast (not including wines, which can jack up your meal considerably). The dishes made with lobster, sardines and scallops are highly recommended. Elegant Italianate decor, outside terrace.

Perraudin   ★★
Inexpensive

157 rue St-Jacques. ☎ *(46)33-15-75.*

Metro Stop: *St-Michel.*

Generations of starving students and their underpaid professors have made this country-style bistro their hangout for the fixed- price lunch. A must for those on a budget.

Polidor
Inexpensive to Moderate

41 rue Monsieur-le-Prince. ☎ *(43)26-95-34.*

Metro Stop: *Odeon.*

One of Paris' national monuments, Polidor has been serving bistro food since 1845. Some of the more famous patrons have included Ernest Hemingway, James Joyce and Jack Kerouac. Inexpensive fixed-price lunches.

Rendez-vous des Chauffeurs ★
Inexpensive

11 rue des Portes Blanches. ☎ *(42)64-04-17.*

Metro Stop: *Marcadet-Poissoniers.*

Closed: *Wed., Thur.*

You'll find few tourists here, only neighborhood regulars enjoying the home-cooking of mom-and-pop owners Roger and Etiennette Lafarge. The produce is fresh off their own farm. Homemade desserts.

Taillevent ★★★★★
Very Expensive

15 rue Lamennais. ☎ *(45)63-39-94.*

Metro Stop: *George V.*

Credit Cards: *V, MC, E.* Closed: *Sat., Sun.*

This Champs-Elysees area restaurant has been in the family of owner Jean-Claude Vrinat since its founding by his father in 1946, and, from that time, has enjoyed a long bask in culinary glory. The wine list itself dazzles with more than 500 choices. All details of creation and presentation are the province of chef Philippe Legendre, former apprentice to Joel Robuchon. His excellent kitchen produces such delights as Breton lobster sausage and a rabbit-and- spinach pie spiced with wild thyme. Guests enjoy all this largesse while seated on comfortable banquettes; reception is friendly, service smooth as silk.

What to Do
Historical Sites

Arc de Triomphe ★★★★
http://www.paris.org/Monuments/ Arc/

place Charles de Gaulle.

Public Transportation: *1,2,6, A.* Metro Stop: *Charles de Gaulle Etoile.*

🕐 *10 a.m.*

Situated in the middle of place Charles de Gaulle (formerly L'Etoile), Napoleon's monument to his long-suffering troops is the beefiest triumphal arch in existence, standing 164 feet above the tomb of the Unknown Soldier (a relighting ceremony takes place each evening at 6:30 p.m.). Time is taking its toll, however, so don't be surprised to see scaffolding at its skirts. Admission: varies.

Cathedrale St.-Denis ★★
place de l'Hotel-de-Ville.

Public Transportation: *13.* Metro Stop: *St.-Denis-Basilique.*

🕐 *10 a.m.–7 p.m.*

Special Hours: *Winter until 5 p.m.*

The Cathedral, burial place of French royalty (from Clovis to Marie Antoinette), was begun in 1137. During the French Revolution, the regal quietude was disturbed by angry mobs, who went on a rampage, exhuming and reburying bodies indiscriminately outside. Fortunately, most of the sculpted tomb art was left undamaged, and these alone are worth a visit. Admission: varies, inexpensive.

Notre Dame Cathedral ★★★★★
http://www.paris.org/Monuments/NDame/*6 place du Parvis-Notre Dame.*

Metro Stop: *Cite.*

🕐 *8 a.m.–7 p.m.*

It's been a top draw for travelers since 1163. You can mount the towers (387 steps, to see the bells and step outside on the roof platform for a peep at the cathedral roof with its gargoyles, the Ile St. Louis below, the Seine and its bridges. Daily organ concerts at 5:45

p.m., free tours on Wednesdays (in English). Admission: for towers, inexpensive.

Palais de Justice
4 boulevard du Palais, Ile de la Cite.

Metro Stop: *Cite.*

🕐 *10 a.m.–5 p.m.*

Hundreds of heads rolled during the Reign of Terror, (beginning in 1793) and many those fateful decisions were handed down from this imposing building, now home to the law courts of Paris. At present, a more benevolent form of justice is meted out, and the public is invited to attend court room sessions. Admission: free.

Pantheon
Place du Pantheon.

Public Transportation: *B.* Metro Stop: *Luxembourg.*

🕐 *10 a.m.–5:45 p.m.*

At the summit of Mount St. Genevieve, the crypt of this national shrine contains the tombs of Victor Hugo, Voltaire, Rousseau, Emile Zola and heroes of liberty. Originally a church built by Louis XV in honor of the patron saint of Paris, it is modeled after the Pantheon in Rome.Admission: inexpensive.

Place de la Bastille
http://www.paris.org/Monuments/ Bastille/

Public Transportation: *1,5,8.* Metro Stop: *Bastille.*

Now a major traffic intersection, this is where the infamous Bastille Prison stood. If you feel like risking your own life to taxis, cars and buses whizzing by, you can pace off the outline of the edifice by following the white periphery painted on the street surface. The July Column (Colonne de Juillet) at its center, honors Parisians killed during the July 14, 1830 uprising, as well as the destruction of the prison Admission: inexpensive.

Sacre-Coeur
35 rue de Chavalier.

Metro Stop: *Abbesses.*

🕐 *6:45 a.m.–11 p.m.*

This oft-painted, tall, white Romanesque- Byzantine church is visible from most of Paris. The view from the dome (Admission, 15F, open 9 a.m.–7 p.m., winter until 6 p.m.) is the stuff of eagles. You can also visit the crypt, where Alexandre Legentil, one of the basilica's builders, literally left his heart. There's plenty of street entertainment and corny souvenirs to buy on the steps of the church. Admission: inexpensive, varies.

The Sorbonne

http://www.sorbonne.fr/

47 rue des Ecoles.

Public Transportation: *10.* Metro Stop: *Cluny- La Sorbonne.*

🕐 *9 a.m.–6 p.m.*

Founded in 1253 to teach theology to a small number of impoverished students, today the Sorbonne is France's leading university, also known as the University of Paris. Cardinal Richelieu ordered the construction of the Church of the Sorbonne in the 17th century; it's the only original building left standing. The crafty clergyman's (who essentially ran the country for Louis XII) tomb is in the church's south transept. Classes are not open to the public. Church open for special events only; call for information.

Tour Eiffel

quai du Branly and ave. Gustave Eiffel.

Public Transportation: *6.* Metro Stop: *Bir- Hakeim.*

🕐 *9 a.m.–12 p.m.*

Special Hours: *Winter hours 9:30 a.m.-11 p.m.*

Reviled during its construction (completed in 1889 for the Universal Exposition) like the Beaubourg and the Louvre Pyramid after it, the Eiffel Tower remains Paris' numero uno tourist destination. There are three platforms from which to see the city. From the third level, which you can reach only by double-decker elevator, (there's often a wait) you can—rarely—see up to 40 miles in every direction. You can also take a stairway still higher, where there's an excellent (and expensive) restaurant, the Jules Verne. After dark-illu-

mination makes it more beautiful than ever. If you don't want to
shell out for the stiff admission fee to the top, you can use the stairs
to the first and second platform. Admission: varies, expensive.

Kid's Stuff

Jardin d'Acclimation
Boulevard des Sablons.

Public Transportation: *1.* Metro Stop: *Les Sablons.*

🕐 *10 a.m.–6 p.m.*

Special Hours: *Saturday, 2–6 p.m.*

Tucked away in a far corner of the Bois de Boulogne is this modest-
size park within a park, with kiddie rides, marionette shows,
(Thursdays, Sat-Sun, holidays) a riding school and a minicar racing
track. Admission: inexpensive.

Parc Zoologique de Paris ★★
Bois de Vincennes. ☎ *43.43.84.95.*

Metro Stop: *Porte Doree.*

🕐 *9 a.m.–5:30 p.m.*

Special Hours: *Sunday to 6 p.m.*

France's largest zoo, located in the 2500 acre Bois de Vincennes, is
also a kind and gentle place, with mostly uncaged animals roaming
as freely as possible, in natural settings. Nearby, on the western edge
of the Bois, *(293 avenue Daumesnil,* 43.43.14.54) is the **Musee des
Arts d'Afrique et d'Oceanie**, with a crocodile room and an interesting, well-stocked aquarium; open 10 a.m.–5:30 p.m., Saturday-
Sunday 12:30–6 p.m., closed Tuesday-Thursday. Includes admission
to the museum; included in the Carte Musees et Monuments.
Admission: varies.

Museums and Exhibits

Georges Pompidou Center
http://www.cnac-gp.fr/english

rue du Renard.

Public Transportation: *11.* Metro Stop: *Rambuteau.*

🕐 *12 p.m.–10 p.m.*

Special Hours: *Saturday-Sunday; 10 a.m.–10 p.m.*

Completed in 1977, this is possibly the most hideous structure ever to be dedicated to the preservation and exhibition of beauty. Unhappily, it will probably stand as an everlasting hymn to modern "intestinology"—architecture so repugnant that it defames France's historic role as an arbiter of taste and erudition. The building notwithstanding, its collections, presentations and quirky tricks of holding up a mirror to life bring a fresh, bright, and idiosyncratic touch to art appreciation. The open space out in front of the Pompidou Center is the site of impromptu performances—music, mime, magic—and there are some pleasant cafes in its multiform shadow. Inside are galleries for temporary art exhibitions, a large performance space, and on the third through fifth floors, the **Musee National d'Art Moderne** (Museum of Modern Art), which includes ragtag environmental pieces among its contemporary paintings, (Braque's "Man with a Guitar") mobiles, (Calder's "Mobile on Two Planes") and sculpture. You may wish to visit **Brancusi's Atelier**, an atmospheric reproduction of the sculptor's studio. Museum hours are the same as the Center. Free admission on Sundays, from 10 a.m.–2 p.m.

Hotel Les Invalides　　　★★★★★
place des Invalides.

Metro Stop: *Invalides.*

🕐 *10 a.m.–5 p.m.*

A vast complex, encompassing four museums and two churches, it has functioned as lodgings and a hospital for wounded military veterans since 1670; hence its name. Near the south entrance is the verdant Jardin de l'Intendant, affording views of the Eiffel Tower. Under the gold-leafed Dome Church, designed by Mansart, lie the entombed remains of Napoleon, in not one, but six coffins. Some of his immediate family members, including his son and brothers Jerome and Joseph, keep him company in death. (Open 10 a.m.–6 p.m., April-September, until 5 p.m.; October- March). Nearby the **Musee de l'Armee**, begun in the 1700s, is perhaps the most impressive and comprehensive of its kind in the world. Naturally, a large portion of one of its two galleries are devoted to the exploits of little general from Corsica. You'll see his death mask and stuffed horse here, as well as uniforms, medals and weapons. The rest of the museum is devoted to war toys from the Stone Age through World War

II (same hours as Napoleon's Tomb). For a small sum, you gain admittance to both museums, plus St. Louis Church and the Musee des Plans et Reliefs; tickets are good for two days.

Musee National du Moyen
Age-Thermes de Cluny
http://www.musee-moyenage.fr/ RMN/mnma/message.html

6 place Paul-Painleve.

Public Transportation: *10.* Metro Stop: *Cluny/ La Sorbonne.*

🕐 *9:15 a.m.–5:45 p.m.*

In this historic tandem you'll discover the 15th century Thermes de Cluny, built upon 3rd-century Gallo-Roman baths, coupled with a comprehensive collection of medieval art and artifacts. Most notable among its displays are some exquisite tapestries, including the 15th and 16th century series known as The Lady with the Unicorn. Admission: varies.

ITRAVELBOOK TIP: IF YOU ARE A STUDENT, A SENIOR, OR TRAVELING WITH A SMALL CHILD, CHANCES ARE YOU'LL BE ALLOWED ADMISSION TO ANY OF PARIS' MUSEUMS ON A REDUCED RATE. LIKEWISE, MANY MUSEUMS OFFER REDUCED RATES FOR THOSE WHO VISIT ON SUNDAY.

Musee Picasso
http://www.paris.org/Musees/Picasso/

Hotel de Sale, 5 rue de Thorigny.

Public Transportation: *8.* Metro Stop: *St. Sebastien-Froissart.*

🕐 *9:30 a.m.–5:30 p.m.*

Located in the Hotel Sale (former home of Aubert de Fontenay, a salt tax collector), this handsome palace of the late 17th century contains several thousand works of art—not all of them by the Spanish artist, but many splendid pieces collected by or given to Picasso by other masters of his time. Admission: inexpensive.

Musee d'Orsay
http://www.musee-orsay.fr:8081/ORSAY/accueilMO/
HTML.NSF/732927420973f9b5c12564280045edf6/
322da73321db3942c1256714004e756 a?OpenDocument

1 rue de Bellechasse.

Metro Stop: *Solferino.*

🕐 *9 a.m.–6 p.m.*

Special Hours: *Thursday to 9:45 p.m.*

The Musee houses a grand collection of art from the frenzied period (1850 to 1910); a teeming cauldron of some 1500 pieces of sculpture, 2300 paintings, 13,000 photographs, art objects, and furnishings in the thousands. Orsay not only received the Jeu de Paume's Impressionist treasures, (one of its main draws) it also became heir to heretofore unseen assemblages from the Louvre's vaults, and other state sources. Admission: varies.

Musee de l'Orangerie ★★★★
Jardin des Tuileries, pl. de la Concorde.

Metro Stop: *Concorde.*

🕐 *9:45 a.m.–5:15 p.m.*

Located in the southwest corner of the Jardin des Tuileries, this museum houses a section one of the most famous series of paintings in the world, Monet's Nympheas, or Waterlilies, which the artist completed towards the end of his life, while in his garden at Giverny. The canvases fill two lower-level rooms in the museum. There's more to see, however: early works by Picasso, some 24 paintings by Renoir (Young Girls at the Piano), Rousseau, Cezanne and others, round out the fabulous Walter-Guillaume Collection. Admission: varies.

Musee du Louvre ★★★★★

http://www.louvre.fr/louvrea.htm

rue de Rivoli.

Metro Stop: *Palais Royale-Musee de Louvre.*

🕐 *9 a.m.–6 p.m.*

Special Hours: *Monday-Wednesday, to 10 p.m.*

The main entrance to the Louvre is via the controversial seven-story inverted metal and glass pyramid designed by I.M. Pei. Whatever your opinion of it may be, there are some definite improvements, including more gallery space, and increased light around the underground reception area. To avoid the inevitable queues, just take a look at the pyramid, don't enter the museum through it—there's a more accessible entrance via the Porte Jaujard (at the far end, near the Tuileries and Seine River). The massif began as the residence of Francois I and as buildings were added and remodeled, it remained a royal residence until the Court relocated at Versailles in 1682. There are six galleries, with more than 300,000 priceless paintings, sculpture and objets d'art. After you've seen Michelangelo's Mona Lisa, the Winged Victory at Samothrace, and the Venus de Milo, head over to the Cour Carree site, a dungeon conceived by Phillippe Auguste in the 12th century, which is a change of pace from gallery hopping. Admission: varies.

Rodin Museum ★★★★
77 rue de Varenne.

Public Transportation: *13.* Metro Stop: *Varenne.*

🕐 *10 a.m.–5:45 p.m.*

Special Hours: *Winter until 5 p.m.*

One of the loveliest small museums in Paris. Situated in the great sculptor's former home, (pretty luxurious digs, they were, too) the 18th-century Hotel Biron, his major works are on display inside or arranged outdoors in a parklike setting. Admission: varies.

Music

ITRAVELBOOK FREEBIE

Free Concerts ★★★
Various locations.

Paris is a spontaneous city—on every street corner individual or group musicians of varying degrees of expertise clamor for your attention. But many prominent theaters, parks, churches, museums and galleries hold regular musical events scheduled throughout the year. Classical concerts and recitals are held weekly at the St-Roch Church, the burial place of Corneille, in the 1st Arr. (rue St-Honore at rue St-Roch; Metro–Tuileries) The church of St-Nicholas-des-Champs (3rd Arr., 252 rue St-Martin, Metro–Arts et Metiers), justifiably proud of its 17th-century organ, shows it off with concerts from time. Aside from daily organ recitals at 5:45 p.m., there are Sunday concerts at Notre Dame Cathedral (see Historical Sites). In the 7th Arr., the Parc du Champ de Mars, a lo-o-ng stretch of green (see Historical Sites). In the 7th Arr., the Parc du Champ de Mars, a lo-o-ng stretch of green (extending from the Ecole Militaire to the Eiffel Tower) was once trampled by the marching feet of every armed force from the Romans to students at the military school; now resounds with the pleasing beat of music from numerous concerts given here in the summer. Popular for its arboretum, the Parc Montsouris, in the 14th Arr. (off ave. Reille, Metro: Cite Universitaire), has a bandstand where summer concerts are given; there's also a man-made lake, surrounded by sculpture.

Parks and Gardens

Jardin des Tuileries ★★★★
place de la Concorde.

Public Transportation: *1, 8 or 12.* Metro Stop: *Concorde or Tuileries.*
🕐 *7 a.m.–10 p.m.*

Special Hours: *October 1–March 31, to 8 p.m.*

A sizable part of the Tuileries was laid out in 1664 by Le Notre, and what was once the private enclave for the royal family is now a popular people's park. Spring is best, of course, and there are lovely views from the south end. Two museums in the park include the not-to-be missed **Musee de l'Orangerie** (see Museums) and the no less important **Jeu de Paume**, (designed by Antoine Stinco) which ceded its Impressionists to the Musee d'Orsay; (see Museums) it has for several years become a salon for top contemporary artists. Admission: free.

Jardin du Luxembourg ★★★
rue de Vaugirard.

Public Transportation: *B.* Metro Stop: *Luxembourg.*

This 60-acre park is really the backyard of the Palais du Luxembourg, built in the 17th century for Marie de Medici, (also headquarters for the Luftwaffe during the Occupation) now the French Senate. Romantic for strolling. (But heavens, not on the grass, please!) Kids love riding ponies and sailing toy boats. Free band concerts on Sunday.

Shopping
Hours
Most of the deluxe establishments stay open Saturdays but are

closed Sundays and perhaps Monday mornings. Hairdressers, however, operate on Monday. Food stores are open all day Saturday; some of them do business on Sunday mornings, too, but many are closed on Monday. Department stores are busy every day, except Sunday, with hours from 10 a.m. to 7 p.m. Boutiques and specialty shops generally open at 10 to 10:30 a.m. and lock up around 6:30 to 7 p.m. Many no longer shutter during the lunch hours, particularly those in areas heavily traveled by tourists (Champs-Elysées, Faubourg Saint-Honore, St-Germain-des-Pres, place des Victoires).

Savings on Purchases

It's important to know that you're entitled to a 13 to 22 percent TVA *(Taxe de Valeur Ajoutee)* refund for items you buy over a certain minimum price. Always ask the salesperson to guide you because this costs the store absolutely nothing, except, perhaps, a little lost time. Request a *Fiche de Douane* and be sure to carry your passport as proof of nonresidence. The form must be shown to the French Customs officials and validated at your point of departure, so keep it handy. This may come back to you through the mails to your home or via a refund to your credit-card account. Be sure to pack the items for which you are claiming a refund near the top of your luggage or in some convenient place where Customs may verify them should they wish.

Bazar de l'Hotel de Ville ★★
52 rue de Rivoli. ☎ *42.74.90.*

Public Transportation: *1, 11.* Metro Stop: *Hotel de Ville.*

🕔 *9:30 a.m.–7 p.m.*

Special Hours: *Wednesday until 10 p.m.*

The basement of this department store is hardware heaven; whatever's broke, this store will help you fix it. Everything from hammer and nails to electrical converters is available here, and there's a knowledgable army of sales staff to answer any queries you might have.

Bouquinistes ★★★
Quai de Montebello.

Metro Stop: *Saint-Michel.*

🕐 *11 a.m.–7:30 p.m.*

It's worthwhile to make a trip out to these bookstalls near Notre-Dame at least once, even if you're not planning to buy; shopping here is like rummaging through Uncle Waldo's attic. Naturally, there's a lot of junk, but who knows? You might get lucky and find a first edition on your first run-through.

Discount Shopping Centers ★★★
Various locations.

Outlets for new or gently-used (worn but once) designer clothing, proliferate in Paris. You'll also find bargain boites teeming with fellow shoppers (with elbows like scimitars) muscling you, ever so gently, out of their way. Almost a mile of clothing, brand new, is sold for a song at the **Marche du Temple**, across from the medieval Square du Temple (2nd Arr., Carreau du Temple, off rue Dupetit Thouars), open 9 a.m.–12 p.m., except Sunday. Only top of the line designer clothing, shoes and accessories for men and women are sold on consignment at **Catherine Baril** (*16th Arr., 14 & 25 rue de la Tour;* ☎ 45-27-11-46, open 10 a.m.–7 p.m., Monday 2–7 p.m., closed Sunday). If you can squeeze into an Alaia, you can do so at considerable discount from **Reciproque**, a nest of consignment stores, at ☎ *89, 92, 95, 97, 101 and 123 rue de la Pompe*, in the 16th Arr., open 10:30 a.m.–7 p.m., except Sunday and Monday, ☎ 47.04.30.28. **Fabienne** a consignment store for men only, also in the 16th Arr., *(77 bis, rue Boileau,* ☎ 45.25.64.26, open 10 a.m.–1:30 p.m., and 3–7 p.m., closed Sunday, Monday and August) features handmade shoes, clothing and accessories. At the four branches of **Tati**, (one in the 11th Arr., at *13 place de la Republique*, open 10 a.m.–7 p.m., Saturday to 7:30 p.m., closed Sunday and Monday) you might get into a fistfight, but it's certainly worth a visit for undeniable bargains, in everything from fabrics to clothing; to say that it's always crowded is an understatement.

Food Markets ★★★
Various locations.

For either sightseeing or survival, Paris' specialty food markets are must-sees. All are closed Monday, unless specified. Some of the best ones are the rue de Mouffetard (5th e, Metro Cardinal Lemoine), one of the city's oldest, bursting with local color and produce; rue de Buci (6th e, Metro Mabillon, open 8 a.m.–7:30 p.m.), food as well as flowers in the nearby **Carrefour de Buci** (*rue de Buci at rue Mazarine*); **Marche St.-Germain**, (rue Mabillon at rue Clement, Metro Mabillon, open 8 a.m.– 7:30 p.m.); **Marche Chateau-d'Eau**, an ancient covered market, vegetarians stay clear of this one; (*10th e, Metro Chateau d'Eau*, open 8 a.m.–7:30 p.m.); **Marche St-Quentin**, historic, similar to old Le Halles market, lots of gourmet goodies (*10th e, 85 blvd. Magenta, Metro Gare de l'Est*, open 8 a.m.–1 p.m., 3:30–7:30 p.m.; Sunday to 1 p.m. only); **Marche de Passy**, fresh foodstuffs and more (*16th e, Metro Passy); rue Poncelet and Place des Ternes*, for meats and deli items (*17th e, off avenue des Ternes, Metro Ternes*, open 8 a.m.–7:30 p.m.).

Galignani ★★
224 rue de Rivoli. ☎ *42.60.76.07.*

Metro Stop: *Tuileries.*

🕐 *9:30 a.m.–7:30 p.m.*

At more than 300 years old, this is possibly the oldest English-language bookstore anywhere in Europe. There are best sellers here, but it is known for big, glossy art books and calendars.

Gault ★★★
206 rue de Rivoli. ☎ *42.60.51.17.*

Metro Stop: *Tuileries.*

🕐 *10 a.m.–7 p.m.*

A playland of marvelous ceramic houses, churches and buildings from France's varied regions. These make splendid home decorations and collector's items of surprisingly low cost. You can also have your name imprinted on the "building" of your choice. Made in St-Paul-de-Vence by two brothers, Jean Pierre and Dominique Gault. Each creation carries a certificate of authenticity. No credit cards.

Haute Couture ★★★★
rue du Faubourg Saint-Honore/Avenue Montaigne.

The hottest areas for fashion, whether for Chanel classics or the razzle dazzle of Christian Lacroix, are in the bejeweled, over-cultured 8th Arrondisement. Many famous boutiques are within whispering distances of each other around the avenue des Champs-Elysées, some on ave. Montaigne or the rue du Faubourg Saint-Honore. Most are open daily except Sunday; opening times vary from 8 a.m. to 10 a.m., and they close between 6 p.m. and 7 p.m. Buy a gently-used designer ensemble at one of the consignment stores (see Discount Shopping), put on a haughty face, and browse. Or you can wimp out and window shop. Here are some addresses: **Christian Lacroix**, *73 rue du Faubourg St- Honore*, ☎ (42.65.79.08) Metro: Champs-Clemenceau—average price for one of his creations is 50,000F; **Chanel**, *42 Avenue Montaigne*, ☎ (42.23.74.12) Metro: Franklin D. Roosevelt—sales staff is fairly approachable; **Yves Saint-Laurent**, *5 Avenue Marceau* ☎ (47.23.72.71), Metro: Alma-Marceau—the aging enfant-terrible of the 60s still has the stuff.

Hotel Druot ★★
9 rue Drouot. ☎ *42.46.17.11.*

Metro Stop: *Le Pelettier.*

🕐 *11 a.m.–6 p.m.*

Special Hours: *Closed between noon-2 p.m.*

If you have a family treasure to sell you can bring it to this auction house for appraisal at the times specified below; auctions are held several times daily. But most travelers will just want to watch the show, or look at the varied objects d'art that will be going on the auction block. An interesting and different way to pass the day, and work on your French. Closed August.

La Samaritaine ★★★
quai du Louvre and rue de la Monnaie. Public Transportation: *7.* Metro Stop: *Pont Neuf.*

🕐 *9:30 a.m.–7 p.m.*

Special Hours: *Tuesday-Friday until 8:30 p.m.*

Supposedly the Sears of France—except that it's housed in an incredible glass and steel Art Nouveau building. Actually four stores in one, "Samar" is a a one-stop amusement center. Starting at the top, you can have a picture-postcard view of Paris that won't cost you a cent. There's also an inexpensive cafe that's open six months a year in good weather (closed April-October). The cafe-terrace is located in Building 2, on the 10th floor. Test out the equipment in the sporting goods department; the staff won't mind. You can get some advice on your cranky rental bike (or have your own fixed if you brought it with you). Practice some reverse chic: typical tradesmen and workers' clothing can be purchased here; it's up to you to put it all together, or surprise an amateur chef with an authentic chef's toque. A great way to remember Paris.

Marche aux Puces dela Porte de Cligancourt ★★★
porte de Cligancourt and porte de St.-Ouen.

Public Transportation: *4.* Metro Stop: *Porte de Cligancourt.*

🕐 *8 a.m.–8 p.m.*

Stalls and displays with everything from secondhand Levis to antique coins—some values if you have the patience to hunt them down. Another flea market of note is in the **Porte de Montreuil**, relatively large, good for used clothing. Mondays are the best days for bargains (*19th e, Metro: Porte de Montreuil, southeast section of the district*, open Saturday-Monday 6:30 a.m.–7:30 p.m.); if you want really cheap prices, save your weekends for the flea market at the de **la Porte de Vanves** (*14th e, avenue Georges Lafenestre, Metro: Porte de Vanves*, open 7 a.m.–7:30 p.m.); although small, the **Place d'Aligre Market**, (*off rue du Faubourg St. Antoine, in the 12th e, Metro*: Ledruc Rollin, open 8 a.m.–1 p.m., Tuesday–Sunday) features books and bibelots at low, low, prices.

Poilane ★★★★★
8 rue du Cherche-Midi. ☎ *45.48.42.59.*

Metro Stop: *Sevres-Babylone.*

🕐 *7:15 a.m.–8:15 p.m.*

This shop sells the world-famous sourdough bread that even Uncle Ernie in Peoria has heard about; lines form outside the shop early in the morning for fresh loaves, cookies and pastries; for ice cream and sorbets, you shouldn't miss **Berthillon**, *31 rue Saint-Louis-en-l'Ile* ☎ (43.54.31.61), Metro: Pont-Marie, with unusual flavors that Baskin-Robbins never even heard of: marron glace, gianduja (hazelnut), kiwi, and kumquat. Open daily except Monday and Tuesday from 10 a.m.–8 p.m.; no cards. For equally unusual chocolates, try **Christian Constant**, *26 rue du Bac, 7th arr, Metro: Bac* ☎ (42.96.53.53), a wizard who is constantly (no pun intended) coming up with wild ideas: bonbons with the essence of flowers, including jasmine, and others made with tea. Many of them are low in sugar. Open daily from 8 a.m.–8 p.m.; On the same street, at No. 44, **Lenotre** ☎ (42.22.39.39), the Roi of patissiers, is also renowned for his chocolates, including palets d'or with buttercream filling; he has shops all over town. Open 9 a.m.–8 p.m., Monday-Saturday, Sunday to 1 p.m. For gourmet goodies, the 8th arr. is host to a trio of greats who have been around since the 1800s. **Fauchon** (since 1886), at *26 place de la Madeleine, Metro:* Madeleine ☎ (47.42.60.11) is the most commonly known; besides prepared foods to go, there's a huge variety of exotic jams (sweet potato, jasmine petal), pastries, charcuterie, and wines. Mail order to anywhere, and it also has a cafeteria. Open daily except Sunday, 10 a.m.–7 p.m., all major cards. **Hediard** (1854,), at *21 place de la Madeleine* ☎ (42.66.09.00), open daily except Sunday, 9 a.m.–6:30 p.m.; and Fouquet, the oldest, (since 1852) at *22 rue Francois-1er, Metro: George V* ☎ (47.23.30.36) open daily except Sunday from 9:30 a.m.–7 p.m.; both have impeccable reputations for unusual and high- quality condiments, chocolates, pastry and packaged items. Hediard has a restaurant on the premises.

W.H. Smith ★★
248 rue de Rivoli. ☎ *42.60.37.97.*

Metro Stop: *Tuileries.*

🕐 *9:30 a.m.–7 p.m.*

Special Hours: *Saturday to 7:30 p.m.*

All the guidebooks to Paris and France you couldn't find overseas are available at this famous bookshop. You can also pick up your magazines and thrillers here. Tickets to cultural events can be purchased, and there's a tearoom upstairs.

Special Tours

Bateaux Mouches ★★★
Pont de l'Alma.

Metro Stop: *Alma-Marceau.*

🕐 *10 a.m.–11 p.m.*

Multi-lingual boat cruises of the Seine, very touristy, but can be fun if you have a good sense of humor. Duration 90 minutes, boats leave every 30 minutes; winter departures 11 am, 12 p.m., 2:30 p.m., 4 p.m., 9 p.m. After 8 p.m., Lunch cruises Saturday and Sunday from April 15-November 15, departs 12:45 p.m. Admission: varies.

Bateaux Parisines Tour Eiffel
port de la Bourdonnais.

Metro Stop: *Trocadero.*

🕐 *10 a.m.–10:30 p.m.*

Glass-topped boats (somewhat more luxurious than the Bateau Mouches) leave every half-hour from the wharf near the Eiffel Tower. The usual tour lasts 90 minutes, but there's also a two-hour lunch cruise or three-hour dinner cruise; jacket and tie required. Admission: varies.

Batobus
Various locations.

🕐 *10 a.m.–7 p.m.*

Special Hours: *No winter service*

Admission: *FR 12.*

A floating taxi service on the Seine. Stops at the Eiffel Tower, Musee de'Orsay, Louvre, Hotel de Ville and Notre Dame. Individual tickets are steep, but a day pass for is a scenic (and less frenzied) alternative to the mouches. Admission: varies.

Theater

Lido Cabaret   ★★★
116 bis, ave. des Champs-Elysées. ☎ *40.76.56.10.*

Metro Stop: *George V.*

Special Hours: *Shows 10 p.m. and 12:15 a.m.*

The Lido stages what is probably the most elaborate spectacle in Europe today— imaginative, grand, dynamic. It stuns the customers with its ensemble of at least 50 dancers, showgirls, seminudes and international headliners. In the spacious 1200-seat venue located in the Normandie Cinema building, the theater-restaurant affords all customers an adequate view of the stage; the slope-away design terminates at a ringside tier that sinks to navel level. Admission:

varies, expensive.

Moulin Rouge
place Blanche. ☎ *46.06.19.*

Metro Stop: *Place Blanche.*

Up at Montmarte, the renowned Moulin Rouge, sketched by Toulouse-Lautrec and later infamous for its cancan, is a sister to the Lido in spirit. Huge, tiered, theater-like hall, the show has enough glitter, feathers and chiffon to bury the Gare du Nord. Shows at 10 p.m. and midnight. Admission: varies, expensive.

Ticket Agencies

FNAC
Forum des Halles, Level 3. ☎ *42.86.87.12.*

Metro Stop: *Chatelet/Les Halles.*

 10 a.m.–7:30 p.m.

Special Hours: *Monday, 1-7:30 p.m.*

If you plan to be in Paris for a reasonable length of time and intend to hit every play, concert and festival, the Carte Alpha or the Carte FNAC will lop off 40 percent of the price of your tickets. This money-saving package can be purchased from FNAC, a music-book-store entertainment center at the above location, with branches all over the city. For theatre goers only, the **Kiosque Theatre** (*8th Arr., 15 place de la Madeleine, Metro: Madeleine,* no phone, open 12:30 p.m.–8 p.m., Tues-Sat, Sunday to 6 p.m., closed Monday) will sell you tickets for half-price; good only for the day of the show.

Museum Pass/Carte Musees et Monuments
Various locations.

Here's a splendid way to see a lot for comparatively little. Sold in increments of one day, three days, and five days, the pass offers immediate entry to 65 museums and monuments (permanent collections only, not valid for special exhibitions), without waiting in long lines. You present your card, and voila, you're in. Here's a sampling of museums: The Louvre, Pompidou Centre, the Musee d'Orsay, Cluny, the Crypt of Notre Dame, and much more. YOU CAN OBTAIN THE PASS FROM THE PARTICIPATING MUSEUMS, ALL

METRO KIOSKS, AND THE TOURIST OFFICE HEADQUARTERS AT 127 AVENUE DES CHAMPS ELYSÉES. TRAVEL AGENCIES ALSO OFTEN SELLS THE PASS IN THE U.S.A. AND EUROPE.

Historical Sites
Yvelines

Chateau de Versailles   ★★★★★
http://www.chateauversailles.fr/*Versailles.*

🕘 *9 a.m.–6:30 p.m.*

Special Hours: *October-April to 5:30 p.m.*

In 1682, Louis XIV and his court left Paris for the Chateau de Versailles, (once his father's hunting lodge) urging his nobles (none too gently) to live with him, effectively curtailing any plans of revolt. Louis XVI and Marie Antoinette lived here in untold splendor until forced to vacate by revolutionaries in 1789. Royalty is long gone, but the magnificence of this national treasure has been preserved. The palace was started by Louis Le Vau, finished later by Jules Mansart. The gardens were laid out by Le Notre. You may look into the Grands Appartements (lavishly decorated by Charles Le Brun), and see your lovely self many times over in the Hall of Mirrors, scene of the Treaty of Versailles in 1919, which effectively ended World War I. 26F; Sunday admission 26F. Set away from the Chateau are the Grand Trianon, a tryst spot for Louis XIV and Madame de Maintenon, and the Petit Trianon, beloved by Marie Antoinette. She also tended a flock of pampered sheep in the hamlet directly behind it. Admission: varies.

Languedoc-Roussilon
Carcassone

With the snow-capped Pyrénées rising behind it, Carcassonne is the greatest fortress city on the Continent. The Ville- Basse is the modern district, and probably of little interest to tourists. However, the medieval Cité has been restored to look as it did in the 13th century—and is among the leading attractions in France. We recommend that you stay in the Old City; the **Hotel de la Cité** offers ample comfort and is built within the actual walls, adjoining the Cathedral.

Where to Stay

Domaine d'Auriac ★★
http://www.relaischateaux.com/site/us/FicheAdherent?RcCode=auriac/

Expensive

route St-Hilaire. Take D104 about 3 km southwest from Carcassonne to Auriac.

☎ *(68)25-72-22.*

Credit Cards: *All Major.*

Rated as a Relais and Chateaux, this is probably the best place for food and lodging in the region. Within there are 23 rooms, all uniquely decorated and with private bathrooms. In summer, meals are served beside the swimming pool on the terraces overlooking the beautifully landscaped gardens.

Hotel de la Cite ★★★
Moderate to Expensive

place de l'Eglise. From Porte Narbonnaise take rue Mayrevieill to rue Porte d'Aude to rue St-Louis.

☎ *(68)25-03-34.*

Credit Cards: *All Major.*

In a former episcopal palace, this luxurious hotel is the most desirable place to stay within the ramparts of the Old City. There are 23 rooms and three suites many of which are furnished with antiques or reproductions and have views of either the city or an interior garden. Even the simpler rooms are freshly painted and have tile baths. The hotel also features an attractive bar with a terrace and a baronial dining room.

Where to Eat

Brasserie Le Donjon ★★
Moderate

4 rue Porte d'Avde. ☎ *(68)25-95-72.*

Credit Cards: *All Major.*

Operated by the Hotel Donjon nearby is this bustling, comfortable brasserie serving cassoulet and a reasonable set-price meal. Also within La Cite is a bistro, **Les Coulisses du Theatre**, in the Dame Carcas hotel, *15 rue St.-Louis* ☎ (68-71-37-37), which offers a set-price lunch. Closed Sundays and from Sept. 15-Mar. 31. Market: fruits and vegetables at pl. Carnot, open Tues., Thurs., Sat. from 7 a.m.–1 p.m.

What to Do
City Celebrations

Festival de Carcassone
http://www.festivaldecarcassonne.com/

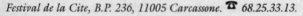

Festival de la Cite, B.P. 236, 11005 Carcassone. ☎ *68.25.33.13.*

Carcassone's fairy-tale medieval city is a lucrative income producer, and the town fathers have craftily planned several events to grease the wheels of commerce. The entire month of July is set aside for a performing arts fete held at the Chateau Comtal. For reservations and ticket information call, ☎ 68.77.71.26. The Bastille Day pyrotechnics show, which can be seen all over the city, probably beats any other July 14 festivity anywhere in France for spectacle. The two-week Medievales (mid-August) takes visitors back to the prettier aspects of the 12th century, with townspeople in authentic costumes hawking their wares. The tourist office, at *15 blvd. Camille Pelletan, place Gambetta,* ☎ (68.25.07.04) will supply details.

Historical Sites

La Cite ★★★★
La Cite. ☎ *68.25.27.65.*
🕐 *9 a.m.–6 p.m.*

La Cite, Carcassone's upper town, has been restored to appear as it looked in the 13th century. The old city is surrounded by a double set of walls (the inner walls are Gallo-Roman) and ramparts built by Louis IX and Philip the Bold (13th century). Guided tours are given daily, literally hitting all the high points, including a walk on the ramparts and into the towers; it's recommended for the first time visitor. Although entrance to La Cite is free, you'll have to pay a fee to get to see inside some of the main sights. These include the Chateau Comtal, the former 12th century palace of the Trencavels that later became a fortress after Carcassone fell under French rule. Happily, there's no charge to visit the beautiful Romanesque-Gothic

Basilique St-Nazaire, where you can admire the vibrantly colored stained-glass windows. Within the church is the Siege Stone, relating the takeover of the city by the Crusaders, a 16th century organ, and the tomb of Bishop Radulf.

Le Nord

Calais

The nearest French town to England, Calais is just 21 miles from Dover, across the Channel. It was once a fishing village, but today it's the second most important passenger port in France. Calais is also the terminus for the world's largest commercial catamaran, called the *Seacat*, which zips in triangles between here, Boulogna and Dover. A convenient ferry point and rest stop for crossings to Dover and other British ports is **Montreuil-sur-Mer**. Across from its ancient citadel is the **Château de Montreuil**, a worthy stopover for its comfort, beauty and cuisine.

Where to Stay

Meurice ★★
Moderate

5 rue Edmond-Roche. Located near parc Richelieu and Notre Dame church. Rated Restaurant: La Diligence.

☎ *(21)34-57-03.*

Credit Cards: *All Major.*

An elegant Old World hotel with modern comforts, it carries on the tradition of Monsieur Augustin Meurice, owner in 1772 of the stagecoach express line, Le Chariot Royale. Accommodations include 40 rooms; all are comfortable and well kept with bath, telephone and TV; many look out on Richelieu Park.

Where to Eat

Acquar'Aile ★★
Moderate to Expensive

255 rue J.-Moulin. ☎ *(21)34-00-00.*

Credit Cards: *V, MC, A, E.*

Perched above the beach, this attractively decorated, polished restaurant serves excellent shellfish, poultry and organ meats. Varied wine list, and the service is first rate. Folks on a budget (or just prudent people) will want to know about the George V hotel's bistro, the Petit George, offering a fixed-price menu. It's located at *36 rue Royale* ☎ (21-97-68-00), closed Sat. for lunch, Sun. dinner.

Le Channel
Inexpensive

3 boulevard de la Resistance. ☎ *(21)34-43-30.*

Credit Cards: *All Major.* Closed: *Tues.*

Located where the harbor meets the sea, this roomy family restaurant serves mostly seafood at reasonable prices. The fixed- price menu, served daily except Sunday is an excellent deal.

Ligny

Chateau de Ligny
Inexpensive to Moderate

4 rue P.-Curie. ☎ *(27)85-25-84.*

Credit Cards: *V, MC, A, E.* Closed: *Sat.*

Classic cuisine with impeccable ingredients, is served in this 13th-century chateau covered with foliage. Though it's somewhat off the beaten path (in the northern reaches, towards Lille or Brussels), you'll be guaranteed a friendly welcome by the owners.

What to Do

The Burghers of Calais ★★★
Hotel de Ville.

Gracing Calais' city hall is one of August Rodin's most famous statues, "The Burghers of Calais." The aged bronze statue depicts six men who offered their own lives to save the city from the conquering forces of Edward III. If you want to see preliminary sketches of the sculpture, visit the **Musee des Beaux Arts et de la Dentelle**, *25 rue Richelieu* ☎ (21.46.62.00 Ext: 6317), closed Tuesday; it also has Dutch and Flemish paintings and fine examples of local arts and crafts. Some worthwhile excursions from here include Boulogne-Sur-Mer, 21 miles southwest, where Caesar, Claudius, Charlemagne,

Napoleon and Hitler contemplated (but not at the same time, thank God) English invasions. All major sites are within the walled city, the Haute Ville: the 19th century Notre-Dame Cathedral, and a medieval Chateau, *rue de Bernet* ☎ (21.80.80), closed Tuesday; a historical museum that was once home to the Counts of Boulogne. **Nausicaa**, at *Bd. Sainte-Beuve* ☎ (21.30.98.98) is not an amusement park with stomach churning rides, but rather, an excellent sea center and aquarium. Open every day except Christmas, New Year and a couple of weeks in January.

Normandy

Though it lies adjacent to Brittany's eastern flank, the province of Normandy is quite different. Its character is softer, its soil is richer, and its prosperity is noticeably greater. Culturally, it is one of the most rewarding regions on either side of the English Channel.

Ironically, this French embankment is the focal point today of all of the fighting that ended in 1066 at Hastings on the British side. The interface for the titanic bicultural squabbling can be witnessed at the intriguing **Musée de la Tapisserie de Bayeux**. The amazing tapestry (actually an embroidery), known as the Mathilde Frieze, is in the former seminary beyond the hospital. This museum undoubtedly is one of the world's finer monuments to self-education; if you devote as little as three hours to the marvelous explanatory displays and the visual aids, you will come away with a real understanding of how two cultures developed from the 11th century onward.

In nearby **Caen**, there are the monumental and classic Norman **St-Stephen's Abbey** *(Abbaye aux Hommes)*, begun in 1064, and the **Abbaye aux Dames**, close by. William the Conqueror is buried in the Choir of the former church. There's a **Peace Museum** here called **Memorial**, which is dedicated to understanding the factors that brought on World War II.

Of course, one of the lasting moments in travel is a visit to the ancient **Abbaye du Mont Saint Michel**, an intellectual and spiritual center standing on a pinnacle of land (which becomes an island at times) and is still utilized as a Benedictine abbey. Despite the crowding from bus package tours, it is one of the most inspiring sites in Europe.

For excursions in the region, there is the redolent follow-your-nose path through cheese country, which takes you into **Auge** and by farms where the wonderful products of Livarot, Pont L'Eveque,

Pave d'Auge and, of course, Camembert are born and bred. You can visit the **Camembert Museum** at **Vimoutiers**. Additionally, there is a **Route du Cidre**, which, naturally, refers to the apple juice pressed from local orchards and developed into cider—some of it resulting in the dynamic and beautiful Calvados of international fame.

Somewhat further afield is the scenic trip through the **Route de la Suisse Normande**, which is south of Caen and moves through harmonious rolling country with interesting chapels and châteaux dotting the circuit.

In quiet salt breezes blowing softly over St-Laurent-sur-Mer, you can stand beside the magnificent polychrome plaque that marks the spot where the first wave of U.S. troops fought their way up the sand banks to achieve what was to become the most earth-shaking mass military movement in the annals of mankind. Below lies the full sweep of Omaha Beach and the sparkling waters of the Channel. To the rear is a beautiful chapel, an impressive rondure with the names of the fallen and a reception center for pilgrims. From there lies the immaculate greensward with tidy white gravemarkers stretching over acres of Norman soil.

If you're driving, strike out first for **Arromanches-les-Bains** (roughly 38 miles from Deauville), the strategic center of the British zone of attack and the site of the "Mulberry" artificial harbor. Visit the fascinating **Musée du Debarquement** (loosely translated as "Invasion Museum"), where battle memorabilia, photos of the commanders, films of the fighting taken by combat cameramen and an ingenious diorama can be seen.

The most dramatic terrain of all is Pointe du Hoc (7 miles from central Omaha), where Colonel Rudder's American Rangers stormed its cliff and seized and held its German fortifications for 48 hours, during which all but 14 of these heroes were killed or wounded—to find later that they had attacked the wrong promontory.

Utah Beach, about 20 miles farther along, holds little of sightseeing interest today—unless, of course, there are personal reasons for visiting it. Two airborne divisions and gliders landed here, as did General Patton. Memorabilia of those events can be seen at the museum at **Ste-Mere-Eglise**.

Caen

Caen is the capital of the department of Calvados and it contains the fortress walls of William the Conqueror and two Romanesque abbeys. The city is a good base for further excursions since the Landing Beaches of Normandy and the Flowered Coast are easily accessible by bus or train. A number of nightclubs cater to the young crowd from the university.

Where to Stay
Hotels and Resorts

Argouges   ★★
Budget to Moderate

21 rue St-Patrice. Located on a main square, near rue Royale.

☎ *(31)92-88-86.*

Credit Cards: *All Major.*

Sheltered behind tall gates, there is a large courtyard and stone, semicircular staircase that lead up to the 18th-century hotel's front entry. Looking out over the garden or front courtyard, the 25 guest rooms all have exposed beams; fabric covered walls; comfortable furniture; and private bathrooms. There are also two charming suites that have a small extra room for children. Additional guest rooms are found in an equally delightful adjacent home. Breakfast is the only meal served. The hotel is open year-round.

Chateau d'Audrieu   ★★
Moderate to Expensive

Audrieu. From Caen take the N13 east for 29 km; then take the D158 for 5 km.

☎ *(31)80-21-52.*

Credit Cards: *All Major.*

This chateau, set in a 50-acre park, offers the most luxurious accommodations at Audrieu. Its 21 well-appointed rooms are decorated with antiques and calla lilies, and all have private bathrooms. There is an excellent restaurant, and some of the produce, such as the raspberries, comes from the hotel's garden.

Lion d'Or
Budget to Moderate

71 rue St-Jean. Located two blocks east of the tourist information center.

☎ *(31)92-06-90.*

Credit Cards: *All Major.*

Like an old French coach inn, the Lion d'Or has a large open courtyard and a mansard roof, and lush flower boxes decorate the facade. Its 26 comfortable rooms, all with private bath, are set back from the street and around the cobbled, flower-filled courtyard. The beamed dining room, looking out on the courtyard, is famous for its cuisine. One meal is required of overnight guests.

Relais des Gourmets ★★★
Moderate

15 rue de Geole. Located at the foot of Chateau de Guillaume-le-ConquÈrant.

☎ *(31)86-06-01.*

Credit Cards: *All Major.*

A charming hotel in a great location near the Chateau. The reception area and lounges are filled with antiques, including a 13th-century closet. Its 24 spacious rooms, with private bath, are soundproofed; many have a view of the garden or the Chateau. Guests can dine on the hotel's terrace where an excellent seafood salad is served. There is also a high-quality restaurant next door, L'Ecaille, that faces the castle of William the Conqueror.

Where to Eat

Daniel Turboeuf ★★★
8 rue Buquet. ☎ *(31)43-64-48.*

Credit Cards: *V, MC, E.* Closed: *Mon., Sun.*

Housed in an old dance studio, chef Daniel Tuboeuf's maison is fast becoming one of the leading restaurants in the city. Norman specialties are served, making good use of superb local ingredients. He combines the ubiquitous tripe with potatoes and apples, and bakes it into a luscious gateau. Excellent wine list.

La Bourride ★★★

Moderate

15-17 rue du Vaugeux. ☎ *(31)93-50-76.*

Credit Cards: *All Major.* Closed: *Mon., Sun.*

Within a lovely half-timbered house across the port is the city's best restaurant. Built on *bourride*, a fish soup made with rich tomato and saffron stock (actually a southern specialty), the restaurant serves five different kinds. Chef Michel Bruneau also cooks up a variety of Norman dishes, including a flavorful andouille sausage mele.

Le Petite Auberge ★
Inexpensive to Moderate

17 rue des Equipes-d'Urgence. ☎ *(31)86-43- 30.*

Credit Cards: *All Major.*

Norman specialties are served at this restaurant near the Church of St-Stephen, at reasonable prices. The seafood and tripe are notable.

Trouville

Le Petite Auberge ★
Moderate to Expensive

7 rue Carnot. ☎ *31.88.11.07.*

Credit Cards: *V, MC, E.*

A traditional bistro within a dice throw of the Casino. Well-prepared stews, shellfish and other uncomplicated dishes at decent prices. Always packed with elbow-to-elbow diners. Also very popular with visitors is a brasserie across from the fish market, **Les Vapeurs**, *160 bd Fernand- Moureaux* (31.88.15.24), across from the fishmarket, naturally serves fish and shellfish (mussels in cream, a specialty) and tons of it; open daily except Wednesday, serving until 1 a.m. Outside dining in season. AE, V. Reservations recommended.

What to Do
Museums and Exhibits

Memorial: Un Musee Pour La Paix/Peace Museum ★★★★
Esplanade Eisenhower. ☎ *31.06.06.44.*
🕐 *9 a.m.–9 p.m.*

Special Hours: *September-May, to 7 p.m.*

Although there are other moving and intelligent exhibits, the highlight of this museum and memorial to peace is a series of spectacularly edited films (real footage interspersed with Hollywood interpretations) that try to explain "why we fight." Free admission for World War II veterans. Explanations in English. The museum is located northwest of Caen's city center on N13. Closer to the center are two abbeys and a castle built by William the Conqueror and his wife, Queen Matilda, who made Caen their home base in the 11th century. The castle, the Chateau de Caen, Esplanade du Chateau, mostly in ruins, houses several interesting museums; the **Beaux Arts** ☎ (31.85.28.63), with a fine collection of 16th, 17th and 19th century art, from the French and Italian Masters to the French Impressionists. **Musee de Normandie** ☎ (31.86.06.24), is a showcase for the crafts and agricultural products of the region, including the famous Camembert cheese, Calvados apple brandy and cider. Both open daily except Tuesday from 10 a.m.–6 p.m. in summer, other times they close for lunch between 12:30 and 2 p.m. Spectacular views of the city can be seen for free from the castle ramparts. There's also a medieval herb garden on the grounds. William and Matilda, who were cousins, built his-and-her Romanesque abbeys, the Abbaye aux Hommes (Men) and the Abbaye aux Dames (Women), in order to appease the Church for marrying against its wishes. Wil's abbey, (Esplanade Jean-Marie Louvel) is notable for its church, the Eglise St.-Stephen, which houses the Conqueror's thigh bone, the only thing left of the great man after his tomb was desecrated by Huguenots in the 16th century. (Church open 8 a.m.–12 a.m. and 2 p.m.–7:30 p.m.) Admission: varies.

Arromanches-sur-Mer
Museums and Exhibits

Musee du Debarquement   ★★★★
http://www.normandy-tourism.org/gb/21SitMo/fiches/musdebar.html

pl. du 6 Juin. ☎ *31.22.34.31.*

One of the most amazing strategies in modern warfare was undertaken in this area on D-Day, June 6, 1944. British troops brought in 500,000 tons of material across the Channel at four miles an hour and constructed a makeshift port at Arromanches harbor (codenamed Mulberry B, but nicknamed "Port Winston"). Meant to handle 9000 tons of material a day, by the end of August, millions of soldiers had been brought in, and tons of equipment and vehicles unloaded. This museum documents the battle plans in detail. It's also worth shelling out 20F to see the film, "The Price of Freedom" at the Arromanches 360° theater on a hill above the museum. Admission: moderate.

Bayeux

Musee de la Tapisserie de Bayeux ★★★★
Centre Guillame le Conquerant, rue de Nesmond. ☎ *31.92.05.48.*
🕐 *9 a.m.–6:30 p.m.*

The Bayeux Tapestry took over 200 feet of cloth, endless spools of thread and lots of womanpower to relate the history of William the Conqueror's subjugation of England in the Battle of Hastings in 1066. What is remarkable about it, other than its sheer size and amazing detail, is that the colors are still vivid after almost 1000 years. Your viewing of the tapestry, which is in five sections, is accompanied by a detailed audiovisual presentation in both French and English. Film in English in the 2nd floor cinema shown every 40 minutes. It's unlikely that a tapestry will be woven to depict the 70-day battle for Normandy (Bayeux was never bombed) so we will have to make do with photos, news articles, and wax soldiers to comprehend what happened from June to August in 1944. These can be seen at the **Memorial Museum of the Battle of Normandy**, *bd. Fabian-Ware* ☎ (31.92.93.41), open 10 a.m.–12:30 p.m., and 2 p.m.–6 p.m., September-June. July-August, open 9 a.m.–7 p.m., with no lunch break. Just a few steps away from the museum is the Bayeux War Cemetery, where almost 5000 soldiers, mostly from Britain, and many from Germany, are buried. Admission: moderate.

Giverny
Parks and Gardens

Musee Claude Monet ★★★★★
Giverny-Gasny. ☎ *32.51.28.21.*
🕐 *10 a.m.–6 p.m.*

Special Hours: *Open April-October, closed between 12 a.m.-2 p.m.*

A dreamworld of pretty pastels, Monet's pink and green house and famous gardens were restored by American enthusiasts; and the French don't mind admitting the fact. For forty years, the artist, nourished by the pristine beauty around him, painted some of his most memorable works. These include the "Water Lilies" series, (*Nympheas*) which can be seen today in the Orangerie in Paris. On display in his studio are some rare Japanese prints from his private collection, but what you think are originals of his work are only reproductions. Still, you won't be disappointed—the decor within is a living canvas—even the kitchen is a sea of bright blue tiles. Admission: varies.

Mont St-Michel
Historical Sites

Abbaye du Mont Saint Michel   ★★★★★
Mont Saint-Michel, 80 miles southwest of Caen. ☎ *33.60.14.14.*
🕐 *9:30 a.m.–5 p.m.*

Special Hours: *Jan-Feb to 4:15 p.m, mid- May-mid Sept. until 6 p.m.*

One of the most visited sights in France, (over 600,000 visitors a year) this beautiful abbey atop a granite island (population: 120) started life as a private chapel in the 8th century by Archbishop Aubert of nearby Avranches. By the mid-18th century, it had grown to its present size, serving as a monastery for a powerful order of Benedictine monks. It was also used as a prison after the Revolution. The island is connected to the mainland by a causeway, and you can reach the abbey via the Grande Rue, a twisty, 12th century street that's a warren of tacky shops. Hour-long guided tours of the Abbey include "The Miracle," a three-story Gothic "mini-monastery" built over a 16 year period in the 13th century. Tours in English daily every hour from 10 a.m. to 12 a.m.; then again at 1:30 p.m. every hour until 5:30 p.m. Directions: Take the train from Caen to the Pontorson-Mont St-Michel station ☎ (33.57.50.50), a 2.5 hour trip. From there take the STN bus 15 to Mont St-Michel (10 minutes). Admission: varies.

Omaha Beach

American Cemetery   ★★★★★
http://www.abmc.gov/no.htm
Omaha Beach, near Colleville-sur-Mer.

Besides the marble crosses of close to 10,000 soldiers, there's a memorial to the fallen with over 1500 listed names.

Ste-Marie-Eglise
Museums and Exhibits

Airborne Troops Museum
Place du 6 Juin. ☎ *33.41.41.35.*

This museum is shaped like the parachutes which dropped fighting men from the 82nd Airborne in this town near Utah Beach on June 6, 1944. The operation was one of the first phases of "Operation Overlord," and the action liberated Ste-Mere- Eglise from the Germans. Within is the Douglas C-47 transport plane that flew the paratroopers in. Open daily, Feb-Mid- November, 9 a.m.–7 p.m.; Mid-November-Mid December; Saturday-Sunday. Admission: free.

Rouen

Rouen is a town of hundreds of medieval timber-frame houses, the cathedral painted by Monet, a marketplace where Joan of Arc was burned and a relatively recently discovered School of the Jews. The **Cathedral Notre-Dame** was razed by fire and only rebuilt in 1201; it took three centuries to finish it (in case you were thinking that construction takes a long time today). The Big Clock (*Gros Horloge*) has but one hand; still you should see it and the Belfry.

Don't miss **Giverny**, where the home, studio and gardens of Claude Monet are open for public viewing. There's also a fine new **American Museum** filled with French Impressionist art. Giverny is not far from the capital, so you may want to return right away. Linger and see the gardens in all the varying light values.

Where to Stay
Bed and Breakfasts

Le Chateau
Budget to Moderate

place de l'eglise.

☎ *(35)34-29-70.*

Credit Cards: *Not Accepted.*

Guaranteed to satisfy anybody's desire for a charming bed and breakfast, this chateau lies across from the church in this small town. Four guest rooms, all cheerily decorated and furnished with complementing wood furniture, overlook the grounds and come with a spacious, private bath. Request a room in one of the turrets on either side of the building, as those are the most charming. Le Chateau receives nothing but accolades from its guests.

Hotels and Resorts

Hotel de Dieppe   ★★
place Bernard-Tissot. Located across from the train station.

☎ 528-1234, ☎ (35)71-96-00, FAX: (35)89-65- 21.

Credit Cards: *V, MC, DC, A.*

Operating since the late 19th century, this hotel has been under the same family management for four generations. The compact rooms are decorated in period or contemporary decor, and each comes with a TV, telephone, bath and double glazed windows to buffer the train noise. Cheerful and helpful, the staff gives a flawless performance.

Hotel de la Cathedrale   ★★
http://www.hotel-de-la-cathedrale.fr/

Budget

12 rue St-Romain.

☎ (35)71-57-95.

Credit Cards: *V, MC.*

An inexpensive hotel with a prime location across from the palace where Joan of Arc was tried and burned behind the cathedral. Behind the timbered facade lie 24 accommodations, each simply furnished and equipped with a TV, telephone and bath or shower. Good for a stopover, the facility is immaculately kept and conveniently located close to the town sights.

Inns

Le Moulin de Connelles   ★★★★
http://www.moulindeconnelles.com/

Moderate to Expensive

40 route d'Amfreville-sur-les-Monts.

☎ (32)59-53-33, FAX: (32)59-21-83.

Credit Cards: *All Major.*

Perhaps the most exquisite accommodations in all of Normandy, Le Moulin is the archetype for all other inns. ithin the classic, gabled Norman structure are seven rooms and six suites, each plushly carpeted, decorated with subtle colors and standard with TV, telephone, minibar and excellent bathrooms. The choice rooms offer views over the river, as does the restaurant which serves sumptuous regional specialties with fixed-price menus. On-site facilities include a heated pool and a tennis court, and the gracious inn lends guests boats to casually tour the Seine. Le Moulin is conducive to changes in travel plans for guests who can't bear to leave this French Shangri-la.

Where to Eat

Gill ★★★
Moderate to Expensive

9 quai de la Bourse. ☎ *(35)71-16-14.*

Credit Cards: *All Major.* Closed: *Sun.*

Situated on the waterfront, this cheerful, tasteful dining establishment (devoid of frills) is the finest restaurant in town. Gilles Tournadre's menu is contemporary, with the bright flashes of invention typical of the genre.

L'Ecaille ★★
Moderate to Expensive

26 rampe Cauchoise. ☎ *(35)70-95-52.*

Credit Cards: *All Major.* Closed: *Mon.*

A nautical theme runs through this cool green dining room with equally soothing decor. At this primarily seafood-oriented restaurant, the sauces and spices are kept to a minimum in order to accentuate the natural flavors of the fish and shellfish. Eating lightly has its reward, however; this way you'll be able to thoroughly enjoy the house-dessert apple souffle with Calvados (apple brandy) sauce.

What to Do
Historical Sites

Cathedrale Notre-Dame
place de la Cathedrale.

🕐 *7:30 a.m.–7 p.m.*

Special Hours: *Monday, 9 a.m.–7 p.m., Sunday 7:30 a.m.–6 p.m.*

If this Romanesque-Gothic cathedral looks familiar to you, you may have seen it in paintings by Monet in the Musee d'Orsay; he did more than 30 of them. He seemed obsessed with it, painting it from different angles and at certain times of the day (ghostly on a gray morning, and framed in shadows in the late afternoon). Its 19th-century steeple is the tallest in the country. Take the guided tour of the deceptively simple interior; Richard the Lion Heart is buried within. Admission: *free, tours extra.*

Eglise Jeanne d'Arc ★★
place du Vieux Marche.

Except for tourists, all is peaceful at this square, where in 1431, Joan of Arc was burned at the stake. A bronze cross commemorates the spot, and a contemporary church nearby is dedicated to her memory. At 33 place du Vieux-Marche is the Musee Jeanne d'Arc, tracing her life and death in wax. During the last weekend in May, the city pays tribute to Joan with theatrical events, markets, concerts and fireworks; call the tourist office ☎ (35.71.41.77), for details.

Provence

Aix-en-Provence

This ancient capital city of Provence dates back to 122 B.C., when it was founded by the Romans. With its stately mansions, tree-shaded boulevards and public squares with their many old stone fountains, it still retains much of the atmosphere of its heyday during the 17th and 18th centuries. Aix-en-Provence continues to be a thriving cultural center. If you're in Provence during the month of July, be sure to catch the *International Music Festival*, held in Aix-en-Provence every year since 1948. The artist Paul Cezanne was born and lived here, immortalizing the surrounding countryside; his studio has been left intact and is open to the public.

Where to Stay

Augustins ★
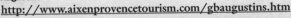
http://www.aixenprovencetourism.com/gbaugustins.htm

Moderate to Expensive

3 rue de la Masse. Located off the Cours Mirabeau on its north side, just a block east of the Place Charles de Gaulle.

☎ *(42)27-28-59.*

Credit Cards: *All Major.*

A majestically restored 12th-century convent, this converted hotel boasts vaulted ceilings, terra cotta floors and stained glass windows. The 32 air-conditioned guest rooms are modestly decorated and include TV, telephone, minibar and private bath. The two rooms with private terraces facing the bell tower are the best choices.

Le Pigonnet ★★
http://www.hotelpigonnet.com/

Moderate to Expensive

5 avenue du Pigonnet. Located at Pont de l'Arc, south of av. de l'Europe; west of train station.

☎ *(42)59-02-90.*

Credit Cards: *All Major.*

Surrounded by gardens on the edge of town, Le Pigonnet charms guests with its Provencal architecture. The view might look familiar to art aficionados, Paul Cezanne painted the Mountain of Sainte Victoire from this garden. The 49 air-conditioned accommodations are all constantly updated and include cable TV, telephone, minibar and private bath or shower.

Where to Eat

Le Bistro Latin ★★
Moderate

18 rue Couronne. ☎ *(42)38-22-88.*

Credit Cards: *V, MC, A, E.*

Classic bistro cookery in one of the friendliest places in town; there's always a nice welcome here. The entrees are popularly priced, but the set menus have the greatest appeal. Aix's most historic eatery is **Les Deux Garcons**, *53, cours Mirabeau* ☎ (42-26-00-51), a brasserie where Cezanne, Camus and other famous folks whiled away the time. Prices are high for the simple fare offered, but it's good for coffee or espresso.

Le Clos de la Violette ★★★
Moderate to Expensive

10 avenue de la Violette. ☎ *(42)23-30-71.*

Credit Cards: *V, A.* Closed: *Sun.*

One of Aix's top chefs, the energetic Jean- Marc Banzo, prepares bright, regional dishes in this beautiful walled villa in a suburban location. There are several dining areas, but the most favored spot is a garden that's a riot of blooms in summer. Market-fresh produce, lamb, oysters and Mediterranean seafood are often featured on his seasonal menus. The fixed-price lunch is a bargain.

What to Do
Historical Sites

Atelier de Cezanne ★★★
http://www.atelier-cezanne.com/

9 av Paul Cezanne. ☎ *42.21.06.53.*

🕐 *10 a.m.–5 p.m.*

Special Hours: *Closed noon–2 p.m.*

The interior of the studio where the father of cubism, Paul Cezanne, spent his last days, appears as if he was about to return at any moment. An unfinished canvas is propped up on an easel, and his coat hangs on a door peg. You can almost smell the coffee brewing. The tourist office, at *2 place du General de Gaulle,* ☎ (42.26.02.93) has devised an interesting walking tour of the city; follow their brochure, which will take you past all of the artist's favorite haunts, ending up at the atelier, just outside of town. Just nine miles north from Aix is the Montaigne St-Victoire, a peak recognizable in much of Cezanne's work. The tourist office is open from 8 a.m.–10 p.m., Monday-Saturday; Sunday from 9 a.m.–10 p.m. Admission: inexpensive.

Music

International Music Festival ★★★★
Palais de l'Ancien Archeveche. ☎ *42.21.14.40.*

🕐 *9 a.m.–7 p.m.*

Special Hours: *Fall-Winter 10 a.m.–6 p.m.*

Some of the world's greatest opera stars, chamber orchestras and guest soloists perform annually at this world-famous festival (July). Performance venues include the Cathedrale de St-Saveur, the Musee des Tapisseries and the Theatre d l'Archeveche. Tickets (downright cheap to astronomical) should be purchased several months ahead of time. Less highbrow entertainment can be enjoyed (it's easier on the wallet, too) in the second week of June, when the Aix en Musique is in full swing. Jazz, rock, and alternative musicians, as well as classical performers pop up in unlikely places, and many events are free of charge. There's also a dance festival of some renown, also held throughout the month of July. Call the tourist office for information.

Nightlife

Le Mistral ★★
3 rue Frederic Mistral. ☎ *42.38.16.49.*

🕐 *11 p.m.–6 a.m.*

Admission: *FR80.*

Popular student hangout (the ones that drive Beemers, that is) with live music until the rooster crows; **Le Scat**, at *11 rue Verrerie* (42.23.23) is, as its name implies, a jazz club, highly recommended, also in the 80F range, patrons don't have to scat until dawn; closed Sunday. Gay Aix repairs to **La Chimere** for dancing and drinking; outside the city limits at *rte d'Avignon,* ☎ (42.23.36.28) open 10 p.m.–6 am; closed Monday.

Arles

Established as a Roman colony in 46 B.C., this historic town has long attracted archeologists and art lovers for its Roman remains and associations with Van Gogh—who painted some of his most celebrated works here, including "Sunflowers" and "Starry Night." Lying on the left bank of the Rhône, the Provencal town is a charming destination in itself, while also offering such attractions as arts festivals, museums, bullfights, a Gothic palace and numerous Roman ruins.

Where to Stay

Calendal ★
http://www.lecalendal.com/

Budget to Moderate

22 place Pomme. Located on a quiet square, about 3 blocks south from the Roman arena (arenes).

☎ *(90)96-11-89.*

Credit Cards: *All Major.*

This relaxing hotel has 27 large rooms with classic Provencal decor. Most of the antique-adorned rooms afford views over the garden, and all come with telephone and private bath. A good choice for a comfortable overnighter.

D'Arlatan ★★
http://www.hotel-arlatan.fr/

Moderate

26 rue du Sauvage. At Place Lamartin enter through the ramparts on rue Septembre, which becomes rue du Sauvage.

☎ *(90)93-56-66.*

Credit Cards: *All Major.*

This hotel is tucked away on a small street in the center of town near the Place du Forum, within easy walking distance of all the city's major sights. Built in the 15th century on the ruins of an old Constantine palace, the structure still has parts dating back as far as the fourth century. The well-appointed and charming rooms are furnished with regional antiques and tapes tries. Modern amenities include a TV, telephone, minibar and private bath. Request a room overlooking the palm- lined garden and the pond. An understated charmer, as discovered by the many loyal return clients.

Jules Cesar ★★★★
Moderate to Expensive

7 boulevard des Lices. Located across from the tourist information center.

☎ *(90)93-43-20.*

Credit Cards: *All Major.*

deally located in the town center, this Relais and Chateaux establishment is situated amid the gardens, buffering it from any of the noise caused by its downtown location. It offers 49 ultra-spacious rooms, each quite comfortable and equipped with TV, telephone, minibar and air conditioning.

Where to Eat

Hostellerie des Arenes
Moderate

62 rue de Refuge. ☎ *(90)96-13-05.*

Credit Cards: *V, MC.* Closed: *Tues.*

On the rue du Refuge near the dual amphitheaters, this homey refuge is thankfully not too touristy, although it's packed tight most nights with hungry diners. The mood is convivial, especially on summer nights when the terrace is open. Pizza is a specialty, but it's expensive.

L'Olivier
Moderate to Expensive

1 bis, rue Reattu. ☎ *(90)49-70-74.*

Credit Cards: *A.* Closed: *Mon., Sun.*

This is one of Arles' best restaurants, and it's accessible to all via a generous set of fixed-price meals, especially on weekdays. You won't get cast-offs either, nor will you leave hungry. The four-course repast includes soup, a fish course, a choice of meat or poultry, ending with one of its excellent desserts.

Le Vaccares ★★★
Moderate to Expensive

place du Forum, entrance rue Favorin. ☎ *(90)96-06-17.*

Credit Cards: *V, MC.* Closed: *Mon.*

Everyone gets a bird's eye view of the goings-on in the market square while dining at this cheerful restaurant. Chef Bernard Dumas serves wonderful traditional specialties like *tapenade* (olive paste with capers, anchovies and olive oil) with Camargue lamb, and herbed mussels. His aioli garlic sauce with anything is not to be missed.

What to Do
City Celebrations

Rencontres Internationales de la Photographie   ★★★
10 rond point des Arenes. ☎ *90.96.76.06.*

Special Hours: *July only*

Shutterbugs the world over take this festival of photography (July) very seriously. Gallery exhibits, slide presentations, workshops and other events are open to the public at reasonable prices. If you think your work is up to snuff, bring your samples along for a consultation. The Arles Festival, also in July, is a month-long drama, music and dance extravaganza made even more dramatic by being staged in the city's impressive Roman ruins (see "Historical Sites").

Historical Sites

Roman Amphitheater   ★★★★
Rond-Point des Arenes. ☎ *90.96.03.70.*

🕐 *8:30 a.m.–7 p.m.*

Special Hours: *Contact tourist office for winter hours .*

All of Arles' important ancient Roman sites are within walking distance of each other, and an all-inclusive ticket called Forfait 2 can be purchased at the tourist office at *blvd des Lices* ☎ (90.18.41.20). Hours for all sites are the same. The amphitheater, still in use today for summer bullfights and as the site of outdoor concerts during the Arles Festival (July), was built in the 1st century. Much of the structure is still intact, and as many as 20,000 people can be seated in the arena. Once used as a fortress, it has three towers, or donjons, that can be climbed for a definitive view of the area. Emperor Augustus' Roman Theater, at *rue du Cloitre,* ☎ (90.96.93.30) should actually be called "The Two Corinthian Columns," because they are the only remnants of the 1st-century theatre-fortress-quarry. A semicircular seating area within the complex is an important Arles Festival venue. Also worth visiting are the thermae, or Baths of Emperor Constantine, within the old imperial palace, at rue Dominique Maisto, near the rue du 4 Septembre. The baths date from the 4th-century A.D. Admission: varies.

Avignon
Along with Arles and Aix-en-Provence, Avignon is one of the

more picturesque and typical towns of Provence. It is situated near the junction of two branches of the Rhône River and ringed by ramparts dating from the 14th century. The **Palais des Papes** is the focal point of the town—and a reminder that Avignon had been the capital of Christendom when the papal court resided here from 1309 to 1377. Today visitors are not only drawn by its historic sites but by its lively contemporary theater-and-dance festivals held every year in the summer.

Where to Stay

Danieli ★

Budget to Moderate

17 rue de la Republique.

☎ *(90)86-46-82.*

Credit Cards: *All Major.*

An intimate hotel with an Italian flair, the Danieli offers 29 rooms. The softly-toned rooms, accented with a bit of art deco style, feature contemporary furnishings, TV, telephone and private bath. A bit of charm is thrown in with this value-minded hotel.

Europe ★★★

Moderate to Expensive

12 place Crillon. Located in front of pte. de l'Oulleridge. Turn inside the ramparts; place Crillon is on the left.

☎ *(90)82-66-92.*

Credit Cards: *All Major.*

Once the home of the Marquis de Graveson, this 16th-century mansion has been operating as a hotel since the late 1700s. The salons are graced with Aubusson tapestries, lovely antiques and original pieces of art. Retreat to any of the 47 guest rooms, decorated with period furnishings and including air conditioning, TV, telephone and marble bath. Overlooking the town and the Palais des Papes, the three rooftop suites are splendid displays of refined elegance. The experience here is capped with a meal in the hotel restaurant, **La Vielle Fontaine**, which serves fixed-price meals in the dining room and in the inner courtyard. A grand hotel with an intimate feeling aroused by the charming staff.

Where to Eat

Christian Etienne
Moderate to Expensive

10-12 rue de Mons.

Credit Cards: *V, MC, A*. Closed: *Sun.*

Besides being one of the best restaurants in town (and one of the oldest), Christian Etienne also has one of the most enviable locations—his patrons face the Palais des Papes while they dine. And what dining! The small but smart menu offers an ever- changing cornucopia of tastes and flavors. The fixed-price meals are perhaps the most creative; one features an entire menu of Provencal vegetables. Marvelous fish and shellfish dishes are available as well.

Le Petit Bedon
Inexpensive to Moderate

70 rue Joseph Vernet. ☎ *(90)82-33-98.*

Credit Cards: *V, MC, DC, A*. Closed: *Sun.*

You might see chefs from the top-flight restaurants eating here on their days off; most of them secretly enjoy the good, simple cooking and the easy prices. What's more, the people are nice and the surroundings are pleasant. The sparkling fish dishes are especially worth ordering; affordable wine list.

What to Do
City Celebrations

Festival d'Avignon
http://www.festival-avignon.com/fr/ index.php3

Bureau du Festival, 8 bis rue de Mons. ☎ *90.82.67.08.*
🕘 *9:30 a.m.–11 p.m.*

Stimulating dance, theatre, film and drama accentuates this important festival held mid July-early August, performances at the Palais des Papes and various cultural centers; tickets range from inexpensive to moderate, also some free events. Fringe festival, called "Off" (July 9-August 3) is slightly cheaper, irreverent and daring; contact Festival Off at place du Palais ☎ (90.82.28.62).

Historical Sites

Palais des Papes ★★★★
place du Palais-des-Papes. *90.86.03.32.*

🕐 *9 a.m.–7 p.m.*

Special Hours: *Winter to 5 p.m. or 6 p.m., depending on month*

If the Palais du Popes looks imposing, standing stalwart above the walled city, it was meant to be that way. The fortress-residence of the Avignon Popes is remarkable for thick brick walls topped by ten stout towers surrounding a central courtyard. Life was tough in the 14th century, and if you weren't prepared, you'd be easily overwhelmed by blackguards, thieves and thugs galore. The empire building began in earnest in 1309, when Pope Clement V decided to move the papal court from Rome to Avignon. The Palais was added on to until the court returned to Rome in 1377. The interior is graced by Gobelin tapestries and frescoes by Simone Martini. Guided tours are given in English daily at 10 a.m. and 3 p.m., extra fee. North of the Palais is the Petit Palais, former home of the Archbishop of Avignon, now a museum brimming with glories from the Renaissance, and sculpture and painting from the School of Avignon. Admission: varies.

Marseille

Marseille, the oldest city in France, dates back to Grecian times, when it was called "Massalia." It's the country's chief port, with a heavy Italian influence, routine hotels, superb restaurants, a bustling atmosphere and plenty of color. Unfortunately the Provencal city also has its fair share of drugs, corruption and crime (hold on to your wallets, especially on La Conebière, the main boulevard heading to the **Vieux-Port**). Still, you shouldn't miss the Vieux-Port, for its salty flavors and perhaps a glass of Tavel at one of its smart cafés. The bouillabaisse found in Marseille is claimed to be the best—and **Chez Fonfon** supposedly serves the best in town. Marseille also boasts some first-rate museums, including the **Beaux Arts**, in the **Palais Longchamp**, and the **Musée Cantini**.

Where to Stay

Concorde Prado ★★★
Moderate to Expensive

11 avenue de Mazarques. About 3.5 km from the train station, near the conference center.

☎ *(91)76-51-11.*

Credit Cards: *V, MC, DC, A.*

Popular with travelers who want to get away from the town center, this quiet hotel sits in a residential area near the harbor. Each of the 81 air-conditioned rooms comes with a TV, telephone, minibar and private bath. Wining and dining options, in addition to room service, include a restaurant and an American-style bar. The hotel has a shopping gallery with 20 boutiques, a 600-person conference facility, various business services and dry-cleaning available.

Concorde-Palm Beach
Moderate

2 promenade de la Plage. Located 2 km east of city center; prom. runs parallel with corniche prest. J.F. Kennedy.

☎ *(91016-19-00.*

Credit Cards: *All Major.*

A well-visited, beachfront hotel fronting Prado Bay, the Concorde is a modern four- story structure catering to both business travelers and vacation travelers alike. The two restaurant options are the grill, **Les Voiliers**, and the more formal restaurant, **La Reserve**. Terrace dining is offered in the warm months. The pool sits in the middle of the deck, adjacent to an umbrella- dotted terrace. The 145 air-conditioned rooms are a meld of cool colors, large windows, cane furnishings and large terraces opening onto the sea. A TV, telephone, minibar and private bath are standard in each. Helpful services include concierge, hairdressing and laundry.

Le Petit Nice
http://www.petitnice-passedat.com/

Moderate to Expensive

corniche President-J.F.Kennedy/Anse-de- Maldorme. Located close to the lighthouse the eastern entrance of Vieux Port; just north of Charles Livon.

☎ *(91)59-25-92.*

Credit Cards: *All Major.*

Easily the finest hotel and restaurant in Marseille, le Petit Nice is situated behind a high wall and iron gates, and sits among a row of private villas hugging the hill above the coast. The vantage point from this property offers fine sweeps of the coast and the islands. The public space keeps a fresh look, with the lobby, lounge, bar and seaside terrace inviting guests to linger and socialize. The 15 air-conditioned rooms have a TV, telephone, radio, safe, minibar, private bath, hair dryer and robes. The attractive restaurant serves creative cuisine to the tables with views of the rocky coast.

Where to Eat

Chez Fonfon

Inexpensive to Moderate

140 rue deu Vallon des Auffes. ☎ *(91)52-14-38.*

Credit Cards: *V, MC, A, E.* Closed: *Mon., Sun.*

This simple restaurant, in an out-of-the- way location with its own bay, is noted for terrific bouillabaisse—some say the best in town. All fish dishes are impeccably fresh. Another good place for bouillabaisse and other seafare is **Chez Loury**, *3 rue Fortia, 1st er* ☎ (91-33-09-73), but at a lower price.

Les Arcenaulx ★★

Inexpensive to Moderate

25 cours d'Estienne-d'Orves. ☎ *(91)54-77-06.*

Credit Cards: *V, MC, DC, A, E.* Closed: *Sun.*

The intelligentsia gather at this elegantly appointed bookstore and restaurant offering a terrific lunch fixed-price lunch. Light regional dishes, marvelous desserts. The best pastries and hot chocolate in town can be found at **L'Atelier du Chocolat**, *18 pl. des Huiles, 1st er* ☎ (91-33-55-00), also light meals. Go for the set menu. For regional cooking at a low price, try **Panier des Arts**, *3 rue Petit-Puits, 2nd eme* ☎ (91- 56-02-32), open until 10 p.m. Then there's **Chez Angele**, *50 rue Caisserie, 2nd eme* ☎ (91-90-63-35), for pizza; lots of young people. Open until 11 p.m., closed Sun. nights and all day Mon. Nearby is **Le Roi du Couscous**, at *63 rue de la Republique* ☎ (91-91-45-46), offering a vegie version of the North African semolina stew.

What to Do
Excursions

Chateau d'If   ★★★
1 mile south of the Port of Marseilles. ☎ *91.59.02.30.*

🕑 *9 a.m.–7 p.m.*

Special Hours: *Winter to 5:30 p.m.*

Just a short boat ride from the port of Marseille, this small isle is
home to the formidable castle-prison immortalized in Dumas'
Count of Monte Cristo. Originally a fortress, it eventually housed
state prisoners, but not the fictional count. Admission: inexpensive,
varies.

Museums and Exhibits

Palais Longchamp
blvd. Longchamp. ☎ *91.62.21.17.*

🕑 *10 a.m.–5 p.m.*

A trio of noteworthy museums are housed in the Palais Longchamp,
a 19th-century building and multi-use complex, with a zoo, gardens
and fountains. The jewel in the crown is the Beaux Arts, with a
definitive collection of Italian, French and Flemish masters (Rubens,
Watteau, Tiepolo). A special salon is set aside for Honore Daumier,
a Marseille-born painter and sharp-penned political caricaturist. Kids
can bolt for their own museum on the ground floor and then take
their parents to the adjoining natural history museum. Admission:
varies. Seniors, free.

Rhone Valley
Bourg-en-Bresse

This farming-and-business center is primarily visited for its
remarkable medieval church and its gastronomic shrines. The most
hospitable accommodations are at **Le Logis de Brou**, which is near
the church and adjoining antique buildings. **Du Prieure** was opened
recently by the former proprietresses of Le Logis. It has 14 rooms
and the ladies' traditional hospitality. But, what you really want to
do in this town is dine.

Where to Stay

Le Logis de Brou
Budget to Moderate

132 bd. de Brou. Located up the street from Prieur and Eglise de Brou.
☎ *(74)22-11-55.*

Credit Cards: *All Major.*

A good overnighter in the center of town, this four-story box-like hotel was built in 1968. Amid landscaped grounds, the 30 rooms can get a bit loud with the busy road just outside the property. All of the rooms are comfortable and simply furnished with antique reproductions, standard with TV, telephone and private bath.

Prieure
Budget to Moderate

49-51 boulevard de Brou. Located near the tourist information center; and a minute's walk from the famous Eglise de Brou.
☎ *(74)22-44-60.*

Credit Cards: *All Major.*

The two French sisters who own this little hostellerie have established it as the most charming place in town. Surrounded by an acre of lovely gardens within 400-year-old stone walls, there are 14 guest rooms with TV, telephone and private bath or shower. Each room is furnished in Louis XV style and restfully quiet. Spring brings the wafting aromas of the blooming flowers into all of the public areas.

Where to Eat

Au Chalet de Brou
Moderate

168 boulevard de Brou. ☎ *(74)22-26-28.*

Credit Cards: *V, MC.* Closed: *Thur., Fri.*

An excellent value in every respect, the food and service here never fail to satisfy the senses and the budget. The Bresse chicken with morels and chardonnay cream sauce and the crepes with mussels best reflect the use of the fresh, local ingredients.

Jacques Guy
Moderate

19 place Bernard. ☎ *(74)45-20-11.*

Credit Cards: *All Major.* Closed: *Mon.*

Traditional fare that's guaranteed to make any local a regular.
Jacques Guy's poached Bresse chicken in a tarragon cream sauce is a
staple that every patron must sample, and the squab with almonds is
sure to delight. The desserts are the specialties here, and every
sumptuous calorie of the warm fruit tarts and the three different
chocolate mousses is worth it.

Le Mail ★★
Moderate

46 avenue du Mail. ☎ *(74)21-00-26.*

Credit Cards: *V, DC, A.*

Join local families for a traditional Sunday lunch at this typical country auberge. The cuisine is delicious though unsurprising, the portions are substantial, and the service is friendly.

What to Do
Historical Sites

Church of Brou ★★★
63 blvd de Brou. ☎ *74.22.26.55.*
🕐 *8:30 a.m.–6 p.m.*

Romantics the world over love this church for the flamboyant,
Carrara marble tombs of Margaret of Austria and her beloved husband, Philibert, Duke of Savoy, who died of a sudden illness short-
ly after their marriage. Guided tours are given of the choir, where
the tombs are kept, along with the finely-carved choir stalls. There's
a small but interesting museum in the Cloisters, with 16th-17th century Dutch and Flemish paintings, and modern art by regional
artists. Admission: inexpensive.

Chamonix

This old-fashioned mountain town lies in a valley at the foot of
the mighty Mont Blanc, the highest peak on the Continent. The first

Winter Olympic games were held here in 1924. Today this leading sports resort not only offers incomparable skiing (its 10-mile Vallée Blanche run is one of the roughest in Europe—and definitely the longest), but also mountain climbing and hang-gliding (for the truly reckless). As a result of all the thousands of international visitors who come here every year, Chamonix has taken on a cosmopolitan feeling, despite its small population of permanent residents.

Where to Stay

Hotel Mont-Blanc ★★★
Moderate to Expensive

62 allee du Majestic. About 500 meters from the train station.

☎ *(50)53-05-64.*

Credit Cards: *V, MC, DC, A.*

A beautiful hotel faintly reflecting the Belle Epoque period, this resort hotel dates to the turn of the century. Its location in the center of Chamonix is sheltered by its gardens, creating a peaceful environment for the 43 rooms. There are a year-round heated outdoor pool, sauna, tennis court and shuttle bus to the ski slopes in the winter. The accommodating staff works hard to keep this one of the finest hotels in town.

Jeu de Paume ★★★
Moderate to Expensive

705 route du Chapeau, Le Lavacher. Located 93 km east of Annecy; from Chamonix take N506 northeast bound about 6 km.

☎ *(50)54-03-76.*

Credit Cards: *All Major.*

Situated in the village of Lavancher, this small hotel snuggles against the mountains with views of Chamonix and the Vallee d'Argentiere. Built in traditional chalet style, this charming hotel has 22 rooms with TV, radio, minibar, private bath and some with balcony. Five of the rooms are suites, and all are wheelchair accessible. Dining and drinking options include a restaurant, bar and 24-hour room serviceA shuttle bus whisks guests into Chamonix for other restaurant choices and shopping. Peaceful surroundings, comfortable accommodations and personal service.

Inns

Albert 1er
Budget to Moderate

119 impasse Montenvers. Located 93 km east of Annecy; near av. Cachat-le-Geant; at the commercial side of town.

☎ *(50)53-05-09.*

Credit Cards: *All Major.*

Since its inception at the turn of the century, this four-story hotel has stood out as one of the choice hotels in Chamonix. Recently renovated in a Tyrolean style, there are 30 charming rooms, each comfortable and well-equipped with TV, telephone and bath. A superb Alpine chalet.

Where to Eat

Atmosphere
Moderate

113 place Balmat. ☎ *(50)55-97-97.*

Credit Cards: *All Major.*

Atmosphere, as its name implies, offers a great view of Mont Blanc, as well as a delicious, untrendy menu and friendly service. For fondue, raclette (potatoes, melted cheese, pickles) and grills in a traditional mountain setting, head for the well-known **La Tartiffle**, *87 rue des Moulins* ☎ (50-53-2- .02). Open daily, except Tues., until 11 p.m. Cheaper still is a cafeteria, **Le Fonds des Gires**, *350 Ave. du Bois du Bouchet* ☎ (50-55-85-76). Sandwiches are available at **Poco Loco**, *45 rue du Dr. Paccard*; in season open until 2 a.m.

What to Do
Special Tours

Telepherique Aiguille du Midi
🕐 *6 a.m.–5 p.m.*

Special Hours: *Winter, 8 a.m.–4 p.m.*

Until you're past the halfway point of this trip (7,544 feet, at the Plan de l'Aiguille), you'll be singing the verses "where little cable cars, climb halfway to the stars." But soon enough, you WILL be seeing stars, and the words will freeze on your lips as the altitude changes drastically upon reaching the craggy needle, the Aiguille du Midi. At 12,606 feet, this is the highest cable car ride in the world, affording the intrepid with uninterrupted views of Mont Blanc, and the Vallee Blanc, Europe's largest glacier (unless obscured by clouds). After a brief recovery, you can hike back to town . Or, continue on to Italy (you'll need a passport) for a moderate sum. Don't forget warm clothes, and try to get an early start. Two shorter and less harrying excursions are to a four-mile long glacier: **the Mer de Glace** (information: ☎ *50.53.12.54*, May–September, 8 a.m.–6 p.m.), reached by rack railway next to the main station, at ave. de la Gare.

Sports and Recreation

Chamonix Mountain Bike ★★
138 rue des Moulins. ☎ *50.53.54.76.*

🕐 *9 a.m.–7 p.m.*

Special Hours: *Winter, closed noon-2 p.m.*

This outfit arranges mountain bike tours and daily bike rentals. For hiking tours as well as bike tours, contact **Compagnie des Guides** *(190 pl. de l'Eglise,* ☎ 50.53.88); bike tours are quite a bit cheaper and shorter. These experienced guides will take you on hiking trips to Mont Blanc and other locations during the summer months.

Lyon

Lyon the nation's second-largest city (when its suburbs are included), resides at the junction of two rivers (the Rhône and Saône) and two worlds (central and northern Europe). At the apex between the Alps and Burgundy, Lyon is a thriving and stimulating city and a hub for banking and publishing. Satolas Airport, with a capacity up to eight million, provides many new services for traffic to and from the nearby ski slopes; a superhighway will help you bypass town traffic if you are heading south to the Mediterranean or up to the hills. The high-speed TGV trains link Lyon to a score of other centers. The city is renowned for its silks—see the marvelous **textile museum**—and its stupendous dining establishments—chocoholics swoon over the rich creations of **Bernachon**, often praised as the finest chocolatier on this globe— as well as its Roman antiquities, châteaux, and cultural attractions that include the fine **Musée Gallo-Romain** and the **Theatres Gallo-Romain**, the last vestiges of the Roman city of Lugdunum, dating to 43 B.C.

Nearby **Courchevel 1850** (the numbers indicate the altitude in meters) is indisputably France's premier spot for winter sports. Its skiing opportunities are thrilling and nearly endless, and, moreover, you don't have to wait in long lines and the runs are perfectly maintained. The recent Winter Olympics also bestowed upon the region a giant Forum, an ice rink, a jump stadium, the improved Altiport (with daily flights to and from Paris plus air-taxi services) and many new bars and restaurants.

Where to Stay
Bed and Breakfast

Saint-Colomban Lodge
Budget to Moderate

7 rue du Hetre-Pourpre.   Exit Ecully, then Ecully-Centre. After church, head towards Tassin. The second street on left.

☎ *(78)33-05-57.*

Credit Cards: *Not Accepted.*

A great escape to a peaceful residential neighborhood just outside of Lyon. Surrounded by a private park, there are five attractive rooms withing this contemporary lodge. Sunny weather translates to complementary breakfast on the terrace; otherwise, the tables in the lounge are set. A good base for touring Lyon while remaining a bit removed.

Hotels and Resorts

Cour des Loges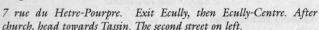
Expensive to Very Expensive

6 rue du Boeuf. In old town; accessible by bus #1 or 31.

☎ *(78)42-75-75.*

Credit Cards: *V, DC, A, E.*

A magnificent transformation of four Renaissance mansions from the 14th, 17th and 18th centuries, this brilliant piece was orchestrated by lyonnais architects and Italian interior designers over the course of a few years. The resulting hotel is the most stylish in Lyon. There are 63 contemporary rooms, each equipped with cable TV, telephone, radio, minibar and private bath. The hotel also offers an indoor pool, a Jacuzzi, a gym, a sauna and several lounges. The tapas bar, wine cellar and terraced gardens cap off this luxury hotel rivaled by no other.

Pullman Perrache
Moderate

12 cours de Verdun. Located near the Lyon- Perrache train station and Place Carnot.

☎ *(78)37-58-11.*

Credit Cards: *All Major.*

This 19th-century renovated hotel is near the Perrache train station and offers some of the best 123 rooms in Lyon. The rooms, all with private bathrooms, have been redecorated in a traditional style. They include many improvements like soundproofing and air conditioning. There are also shops, a piano bar and a winter garden in the hotel. The hotel and restaurant are open year-round.

Inns

Hotellerie Beau Rivage
http://www.hotel-beaurivage.com/ english/accueil.htm

Moderate to Expensive

2 rue de Beau-Rivage. Located 11 miles (18 km) southeast of Vienne on N86.

☎ *(74)56-67-27.*

Credit Cards: *All Major.*

This Relais and Chateaux inn offers 20 well-furnished rooms decorated in an old-fashioned way, and all have private bathrooms. The cuisine is exceptional and traditional, and garden dining is available. The inn and restaurant are open year- round.

Courchevel 1850

Byblos des Neiges
http://www.byblos.com/ pop_home.html

Expensive to Very Expensive

au Jardin Alpin. Located 51 km southeast of Abertville; next to the Jardin Alpin.

☎ *(79)08-12-12.*

Credit Cards: *All Major.*

In this ski town known as much for its high taste and high profile as it is for its high elevation, the Byblos des Neiges blends in perfectly. A virtual snow palace in the forest, this tops the list of luxury hotels in Courchevel. The 78 plush rooms have TV, telephone, radio, minibar and bath; most come with loggia and panoramic windows to open up the snug space. There are two restaurants, one featuring elaborate seafood platters and the other serving lunch buffets, and a piano bar.

Inns

Bellecote   ★★★
Moderate to Expensive

route de l'Altiport. Located 51 km southeast of Abertville; beside the Jardin Alpin; next to the Bellecote.

☎ *(79)08-10-19.*

Credit Cards: *All Major.*

Beside the Bellecote run, this seven-story chalet sits on a solid stone foundation. In addition to the exotic objects adorning the 53 wood-paneled rooms, each comes with TV, telephone, minibar, bath and terrace. Its central location affords easy access to the ski slopes, and there is a heated indoor pool, a health club and a sauna.

Vonnas

Georges Blanc   ★★★★
Expensive

Vonnas. Located on the banks of the River Veyle.

☎ *(74)50-00-10.*

Credit Cards: *All Major.*

Georges Blanc's Relais and Chateaux 19th-century country inn sits on the banks of the romantic River Veyle. The 30 airconditioned guest rooms vary from basic to luxurious, and each has a private bath. The culinary masterpieces created by George Blanc are among the finest in the world. From appetizers of frog legs, to any wine from the select list to the superb desserts, every course is gastronomic euphoria. Reservations are required for a chance to experience this legend.

Where to Eat

Bernachon ★★★
Moderate

42 cours F.D.-Roosevelt. ☎ *(78)52-23-65.* Closed: *Mon., Sun.*

Here you'll find the best hot chocolate in the world (great for breakfast) made from house-roasted cocoa beans; also offered are bonbons and pastries, as well as daily lunch specials.

La Tour Rose ★★
Moderate to Expensive

22 rue du Boeuf. ☎ *(78)37-25-90.*

Metro Stop: *St.-Jean.*

Credit Cards: *All Major.* Closed: *Sun.*

This inn and restaurant is a multilevel structure incorporated into a medieval convent in Lyon's Old Town. Favored by the arts community, it is the baby of chef, caterer and party planner Philippe Chavent. Asian flavors and spices are often employed, including ginger, seaweed, sesame oil and hibiscus flowers. The desserts are delicate and different. It's very expensive, but he's made up for that by opening a wine bar, **Comptoir du Boeuf**, at *2 place Neuve-Saint-Jean* ☎ *(78-92-82-35)*, which serves hearty dishes for a smaller sum. Wines by the glass, terrace dining.

Le Bouchon de Fourviere ★★
Inexpensive to Moderate

9 rue de la Quarantine. ☎ *72.41.85.02.*

Closed: *Sat., Sun.*

Welcome to bouchon (bistro) country—Lyon has middling to excellent bistros all over town with hearty cooking at easy prices. Frequented by journalists, La Bouchon de Fourviere offers three-course set meals, including dessert. Open until 10 p.m.

Le Vivarais ★★★
Moderate

1 place du Dr-Gailleton. ☎ *(78)37-85-15.*

Credit Cards: *All Major.* Closed: *Sun.*

This bouchon (bistro) is favored by well-heeled members of Lyon's business community, who can expect unstinting quality at reasonable prices. Robert Duffaud, the chef, worked for years with Alain Chapel, and he believes in procuring the freshest ingredients possible from the best suppliers in town. You can taste a wide sampling of his skill in the FR100 fixed-price menu, which often includes a local sausage served with Le Puy lentils.

Leon de Lyon   ★★★★

Expensive to Very Expensive

1 rue Pleney. ☎ *(78)28-11-33.*

Metro Stop: *Hotel-de-Ville.*

Credit Cards: *V, MC, A, E.* Closed: *Sun.*

Second only to Paul Bocuse in stature, chef Jean-Paul Lacombe may truly be the culinary lion of Lyon, now that the former is frequently absent. An inventive artisan, Lacombe takes humble Lyonnnaise favorites like pigs' feet and stuffs the meat into a potato, together with foie gras, truffles and champignon mushrooms. His dining room is tasteful and comfortable, with leather chairs and pretty stained-glass windows. The service is self-assured, and the reception is welcoming. Other top-class establishments are **Nandron**, *26 quai J.- Moulin* ☎ (78-42-10-26), popular with wealthy businesspeople; sublime quenelles de brochet with sauce Nantua, quail eggs en cocotte with truffles, Bresse chicken grandmere; open daily, except Sat. from noon–2 p.m. and 7:30–10 p.m. Closed July 24–Aug. 23, all cards, reservations recommended. Metro: Cordelier. **Pierre Orsi**, *3 pl. Kleber* ☎ (78-89-57-68), is the perfect place for a birthday, anniversary or any sentimental occasion. The chef makes everyone feel welcome, and the waitresses in long floral-printed dresses take their jobs very seriously. Turn-of-the-century decor; specialties include Bresse pigeon with garlic, and wild mushrooms and lobster in puff pastry. Open daily, except Sun. evening; 12:15 a.m.–1:30 p.m. and 8 p.m.–9:30 p.m., closed Aug. 10-20. AE, MC, V, reservations required. Metro: Place Kleber.

Marche du Quai St-Antoine
Inexpensive

quai St-Antoine.

Metro Stop: *Hotel de Ville.* Closed: *Mon.*

Fill a picnic basket with cheese, sausages, fruit and veggies from this daily farmer's market facing the Rhone River. Just north of the city center, the Parc de la Tete d'Or is so big (300 acres) that there's more than enough space to enjoy your meal in relative peace and quiet.

Collonges-au-Mont d'Or

Paul Bocuse ★★★★★
Very Expensive

50 quai de la Plage. ☎ *(72)27-85-85.*

Credit Cards: *All Major.*

This world-famous establishment is located in a sprawling converted house on the banks of the Saone River, a 15-minute car trip from Lyon. Paul Bocuse has long been known as the culinary lion of the region, but because of many other business ventures, he is often out of the country, leaving the restaurant to be run by his long time associates, Roger Jaloux and Christian Bouvarel. This disturbs many critics, who claim these absences have led to indifferent service and amateurishly prepared dishes. Be that as it may, it has not been stripped of its three-star Michelin rating, nor does it lack support from fans (you have to book way ahead of time). His classic creations are still extremely popular, like Bresse chicken served in a pig's bladder or truffle soup under a puff-pastry beret.

Courchevel 1850

Chabichou ★★★
Moderate

quartier Les Chenus. ☎ *(79)08-00-55.*

Credit Cards: *V, MC, DC, A, E.*

Cuisine of the Savoie region is served either on the terrace or in the dining room with big picture windows and a glass roof; wherever you dine, the views are amazing, especially in winter.

La Chalet de Pierres
Inexpensive to Moderate

au Jardin Alpin. ☎ *(79)08-18-61.*

Credit Cards: *V, MC, E.*

Inexpensive for the area, and highly popular with the pre- and apres-ski crowd, who can swish in directly from the Verdon ski slope outside. Good protein-rich meat dishes are served to get the blood going (steaks, chicken) as well as daily specials, and there's a dessert bar. Less expensive is the **Bel Air 1650**, at the top of the Montriond lift ☎ (79-08-00-93), with hearty set meals.

Roanne

Troisgros ★★★★★
Expensive

place de la Gare. ☎ *(77)71-66-97.*

Credit Cards: *All Major.* Closed: *Wed.*

The "trois" in Troisgros is practically just an "un" now, with Michel, son of Pierre (brother of the deceased Jean) running the kitchen. Along with foie gras with Breton lobster and pigeon with zucchini chutney on the usual menu are seasonal "events" like Michel's "Entre-Deux" lasagne of truffles (summer only) on a bed of baby peas.

What to Do
Historical Sites

Theatres Gallo-Romains ★★★★
17 rue Cleberg. ☎ *78.25.94.68.*

Still in use today for everything from rock to opera, these dual amphitheaters are the last vestiges of the great Roman city of Lugdunum (43 BC). Both in remarkable repair, the larger Grand Theatre is the oldest of its kind in France. Below the theaters is an excellent archaeological museum, the Musee Gallo-Romain, showcasing an Aladdin's cave of ancient money, jewelry, mosaics, weapons and other essentials of Roman living. Admission: inexpensive, varies.

Museums and Exhibits

Musee Historique des Tissus ★★★
34 rue de la Charite. ☎ *78.37.15.05.*

🕐 *10 a.m.–5:30 p.m.*

Special Hours: *Free on Wednesday*

Yes, tissues. After a visit here you'll learn everything there is to know about why Lyon was once the center of the silk industry. The dazzling display of antique and contemporary embroideries and tapestries will make you want to go out and buy a loom and start spinning. The Musee Lyonnais des Arts Decoratifs next door is a worthy complement to its fabulous neighbor. Both museums are included on one ticket and share the same hours.

Musee des Beaux Arts ★★★★
Palais St-Pierre, 20 place des Terreaux. ☎ *78.28.07.66.*

🕐 *10:30 a.m.–6 p.m.*

Lyon's fine art museum is a mini-Louvre, and much more accessible. Located in a former convent where nuns taught noble schoolgirls in the 17th century, the Beaux Arts features an impressive collection of Egyptian and Near Eastern antiquities on its ground floor. There's a multi-period assemblage of paintings, drawings and sketches on the first and second floors. Objets d'art and sculpture round out the collection, including some important Rodin pieces in the courtyard. At the time of this writing, some exhibits may be closed due to renovation. The Musee d'Art Contemporain, which once shared space with the Beaux Arts, has moved from the Palais to quai Charles de Gaulle, near the Jardin Tete d'Or. Admission: moderate.

Vienne
Historical Sites

Temple d'Auguste et Livie ★★★
place du Palais.

Not far from Lyon (about 20 minutes) is this Rhone-side wine and gastronomic center with ancient sites that rival its neighbor to the south. Strategically placed in the center of town is this graceful temple, built in 25 BC (the Romans conquered the city in the 1st century BC) with well- preserved Corinthian columns. Another temple, dedicated to the goddess Cybelle, lies in ruins nearby, located off the place de Miremont. A working amphitheater, the **Theatre Romain**, based at the foot of Mont Pipet, off rue de Cirque, is used today for rock concerts and the Jazz a Vienne festival, which takes place in the first two weeks of July. The theatre seats about 8000 people; when it was first built, over 13,000 gladiatorial spectators were accommodated. Admission: varies.

Megève

Megève is a sunny ski center, just a few miles from the more challenging slopes of Chamonix. The site of the renowned **Ski School**, this charming and cosmopolitan resort also offers rock climbing, tennis and horseback riding, as well as nightclubs, dancing, discos and a casino.

Where to Stay
Inns

Chalet du Mont d'Arbois   ★★★
http://www.chalet-montarbois.com/

Expensive

route du Mont-d'Arbois. Located 70 km southeast of Geneva; near Calvaire, at the bottom of a meadow.

☎ *(50)21-25-03.*

Credit Cards: *All Major.*

Two words to describe this Rothschild-family chalet—rustic and luxurious. Built in 1928, Nadine de Rothschild designed the interior and runs the entire show. Overlooking Megeve, the chalet offers fine views from the 20 well-appointed rooms that are furnished with bleached pine, antiques, comforters, TV, radio, telephone, bath and some with balcony. The public rooms reflect the rustic side of the chalet, with exposed beam ceilings, fireplaces and antiques. The house restaurant serves the best gourmet meals in town, and the wine list features some bottles from the Rothschilds' vineyards in Bordeaux. The accommodations, service and food make it worthy of its Relais and Chateaux status.

Where to Eat

Les Fermes de Marie

Moderate to Expensive

Chemin de Riante-Colline. ☎ *(50)93-03-10.*

Credit Cards: *V, MC, A, E.*

This farmhouse restaurant-hotel is one of Megeve's top spots. The cuisine is hearty, designed to be fuel for the energetic skiing that takes place here. A full range of fish and meat dishes is offered, including frogs' legs with garlic sauce. Great desserts, the kind that bring back childhood memories, can be worked off in the hotel spa.

Michel Gaudin ★★★

Moderate

Carrefour d'Arly.

Credit Cards: *V, MC, E.* Closed: *Tues.*

This simple restaurant with a rough-hewn atmosphere serves some of the best regional cooking in the area, and at reasonable prices.

GERMANY

Germany is an excellent introduction to Europe for the first-time traveler. English is widely spoken, the country is clean and functional, and the tourism infrastructure is well established. The Germans take their tourism seriously, and, with 80 million eager German tourists, you can imagine the summertime crowds. Despite the setbacks the Germans have faced in two wars, they have meticulously restored their once-bombed historic areas and have replanted forests. The smaller villages still retain their quaintness and scenic treasures, if not with a little overbuilding of tourist facilities. The downside is that Germany can seem a little too modern, too efficient, too expensive and just too Teutonic after a couple of weeks. You may long for a little chaos and serendipity. The solution is to plan your trip to give you days in the city and evenings in some of the older, more remote towns. For those of you who are driving, tourism in Germany can even be broken into *ruts* (or roads). Keep in mind that you will be amongst rows of shiny tourist buses and crowds of eager fellow-travelers.

The Romantic Road

This is the most scenic southern route from the mountainous border near **Garmisch Partenkirchen** to the forests of **Würzburg**. The walled towns of **Rothenburg ob der Tauber**, **Dinkelsbül** and **Nördlingen** are highlights.

The Rhine

Whether by land or water, the Rhine is Germany's number-one tourist drive. From **Cologne** (the cathedral and shopping), winding down through the **Koblenz** (where you turn right to tour the less crowded Mosel river), past the touristy wine center of **Ruedeshiem** (have lunch at the Hotel Krone in **Assmannshausen** instead), go up into the hills to seek out little-known vintages and finally to **Wiesbaden** and then **Worms**.

The Black Forest

Tucked away in the southwest, start in **Baden-Baden** and head south to the sources of the **Danube** spas and breathtaking scenery. You may feel like bringing home a pair of *lederhosen* (leather shorts).

BERLIN

1 Charlottenburg
2 Castle

The Alpine Road

Just below **Munich** is Germany's winter-sports heaven. **Garmisch-Partenkirchen** is your starting point, with visits to the painted alpine village of **Mittenwald** (Emperor Ludwig's masterpiece of fantasy) and **Neuschwanstein Castle** and ending up in Hitler's favorite alpine getaway in **Berchtesgaden**.

The Baltic Road

Flat, cold, blustery and gray most of the year, the **Baltic** road areas are favorite holiday destinations of the sun-starved Germans from Hamburg and Lübeck. During the off season, you will find the solitude of the areas refreshing.

The Fairy-Tale Road

If you're heading south from **Bremen** to **Frankfurt,** you may want to take a little fantasy tour. For those who grew up on the tales of the brothers Grimm, **Bremen** is remembered for its fabled musicians and Hamelin as the home of the Pied Piper. Even the dark forests of **Reinhardswald** may have been the setting for *Hansel and Gretel*. **Sababurg castle**, north of **Kassel**, is supposedly the inspiration for the castle in *Sleeping Beauty*.

Thüringia Road

This popular route takes you north from **Mannheim** through the historic cities of **Anspach, Nürnberg, Bamberg** and **Coburg** and ending up in **Wiemar** below the cool forests of **Thüringer Wald.**

Keep in mind that transportation in Germany is superlative. The main roads are fast; even the smallest are well-paved and marked. The trains leave the station as the second hand hits the top of the clock's dial. You can choose clean, professional taxis, efficient railways, air, ferries or the legendary high-speed autobahn. There is even a network of intelligently designed hiking trails for the athletic. Germans like to follow rules and will expect you to do so as well, whether driving (slower cars stay to the right), walking (no jay walking), waiting in line (no pushing or cutting in) or making reservations (you book, you pay).

You don't have to like beer and tubas to enjoy Germany. Many make pilgrimages to visit the manufacturers of their favorite collectibles. Famous companies from Mercedes to Leica have tours and museums.

Highlights of travel in Germany include visiting castles and old villages, hiking, the Rhine, beer drinking, wine tasting and hearty food. On the downside, Germany is expensive, somewhat regimented and strangely lacking in other cultural influences. Efficient, dependable, and consistent, Germany is an excellent starting and ending point for a European tour.

Sightseeing

The Germans are well-traveled people, both in and out of their country. They zip along in polished space-age buses, each day split into microseconds of cultural enlightenment. Needless to say, during the summer, this enthusiasm for hitting the road can make the more scenic areas of Germany look like the parking lot of the Super Bowl. Don't limit yourself to motorized transportation. Germany is one of the best countries in the world for plain old hiking.

Historic Structures

Bavarian castles, particularly **Neuschwanstein**, **Herrenchiemsee**, **Linderhof** and the **Residence Palace at Würzburg**. (Check the German Federal Railways about combined rail-bus tours during weekends in summer.) From Munich, there's an easy low-cost excursion to the **Cloister of Andechs**—first by subway to *Herrsching am Ammersee*, then from the exit by bus to your destination. It's a Baroque joy!

Churches and **cathedrals** are eternal attractions. The granddaddies are at **Ulm**, **Würzburg**, **Munich**, **Freiburg**, **Mainz**, **Worms**, **Speyer**, **Cologne**, **Bremen**, **Marburg**, **Limburg**, **Regensburg**, **Treves** and **Aachen**. Try to include the **Neckar Valley** and the university town of **Heidelberg**, as well as **the Hag** development and "Bottcherstrasse" in **Bremen**.

The **medieval castles** along the **Moselle** route are especially beautiful whether you are driving or loafing aboard one of the tiny steamers. The **Rhine**, **Danube**, **Ahr**, **Lahn**, **Main** and **Weser** are also studded with ancient fortresses.

If you are pressed for time, try one of the numerous **bus tours** that cover many of the nation's most scenic regions such as Garmisch-Partenkirchen, Mittenwald, Bad Tolz, Tubingen,

Oberammergau, Rosenheim, Baden-Baden and many forested, lake and alpine climes. They offer wonderfully low rates, modern equipment and magnificent scenery. The **"Romantic Road"** tours between Wurzburg and Fussen in the Allgau Alps (summer only) and the **"Castle Road"** tours from Mannheim via Heidelberg and Rothenberg to Nürnberg are outstanding too. These tours stuff more into one day than most postdoctorate courses in Teutonic culture.

The **motorboat rides** on the Neckar between Heidelberg and Neckarsteinach, on the Moselle between Coblenz and Cochem, or between Trier (summer only) and other points and on the Danube between Passau and Linz. Take a river-ride on a *platten* (flat-bottom barge) on the Salzach, an Inn tributary, or float on a raft down the Isar.

Bayerischer Wald is a 30,000-acre national park nestling along the Czech border near Regen. This first legally designated wilderness in Germany abounds with wolf, lynx, otter, red deer, bear, beaver, alpine marmot and two rare species of owl, Ural and pygmy. Some captive fauna are available for lazy shutterbugs.

Son ét Lumière ("Sound and Light") or similar spectacles are available at some historic sites. One outstanding example is at **Schloss Herrenchiemsee**, a copy of Versailles Palace on an island in the **Chiemsee**, about 46 miles down the fast autobahn from Munich. The castle is fully furnished with its original treasures and illuminated by more than 4000 wax candles. Chamber music is played, the pools and gardens are on show, but the pornographic pictures of Mad King Louis (Ludwig II of Bavaria, whose eccentricities were taken for madness by locals) are not. Shows are held every Saturday evening from May to September; book in advance at American Express in Munich. Arrive before 5:30 p.m., after which the palace tours end for the day; no photography permitted.

On a completely different note is the museum in the crematory of **Dachau** concentration camp, a 45-minute subway and bus ride from Munich, where at least 30,000 human beings were cremated. Surviving inmates representing 21 nations established this monument to atrocity. Documents, orders and photographs relating to the torture and extermination of prisoners are displayed.

Festivals

Keep in mind that Germans like to party as hard as they like to work. The colorful, boisterous pre-Lenten festivals called *Karneval* are held in **Cologne** and **Mainz**. The **Christmas markets** found in every major town and village are a treat.

There are the **Richard Wagner Festival** at Bayreuth during July and August, the **Munich Opera Festival** during the same period, plus concerts by the Berlin Philharmonic Orchestra the year round. More folk festivals, home festivals, jubilees, fairs, religious events, expositions, congresses and conventions are held throughout Germany than anyone can attend. Ask the **German National Tourist Association** or your nearest **German National Tourist Office** (New York, Los Angeles, Montreal and Toronto) for their excellent programs of these topical events. For popular events, purchase tickets ahead.

Weather forecasts, road conditions and information on Germany and its people are broadcast in English and seven other languages during the tourist season over the South German Radio Station in Stuttgart. Reports are featured daily from 10:00 a.m.-10:45 a.m.

Hobbyists, efficiency experts and industrial spies will be especially interested in knowing that Germany's **"Open House"** program flings wide the doors of hundreds of the nation's factories and workshops. The German National Tourist Information Office in New York or Toronto will provide a long list of the names and addresses of these hospitable companies or ateliers.

Transportation

Airlines

Lufthansa (http://www.lufthansa.com/index_en.html) is a sound carrier over the Atlantic, offering above-average attention to the business traveler and predictably Teutonic cuisine. Frankfurt Airport links into the intercity rail network with frequent departures to all European destinations. German airports have excellent connections, as well as plenty of luggage carts, short walks to train stations and range of stores and services.

Trains

The German Federal Railways system surpasses almost any other rail system in Europe today. There's a money-saving German Rail Pass (Flexipass) for unlimited travel all over united Germany; it is valid for one month and comes in five-, 10-, or 15-day (nonconsecu-

tive) packages that are very convenient. They can be reached at
http://www.alleuroperail.com/germany-eurail.htm. (Passes
also are valid for buses along the **Romantic Road**, the **Castle Road**,
or on the **Rhine** for day trips. Plus you receive free admission to the
Museum of Transport in Nuremburg.) Youth Pass are available as
well. All can be purchased via airlines, which can incorporate the fare
into the overall ticketing. Some plans include a rental car or even a
bike if you want to explore beyond the national trackage. All intercity services carry first *and* second class; what's even better is that
they now run every hour in a similar fashion to subway passage.
Networks link 40 cities on rapid transport to the major international gateway at Frankfurt Airport. The Hamburg-Munich route has 25
new supertrains, which run up to 165 m.p.h.; this is only phase one
of a general modernization program. Trains are punctual, clean and
comfortable and feature nonsmoking sections similar to those on
Lufthansa airliners. DB (for *Deutsche Bundesbahn*) sleepers offer
adjustable air conditioning, broad beds with foam-rubber mattress-
es, quilts, folding walls, electric razor outlets, shower-baths and
many other innovations; light-bite rolling "bistros" and DB diners
are efficient and reasonably priced. Intercity electric locomotives can
average 135 m.p.h. on certain runs. The color scheme for DB is red
for locomotives, red and gray for intercity coaches, blue and gray for
express coaches and green and gray for local haulage. The *Komet* is
an express sleeper covering the dreamlands between Hamburg and
Basel; in season some cars will give you a wake-up call in Chur or
Brig (East and West Switzerland, respectively). "Bunk cars"
(*Liegewagen*) are available to budgeteers on many intra-German and
some international night runs. They're sort of "Economy
Pullmans," with no curtains and three decks of six bunks per compartment—passengers sleep (if they can) in their clothes. These
bunk cars are far, far better than sitting up. You also can enjoy
overnight baggage delivery to your destination, so ask as you check
in.

Almost all German railroad tracks have undergone the so-called
"seamless-welding process"; the rhythmic clickety-clack of the
wheels is a nostalgic memory nearly everywhere. On medium-short
hauls, the better trains are now beating the airliners' time—airport-
to-city coverage considered. All fast intercity trains offer coin telephone service en route.

To minimize luggage problems, ship heavy pieces by registering
them through to your destination. As all of Germany offers this service, you can forward your possessions direct to your lodgings; it

costs only a little more than the railway shipping charge.

Buses

Most long-haul buses, particularly in sightseeing districts, are modern and comfortable. Many offer adjustable chairs, nonsmoking zones, a public-address system, lavatories, radio loudspeakers and huge windows for maximum visibility. The German Federal Railways runs the show, so inquire there; private bus tour companies are another matter.

Tour Services

ADAC and AvD, the two most important German automobile clubs, offer tour information in most cities. In the ports of Hamburg and Bremerhaven and at a number of key frontier crossings, the auto clubs and the German Tourist Association have set up special no-charge bureaus to help foreign visitors plan their trips. There's also a free motorists' aid service for outlanders stranded on the auto-bahns. Just flag down a red or yellow patrol car, or get to one of the telephones set seven miles apart throughout the network. In the Alps, the ADAC rents snow chains to winter visitors; your small deposit is refunded when you return them.

Roads

You drive on the right side of the road. Signs are posted in kilo-meters. On the autobahn, government-recommended speed limits are 139 khp (80 m.p.h.), although no formal top limit exists. Most non-German drivers are more comfortable using the slower lane when on the autobahn. Seat belts must be worn at all times by passengers in both the front and back seats.

Car Rentals

All the multinationals are everywhere, of course, but you might try **Sixt-Budget** (http://www.e-sixt.com/), which offers mod-est-to-luxury cars—even sports versions—at rates that are guaranteed on a dollar basis. Headquarters: Dr. Carl von Linde Strasse, 8023 Munich-Pullach; (089) 79107-1.

Food

Germans like their food filling, plentiful and inexpensive. There is little pretension in German cooking. The Germans have found ways to use about every part of the porker from *Schnitzel* (pork) to *Eisbein* (pig trotters) and even *Schweinhaxe* (pig knuckles). Germans also like venison (frequently imported from New Zealand), clear soups with dumplings, *Sauerkraut* (pickled shredded cabbage) and pickled fish.

Americans take quickly to German breakfasts, usually consisting of a boiled egg, sliced cold meats, cheeses, fresh breads and strong coffee. Hearty and filling, they will take you right through lunch.

In taverns, cafés and beer halls or wine gardens—not deluxe establishments—national custom dictates that tables be shared by two or more parties if the place is crowded. Quite often you might find yourself sitting with strangers—fortunately, most of the time in a courteous but remote "please pass the salt" relationship, rather than one of compulsory small talk.

Although you can find 1500 types of *wurst* (sausage) and 300 types of bread, German cooking can be light, delicate and highly inventive. If in doubt about a good place to eat in a strange town, head for the nearest *Ratskeller*. The word means "council cellar," and it's the place (usually the cellar of the Town Hall) where, in the Middle Ages, municipal officials received guests. There is one in most communities; part of the Ratskeller is known as the *Ratstrinkstube* (council drinking room). The tradition of quality is stoutly upheld in most of these.

Drinks

Wine

Most connoisseurs (if they weren't born in Burgundy, Bordeaux, or Champagne) agree that Germany makes the finest white wines of the world. With typically Teutonic attention to detail, every bottle character bears its full pedigree on the label—type, year, district, grower, shipper and often even the condition of the grape at the picking. There are 11 wine-growing regions in Germany: Ahr, Mosel-Saar-Ruwer, Mittelrhein, Rheingau, Nahe, Rheinhessen, Rheinpfalz, Hessische Bergstrasse, Franken, Wurttemberg and Baden. And there are six (ascending) tiers of ripeness: *Kabinett, Spatlese, Auslese, Beerenauslese, Eiswein* and, finally, the princely

Trockenbeerenauslese. "Riesling" is a generic term for any wine of the Riesling grape, as opposed to the Sylvan grape. Moselle, Rhine, Ahr, Franconia, Palatinate and others are named for their specific districts or valleys, although technically they could be called Rieslings. Steinwein is harsh and rough; most visitors prefer others. Hock, derived from "Hochheimer," is erroneously used by many British drinkers as a blanket appellation for all Rhines and similar types; the vineyards for this are actually on the north bank of the Main.

German "champagne," called *Sekt*, is frequently sparkling Rhine or Moselle wine. Remarkable strides have been made in recent years to improve its quality. Today selected labels of the *brut* types have an urbane and noble character. Mumm Dry (no relative of the French brand of the same name) is an excellent candidate for your white; Henkell Rose is a delightful pink nectar. (The Henkell cellars in Wiesbaden produce much of their *Sekt* from French wines, incidentally. This house is famous and excellent.) Many other so-called German "champagnes" are still cloyingly sweet, less bubbly than their French originals and repulsive to the knowledgeable international palate.

Beer

You can drink your way through Germany. If you drank a different beer every day, you'd have to stay there more than 13 years and it would set you back about $6250. The 5000 different brews average about $1.25 per large mug. There are Helles or Export or simply Ex (light), Pilsner or Pils (light in color but stronger), Dunkles (dark), Weisse (extra light), served in Bavaria chiefly but available elsewhere, and the different Berliner Weisse (Berlin wheat-malt specialty, which is light and lemony). The Bockbier season is January to March; this dark, rich beer is one of the most delicious of all. The best-known brews are those of Munich, Frankfurt, Dortmund, Donaueschingen (Fuerstenberg), Nurnberg (Siechen and Tucher), Wurzburg and Kulmbach. (The last is famous for being frozen into an iceblock that packs a nine percent alcoholic punch after the solidification!) As a curiosity, you might like to try a stein of Weihenstephan. This brewery, in Freising, has been running continuously for almost a thousand years; the yeast in your potion first saw the light of day in the 11th century.

Telephone

Access code to USA: 001. To phone Germany: 49; time difference (Eastern Daylight) plus 6 hours.

CURRENCY USED: Euros.

Tipping

In all German hotels there is an automatic service charge of 10 to 15 percent of the price of the room. Now it is usually lumped into your overall bill rather than itemized separately. For meal service in hotels and restaurants the service bite is 10 to 15 percent; it need not be noted on the overall billing. For drinks most anywhere a separate tax (*Getrankesteuer*) is levied, but it does not often appear on your tab; generally this is 10 percent, but in Munich and Stuttgart it is 20 percent. You're still expected to shell out something for the bartender, however.

Lodging

German hotels are probably the most restful for travelers. They're not as tiny and spartan as Scandinavian accommodations and cleaner and more modern than southern facilities. Business hotels are very expensive, but some of the best values in accommodations can be found in the suburbs. Just make sure you know the closest streetcar or cross street after a late night of carousing. The tourist offices in large towns will help you find a room within your price range, but don't be surprised if you find everything booked up during peak season. Out in the country, there is a wide range of alpine lodges, homestays, resorts and spas.

For More Information

German National Tourist Office

http://www.germany-tourism.de/

122 East 42nd St., New York, NY 10168, ☎ *(212) 661-7200.*

11766 Wilshire Blvd., Suite 1750, Los Angeles, CA 90025,

☎ *(310) 575-9799.*

Bavaria

Berchtesgaden

Though the valley drive to arrive here is one of the most breath-taking routes anywhere in Europe, travelers usually pause only briefly. Of course, you'll want to visit Hitler's **Eagle's Nest** atop the looming Mount Kehlstein. The Nazi Chief's alpine redoubt at near-by *Obersalzberg* (on a slope above Berchtesgaden) has been totally demolished in a postwar effort to remove all memory of the *Fuhrer*.

Where to Stay

Hotels and Resorts

Hotel Fischer ★

Budget

Konigsseerstrasse 51.

☎ *(08652) 95-50.*

Credit Cards: *MC.*

Each of the 54 bedrooms in this fairly new hotel is decorated in a different regional theme. Room rates include a buffet breakfast. The hotel is within walking distance of the train station. There is a restaurant, bar and solarium. Good, basic accomodations.

Hotel Watzmann

Moderate

Franziskanerplatz 2. Just opposite the chiming church in the old town

☎ *(08652) 20-55.*

Credit Cards: *V, MC, DC, A.*

This Bavarian landmark was a favorite of American servicemen, who enjoyed the warm hospitality of the English-speaking Piscantor family, not to mention the two dining rooms and large outdoor terrace. The guest rooms were recently refurbished, but still only 17 of the 38 rooms have private baths. The low-end rates are rooms without shower, and the prices are a little higher in the summer. All of the rooms, however, are clean and comfortable; family suites also are available. No amenities besides the eating areas. Rooms don't come with TV or phone.

Vier Jahreszeiten

http://www.hotel-vier-jahreszeiten.de/

Budget to Moderate

Maximilianstrasse 20.

☎ *(08652) 50-26.*

Credit Cards: *V, MC, DC, A.*

A quaint, family-run establishment that's been redone over the years to provide guests with a pleasant stay in Bavaria. Some of the new guest rooms are more like suites, complete with sitting areas and balconies. Some of the 59 rooms have TVs. Rates include a buffet breakfast. The restaurant is excellent; there is a terrace for outside dining.

Inns

Geiger

Moderate to Expensive

Berchtesgadenstrasse 11.

☎ *(08652) 96-53.*

Credit Cards: *V.*

This charming Bavarian chalet has been a favorite of tourists for more than a century. While there is all the authentic atmosphere of country living, there are also all the amenities of a fine city hotel, plus the sweeping vistas of the Alps. All 50 rooms have mountain views. Rates, which include continental breakfast, depend on whether there is a balcony and the bathroom arrangements. All the rooms have central heating and a phone. There are dining rooms, a massage salon, solarium and game room.

What to Do

Museums and Exhibits

Kongliches Schloss Berchtesgaden

Schlossplatz 2. 2085.

🕐 *10 a.m.-1 p.m.-2 p.m.-5 p.m.*

Special Hours: *Oct.-Easter 10 a.m.-5 p.m., closed Sun.*

When the abbey that housed the monks who founded Berchtesgaden was secularized in 1809, it became a residence of the ruling family of Bavaria. When they were overthrown, it was turned into a museum. Ironically, one of the prime movers behind the present-day museum was Crown Prince Rupert of Bavaria, who helped assemble the collection of sacred art, including works by the woodcarver Tillman Riemenschneider, Nymphenburg porcelain from the royal collection, and decorative Italian furniture. Don't miss the medieval cloisters and dormitory from the former abbey. Admission: inexpensive.

Garmisch-Partenkirchen

Garmisch-Partenkirchen is an Alpine resort with strong tourist appeal and backup facilities sprouting everywhere—so much so, in fact, that a lot of its charm is swiftly vanishing. The U.S. military colony is so ingrained into this locality that the rich Teutonic flavor of yore is almost lost. It offers a magnificent panorama of the German and Austrian Alps; bracing climate; restyled casino; winter sports galore, with ski runs and lifts, bobsledding, cable cars, a glass-lined public swimming pool and much more. Take the train for a short roll out to Eibsee, then whistle up the 12-minute cable ride to the 9730-foot crown of Zugspitze Mountain; it's an eyeful you'll never forget.

Where to Stay

Hotels and Resorts

Alpenhotel Waxenstein   ★★★

http://www.waxenstein.de/

Moderate

☎ *(08821) 80-01.*

An Alp's-worth of high-fashion hotel baubles in a low-profile, stucco-and-wood chalet-style building. Exquisite garden and pool area, inviting public rooms. The bedchambers are deluxe, and the cuisine is superior.

Clausing's Posthotel

http://www.clausings-posthotel.de/

Moderate

Marienplatz 12.

☎ *(08821) 70-90.*

Credit Cards: *V, MC, DC, A.*

Clausing's Posthotel in the Garmisch section attracts a chiefly European clientele. Those looking for that Old World atmosphere will most likely find it here. The former postal station, which has been in the Clausing family for five generations, is on a noisy main street, not far from boutiques or ski facilities. Zugspritze looms right before the front guest rooms, but those in the back can afford a quieter night's rest. The 42 rooms all come with bath or shower, central heating, TV and radio.

Grand Hotel Sonnenbichl

http://sonnenbichl.de/

Moderate

Burgstrasse 97. Take Route 23 toward Oberammergau

☎ *(08821) 70-20.*

Credit Cards: *V, MC, DC, A.*

This hotel has much to offer those who don't mind being somewhat out of the town center. There are 93 rooms, three restaurants, a bar, a solarium, whirlpool, sun terrace, massage rooms and a beauty farm. Rates include a continental breakfast. Other conveniences are room service, laundry and dry cleaning.

Reindl's Partenkirchner Hof

http://www.reindls.de/

Budget to Moderate

Bahnhofstrasse 15.

☎ *(08821) 58-02-5.*

Credit Cards: *V, MC, DC, A.*

Rich in Alpine personality, Reindl's boasts one of the best locations in the valley for the medium budget. The 65 rooms, which come with TV and phone, have been configured so each has a view of the mountains and town.

Inns

Gasthof Fraundorfer ★★

Budget to Moderate

Ludwigstrasse 34.

Public Transportation: *Bus 1.* Metro Stop: *Eibsee.*

☎ *(08821) 21-76.*

Credit Cards: *V, MC, A.*

The Fraundorfer family has been running this inn since 1820, and the pride shows. Located on the main thoroughfare in the historic section of town, its guests will find plenty of shops and restaurants nearby, but the best meal may be the home-cooked country-style spread in the Fraundorfer dining room. In addition to the food, there are nightly dances (except Tuesdays) and special nights of Bavarian entertainment that includes yodeling. All 33 rooms have central heating, phone and TV. Rates include a buffet breakfast.

What to Do

Nightlife

If gambling is your thing, try **Spielbank Garmisch-Partenkirchen** at *Am Kurpark 10* where you can play roulette, baccarat, or black jack. Slot machines are also enjoying a vogue. Like most ski resorts, the town has an active disco scene which changes from year to year.

Parks and Gardens

Garmisch-Partenkirchen

Garmisch-Partenkirchen earned its 15 minutes of fame in 1936, when it played host to the Winter Olympics. Today, its Ski Stadium, a relic of the Olympics, is a venue for the World Cup Ski Jump held every New Year's day. But the Zugspitze mountain is far and away the most popular attraction in Garmish-Partenkirchen. Those who want to go easy on their feet can make the ascent up Germany's highest peak by cable car or by cog railway. The cog railway leaves from the town railway station; the cable car leaves from Eibsee, just a short distance out of town on the road towards Austria. If you wish, you can take the cable car one way and the cog railway the other, all on the same ticket. But the trek on foot may be worth the sweat; 150 marked trails wind through beautiful mountain lakes and waterfalls, with rare species of rock flowers peppering the path along the way. The **Philosophers' Way** (Philosphenweg) starts behind St. Anthony's Church and offers unsurpassed views of the surrounding countryside and the Zugspitze. Numerous ski trails and lifts make this a mecca for skiers from all over the world. But make sure to bring a map and check the local weather conditions. If it does get stormy, or you're just flat-out pooped, one-way tickets are available.

Sports and Recreation

Food
After a hard day skiing or hiking, people need good, filling food, and the restaurants in Garmisch are pleased to oblige. **Riendli's Restaurant** *(Bahnhofstrasse 15)* serves lunch and dinner daily. Their chef has trained in the kitchens of some of the finest hotels and takes advantage of the best seasonal foods available. Look for sauces with local mushrooms as an ingredient. The wine list also includes some excellent French wines. **Flösserstuben** *(Schmiedstrasse 2)* has a few Balkan items on its menu in addition to local specialties, while **Restaurant-Cafe Flösserstuben** *(Frickenstrasse 2)* likes to serve game and cheeses made from the milk of the cows that graze in the nearby meadows.

Munich

The Bavarian capital is the southern apex of industry, commerce and at least one foreign visitor for every one of the 2.3 million permanent population. Its modern airport, 15 miles northeast of town (connected with a rapid rail link), handles 12 million travelers a year. The typical Bavarian is a hardy, fun-loving host; the city's booklet (Munchen) contains six full pages of museums for every period and interest. Taxis, buses and a newly expanded subway system can deliver you almost anywhere in and around the town. For up-to-the-minute info, go to **http://www.muenchen-tourist.de/englisch/**

Where to Stay

Hotels and Resorts

Acanthus

http://www.lodging-germany.com/ munchen/acanthus.htm

Budget to Moderate

Blumenstrasse 40.

☎ *(089) 23-18-80.*

Credit Cards: *V, MC, DC, A.*

Retired Lufthansa stewardess Carola Gunther and her husband, Jorg, bought the former Hotel am Sendlinger Tor in 1989, and their personal touch is obvious everywhere. The 36 bedrooms, all upstairs, are divided into two styles, the Rustikana, which has a more contemporary flavor, and the more expensive Alba Rose, which makes heavy use of antiques, wallpaper and English-style fabrics. Located near the gate to the old town, Acanthus also has a 24-hour bar. It doubles in the mornings as a breakfast room, where guests are treated to an impressive buffet that includes home-baked bread.

An Der Oper

http://www.hotel-an-der-oper.de/ inde_eng.html

Moderate

Falkenturmstrasse.

Public Transportation: *Tram 19.*

☎ *(089) 290-0270.*

Credit Cards: *V, MC, DC, A.*

This hotel takes its name from its proximity to the opera, which also affords the visitor convenient sightseeing and shopping. The staff will help guests obtain tickets to the opera. There are 55 large, comfortable rooms, so there's no sensation of mass commercialism. Rates include a continental breakfast.

Bayerischer Hof Palais Montgel

http://www.bayerischerhof.de/

Promenadeplatz.

Public Transportation: *Tram 19.*

☎ *(089) 21-20-0,* FAX: *223-6800.*

Credit Cards: *V, MC, DC, A.*

A mid-city champion that keeps improving with age, the Bayerischer Hof is a prizewinner that garnered the *Prix d'Excellence* for European hostelry. The 440 rooms have been recently refurbished. Dining options include the Garden Restaurant with summer terrace and winter garden, a piano bar and a totally refreshed nightclub. All front units have been lovingly clad in Laura Ashley attire. Other amenities include a **Trader Vic's** restaurant, an 850-capacity festivity hall, a 200-ton, sliding-roofed swimming pool, a health center with adjoining bar and a solarium. The adjoining **Palais Montgelas** is an elegant classic, serving as sort of a Bavarian cousin to the Waldorf Towers. The tariffs there are only slightly more than in the main building, but from private receptionist to golden bathroom taps, everything here is exclusive. In the cellar there's the finest and liveliest nightclub in Bavaria with room for 200.

Excelsior

http://www.excelsior-muenchen.de/

Budget to Moderate

☎ *(089) 55-13-70.*

This hotel near the train terminal is a surprising island of quiet. The spotless units, including penthouse suites, encircle a peaceful courtyard; most of the 113 rooms are cheery, while others very smartly elegant.

Intercity

Budget to Moderate

Bayerstrasse 10.

Public Transportation: *U-Bahn, S-Bahn.* Metro Stop: *Hauptbahnhof.*

☎ *(089) 54-55-60.*

Credit Cards: *V, MC, DC.*

Actually located inside the train station, this hotel continues to win a following for its Old World charm and modern comfort. Don't be thrown by its location. All 203 rooms are soundproof and air conditioned. Immaculate maintenance. Room rates include a buffet breakfast.

Platzl ★

http://www.platzl.de/
Moderate

Platzl 1.

☎ *(089) 23-70-30.*

Credit Cards: *V, MC, DC, A.*

This a perfect base for exploring Old Munich. Right across the street is the Hofbrauhaus, with Marienplatz just a few blocks away, the hotel is also next door to the famed Bavarian folk theater Platzl Buhne. The Platzl's 170 rooms, decorated in rustic Bavarian, are soundproof. Rooms also have phones.

Rafael

http://www.abnet.at/hotel-de/muenchen/bayrischerhof/english/ infos.htm
Moderate to Expensive

Neuturmstrasse 1.

Public Transportation: *Tram 19.*

☎ *(089) 29-09-80.*

Credit Cards: *V, MC, DC, A.*

This relative newcomer appeal to a highly discerning audience of world travelers. Consequently, most of its 74 accommodations are devoted to luxury suites. A traditional building from the late 19th century in the center of historic Munich, the hotel is thoroughly modernized. Check out one of the suites stocked with four phones, color TV with VCR and fax machine. Other conveniences include an in-house butler, concierge, 24-hour room service, laundry, baby sitting, valet parking, foreign-money exchange and boutique.

Inns

Gastehaus Englischer Garten

Budget to Moderate

Liebergesellstrasse 8. On western edge of Englischer Garten, five-minute walk from U- Bahn.

Public Transportation: *U-Bahn 3 or 6.* Metro Stop: *Munchener Freiheit.*

☎ *(089) 39-20-34.*

Credit Cards: *Not Accepted.*

In the suburbs of Schwabing, this ivy-covered 19th-century building, was once a mill but is now one of Munich's most popular lodgings. There are 27 rooms, but half are in a cheaper, but less appealing, annex across the street. Nice personal touches in the decor have been added by Frau Irene Schluter-Hubscher, the owner for the past two decades. Breakfast is served in the hotel's own garden area alongside a stream. Be sure to make reservations far in advance.

Where to Eat

A. Boettner

Moderate to Expensive

Theatinerstrasse 8. ☎ *(089) 22 12 10.*

Public Transportation: *U-Bahn.* Metro Stop: *Marienplatz.*

Credit Cards: *V, MC, DC, A.*

Boettner is a family-run establishment in business since 1901. Its menu has evolved with the times; today it leans towards nouvelle German. They do wonderful things with lobsters and goose liver—but be prepared to pay.

Aubergine

Expensive to Very Expensive

Maxmilliamplatz 5. ☎ *(089) 59 81 71.*

Public Transportation: *Tram 19.*

Credit Cards: *V, MC, DC, A.*

Aubergine is known as much for the personality of its owner/chef Eckart Witzigmann as for its cuisine, which is of the Paul Bocuse school—not surprising since Witzigmann trained in Bocuse's kitchen. In keeping with this tradition, the menu is revealed for the day when the owner returns from the produce market with the best and freshest of the local produce. Witzigmann is particularly creative in using the local wild mushrooms in season and in the creation of sauces of local fruit to complement game.

> ITRAVELBOOK TIP: NO ONE NEED GO HUNGRY IN MUNICH. THERE ARE NUMEROUS SNACK BARS IN THE S-BAHN AND U-BAHN STATIONS, AND SMALL CAFES SELL AN UNENDING SUPPLY OF VARIOUS SOUPS *(SUPPEN)* WITH OR WITHOUT *KNÖDEL* (DUMPLINGS). *LEBERKNODEL* (LIVER DUMPLING) WITH SOUP OR SAUERKRAUT CAN BE LIFESAVING ON A WINTER DAY. BUTCHER'S SHOPS *(METGEREI)* VERGE ON BEING DELI'S IN MUNICH. VERY OFTEN THEY HAVE A SELECTION OF *LEBERKASE*, WHICH IS SIMPLY AN ELEGANT MEATLOAF OR TERRINE. IT CAN BE BOUGHT IN 100 GM. PORTIONS ALONG WITH A ROLL. EACH *METGEREI* HAS ITS HOUSE VERSION OF SWEET MUSTARD *(SENFF)* WHICH IS SPREAD OVER THE *LEBERKASE*. EAT AT THE STANDUP COUNTER.

Haxnbauer

Inexpensive

Munzstrasse 8. ☎ *(089) 22 19 22.*

Public Transportation: *U2, U3, S-Bahn.* Metro Stop: *Marienplatz.*

Credit Cards: *V, MC, DC, A, A.*

Specialties of the house are *Schweinhaxen* (pork hocks), *Kalbshaxen* (veal hocks), and more recently *Truthahaxen* (turkey legs), all spit-roasted to crisp, brown perfection. *Apfelkuchen* for dessert.

Rathskeller Munchen

Inexpensive to Moderate

Marienplatz 8. ☎ *(089) 22 03 13.*

Public Transportation: *U-Bahn.* Metro Stop: *Marienplatz.*

Credit Cards: *V, MC, A.*

It seems as if every *Rathaus* in Germany has a *keller* (basement), and Munich is no exception. Good, well-prepared food (the soup of the day is invariably tasty) and Bavarian music are offered. Lots of dark wood panelling and chairs.

Zum Alten Markt

Moderate

Dreifaltigkeltsplatz 3. *(089) 29 99 95.*

Public Transportation: *Bus 52.*

An affordable Aubergine-type restaurant, the chef makes good use his proximity to the produce market. Traditional dishes such as roast goose and pork loin are cooked with loving care and panache. The decor is inviting, complete with carved ceilings from an old castle. In the summer it's possible to eat outside.

What to Do

City Celebrations

Oktoberfest   ★★★★★

http://www.oktoberfest.de/en/

Surprisingly, the *Oktoberfest*, instead of being a harvest festival, is more like a giant midway with an extraordinary selection of whirling, spinning, vertigo-causing rides. The festival begins in September and runs 16 days until the first Sunday in October. There are activities all over the city, but the main action takes place at the *Theresienwiese*, a huge fairground near the Hauptbahnhof. There is also a surfeit of impossible skill tests (shoot the moving duck and win a stuffed animal). Huge tents are set up, where the serious carousing takes place. Some of the tents feature painted villages on the walls and skies complete with clouds and free-hanging lanterns that double as stars. Seating is at long wooden tables with wall-to-wall camaraderie; if you didn't know your neighbor when you came in, you will when you leave. Outside there are innumerable stalls selling food. Sausages (over half a million sold) and spit-roasted meat are traditional fare, washed down with around six million liters of beer. The drinking-and-driving problem is neatly solved by prohibiting parking around the Theresienwiese. To get there, follow the crowds on foot or take the U-Bahn to Theresienwiese (Lines 4 and 5). Lines 3 and 6 to Goetheplats or Poccistrasse are alternatives when Lines 4 and 5 are too crowded. They drop you close to the southern end of the grounds.

Historical Sites

ITRAVELBOOK FREEBIE

Assamkirche ★★★★

Sendlingerstrasse.

Public Transportation: *U-Bahn and S-Bahn.* Metro Stop: *Marienplatz.*

🕐 *6 a.m.–6:30 p.m.*

Look up to the ceiling and you'll see the life and death of this church's actual namesake depicted in frescos and stucco. But to locals, St. John of Nepomuk, who drowned in the Rhine, is second fiddle to Cosmas Damian Assam, the man who created these frescos, and his brother Egid Quirin Assam, a sculptor and stucco craftsman. Locally referred to as the Assamkirche, this church is one of the Assam brothers' masterpieces. Admission: free.

Frauenkirche (Church of Our Lady) ★★★★★

Frauenplatz 12.

Public Transportation: *U-Bahn and S-Bahn.* Metro Stop: *Marienplatz.*

🕐 *6 a.m.–6:30 p.m.*

Yet another casualty of World War II, this Munich cathedral and its onion-shaped domes has been fully restored after suffering extensive damage from allied bombings fifty years ago. Photographs in the nave show the condition of the cathedral immediately after the bombing. Today, the renovated Frauenkirche is a pleasant mix of the old and the new: Erasmus Grasser's 500-year-old wood carvings representing the Apostles, the Old Testament Prophets and assorted saints sit above modern choir stalls. The exterior of the church is somber red brick that has darkened over the years, while the interior, in contrast, is blazing white. In the north chapel, a stained-glass medallion dating from the late 1300s has been restored to its origi-

nal place. The Bishops of Munich and minor members of the
Wittlesbach family are buried in the Bishops' and Prince's Crypt.
You can also catch an excellent view of the city from the cathedral's
observation deck, accessible by Elevator.

Marienplatz

Named after a 300-foot gilt statue of the Virgin Mary, patron saint
of the cities, standing in the middle of the square, Marienplatz is the
center of life in Munich. At the north side of the square is the **Neues
Rathaus,** built at the end of the 19th century. The Neues Rathaus
is best known for it's **glockenspiel**, which is an attraction in itself.
Three times a day *(11 a.m., noon and 5 p.m.)* an army of enamelled
copper figures perform the *Schaffertanz,* followed by the reenact-
ment of a tournament that celebrated royal weddings in the 15th
century. When it's all over, a mechanical rooster crows. Legend has
it that after World War II an American GI, distressed by the condition of the figures, "liberated" some paint and donated it to the
caretakers of the building. As a reward, he was allowed to ride one
of the horses in the jousting scene, earning wild applause from the
citizens in the square. The Marienplatz is also the scene of the
Cristkindlmarkt (Christmas Market) which sets up at the end of
November and runs until Christmas Eve. Stalls sell almost anything
you can think of that has to do with Christmas, but the fair is especially well-known for its handmade Christmas ornaments and decorations. *Gluhwien* (mulled wine) and *lebkuchen* (gingerbread) are
also good sellers.

Palace (Residenz) and Treasury (Schatzkammer)

Max-Joseph-Platz 3. ☎ *(089) 29 06 71.*

Public Transportation: *U-Bahn.* Metro Stop: *Odeonsplatz.*

🕐 *10 a.m.–4:30 p.m.*

Special Hours: *Closed Mon.*

It is impossible to say anything about Munich without mentioning
the Wittlesbach family, who ruled Bavaria for more than 800 years
until forced to adbicate the throne in 1918. The Residenz was the
principal seat of the family and parts of it date from the late 14th
century. Today, the **Residenz Museum** occupies the southern section of the former palace, and it consists of approximately 100
rooms of art and furniture collected by the royal family. It takes at

least a day to see the entire collection. You can do it on your own, or you can take two tours, one in the morning and one in the afternoon. On the second floor are the so-called (and rightly so) **"rich rooms"**, majestic examples of Rococo carried to the extreme. Also on the upper level is the Wittelsbach collection of Far Eastern porcelain and another of Oriental rugs. Some of the rooms have been restored as they were when the palace was indeed a residence. Take note of the Electorís bedroom with its immense chandelier and ornate bed. The **Schatzkammer** (Treasury) contains the crown jewels of Bavaria and other bibelots of the Wittlesbachs, including the magnificent cross created for Queen Giselle of Hungary in the early 11th century, and the world-renowned statue of St. George Slaying the Dragon (16th Century). The statue is solid gold, but the gold is hardly visible under the encrustation of rubies, diamonds, emeralds and other precious and semiprecious stones. There is an entire room dedicated to the preservation of the jewel-covered articles that the royal family used in their religious devotions— icons, innumerable crucifixes, prayer books, receptacles, altars, and baptismal fonts. The **Altes Residenztheater** is the work of Francois Cuvilliés, a Belgian dwarf who was brought to the court for the amusement of the ruler. Cuvilliés possessed enough talent that he became a military cadet and even was made a member of the *Electorís* personal regiment. There he came to the notice of Max III Joseph, who recognized his artistic talent and paid for his education as an architect. Cuvilliés is responsible for many of the most important Rococo interiors in Munich. Admission: inexpensive.

Museums and Exhibits

Alte Pinakothek

Barer Strasse 27. ☎ *(089) 217 91.*

The Alte Pinakothek is arguably one of the five best museums in the world. Here, you'll enjoy a smorgasbord of fine art spanning the 13th to the 17th centuries. Seems the Wittelsbachs collected lots of anything they found even remotely interesting. For that same reason, the museum is weak in certain areas: if the monarch of the moment or one of his relatives wasn't interested in a work, it was ignored, no matter how fine it may have been.

Antikensammlungen (Museum of Antiquities)

Konigsplatz 1. ☎ *(089) 59 83 59.*

🕐 *10 a.m.–4:30 p.m.*

Special Hours: *Wed. Noon-8:30 p.m.; closed Mon.*

Located next door to each other, the Glypothek and
Antikensammlungen complement each other perfectly. The
Antikensammlungen has its roots in the collection of Greek vases
(more than 600) amassed by King Ludwig I. There is also a fine display of Etruscan art, including bronzes and glass. The collection of
Roman, Etruscan and Greek jewelry is almost contemporary in its
design. The Glyptothek rounds out the survey of surviving Classical
art with its collection of sculpture. The nucleus of the collection is
the body of work obtained by Ludwig I, who had visions of making
Munich into a modern Athens—hence the preponderance of art
from the Hellenistic period and Roman copies of Hellenistic statues.
Admission: varies, inexpensive.

Deutsches Museum

http://www.deutsches-museum.de/

Museuminsel 1. ☎ *(089) 217 91 or 217 94 33.*

Public Transportation: *Tram 18, S-Bahn.* Metro Stop: *Isartor.*

🕐 *9 a.m.–5 p.m.*

Special Hours: *Closes at 1 p.m. 2nd Wed. in Dec.*

This is not a museum to just browse through; its 13 km makes it the
largest museum of technology in the world. Decide in advance what
particular branch of science you want to concentrate on: computer
science, mining, geology, astronomy, physics, etc. The museum is a
wondrous gathering of live demonstrations; historic artifacts—such
as the bench where Hahn and Strassmann split the first atom or the
world's first automobile (an 1886 Benz); hands-on experiments;
walk- through exhibits (check out the gold mine); an exhibition that
answers every question anyone has ever asked about astronomy and
more interesting stuff, pleasant and multilingual staff answer questions. Great for kids. Admission: varies.

Schloss Nymphenburg ★★★★★

http://www.schloesser.bayern.de/ seiten/objekte/mu_ny.htm

Schloss Numphenburg 1. ☎ *(089) 17-908-668.*

Public Transportation: *U-Bahn 1, Tram 12, Bus 41.* Metro Stop: *Rotkreuzplatz, Amalienburgstra.*

🕐 *9 a.m.-12:30 p.m.–1:30 p.m.-5 p.m*

Special Hours: *Oct.-Mar. 10 a.m.-12:30 p.m.; closed Mon.*

In 1662, the Electress Henriette Adelaide gave birth to a son after 10 years of marriage. Her husband showed his gratitude by building her a small country palace west of Munich. The original name for the building was *Castello delle Ninfe.* More than 150 years later, after the architectural ministrations of generations of Wittlesbachs, it emerged as *Schloss Nymphenburg* and had as many eccentricities as the family that owned it. The exterior of the palace is fairly subdued, but inside practically every surface is decorated in some way or another. This is especially evident in the Great Hall, which was used for state dinners and concerts. Smaller rooms contain tapestries and furniture of the period. The Wittlesbach men were great believers in the *droit de seignor,* and the *Schonheitengalerie* (Gallery of Beauties) of Ludwig I commemorates 36 of the most beautiful women of his time. Among the portraits is one of Lola Montez, the Spanish dancer (she was actually English) whose scandalous affair with Ludwig brought about a revolution. **The Marstallmuseum,** housed in the former royal stables, is comprised of the state carriages of the Bavarian royal family. The coronation coach of the Elector Karl Albrecht is a flight of fancy built in Paris in 1740. Every possible surface is adorned with every possible motif from ivy leaves to dolphins, and the panels contain oil paintings showing scenes from Greek myths. Take a look at the royal hunting sleighs—even the runners are decorated. Last but not least are the carriages and sleighs of Ludwig II. His coach looks like something out of a fairy tale, and his sleigh is just as elaborate. Admission: inexpensive.

Nightlife

Hofbrauhaus ★★★★

Am Platzl 9. ☎ *(089) 22 16 76.*

Public Transportation: *U-Bahn and S-Bahn.* Metro Stop: *Marienplatz.*

🕐 *9 a.m.–Midnight*

On an average day at the Hofbrauhaus, approximately 18,000 pints of beer are served within the building's 16th century walls to as many as 4500 beer drinkers. The cavernous *Bierschwemme* on the first floor is the most rowdy, and usually resounds with ompah bands and drinking songs, with obliging dirndl-clad waitresses scurrying about. But don't get too deep in your cups—an intoxicated tourist is easy prey here. And besides, patroling policemen will remove you if you get too rowdy. Adolph Hitler and his German Worker's Party held a meeting at the Hofbrauhaus; a fistfight broke out and Hitler got thrown in the slammer, where he wrote a best-seller. The rest of Hitler's history, we know. Admission: free.

Mathaser Bierstadt

Bayerstrasse 5. ☎ *(089) 59 28 96.*
🕐 *9 a.m.–1 a.m.*

The biggest beer hall in town also serves a respectable meal—start your day off with a Bavarian breakfast of Weisswurst (white sausage) and beer, or try the ham hocks with sauerkraut and potatoes. This is multilevel partying; street level is a tavern, above that is another beer hall, and the rooftop garden is loads of fun in the summertime. If you are really pressed for time, you can eat on the sidewalk at a standup counter. Other beerhalls include the **Lowenbrukeller** *(Nymphenburgerstrasse 2)* and **Hirschgarten** *(Hirschgartenalee 1,* supposedly the largest beer garden in Europe. Young people congregate at the **Chinesischer Turn** next to the pagoda in the **Englischer Garten** (the large park in downtown Munich). For a sophisticated evening and dancing to a live band, try the **Bayerischer Hof Night Club** in the Hotel **Bayerisher Hof**, *Promenadeplatz 2 - 6,* ☎ 212-09-94. There is no cover charge in the piano bar, but there is for the club itself on weekends. This is a nice place; bring your money and your nice clothes. Jazz clubs, such as the **Unterfahrt** *Kirchenstrasse* ☎ *96, 448-27-94, S-Bahn or U-Bahn: Ostbahnhof* are more relaxed. Table candles and wood paneling give the Unterfahrt a warm appeal. Listen to jazz from the '50's and '60's and some cutting-edge music from today. **Muncher Jazz-Zeitung** is indispensable for an up-to-date listing of what is happening on the jazz front. For rock, heavy metal, etc., look for posters on the bulletin boards, doors, walls and other flat surfaces around the university. The **Schwabing** district also has its share of night spots ranging from tourist traps to discos to smoky cellars. *Prinz,* published monthly, is available at newsstands and has complete listings of what's hip. Admission: varies.

Shopping

Dirndl-Ecke ★★★

Am Platz 1. *(089) 22 01 63.*

Go native and buy some traditional Bavarian clothing for men, women and children at Dirndl-Ecke, conveniently located just one block from the Hofbrauhaus. This is the real thing, not just tourist fun.

Viktualiennmarkt ★★★★★

Viktualiennmarkt.

Public Transportation: *U-Bahn and S-Bahn.* Metro Stop: *Marienplatz.*

Special Hours: *varies.*

The famous open-air market sells almost any gastronomic delight. Look but don't touch is the rule for the produce. A beer garden is attached to the market but is open only in the summer months. The streets and alleys around the market sell all sorts of snacks and pastries.

Wallach ★★★

Resiidenstrasse 1. *(089) 22 08 71.*

Carefully selected objects old and new boast faultless craftsmanship. There is no kitsch in sight. Prices are not cheap, especially in the face of a falling dollar, but money here is well spent.

Oberammergau

The legendary *Passion Play,* portraying the last days of Christ's life, has made the town famous; it is given every decade. Meanwhile, whittlers feverishly carve out shelves (nay, warehouses) of passionate souvenirs that are sold at prices higher than in the neighboring villages.

Black Forest

Baden - Baden

This most historic of all spas is famous for its Lichtentaler Allee, Roman baths and thermal ablutions at Caracalla Therme. The three-story Congress Hall, with its main-floor restaurant and flowering terrace, is at nearby Augustaplatz; the more youthful, jazzed-up casino, with a recreational wing, spa gardens, racetrack and other enticements, is drawing fun-loving vacationers. The town's "Grand Week" of big-time horse racing (late August to early September) is internationally known.

Where to Stay

Am Markt   ★★★

http://www.hotel-am-markt-baden.de/

Budget

Marktplatz 17-18. Take Bus 1 or 3 from the Hauptbahnhof to Leopoldsplatz

☎ *(07221) 22-74-7.*

Credit Cards: *V, MC, DC, A.*

For those looking for nothing more than a clean, comfortable room in a good location, the family-run Am Markt is the place. It's in the center of the oldest part of Baden-Baden, right on a cobblestone square across from a church and the town hall. The hotel isn't far from the Roman baths, the casino or any other major attractions, but the only noise here is the chiming of the church bells. There are 27 rooms, 20 with bath or shower. Pets are welcome.

Bad-Hotel zum Hirsch   ★★

Budget to Moderate

Hirschstrasse 1.

☎ *(7221) 93-90,* FAX: *223-5652.*

Credit Cards: *V, MC, A.*

This 300-year-old hotel, the oldest in the area, has attracted the likes of Balzac, Paganini and the Rothschilds. Each guest room is individually furnished in country-home style. Room rates include buffet breakfast. Rooms have central heating, phone, TV and radio. Amenities include a newsstand, dry cleaning, laundry, social program and adaptor plugs.

Brenner's Park-Hotel & Spa

http://www.brenners.com/entrance.htm

Expensive

An der Lichtentaler Allee.

☎ *(07221) 90-00*, FAX: *323-7500*.

Credit Cards: *V, MC, DC, A*.

Everything about Brenner's is first rate, from the wooded location facing the River Oos to the lounge where music plays nightly to the 100 opulent guest rooms. The rates include continental breakfast, but at Brenner's, who's counting Euros? There is a Roman indoor swimming pool with a view of the park, a party room, beauty parlor, solarium, masseur, two restaurants, miniature golf and riding. On top of this, the service is fast and friendly.

Kurhotel Quisisana

Moderate

Bismarckstrasse 21.

☎ *(07221) 36-90*.

Credit Cards: *MC, A*.

Those who come to Baden-Baden looking for the cure just might find it here. Health seekers can partake in group calisthenics, receive skin and muscle treatments from the masseuse, enjoy a therapeutic bath or spend time in the solarium, sauna or indoor pool before partaking of a meal from the world-class kitchen. Many of the rooms are decorated in English country style. The hotel is in the middle of a park, but it's only an eight-minute walk to the center of the spa.

Steigenberger Avance Badischer

Moderate to Expensive

Langestrasse 47.

☎ *(07221) 93-40*, FAX: *223-5652*.

Credit Cards: *V, MC, DC, A*.

Experience what it was like when the rich and famous of the 19th century came to Baden-Baden to "take the cure." Originally a Capuchin monastery, the main building was converted into a spa hotel in 1809 with a four-story-high colonnaded hallway, great stair-case and encircling balustraded balconies. While the 145 guest rooms are modern, the public rooms retain that Old World feel. Outside is a garden, flower beds and lawn around a stone fountain. There is swimming in either the open-air pool or the thermal-spring pool. Room rates depend on the size and view. The rooms in the old monastery building have thermal water in the baths. Rates also include a buffet breakfast.

Where to Eat

Munchner Lowenbrau   ★

Inexpensive

Gernsbacherstrasse 9. ☎ *0721/2 23 11.*

Public Transportation: *Bus 1*.

Specialties: *Soup and sausage*. Credit Cards: *V, MC, DC, A*.

Of course, here, the house beer is Lowenbrau. If you can't make it to Munich this trip, try to spend some time here—this is a real Munich beer hall set down on the edge of the Black Forest.

Park-Restaurant

Expensive

Schillerstrasse 6. Specialties: *0721/90 00*.

Credit Cards: *V, MC, DC, A*.

Reservations required.

Located in the premier hotel in Baden-Baden, this is the premier restaurant. The kitchen uses only top ingredients, and the chefs are top-rate. And you can expect to pay accordingly—but it's worth every penny. Pate de foie gras accented with a hint of cognac and slices of black truffles is a worthy appetizer for the lobster thermidor, perfectly cooked in classic manner with no attempt to improve or embellish it. Reservations are required, and gentlemen should wear coat and tie.

Sports and Recreation

Caracall-Therme

Romberplatz 11. Specialties: 0721/27 59 40.

Public Transportation: *Bus 1.*

🕐 *8 a.m.–10 p.m.*

The Caracalla-Therme is a more modern facility than the Friedrichsbad and, unfortunately, lacks the Belle Epoque ambiance. Nevertheless, if you want to sample the spa experience, it provides an attractive setting that lets you choose what treatments you want and in what order. **Note:** Bathing suits are obligatory in the pools, but you must take them off if you use the saunas. Admission: inexpensive.

Friedrichsbad

Romerplatz 1. Specialties: 0721/27 59 21.

Public Transportation: *Bus 1.*

🕐 *9 a.m.–10 p.m.*

Special Hours: *Sun. open at 2 p.m., admission ends 7 p.m.*

Built in the 1870s, Friedrichsbad is Cecil B. DeMille's version of a European Spa, and the irascible Mark Twain is reputed to have been a satisfied customer. The facility prides itself on its marble pools set beneath gilded domes supported by Rococo pillars. Friedrichsbad uses the Roman-Irish method of treatment involving alternate hot and cold baths in 15 different rooms, as well as deluging the bather with water from all angles. For a few Euros extra, you get a soap-brush massage, which is a lot better than it sounds and doesn't last long enough. As a final touch, you are swathed in heated towels and left to meditate and recover before going out and tackling the world again. **Note:** You will be required to disrobe for certain portions of the treatment. Admission: moderate.

Freiburg

Freiburg-im-Breisgau (to eliminate confusion with the Freiberg located in Eastern Germany) is off the tourist trail but is well- worth a visit. Founded in the 12th century, Freiburg suffered extensive damage in World War II. Today, the town has been restored and it offers charming medieval vistas and world-famous **Munsterplatz.** Stay at the **Colombi Hotel,** and dine at the hotel's **Hans-Thoma-stube.** Or try the intimate **Rappen**, which has steeply pitched roofs and dormer windows. Don't miss visiting the **Gothic Freiburg Cathedral**, with its 12 chapels.

Where to Stay

Colombi Hotel   ★★★

http://www.colombi.de/

Moderate

Rotteckring 16.

Public Transportation: *Tram 10, 11 or 12.* Metro Stop: *H. Rated Restaurant: Hans-Thoma-Stube/Falkenstube.*

☎ *(0761) 21-06-0.*

Credit Cards: *V, MC, DC, A.*

There are seven floors of comfortable modernity in the 92 rooms at this quiet downtown locale. It's popular with the business set, but tourists will feel right at home as well. The top hotel in town also houses the city's best restaurant. The Hans-Thoma-Stube/Falkenstube (Hans Thoma is a famed Black Forest painter) is two restaurants in one created out of a pair of 18th-century farm-house guest rooms. The Hans Thoma half is the more informal eatery; it gets much more upscale at the Falkenstube.

Oberkirchs Weinstuben

Budget to Moderate

Munsterplatz 22.

Public Transportation: *Tram 10, 11 or 12.*

☎ *(0761) 31-01-1.*

Credit Cards: *V, MC, DC, A.*

Located on a small square in the center of town near the Gothic cathedral. Try to get one of the nine rooms directly above the wein-stube. The other 17 are in another building around the corner. While all have been recently renovated, the ones in the main building are worth the extra charge. All come with central heating, phone and TV. The restaurant is famed for its regional specialties, especially the game dishes, served in wood-paneled ambience.

Park Hotel Post ★

Budget to Moderate

Eisenbahnstrasse 35.

Public Transportation: *Tram 10, 11 or 12.*

☎ *(0761) 31-68-3.*

This Baroque building in the center of town, close by the key sights and the train station, has been a hotel since the turn of the century and continues to offer Old World service. Its unique exterior with stone balconies and copper-domed tower has made it a historic landmark. There are 41 rooms with TV. Rates include a continental breakfast.

Zum Roten Baren ★★★

http://www.roter-baeren.de/

Moderate

Oberlinden 12.

Public Transportation: *Tram 1.*

☎ *(0761) 38-78-70.*

Credit Cards: *V, MC, DC, A.*

Zum Roten Baren possibly is Germany's oldest hotel, having served guests since 1311, and parts of the building itself date back to 1120, making it as old as Freiburg. The 25 bedchambers have central heating, TV, phone and radio.Make sure and visit the wine cellars that go back to the 12th century. Rates include a buffet breakfast.

Inns

Rappen ★★

Budget to Moderate

Munsterplatz.

Public Transportation: *Tram 10, 11 or 12.*

☎ *(0761) 31-35-3.*

Credit Cards: *V, MC, DC, A.*

Those looking for atmosphere can stop at this 23-room inn right on the market square next door to the Gothic cathedral in the pedestrian-only old town. The guest rooms come with central heating, and most have a phone and TV. Rates include a buffet breakfast. There is a garden terrace and a sidewalk terrace that attract crowds on summer nights.

Where to Eat

Oberkirchs Weinstuben ★

Inexpensive

Munsterplatz 22. ☎ *2 91 03.*

Credit Cards: *V.*

Much of the game served at Oberkirchs has been bagged by the owner, who has a special interest in its preparation. The saddle of venison with rosemary and a red wine/black peppercorn sauce is memorable. Fresh trout with butter and herbs and a side of the house fried potatoes are also very satisfying. In the summer, tables are set up on the terrace.

Weinstube zur Traube

Moderate

Schusterstrasse 17. ☎ *3 21 9.*

Public Transportation: *Tram 10, 11, 12.*

Credit Cards: *V, MC, A.*

Game, meat and fish are the best choices on the menu at this 600-year-old tavern. Goose liver, so beloved of all Germans, is particularly well prepared in a terrine with green peppercorns and a cold port wine sauce.

Ettlingen

Ratsstuben

Inexpensive to Moderate

Kirchgasse 1-3. 14 75 4.

Credit Cards: *V, MC, DC.*

Near the Alb river, this restaurant was once used to store salt. The menu changes with the seasons but there are no nouvelle touches here—just good, traditional food prepared with attention to detail. The service is attentive and the atmosphere welcoming.

What to Do

Museums and Exhibits

ITRAVELBOOK FREEBIE

Freiburg Munster (Cathedral) ★★

Munsterplatz. 31 099.

Public Transportation: *Tram 10, 11, 12.*

🕐 *10 a.m.–6 p.m.*

Special Hours: *Tower to 5 p.m., Sun. open at 1 p.m., closed Mon.*

The Freiburg Cathedral is mainly Gothic, although it has Romanesque beginnings, and its builders procrastinated long enough that it has some Renaissance touches. The graceful pulpit, its stairs winding around one of the columns in the nave, is an especially fine example of Renaissance artisanry. The carved figures beneath the stairs are portraits of the citizens of Freiburg. The stained-glass windows are unusual. The oldest of them are the small round ones in the south transept. Others were donated by the town guilds, which explains why pretzels, wheels, scissors and other tools have made their way into the window designs. Each of twelve chapels surrounding the chancel contains important works of art. Look for the Rococo baptismal font by Wenzinger in the Sturzel chapel and the altarpiece in the University Chapel. The two side panels on the altar, illustrating the Nativity and the Adoration, are by Hans Holbein the Younger. The Spire of the cathedral is often described as the finest tower in Christendom. It is a masterpiece of pierced stonework. Do your best to be there at night when it is lit from the inside. Admission: free.

Shopping

The Munsterplatz

The market on Munsterplatz is one of the most famous in Germany. Get there early on a summer morning, before the heat of the day, when an astounding array of fresh produce and flowers is displayed beneath wide umbrellas. Homemade cakes, pastries, and sausages are in another area, and along the south wall of the cathedral you'll find a selection of local crafts. Interspersed are street musicians, their tunes punctuated by the tolling of the cathedral bells.

Bodensee

Constance

This ancient city of religious, military and political importance since before the 10th century takes its name from the lake at its doorstep (The Germans call the lake the Bodensee) and at one time, a Roman fort stood at the lake's spillway into the Rhine. After a brief walk along the bridge and through the Old Town, you will have absorbed its better part—a foray which should take less than an hour. The **Insel**, with roots going back to the 13th century as a Dominican cloister, is the best hotel. Sightseeing here should include a browse through the town and a look at the port with its lighthouse and towering entry pillar. Then stroll to the nearby Rathaus; be sure to see both sides, one with a covered staircase and the other without. Surrounding the center are numerous inns, shops with cheveroned shutters, fish terraces and the usual plethora of tour buses in high season. What draws most travelers to the lake is the romantic garden on the island of **Mainau**, which can be reached by car, by foot and by lakeboat. The natural paradise occupies more than 100 acres of ever-changing pageantry—600,000 new bulbs every autumn, 200,000 pansies and primroses, 200 manifestations of dahlias, hyacinths, daffodils, palms, bananas and an exotic array of unexpected subtropical plants. Viewers will discover more than 30,000 rose bushes of 1200 varieties!

Where to Stay

Hotel Reutemann und Seegarten

Budget to Moderate

Seepromenade.

☎ *(07351) 50-55.*

Credit Cards: *V, MC, DC.*

The Reutemann und Seegarten itself is two distinct hotels operated as one. Each has its advantages. The Reutemann is known for its large rooms and tile baths with big tubs. There also is a dining room. The prettier Seegarten has flower-bedecked balconies. Together they offer 64 rooms, many with outstanding views of Lake Constance, and each has a lakeside garden with an abundance of flowers and plenty of furniture for sunning. Rates include a continental breakfast.

Steigenberger Insel Hotel ★★★

Moderate to Expensive

Auf Der Insel 1. Rated Restaurant: Dominikaner Stube.

☎ *(07351) 12-50*, FAX: *223-5652.*

Credit Cards: *V, MC, DC, A.*

The Dominicans never envisioned anything like this when they built their monastery on the shores of the Bodensee in the 13th century. Today's Insel has integrated parts of the original cloisters where Jan Hus was held before his execution and Graf Zeppelin was born. Guest rooms are huge; some are furnished with sofas, armchairs and coffee tables. Many have views of the lake. Rates include continental breakfast.

Where to Eat

Lowen

Moderate

Marktplatz 2. ☎ *(07351) 4 30 40.*

Credit Cards: *V, MC, DC, A.*

Lowen has been here since 1390, and it wears its age well. The cooking is simple and portions ample. Lake fish is always on the menu. Poached felchen (a cousin of the salmon) in a fresh basil sauce is delicious. The *Pfannkuchen* with sultanas in a brandy sauce bears a fleeting resemblance to crepes suzette but without the glitz.

Restaurant Hoyerberg Schlossle

Moderate

Hoyerbergerstrasse 64. ☎ *(07351) 25 29 5.*

Credit Cards: *V, MC, DC, A.*

Even if the food wasn't outstanding, people would come here for the atmosphere. Originally a private palace, the facility was later a private home and finally a restaurant. Salads made from local greens and dressed with a light vinaigrette are a good way to start the meal. Lake perch in a champagne sauce is recommended when in season.

What to Do
Historical Sites

Meersburg

Two castles overlook **Meersburg**, and its houses are picturesque, especially in the summer, when window boxes overflow with flowers. The **Altes Schloss** is the oldest inhabited castle in Germany. You can see the dungeons, instruments of torture, suits of armor, sculleries, etc. The **Zeppelin Museum** is interesting if you're an aviation nut. Count Zeppelin was born nearby, and there are some interesting artifacts of his life as well as remnants of the Hindenburg.

Richenau Island ★★★★

Located northwest of Constance on the Untersee, **Richenau Island** is worth visiting for its three Romanesque churches, relics from the time when the island's monastery housed more than 700 monks and reigned as one of the major learning centers in the area. Today, the island is largely given over to intensive flower and vegetable farming. The St. George church was built in the 9th century. It contains some superb 10th-century murals illustrating the miracles of Christ. Its most famous relic is the skull of St. George. The **Munster,** or main abbey, is located at **Mittelzell.** It is the main village on the island,

and has an interesting **Schatzkammer** (treasury), which contains some ecclesiastical plates and numerous reliquaries. The star of the collection is a 5th century ivory goblet carved with scenes of Jesus's miracles. Behind the Munster is a medieval herb garden. The third church, **St. Peter and St. Paul,** is a mini-history of ecclesiastical architecture in Germany. It began as a Romanesque church, has a few gothic touches, with some respectable Rococo stucco rounding things out.

Parks and Gardens

Mainau Island   ★★★

🕐 *7 a.m.–7 p.m.*

Special Hours: *Nov.-Feb. 9 a.m.-5 p.m.*

The island is owned by Count Lennart Bernadotte, who lives in the castle, once the property of the Knights of the Teutonic Order. The castle itself is not open to the public, but its spectacular gardens are, and they are worth seeing. The unusually mild climate makes it possible to grow orange trees, palm trees, hibiscus and other exotic plants, many of which have been brought from abroad by members of the Swedish Royal Family (Count Lennart is a cousin). Access to the island is by boat or by causeway. Be advised that the island can be very crowded during the summer (at times 30,000 visitors per day). There are four restaurants on the island, and you can beat the crowds by eating there in the evenings. Not only will your admission fee be returned to you, but by the time you leave, there will be considerably fewer people. Admission: moderate, varies.

Central
Frankfurt

Frankfurt is home to the busiest airport in Europe (an international flight leaves every five minutes). The fifth biggest city, Frankfurt is also the banking mecca, the leading Trade Fair center, and an important railway terminus. Don't miss the **Dom,** a thirteenth century church, or the rebuilt but attractive buildings of the **Romerberg** on the north bank. Frankfurt is also is known for the **Applewine taverns** packed among the discos and restaurants of the nightlife area of **Sachsenhausen** (just across the Main river from the **Romerplatz.** Just look for the traditional pine wreath on the door, grab a seat on the wooden bench and don't be shy—Frankfurters are social drinkers, and *Ebbolwoi* is the drink of choice. The Flohmarkt or **flea market** every Saturday morning along the river is worth a visit. Sachsenhausen is also home to most of the 11 museums that have impressive exhibits on film history, architecture, sculpture, folk art, communications, ethnology, crafts, Jewish culture, and even the post office. If you have time to see only one, stop in at the **Stadel**, one of the best art galleries in Germany.

BE SURE, ESPECIALLY DURING TRADE FAIRS AND CONGRESSES, TO HAVE WRITTEN, EMAILED, OR FAXED CONFIRMATION FOR YOUR ACCOMMODATIONS. If you have a choice, try to get out of Frankfurt where the rates and the scenery improve dramatically.

Where to Stay

An Der Messe

Moderate to Expensive

Westendstrasse 104.

Public Transportation: *Bus 32.*

☎ *(069) 74-79-79*, FAX: *221-6509.*

Credit Cards: *V, MC, DC, A.*

The aptly named "At the Fairgrounds" is five minutes by foot from the fairgrounds, as well as the university, the train station and the banking district. TV and radio. 46 clean, modern rooms. Rates include breakfast. No restaurant.

Arabella Sheraton Grand Hotel

http://www.arabellasheraton.com/content_10100/id_33600/gra/33612_gra.html

Moderate to Expensive

Konrad-Adenauer-Strasse 7.

Public Transportation: *U-Bahn.* Metro Stop: *Konstablerwache.*

☎ *(069) 29-81-0.*

Credit Cards: *V, MC, DC, A.*

This hotel offers a splendid shelter for luxury pilgrims. Located in the heart of the city near the main shopping center, it contains 378 bedrooms and noteworthy restaurant restaurants. Other conveniences include 24-hour room service, laundry, baby sitting, foreign-money exchange and parking.

Gravenbruch Kempinski

http://www.kempinski-frankfurt.com/

Expensive

63243 Neu Isenberg. Just off B459

☎ *(06102) 50-50*, FAX: *426-3135*.

Credit Cards: *V, MC, DC, A.*

Situated beside a man-made lake ringed by willows, this 288-room resort leaves nothing to chance.The 288 bedchambers vary widely in style, but most are outfitted with traditional English furnishings. There are ground-floor units with direct access to the gardens, and all the rooms have views of either the surrounding park or the lake. Try not to miss the Sunday multi-course brunch. The hotel is just a few seconds off the north-south autobahn intersection called Frankfurter Kreuz (a handy pull-off for motorists).

Maingau

Budget to Moderate

Schifferstrasse 38-40.

Public Transportation: *Tram 16; Bus 62.*

☎ *(069) 61-70-01.*

Credit Cards: *V, MC, A.*

For those interested in checking out Frankfurt's famed apple-wine district, this is the place. It's right across the river from downtown, next to a small park, but it's even closer to the **Sachsenhausen** quarter and its string of apple-wine establishments. All 100 wood-furnished rooms come with TV, and there is a restaurant on the premises. Room rates include a buffet breakfast. Children are welcome.

Movenpick Parkhotel Frankfurt

Moderate to Expensive

Wiesenhuttenplatz 28-38.

Public Transportation: *S-Bahn 15.*

☎ *(069) 26-97-0,* FAX: *333-3333.*

Credit Cards: *V, MC, DC, A.*

Not far from the main train station, greets guests with a handsome entrance. The 299 rooms are agreeable, but not luxurious. As expected, the rooms with a personal touch are in the tower, while those in the new wing are more modern. The superb **La Truffe** dining room is ideal for business tete-a-tete.

Mozart

Moderate

Parkstrasse 17.

Public Transportation: *U-Bahn 1, 2, 3.*

☎ *(069) 55-08-31.*

Credit Cards: *V, MC, DC, A.*

The picture-postcard exterior with its marble front is almost matched by the white-and-pink interior. The breakfast room itself looks like it came right out of the 1700s. Rates for the 34 rooms include a buffet breakfast.

Schlosshotel Kronberg

http://www.schlosshotel-kronberg.de/ english/

Moderate to Expensive

Hainstrasse 25.

☎ *(06173) 70-10-1.*

Credit Cards: *V, MC, DC, A.*

This original Tudor castle of Empress Friedrich III, the eldest daughter of Queen Victoria and mother of Kaiser Wilhelm II, still retains its grand terrace, its priceless tapestries, its art masterpieces (Titian and Holbein paintings are in the dining room) and its beautiful furnishings that so deftly have been combined with up-to-the-minute amenities. Strange as it may seem, prices are lower here than at other top-line, more centrally located Frankfurt hotels, offsetting to a degree the cost of taxi links to town. Past visitors included the likes of Victoria herself, Edward VII and Czar Nicholas II. Recognizing its roots, an English tea is served weekends in the library, just one of a number of high- ceilinged grand halls. Outside is an Italian garden, part of the surrounding 56-acre park. Tennis and swimming are available nearby. All 57 rooms have central heating, phone, hair dryer, TV and radio. Facilities include a bar, sitting room with open fire, salon and conference room. Pets are welcome, but only in the bedrooms.

Steigenberger Frankfurter Hof

http://www.steigenberger.de/servlet/PB/menu/1000356_11/index.html

Expensive

Am Kaiserplatz.

Public Transportation: *U-Bahn 1, 2 or 3.*

☎ *(069) 21-50-2*, FAX: *223-5652.*

Credit Cards: *V, MC, DC, A.*

Easily one of Europe's finest hotels, the Frankfurter Hof, improves almost daily under the expert guidance of general manager Bernd Ludwin. His connoisseur's attention to wine and gastronomy are special credits to this establishment. There are many new rooms, a splendid presidential suite (the ultimate in security) and two fresh deluxe spreads. Centrally located near the Hauptbahnhof and Altstadt, this 1876 neo-Baroque building was headquarters for Allied occupational forces. All 357 bedchambers have hush-the-traffic windows and color TV. Good parking facilities are available.

Where to Eat

Adolf Wagner

Moderate

Schweizerstrasse 71. ☎ *(069) 61 25 65.*

Public Transportation: *Tram 16.*

Ebbelwoikneipen, or apple-wine taverns, have been a fixture in Frankfurt. Many are concentrated in the *Sachsenhause*-district, where they are frequented by locals and G.I.'s alike. Look for a pine wreath hanging over the door. Inside will be an establishment serving

Ebbelwei, Ebbelwoi, or *Stoffche* depending on whom you are talking with. Be warned that the wine comes in varying strengths from *Susser,* which has hardly any kick to it, to *Rauscher* which can turn strong persons weak. Stick with *Alte* or *Helle,* which fall somewhere in the middle if taken with discretion. The typical accompaniment is *Handkas mit Musik,* or white cheese with onions, which have been marinated in vinegar, oil and caraway. Portions are enormous, so you might decide to split one. The place is always crowded, so be prepared to share your table. If things get too crowded don't be afraid to move on; there are lots of good *kneipen* on this street.

Bistorant Die Leiter

Moderate to Expensive

Kaiserhofstrasse 11. ☎ *(069) 29 21 21.*

Credit Cards: *V, MC, DC, A.*

Right across the street from Yves St. Laurent, this is a good place to recoup your strength after shopping or gather your forces for the onslaught. It's a favorite haunt of advertising types, artists and actors. The cooking is light with dishes such as grilled lobster, scampi, and salmon carpaccio. The pastry chef does nice things with fresh fruit in season—including tarts, and *kuchen.*

Die Gans ★★★★

Moderate

Schweiszerstrasse 76. ☎ *(069) 61 50 75.*

Public Transportation: *U-Bahn.* Metro Stop: *Schweizerplatz.*

Credit Cards: *V, MC, DC, A.*

Die Gans is casual enough to feel comfortable but stylish enough to make you feel you have been somewhere respectable. Dishes range from the traditional roast goose with red cabbage and potato dumplings to seafood pastas to well-prepared game.

Erno's Bistro

Moderate to Expensive

Liebigstrasse 15, Westend. ☎ *(069) 72 19 97.*

Credit Cards: *V, MC, DC, A.*

Frequented by the financial crowd from the nearby stock exchange, Erno's Bistro is definitely upmarket. The cuisine is ultra-sophisticated and changes daily. The fish is flown in from Paris or the Baltic. Other than that, the menu relies on fresh produce from the surrounding countryside.

> **ITRAVELBOOK TIP:** ERNO'S OFFERS A FIXED PRICE MENU WHICH REALLY IS A BARGAIN. YOU GET PORTIONS OF THE HOUSE SPECIALTIES FOR A FRACTION OF THE PRICE YOU WOULD PAY IF YOU ORDERED A LA CARTE. THIS HOLDS TRUE FOR MANY OF THE BETTER RESTAURANTS IN THE CITY.

Romer Bernbel

Inexpensive

Romerplatz 20-22.

Metro Stop: *Romer.*

Credit Cards: *V, MC, DC, A.*

Right on the square, this is a great place to enjoy a beer or *Ebbelwoi* (local apple wine) and watch the world go by. Snacks in the form of grilled sausages on a fresh roll are available as are unpretentious, well-prepared meals.

University Mensa

Inexpensive to Moderate

Bockenheimer Landstrasse 133.

Public Transportation: *U-Bahn 6 or 7.* Metro Stop: *Bockenheimer.*

The Mensas (university dining halls) are found throughout Germany, and although the quality of the food may vary widely, they are always cheap. This Mensa is a particularly good one and offers three main dishes, one of which is vegetarian, every day.

What to Do

Amusement Parks

Zoologischer Garten (Zoo)

http://www.zoo-frankfurt.de/

Alfred-Brehm-Platz 16. ☎ *(069) 222 33 715.*

Public Transportation: *U-Bahn 6 or 7.*

🕐 *8 a.m.–5 p.m.*

Special Hours: *Apr.-Sept. 8 a.m.-7 p.m.*

One of the finest zoos in the world, the Zoologischer Garten's mission is to educate visitors about its animals through exhibits. The African Veldt Enclosure is home to numerous species of antelope and ostriches. There is also a bear castle, and a darkened exhibit where you can see nocturnal animals. Children love the animal nursery where they can see zookeepers care for young creatures. Admission: moderate.

Historical Sites
ITRAVELBOOK FREEBIE

Dom (Cathedral)   ★★

Complatz. ☎ *(069) 28 92 29.*

Metro Stop: *Romer.*

🕐 *7 a.m.–7:30 p.m.*

The Cathedral (Dom) is on the Eastern end of the Romerberg. A church has been on this site since the 13th century, although the present building was constructed much later. This was the location of the coronations of the Holy Roman Emperors, who would emerge, in all their glory, from the Marienportal and proceed across the square to the Römer for their coronation banquet. The Gothic carvings on this entrance to the Dom are especially well executed. If you have the time (and aren't going to Cologne), try to see the Altar of Mary Sleeping *(Maria Schlaft)* and the murals depicting the life of St. Bartholomew. They are the work of masters of the School of Cologne (the Bartholomew murals have been restored) and are good examples of this late medieval/early Renaissance type of painting. *The Wahlkapelle*, to the side of the choir, is the room to which the seven electors would withdraw when the time came to elect a new Holy Roman Emperor Attached to the cathedral in the remains of the cloister is the Cathedral Museum *(Dommuseum)*. The display of vestments worn at the coronation of the Holy Roman Emperors is extremely interesting and contains wonderful examples of ecclesiastical needlework. Admission: free.

Höchst ★

Public Transportation: *S-Bahn 1 or 2.*

Höchst is one of the few areas near Frankfurt that escaped bombing during World War II. You can still see original half-timbered buildings and cobblestone streets. In the summer the ubiquitous window boxes brim with flowers and there are some lovely cafes for lunch. An excursion here makes a nice break from the noise of downtown Frankfurt. Before it was engulfed by the larger city, Höcht was a town in its own right with the requisite public buildings. The Höchster Schloss on Bolongarostrasse, which dates from the mid-14th century, was the residence of the Archbishop of Mainz as well as the customs house for the area. Today it houses a museum of local history (admission free). It's worth taking the time to see the *Justriniuskirche* (Church of St. Justinian), *the oldest building in the Frankfurt area.* As the church evolved over the centuries, it acquired an interesting blend of Romanesque and Gothic architecture.

Museums and Exhibits

Goethe-Haus ★★

http://www.goethehaus-frankfurt.de/ willkommen.html

Grosser Hirschgraben 23-25. ☎ *(069) 28 28 24.*

Public Transportation: *U-Bahn, S-Bahn.* Metro Stop: *Hauptwache.*
🕒 *9 a.m.–6 p.m.*

Special Hours: *Sun. 10 a.m.-1 p.m., Oct.-Mar. 9 a.m.-4 p.m.*

Goethe was born in a house on this site in 1749. The original house was destroyed in World War II, after being open to the public since 1863; the present building is a meticulous reproduction of the original. The house mixes Barouque, Rococo, and neoclassical architectual styles, and also contains artifacts pertaining to other family members. Visitors can view Goethe's father's art collection and visit his mother's workroom. Admission: inexpensive.

Jewish Museum ★★

http://www.juedischesmuseum.de/

Untermainkai 14/15.

Public Transportation: *U-Bahn.* Metro Stop: *Theaterplatz.*

🕐 *10 a.m.–5 p.m.*

Special Hours: *Wed. to 8 p.m.; closed Mon.*

Admission: *free.*

This recently opened museum details the history of Frankfurt's Jewish Community, which at one time was the second largest in Germany. The exhibits go beyond religious artifacts, successfully presenting this community in the context of its times. The museum is housed in the former *Rothschild* mansion and is worth seeing for this alone.

ITRAVELBOOK FREEBIE

Museum of Applied Arts

http://www.rma.de/eng-rmaweb/kultur/museen/museum-angewandte-kunst.htm

Schaumainkai 43. ☎ *(069) 606 01.*

Public Transportation: *U-Bahn 1, 2, 3.*

🕐 *10 a.m.–5 p.m.*

Special Hours: *Wed. to 8 p.m.; closed Mon.*

A monument to good taste, the *Museum fur Kunsthandwerk* contains beautifully crafted objects from all over the world. The collection is divided into four sections: the European, the Far Eastern, the Islamic, and Books and Graphics. In the European Section, the 15th- and 16th-century glasswork is particularly fine. German porcelain is well-represented, and there are some wonderful *Jugendstil* pieces of furniture. The Islamic Section has an excellent collection of Oriental rugs as well as lovely glassware from the late Byzantine period. The Far Eastern Section contains an exceptional collection of Ching porcelain, lacquer work and blue-and-white export ware. Tibet is represented by unusual bronze statues in styles seldom seen in the West. Also connected with the museum (and also free) is the **Ikonen-Museum** located around the corner at Brückenstrasse 3-7. It contains an attractive collection of about 200 18th and 19th century Russian icons—one of the best collection outside of Russia. Admission: free.

Nightlife

The residents of Frankfurt are the most affluent in Germany; they don't mind spending their money on entertainment. To find out what's going on, buy the *Frankfurter Journal*, available at all news-stands. Frankfurt is home to the *Radio-Sinfonie Orchester Frankfurt*, which performs at the *Alte Oper* on Opernplatz ☎ (1340 400). Opera and ballet productions, on the other hand, take place at the **Stadtische Buhnen** *on Theaterplatz* ☎ ((069) 236 0611). Local and touring companies perform, and productions are often lavish. Good seats can be quite expensive but are worth it. Like anywhere else, clubs come and go, but **Jazzkeller** *on Kleine Bockenheimer Strasse 18a* ☎ (288 537) has been around for a long time and shows no signs of closing. There are many jazz clubs on this street, and you might want to use Jazzkeller as a starting point. **Saschenhausen** is usually associated with the apple wine taverns, but **Jazz Life Podium** *at Rittergasse 22* ☎ *(62 63 46)* is a poor man's Jazz Keller. Many groups have started out here—you might get lucky and hear a famous group on the way up.

Cafes

Like all German cities, Frankfurt has a lot of cafes serving coffee, pastries, light snacks and newspapers. You are usually welcome to come and sit, write postcards, talk and read the papers. **Cafe Lilliput**, *Sandhofpassage, Neue Krame* ☎ *(285-727)* is just off the Römerberg and is a little cheaper than you might expect, given the location. **Cafe Laumer**, *Bockenheimer Landstrassse 67* ☎ (72 79 11) serves good breakfasts and comes into its own during the **Book Fair,** when it is filled with agents from all over the world. It also serves light lunches. They also have a terrace which is popular in the summer months. **Sonus** *at Bockenheimer Anlage 1a* ☎ *(*(069) 596 2525)* is just off the financial district and feeds many functionaries from the surrounding banks and other institutions. The decor is spare with a lot of tiles and palm trees. Good, medium-priced lunch-es and the mandatory tarts, torts, *kuchen*, etc.

East

Berlin

No longer divided by the infamous Wall, Berlin has been, since 1999, the official capital of a united Germany. A city that can (and does) stand side-by-side with its glamorous European counterparts -- Rome, London, Paris, Milan -- Berlin is packed with the kind of cultural energy that it had when it was in its wilder heyday, prior to the Second World War. Berliners are, by their nature, outspoken, brash, and often the subjects of their countrymen's ridicule. But make no mistake: the stolid juxtaposition of *Macht und Geist* (power and intellect) that set Berliners apart from the rest of their countrymen continues to do so, albeit in a more welcoming manner than it has in the past. Much like New Yorkers, Berliners have been through and seen it all: the result is an ironic, often mordant sense of humor similar to that of their neighbors across the Atlantic. Visit the city for its vibrant restaurants and nightlife; its thriving cultural community; its vast history. It is not to be missed.

Town Transport, Taxis and Car Rentals

Throughout the united metropolis and suburbs, there are miles of subways (U-bahn) and elevated rails (S-bahn) that cover all the districts you'll need. Buses operate, too, plus double-deckers that run all night. Tourist tickets are sold at bargain rates. The city is accommodated by a 6000-taxi fleet; half of them are linked to a central exchange by radio-telephone. When the city was isolated, it was pointless to rent a car since travel was so limited. Today hotels, the airport and travel agencies represent the multinational services, plus local rental companies, which often are cheaper.

Travel Information

The **Berlin Tourist Office** (**http://www.germany-tourism.de/**, *Europa Center,* ☎ *(030) 262-6031, Mon.–Sat. 8 a.m.–10:30 p.m., Sun. 9 a.m.–9 p.m.*) maintains branches at key points to dispense advice, brochures and every type of assistance. Some of the localities include the **Hauptbahnhof**, the **Brandenburg Gate** and **Tegel Airport.**

Where to Stay

Hotels and Resorts

Brandenburger Hof

http://www.brandenburger-hof.com/

Moderate to Expensive

Eislebener Strasse 14.

Public Transportation: *U-Bahn*. Metro Stop: *Augsburgerstrasse*.

☎ *(030) 214-050.*

Credit Cards: *V, MC, DC, A.*

Tranquillity reigns in this five-story hotel that was built in 1991 to resemble the turn-of-the-century mansions around it. The Old Berlin style goes beyond its five-story facade, too. The 88 rooms are large and well-lit, thanks to balconies in some and bay windows in others. Room rates include breakfast.

Curator ★★

Moderate

Grolmanstrasse 41-43. U-Bahn to Uhlandstrasse; S-Bahn to Savignyplatz

☎ *(030) 88-42-60.*

A modern hotel targeting the tourist and business traveler, the Curator offers 100 rooms with king-size beds and phones in the bathrooms. Located between Savignyplatz and Kurfurstendamm, in an area of boutiques and cafes, this seven-story edifice has a lobby bar and restaurant and roof terrace for sunning.

Grand Hotel Esplanade ★★★

http://www.esplanade.de/frameset- ie.html

Moderate to Expensive

Lutzowufer 15. On the Landwehrkanal, a few minutes on foot from the Tiegarten

Public Transportation: *106, 129, 219, 341*. Metro Stop: *Lutzowplatz*.

☎ *(030) 26-10-11,* FAX: *223-5652.*

Credit Cards: *V, MC, DC, A.*

For those who like modern, the Esplanade is the place to be. But you'll also enjoy the old-fashioned service and comfort, and the views of the Landwehrkanal from many of the rooms. The hotel is right on the canal, only a few minutes from downtown and the Tiegarten. Rates include a buffet breakfast.

Hecker's Hotel

http://www.heckers-hotel.com/

Budget to Moderate

Grolmanstrasse 35.

Public Transportation: *U-Bahn.* Metro Stop: *Uhlandstrasse.*

☎ *(030) 88-90-9.*

Credit Cards: *V, MC, DC, A.*

Right off the busy Kurfurstendamm, close by the nightlife of Savignyplatz, this hotel is a pleasant surprise. Hecker's offers 42 rooms, four junior suites and six studios with kitchenettes. Each room has a king-size bed, central heating, phone, hair dryer, TV and radio, not to mention huge closets and soundproof doors. The restaurant, Hecker's Deele, stays open late and is known for its regional German dishes.

Landhaus Schlachtensee ★★

http://www.hotel-landhaus-schlachtensee.de/

Budget

Bogotastrasse 9.

Credit Cards: *V, MC, DC, A.*

This three-story former villa, built in 1905, now provides a country-living experience only seven miles from town. The hotel offers swimming or boating on neighboring Schlachtensee and Krumme Lanke lakes.The 19 rooms are adequate and the bathrooms modern. Pets are accepted, but it is not wheelchair accessible. Rates include a breakfast buffet, which is best taken out on the terrace if the weather permits. The service is first-rate, one of many reasons to make reservations at least a month in advance. Rooms have central heating, phone, hair dryer, TV, radio, trouser press.

Maritim Grand Hotel

Expensive

Friedrichstrasse 158-164. U-Bahn: Franzolsche Strasse; S-Bahn: Friedrichstrasse

☎ *(030) 23-27-0*, FAX: *843-3311*.

Credit Cards: *V, MC, DC, A.*

An impressive tribute to capitalism in what used to be downtown East Berlin, the Maritim Grand is another reason to be glad the Wall came down. This hotel was made to satisfy every whim and to do it with class. Only three blocks east of the Brandenburg Gate, the Maritim has 349 rooms, four restaurants, winter garden, beer room, bars, concert cafe, solarium, shopping arcade, hairdresser, theater ticket office, foreign-money exchange.

Riehmers Hofgarten ★★

Yorckstrasse 83.

Public Transportation: *Bus 119.* Metro Stop: *Mehringdamm.*

☎ *(030) 781-01-1.*

For a unique hoteling experience, try this 21-room mansion in the section of Kreuzberg known for its art colony. It's close to Viktoriapark and not far from the Mitte section of town. The building was constructed in 1892; the rooms are large and well-appointed. Rates include a big breakfast. Bus 119 from the Kurfurstendamm goes right by.

Where to Eat

Alt-Luxemburg ★★★

Moderate

Windscheidstrasse 31, Charlottenburg. ☎ *(030) 323 8730.*

Public Transportation: *U-Bahn 1.* Metro Stop: *Sophie Charlotten Platz.*

Credit Cards: *V, DC, A.*

Small and intimate, seating only 35, this venerable restaurant advertises itself as international, but the menus lean heavily towards classic and nouvelle French. Expect new adaptations of old favorites.

Ax Bax ★★★

Moderate

Liebnizstrasse 34. ☎ *313-8594.*

Public Transportation: *S-Bahn*. Metro Stop: *Savignyplatz*.

Credit Cards: *V, MC, DC, A*.

You have to look for this place—it's marked only by a small neon sign and the menu outside the door. The menu is roughly based on the boundaries of the old Austro-Hungarian Empire, and there is an interesting cold buffet with a good assortment of herring dishes. If you want to be seen by anyone who is anyone in literature and the arts, book a table in advance and come around 9 p.m.

Baharat Falafel

Inexpensive

Winterfeldstrasse 37.

Public Transportation: *U-Bahn 1, 4*. Metro Stop: *Nollendorfplatz*.

The speciality of the house is the falafel served in fresh pita bread. Toppings include fresh vegetables and a choice of yogurt, manto, chile or sesame sauces.

Cafe Buchwald

Inexpensive to Moderate

Bartingallee 29. ☎ *(030) 391 5931.*

Cafe Buchwald is one of the few cafes to have survived World War II intact. Inside, the specialty of the house is *Baumkuchen*, a rich, multilayered butter cake. The menu is limited to coffee and pastries.

Cafe Einstein ★★★

Inexpensive to Moderate

Kurfurstenstrasse 58. ☎ *(030) 261 5096.*

Public Transportation: *S-Bahn, U-Bahn 1, 4*. Metro Stop: *Savignyplatz, Nollendorfplatz*.

Credit Cards: *V, MC, DC*.

Cafe Einstein has an intellectual clientele, elegant decor, nouvelle cuisine and a seemingly unending supply of German, French, and English magazines and newspapers. The waiters have been known to wear tuxedos and eye makeup. An excellent place for people-watching, and for being watched.

ITRAVELBOOK FREEBIE

Topography of Terror ★★★

🕐 *10 a.m.–6 p.m.*

Special Hours: *Closed Mon.*

Continue west on Zimmerstrasse and you will come to the Topography of Terror museum/monument built on the site of the former Gestapo and SS headquarters. In addition to the monument, there is a small exhibition of photos and histories of some of the Gestapo's victims. Admission: free.

Cafe Voltaire ★

Inexpensive

Stuttgarterplatz 14.

Public Transportation: *S-Bahn 3, 5, 8, 9.* Metro Stop: *Charlotten burg.*

Cafe Voltaire serves breakfast from 5 a.m. to 3 p.m. for just a few Euros. The servings are gargantuan, and a late breakfast can tide one over until a smaller meal in the evening—one way to economize a in the face of a strong Deutsche Mark.

Grand Slam ★★★★

Expensive

Gottfried-von-Cramm-Weg 47, Grunewald. *(030) 825 3810.*

Public Transportation: *Bus 19.*

Credit Cards: *V, MC, DC, A.*

One of the best restaurants in town. Game birds and the local freshwater fish such as lake perch and red mullet are specialties. The fixed-price menu includes the house Grand Slam cocktail—peach schnapps and champagne with a few secret ingredients.

Loretta's Biergarten ★

Inexpensive to Moderate

Lietzenburger Strasse 89.

Public Transportation: *U-Bahn 3, 4.* Metro Stop: *Ku'damm.*

Credit Cards: *V, MC, DC, A.*

Lots of lights in the trees, caves, girls in colorful costumes—if Walt Disney ever designed a beer garden, this would be it. A little on the expensive side, but the beer is good and the plates of sauerkraut and bratwurst are ample, as are the waitpersons. Lots of fun if you're in the mood.

Zur Letzten Instanz

Moderate

Waisenstrasse 14. ☎ *(030) 242-5528.*

Public Transportation: *S-Bahn.* Metro Stop: *Klosterstrasse.*

Credit Cards: *V, DC, A.*

Established in 1621, this is one of the oldest restaurants in Berlin, and so is its menu. Don't look for any nouvelle touches here. Sample an honest platter of spareribs and sauerkraut. Not far from the Supreme Court, Zur Letzen Instanz is a favorite with judges and lawyers.

What to Do

Historical Sites

Brandenburg Gate

Unquestionably the symbol of Berlin and the city's rising and falling fortunes. The statue atop the arch represents Nike driving her chariot to victory. Notice that she is driving towards the West. The irony in this was not lost on Berlin residents during the period when the Wall ran a few yards in front of the gate.

Checkpoint Charlie

Continuing south on Friedrichstrasse look for the sign saying "You are now leaving the American Sector." This was the location of Checkpoint Charlie, which during the Cold War Era was a foreigner's main entrance and exit into or out of East Germany.

Humboldt University

Founded in 1810 by Wilhelm von Humboldt, brother of the noted geographer and explorer Alexander von Humboldt, for whom every German secondary school abroad is seemingly named, the Humboldt University has had noted German intellectuals from Einstein to the Brothers Grimm serving on its faculty. In the 1930s it was so independent in its thinking that Goebbels chose the Bebelplatz (the square in front of the Humboldt) as the site for his **Buchverbrennung** on May 11, 1933. At that time, thousands of books deemed decadent and immoral by the Nazis were burned to symbolically purify the thoughts of their opponents. The rest is history.

Jewish Quarter

Take Monbijoustrasse east from the tip of **Museum Island**, and you will find yourself on **Oranienburgerstrasse,** the main street of Berlin's Jewish Quarter before World War II and the site of great brutality during the **Kristallnacht** (the night of broken glass). Though by the end of World War II it was a ghost town the Quarter currently is undergoing a revival of sorts and is becoming a center for the kind of nightlife that begins at midnight and ends at dawn. Hip spots change from week to week, so just look for the place with the biggest crowds and the loudest music.

Potsdamerplatz

Public Transportation: *U-Bahn*. Metro Stop: *Kurfurstenstrasse*.

Walk south from the Soviet Memorial across the narrow end of the park, and you will find Potsdamerplatz, before the war one of the busiest squares in Berlin. Today it is a rather bare expanse. It's chief claim to fame is the fact that three of the former sectors—the British, the American and the Russian—used to meet in the square. As a result, the Wall used to run right across the middle of it. You can also find the remains of one of the entrances to Hitler's bunker. Future plans for the square include the construction of embassies and headquarters for multinational companies.

The Reichstag

Platz der Republik.

Located just to the north of the Brandenburg Gate, the Reichstag was intended to be the seat of the Prussian Diet, Germany's first elected parliament. The building gained notoriety when it was gutted by fire in 1933. The cause of the blaze has never been determined, but the Nazi's placed blame on the Communists who had won around 3 percent of the votes in recent elections and posed a real threat to their aspirations. The accusation was used as pretext to outlaw the Communist Party and was one of the first acts taken by Hitler in his ascent to absolute power. In the closing hours of World War II, some of the heaviest fighting of the war took place around the Reichstag, and Hitler committed suicide in his bunker a few blocks away.

Unter den Linden

In Pre-Nazi Germany, Unter den Linden was the grand boulevard running through the center of Berlin. Shaded by magnificent lime trees (linden) planted by the Elector Friedrich-Wilhelm and lined with buildings designed to glorify the Hohenzollren dynasty, it was a promenade for the cosmopolitan population of the capital of a world power. Unfortunately, it drew the attention of Hitler, who saw its possibilities as a parade ground for his armies and a staging area for massive rallies. The lindens were chopped down and the ground covered with pavement. A few of the trees were replaced by the Communists, but it was not until reunification that the replanting was complete. In another hundred years or so, Unter den Linden should be back to normal.

Museums and Exhibits

Antikensammlung

http://www.smb.spk-berlin.de/ant/

Schlossstrasse 1. ☎ *320-91-215.* Public Transportation: *U-Bahn.* Metro Stop: *Richard Wagner Platz, Sophie C.*

🕐 *9 a.m.–5 p.m.*

Special Hours: *Sat., Sun. open at 10 a.m.*

In the western guardhouse of the palace, just across from the Egyptian Museum, is one of the world's most comprehensive collections of classical decorative art. Ivory carvings, glassware, pottery, amphora and marble sculptures are just the beginning. Of special interest is the bronze statue of the goddess Diana in her persona of Luna. Admission: inexpensive.

Bauhaus-Archiv

http://www.bauhaus.de/

Klingelhoferstrasse 14.

Public Transportation: *U-Bahn, Bus 100,187,129,341.* Metro Stop: *Nollendorfplatz.*

🕐 *11 a.m.–7 p.m.*

Special Hours: *Closed Mon.*

Berlin was the birthplace of the Bauhaus movement, which flourished from its foundation by Walter Gropius in 1919 until its suppression by Hitler in 1930. Representative samples of everything having to do with Bauhaus are found in this museum, which will give you a new appreciation of how good ideas can go wrong in their mass application. Admission: inexpensive.

Bodemuseum

Monbijoubrucke, Bodestrasse 1-3, Museuminsel. 20355 0.

Public Transportation: *S-Bahn.* Metro Stop: *Hackescher Markt.*

🕐 *9 a.m.–5 p.m.*

Special Hours: *Closed Mon., Tues.*

The Bodenmuseum's original collection of Egyptian artifacts was broken up during World War II. The best exhibits, including the bust of Nefertiti, found their way to the museum at Charlottenburg. What remains is well worth seeing and suffers only in comparison to the past. For a change of pace, visit the Numismatic Gallery which has examples of coins struck at the Brandenburg mint from the 13th century to the present. An adjoining gallery specializes in medals. The Bode once housed a preeminent collection of Rubens, most of which is now gone. The paintings were victims of their own grandeur—they were simply too big to move and were destroyed by fire during the last days of the war. A must for nostalgia buffs is the museum cafe. It's located in the balcony under the main dome. If you like high ceilings, palms, discreet gold trim and a quiet place to enjoy coffee and pastries, this is the place for you. Admission: inexpensive.

Gemaldegalerie (Picture Gallery)

Arminalee 23-27.

Public Transportation: *U-Bahn 2*. Metro Stop: *Dahlem-Dorf*.

🕐 *9 a.m.–5 p.m.*

Special Hours: *Sat., Sun. open at 10 a.m.*

Only in Berlin does the *Gemaldegalerie* receive only ho-hum notice in comparison with other museums in the city. It has an exceptional Early German Collection which includes works of Drer, Cranach the Elder (don't miss the risque *Fountain of Youth* depicting the trans-mogrification of elderly women into nubile girls), such as pieces by Altdorfer and Holbein. The Dutch and Flemish section is an art history lesson in itself, with works by Breugel, van der Weyden, de Hooch and other masters. There are also the obligatory Rembrandts (15, count'em!), including self- portraits of the artist and portraits of both his wives. Not to be outdone, the Italian collection contains Canalettos, numerous Boticellis, Titians, Giottos, Fra Filippo Lippis and no less than five Raphael *Madonnas*. The Sculpture Gallery, also a part of the museum, has Byzantine and European sculpture ranging from the 3rd to the 18th century. It is particularly famous for its collection of medieval German carvings, including works by Tillman Riemanschneider and Hans Multscher. Don't miss Donatello's bas relief of the Madonna and Child. **The Ethnographical Museum** *(Museum fur Volkerkunde)*, with its ritual masks and tribal weapons, is housed in the same building as the Gemaldegalerie. In fact, the top floor of the museum is devoted solely to East Asian artifacts, and the surplus, which includes ethnic art from Africa, the South Seas and South America, is scattered about on other floors. The collection of Mayan and Inca ceramics is not to be missed. The museum complex also includes the **Museums of Far Eastern** Art, **Islamic Art and Indian Art.** Admission: inexpensive.

Markisches Museum

Am Kollnischen Park 5. ☎ *(030) 270-0514.*

Public Transportation: *U-Bahn*. Metro Stop: *Markisches Museum*.

🕐 *10 a.m.–6 p.m.*

Special Hours: *Closed Mon.*

This museums contains artifacts pertaining to the history of the city, including a special section devoted to the history of Berlin theater and an exceptionally interesting exhibit of musical instruments. The mechanical musical instruments, can be activated for a small extra fee. Next door to the museum is the **residence** of Tilo, Maxi and Schnutte, the three bears who are the mascots and symbol's of Berlin. Admission: inexpensive.

New National Gallery

Potsdamer Strasse 50. ☎ *(030) 2666.*

Public Transportation: *U-Bahn.* Metro Stop: *Kufurstenstrasse.*

🕐 *9 a.m.–5 p.m.*

Special Hours: *Sat., Sun. open at 10 a.m.*

This ultramodern building designed by architect Mies van der Rohe was built in the 1960s. The museum collection specializes in works from the 19th- and 20th-centuries and is famous for its collection of French impressionists and German artists such as Munch, Beckman and Klee. It also has its share of Picassos and representatives of the Bauhaus. Admission: inexpensive.

Pergamonmuseum

Kupfergraben, Museuminsel. ☎ *(030) 203 55 444.*

Public Transportation: *S-Bahn.* Metro Stop: *Hackescher Markt.*

🕐 *9 a.m.–5 p.m.*

Special Hours: *Closed Mon., Tues.*

The museum is divided into five sections: the **Antiquities Collection,** the **Middle East Museum,** the **Islamic Museum,** the **Far East** collection and the **Museum of Popular Art.** The Pergamon takes its name from the Pergamon Altar excavated in Turkey at the end of the 19th century. This altar is really the size of a small temple—its frieze is more than 400 feet (120 meters) long. There is an interesting photographic exhibit that shows the altar in the process of being dismantled. The Middle East Museum serves as a reminder of the preeminent position held by German scholars prior to World War II in the study of ancient civilizations. It contains artifacts from the empires of the Assyrians, the Babylonians, the Persians and the Hittites. Among the principal exhibits is the processional way which led to the Ishtar Gate in ancient Babylon and the throne room of Nebuchadnezzar. The Islamic Museum contains entire houses and streets, portions of desert fortifications, gates and mosaics. On a smaller scale there is an incredible collection of Oriental rugs and jewelry. If you still have energy and the time, the Far Eastern Collection displays Chinese and Japanese carvings, rugs, robes, armor— you name it. Sadly, the Museum of Popular Art lost most of its collection when it was almost completely destroyed by fire during the war. What survives presents a detailed and fascinating picture of life in a working-class household in Berlin at the end of the 19th century. Don't miss this museum complex and plan to spend the day. Admission: inexpensive.

Schloss Charlottenburg

Public Transportation: *U-Bahn, Bus 109,121,145,204.* Metro Stop: *Richard Wagner Platz, Sophie-C.*

🕐 *9 a.m.–5 p.m.*

Special Hours: *Sat., Sun. open at 10 a.m.*

One of Berlin's most elegant buildings, Schloss Charlottenburg was commissioned by the Elector Frederick as a summer residence for his wife, Sophie. Unhappily, funds for the project ran out, so work proceeded in fits and starts until it was finished in the 1840s. The building was bombed in 1943, and what you see now is an expert restoration based on original plans. The interior of the restored palace is accessible only on guided tours, conducted in German (a pamphlet in English is available at the ticket counter), and in the summer it may be almost impossible to obtain tickets. Nevertheless, the palace exterior is interesting and the gardens are also worth visiting, even if you don't get inside. If you should be fortunate enough to get on a tour, you will be shown the royal living quarters: the Reception Chamber with its mirrors, vaulted ceilings and tapestries depicting the subjects of Plutarch's Lives, and the Porcelain Chamber, decorated on every surface with Oriental porcelain pieces. They hang on the walls, stand on pedestals, are embedded in the plaster, and are suspended from the ceiling. The effect is further heightened by the use of mirrors. The new wing, or **Knobelsdorff-Flugel** as it is properly known, is the location of the apartments of Frederick the Great. They contain an extensive collection of paintings of him or commissioned by him, all interspersed with furniture from the same period. The **Schinkel Pavillion** is located at the back of the Knobelsdorff-Flugel. It was originally a summer house but is now the repository of a respectable collection of sketches and paintings from the early 1800s. Many of them are by the architect Karl Friedrich Schinkle, the building's namesake. **The Belvedere** is at the far end of the palace gardens and overlooks the **River Spree**. It was a favorite spot for the royal family to take tea in the summer. Today it houses a noteworthy collection of German porcelain, much of it from the 1700s. Admission: inexpensive.

Music

Philharmonie (Philharmonic Hall)   ★★★★★

Matthaikirchstrasse 1. ☎ *(030) 25 48 80.*

Public Transportation: *Bus 129.*

The Philharmonie is an ultramodern concert hall with an orchestra pit uniquely set in the center of the building. This is the home of the Berlin Philharmonic Orchestra. If you are able to attend a performance in the Philharmonie, don't be afraid to buy cheap seats; because the audience surrounds the orchestra, all seats in the auditorium are great (none is more than 100 feet from the conductor). Performances sell out quickly. Admission: inexpensive to very expensive.

Nightlife

E'Werk   ★★★★

Wilhelmstrasse between Leipzigerstrasse and Nieder.

Public Transportation: *U-Bahn.* Metro Stop: *Mohrenstrasse.*

Special Hours: *Open weekends 11 p.m. Fri.- Sun. Noon.*

E'Werk takes its name from the building in which it is located—an abandoned electrical plant built during the Third Reich and then left by the Russians to deteriorate. The original hardware, including generators, chains, cables, insulators and wire fences, is still in place and makes a fitting venue for the avant garde musicians who perform here. One group had a member who "played" a chainsaw by running it against exposed pipes—the display of sparks was spectacular and gave a whole new dimension to the term heavy metal. This is said by many to be the finest club in Europe. Admission: moderate.

Nightlife

Unfortunately, the prewar cabaret scene so well depicted by Christopher Isherwood is long gone, and if you are offered the chance to see some real cabaret you will probably wind up disappointed. Today's nightlife is loud, rather raunchy and in a constant state of flux. *Die scene* changes from week to week. For what's going on now, look for the magazines *Tip* and *Zitty* which come out in alternate weeks. They're both in German, but with a little imagination and some help from pictures, you shouldn't have too much trouble figuring out what's going on.

Parks and Gardens

Gendarmenmarkt

A copy of the **Schauspielhause Theater** (the original was destroyed by World War II bombing) is located in the center of the Gendarmenmarkt, possibly Berlin's most elegant square. Twin Protestant **cathedrals** sit on opposite sides of the square. The Franzsischer Dom (French cathedral) served the needs of the French Huguenot community that sought refuge from religious persecution in France. The Deutscher Dom (German cathedral) served the needs of the German Lutherans. To get there, take Charlottenstrasse south from Unter den Linden.

Tiergarten

Public Transportation: *S-Bahn.* Metro Stop: *Tiergargen.*

Tiergarten was originally the private hunting preserve of the Electors of Prussia. Frederick the Great opened it to the public in 1742, and today it is a pleasant green space in the middle of the city, complete with lakes and groves of trees. During the war, trees were cut for firewood, and the lawns were turned into vegetable gardens to feed the populace of Berlin. What remained was bombed. The present-day plantings took place after the war. The Strasse des 17 Juni runs east-west through the park to the Brandenburg Gate, where it becomes Unter den Linden and runs into East Berlin.

Zoologischer Garten (Zoo)

Hardenbergplatz 8. ☎ *(030) 25-40-10.*

Public Transportation: *S-Bahn*. Metro Stop: *Zooligischer Garten*.

🕐 *9 a.m.–6 p.m.*

The oldest zoo in Germany is located at the southeastern corner of the Tiergarten. Along with the rest of this area, it suffered extensive damage from Allied bombing in World War II. Today the zoo participates in numerous programs for the breeding and preservation of endangered species. It also contains a terrarium famous for its crocodiles, plus an aquarium that is home to thousands of species of fish, amphibians and reptiles. Admission: moderate.

Shopping

Kunsthaus Tacheles

Oranienburger Strasse 53-56.

Kunsthaus Tacheles is an abandoned factory or department store, depending who you ask, taken over by squatters and turned into a center for fringe elements of the art scene. Inside are artists, studios, bars, discos, galleries, cafes, a cinema, a theatre and several book shops—all trying to outdo each other in an unstated and unsubtle contest to shock the unwary. Look for a large building covered with graffitti and scrap metal sculptures.

Special Tours

Guided bus excursions originate from the intersection of Kurfurstendamm and Uhlandstrasse, from Kurfurstendamm and Joachimstalerstr. lasse, from the Kaiser-Wilhelm Memorial Church, and from the corner of Meinekestrasse at the Kurfurstendamm. They include so much history that any first-time visitor should take a tour as part of a Berlin visit.

A sample itinerary is the six-hour spin to neighboring Potsdam by motor coach. Composed of a shuffle through Frederick the Great's crumbling Sanssouci Castle (you don enormous felt slippers so that your shoes won't mar the flooring) guests also visit the Tudor-style Cecilienhof Mansion, where the Potsdam Agreement was signed in 1945. Dresden, Meissen and Leipzig also can be absorbed on a two-day swing. A rewarding day-long outing in spring, summer or autumn is to Spreewald.

Boat Tours

A boat ride on one of the many lakes or rivers in the huge forest areas outside the city center to the west is a pleasant alternative to a bus tour. Most foreign visitors are unaware of these expansive forests and waterways, so you'll be more likely to spend this time with a high concentration of native Berliners. More than 70 boats a day ply the waters of the **Havel River, Tegeler See** and **Wannsee,** and they stop at all the best places. You can even glide over to **Potsdam** by boat. The biggest of many shiplines is **Stern and Kreisschiffahrt,** *Sachtleben Strasse 60* ☎ (030) 803-8750 or ☎ (030) 810-0040.

Stern-und Kreisschiffahrt
☐ *Pushkinalee 60-70.* ☎ *(030) 61-73-900.*

Among the best-known river-excursion companies. One of their newer offerings is the **Historische Stadfahrt** which takes passengers along the **Spree.** The trip takes about three hours and offers good views of the **Pergamon Museum,** the **Reichstag** and the **Royal Library,** and transverses what used to be the Soviet zone. Another interesting alternative is the **Seerunderfahrt,** a five-hour tour. It leaves every morning at 11:30 a.m. and circles southeastern Berlin on the Spree and Dahme rivers, the Langersee, the Seddinsee, the Muggelsee and the Grosser Muggelsee. Many visitors elect to get to **Potsdam** by boat. The trip requires about five hours travel time each way. There are many stops along the slow route; you many even have to change boats. Another option is to take the boat to Potsdam and then take the train back to Berlin. Boats for this excursion leave from **Treptow** on the eastern edge of Berlin.

Theatre

German State Opera   ★★★★
Unter den Linden 7. ☎ *(030) 200-4262.*
🕐 *Noon–5:45 p.m.*

Continue east on Under den Linden. On the south side of the street is the Staatsoper. This is the oldest opera house in Berlin and is still home to a performing company. Like so many of Berlin's buildings, the State Opera's design began as a Greek temple of classic simplicity, but inevitably took on some Rococo embellishments courtesy of architect Georg von Knobelsdorff. The result is a pleasing, if not slightly eccentric, whole. The productions are lavish and sell out quickly. Prices are usually lower than in West Berlin.

Neckar Valley
Heidelberg

Heidelberg boasts an enchanting situation astride a riverbank. It is simultaneously historic and modern, alive and tranquil, but always bewitching for its Old World beauty. In autumn when the leaves turn color, "Heather Hill" is a picture of dreamlike splendor. At night, the lights evoke the sensation of a theater setting— and to stroll anywhere is to turn the clock back five-hundred years. The city contains the world's largest **wine barrel** (58 thousand gallons), **Karzer Prison** for obstreperous 15th-century students of its celebrated university and the **127-foot TV tower** (observation platform open to the public). Heidelberg is guilty of nothing except an excess of historic charm; the only thing wrong with it is the rabble of Japanese, French, Italian, Belgian, Scandinavian, Indian, Greek, North American, Latin American and Hottentot tourists who throng it in season. But in good weather during the slowest months—*wunderbar!*

Where to Stay

Der Europaiche Hof-Hotel Europ ★★★★

Moderate to Expensive

Friedrich-Ebert-Anlage 1.

Public Transportation: *Tram.* Metro Stop: *Bismarckplatz.*

☎ *(06221) 51-50*, FAX: *223-6800*.

Credit Cards: *V, MC, DC, A.*

This family-run hotel is continuously updating in the most tasteful of traditional Germanic themes. Its latest addition is a 33-room wing with shops, conference salons and cellar garage. There are 135 units, all excellent and each different. Those in the original 1865 building are especially spacious. The high-end rooms even come with Jacuzzis. Fine, too, is the cuisine served in the elegant Europ-Treff or in the cozy Kurfursten-Stube. The attractive bar is another famous meeting place.

Hollander-Hof

Budget

Neckarstaden 66.

☎ *(06221) 12-09-1.*

Credit Cards: *V, MC, DC, A.*

This 40-room riverside hotel is located at one end of the ancient Alte Brucke, right in the middle of the city. The original building, a guesthouse dating back to medieval times, was destroyed by fire in 1693. The new facility dates from the 19th century, but the rooms are up to date, and hair dryers and radios.

Romantik Hotel zum Ritter St.

http://www.ritter-heidelberg.de/

Moderate to Expensive

Hauptstrasse 178. If driving, follow signs to Parkhaus 12. Hotel is a few blocks from there.

Public Transportation: *Bus 10, 11 or 12.*

☎ *(06221) 24-27-2,* FAX: *826-0015.*

Credit Cards: *V, MC, DC, A.*

Its first cornerstone planted in 1592, this is one of the landmarks of downtown. There are 39 rooms some furnished with 19th-century antiques and others with a more up-to-date motif. All come with TV and phone. The atmospheric dining room doesn't look like it's changed much since the 16th century. Room rates include a buffet breakfast.

Where to Eat

Zum Roter Ochsen

Moderate

Hauptstrasse 217. ☎ *(06221) 2 09 77.*

This is a typical German bar. There is some music, singing and a lot of beer. The food is heavy and servings are titanic—as are the prices. Why bother with this place? Because you'd feel dumb if you went to Heidelberg and didn't go to a student tavern. If it's too crowded here, just go on down the street to **Zum Seppíl,** which is almost the same thing.

What to Do

Historical Sites

Heidelberg University   ★

Universiitatsplatz.

There are two universities in Heidelberg, the Alte-Universitt (Old University) and the Neue Universitt, a newcomer formed in 1932. It is the Alte-Universitt or, as it is more properly known, the Ruprecht-Karl-Universitt, that most people associate with the city. The Alte Universitt was founded in the early 1300s by teachers and students who fled the political upheavals at the University of Paris and has existed in one form or another ever since. In the late 1800s and up until the 1930s it was the equal of any in the world. However, the rise of the Nazi Party and the persecution of its opponents led to a brain-drain of unprecedented proportions, from which the university has never recovered. Today it draws its students largely from the surrounding areas. It offers a sound education but is a shadow of its former self. The Alte-Universitt's building is open, and you can wander around. But function has won over form, and the interior is not that interesting or noteworthy.

ITRAVELBOOK FREEBIE

Heidelberger Schloss

Public Transportation: *Bus 11 or 33.* Metro Stop: *Kornmarkt.*

Heidelburger Schloss looks like a ruined castle right off a picture-postcard. Construction on the castle began in the 1300s and continued by fits and starts until 1764, when lightning struck the powder magazine in one of the towers. A large portion of the tower was blown away, and the rest burned, leaving an intriguing ruin with elements ranging from Gothic to high Renaissance. Heidelberger Schloss met its fate just in time to be taken up by the Romantics, who were fascinated with anything old and abandoned. Just about all the important Romantics seemed to have passed through the Heidelberger Schloss, and the castle is memorialized in operas, plays, poetry, literature and endless paintings. Very often it is depicted in the last rays of a setting sun, that depends naturally red sandstone walls and darken the green and foreboding woods surrounding it. Certain parts of the castle have been restored, but admission to them is restricted to guided tours. If you have the time, take the tour, but you can get a feel for the place just by walking around the grounds. Don't miss the courtyard, which is surrounded by splendid Renaissance facades and graceful arches. The walls and statuary have long since been covered with creepers, while massive trees force their way between the paving stones. No visit to the schloss would be complete without a visit to the **Grosses Fass** (Great Cask), which is supposed to hold 331,726 liters of wine. Pipes connect it to the adjacent King's Hall, where consumption is calculated to have reached more than 2000 liters per day. This is where the dwarf Perkeo held sway as guardian of the Cask. One wonders if he was the person best suited to this job, since legend tells us that his daily consumption of wine was 18 bottles per day (and he died from the after-effects of drinking a glass of water). A pharmacy and laboratory from the 18th- and 19th-centuries have been meticulously recreated, complete with scientific instruments, strange looking beakers and skulls. An alchemist's laboratory has been recreated in the **Apothecary's Tower** if you are curious about turning base metal into gold. If at all possible, try and time your visit to coincide with one of the summer's monthly illuminations of the castle. At night, floodlights shine on the castle from below and fireworks are set off on the terraces.

North

Hamburg

With approximately 1.6 million population, Hamburg is Germany's first seaport and the nation's second city. The skyline is dominated by an 890-foot-tall TV spindle that has a rotating restaurant. Dine in the famous **Ratsweinkeller**, stroll through **Planten un Blomen Park,** shop along Alster Lake, take a whirl through that naked, rowdy **Reeperbahn** night district, visit a **Doll Museum** with 300 *puppen* and 60 tiny houses, see the early Sunday morning trading at the **St. Pauli Fischmarkt,** then ride a steamer to **Blankenese** on the Elbe River, or to the war-famous island of Helgoland and see **Hagenbeck's** renowned zoo with its Troparium to display its apes, snakes, crocodiles and other exotic critters in natural surroundings. As a city of art, Hamburg has few peers. Visit the Kunsthalle, the Kunsthaus, the Kunstverein and the Deichtorhallen. You'll find more than 200 superb private galleries, many containing pieces which have come over from the East and are relatively cheap. Auction houses such as Hauswedell and Nolte (both locally based) plus branches of Sotheby's and Christie's are booming. It's a fascinating market.

Where to Stay

Alster-Hof ★

http://www.alster-hof.de/english/ index_eng.html

Budget

Esplanade 12.

Public Transportation: *U-Bahn.* Metro Stop: *Gansemarkt.*

☎ *(040) 35-00-70.*

Credit Cards: *V, MC, DC, A.*

Has 117 varying accommodations, two penthouse suites and 21 rooms with the most minuscule baths outside a U-boat. Maintenance is good. Rooms come with TV and phone. Rate includes a continental breakfast. There is no restaurant.

Atlantic Hotel Kempinski ★★★★★

http://www.kempinski.atlantic.de/ juk/jframeie.htm

Moderate to Expensive

An der Alster 72.

Public Transportation: *U-Bahn*. Metro Stop: *Hauptbahnhof.*

☎ *(040) 28-80-0,* FAX: *426-3135.*

Credit Cards: *V, MC, DC, A.*

Comfortable and elegant, this hotel provides a faintly robust air of
executive domain. The lobby is a gracious restoration of the Atlantic
of 1909—and a pleasure to behold. There is the Die Brucke restaurant for quick meals, the Edwardian- modern Rendezvous Bar with
piano music, a dining room with orchestrated dinner dancing, a
superb grill, air conditioning in all public quadrants, an indoor pool-
massage-sauna complex and 256 rooms featuring some glorious
suites.

Aussen Alster

http://www.aussen-alster.de/

Moderate

Schmilinskystrasse 11.

Public Transportation: *U-Bahn*. Metro Stop: *Hauptbahnhof.*

☎ *(040) 23-00-02,* FAX: *528-1234.*

Credit Cards: *All Major.* Credit Cards: *V, MC, DC.*

This hotel has a peaceful location on a residential street within walking distance of the train station, 12 intimate rooms and personalized
service. Rates include a continental breakfast. Room and laundry
service are available. There also is a boat docked at the nearby
Aussenalster that guests can use for sailing.

Elysee

http://www.elysee-hamburg.de/wms/ elysee/index.php3?lan-
guage=2

Moderate to Expensive

10 Rothenbaumchaussee.

☎ *(040) 41-41-20.*

Credit Cards: *V, MC, DC, A.*

The Elysee exudes a youthful ambience that will be noted in the lobby each afternoon and evening, when live music stirs the air. The hotel has 305 rooms, two restaurants, plus a Bodega and the toe-tapping Bourbon Street Bar.

Garden Hotel Poseldorf

✉ *Magdalenenstrasse.*

Public Transportation: *U-Bahn.* Metro Stop: *Halalerstrasse.*

☎ *(040) 41-40-40.*

Í *DM230–DM300.* ÍÍ *DM360–DM420.*

Credit Cards: *V, MC, DC, A.*

This place seems aimed toward the upwardly mobile young executives, models, theater people and the frolicsome movers and shakers of modern Germany. The botanical feature in its name imparts a more residential than commercial tone to hotel's overall aura. The Harvestehude area surrounding Magdalenenstrasse is likewise quiet and more private than the midcity precincts, although it's only a mile from downtown. The 61 rooms, each with its own decor, have been created out of three 18th-century town houses. Among the many modern touches are marble baths, cable TVs, VCRs and hair dryers. Rates include a continental breakfast, which is served in the winter garden. Room service, laundry and dry cleaning are available.

Hotel Abtei

http://www.abtei-hotel.de/

Moderate

Abteistrasse 14. NW of Alster, three kilometers from city center.

☎ *(040) 442-2905.*

Credit Cards: *V, MC, DC, A.*

This small, family-run hotel not only looks just like other mansions in the exclusive Harvestehude residential area of Hamburg, it makes guests feel royally rich. The 12 bedchambers, each with bath, have high ceilings and antique furnishings.

Mellingburger Schleuse

Moderate

Mellingburgredder 1.

☎ *(040) 062-4001.*

Credit Cards: *V, MC, DC, A.*

This is the perfect spot for the outdoor enthusiasts visiting the Hamburg area. Twenty minutes from the center of the city, the Mellingburger is in the woods on the Alsterwanderweg hiking trail. The 250-year-old thatch-roofed lodging offers 37 rooms and a small restaurant specializing in northern German cuisine.

Radisson SAS Hamburg Plaza

Moderate to Expensive

Marseiller Strasse 2.

☎ *(040) 350-20,* FAX: *221-2350.*

Spliced neatly into the municipal convention center, this properly boasts of being the nation's highest hostelry. SAS, which caters chiefly to business travelers, runs this show, which is plainly a massive commercial enterprise. Its corridors lead to 563 look-alike units. Most are cookie-mold-standard doubles or twins, but some of the views of the city are outstanding. There are four restaurants, a communications center and bars.

Travel Hotel Bellevue

http://travel.bellevue.de/home

Moderate

An der Alster 14.

Public Transportation: *Bus 108.*

☎ *(040) 24-80-11.*

Credit Cards: *V, MC, DC, A.*

This neighbor to the Prem boasts 78 bedchambers. The neighborhood is a good one, which is one reason it attracts so many celebrities. The hotel is on the lake and close to the rail station. The Pilsner Urquell Stuben is noted for its cuisine; the INA bar for its live organ music. Rooms come with trouser press and hair dryer. Rates include a buffet breakfast.

Where to Eat

At Nali

Inexpensive to Moderate

Rutschbahn 11. ☎ *(040) 410 3810.*

Credit Cards: *V, MC, DC, A.*

This is a Turkish restaurant where the Turks go to eat. There is nothing fancy about this place, but the food is consistently good and so is the service. Portions are ample. Try the classic babaganoush with oven fresh pita bread, order eggplant grilled with a little bit of olive oil and a judicious addition of fresh herbs. There are all kinds of strange-looking pastries made with lots of honey and nuts. Dress is informal. With these prices and this kind of food, it's always crowded.

Colln's Austernstuben

Moderate

Brodschrangen 1-5. ☎ *(040) 35 60 59.*

Public Transportation: *U-Bahn.* Metro Stop: *Rathausmarkt.*

Credit Cards: *V, MC, DC, A.*

Austernstuben means "oyster bar" in German, and Colln's Austernstuben was exactly that when it opened its doors sometime in the 1760s. The place has gone through several transformations since then, but today it's a Hamburg tradition. Oysters are still a house specialty, but the kitchen does much more. The chef has a wonderful way with puff pastry, which is not limited to the dessert menu.

L'Auberge Francaise

Moderate to Expensive

Rutschbahn 34. ☎ *(040) 410 25 32.*

Credit Cards: *V, MC, DC, A.*

This is a classic French restaurant in the heart of the most German of seaports. Local fish from the Baltic are always on the menu. If your arteries can take it, try the goose liver prepared in a number of ways or the equally delicate calf's liver in assorted sauces. The service is discreet and faultless. Coat and tie required.

O Pescador ★★★

Moderate

Ditmar Keohl Strasse 17. ☎ *(040) 319 3000.*

Public Transportation: *U-Bahn.* Metro Stop: *Landungsbruken.*

Close to the docks, this restaurant is frequented by seafaring types seeking large portions. It's always crowded, so you may be asked to share your table. Grilled swordfish with *cheiro verde* (parsley sauce) and plain boiled potatoes is hard to beat. There's also a good *bacalao* (dried cod) in a cream sauce with a little bit of tomato and basil (in season). Stick to the simple things and you can't go wrong. Reservations aren't accepted, so you may have to wait at the bar.

Peter Lembcke ★★

Moderate

Holzdamm 49. ☎ *(040) 24 32 90.*

Public Transportation: *U-Bahn.* Metro Stop: *Hauptbahnhof.*

Credit Cards: *V, MC, DC, A.*

Located on the second floor of an older building, Peter Lembke has an unprepossessing exterior, but the food and service are warm, friendly and consistently good. The eel soup, specialty of the house, blends fruit and the unexpected flavor of dill. Fish from the nearby Baltic make their appearances in various guises, depending on the inspiration of the chef. Coat and tie are required.

What to Do

Historical Sites

ATG-Alter-Touristik ★★★★★

Am Angleger Jungernsteig. ☎ *(040) 34-11-41.*

Public Transportation: *U-Bahn*. Metro Stop: *Landungsbruken*.

Special Hours: *Closed Dec.-Feb.*

Hamburg has been a seaport for over a thousand years, and one of the best ways to get a feel for the city is to take a tour of the harbor. There are more than 33 docks and berths for over 500 ships. In any given month, 1500 ships from all over the world will arrive and depart from the port, and the money generated from this commerce has made Hamburg one of the wealthiest cities in Germany. If you can take the tour after dark, even better. Bear in mind that Hamburg's dock area endured some of the heaviest bombings during World War II. In one night in 1943, more than 46,000 people, mostly dock workers living in tenements, died in a fire-storm caused by bombs. Admission: moderate.

Museums and Exhibits

Erotic Art Museum ★

Bernhard-Nocht-Strasse 69. ☎ *(040) 313 429.*

Public Transportation: *U-Bahn*. Metro Stop: *St. Pauli*.

This museum houses what you'd expect, all items tastefully displayed. The collection, four floors worth, displays an astounding quantity of articles that have at one time been considered titillating. Some still are; others will simply evoke a smile. Admission: inexpensive.

Kunsthalle

Glockengeisser Wall 1. ☎ *(040) 2486-2614.*

Public Transportation: *U-Bahn*. Metro Stop: *Hauptbahnhof.*

Special Hours: *Thurs. to 9 p.m.; closed Mon.*

As the premier art collection in Northern Germany, the Kunsthalle ranges from the Middle Ages to the present day. Meister Bertram, one of the first of the medieval artists to be remembered by name, is represented in the *St. Petri Altar,* consisting of 36 painted and gilded panels. The Kunsthalle displays Rembrandt's *The Presentation at the Temple*, painted when the artist was only 21. The collection of 19th-century German paintings is especially fine, with representative works by such artists as Caspar David Friedrich, Wilhelm Leibl and Max Liebermann. The *Cafe Lebermann* in the museum's Suerhalle is a good place to rest your feet while enjoying delicious cakes and pastries. Admission: inexpensive.

Museum fur Kunst und Gewerbe

Steintorplatz 1.

Public Transportation: *U-Bahn.* Metro Stop: *Hauptbahnhof.*

Special Hours: *Closed Mon.*

An excellent collection of applied arts ranging from medieval carvings to porcelain to musical instruments. You'll also find a world-renowned collection of *Jugendstil* (Art Nouveau) furniture so extensive that excess pieces are used as furniture in the museum cafe. There is also a real Japanese tea house. Admission: inexpensive.

Nightlife

Cotton Club

Alter Stenwig 10. ☎ *(040) 34 38 78.*

🕐 *8 p.m.–1 a.m.*

You might like to drop into this fixture in *die szene*, the Cotton Club. It's an old, established jazz club often featuring groups from other European countries as well as the United States. Admission: varies.

Die Insel

Alsterfer 35. ☎ *(040) 410 69 55.*

Die Insel is located in a lovely multistory townhouse near the Kennedy-Brucke. The champagne bar is a popular gathering place for artistic and journalistic types (Hamburg is the media capital of Germany). The restaurant is also a popular place to come after the theater, but a fixed-price meal with upwards of five courses can set you back about $100. The food and the atmosphere are great. Admission: varies.

Theatre

Hamburg has an **opera company** that constantly tries to outdo Munich for the number one position. The **ballet company** under the direction of John Neumeier (an American) is also top flight. Both perform in the **Hamburg Opera**, *Dammtorstrasse* ☎ ((040) 35 17 21). Tickets sell out well in advance but are worth trying for. The city supports no fewer than three symphony orchestras: the **Hamburg Philharmonic,** the **Hamburg Symphony** and the **NDR Symphony** (this one is known for performances of "modern" music). They all perform at the **Musikhalle, Karl-Muck-Platz** ☎ (040) 34 69 20). Hamburg is a bulwark of the Lutheran church and, as such, has a strong tradition of organ and choral music. Church concerts are frequent (especially around Christmas and Easter) and some of the "amateur" choirs offer surprisingly polished performances. A donation to the church may be requested, or admission is often free. The citizens of Hamburg are also ardent theater goers; if you speak German, you have your pick of nearly 20 live productions every night. The **State Theater** performs in two houses, the *Deutsches Schauspielhaus, Kirchenalee 39* ☎ (24 87 13) and the **Thalia Theater,** *Gerhard- Hauptmann-Platz* ☎ (040) 32 26 66). If you really want to know what's happening now, check out the magazines *Prinz* and *Szene* —they carry an exhaustive listing of what's going on with the hip crowd, where, and for how much. *Hamburger Vorschau* presents much the same material.

The Rhine

Aachen

Aachen, also called **Aix-la-Chapelle**, is known as the city of Charlemagne. Developing gracefully over 2000 years, Aachen is the union of Belgium, Holland and Germany. The **Cathedral** (Dom) and the **Rathaus** are its focal points, and they overlook the open market The church—magnificently ornate—contains the burial place of the mighty conqueror, while the Rathaus is built upon the foundations of Charlemagne's palace. The church **Treasury**, houses one of the richest ecclesiastical collections north of Rome. Children should head straight for the **Puppet Fountain** in the market, which is composed of brass articulated dolls.

Where to Stay

Hotels and Resorts

Am Marschiertor ★★★

Moderate

Wallstrasse 1-7.

Public Transportation: *Bus 1, 11, 21.*

☎ *(0241) 31-94-1.*

Credit Cards: *V, MC, DC.*

There is plenty to appreciate at this 50- room hotel near the city's historical area, particularly the coziness and quiet. There is a courtyard with a view over the Altstadt and the cathedral. Rates include a buffet breakfast.

Aquis Grana City Hotel   ★★

Budget to Moderate

Büchel 32.

Public Transportation: *Bus 1, 11, 21.*

☎ *(0241) 44-30.*

Credit Cards: *V, MC, DC, A.*

Here's everything you need in a modern hotel without sacrificing any warmth. Located on a downtown street corner, there is a direct entrance to the spa facilities Thermalhallenbad Römerbad. There are 94 rooms and two suites. Rates include a buffet breakfast, and there is a good restaurant on the premises. The hotel also has a hot tub.

Danmark   ★

Budget

Lagerhausstrrasse 21.

Public Transportation: *Bus 1, 11, 21.*

☎ *(0241) 3-44-14.*

Credit Cards: *V, MC, DC, A.*

Some consider the 37-room Danmark the best bargain in Aachen. It's only a two-minute walk from the rail station and only a 10-minute walk from the center of town. Families can take advantage of the triple-room rate that, like the other rates, includes a continental breakfast.

Hotel Baccara

Budget

Turmstrasse 174.

Public Transportation: *Bus 3, 13, 23.*

☎ *(0241) 8-30-05.*

Credit Cards: *V, MC, A.*

This centrally located hotel is within short walking distance of downtown. Modern and clean. Some of the 33 rooms come with private balconies, and the rates include a buffet breakfast.

Krott ★

Budget to Moderate

Wirichsbongardstrasse 16.

☎ *(0241) 48-37-3.*

Credit Cards: *V, MC, DC, A.*

The family-run Krott offers 22 rooms, all with baths, in the middle of town, within walking distance of most sights. The hotel offers a restaurant, solarium and hot tub.

Steigenberger Hotel Quellenhof

Moderate to Expensive

Monheimsallee 52. Near Kurpark and casino

Public Transportation: *Bus 1, 11, 21. Rated Restaurant: Park restaurant Quellenhof.*

☎ *(0241) 15-20-81,* FAX: *223-5652.*

Credit Cards: *V, MC, DC, A.*

Royal treatment has always been a feature at the Quellenhof. Built in World War I as a home for the Kaiser, the hotel is expensive, but worth it. There are 165 rooms with high ceilings in a quiet setting near the Kurpark and casino. Don't miss a meal at the Parkrestaurant Quellenhof, one of northern Germany's best. One of several restaurants available. There also is a solarium and parking.

Where to Eat

Ratskeller and Postwagen ★

Inexpensive to Moderate

Am Markt. ☎ *(0241) 3 50 51.*

Public Transportation: *Bus 1, 11, 21.*

Credit Cards: *V, MC, DC, A.*

Two for the price of one. The Rathskeller serves full meals. The Postwagen is a tavern which serves drinks and very large plates of cold cuts and potato salad. Both restaurants have been here for centuries and have lots of atmosphere—especially Postwagen, which has tiny wood-panelled rooms on various levels.

Restaurant Gala ★★

Moderate

Monheimsalee 44. ☎ *(0241) 15 30 13.*

Public Transportation: *Bus 13.*

Credit Cards: *V, MC, DC, A.*

Located at the same address as the casino, Gala has class. Crystal pendants distribute light on the wood paneled walls and oil paintings, several of which are originals by Salvador Dali. Every dish is made from scratch, and fresh ingredients are trucked in from Paris every morning. The chef combines the best of French and German cuisine, and the result is enviable.

What to Do

Historical Sites

Dom (Cathedral)

Munsterplatz. ☎ *(0241) 477 09 27.*

Public Transportation: *Bus 1, 11, 29.*

Aachon's cathedral is furnished in a manner worthy of the 32 Holy Roman emperors, successors to Charlemagne, crowned here. In addition to Charlemagne's throne, the cathedral possesses a chandelier donated by Barbarossa and a gold shrine containing the remains of Charlemagne. Admission: free.

Rathaus (Town Hall) ★★

Am Markt . ☎ *(0241) 432 73 10.*

Public Transportation: *Bus 1, 11, 21.*

Special Hours: *Sat., Sun. open at 10 a.m.*

The Rathaus, built on the site of the great hall of Charlemagne's palace, is located across Katschof Square from the Cathedral. After their coronations, it was the custom of the Holy Roman Emperors to proceed across the square to the Empire Hall on the upper floor of the Rathaus, where they enjoyed their coronation feasts. The Rathaus also houses a collection of exact replicas of the Austro-Hungarian crown jewels, which are now kept in Vienna. Along the north wall of the building are statues of the fifty Holy Roman Emperors crowned in Aachen before the coronation site was moved to Frankfurt. An imposing bronze statue of Charlemagne is the focal point of the fountain in the square separating the Rathaus from the cathedral. The Rathaus itself suffered heavy damage during World War II but has been faithfully restored. Admission: inexpensive.

Museums and Exhibits

Couven Museum ★

Huhnermarkt. ☎ *(0241) 432 44 21.*

Public Transportation: *Bus 1, 11, 21.*

Special Hours: *Sat. open to 1 p.m.; closed Mon.*

The Couven Museum is located away from the city center but it is well-worth a visit. Housed in a restored, Rococo house that belonged to a merchant, the ground floor of the museum represents a dispensary as it would have been during the 1600s; the second floor has an extensive collection of furniture and artifacts pertaining to every day of life in the same period. Take care to observe the carved wooden chimney, which is an especially fine example of its kind. Admission: inexpensive.

Domschatzkammer

Klostergasse, around the corner from the cathedral.
☎ *(0241) 477 09 27.*

Public Transportation: *Bus 1, 11, 21.*

The Cathedral Treasury at Aachen contains the largest collection of ecclesiastical plates in Germany. Among its treasures is the Lothair Cross from the 10th century. A true masterpiece of medieval workmanship, the cross combines gold filigree, pearls and precious stones. From a slightly later period, the Golden Bookcover shows a Byzantine influence in the ivory panel which depicts the Virgin and Child. Admission: varies.

Nightlife

Spielbank (Casino)

Monheimsalee 44, facing Kurbad Quellenhoff. ☎ *(0241) 18-080.*

Special Hours: *Fri., Sat. open to 3 a.m.*

Though not in a class with the casino at Baden-Baden, the Aachen casino keeps up appearances by requiring men to wear coats and ties at the gaming tables. Women must dress accordingly. Gamblers must be 18 or over and must present their passports to gain admittance. Roulette, blackjack and baccarat are the games of choice, although there are slot machines. Admission: varies.

Cologne

Cologne's modern midtown towers contrast dramatically with its beautifully preserved cathedral, a magnificent structure, the largest Gothic building in the world. You can't appreciate the colossal size and the detailed craftsmanship of the stonework without making the climb (20 minutes, 509 steps) up to the topmost belfry. The views alone are spellbinding. In recent years a dozen Romanesque churches, which have been restored are now open to the public. **St. Pantaleon**, with its 10th-century cloister, is often said to be the oldest in Germany. The massive unveiling has made Cologne one of Europe's most important centers of medieval architecture and ecclesiastical art. The big draws otherwise are the radically daring **Museum Ludwig,** the infinitely rich and rewarding Wallraf-Richartz collection, the **theater-opera** house, the playhouse, the **Roman Germanic Museum** surrounding the Dionysos Mosaic and containing fabulous Roman glassware, plus a splendid gem display and **Phantasialand**, the local answer to the Disney realms.

Where to Stay

Altstadt-Hotel

Moderate

Salzgasse 7.

Public Transportation: *U-Bahn.* Metro Stop: *Hauptbahnhof.*

☎ *(0221) 25-77-851.*

Credit Cards: *V, MC, DC, A.*

This small but comfortable haven in the old section of Cologne, not far from the Rhine, offers 28 individually decorated rooms with bath. Rates include a buffet breakfast, though no restaurant exists on the premises. Rooms come with radio and TV. Advance reservations recommended.

Dom-Hotel

Moderate

Domkloster 2A.

Public Transportation: *U-Bahn.* Metro Stop: *Hauptbahnhof.*

☎ *(0221) 20-24-0.*

Credit Cards: *V, MC, DC, A.*

This is one of the better traditional hostelries in the region. It is professionally maintained and offers modernized baths, color TV and English video. In this traffic-dense town, its 650-car underground garage with direct entry to the hotel comes as a blessing to anyone on wheels. There is a cheery winter garden restaurant with a pleasant summer terrace. Some of the 126 rooms are on the Domplatz and have breathtaking views of its Gothic splendor. Ask about the hotel's weekend package. Also on the premises are a bar and conference facilities.

Haus Lyskirchen

Moderate

Filzengraben 26-32. U-Bahn: Heumraktplatz

Public Transportation: *Trams 1, 2, 7.*

☎ *(0221) 20-97-0.*

Credit Cards: *V, MC, DC, A.*

A medium-size lodging with up-to-date amenities, this hotel is
located only four blocks from the cathedral. It offers a countrylike
atmosphere thanks to its gabled exterior and wooded interior.
Rooms have color TV, radio, hair dryer and trouser press. There are
two restaurants, a pub, solarium and underground parking. Rates
include a continental breakfast.

Stapelhäuschen Das Kleine

Moderate

Fischmarkt 1-3 am Rheinufer.

Public Transportation: *Bus 136.* Metro Stop: *Heumraktplatz.*

☎ *(0221) 25-77-862.*

Credit Cards: *V, MC.*

Get a feel for medieval Germany from this colorful antique structure
on cobbled Fish Market Square, a waterfront locale where
Benedictine monks sailing from Scotland sold their fish. The original Stapelhäuschen was built in the 12th century. It became a hotel
in 1950, when two neighboring houses were combined. There are
33 rooms, 14 with bath, a restaurant and a bar. Rates include a continental breakfast. Only minutes from the cathedral.

Alte Thorschenke

Moderate to Expensive

Bruckenstrasse 3.

☎ *(02671) 70-59.*

Credit Cards: *V, MC, A.*

Old World charm is personified in this 14th-century inn by the
Mosel River. Many of the 45 rooms have four-poster beds, including ones occupied by Maria Theresa, Napoleon and Goethe. To capture the full flavor of "Thor's Old Inn" get one of the rooms
accessed by the old spiral wooden staircase. Even these rooms have
central heating, and some have phone, TV, radio and hair dryer. The
rustic, all-wood dining room, where you order wine from the 500-

year-old winery, is adorned with hunting trophies. The entire inn is full of old paintings and artwork. Pets are allowed, and room rates include a buffet breakfast. Closed from Jan. 5 to March 15.

Where to Eat

Alt Koln am Dom

Inexpensive to Moderate

Trankgasse 7-9. ☎ *(0221) 13 74 71.*

Public Transportation: *U-Bahn.* Metro Stop: *Hauptbahnhof.*

Credit Cards: *V, MC, DC, A.*

Obliging waitresses serve good German food such as Wiener Schnitzel, smoked bacon pancakes, and lots of sausage and sauerkraut.

Ambiance am Dom

Am Hof 38. ☎ *(0221) 29 91 27.*

Public Transportation: *U-Bahn.* Metro Stop: *Hauptbahnhof.*

Credit Cards: *V, MC, DC, A.*

This is not your typical hotel dining room. The chef is attuned to the changing seasons, and the menu specialties are composed of what is best in the market that day. Recipes are based on classic French techniques adapted to local traditions.

Die Bastel ★★★

Moderate

Konrad Adenauer Ufer 80. ☎ *(0221) 12 28 25.*

Public Transportation: *U-Bahn.* Metro Stop: *Ebertplatz.*

Credit Cards: *V, MC, DC, A.*

For once the food is as good as the view: an old watchtower jutting out into the Rhine. The menu is Franco-German with the best of both worlds. Try the refined sauerkraut salad with toasted caraway seeds and warm walnuts. Dinner and dancing on Saturday. Reservations are wise, especially on weekends.

Rino Casati   ★★★★

Moderate to Expensive

Ebertplatz 3-5. ☎ *(0221) 72-44-08.*

Public Transportation: *U-Bahn.* Metro Stop: *Ebertplatz.*

Credit Cards: *V, MC, DC, A.*

This is the best Italian restaurant in Germany. All pasta is made on the premises. The wine list is extensive—mostly from Italy and France. Expect to pay accordingly. Reservations are a must.

What to Do

City Celebrations

Carnival

Somehow or other, the Reformation missed Cologne, which remains a largely Catholic city that takes Carnival very seriously. Officially, the season begins on November 11, when the mayor makes a speech and announces who has been selected as Prince of the Carnival in the coming year. Things pick up speed on New Year's Eve, when the yearly series of *Sitzungen* begin. Sitzungen are parties which are held to raise money to finance the carnival parades during Holy Week. They can be anything from gatherings at the local pubs to jet-setting balls. On the Thursday before Ash Wednesday, the mayor hands over the keys of the city to the Prince of Carnival, and from then on anything goes. The pubs (look for the straw dummies that are hanging outside of them) stay open 24 hours, and revelry reign although shops and offices do their best to maintain business hours. The *Rosenmontagzug* (Rose Monday Parade) is the culmination of all this activity. Flowers, candies and miniatures of eau de cologne are thrown into the crowd. The final ball of the season is held on Tuesday, at which point the Prince gives back the keys to the city to the mayor, and everyone goes home to sleep it off until next year. Book your room well in advance. It's a good idea to have written confirmation in hand.

Historical Sites

Dom (Cathedral)   ★★★★★

Domkloster. ☎ *(0221) 25 77 650.*

Public Transportation: *U-Bahn*. Metro Stop: *Hauptbahnhof*.

Many historians consider Cologne Cathedral to be the most perfect example of Gothic architecture in the world. Over 90 percent of Cologne was destroyed by Allied bombing during the war, but orders were given to spare the Dom. Early postwar photos of the city show the cathedral towering over the rubble. The most important religious object housed in the Dom is the *Shrine of the Magi*. The gold reliquary in the shape of a basilica is covered with jeweled votive offerings of the faithful and holds what are purported to be the bones of the Three Kings. They were brought to Cologne from Milan in 1164, and there are still numerous taverns and inns along their route whose names refer to the Drei Konigen. These holy relics soon became the object for numerous pilgrimages, and the impetus for the cathedral's construction in 1284. Notice the windows in the Dom. They represent every major period in the development of stained glass and include the biblical windows of the 13th-century, Renaissance windows and, more recently, the Bavarian windows donated by King Ludwig in the mid-1800s. The *Geron Crucifix* is housed in the *Chapel of the Cross*, located under the organ loft. This cross, which dates from the 10th century, is the oldest life-sized depiction of the crucifixion in the world and is still an object of religious veneration. Directly across the chancel from the Chapel of the Cross is the Lady Chapel, which contains the famous Lochner triptych. When closed, it shows the Annunciation; when opened, it depicts the Adoration of the Magi. The Dom has a *Schatzkammer* (Treasury), which is open to the public. It contains the relics of 18 saints, a fragment of St. Peter's staff and a collection of church plate in solid gold and silver. Admission: free.

Museums and Exhibits

Church of St. Ursula

Ursula Platz.

The crown on the spire of the church commemorates the fact that St. Ursula was an English princess. Legend tells us she led 11,000 virgins into battle against the Huns sometime around the year 400. All of the nuns, including Ursula, were slaughtered and buried on this site. Around the year 1100, a church was constructed, and the bones were dug up and used to form mosaic patterns which adorn the walls. The femurs have been used to spell out Latin mottos. Admission: free.

Museum of East Asian Art

Universitatstrasse 100.

Public Transportation: *Tram 1, 2 from Neumarkt.*

Special Hours: *First Thurs. of the month open to 8 p.m.*

This museum specializes in the art and history China, Japan and Korea. The collection of Japanese woodcuts is extensive, and the collection of Korean ceramics is considered to be the best outside of Korea. The building is modern and designed by Kunio Mayekawa. The Japanese garden that borders on the river is an especially popular place. Admission: inexpensive.

Römisch-Germanisches Museum

http://www.museenkoeln.de/rgm/

Roncalliplatz 4. ☎ *(0221) 221-4438.*

Public Transportation: *U-Bahn.* Metro Stop: *Hauptbahnhof.*

Special Hours: *Sat., Sun. open at 11 a.m.*

The Romisch-Germanisches Museum is an upstart in museum circles. It houses a magnificent 100-square-yard mosaic that was discovered during excavations for construction of an air-raid shelter during World War II. The mosaic is almost 10 meters by 10 meters and portrays graphic events in the legends of Dionysus, the Greek god of wine and revels. On the south side of the building, you can see a restored stretch of the original Roman road that once led up from the river. Admission: inexpensive.

Wallraf-Richartz Museum (Museum Ludwig)

Bischofsgartenstrasse 1. ☎ *(0221) 221-2379.*

Public Transportation: *U-Bahn.* Metro Stop: *Hauptbahnhof.*

Special Hours: *Sat., Sun. open at 11 p.m.*

The Wallraf-Richartz-Museum includes works from the 13th-century through the 19th-century. As might be expected, the emphasis is on the German, Dutch and Flemish schools, but the Italian masters of the High Renaissance are also well represented, as are the French Impressionists. Don't miss the triptychs by the Master of Saint Veronica and the Master of the Life of the Virgin. There are representative works by artists as diverse as Titian, Canaletto, Tintoretto, Murillo, Degas, Renoir and Delacroix, as well as self-portraits by Rembrandt and Rubens. What the collection lacks in depth, it makes up for in scope, and it is well worth an afternoon. The Museum Ludwig, located on the top floor of the complex, is devoted to 20th-century art. It is especially well known for its collection of Russian avant-garde art from the period 1910 through 1930. There is also a room dedicated to various works of Picasso, as well as the cubists Leger, Braque and Gris. The collection is constantly expanding and now includes the works of Roy Lichtenstein and a representative sample of Andy Warhol's cans of tomato soup. Often overlooked is the collection of prints and drawings on the first floor. Among the works are sketches by Leonardo da Vinci, Raphael, Rembrandt, and others, some of which are "roughs" for pictures which are displayed elsewhere in the gallery. Admission: varies.

Nightlife

Nightlife

Cologne is home to the world-famous *Cologne State Opera*

☎ *0221-84-00,* Oper de Stadt Koln located at Offenbachplatz. If you are even faintly interested in opera, try for tickets. The Philharmonie orchestra holds forth at *Bichofsgartenstrasse 1* ☎ *(0221) 204-080,* and regularly attracts internationally known artists. Unfortunately, *Die Szene* is not as well developed in Cologne as it is elsewhere, and there doesn't appear to be much that can compete with the smoky, heavy-metal happenings in Berlin. What there is appears to be happening in the **Quartier Lateng** near **Zulpicher Platz**. The magazine *Stadt Revue,* sold at newsstands for DM3.50, has listings of just about anything that's going on in town.

Düsseldorf

Although 80 percent of the city was destroyed during World War II, Düsseldorf today is Germany's center for high fashion and advertising. This large, wealthy town is 25 miles north of Cologne. The airport offers a rail spur to midtown, and this melds conveniently into the continent's express Intercity system of trains. The main street, called "Kö," runs along a lovely waterway and offers many hotels, good restaurants, **Benrath Castle**, scads of churches and art galleries, a revolving 540-foot tower *(Rheinturm)* that is part of an intricate geophysical clock system, a modern four-story apartment-style bordello, and handsome environs, one of which includes the **Minidomm**, elf-size scale models of world-famous architectural wonders from Gothic cathedrals to Kennedy Airport (*open daily from 9:00 a.m.–11:00 p.m.*; between Dusseldorf and Mulheim). While the Kunst (Art) Museum is noteworthy, those with specialized tastes might enjoy the fabulous glass exhibition next door at Ehrenhof 1; the range runs from antiquity through Tiffany to contemporary pieces by Steuben, Kosta and other greats.

Where to Stay

Hotels and Resorts

Am Rhein Schnellenburg

Moderate

Rotterdamerstrasse 120. Less than four miles from center of town, opposite Nord Park, on Rhine

Public Transportation: *Bus 722.* Metro Stop: *Messe Center.*

☎ *(0211) 43-41-33*

Credit Cards: *V, MC, DC, A.*

The attractive, family-run Schnellenburg is on the Rhine River less than four miles north of the center of town, close to the airport and just a short walk to the convention center and Japanese Garden. River viewing is possible from some of the 49 guest rooms and the restaurant's terrace. Sight-seeing boats stop at the hotel's private pier. Also on the premises are a bar and lounge.

Breidenbacher Hof

Expensive

Heinrich-Heine-Allee 36. Tram 76, 78 or 705.

Public Transportation: *U-Bahn.* Metro Stop: *Heinrich-Heine-Allee.*

☎ *(0211) 13-03-0.*

Credit Cards: *V, MC, DC, A.*

A classic that is lavishly outfitted in sparkling attire, this hotel, from cellar to roof, is a little jewel. For traditionalists—as opposed to modernists—nothing in the city proper can beat it. Built in the early 1800s and updated several times since, it is located between

Konigsallee and the Altstadt (Old Town). This is the favorite spot for visiting royalty and celebrities. The elegant reception and lobby salon exotica from the Orient; bar-lounge with wood- paneling, black leather and pastoral paintings; marvelous, cozy Eck restaurant with imaginative selections on a small menu; a grill-lounge with cognac-colored walls and fine Italian mahogany furniture. The hotel offers a quartet of gorgeous suites among the 132 antique-filled rooms. For guests' convenience there are car-rental facilities, 24-hour room service, a laundry and dry cleaning.

Eden

Moderate to Expensive

Adersstrasse 29-31. Tram 709 or 719; Bus 834 Rated Restaurant: Bierstube.

☎ *(0211) 38-97-0.*

Credit Cards: *V, MC, DC, A.*

Close to the shopping on Konigsallee and only five minutes from the main rail station, Eden provides comfort and convenience. Besides the Bierstube restaurant, there is a lobby bar, hairdresser and flower shop on the premises. Newly renovated conference rooms also are available.

Gunnewig Uebachs

Budget

3-5 Leopoldstrasse.

☎ *(0211) 36-05-66.*

This Gunnewig entry attracts an older clientele of loyal wayfarers. They like the hotel's overall feeling of cleanliness and puffy-pillow snap. A restaurant and bar are located on the premises, and guests can take a short walk and use the Savoy facilities.

Steigenberger Park-Hotel

Moderate to Expensive

Corneliusplatz 1. Tram 78 or 79; Bus 778 Rated Restaurant: Menuett.

☎ *(0211) 13-81-0,* FAX: *223-5652.*

Credit Cards: *V, MC, DC, A.*

The lobby, lounges and especially the suites are exceptional. The
hotel is within walking distance of Konigsallee, the Altstadt,
Hofgarten Park and the German Opera on the Rhine. All 160 rooms
have quality furnishings, full carpeting and good baths; streetside
units are soundproofed. Rooms come with TV and radio. Also available are 24-room service, a laundry, dry cleaning, shoeshine service
and a car-rental desk.

Burghotel

Budget

Laufenstrasse 1.

☎ *(02472) 23-32.*

The family-run lodging, with 13 nicely furnished rooms, is full of
antiques. The rooms have central heating, but only a few have TV.
The restaurant serves international cuisine along with regional Eifel
dishes. Parking is available, which is a plus in the narrow streets. The
hotel is closed from October to June and Wednesdays. Room rates
include breakfast.

Haus Rolshausen

Budget to Moderate

5108 Monschau.

☎ *(02472) 20-38.*

Credit Cards: *MC, A.*

Charming—this friendly five-story guest house is a pleasant base for
exploring the old town of Monshau. The house is over 400 years
old, but you would not know it from the neat, modern bedrooms.
Vaulted wine cellars for sitting, narrow beamed room for breakfast.
All 19 rooms have shower, central heating, phone, radio; some
rooms have TV. Closed Mon. Languages include English.

Where to Eat

Zum Schiffchen ★

Inexpensive

Hafenstrasse 5. ☎ *(0211) 13 24 21.*

Public Transportation: *Tram 705.*

Credit Cards: *V, MC, DC, A.*

Reservations required.

There is documented proof that Napoleon really did eat here, or if he didn't eat, he certainly had a beer here. Served for two is an order of the boiled beef with judicious quantities of house mustard and horseradish.

Zum Schlussel ★

Inexpensive to Moderate

Bolkerstrasse 43-47. ☎ *(0211) 32 61 55.*

Public Transportation: *U-Bahn.* Metro Stop: *Opernhaus.*

Zum Schlussel successfully manages to bring a country Gasthaus into the middle of downtown Dusseldorf. The food is triumphantly peasant fare, and portions are big enough for people who plan to plough fields after lunch. On a cold day, a bowl of the chef's soup will revive a frozen soul. Desserts are the stuff Mom used to make—apple strudel, kuchen, and more.

Rats-und Zunftstuben Helig Gei

Moderate

Rentengasse 2. ☎ *(0211) 22 29 56.*

Credit Cards: *V, MC, DC, A.*

Atmosphere in spades—part of the building was constructed by the Romans. Typical Bavarian fare mixed with some nouvelle. Try the rabbit in marsala sauce or a trout mousse. The wine list is respectable, with some interesting local vintages.

What to Do

Museums and Exhibits

Heinrich-Heine-Institut ★

Bilkerstrasse 12-14. ☎ *(0211) 899 55 71.*

Public Transportation: *Tram 704, 707.*

Special Hours: *Closed Mon.*

The institute library has more than 10,000 volumes pertaining to the life and works of Germany's great lyric poet, as well as many manuscripts in his own hand. Admission: inexpensive.

Kunstmuseum Düsseldorf ★

http://www.kunstmuseum.org/

Ehrenhof 5. ☎ *(0211) 899 24 60.*

Public Transportation: *Tram 725.*

Special Hours: *Closed Mon.*

The Kunstmuseum possesses a comprehensive collection of all types of art, from medieval times through the 19th century. It is especially strong in the work of the Düsseldorf School and the German Romantic School. There is a collection of 80,000 prints and drawings. Decorative arts are well represented in the Persian bronzes and enamels. Admission: varies.

Kunstsammlung Nordrhein-Westfalen ★★

Grabbeplatz 5. ☎ *(0211) 838 10.*

Public Transportation: *Bus 705, 717.*

Special Hours: *Closed Mon.*

The collection is a who's-who of 20th-century art. Dali, Mir, Rauschenberg, Lichtenstein, Warhol—they're all here. The museum has no fewer than 94 of Paul Klee's paintings. Admission: varies.

Nightlife

Nightlife ★★★

Düsseldorf is wealthy enough to support a healthy night life, and you'll find plenty to do in the Altstadt between the Kö and the Rhine. **The Irish Pub** at *Hunsruckenstrasse 13* (13 31 81) is just what it says— an Irish Pub complete with televised soccer matches, Guinness and a lot of good music. For a change of pace, try getting tickets to the **Deutsche Oper am Rhein**, *Heinrich-Heine-Alee 16A*. Performances usually are sold out well in advance, but you just might get lucky.

Shopping

Shopping ★★★★

Düsseldorf is the most fashionable city in Germany, and the Königsalee (the Kö to the cognoscenti) is the most fashionable street in Dusseldorf—the Rodeo Drive of the Ruhr, if you will. Sidewalk cafes are sprinkled between the chic boutiques and department stores. The Kö Galerie is a superior mall where shoppers can listen to live piano music while they make their purchases.

Historical Sites

Dom (Cathedral) ★★★★★

Domstrasse 3. *(0211) 25 33 44.*

Public Transportation: *Tram 1, 7, 13, 17, 23.*

🕐 *9 a.m.–6:30 p.m.*

Special Hours: *Sat. to 4 p.m., Sun. 1 p.m.-5 p.m.; museum 10 a.m.*

St. Martin's Cathedral is considers one of the most important in Germany. The archbishop of Mainz dates from the 700s, and the tombs of the archbishops line the walls of the nave. The Romanesque basilica dates from the late 900s. An outstanding example of Romanesque style of architecture, although does have Gothic and Renaissance elements. It sports no fewer than six steeples. Take time to look at the bronze doors at the main entrance. They date from AD. 988 and the rings in the lions' mouths are immunity rings. Anyone who was fleeing would be granted refuge if he grasped one of the rings. When Napoleon conquered the city, he carried off anything that wasn't nailed down, and today the most important art works in the cathedral are the carvings on the pillars and tombs of the archbishops. On the north side of the nave is the entrance to **St. Gotthard's chapel,** once a separate church but now incorporated into the cathedral. It is an example of the Doppelkirche, or church and features two levels. The archbishops and other members of the nobility worshipped on the upper level, while commoners worshipped on the lower level. A door on th south side of the nave leads into the former cloister, which has now become the **Diocesan Museum.** It contains the numerous reliquaries and pieces of silver plate. Admission: free.

Museums and Exhibits Gutenberg Museum

http://www.gutenberg.de/

Liebfrauenplatz 5. ☎ *(0211) 12 26 40.*

Public Transportation: *Bus 1, 7, 13, 17, 19.*

🕒 *10 a.m.–6 p.m,*

Special Hours: *Sun. 10 a.m.-1 p.m.; closed Mon.*

Johannes Gutenberg's workshop disappeared long ago, but a reproduction has been built on the northeastern corner of Liebfrauenplatz across from the Dom. The workshop forms the nucleus of the museum and contains numerous artifacts connected with Gutenburg's life and the history of printing. The greatest attractions in the museum are two copies of the Bible. Although these are considered to be the first books ever printed using moveable type, portions of them were still done by hand. Admission: free.

The Romantic Road

This fascinating route was a vital and thriving lifeline during the Middle Ages, when a military link between fortresses was imperative for survival. The word "Hof," which is suffixed to the names of so many modern German hotels, literally derives from the walled and safe "courtyard" where travelers could rest while passing from stronghold to stronghold. Initially, they slept in their carriages or under their horses. Soon drink was provided. Later food was served. Finally overnight shelters were constructed. When the wars ended and transportation lanes were shifted, these great installations became superannuated. Not until recent times did historic interest regenerate their unique touristic allure.

The Romantic Road begins in Wurzburg and makes its way through towns like Bad Mergentheim, Rothenberg, Dinkelsbuhl, and Augsburg to end in the Tyrol at Fussen. The towns along the road have little in common historically and culturally. Nevertheless, the road has been promoted to such an extent that it has become an attraction in itself and has inspired several imitations including the Fairy Tale Road (sites associated with the Brothers Grimm) and the Classical Road, which promotes areas associated with the works of Schiller and Goethe. It is possible to drive the Romantic Road in a day or take one of the buses that follow daily routes along it, but this is one trip that is better taken alone and at your own pace, with plenty of time to explore the smaller villages and roads which lead off into the mountains. Because the Romantic Road is so popular, there is no shortage of places to eat along the route.

Augsburg

Augsburg has been inhabited since Roman times and takes its name from the emperor Augustus. Augsburg greatest period came during the Renaissance under Jacob Fugger the Rich ☎ (1459–1529), who was the financial brains behind the Emperor Charles V. Such was the influence of the family that after Jacob's death, his son Anton was offered control over the revenues coming into the Imperial coffers from Chile and Peru. Feeling that the risks were too great, he declined the offer.

Where to Stay

Dom Hotel ★★

http://www.domhotel-augsburg.de/

Moderate

Frauentorstrasse 8.

Public Transportation: *Tram 1.*

☎ *(0821) 15-30-31.*

Credit Cards: *V, MC, DC, A.*

Across the street from the cathedral, this 43-room hotel, belonged to the town administrator in the 15th century. All of the rooms are fine, but those on the top floor have sloping beam ceilings and views of the city. Rooms come with phone and TV.

Hotel am Rathaus

Budget to Moderate

Am Hinteren Perlachberg 1.

Public Transportation: *Tram 1.*

☎ *(0821) 50-90-00.*

Credit Cards: *V, MC, DC, A.*

This hotel gets its name from being right behind Augsburg's historic
city hall. It's not nearly as old, however. The three-story building is
of 1986 vintage while the lobby reflects some Old World charm but
the 32 rooms are on the modern side, with phone and TV.

Romantik-Hotel Augsburger Hof

Budget to Moderate

Auf dem Kreuz 2.

Public Transportation: *Tram 1.*

☎ *(0821) 31-40-83.*

Credit Cards: *V, MC, DC, A.*

This Renaissance-style mansion, dating to 1767, is a historic landmark, so more care than usual was put into its refurbishment in
1988. Situated in the middle of town, it's a perfect base for visiting
the major sights on foot. There are 36 rooms reflecting the recent
remodeling, a formal restaurant, Stube and an inner courtyard.
Room rates include a buffet breakfast.

Steigenberger Drei Mohren   ★★★

http://www.steigenberger.de/servlet/PB/menu/1003803_11/

Moderate

Maximilianstrasse.

Public Transportation: *Tram 1.*

☎ *(0821) 50-360.*

Credit Cards: *V, MC, A.*

The renown of the original "Three Moors," established in 1723,
was such that it attracted guests of the magnitude of Mozart, the

Duke of Wellington, Goethe and Paganini. All that went up in flames, however, in World War II during an Allied bombing. The new Drei Mohren wasn't rebuilt until 1956, but its reputation as a first-class hotel remains intact. The 110 rooms come with TV and phone, and a buffet breakfast is included in the rate. Room service, laundry and dry cleaning are available.

Where to Eat

Fuggeri-Stube ★

Inexpensive to Moderate

Jacobstrasse 26.

Credit Cards: *V, MC, DC, A.*

Just outside the Fuggerei, this tavern is actually built into the walls surrounding the housing project. Pork and Spatzle is not fancy, but it is tasty. This is also a good place for a schnapps on a cold winter afternoon.

What to Do

The Fuggerei

Established in 1519 by the Fuggerfamily to provide having for poor Augsburgers, the Fuggerei, still exists to the east of the Rathaus on Jackoberstrasse. It is a walled enclave with its own church and civic infrastructure. The gates are still closed at dusk, and the gabled houses on the eight streets are the original ones constructed by Jacob the Rich. To live in the Fuggerei one must be a resident of Augsburg, Catholic, poor through no fault of one's own, and pledged to pray daily for the souls of the Fuggers. Rent is considered to be the modern equivalent of the rent established by Jacob—one Rhenish guilder per year. The settlement is still administered by the Fugger family. Mozart's great-grandfather lived in house No. 13 after having incurred the displeasure of his contemporaries for burying an executioner. His house is still occupied, but the house next door, No. 14, has been restored and is open to the public (Mar–Oct., 9–6,). The houses are small by today's standards but surprisingly comfortable and much sought after. Southeast of the Rathaus on Annastrasse is St. Anne's Church, formerly a Carmelite monastery. Martin Luther stayed here when he came to Augsburg in 1518 to be examined by the Inquisition. In the same year, the

Fugger family constructed their own chapel which dominates the interior of the church and is held to be one of the best examples of Renaissance design in Germany. Today, the church is Lutheran, and a portrait of Martin Luther and his protector, Johan-Friedrich, the Prince-Elector of Saxony hangs in the sanctuary. The **Dom** is directly north of the Rathaus on Hoheweg. Eclectic is a weak word to describe the mixture of architectural styles which are to be found in this building. Construction began in 1060, and the high altar was constructed in 1962! Take time to examine the Prophet Windows— the oldest cycle of stained glass in the area. A series of paintings by Holbein the Elder depicting the life of the Virgin is on display in the Dom. The bronze doors on the south portal date from the 12th century. The Bishops of Augsburg have been buried in the crypt beneath the Dom since the 900s. The **Mozarthaus**, *(Frauentorstrasse 30)* where Leopard Mozart, Wolfgang's father, was born is a short walk to the north of the Dom. It is open to the public as a memorial and museum.

Fussen

Fussen is the southern end of the Romantic Road. Today its importance is largely as an accommodation center for tourists who are visiting Ludwig's royal castles, but it has its own interesting—if less spectacular—history. Its castle, the **Hohes Schloss**, is one of the most perfectly preserved Gothic castles in the region. It stands on the site of a Roman fortress that guarded the main trading route from Rome to the Danube. The castle was the seat of the local Bavarian rulers until the Emperor Heinrich VII mortgaged it to the Bishop of Augsburg for 400 pieces of silver. The debt was never repaid, and the city became the property of the Bishops, who used it as their summer palace until the early 18th century.

Where to Stay

Sonne

Budget

Reichenstrasse 37.

☎ *(08362) 60-61.*

Credit Cards: *V, MC, DC, A.*

Sonne means "sun," and this is an appropriately bright, cheerful and modern hotel in Bavarian style with traditional furnishings. Located in the center of Fussen, this hostelry has 32 comfortable, rustic rooms and a cafe.

Hotel Lisl and Jagerhaus ★

Budget to Moderate

Neuschwansteinstrasse 1-3.

Public Transportation: *Bus: Fussen Bus.*

☎ *(08362) 88-70.*

Credit Cards: *MC, A.*

Pool.

Situated in the valley between the royal castles Neuschwanstein and Hohenschwangau this 53-room hotel is compiled of the original villa on one side of the street and an annex on the other side, but each has a garden and high-ceilinged rooms with views of the castles. There are two dining rooms and a restaurant. The guest rooms have a TV and phone. Rates include a buffet breakfast.

Hotel Muller

Moderate

Alpseestrasse 16.

Public Transportation: *Bus: Fussen bus.*

☎ *(08362) 81-99-0.*

Credit Cards: *V, MC, A.*

Family-run Hotel Muller would be worth a stop if for no other reason than to dine in the winter and enjoy the view of floodlit Neuschwanstein Castle. This 48-room Alpine resort was remodeled in 1984 and it's right at the base of the fantastic Neuschwanstein and only a short hike through the woods to the more stolid Hohenschwangau Castle. The rooms come with TV and phone and a continental breakfast. Because of its locale, tour groups are not uncommon. Closed from Nov. 20 to Jan. 1.

What to Do

Historical Sites

Hohenschwangau Castle ★★★

Alpenseestrasse 24. ☎ *(08362) 81 727.*

Special Hours: *Oct.-Mar. 10 a.m.-4 p.m.*

Parts of Hohenschwangau date from the 12th century, when it was associated with the Knights of Schwangau. When the order declined in importance, so did the castle. Eventually, it came into the possession of Ludwig II's father, Maximilian II in 1832. Maxmillian restored it and Ludwig spent his boyhood here. The castle is decidedly Gothic in style, and it is easy to see how Ludwig came by his penchant for the tales of medieval Germany and its mythic heroes. One of the most interesting rooms is the Hall of the Swan Knight, which has murals illustrating this legend before embellishments by Richard Wagner and Ludwig. The furniture in the room is an interesting combination of Gothic, Biedemier and decorative pieces of varying periods presented to the ruler by grateful subjects. In the Hall of the Heroes, notice the bronze pieces decorating the long tables. They represent scenes from the Nibelungen legend. Did they influence Ludwig and Wagner, or was it the other way around? Ludwig was a creature of the night. He loved to ride by the light of the moon and stars and he carried this fixation into his bedroom. It is on the third story of the building, with an incredible view out over the valley to his castle, **Neuschwanstein**. Like many Gothic chambers it is decorated with stars on the ceiling. Ludwig's chamber the stars and moon are, lit from behind by lanterns. This is one of the most popular tourist spots in Germany, especially in the month of August. The crowds are moved with dispatch and efficiency, but you may experience long waits. Admission: varies.

Neuschwanstein ★★★

http://www.neuschwanstein.net/

Neuschwansteinstrasse 20. ☎ *(08362) 81 127.*

Special Hours: *Oct.-Mar. 10 a.m.-4 p.m.*

By the time Ludwig began construction on Neuschwanstein, he was well in the grip of legends and, best of all, operas which depicted German legends. It should come as no surprise that, as a patron and friend of Wagner, Ludwig consulted a theatrical set designer when selecting the location for his castle. If the castle itself looks familiar, it's because it was selected by Walt Disney as the archetypal castle to be immortalized in Fantasyland. Construction on this flight of fancy began in 1869 and continued until Ludwig's death in 1886 when all work stopped. Admission to the castle is by guided tour only. There are acres of woven tapestries, murals, colored marble, gilded stucco and wooden carvings. On the third floor, there is an artificial grotto complete with stalactites and stalagmites, and an adjoining winter garden with murals illustrating the legend of Tannhauser. From there the visitor passes into the Great Hall, its decor inspired by Lohengrin (more swans). The castle departs from the Germanic themes and explodes in a riot of Roman-Byzantine decorative excess. Ludwig was deposed and died (under mysterious circumstances) before his throne could be installed in the throne room. The fourth floor of the castle is given over to the Sangersaal or Minstrel's Gallery. The decorative ceiling is especially noteworthy, as are the chandeliers and candelabra with their sparkling bits of colored Bohemian glass. Access to Nueschwanstein is not easy. Cars must be left in the parking lots, and visitors must walk the rest of the way (about 1 km. uphill), go by horsedrawn carriage , or take the bus to the Marienbruke, which overlooks the castle. From the Marienbruke it's about a 10 minute walk to the castle. Be advised that this walk is very rough and steep, but the view is spectacular. Admission: varies.

Rothenburg ob-der-Taube

Rothenburg may be more photogenic than any other place in Germany. A good place to start any tour of Rothenburg is by taking the walk around the city walls. The city is located on an ox bow of the Tauber. On three sides you can look down into the river valley, and on the fourth side there is a dreamy view over the roofs, gables, cupolas and spires of the medieval city. Actually, much of what you see is an excellent reconstruction of what was destroyed during the war, but the restoration is impeccable. The town inside the walls, has been declared a monument and no cars are allowed. The result that, despite the unseemly number of tourists who visit it, Rothenburg preserves the feel of a medieval town. Spend a morning or afternoon walking around or taking pictures.

Where to Stay

Burg-Hotel　★★★

Moderate

Klostergasse 1-3.

☎ *(09861) 50-37.*

Credit Cards: *V, MC, DC, A.*

Gabrielle Berger has turned this 14-room lodging, actually built on top of the old city wall in the 12th century, into a designer hotel. Every room is different, from old-fashioned to modern, but all in a fashionably elegant style. The views are what one would expect from its high position on the edge of the Tauber valley. Guest rooms have TV, radio, central heating, phone and hair dryer. Rates include a buffet breakfast. Pets are accepted.

Goldener Hirsch　★★★★★

Moderate to Expensive

Untere Schmiedgasse 16-25.

☎ *(09861) 70-80.*

Credit Cards: *All Major.* Credit Cards: *V, MC, DC.*

This hotel has viewful accommodations with public rooms and 72 living quarters where the emphasis is on luxury. The building is authentic, but it wasn't the 17th-century inn it now resembles. Still plenty of history here, however, along with comfort.

Hotel Baren　★★★★

Moderate to Expensive

Hofbronnengasse 4-9.

☎ *(09861) 60-31.*

Credit Cards: *V, MC.*

Built in 1577, the building has 15-inch oak beams, crystal chandeliers, a sitting room with an open fireplace and, perhaps most special, Fritz Muller's handiwork in the kitchen. Besides Restaurant Barenwirt, guests can spend time in the paneled bar, breakfast room and—something unusual in this town noted for its antiquity—an indoor pool. The guest rooms, which have central heating, phone and TV, also display the personal touch of the Mullers. Rates include a buffet breakfast.

Eisenhut

http://www.eisenhut-rothenburg.com/

Expensive

Herrengasse 3-5.

☎ *(09861) 70-50.*

Credit Cards: *V, MC, DC, A.*

This family-run hotel is almost as famous as the city it's been a part of for some 500 years. Entering the doors is like stepping back into medieval history: In a lodging full of rooms with beamed ceilings and impressive woodwork, the three-story- high dining hall is the star attraction. The 79 bedchambers have been individually decorated with many new baths and TVs and phones. An annex, also beautifully antique, is across the street, but does not offer a valley view. Other facilities include a piano bar and beer garden. The mood here is Old World through and through. Room rates include a buffet breakfast.

Gasthof Glocke

Moderate

Am Plionlein 1. Rated Restaurant: Gasthof Glocke.

☎ *(09861) 30-25.*

Credit Cards: *V, MC, DC, A.*

The Glocke, situated in the south end of town, is a hotel of more recent vintage that offers guests a variety of conveniences along with noteworthy guest rooms. There are three dining rooms, one for the highly touted Gasthof Glocke restaurant, which has its own wine cellar. The hotel also offers a terrace, TV room, wine bar, children's game room and conference facilities, which attract some tour groups. Rooms come with TV and radio. Rates include a continental breakfast.

Gasthof Hotel Kloster-Stuble ⭐⭐⭐

Moderate to Expensive

Heringsbronnengasse 5.

☎ *(09861) 67-74.*

Credit Cards: *MC.*

Being out of the way in Rothenburg isn't the same as being out of the way in a big city. The Kloster-Stuble is just a short walk from the market square, but it's far enough to avoid the noisy bustle of all the foot traffic around the major sights. And being out of the way doesn't mean the Kloster-Stuble doesn't have good views. It's situated close to the old city wall, so most of the 13 guest rooms, which were remodeled in 1987, look out over the Tauber valley or the far end of the city. There also are two terraces for enjoying the views. Pine is the wood of choice throughout. Facilities include a restaurant and stube. Pets are accepted.

Romantik Hotel Markusturm

Moderate to Expensive

Rodergasse 1.

☎ *(09861) 20-98.*

Credit Cards: *V, MC, DC, A.*

Those who have seen a photograph or painting of Rothenburg's famous old clock tower, *Markusturm* (St. Mark's Tower), inadvertently have seen the Romantik Hotel Markusturm. It's right there to the right of the picture, up against the tower wall where it has been since it was built in 1264. There is nothing dated about the accommodations, however. The decor varies in style, but the 24 rooms all have central heating, TV, radio, phone and hair dryer. Rates include a buffet breakfast. Pets are accepted.

Dinkelsbuhl

Blauer Hecht

Budget

Schweinemarkt.

☎ *(09851) 8-11.*

Credit Cards: *V, MC, DC, A.*

This three-story 17th-century building that became a brewery-tavern has been recently remodeled. And there still is a backyard brewery. There also is a restaurant featuring regional dishes. The 44 rooms come with TV and phone. Room rates include a continental breakfast.

Eisenkrug ★★

http://www.hotel-eisenkrug.de/

Budget to Moderate

Dr.-Martin-Luther-Strasse.

☎ *(09851) 60-17.*

Credit Cards: *V, MC, DC, A.*

The 1620 building is in the center of town near the wine market. The pink walls, forest green shutters and flower-filled windowboxes at every window on all five floors make this hotel one of the prettiest pictures in town. It's just as picturesque inside, with the heavy use of flowery wallpaper and antiques in its 12 guest rooms. The Zum Kleinen Obristen restaurant is well-known in the area for its Franconian- Swabian fare. The hotel offers a wine cellar, bar and small terrace. Rooms have central heating, phone and TV. Rates include a continental breakfast. Pets are allowed for a fee.

Nördlingen

Kaiser Hotel Sonne

Moderate to Expensive

Marktplatz 3.

☎ *(09081) 50-67.*

Credit Cards: *V, MC, DC, A.*

Not everywhere can an everyday tourist sleep in the same lodgings that have put up kings, princes and even emperors. But such is the case with the Sonne, which dates back to 1405. The guest list includes Frederick II, Frederick III, Maximilian I and Charles V. Goethe also slept here, and among the more mundane celebrities have been numerous American astronauts. Located next to the Rathaus and cathedral, the hotel retains its medieval flavor despite recent renovations. The vaulted cellar wine-tavern probably hasn't changed that much from the 15th century. There are 40 bedrooms and four dining rooms. Rates include a continental breakfast.

Where to Eat

Restaurant Barenwirt

Moderate to Expensive

Hofbronnengasse 9. 60 31.

Credit Cards: *V, MC.*

There has been a restaurant at this site since 1577, and today the Barenwirt is considered one of the best in the city, if not in all of Germany. It's impossible to predict the menu because it changes daily, depending on what's available locally. But expect something along the lines of fresh pork medallions in a wine sauce served with refined dumplings on the side. The house wine is always good.

Tillman Riemenschneider

Inexpensive to Moderate

Georgengasse 11.

Credit Cards: *V, MC, DC, A.*

Located in one of the best hotels in town, this restaurant combines old-fashioned service and old-fashioned food served in generous portions. Herring appetizers, with dill and sour cream, are delicious with dark bread. Try following that with a simply poached fish or a baked pork loin with baked apples.

What to Do

Historical Sites

Schloss Harburg

★★★

Schloss Harburg is located between Norlingen and Donauworth. It has belonged to the counts of Oettingen since 1295 and is considered to be one of the best preserved castles in Germany. It is open to the public, and many of the works of art collected by the family

are displayed. Among the exhibits are more carvings by Tilman Riemenschneider, illuminated prayer books and manuscripts and various ecclesiastical artifacts, including an incomparable 12th- century
crucifix carved from ivory.

Museums and Exhibits

Mittelalterliches Kriminalmuseum

Burggasse 3.

Special Hours: *Nov.-Mar. 2 p.m.-4 p.m.*

Four floors dedicated to the medieval concept of justice.
Instruments of torture, law books, documents, manacles and meth-
ods of execution. The building is the former seat of the Order of St.
John of Jerusalem, another of the medieval military orders.
Admission: inexpensive.

ITALY

Italy's ingratiating climate is as diverse as its landscape. Along the Italian Riviera, it's subtropical, similar to upper (not lower!) Florida at its most delightful. Around Sicily and the southern coast, you'll bask in typical Mediterranean surroundings. The Adriatic side is cooler than its western twin. The Po Basin, across the North, has seasonal extremes and is similar to the mid-Atlantic climate. Around Rome, Naples, Pescara, Bari and Taranto, conditions are fairly pleasant throughout the year. But keep out of the high Apennines and Alps from September to May, unless you have skis. April to October are the best tourist months.

Apart from the sometime government of Italy itself, three independent domains, each with its separate leader, laws and diplomats, function within the borders of Italy—the Vatican, the Sovereign Military Order of Malta and the Republic of San Marino.

Patriarch of the **Vatican** is the Polish-born Supreme Pontiff, John Paul II. His papal state of 108 acres and 890 people operates under extraterritorial rights. As spiritual head of the Catholic Church, he is responsible only to his tenets, his followers and himself. The flag is white and yellow, charged with crossed keys and triple tiara. A complete coinage is struck every year; examine your change in Rome for Pius XII coins, because the early ones are collectors' items. (For further information, turn to "Vatican City.")

The **Sovereign Military Order of Malta** (better known as "Knights of Malta"), with headquarters on via Condotti and a villa—its demesne—on Aventine Hill in Rome, sends its own ambassadors to many Catholic countries, issues its own "SMOM" license plates and performs many other functions of separate statehood. The total population is 40. The nation boasts its own stamps, which are prized by many collectors. It is smaller than Vatican City, but potent both ecclesiastically and politically.

In thumbnail form, here are some jottings about **San Marino**, the world's most ancient and smallest republic, which is now almost 17 centuries old; its birthday is September 3.

Location • Only 23.4 square miles of property in the Apennines, entirely surrounded by Italian soil, 20 minutes by car from Rimini and the Adriatic Sea via the Superstrada. The District of Columbia is three times as large.

Altitude • More than 2200 feet, with a glorious view as far as the Venice lagoon and Slovenian coast when the sky is clear.

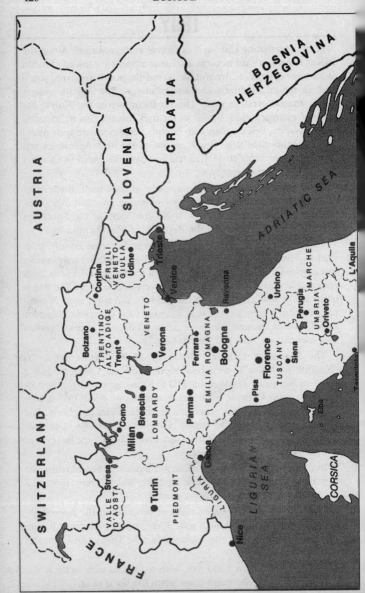

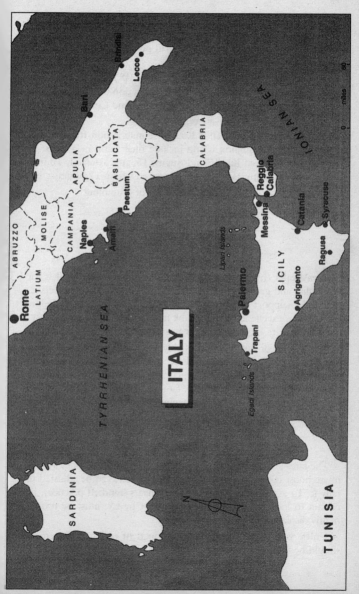

Population • About 19,000 (its out-of-country citizenry is even more voluminous—22,000).

Industries • Postage stamps, fingernail polish, furniture, tourism, leather, and clothes clothes clothes.

Armed Services • There's a standing army of 180 stalwarts—but because it's such a peaceful nation, they often don't do much. You'll also be relieved to know that the republic's Grand Council ratified a pledge not to acquire nuclear weapons.

Number of foreign tourists • Roughly a million non-Italian sight-seers per year; 2.5 million if you include their Latin neighbors; in high season, between July 15 and August 15, approximately 10,000 per day (but as many as 80,000 have arrived within 12 hours).

Currency • The EURO, albeit with a lot of grumbling.

Language • Italian.

Transportation
Airlines

Air Alitalia (**http://www.alitalia.it/**) has a wonderful flair for hospitality and graciousness once you get aloft, but the desk services and the support systems are *average* (at best) or certainly below the levels of excellence displayed by flight crews. The carrier is trying hard now to improve matters at ground zero.

If you fly in or out, you'll probably use Rome or Milan airports. The first is a long haul from midcity, and transport can range from 40 minutes to 1-1/4 hours, depending on traffic and rush-hour congestion. Agree on your taxi fare beforehand—always! Milan, sometimes in a state of chaos, is beginning to realize it is one of the most important business hubs in the world.

Taxis

The fares are jumping so fast and so often that sometimes a legitimate boost is correctly added before the meters can be adjusted to tally it. To avoid being conned (which nears standard practice), be certain to look for the *official* notice that by law must be prominently displayed.

Unless your driver is extraordinarily patient or kind, 10 percent should be the maximum tip.

Trains

Your best chance of a seat is in first-class. *Make sure of it by reserving in advance, whenever reservations are possible.* If you have no reservations and are leaving from the point where the train is made up or cars are being added, plan to arrive at the station 30 minutes before departure time, to assure yourself of a space when the gates are opened for entry. First class is definitely worth the difference.

In winter, snow seems to impede the high-speed **ETR 450s** that otherwise zip between Rome and Milan. In all seasons, however, these rockets swing and sway in the turns, sometimes causing motion sickness.

> ITRAVELBOOK TIP: WHEN YOU BOOK A TRAIN TICKET, MAKE SURE TO BUY AT LEAST A SECOND-CLASS RESERVED SEAT. OTHERWISE, YOU'LL BE SITTING ON LUGGAGE RACKS.

Some of the single-compartment sleepers are the best around. The cheapest sleeping accommodation is called the *Carrozze Cuccette*—ordinary coaches fixed up with bunks. Again—be certain to reserve them beforehand.

You may save money by buying a Tourist Ticket (valid for eight, 15, 21, or 30 days and permitting advance seat reservation), a "circular" ticket (a minimum of 600 miles within 60 days), or a "family" ticket (minimum of four). And don't forget to check into the Eurailpass.

Be extra careful of theft in rail stations, especially Rome's *Termini*, where, according to police, illegal immigrants are targeting tourists in droves. This could be true of any crowded places, so beware.

Food

Discounting the North, where rice is king, Italy loves its pasta. To cut back on expenses, either of these plus a salad can serve as a pretty filling meal.

But if you are not economizing, **Italian white truffles** are the most scrumptious in the world—infinitely superior in my opinion to the coarser black variety grown in France. Specially trained dogs are used in Alba, south of Turin, the global capital of this delicacy, to sniff out their earthen hiding places and to root them up.

Risotto is marvelous. It has innumerable versions. The basis is towel-rubbed rice, simmered in bouillon or chicken broth until the kernels are dark and tasty. With this are mixed mushrooms, peppers, onions, saffron, butter, cheese, veal, chicken, pork, lobster and beef.

Polenta is a staple of the North. It's a cornmeal porridge, white or yellow, so heavy in texture that it stands up by itself. It isn't particularly interesting in taste, but it comes into its own when used to mop up a rich gravy. Incidentally, northern cooking leans heavily on butter; the prime ingredient throughout the South is olive oil.

Prosciutto, dark spicy local ham served in wafer-thin slices, is an excellent cocktail appetizer. It's wonderful with fresh figs or a slice of melon—but be sure to order it *crudo* (raw), or they might serve it *cotto* (cooked).

Stick to bottled water in rural or village areas of Italy. In the larger cities, tap water is pure. Most people are never bothered by the water but invariably blame it for indigestion after downing cocktails, wine, cognac and gigantic repasts served in tropical surroundings. Popular sparkling brands of bottled water are **San Pellegrino** and **Crodo**; **Fiuggi** and **Sangemini** are the best bets without gas (said to be the remedy for kidney stones).

You may order half *(mezza)* portions of pasta—a useful trick to save money while saving room to sample more new dishes.

If you are traveling by car, the *autostrada* pit stops are clearly the pits. The huge Pavesi pull-offs even offer public microwave ovens so that you can heat your own grub. (At one recent stop near Orvieto, the only thing that had warmth was my Coca-Cola.) So, should you want to enjoy a meal, you'd better drive off the superhighway and into a town.

Meal hours: In Rome and the South, breakfast, 7–9 a.m.; lunch, 1–3 p.m.; dinner, 9:30–11 p.m. From Rome northward, dinner is often earlier.

Drinks

Grappa, vermouth and brandy are the national hard drinks. **Grappa**, popular in the North, is a raw, harsh, high-proof beverage made from the leftovers of the ordinary distillation process; **Friuli** is one of the best. If you are tired of the enamel on your teeth, try **Centerba**, made as the name implies, from 100 herbs and a generous supply of alcohol. It's a digestif from Tocco Casauria near Pescara. A more mellow one (perhaps because it is made from only 79 herbs) is **Amaro Siciliano**. As for brandy, **Vecchia Romagna** and **Rene Briand** are the only brands we can recommend. A drink that delights most visitors is **Sambuca** *(anisette)* when it is served *con* *mosche* (with "flies," which are floating coffee beans).

Italy is a wine country. She has moved ahead of France as the largest producer in the world, even though the Gauls still drink more on a per capita basis; she dedicates 55 percent of her farmland to the glories of the grape.

Taste, of course, is a very personal thing. The "fashion" of the instant is **Prosecco**, a cheerful sparkling white from the Veneto district; it's wonderful as refreshment or with shellfish. Order a chalky red called **Villa Antinori** or the softer **Tignanello** (also Antinori) as quality Chiantis that are reliable and universal. (Pay no attention to the irrelevant fact that the Antinori production is not registered in the regional "Classico" category; the house provides some of the greatest rewards to be discovered in a corked bottle.) Soave Bertani, though common, is a gentle white, while the ever-popular Bolla company produces a soothing rosé beverage.

Bardolino (a red from Verona), Verdicchio (a white from the Adriatic slopes) and Rosatello (a rosé) are excellent alternatives. If you favor greater softness in a red, try a Torgiano Rubesco from Umbria. Most bottlings beyond five years of age are fine companions for meat or fowl. Picolit, from the northeast, is a cheerful white. Barolo, a rich ruby pressing from the Piedmont, is not too flexible, but it is satisfying given the complementary foodstuffs. Some would opt for something lighter, like Barbera, for instance. The Lambrusco from Emilia and the Recioto from Verona are bubbly reds that drinkers of American sparkling burgundy might enjoy. Asti Spumante is similar to a sugar-fed champagne; the dry types called *spumante metodo champenois* are rapidly replacing French imports these days.

If you don't choose a light white wine as is the custom today for an aperitif, the standbys remain Martini and Cinzano (red or white), the mellow dark Punte Mes and the Ferrari-red Campari (try the last mixed with orange juice and ice on a summer day).

The best tonic in the world for overeating, flatulence, gas pains, picking yourself up off the floor when you've mixed oysters and bananas—practically any stomach ailment up to chilblains or ulcers—is an Italian bitters called **Fernet Branca**. The taste is horrible, but the effect is atomic. This hideous black liquid can save your digestion and your temper. Try any bar; it's less than soda pop.

ITRAVELBOOK TIP: ANY RED WINE BEARING THE DATE 1997 IS WORTH ITS WEIGHT IN GOLD.

Tipping

Aside from the hotels and restaurants, generally tip 10 percent. Hotels automatically add 18 percent to your bill for a "service charge." This is sometimes a racket, because the employees who have helped you don't always see it, despite union laws that insist that they must.

Always tip everybody for small services, because Italians consider it gainfully earned income.

For More Information

Italian Government Travel Office (also known as "ENIT")
http://www.italiantourism.com/
630 Fifth Ave., Suite 1565, New York, NY 10111
(212) 245-4822; FAX *(212) 586-9249;*

One of the most helpful touring organizations in the world is located in Italy. It's called **Compagnia Italiana di Turismo** (CIT) with 50 offices in Italy and 49 in foreign cities. The Rome head-quarters are located in *piazza della Repubblica 64*.

Campania

Amalfi

An important maritime republic during the Middle Ages, Amalfi is also the target of dozens of daily bus tours from Naples, which pause here for refreshment on the spectacular (but not too difficult) coastal drive in and around Sorrento.

Where to Stay

Hotels and Resorts

Excelsior Grand Hotel

http://www.exvitt.it/
Moderate to Expensive
Localita Porgerola A twisty 15 minutes up from Amalfi to Porgerola.

☎ *(89) 830-015,* FAX *(89) 830-255.*

Credit Cards: *All Major.*
If awards are ever given for tranquility, this first-class hotel, perched

above Amalfi, should win a Peace Prize. It has a modern ambience in a sawtooth layout and is decorated in the strange Italian meld of 19th- and 12th-century themes. There are 97 seafront units all with bath or shower, central heating; seven suites; restaurant; some room service; two bars; rooftop garden; free parking.

Il Saraceno Grand Hotel

http://www.saraceno.it/

Moderate

Conca Dei Marini Located just below the highway at Conca Dei Marini.

☎ *(89) 831-148,* FAX *(89) 831-595.*

Credit Cards: *All Major.*

This resort hotel is is comprised of 56 adequately sized doubles with bath or shower, TV, waterfront terraces; six suites; two restaurants, one a vaulted restaurant-grill with tiled floor and the other on the beach in original castle; gilt cave-dwelling bar; lower-level saltwater pool; private beach; mini-chapel; free parking.

Where to Eat

Da Gemma

Moderate to Expensive

Via Fra Gerardo Sasso 9, ☎ *(089) 871345.*

Credit Cards: *V, MC, DC, A, YE.*

Closed: *Wed.*

Delectable fresh seafood on pasta or en casserole draws a repeat clientele to this unpretentious and welcoming restaurant. Its rooftop patio, open to the breezes, is a definite plus. Although portions can be hefty, and the cuisine hearty, the kitchen here is not averse to preparing a simply dressed whole fish or filet for your dining pleasure. It's within strolling distance of the Duomo.

La Caravella

Inexpensive

Via Matteo Camera 12, ☎ *(089) 871029.*

Credit Cards: *V, A.*

Closed: *Tues.*

This place draws raves for sublime pasta specialties stuffed with the day's catch and a potpourri of spices. The friendly proprietor is usually on hand for a chat and a tempting description of the menu specials, which may include veal as well as fish and shellfish. Save some room for the home- baked desserts. La Caravella has a quiet ambience, and diners can enjoy supper here in air-conditioned comfort after a day at the beach.

What to Do
Excursions

Emerald Grotto ★★★

Seven miles west of town, toward Sorrento.

🕐 *10 a.m.–4 p.m.*

Special Hours: *8 a.m. to 6 p.m. June-Sept., 9 a.m. to 5 p.m. Mar.-May.*

Not quite as famous as the Blue Grotto of nearby Anacapri, this aptly named natural attraction can evoke its share of thrills and chills. Getting there is half the fun. After a ride in an elevator that descends from the road, you board a boat that takes you to the grotto. The stalagmites (some of them underground) and surrounding waters turn a jewellike green from reflected light entering the caverns. Admission: varies.

Historical Sites

ITRAVELBOOK FREEBIE

Duomo di Sant' Andrea ★★★★

Piazza del Duomo.

🕐 *6 a.m.–8 p.m.*

Special Hours: *Closed from 1:30 to 2:30 p.m.*

Both a holy site and a marvel of ancient Arab-Moorish architecture, with a facade emblazoned with intricate mosaics, the Duomo crowns the piazza of this ruggedly beautiful coastal town. Its bronze doors, embossed with biblical scenes, were cast in Constantinople in the late 11th century. The body of Sant' Andrea, the city's patron saint, is buried in the cathedral's crypt.

Capri

Capri and the upper-level Anacapri remain the "in" scene for international travelers. By spending millions on comfort and style, the island has secured its continuing success. And even with their prosperity, the inhabitants are not spoiled. You can sit all evening in the *piazzetta* and sip a drink, but outright loitering has been banned. After dark, the creeping flow of neon has also been contained with discretion and strict ukase. The cuisine is Mediterranean and varied, the shopping is on the leading edge of international chic, the hotels are among the finest in the nation (if money is no object, we recommend the **Grand Hotel Quisisana**) and the scenery is as unspoiled as when the ancients first scrambled up its cliffs—or tossed their enemies off them. The hypnotizing **Blue Grotto**, reached by skiff from Marina Grande or by bus from Anacapri, remains an eternal attraction. Among antiquities, there's the 14th-century Certosa di San Giacomo, Tiberius' Villa Jovis and the church of Santo Stefano (17th century). There's a funicular from main port to main village; chair lift to mountain peak above Anacapri for a spellbinding view; from May 1 to September 30, private cars are banned from the tiny isle; taxis and buses are available throughout the year; one small, so-so beach at Marina Piccola; fast inexpensive hydrofoil service (40 minutes) which skims atop the waves from Naples to Capri and returns in half the time of the even less expensive—but much more crowded—regular service. In spring or fall there's greater tranquillity, but many visitors enjoy the hubbub of humanity in midsummer. The town is quiet during the windblown winters. Up at Anacapri the big draw is Axel Munthe's Villa San Michele. If you feel inspired, mornings are best, before the throngs roll in from Naples and Sorrento.

Where to Stay

Gatto Bianco Hotel

Budget to Moderate
Via Vittorio Emanuele 32

☎ *(81) 837-0446,* FAX *(81) 837-8060.*

Credit Cards: *All Major.*

A small colorful hotel in a quiet, yet central area. Its decor is a melange of conventional and supermodern design concepts. There are 37 rooms with bath or shower, TV, panoramic views; three suites; many terraces; restaurant with garden; breakfast room; bar; nightclub; business center. Open Apr. 1 through Nov. 2.

Grand Hotel Quisisana

http://www.quisi.com/
Expensive
Via Camerelle 2 Close to the Piazza.

☎ *(81) 837-0788*, FAX *(81) 837-6080*.

Credit Cards: *All Major*.

The Quisisana never diminishes in its mandate for excellence. Its attractive lobby opens to the patios and terraces; 150 rooms with bath/shower, TV, hair dryer; some have Jacuzzi; 15 suites; wheelchair accessible; a romantic restaurant by the palm-grove pool and an indoor restaurant; handsome bar with live music; nightclub; gym; massage. Open Apr. through Oct.

Hotel Punta Tragara

http://www.hoteltragara.com/
Moderate to Expensive
Via Tragara 57 About 1-1/2-hour ferry ride from Naples.

☎ *(81) 837-0844*, FAX *(81) 837-7790*.

Credit Cards: *All Major*.

A casually sprawling cliff-hugger, this persimmon-colored hotel was designed by Le Corbusier and, during WWII, used temporarily by Eisenhower as a command headquarters. Now a beautifully tranquil hotel, it is found at the end of the footpath (about 15 minutes' walk from midvillage) overlooking the majestic Faraglioni. It maintains 35 units; 30 suites decorated in rich to almost heavy furnishings mixed with 16th-century antiques; all with bath, climate control, hair dryer, sitting room, terrace or balcony overlooking the sea. Sitting on the private balcony at twilight is pure bliss. Especially suited to couples. Open Mar. 28 through Oct. 30.

La Pineta Hotel

Moderate
Via Tragara 6 Located near the village of Capri.

☎ *(81) 837-0644*, FAX *(81) 837-6445*.

Credit Cards: *All Major.*

Situated on one of the most enchanting walks on the island, this terraced hotel offers comfort, tranquility and privacy. The rooms are excellent, and some are even more handsome than those at the Quisisana; 50 rooms with bath, TV, some with a balcony, air conditioning (fee); seven suites; bar, beach strip at Marina Piccola with cabanas; lunching facilities at Ristorante delle Sirene. The view from the pinewood facing the sea is superb.

La Residenza

Budget to Moderate
Via Federico Serena 22 Close to the Piazzetta and funicular railway.

☎ *(81) 837-0833*, FAX *(81) 837-7564*.

Credit Cards: *All Major.*

All the rooms in this modern, Mediterranean-style hotel have bath, TV, and some have an ocean view; 16 balconies; restaurant; rooftop terrace. Mother Nature is outside your window at her most exquisite.

San Michele Hotel

http://www.sanmichele-capri.com/
Moderate
Via G. Orlandi Located on the Anacapri-Capri bus route.

☎ *(81) 837-1427*, FAX *(81) 837-1420*.

Credit Cards: *All Major.*

Almost across the road from the Europa Palace Hotel, this modern hotel overlooks the Bay of Naples. It offers 59 rooms with bath, TV; restaurant with panoramic views; bar; popular nightclub; a fabulous terrace; solarium; private garden; free parking. Unfortunately, this hotel is at a disadvantage due to its suburban location. However, a bus stop on the Anacapri-Capri route is immediately outside, providing frequent, easy transportation.

Where to Eat

First a word about the food, much of which is brought to the island by ship. Fish is mainly frozen—even though you will watch sailors netting their catches from your restaurant terrace. When it is fresh, the price is spine-tingling by the time it reaches your table. Seafood *antipasti* are staples; try local *caciotta* and *mozzarella* cheeses; and don't miss a sip of the Capri liqueur made from laurel.

Da Gemma ★★★

Moderate

Via Madre Serafina 6, ☎ *(081) 837-7113.*

Public Transportation: *Capri Funicular.*

Credit Cards: *V, MC, DC, A, YE.*

Closed: *Mon.*

Beloved by artsy and literary types, this favorite is found perhaps 50 steps up the arch-covered footpath from the central plaza. There are two sections, one a year-round tavern and the other a seasonal patio (closed Nov. 1 through Dec. 15); the former comprises a series of rooms enclosing an open, sunken kitchen, where pizzas are cooked on a traditional oven while you watch. These pies are terrific and good for fish-haters; otherwise, enjoy broiled, boiled and sauteed seafood, usually prepared in a hearty manner.

Da Paolino ★★★

Moderate

Via Palazzo a Mare 11, ☎ *(081) 837-6102.*

Credit Cards: *V, MC, A.*

This restaurant is just a short taxi ride to the Marina Grande area and is my favorite for cuisine, even though it may not be the most conveniently located. The arbored dining area is redolent of the lemon groves where the property is situated. Pasta dishes—especially ravioli and spaghetti with radicchio, basil and cheese—are among the best to be found in the south of Italy. A sunny, charming spot.

What to Do
Excursions

Blue Grotto ★★★

Marina Grande Harbor, *81-837-0686.*

Public Transportation: *Marina Grande.*

🕐 *9 a.m.–5 p.m.*

Try to catch a morning boat ride (if the weather is calm) to the still spectacular natural grotto, formed from jagged limestone cliffs off the coast of Anacapri. The incredible hues of blue are caused by refracted light. There are many drawbacks to this adventure, however. Because of its incredible popularity, tourists and their inevitable paraphernalia are constantly hustled in and out of small boats by aggressive oarsmen. Additional fees are charged to enter the grotto, an adventure which lasts all of five minutes. Admission: varies.

Historical Sites

Villa Jovis ★★★

Monte Tiberio.

🕐 *9 a.m.–5 p.m.*

Crowds in Capri getting to you? Trek to the top of Monte Tiberio on the eastern end of the island, where the ruins of mad Emperor Tiberius' lair, the Villa Jovis, await. This is just one of the many villas he built to alleviate ennui and where he eventually retired in A.D. 27. Imagine yourself throwing your annoying traveling partner off the steep cliff into the sea, as Tiberius might have done. Others can envision themselves as king of the hill with an eagle eye view of the countryside from the top. **WARNING: THE WALK IS STRENUOUS AND ALMOST AN HOUR IN LENGTH.** Admission: varies.

Anacapri
Excursions

Chairlift to Monte Solaro ★★

Piazza della Victoria.

🕐 *9:30 a.m.–6 p.m.*

A chairlift whizzes visitors all the way to the top of Monte Solaro, Anacapri's highest point (1950 ft.); for less than $8, this is the best carnival ride ever. The trip takes 12 minutes, and you're rewarded with breathtaking views of the Bay of Naples and surrounding islands at the summit. Admission: inexpensive.

Historical Sites

Villa San Michele

Via Axel Munthe, Capodimonte 34, ☎ *81-837-1401. Five minutes from piazza Monumento.*

🕓 *9 a.m.–6 p.m.*

Some of the best views on the island are seen from the gardens of this handsome villa that was the home of Swedish writer Axel Munthe, author of *The Story of San Michele*. One of Emperor Tiberius' villas was built on the foundation; think of the strange dreams Munthe must have had!

Cervinia

Nestled at the southern base of the Matterhorn (Cervinia is the Italian name for the famous mountain), here is one of the unsung alpine centers of summer and winter sport in Europe. Now that its lifts are among the most modern on the continent and its prices are among the lowest, it is an ideal destination for skiing families or climbing groups. The swift and convenient lift system connects to the top of the Swiss side, so if you wish to drift down to Zermatt for lunch, all you have to do is snap on your skis. The Aosta-veering slopes, which run between 2000 to 3000 meters in altitude, seem to receive snow earlier in the season than the north-facing bowl of the Monte Rosa. The town itself is an architectural hodgepodge of various Italian Modern schools clashing with Mountain Rustic. There are bobsleds, ice skating, tennis and golf all around the area. The tourist office can handle all hotel bookings for you: **Azienda Autonoma Di Soggiorno**, *11021 Breuil-Cervinia* 749136 or 949086; FAX 949731. While the town is on the Swiss frontier, it is about 80 miles by car from Geneva or 70 miles from Turin. Train connections are via Chatillon, 15 miles away; buses arrive from Turin, Aosta and Milan.

Where to Eat
Breuil-Cervinia

Les Neiges d'Antan   ★

Inexpensive

Perreres, ☎ *(0166) 948-775.*

4km from Breuil,
Located at Les Neiges d'Antan.
Credit Cards: *All Major.*

The homey food served at this chalet-style hotel may be the perfect thing after a hard day of skiing or hiking. Perhaps the only sound heard except for contented chewing noises is the wind whistling outside. Local Valdostan wines and cheeses round out a satisfying meal of beef and polenta.

What to Do
Sports and Recreation

Plateau Rosa   ★★★★

Professional skiing events go on regularly in this area, with almost 200 km of ski runs. Take a cable car and lift from the Plateau Rosa to the top of Piccolo Cervino (Little Matterhorn). Awesome downhill trails go all the way to Switzerland. There are also undemanding walks from the Plateau to nearby lakes and less imposing mountain tops. For complete information, contact **Breuil-Cervinia tourist office** at *via J.A. Carrel 29* ☎ *(0166) 949136,* FAX *949731.*

Naples

Napoli, the nation's third-largest city, continues to provoke both irritation and pity. With all its exquisite natural assets, it's a shame that corruption has taken a toll and prevented progress for citizens who would like to see their city at its best. The airport has improved, and many features cast a spell of sunlit invitation. Poverty is more visible here than in northern cities, so you can expect to witness those side effects.

Attractions include **Vesuvius**, the new digs at nearby **Oplontis**, **Ercolano**, one of the world's most magnificent bays, the **Castel**

Nuovo (Anjou Castle) and the former **monastery of San Martino**, the **Museo Archeologico Nazionale** (some of the best Greek and Roman art was taken here for protection from theft at the digs), the **Museo e Gallerie di Capodimonte** (paintings by Botticelli and Michelangelo, among many others), the **San Carlo Opera House**, 499 churches—a score of wonders. **Pompeii** is covered separately.

Where to Stay

Britannique Hotel

Moderate
Corso Vittorio Emanuele 133 Just 1 mile from Mergellina train station, 4 miles from airport.

☎ *(81) 761-4145,* FAX *(81) 669-760.*

Credit Cards: *All Major.*
The location of this hotel with its panoramic views of the Gulf of Naples makes it worth considering, even though you will probably need a car here. It is a former 19th-century villa that maintains its traditional decor. It has 90 rooms with bath, TV; 10 suites with kitchenette; restaurant; bar; private garden; lounges; parking.

Excelsior Hotel

Expensive to Very Expensive
Via Partenope 48 In old town center; 1 mile from train station.

☎ *(81) 764-0111,* FAX *(81) 764-9743.*

Credit Cards: *All Major.*
Dating to the early 1900s, this hotel remains the favorite of returning travelers to this area. It is so far ahead of other hotels here, there is no other that can compete with it. All 136 classically elegant rooms have bath or shower, climate control, soundproof double windows on all sides, TV, many with a balcony or terrace that overlooks the bay and Mount Vesuvius; eight stunning suites, plus the splendid "Royal"; wheelchair accessible; restaurant serving sumptuous cuisine; room service; bar; diet menu available; massage; concierge; shuttle bus to the train station. The service is flawless. The director is of great help to any traveler here and shows concern for his guests.

Grand Hotel Parker's

http://www.grandhotelparkers.com/

Corso Vittorio Emanuele 135 Downtown overlooking the gulf; 1 mile from train station.

☎ *(81) 761-2474,* FAX *(81) 663-527.*

Credit Cards: *All Major.*

This 19th-century downtown hotel with a view overlooking the gulf is another worthwhile choice. It offers 80 tastefully decorated rooms with bath, marble fixtures, bidet, bathrobe, hair dryer, TV, fax hookup on phone; 10 suites; rooftop restaurant; rooftop bar; tea room; supervised children's program; laundry; parking (fee).

Where to Eat

Casanova Grill

Moderate

Via Partenope 48, 80121, ☎ *(81) 417-111).*

Located at Excelsior.

Credit Cards: *All Major.*

This first-rate restaurant in the Hotel Excelsior is the most consistently dependable choice for lunch or dinner in the entire region. The Casanova Grill's cuisine is Mediterranean in style. Top-quality cookery, service and hygienic standards are scrupulously observed here, and the fare is uniformly excellent. The bar is good for snacks.

Ciro

Inexpensive

Via Santa Brigida 71, ☎ *(081) 552-4072.*

Credit Cards: *V, DC, A.*

Closed: *Sun.*

A refined trattoria, as well as pizza and pasta house, in the Santa Lucia Basin, it stays open later than many establishments in the city.

Try the spaghetti with clams and the grilled shrimp. If you don't favor olive oil, especially on your pizza, be sure to advise your waiter to go easy.

Giuseppone a Mare

Moderate

Via Ferdinando Russo 13, ☎ *(081) 575-6002.*

Credit Cards: *All Major.*

Closed: *Sun.*

Situated on the sea on an open-air terrace, this is a great spot for relaxing on a sunny day. Extra-fresh fish every day, vended from table to table by a blue-sweatered *ostricaro,* or oysterman. It's rather on the simple side in furnishings, but there's an ocean view, it's clean, bustling and busy, and the pizza's a dream.

What to Do
Excursions

Vesuvius

East side of the Bay of Naples, ☎ *81-850- 7255.*

Metro Stop: *Ercolano.*

Although its last major eruption was in March 1944, the population-choked areas near this legendary volcano that buried Pompeii and Herculaneum await the next "big one" (the volcano is still active). There is a bus service that leaves from the Ercolano station to a parking lot near the trail to the crater's rim. You can either walk (an hour-long, rocky trek) or take a cable car in summer (Apr. through Sept., 10 a.m.–5:30 p.m.), but check with the tourist office for schedule changes. The guide's fee and round-trip tickets are included in the admission price. The landscape is undoubtedly eerie (and watch out for sulphurous fumes). Admission: varies.

Historical Sites

Ercolano (Herculaneum)

Take Bus 255 from piazza Municipio.

Public Transportation: *piazza Municipio.*

🕘 *9 a.m.–5 p.m.*

It's possible to combine a trip to the rim of Vesuvius with a visit to the ancient city of Herculaneum buried in A.D. 79, in one day. Though dwarfed by the more famous Pompeii, the remains of Herculaneum depict the day-to-day doings of a Roman town more vividly than the former, mainly because it was covered over by mud, not ash. Admission: varies.

Monastery of San Martino

Largo San Martino 5, ☎ *81-578-1769.*

Take the Funicular Centrale from via Toledo.
Public Transportation: *49 or 42.*

🕘 *9 a.m.–2 p.m.*

Special Hours: *Sun. until 1 p.m.; closed Mon.*

The most fabulous view site in all of Naples may be from the balcony (the Certosa) of this former Carthusian monastery that now houses antiques and artifacts reflecting the glory days of the city. Although many visitors may be museum-phobic by now, the paintings by Neapolitans Ribera, Stanzione and Vaccaro, a maritime display and the holiday creches by Cuciniello in the former cloisters are all worth a look. Admission: varies.

Museums and Exhibits

Castel Nuovo (Anjou Castle)

Piazza del Municipio.

🕘 *9 a.m.–7 p.m.*

Castel Nuovo was built in the late 13th century for Charles of Anjou; later it was occupied and rebuilt by Spanish rulers of the House of Aragon. Today, the three towers that comprise the building are surrounded by several moats. Worthy of note is the Renaissance-era arch at the entrance designed by Francesco Laurana, built to commemorate the triumphant capture of the city by Alfonso I. The Museo Civico within is open to the public, although the Castle itself is now used for civic business. Admission: varies.

Museo Archeologico Nazionale

Piazza Museo 18-19, ☎ *81-440-166.*

Metro Stop: *Piazza Cavour.*

🕐 *9 a.m.–7:30 p.m.*

Special Hours: *Sun. only open until 1 p.m.*

This must-see museum contains the Farnese collection of antiquities
from digs at Pompeii and Herculaneum, taken from the sites for
protection from poachers. Galleries on the mezzanine reveal a collection of mosaics depicting the lives of ancient Romans; upstairs
there is a vast array of murals lifted from Pompeiian villas.
Admission: inexpensive.

Shopping

Fiera dell'Antiquariato

Villa Communale 1,via Caracciolo.

🕐 *7 a.m.–1 p.m.*

Special Hours: *Open only Sat., Sun.*

Bargain hunters from all over the city come to check out what's
newly old at this antiques and collectibles market in the municipal
park. The affair happens twice a month, alternating on Saturdays
and Sundays. There's a regular flea market held every Monday and
Friday morning near the Central Railway Station at Corso Novara,
and on Corso Malta in the Poggioreale District.

Theater

San Carlo Opera House
http://www.teatrosancarlo.it/
Via Vittorio Emanuele III.

🕐 *9 a.m.–4:30 p.m.*

Built by the Bourbon monarch Charles III in 1816, this historic theater hosts some of the most distinguished opera singers in the world.
In Italy, only Milan's La Scala comes close to it in importance.

Pompeii

With Vesuvius' eruption in A.D. 79, more than 17 feet of ash rained down on Pompeii, burying the city of 20,000 for centuries. It wasn't until 1748 that it was rediscovered, with excavations continuing to this day. A quick trip involves a full day in the ruins, but several days would give you time to pause at the forum, the open and covered theaters, as well as in the earliest research areas. Later archaeology uncovered such beauties as the *Vettii House, the Villa of Diomedes, the Golden Amorettes, plus "The Mysteries"* and yet another amphitheater. The paths are endless and each mosaic, shop, or hearth is fascinating. Herculaneum (Ercolano) also was victimized and preserved by Vesuvius. It is nowhere near as impressive as Pompeii. A museum now exists even if work has slowed due to hardening earth. (This city was covered by mud rather than ashes and, hence, is very well preserved.)

Where to Stay

Campgrounds

Camping Zeus ★★

Budget

Viale Villa dei Misteri Next to the Villa dei Misteri station.

☎ *081 861 5320.*

Usually not too crowded at these campgrounds. Highlights include a pool, restaurant and convenient location.

Where to Eat

Anfiteatro ★★

Moderate

Via Roma 125, ☎ *(081) 863.1245.*

Credit Cards: *All Major.*

Owner Mario Scisciola runs an honest establishment offering peasant-style fish dishes like baccala, a salt cod, or some toothsome seafood pastas. His refreshing restaurant is a bit away from the city center, where an abundance of eateries try to rook a few bucks from exhausted tourists.

Il Principe   ★★

Moderate

Piazza Bartolo Longo 8, ☎ *(081) 850.5566.*

Credit Cards: *All Major.*

This prosperous-looking establishment on the main square proffers
sophisticated cooking for a reasonable price. There's outside dining
on tables facing the Basilica, for an amusing vista of the surrounding
scene. Inside, the theatrical but tastefully decorated restaurant is
comfortable and easy on the eye. The cuisine is excellent; basically
Mediterranean-style seafood and continental dishes.

What to Do
Historical Sites

Pompeii   ★★★★

Piazza Esedra, ☎ *81-861-1051.*

Special Hours: *Closes 1 hour before sunset.*

Before Vesuvius put it to sleep prematurely in A.D. 79, Pompeii was
a popular Roman resort with vacation villas, luxury baths--the
works. Although some residents were able to return after the eruption, removing some valuables, today visitors can see the sites of several homes. One of interest is the House of the Vettii, an upper-mid-
dle-class domicile owned by two brothers, apparently collectors of
erotica and exotica--a statue of Priapus at the entrance reveals much
by saying little. The Forum, the city's promenade point, is interesting, although largely unrestored after being heavily damaged. Your
dreams may be disturbed by the plaster casts of animals and people
fully aware of their fate and unable to change it. Admission: varies.

Positano

Positano, in the opinion of many, is the star attraction of the
Amalfi Drive and of the entire area near Naples. The houses in this
picturesque village climb straight down the mountainside, like
mountain goats; so will you, every time you go for a swim in the sea.
(Fortunately, many hotels now boast pools and/or cliffside elevators.) If you're planning to spend the night in this region, it's a sen-

sible stop—and there are a number of marvelous hotels.

Where to Stay
Hotels and Resorts

Casa Albertina Hotel

http://www.casalbertina.it/ welcome_eng1.htm
Moderate
Via Tavolozza 3 Near the town center.
☎ *(89) 875-143*, FAX *(89) 811-540.*

Credit Cards: *All Major.*

This family-run hotel is only a few minutes from the beach, but its location allows peace and quiet even during the busiest season. It has 21 pleasantly furnished rooms with bath and shower, air conditioning (fee), TV, central heating, balcony overlooking the sea; three suites; delightful rooftop terrace restaurant with panoramic views; elevator; solarium. The service is warm and friendly, and the staff would be pleased to arrange a sea excursion. This hotel is located a number of steep steps up a hill, but porter service is available.

Hotel San Pietro Di Positano

http://www.besthotelsresorts.com/ ilsanpietrodipositano.htm
Expensive
Via Laurito 2 Just 1/2 mile south of Positano on the Amalfi drive.
☎ *(89)875-455*, FAX *(89) 811-449.*

Credit Cards: *All Major.*

A luxurious hotel taking its name from the chapel on its cliffside. Here is one of the ultimate secluded spots you will find; this romantic site is flanked by flowers of every kind imaginable and offers breathtaking views of the sea. The hotel's 60 rooms and six suites are decorated in exquisite taste and furnished with antiques. Each room has bath, fridge, terrace overlooking the sea, some with a Jacuzzi; plant-lined restaurant with two grills, a pizza oven and of course a spectacular vista; room service is limited; private beach with elevator access awesomely set among stone caverns and linked to a sun terrace with bar service; business center; free parking. A quiet dream spot, with a remarkable staff. Open from Apr. through Oct.

Le Agavi

http://www.agavi.it/
Moderate to Expensive
Belvedere Fornillo Near and above town entrance.

☎ *(89) 875-733*, FAX *(89) 875-965*.

Credit Cards: *All Major.*
An ultraquiet, clean cliff-hanger, where the rocks are sometimes the walls of your room. The hotel offers 70 lovely rooms with bath, TV; restaurant; elevator to private beach; wonderful pool. For peace and quiet and magnificent views of coast and sea, this charming hotel is an excellent choice.

Poseidon Hotel

Moderate to Expensive
Via Pasitea 148 Above the town; 10 minutes from the beach.

☎ *(89) 811-111*, FAX *(89) 875-833*.

Credit Cards: *All Major.*
A Mediterranean-style hotel in an off- beach setting, on a hillside facing the Gulf of Salerno. The vistas of the town and the bay are lovely here, as is the relaxing garden terrace. There are 48 large rooms with bath or shower, hair dryer, TV; three suites; restaurant serving above average cuisine; bar; health center; massage; terrace freshwater pool with a view; good parking space. Open Apr. to beginning of Nov.

Where to Eat

Buca di Bacco   ★★★

Moderate
Via Ramp Teglia 8, ☎ *(089) 875.699.*

Credit Cards: *All Major.*
Beachside restaurant, with tempting displays of appetizers, rare fruits

and salads beckoning you inward. Start with a cool drink in the downstairs bar, and repair to a pretty terrace under a canopy to watch the waves while you dine. The restaurant makes its own pasta, but seafood salads are favored by many.

La Cambusa ★★

Moderate

Sulla Spiaggia, ☎ *(089) 875.432.*

Credit Cards: *All Major.*

Busy and colorful harborside eatery with an outdoor patio for cocktails or dining. Nautically decorated exterior, interesting knickknacks. Owners Luigi and Baldo are more than amiable; they'll be calling you by name the next time you see them. Fare is seafood, pasta, the works. Specialty is spaghetti with zucchini, and they're knowledgable in the fish grilling department.

Sorrento

Sorrento is a town of overwhelming beauty set high along Mediterranean cliffs. In winter it's sleepy; in summer it's abuzz with visitors. This city is the largest, greatest and most celebrated center in the world for inlaid furniture and similar artistic accessories. The range of its products is astonishing. Utilizing skills which flowered here ages ago, every single piece from the most modest fruit basket to the most elaborate baroque highboy is 100 percent inset by hand. To see these displays is a unique experience.

Where to Stay

Grand Hotel Ambasciatori ★★★★

http://www.manniellohotels.it/ambasciatori/ukframe.html

Via A. Califano 18 Located 500 meters from train station.

☎ *(81) 878-2025,* FAX *(81) 807-1021.*

Credit Cards: *V, MC, A.*

Sitting on a cliff over its own stretch of sand, this hotel houses 103 rooms with bath/shower, climate control, TV; eight suites; wheelchair accessible. Heavily wooded and tiled lobby; matching bar with sloping ceiling; airy sea-view dining room; lush enclosed garden; elevator to private beach; free parking.

Grand Hotel Cesare Augusto ★

Budget to Moderate
Via degli Aranci 108 Located 100 yards behind Piazza Tasso, 200 yards from train station.

☎ *(81) 878-2700*, FAX *(81) 807-1029.*

Credit Cards: *A.*
It's a beauty for modern metropolitan tastes rather than for resort-type amenities. There are 120 rooms with bath, shower, some with air conditioning; two suites; enormous dining salon with mediocre cookery; woody, almost Scandinavian, Taverna dei Mulini; ice-cool bar. Rooftop pool, plus solarium with snack service. Bid for the 4th or 5th floors, the only ones high enough for a sea view. Excellent, if you don't insist on a waterfront address; conscientious staff.

Grand Hotel Excelsior Vittoria

http://www.ila-chateau.com/vittoria/
Expensive
Piazza Tasso 34 Located 29 miles south of Naples.

☎ *44-UTELL, (81) 807-1044,* FAX *(81) 877- 1206.*

Credit Cards: *All Major.*
This resort of world renown is perched on a rocky crag overlooking the Bay of Naples. Accommodations include 106 rooms and large suites all with bath, TV, some with balcony; room service; dining room serving excellent food; bar; large pool. Open year-round.

Where to Eat

Don Alfonso

Moderate to Expensive
Piazza Sant' Agata, ☎ *(081) 878.0026.*

Closed: *Mon.*

Southern Italian cuisine with a touch of Francais is prepared in this *haute mama i papa ristorante* located a little ways from Sorrento. The setting is the postcard-pretty village of Sant'Agata sui Due Golfi, and you must have a car to get there, as it is some 9km from the city. For the extra trouble and high prices, you will be suitably pampered by a well-trained staff, watched over (unobtrusively by the owners) and fed some fine fare on the order of rabbit in herbs or oyster risotto.

La Favorita O'Parrucchiano ★★

Moderate

Corso Italia, ☎ *(081) 878.1321.*

Credit Cards: *V.*

Try this winning establishment with reasonable prices and a table overstuffed with luscious antipasti, which you can pick and eat from all night. There's a garden to have supper in when the weather is suitable; inside the dining room is a like a cozy pub with a curved ceiling. Good pasta and pizza are also available.

What to Do
Museums and Exhibits

Correale Museum
http://www.sorrentoweb.com/uk/correale/
Via Correale.

🕐 *9:30 a.m.–5 p.m.*

Special Hours: *Sat., Sun. open only until 12:30 p.m.; closed Tues.*

Every town in Italy must have its museum, so Sorrento has assembled an amusing museum of memorabilia in an 18th-century castle. Good place to absorb local color. There is a nominal admission charge.

Shopping

A. Gargiulo Jannuzzi ★★★★

Piazza Tasso, ☎ *81-878-1041.*

🕐 *8 a.m.–10 p.m.*

This enormous three-level showroom stopped us in our tracks: a monumental collection of inlaid furniture by a world-famous, established firm. Examples include nesting tables, dining sets, chests of drawers and tea carts. Smaller, shippable items like cigarette, music, jewelry and cigar boxes, are great suitcase stuffers. On the upper level is a showcase of beautiful, moderately priced embroidered table linen, blouses, handkerchiefs and the like. Most have been hand-made in convents or by orphaned children. Free brochures; world-wide shipment; guaranteed delivery; continuously open 365 days a year.

Emilia Romagna

Bologna

Bologna, boasting about 500,000 residents, is the seat of the oldest university in the world (the word "university" was coined here) and the richest, highest-caloried fodder of the nation. Bologna is famous for its kitchens, university and arcaded streets. Busy modern pace amid marvelously antique atmosphere; more than 20 miles of arcaded walks; leaning towers; splendid palaces designed by masters such as Vignola; villa and mausoleum of Guglielmo Marconi. The city has 10 museums with treasures from Etruscan to modern times. At the **National Gallery** you'll find works by 56 great painters, including Raphael's *St. Cecilia*, and the **Museo Civico Archaeologico** is an Egyptologist's dream. Also not to be missed are the city's fabulous food shops and markets.

Where to Stay

Grand Hotel Baglioni   ★★★★

http://www.baglionihotels.com/iframeset.htm?id_hotel=2&id
_lingua =1

Moderate to Expensive

Via Indipendenza 8 One block from Piazza Maggiore, 1/2 mile from central train station.

☎ *(51) 225-445*, FAX *(51) 234-840*.

Credit Cards: *All Major.*

On Bologna's main but traffic-free street this 16th-century palace is wonderfully situated. There are 125 rooms with marble bath/shower, TV, hair dryer; eight suites, all with a Jacuzzi; two restaurants, including I Carracci, which is considered to be one of the most elegant in Bologna; bar; business center; free parking. A refined, classic hotel.

Internazionale Hotel

Budget to Moderate

Via Indipendenza 60 Centrally located near Convention Hall and Trade Fair Center.

☎ *(51) 245-544,* FAX *(51) 249-544.*

Credit Cards: *All Major.*

This hotel is actually a two-part structure, one dating from the 16th century and the other from 1972. There are 143 large rooms with bath, TV; more than half of the accommodations are singles; wheelchair accessible; bar; ample parking garage space, which is an important factor in this cluttered town. There is no restaurant in the hotel, but plenty to be found in the area.

Where to Eat

Cordon Bleu

Moderate to Expensive

Via Saffi 38, ☎ *(051) 649-822.*

Credit Cards: *All Major.*

Closed: *Sun.*

Despite its Gallic-sounding name, Cordon Bleu is noted among many for its classic Emilia-Romagnan cuisine from the Renaissance period. Specials change frequently, but always include prime meats and fish, with top of the market fresh fruits. The wine list spans the boot of Italy. Unusual for a hotel dining room—many local gourmets give this salon a frequent look-see.

Franco Rossi

Moderate

Via Goito 3, ☎ *(051) 238-818.*

Credit Cards: *All Major.*

Closed: *Sun.*

The staff and personable owners provide a warm welcome to this intimate trattoria that's built a strong reputation for top-notch pastas and risottos. Whether it's a simple *tagliatelle* (ribbon pasta) in the rich Bolognese style or a filet of beef emboldened with balsamic vinegar from neighboring Modena, most meals will satisfy discerning diners.

Il Bitone

Moderate

Via Emilia Levante 111, ☎ *(051) 546-110.*

Credit Cards: *All Major.*

An inn with lots of charm and frequented by many of the city's chicest guests. The antipasto and the wild mushroom salad (in season) are fine light starters. End it all with a marvelous *zabaglione*. In the summer, it's de rigueur to be seated in a lovely garden for a delightfully al fresco lunch.

What to Do

Historical Sites

ITRAVELBOOK FREEBIE

Archiginnasio

Via Farini.

🕘 *9 a.m.–1:45 p.m.*

Special Hours: *Closed Sun.*

Admission: *free.*

Built in 1565, the Archiginnasio is a fine example of Baroque architecture. Part of the original University of Bologna, which was founded in 1088, this arresting structure holds within its walls the Teatro Anatomico, an old operating theater, with an ornate profes

Torre Degli Asinelli

Piazza di Porta Ravegnanna.

Public Transportation: *Bus 25 or 30.*

🕐 *9 a.m.–6 p.m.*

These two crazily leaning towers are the result of competition between blue-blood families of the 12th century—the taller the towers built, it was said, the more powerful the family. The tallest, Asinelli, rises some 320 feet, and is reached by 500 or more stairs. Those reaching the observation deck are rewarded by a panoramic view of the city and outlying areas. Admission: inexpensive.

Museums and Exhibits

Museo Civico Archaeologico

http://www.comune.bologna.it/bologna/Musei/Archeologico/

Via Archiginnasio 2, ☎ *51-221-1896.*

🕐 *9 a.m.–2 p.m.*

Special Hours: *Open only until 12:30 p.m. Sun.; closed Mon.*

This fascinating museum is not only loaded with mummies and bas reliefs from the tombs of Egyptian pharaohs, but it contains some of the finest collections of Etruscan artifacts you'll find anywhere. A few notable treasures within its walls are sculpture, urns, pottery and jars from the 5th and 6th centuries B.C. and the Roman Phidias' head of Athenia Lemnia. Admission: varies.

Pinacoteca Nazionale

Via Belle Arti 56, ☎ *51-223-849.*

🕐 *9 a.m.–2 p.m.*

Special Hours: *Sun. open only until 1 p.m.; closed Mon.*

Besides being the gastronomic capital of Italy, Bologna also boasts one of the finest art museums in Europe. The stellar collection includes Bolognese art from the 14th through the 18th centuries. Art mavens and scholars flock to see Raphael's *St. Cecilia in Ecstasy*, Guido Reni's Pieta as well as works by Flemish and French artists. Admission: varies.

Special Tours

Specialty Food Shops

Off Piazza Maggiore.

Italians flock to this city for its outstanding food stores and markets, some of which lie within a short walk from the bustling Piazza Maggiore and the twin towers. Dazzling sights and smells emerge from fish, bread and cheese shops, with names like Pescheria Brunelli or Tamborini. Wheels of parmiagiano cheese from nearby Parma and the prized balsamic vinegar from Modena vie for space with hanging salamis and suckling pigs. The fun here is fighting for a select whole fish with crowds of other shoppers as competition.

Latium

Rome

Roma is said to have been founded in 753 B.C., when Romulus, son of the god Mars, yoked a bullock and a heifer to a plowshare, marked out a boundary and built a wall. Be that as it may, the city has at least 2500 years of unparalleled cultural accomplishment. in Milan, Turin and other Italian cities. To reduce the contaminants produced by traffic, cars are allowed on city streets only every other day, depending on whether plate numbers end in odd or even figures. This includes rental vehicles, too. (Shifty locals often have two cars with different plate endings in order to circumvent this restriction.) Parking meters (3-hour limit) now tick on 62 streets in Rome's midsection. Too many ticks and you'll pay up to $164 in fines. Since the banning of vehicles from five of its main piazzas, the Eternal City is becoming a much more pleasant place to stroll.

Where to Stay

While your room rate may be quoted to you as a fixed sum, many places have sharply jacked up the prices of amenities such as drinks, laundry and room service items. Ask what is included; generally, it is a Continental breakfast, but sometimes you'll be socked extra for air conditioning.

> **ITRAVELBOOK TIP:** IT WAS OUR UNFORTUNATE EXPERIENCE TO ARRIVE AT OUR HOTEL WITH A PRINTED CONFIRMATION IN HAND, ONLY TO BE INFORMED THAT THE HOTEL CANCELLED OUR RESERVATION ... AFTER WE LEFT THE STATES. IN FACT, THE HOTEL FOUND THAT THEY COULD GET MORE FOR THE ROOM THAN THEY CHARGED US, AND THUS GAVE THE ROOM AWAY TO OTHER GUESTS, AT A HIGHER RATE. THE RESULT WAS A DISASTROUS STAY IN AN EXHORBITANTLY-PRICED, FILTHY, GROUND-LEVEL PRIVATE APARTMENT IN TRASTAVERE, WHICH WE SHARED WITH SEVERAL CATS, NO DOUBT A FEW RODENTS, AND A MILDEWED ELVIS PILLOW (THE IMAGE WAS A STILL FROM VIVA LAS VEGAS). THE LESSON WAS CLEAR: RATHER THAN TRY TO SAVE EUROS, LOOK FOR AN EXTREMELY REPUTABLE HOTEL, AND IF POSSIBLE, RESERVE WITH EITHER A VISA OR AMERICAN EXPRESS CARD.

Atlante Star Hotel ★★

Moderate

Via Vitelleschi 34Just 300 yards from St. Peter's Basilica and the Vatican.

Metro Stop: *Ottaviano.*

☎ *(6) 687-3233*, FAX *(6) 687-2300.*

Credit Cards: *All Major.*

This hotel stands eyeball-to-eyeball with the Vatican, and certainly one of the most spectacular vistas in Christianity can be found from its scenic rooftop restaurant, Les Etoiles. You must not miss an opportunity to dine here, especially at sunset. Accommodations consist of 80 rooms with bath, phone, TV; 10 suites; bar; business center; free parking. Complimentary pickup service from the airport.

Atlantico Hotel ★★

Budget to Moderate

Via Cavour 23Just 150 meters from train station; near via Veneto and Opera.

☎ *(6) 485-951*, FAX *(6) 474-4105.*

Credit Cards: *All Major.*

A pleasant hotel in a good location. Its 83 rooms are comfortably simple with bath, TV; breakfast room; room service; lounge; bar; parking (fee); restaurant dining in the adjoining Mediterraneo Hotel. A kindly staff.

Bernini Bristol Hotel

http://www.sinahotels.com/hotels/bristol/

Moderate

Piazza Barberini 23 At entrance to via Veneto; near Spanish Steps; 1/2 mile from train station.

☎ *(6) 488-3051*, FAX *(6) 482-4266.*

Credit Cards: *All Major.*

Here you will find impressive accommodations in a comfortable and unpretentious atmosphere, and in a convenient location. There are 126 rooms with bath, climate control, TV, some with balcony, some with Jacuzzi; 16 suites, most of which have a private terrace; restaurant; lounge.

Carriage Hotel

Moderate

Via delle Carrozze 36 In old Rome at base of Spanish Steps; 2 miles from Termini train station.

Metro Stop: *Piazza di Spagna.*

☎ *(6) 699-01224*, FAX *(6) 678-8279.*

Credit Cards: *All Major.*

A hotel with a unique personality near the Piazza di Spagna. All 27 rooms and four suites have bath, TV, floral wallpaper. The rooms with wraparound terrace are the most in demand with their spectacular view, but if these are not available you can still enjoy your breakfast on the terrace with the Eternal City as your backdrop. This candidate has no restaurant and almost no other public amenities, but its location and character make it a worthy choice.

Gregoriana Hotel

Moderate to Expensive

Via Gregoriana 18 Near Spanish Steps; 10 minutes from train station.

Metro Stop: *Piazza di Spagna.*

☎ *(6) 679-4249*, FAX *(6) 678-4258.*

Credit Cards: *Not Accepted.*

Just below the Hotel Hassler and on a legendary street, off the top of the Spanish Steps, is this little gem. Formerly a convent, it is a beloved magnet for many in the Italian fashion industry. It has only 19 smallish rooms with private bath or shower, radio, phone, TV; breakfasts served in rooms; virtually no lobby; elevator.The maintenance here is superb, as is the hospitality of its staff, which has gained this hotel a loyal following. There is no restaurant, but many to choose from nearby. Certainly in one of the best neighborhoods in Rome.

Hotel Cicerone

http://www.travel.it/roma/cicerone/

Moderate to Expensive

Via Cicerone 55/cNear Vatican; 4 miles from train station.

☎ *(6) 3576*, FAX *(6) 688-01383.*

Credit Cards: *All Major.*

Located in a relatively quiet district near the Vatican, this hotel is commercial but good as an alternate choice. The decor in the angular lobby creates a subdued ambience. The 260 agreeable bedchambers have small bath, TV and thoughtful touches such as shower caps, shoeshine cloths and more, but storage space is inadequate; 10 suites; restaurant; large coffee shop that seats 250, open from 6:30 a.m. to noon; light fare available in American bar during the afternoon and evening; parking garage.

Hotel Excelsior Rome

Expensive to Very Expensive

Via Vittorio Veneto 125 ☞ *Via Veneto district; 5 minutes from train station*.

☎ *221-2340, (6) 4708,* FAX.

Credit Cards: *All Major.*

This hotel is certainly a famous landmark in its proud and busy location on the Via Veneto. It is a luxury redoubt perfectly suited to its midtown location. There are 327 beautifully decorated and furnished rooms with enlarged baths, including twin basins, separate nonskid tub and shower rooms, TV; 45 suites; savory food served in the small off-lobby restaurant; room service; soundproof double windows wherever you look. The maintenance here is immaculate. Tariffs range from the reasonable group levels to the stratosphere for rooms and suites that outshine some of the other luxury hotels.

Hotel Flora   ★★★★

Expensive

Via Vittorio Veneto Located at entrance to the Borghese Gardens.

☎ *44-UTELL, (6) 489-929,* FAX *(6) 482-0395.*

Credit Cards: *All Major.*

Smack on the via Veneto, here is an excellent, unostentatious hotel with a very favorable location. The hotel has been smartened nicely. The furnishings and decor of the interior are comfortable with warm oriental rugs, polished marble, antiques and period furniture. The 175 rooms and eight suites are all with bath, high ceilings, plenty of closet space, TV, many with views of Villa Borghese; restaurant serves pleasant but not memorable cuisine; bar; room service; laundry. The genteel aura and attentive service maintain a regular following for this hotel.

Hotel Giulio Cesare   ★★★★

http://www.hotelgiuliocesare.com/ reservation.htm

Moderate to Expensive

Via Degli Scipioni 287 Near Piazza di Spagna and city center.

☎ *(6) 321-0751,* FAX *(6) 321-1736.*

Credit Cards: All Major.

From its rooftop garden, this lovely hotel provides a splendid view of the Vatican and the Borghese. There are 90 rooms with bath, bidet, hair dryer, TV; piano bar; concierge; laundry/dry cleaning service; free parking. The service and cuisine are very notable. Avoid the basement lodgings.

Hotel Hassler

http://www.hotelhasslerroma.com/

Very Expensive

Piazza Trinita dei Monti 6In city center; at top of Spanish Steps; 4 miles from Termini train station.

☎ *(6) 678-2651,* FAX *(6) 678-9991.*

Credit Cards: *All Major.*

A favorite of many for its intimacy and flair, this establishment is expertly run by Roberto Wirth, whose family has been at the helm here for generations. If you want a convenient address in Rome's finest quarter with a view, then look no further. The subtle homeyness here is hard to duplicate anywhere in the city. It offers a roof garden with magnificent views over Rome and a marvelous window-wrapped dining room serving Roman cuisine; an outdoor patio with the Imperial bar in its court, a genteel interior bar with large adjoining lounge, a reading room in soft greens, perfect maintenance and extra- smooth service. Stunning view from the upper floors; fine hairdressing salon; many rooms widened by clever architectural techniques and built-in furnishings; hand- painted murals added to some walls; 100 rooms with bath, some with balcony and/ or Jacuzzi; 14 suites. The top spots are the San Pietro, the Presidential and the Medici Suites, all with glorious views of the city. The effort here is so cordial and zealous that the Hassler even will arrange golf and lunch for guests at a beautiful nearby club. Hosting at its best.

Hotel Lord Byron

Expensive

Via Giuseppe de Notaris 5In the Parioli district; 1 mile from Spanish Steps; 3 miles from Vatican City.

Metro Stop: *Piazza Flaminio.*

☎ *(6) 322-0404,* FAX *(6) 322-0405.*

Credit Cards: *All Major.*

An Art Deco villa situated on a fashionable residential hilltop whose small scale makes it seem more like a private (and extremely expensive) home than a hotel. The 37 handsomely appointed rooms have marble bath, hair dryer, bidet, climate control, bar, some also with balcony or patio; eight suites; executive floor; nonsmoking available. This is perfection.

Hotel Majestic

Moderate
Via Veneto 50In Via Veneto district; 1/2 mile from train station.

☎ *(6) 486-841,* FAX *(6) 488-5657.*

Credit Cards: *All Major.*

Its location in the center of the Via Veneto district makes this hotel a perfect choice for tourists. It has bounced back from the 19th century with amazing flair, successfully introducing modern conveniences without forgetting its neoclassic beginnings. Each room's decor is pleasingly different from the other. There are 95 rooms with marble bath and whirlpool, TV; some have a terrace and solarium; eight suites; ten junior suites; charming restaurant, which is moved outside onto the terrace in the summer. Although the prices have certainly gone skyward, manager Silvano Pinchetti has brought his considerable skills to bear and the rewards are especially worthwhile.

Hotel de la Ville

Moderate to Expensive

Via Sistina 67 At top of Spanish Steps; 1 mile from train station.

☎ *327-0200, (6) 673-31,* FAX *(6) 678-4213.*

Credit Cards: *All Major.*

This first-class neoclassical hotel boasts breathtaking views and an ideal address next to the Hotel Hassler. The lobby is quiet, uncluttered and uncommercial, which is appreciated after a long day of sightseeing. The accommodations include 192 soundproof rooms with bath, TV (with English programs), radio, direct-dial telephones; 23 suites; room service; restaurant; a marvelous cool inner courtyard for summer dining and sipping; calm Patio Bar for light meals; 6th-floor solarium puts all of Rome at your feet; business center; free parking. The staff goes all out to make your stay a happy one. This is a splendid choice for vacationers.

La Residenza

http://home.venere.it/roma/ la_residenza/
Moderate to Expensive
Via Emilia 22-24Off via Veneto; near U.S. embassy; near Villa Borghese.
Metro Stop: *Piazza Barberini.*

☎ *(6) 488-0789,* FAX *(6) 485-721.*

Credit Cards: *All Major.*
Located on a very quiet side street off via Veneto, this former townhouse, turned hotel, makes an ideal accommodation choice. Its furnishings are elegant, yet homey, with the use of oriental rugs and oil paintings hanging on the walls. The 27 rooms and six suites are delightfully furnished and have bath, hair dryer, bathrobe; breakfast room; bar; rooftop terrace for summer enjoyment; parking. The service is wonderful.

Massimo d'Azeglio Hotel

Moderate

Via Cavour 18 Located 150 meters from train station, 10 minutes from via Veneto and Opera.

☎ *(6) 487-0270,* FAX *(6) 482-7386.*

Credit Cards: *All Major.*
Here is a solid value in a convenient location. All 210 rooms are comfortable with smart marble baths, TV, double windows to quiet street exposures, although some facets are still noisy; modern, pleasant lobby; breakfast room; room service; wine cellar. The dining room is serene, cozy and attractive with cuisine that is just terrific. Top quality at decent prices.

Panama Hotel ★

Budget to Moderate

Via Salaria 336   Next to Villa Ada Park in Villa Savoia at north entrance to the city.

☎ *(6) 855-2558,* FAX *(6) 841-3929.*

Credit Cards: *All Major.*

This small hotel is tranquil and cozy with a colorful lobby. Accommodations include 43 small, well-groomed rooms with bath or shower, TV, most overlooking a shady little garden; #101 is the largest double; attractive restaurant, bar and downstairs grill; parking area plus a small garage. No groups admitted here. Service is unusually good for its informal style.

Where to Eat

Some of the best dining currently to be found in Rome will be in a selection of leading grand hotels or discreet intimate ones. Because of labor problems and spiraling costs, these better-organized institutions can provide outstanding service, refinement, and quality ingredients—and very often the setting and view will be much more inspiring than at the independent entries; advance reservations are necessary at most of the following. Nevertheless, delicious, inexpensive meals can be had at tiny holes-in-the-wall: across the Tiber in Trastevere are located some of the newest, the tastiest, and the most inexpensive restaurants there are to be had in Rome. Rome is a food-lover's city. Therefore, it would be impossible to list all of our favorites here!

Ambasciata d'Abruzzo

Moderate to Expensive

Via Pietro Tacchini 26, ☎ *(06) 806.8256.*

Credit Cards: *All Major.*
Closed: *Sun.*

In the Parioli district, this restaurant is usually crammed with locals, as a jovial proprietor and his staff keep bellowing, "Mangia, mangia, mangia!" ("Eat, eat, eat!") and similar encouragements. Even as the host carries platters to his patrons, he spoons free bites to other clients along his happy route. The moment you sit down, a basket with 17 types of sausage is placed on your table, plus a cutting board, bread, cheeses and knives. Then you are given a stack of plates and told to take anything (and as much) as you want from the terraces of antipasto; There are 35 different preparations, and they are delicious! Serious gourmands then go on to roasts, fowl, trout and a menu so long that our vision blurred just glancing at it. It's absolutely imperative to reserve in advance, especially on a Saturday afternoon.

Cucurucu ★★★

Moderate

Via Capoprati 10, ☎ *(06) 325.2571.*

Credit Cards: *All Major.*

Found in a rust-colored building along the Tiber, about five minutes by taxi from the center. In the summer the garden dining is captivating; in winter the stucco-walled interior spreads over several rooms, the nicest being before a crackling hearth. You'll be rewarded with very honest Italian cuisine, coupled with helpful and generous attention. One of the most reliable bets in town.

Da Mario ★★

Inexpensive to Moderate

Via della Vite 55-56, ☎ *(06) 678.3818.*

Piazza di Spagna.

Specialties: Game, ribolitta.

Credit Cards: *All Major.*

Closed: *Sun.*

Only one room, sometimes one waiter (understandably, service a little brusque) and wonderful Tuscan cuisine. Not much decor, lots of sawdust, raffia and mended tablecloths. Mario is dependable for wild game in season and *Florentine bistecca.* Another favorite is the *ribolitta,* an everything-in-one-pot vegetable soup.

Enoteca Cavour 313

Inexpensive

Via Cavour, 313, ☎ *67.85.496.*

Closed: *Sun.*

A popular wine bar, with more than 600 wines to choose from, and a nibbler's heaven. The menu consists of a variety of starters, salads, cheeses and especially tempting desserts. The Enoteca provides a welcoming atmosphere where you are likely to rub shoulders with a vast stratum of Rome society.

George's ★★★

Expensive

Via Marche 7, ☎ *(06) 484.575.*

Piazza Barberini.
Credit Cards: *All Major.*
Closed: *Sun.*

This old standby is Gallic rather than Italian in tone. The boudoir-like dining salon is crowned with a satin-lined, tented ceiling; tables are set with discreetly lit lamps and fresh flowers. There's a lovely garden terrace open in good weather, and smooth dinner music plays in the background. The staff speaks English and pays attention to myriad details. Oysters, salmon, veal and beef are featured in the cuisine. Two people can casually wave ciao to $75 at lunch.

Giolitti

Inexpensive

Via degli Uffici del Vicario, ☎ *(06) 699.1243.*

By 9 a.m., there are lines out the door at this old-fashioned *gelateria* that features some very original flavors, including champagne. Lunches are served, but most people are really interested in what new tastes in frozen fantasies the artists in the back room are dishing up. It has some strong competition though, from the Della Palma nearby.

Hassler Roof

Very expensive

Piazza Trinita dei Monti 6, 00187, ☎ *(6) 678-2651. Located at Hassler.*

Credit Cards: *All Major.*

The Hassler Roof is easily the most breathtaking perch to occupy at any time of day (brunch is exceptional, and justifiably popular) or night in the Eternal City. Not only are the aesthetics sublime, but so is the cuisine. Almost single-handedly, proprietor Roberto Wirth has brought back Roman cuisine to Rome. The emphasis here is eternally delicious.

Il Matriciano

Inexpensive to Moderate

Via del Gracchi 55, ☎ *(06) 321-2327.*

Lepanto.

Credit Cards: *All Major.*

An ideal location for dining after a day at St. Peter's Basilica; no particular scenic charm or haute cuisine, but fine for stick-to-the-ribs country food. Soups thick with vegetables and beans, pasta with a lusty bacon and tomato sauce. There's sidewalk dining and plenty of shade; superswift and cheerful attention.

La Campana

Moderate

18 Vicolo della Campana, ☎ *(6) 686.7820.*

Credit Cards: *All Major.*

Closed: *Mon.*

A beloved, unpretentious Roman trattoria, specializing in traditional cuisine. Spaghetti Puttanesca is a favorite, as is braised oxtail and lamb. This restaurant has a loyal following that's growing daily through word of mouth. Late night dining is a boost as well. It's a good place to try wild boar if you're game.

Le Restaurant

Moderate to Expensive

Via V. Emanuele Orlando 3, 00185, ☎ *(04) 474.7307.*

Located at Le Grand Hotel.
Piazza della Republica.
Credit Cards: *All Major.*

A grand dining parlor, simultaneously fresh and elegant. This hotel has always drawn the aristocracy of the globe, so on almost any day you will find its tables occupied by front-page personalities. They have come for good reason, because the cuisine, attention and character are insurmountable. The view, however, is rather limited.

Otello alla Concordia

Moderate to Expensive

Via della Croce 81, ☎ *(6) 679.1178.*

Piazza di Spagna.
Credit Cards: *All Major.*
Closed: *Sun.*

A lively, fashionable restaurant with an arresting centerpiece, a fountain of real fruit in the middle of the room. This whimsy provides a general mood of fun at this crowded spot. Celebrities, locals and lots of tourists pack the place (200 seats) for spaghetti with clams, bresaola, baby lamb or swordfish. It's owned by three sisters who run a tight ship and are known for gabbing with guests. On the Via della Croce, just outside, diners can browse later in the boutiques and food shops.

Piccolo Arancio

Moderate

Vicolo Scanderbeg, 112, ☎ *(06) 67.86.139.*

Credit Cards: *All Major.*
Closed: *Mon.*

A caring and convivial spot near the Trevi Fountain, this restaurant is one branch of a small culinary empire owned by the Cialfi family, some of whom are usually in evidence. The decor is subtle and understated, the tables set with a minimum of froufrou. Pastas are stars here as well as zucchini and artichokes cooked in the *giudia* style (flattened and skillfully fried, with lovely results). Desserts are homemade.

Piperno a Monte Cenci

Moderate to Expensive

Via Monte Cenci 9, ☎ *(06) 654.0629.*

Near Palazzo Cenci
Credit Cards: *All Major.*
Closed: *Mon.*

A non kosher pride of the Jewish-Italian quarter of the Eternal City, this spot has been famous since 1844 for its specialty, *carciofi alla giudia*, or artichokes, pressed flat, and quickly deep-fried; the humble vegetable emerges golden brown, the leaves crisp, and the heart sweet and soft. The restaurant is operated by a vigorous and competent young couple, who have improved it so dramatically that now at nearly every meal the house is full. No-nonsense, brusque service, noisy and bustling; simple, old-fashioned furnishings.

Relais Le Jardin

Moderate to Expensive

Via G. de Notaris 5, 00197, ☎ *(6) 361.3041.*

Located at Hotel Lord Byron.
Credit Cards: *All Major.*
Closed: *Sun.*

Relais Le Jardin, on the ground floor of the Lord Byron Hotel, only has a few tables, but they are always filled with the gustatory conoscenti of Rome and visitors of world renown. There is a lighthearted cheer that pervades throughout, obviously encouraged by selections from one of Italy's most prestigious wine cellars.

Sabatini I

Expensive

Piazza Santa Maria in Trastevere, ☎ *(06) 581.2026.*

Credit Cards: *All Major.*

Situated on a large hedged terrace on piazza Santa Maria, this is one of the most popular trattorias on the edges of the Trastevere. The door faces a handsome open grill glowing with charred wood and sizzling with roasts, chops, fish and fowl; interior hall has leaded windows and three enormous ancient timbers supporting a raftered ceiling. This restaurant is especially popular in summer; reservations are recommended, but a wait may still be required.

Taverna Flavia di Mimmo

Moderate

Via Flavia, ☎ *(06) 474.5214.*

Piazza della Repubblica.
Credit Cards: *All Major.*
Closed: *Sun.*

Amid walls lined with photos of celebrated guests, it fills its clientele with celebrated cookery. Simple interior of several interlocking rooms; bottle-green color scheme; generally folksy service. The pasta, white truffles, grilled scampi, sauteed brains with a light garlic flavor and the house wine were all above average. If fresh peas are in season, be sure to order a side dish. Very good, but always total up your bill here.

Taverna Giulia

Moderate

Vicolo dell' Oro 23, ☎ *(06) 686.9768.*

Credit Cards: *All Major.*
Closed: *Sun.*

Made up of three rooms linked together in a lovely white house (near the Pope's big white house) beside the river, this is one of Rome's top gathering places for good food at good value. The dark wood beams and the animated atmosphere are a perfect setting for the delicious Genoese-Ligurian preparations. Excellent pasta, especially topped with pesto sauce, and a creme brulee so heavenly, the clergy visit the place frequently.

Tre Scalini ★★★

Moderate to Expensive

Piazza Navona 30, ☎ *(06) 687.9148.*

Credit Cards: *All Major.*

Closed: *Wed.*

Named for the Three Steps that have been immortalized by Garibaldi, this cafe is situated on a large and lovely square, where all but walking traffic has been banned. So, it's a delight to sit under the awnings of the sidewalk terrace here sipping coffee and sampling a dish of its famous ice cream.

What to Do
Historical Sites

Arco di Constantino (Arch of Constantine) ★★★

🖃 *Next to the Colosseum.*

Public Transportation: *B.* Metro Stop: *Colosseo.*

Erected in A.D. 315 to commemorate a victory by Emperor Constantine, this was the largest of many triumphal arches in ancient Rome. Admission: inexpensive.

Basilica di San Giovanni in Laterano (St John ★★

🖃 *Piazza San Giovanni in Laterano 4,* ☎ *6- 698-6433.*

Metro Stop: *Colosseo.*

🕐 *7 a.m.–6 p.m.*

Before the papacy was installed in the Vatican, St. John's was the residence of the pope and still is the Cathedral of Rome. Built in A.D. 314 by Constantine, the venerable cathedral has survived disaster after disaster, both natural and man-made. In 1993, a terrorist bomb destroyed part of the facade and the inner courtyard. Naturally, parts of the structure have been rebuilt many times, but the Baptistry remains largely the same as it was in Constantine's day. Pilgrims

climb the 28 steps of the Scala Santa in front of the church on their
knees to commemorate the day Christ walked down the same steps
(it's believed) after being tried by Pontius Pilate. Admission: inexpensive.

ITRAVELBOOK FREEBIE

Chiesa Di San Pietro in Vincoli

✉ *Piazza di San Pietro in Vincoli*, ☎ *6-488-2865.*

Metro Stop: *Piazza Cavour.*

🕐 *7 a.m.–6 p.m.*

Special Hours: *Sun. open until 7 p.m.*

Under the central altar of this 5th-century church are the chains that
bound St. Peter after his arrest in Palestine, but its greatest treasure
is Michelangelo's sculpture of Moses, adorning the tomb of Pope
Julius II.

Colosseo (Colosseum)

Piazzale del Colosseo, via dei Fori Imperiali, ☎ *6-700-4261.*

Public Transportation: *B.* Metro Stop: *Colosseo.*

🕐 *9 a.m.–7 p.m.*

Special Hours: *Wed., Sun. open until 1 p.m.; closed from Jan. 16-Feb.
15.*

Known to citizens of ancient Rome as the Flavian Amphitheater, the
Colosseum was built during the years A.D. 72-80 under Emperors
Vespasianus and Titus. Imagine 50,000 people gleefully seated, waiting for you to die! Bored emperors would often order the place
flooded for mock naval battles. The present structure's original marble facade was mined for constructing other monuments, including
St. Peter's Basilica. In the 18th century, Pope Benedict XIV declared
the Colosseum sacred, which stopped further destruction. Admission: varies.

Fontana di Trevi (Trevi Fountain)

✉ *Piazza di Trevi.*

A coin tossed into what is probably the world's most visited fountain, face away from it when you pitch the money, is supposed to guarantee your return to Rome. Toss a second one, and you get to make a wish! The newly restored Trevi Fountain was slowly constructed from 1732-1751, by Nicolo Salvi from a design by Bernini. Most warm afternoons and certainly evenings, the youth of Rome gather on its flanks for socializing. Pigeons, however, do not. During a three-year cleaning and patching, workmen installed a low-voltage electric-shock system to discourage fowl play.

Foro Romano (Roman Forum)

📧 *Via dei Fori Imperiali, near the piazza Ven,* ☎ *6-678-0782.*

Public Transportation: *B.* Metro Stop: *Colosseo.*

🕐 *9 a.m.–7 p.m.*

Special Hours: *Sun. open only until 1 p.m.*

Just behind Rome's Campidoglio (city hall) are the ruins of the Forum of ancient Rome. Although called the Forum, the complex was made up of several forums, containing shops, temples and various public institutions. Much of the Fori today is in ruins, except for the solidly built Curia, where the Roman Senate debated, but some prominent landmarks still remain, including 10 marble columns of the Temple of Antoninus and Faustina, the Arch of Titus and Arch of Septimius Severus, which the emperor built in A.D. 203. The popular Temple of the Vestal Virgins is comprised, sadly, of headless statues and a pedestal. Admission: varies.

Hadrian's Villa

📧 *Via di Villa Adriana. Four miles southwest of Tivoli.*

Public Transportation: *2 or 4.*

🕐 *9 a.m.–7:30 p.m.*

Special Hours: *Closes at 4 or 5 p.m. in winter.*

Emperor Hadrian was among Rome's most active builders, and one of his pet projects was a magnificent villa begun in A.D. 120. It was intended to be a self-contained world with recreations of the most beautiful and/or luxurious examples of architecture that Hadrian had come across in the course of his many journeys throughout the empire. What's left of this imperial dream, four miles southwest of Tivoli (near the Villa d'Este), are ruins and a few reconstructions, and a model of the villa near the entrance. Admission: inexpensive.

La Scalinata di Piazza di Spagna ★★

✉ *Piazza di Spagna.*

☞ *Near the Trevi Fountain.*

The natural starting-out point for visitors to Rome, the Spanish Steps were built of Travertine marble by de Sanctis in 1726. At the foot of the Steps is the boat-shaped fountain by Pietro Bernini, father of the prolific Gian Lorenzo Bernini. At the top is the Church of Trinita dei Monti, with yet another fine view of the city; the interior isn't especially noteworthy, but the facade is.

Ostia Antica ★★

✉ *Viale dei Romagnoli 717,* ☎ *565-0022.*

☞ *Take Lido train to Ostia Antica (every half-hour).*

Public Transportation: *B.* Metro Stop: *Magliana.*

🕐 *9 a.m.–7 p.m.*

Special Hours: *Oct. through Feb. 9 a.m.–5 p.m.*

The archaeological sites, about 45 minutes from downtown Rome near the mouth of the Tiber, were founded as an early port settlement in 4 B.C. Interesting monuments include the Piazzale delle Corporazioni, the ancient stock exchange; mosaics explain the various businesses that flourished there. Admission: inexpensive.

Pantheon ★★★★

✉ *Piazza della Rotunda,* ☎ *6-369-831.*

Public Transportation: *64, 170 or 175.* Metro Stop: *Largo di Torre Argentina.*

🕐 *9 a.m.–2 p.m.*

Special Hours: *Sun. open until 1 p.m.*

Admission: *free.*

This magnificently preserved monument was begun in 27 B.C. by Marcus Agrippa as a temple of Mars and Venus and rebuilt in A.D. 2 by Hadrian after it had been damaged in a fire. The facade sports Corinthian columns, a deep porch and domed roof. Inside is a huge, acoustically perfect rotunda lit naturally from a nine-yard-wide central oculus high above in the cupola. The marble floor of the rotunda is empty, but around the curvilinear sides of the immense enclosure are chapels containing the tombs of Italian kings, including that of Victor Emanuel II, the first sovereign of a unified Italy. To many people, however, the most important tomb here is that of the painter Raphael, who is buried between the 5th and 6th chapels.

Piazza Navona ★★

📧 *Off Corso del Rinascimento.*

This elongated, elliptical piazza was built over the site of the Circus Domitian, which was a race course during the Roman age. Of today's trio of monuments here, the central one is the celebrated Fountain of Four Rivers (1651) by Bernini. Christmas brings a street fair specializing in handmade holiday gifts and foodstuffs.

Piazza del Popolo ★★

📧 *Near via del Corso.*

Scrubbed in a total renovation program, the square is now bright and clean. In the center is the Flaminian Obelisk (1200-1232 B.C.) on a pedestal embellished by lions spouting water from their mouths. Newly illuminated, it is captivating at night. The piazza has three notable churches, Santa Maria del Popolo, with frescoes by Pinturicchio and paintings by Caravaggio on the walls, Santa Maria di Montesanto and Santa Maria dei Miracoli. No vehicles are allowed, but there are vast migrations of tourists day and night.

Santa Maria Maggiore and San Paolo Fuori le ★★★

📧 *Piazza di Santa Maria Maggiore,* ☎ *6-483-195.*

☞ *Take Via Cavour up to the Termini.*

Metro Stop: *Stazione Termini.*

🕐 *7 a.m.–8 p.m.*

Special Hours: *Oct.-Mar. open only until 7 p.m.*

This much-restored church, originally built in the 5th century, contains many cultural and religious treasures. The simple tomb of Bernini, the great architect, is situated near the right side of the altar of the Pauline Borghese Chapel, while Pope Sixtus V's tomb rests in the Sistine Chapel (not the one in the Vatican). Mosaics in the basilica's 5th-century nave portray scenes from the Old Testament.

Via Appia Antica (Appian Way)

Begins at Porta Capena, on the outskirts of Rome.

Extending from Rome to the port of Brindisi, this 360-mile route provided the ancient Romans with their first direct link to the Orient. Reached from the Porta Capena, just on the outskirts of Rome, it turns into S7 after a few miles. Alongside the Appian Way are tombs and monuments in various states of preservation, and, more recently, the villas of film stars and other notables. Drive through at night when the 2000-year-old walls are illuminated, showing the burial niches of slaves set free from the time of Augustus.

Museums and Exhibits

Capitoline Hill

Piazza del Campidoglio, ☎ 6710-2475.

Public Transportation: *46, 89 or 92.*

Special Hours: *Closed Mon.*

The bronze equestrian statue of Marcus Aurelius that crowned the center of the Campidoglio has been restored and is now safely within the confines of the Capitoline Museum. This 500-year-old palazzo, as well as the adjoining Palace of the Conservatori, designed by Michelangelo, focuses on Roman sculpture as well as on Oriental art, including religious objects from conquered provinces. Don't miss *The Dying Gaul*, a replica of a third-century Greek bronze

Admission: varies.

Galleria Borghese

http://www.galleriaborghese.it/
Piazzale del Museo Borghese, off via Pinciano.
Public Transportation: *910.*

🕘 *9 a.m.–2 p.m.*

Special Hours: *Sun. open only until 1 p.m.; closed Mon.*
Housed in the lovely Villa Borghese, this is among the finest museums in Rome, with works by Titian, Correggio, Caravaggio, Botticelli, Raphael, Canova (Conquering Venus), Bernini and others. The surrounding park is a car-free refuge with a puppet theatre, artificial lakes, bridle paths and a zoo. Boats can also be hired on Giardino del Lago. The Puppet Theatre, on Pincio Square, amuses with a daily rendition of Punch and Judy. Admission: inexpensive.

Palazzo Barberini

▣ *Via delle Quattro Fontane.*

🕘 *9 a.m.–2 p.m.*

Special Hours: *Closed Mon.*
This 17th-century palace is named for the wealthy Barberini dynasty of which Pope Urban VIII belonged. The building was designed by the trio of Maderno, Borromini and Giovanni Bernini. The National Art Gallery within contains paintings from the Corsini Palace, works by Raphael, Tintoretto and Titian. Adjacent is Bernini's Fountain of the Triton. Admission: inexpensive.

Palazzo Venezia (Piazza Venezia)

▣ *Piazza Venezia.*

🕘 *9 a.m.–1:30 p.m.*

Special Hours: *Sun. open until 1 p.m.; closed Mon.*
Once a papal residence and later the home base of Benito Mussolini

(he declared war on France and the United States from the balcony as his followers bellowed below). The 15th-century palace is now a decorative arts museum that contains paintings, sculpture and varied objects of the Renaissance and Baroque periods. Admission: varies.

Nightlife

Alexanderplatz

✉ *Via Ostia 9,* ☎ *6-372-9398.*

🕐 *9 a.m.–2 a.m.*

Special Hours: *Closed Sun.*

Alexanderplatz is a jazz emporium (the locals really go for this American art form) and restaurant that jams every night with live talent. It's reasonably priced; typical night-on-the-town; let's-get-happy drinks. The food, if you care for it, is mostly light pastas. Admission: varies.

Alien

✉ *Via Velletri 13-19,* ☎ *6-841-2212.*

🕐 *11 p.m.–4 a.m.*

Special Hours: *Closed Mon.*

Post apocalyptic trappings decorate this dance club, where you can dance to two different kinds of music in two different rooms. The larger is dedicated to house or underground, while retro-rock and blues is relegated to the back room. Lots of fun, though the drinks are overpriced. Admission: varies.

Chiodo Fisso

✉ *Via Dante Aligheri,* ☎ *55-238-1290.*

☞ *Near American Express.*

🕐 *9 p.m.–3 a.m.*

The attraction here is the live American-style folk guitar music in the back, sung in Italian. But it's not amateur night--some of the top local musicians are known to play. Peaceful setting, with classical decor, though expensive drinks. Admission: varies.

La Cabala

✉ *Via dei Soldati 25,* ☎ *6-686-4221.*

🕐 *10:30 p.m.–4 a.m.*

Special Hours: *Closed Sun.*

If you've got a wad of cash in your pocket, venture up one flight of stairs to this disco connected to the formal Hostaria dell'Orso dining room in a 14th-century structure. If you do come to dance, look your best, everyone else does. Admission: varies.

The Hangar ★★★

✉ *Via in Selci 69,* ☎ *6-488-1397.*

🕐 *10:30 p.m.–4 a.m.*

Special Hours: *Closed three weeks in Aug.*

This gay bar is also popular with women and straights, who are all welcome. The music is hot and loud, and the atmosphere is decadent: the place used to be Empress Messalina's (driven mad by nutty Nero) home base.

Shopping
Shopping Hours

There are so many local variations that it's wise to check first with the concierge of your hotel. Wherever the siesta custom is observed (Rome, Naples, the South), most stores are open from 9 a.m. to 1 p.m. and from 4 p.m. to 7:30 or 8 p.m. Everything is open at 3 or 3:30 p.m. in Milan, Turin, Genoa, Bologna and Venice. Often shops are closed in August; frequently during summer months, Saturday evening closings substitute for Monday mornings.

Best Areas

The piazza di Spagna and all the streets off of it such as via Condotti, via della Croce, via Borgognona (now a delightful pedestrian mall), via Bocca di Leone, via Frattina, via del Babuino and via Due Macelli; at the top of the Spanish Steps the via Sistina; via del Corso (running from piazza del Popolo to piazza Venezia); via Veneto and the many streets that crisscross it on either side; via Barberini; via Bissolati; via Nazionale (cheaper shops) and via Cola di Rienzo (extending, on the other side of the Tiber more or less across from the piazza del Popolo, to the Vatican) where prices are on an even lower scale and bargaining is common.

Antiques

Via Giulia is a good street for general hunting, so are via Margutta, via del Babuino and via dei Coronari (with a Settimana dell' Antiquariato three times a year). Piazza Fontanella Borghese also offers jewelry. Watch out for counterfeits.

Art Galleries

Gallerias Schneider, owned and operated by Americans, handles some of the top Italian painters. **L'Obelisco, Barcaccia** and **Il Camino** are well known. There are more than 50 salons in the capital.

Books

The Lion Bookshop *(via del Babuino 181)* has large stocks of reading matter— or try either the **American Book Shop** *(via delle Vite 57)* or the **English & American Bookshop** *(via Torino, close to the Opera House)*, which are also versatile.

Haute Couture and Deluxe Ready-to-Wear Designers

Valentino, Princess Irene Galitzine, Fontana, Mila Schon, Lancetti, Versace, Krizia, Biagiotti, Genny, Trussardi, Complice, Basile, Ferre, Armani, Riva, Tiziani, and Albani have exalted reputations currently. Capucci, Andre Laug, Soprani, Balestra and Antonio de Luca are also in there pitching. You can expect to be rocked an Arabian princess' fortune. Emilio Pucci is enjoying a renaissance. Fantasia has lovely accessories at high tariffs.

Knitwear

Our choices are **Missoni** (via Borgognona 38B), **Albertina** (via Lazio 20), **Laura Biagiotti** (via Vittoria 30) and **Trico** (via delle Carozze). **Laura Aponte** (via Gesu e Maria 9) had a small and poor selection when we were there.

Shoes

For women, **Lily of Florence**, *via Lombardia 38* (see "Florence"), is the exclusive purveyor of the famous Petra line. **Raphael** *(piazza di Spagna and via Veneto)* and **Fragiacomo** *(via Condotti 35)* are pacesetters. **Tanino Crisci** *(via Condotti)* is a classicist. **Grilli** *(via del Corso 166)* and **Giust** *(via Sistina 79)* are somewhat less costly. **Tradate** (via del Corso) is definitely cheaper and displays some good models. So does **Cardinali** *(via di Propaganda Fide, near the Spanish Steps)*. **Via dei Giubbonari** and **via Arenula** near the Jewish quarter boast more than 20 shoe shops.

Silks and Other Materials
By The Yard

Galtrucco, *via del Tritone 14*, has everything. **Polidori** *(via Borgognona and via Condotti)* and **Bises** *(via Fleming 53, via del Gesu 63* and at *"Valentino Piu" via Condotti 13)* carry the wonders of the Italian textile industry—many couture fabrics.

Angelo

Via Bissolati 34/36, ☎ *6-474-1796.*

🕘 *9:30 a.m.–7:30 a.m.*

Special Hours: Closed Sat., Sun.

Angelo Vittucci, with his partners, Aldo Uggeri and Carlo Illari, made an instantaneous success when they opened this elegant house in 1963. And with their taste, imagination and own special dash, how well they deserve it! Superior handworked suits in silks, worsted, tropicals and others; unique foulard linings; additional full line of chic ready-made suits at lower prices; all haberdashery imaginable; finished delivery in three-to-four days; the shop ships worldwide. Ready-to-wear line is especially fine for cashmeres.

Cardinali

📧 *Via di Propaganda Fide, near the Spanish St.*

Via dei Giubbonari and via Arenula near the Ghetto boast over 20 shoe shops.

Discount System

📧 *Via del Viminale 35,* ☎ *6-474-6545.*

🕐 *9:30 a.m.–7:30 p.m.*

Special Hours: *Mon. opens at 3:30 p.m.; closed Sun.*

Top-name designer clothing and accessories are the ticket here, sold at 50 to 70 percent of retail. Savvy men and women who aren't too fussy can buy what the fashion houses consider "goofs," but most people wouldn't be able to tell the difference.

Perruzzi Brothers

📧 *Ponte Vecchio 60,* ☎ *55-292-027.*

🕐 *9:30 a.m.–7:30 p.m.*

Special Hours: *Closed Sun.*

Specializing in handmade silver jewelry and flatware, this shop has been in existence for more than a hundred years. Its clientele is discerning and its reputation stellar.

Polidori

📧 *21 Via Condotti,* ☎ *6-678-4842.*

Davide Cenci (suits, coats), Medison (shirts) and Polidori are all master cutters, too, but Brioni and Angelo are tops. Move warily among the smaller, less famous, less costly stylists, because they are all too apt to take advantage of you. In all custom- made garments, always, always find time for three fittings. A minimum of two fittings normally does not work.

Prado

📧 *Via Sicilia 26-28.*

This island is primarily known for the products of its glass factory, which makes for an intriguing visit (when you arrive at Murano, disembark at Colonna, the first *vaporetto* stop). If you still have time, visit the 12th-century Basilica of S. Maria e Donato.

The Lion Bookshop

📧 *Via del Babuino 181,* ☎ *6-322-5837.*

🕙 *9:30 a.m.–7:30 p.m.*

Special Hours: *Closed throughout Aug.; closed Sun.*

Not quite the place for a paperback bestseller, the regal Lion has for many years sold literary works by American and English writers. Good children's section, volumes about Rome and her history, food, wine and other essentials, also international guidebooks; large stock of videos in English. The satellite store, The Lion Two, is located at *via della Fontanella 7 (*☎ *361.30.37).*

Via del Babuino

📧 *Connects the Piazza di Spagna and Piazza del Poppo.*

Once a deluxe warren of antique stores and art galleries, it has been taken over by fine boutiques, their storefronts graced with the names of famed Italian designers; all the greats dwell easily side by side. **Giorgio Armani**, who moved his haute couture shop here in the early '80s, is at #102 (open Tues. through Fri. 10 a.m.–7 p.m., Mon. 3:30 p.m.–7:30 p.m.); his Emporio at #119 features men's wear at 30 to 40 percent off U.S. prices. **Kenzo's** outre designs can be found at #124A, and **Gente** (#82) beckons a younger, affluent crowd with creations by Dolce & Gabbana and Romeo Gigli. If you don't come to buy, it's a great area for gawking; some of the most fashionable Romans do their slumming here.

Special Tours

Trastevere

Public Transportation: *23.* Metro Stop: *Vatican.*

If you are walking, you can reach the Trastevere by crossing the Tiber by the 2000-year-old Ponte Fabricio to the Tiberine Island and then on Ponte Cestio to the other side of the river. This popular quarter of Rome has been a residential area since ancient times, and is today one of the liveliest and most colorful. One of the oldest churches in the city, Santa Maria in Trastevere, watches kindly over a neighborhood that jumps with mom-and-pop trattorias, wild experimental theatre companies, art galleries and crafts shops.

Janiculum Hill
Parks and Gardens

Janiculum   ★★★

✉ *Janiculum Hill.*

Bus 41 from Ponte Sant'Angelo.

Public Transportation: *41.*

For a splendid view of the Eternal City, stroll along the Janiculum Promenade, where you can see the Tiber with the Castel Sant'Angelo, the Colosseum and much more. The equestrian statue is of Garibaldi, the patriot who fought for the unification of Italy. A very popular vantage point, often overlooked.

Tivoli
Historical Sites

Villa d'Este

✉ *Piazza Trento, vialle delle Centro Fontane.*

Public Transportation: *Linea B.* Metro Stop: *Rebibbia.*

🕐 *9 a.m.–6:30 p.m.*

Special Hours: *In winter open only until 4 p.m.*

This creation in Tivoli *(20 miles from Rome,* ☎ *0774-22070)* was built for Cardinal Ippolito d'Este around 1550. With hundreds of fountains and luxuriant, irrigated landscaping, it was meant to reflect the glory of one of the great families of the Renaissance. Try to include a sumptuous lunch at **Sibilla**, a villa commissioned by Hadrian (0774-20281; closed Mon., a bit of a tourist trap, but the food is good).

Trastavere
ITRAVELBOOK FREEBIE

Santa Maria in Trastavere ★★

✉ *Via Santa Cecilia.*

🕐 *8 a.m.–midnight*

Special Hours: *Closed between 12-4, reopens 4-8pm*

This exquisite church, dedicated to the patron saint of music, is one of the oldest churches in Rome, dating back to the 3rd century. Besides paintings and frescoes, the church contains a celebrated statue of the saint by Maderno. It's especially pretty when illuminated at night, showcasing 13th- and 14th-century mosaics and a Romanesque campanile.

Museums and Exhibits
West of Tiber
Shopping

Porta Portese Flea Market

✉ *Via Porteneuse.*

🕐 *6 a.m.–2 p.m.*

Garage sale aficionados will enjoy plowing through what a typical Roman (and a growing number of immigrant) household throws away at this well-known flea market south of the Trastevere district. Come early (preferably before 8 a.m.) for the best buys. Wear a money belt.

Vatican City

Standing on the side of a hill on the west bank of the Tiber, it is separated from Rome and Italy only by a wall. The pope is absolute monarch, with full legislative, executive and judicial powers.

Dominating the city is the **Basilica of St. Peter**, largest in the world and sited in the smallest independent state in the world. Close by is the Apostolic Palace, home of His Holiness and site of the famous **Vatican Museum**; while many go only for the religious art of classical periods, don't pass up the 55-room modern art section with acres of beauties by Matisse, Marini, Shahn, Kokoschka, Miro, even Lurcat tapestries. It is the biggest residential castle in existence, with 1400 rooms that cover some 13.5 acres. Within are also the City Governor's Palace, a post office, a tribunal, a mosaic factory, a barracks, an observatory, a railway station, a power plant, a newspaper, a pharmacy, a TV station and the super-radio station over which are broadcast the pope's messages to six continents. A self-service restaurant for visitors is located in the basement in front of the main picture gallery, with a tree-shaded terrace at ground-floor level; there's a snack bar in the modern art segment too. Sampietrini is the name given to those who maintain the Basilica but do not live here. The ranks of the famed Swiss Guard, a colorful and elite corps whose red, yellow and blue pantaloons were designed by Michelangelo, is being phased out; their replacements are the plain-blue-uniformed Vatican **gendarmerie**. The papal apartment is newly opened in the **Lateran Palace**. Robes, uniforms and arms are on display; the frescoes are in splendid condition from the 16th century, the period before the pope took up residence in the Vatican.

St. Peter's is the core of the enclave. The dome, Michelangelo's work, is almost as high as the tallest Egyptian pyramid; from doorway to altar, you could tuck in the towers of New York's Waldorf-Astoria with room to spare. In the museums, chapels and libraries of the Vatican you'll find Raphaels, Michelangelos, Peruginos, Botticellis, tapestries, liturgical vessels and priceless manuscripts. An elevator will whisk you to the base of the dome; from there you can climb the winding stairs to the pinnacle for a splendid view of the meandering Tiber and Rome. Then take the walk around the inside upper periphery, put an ear close to the wall and listen to people talking hundreds of feet away. St. Peter's alone is worth a special trip across the ocean. The Sistine Chapel—magnificently refreshed, revealing vibrant original polychrome—is closed to visitors on Saturday afternoon and Sunday as well as on holidays.

Audience with the pope: The best way to arrange this is through a letter from your Bishop to *Rt. Rev. Msgr. Benjamin Farrell, J.C.D., Casa di S. Maria dell'Umilta, via dell'Umilta 30*. Small group or individual meetings are becoming more and more difficult to arrange, though His Holiness grants a few almost daily. Apply as soon as you arrive in Rome; the Casa is only 2 blocks from the Trevi Fountain, a bonus to sightseers who are in the area. I'm also told that the Paulist Fathers at the Church of St. Susanna are extremely helpful in this respect.

On Wednesdays an enormous audience is held in St. Peter's for which tickets are usually available a day ahead, provided you don't require reserved seats. There are three classes: The first two permit you to sit in grandstand structures flanking the main altar, while the third is simply admission for standing room. For tickets to this (as well as to the excavations beneath St. Peter's), apply to the same source mentioned above. Thousands flock to these gatherings, so get there early. For special audiences (Baciamano), ladies should wear black dresses, high necklines, long sleeves and veils (now optional, but more courteous), while men should appear in dark suits with dark ties. Dress requirements for the Wednesday services are nearly as rigid, although they are constantly violated by scores of unknowing travelers. The Papal address is condensed and translated in English, French, German and Spanish. The big assemblages are scheduled from October to July, moving to the summer residence in Castel Gandolfo from July to late September. Transportation to St. Peter's is provided at nominal cost; hotel pickup and round trip are available through SITA (the "coaching" arm of CIT), American Express and Thomas Cook, also for relatively few lire.

You'll hear cheers, loud clapping and cries of "Viva Il Papa!" from European student priests and other spectators when the pope is carried into the Basilica by the *uscieri*. It provokes the same effect as the final bell in a heavyweight championship fight at Madison Square Garden.

What to Do
Historical Sites

Basilica of St. Peter ★★★★★

 Piazza di San Pietro, ☎ *6-698-4466.*

🕐 *7 a.m.–7 p.m.*

Special Hours: *Sept. through Mar. open only until 6 p.m.*

The largest cathedral in the world, the Basilica was built over the site of St. Peter's grave, according to popular belief. Unforgettable sights are Michelangelo's dome, almost 500 feet high, which can be scaled; his Pieta, now behind glass, after a fanatic's attack, and Bernini's canopy, which protects the pope's altar and the Tomb of the Fisherman. There's an elevator to the base of the dome and a stairway to the top; hardy folks can take the stairs all the way if they dare. Admission: inexpensive.

Museums and Exhibits

Vatican Museums

http://www.christusrex.org/www1/ vaticano/0-Musei.html
Viale Vaticano.

Metro Stop: *Ottaviano.*

🕔 *8:45 a.m.–1:45 p.m.*

Special Hours: *Open until 4:45 p.m. in summer; closed Sun.*

There is one entrance to the Vatican Museums on Viale del
Vaticano, about 20 minutes on foot to St. Peter's Square. There are
four different itineraries and color-coded maps to direct visitors to
their preferred destinations. You will need at least two to five hours
to see the highlights, which include the Sistine Chapel and
Michelangelo's ceiling; the Pinacoteca; Egyptian-Gregorian
Museum, Pius Clementius Museum, the Vatican Library, the Borgia
Apartments, and more. For a breather, tour the Vatican Gardens,
almost 60 acres of lush woods, flowers, paths, fountains, and Pope
Pius IV's summer house. Admission: varies.

Music

Accademia Nazionale di Santa Cecilia

✉ *Via di Conciliazone 4,* ☎ *6-679-0389.*

🕔 *9 a.m.–7 p.m.*

The distinguished symphony orchestra performs an annual program
of music in two venues: June-July outdoors at the Villa Giulia
amphitheater under the stars, and, in the winter, in its own concert
hall. Check local listings; sometimes concerts are held in spectacular
locations around the city. Admission: varies. Call in advance.

Liguria

Portofino

Portofino has one of the dreamiest natural settings—a tiny, cliff-
lined harbor of unsurpassing charm and intimacy, over which broods
a castle and the Hotel Splendido. Spring and fall are the best times

to go; in summer it's often akin to Times Square, so crowded that the excursionists, the gays and the souvenir vendors nearly trip over one another along the quay. Even driving into the port area can take an hour to cover 200 yards of roadway. A *must* to visit—but pick your season.

Where to Stay

Hotel Eden   ★

http://www.itwg.com/ itw14073.asp?LAY=US654
Budget to Moderate

Vico Oritto 18 In center of town; 150 feet from the harbor.

Rated Restaurant: Ristorante da Ferruccio.

☎ *(185) 269-091,* FAX *(185) 269-047.*

Credit Cards: *All Major.*

This charming small hotel, set in a pleasant garden, is actually the least expensive here. It offers only nine rooms, some with private bath, TV, telephone; well-known restaurant where regional cuisine is served; veranda with a lovely view.

Hotel Splendido   ★★★★★

http://www.splendido.orient- express.com/
Expensive

Salita Baratta 13 Two miles from train station; on private road; 22 miles east of Genoa.

☎ *237-1236,* ☎ *(185) 269-551,* FAX *(185) 269- 614.*

Credit Cards: *All Major.*

A favorite of royalty and "the famous," this classic hotel offers one of Europe's most magnificent vistas. It is situated in a private park at the top of a private road above Portofino. There are 63 uniquely and delightfully furnished rooms with bath, shower, hair dryer, some with private Jacuzzi and minibar, fridge, TV, balcony; 21 suites; dining room has panoramic views and serves regional cuisine; bar; heated saltwater pool with barbecue and bar area; laundry; baby-sitting service available; beauty center. Quality appointments throughout.

Service is efficient and warm. Open Apr. 14 through Jan. 2.

Where to Eat

Da Puny

Moderate

Piazza Martiri delli Olivetta, ☎ *(0185) 269.037.*

Closed: *Thurs.*

This bastion of chic is a portside charmer, with a good vantage point for perusing the passing parade; eclectic decor. Fish will put hair on your head and a song in your heart, especially the fish baked in crusted salt.

Hotel Splendido

Expensive

Viale Baratta 13, ☎ *(0185) 269.551.*

Credit Cards: *All Major.*

The cuisine is deluxe in every respect, and its setting is magnificent, especially from a terrazzo above the sea; the view is even better than the food, which is superb. Excellent lunches, from soup to service to *saltimbocca.*

Il Pitosforo ★★★

Expensive

Molo Umberto I no. 9, ☎ *(0185) 269.020.*

Credit Cards: *All Major.*

Closed: *Tues.*

This enchanting harborside nest holds the lead among dining candidates. Situated farthest out on the bayfront, two stories above street level, it has a small interior restaurant and a 20-table, semi open terrace commanding a lovely view. Service is friendly to boot; the menu is regional and substantial; VERY costly by local standards. Best vintage is a Bianco Secco Portofino, dry and agreeable with an amusing label. Tops in the village.

What to Do
Excursions

Old Castle/Church of St. George

🕐 *10 a.m.–6 p.m.*

Special Hours: *Closed Mon.*

Portofino is so minuscule, one can see the sights in a day. The village's two prime historical sites are the Church of St. George, and a castle (time schedule for castle only) built as a fortification against Turkish attacks. The church can be reached by walking up a flight of steps from the port. The view of the port from the top is definitely rewarding. You can visit the castle on a walking tour of the peninsula, passing villas and gardens; if you have stamina, continue on for another hour to the Faro, an old lighthouse at the tip of the peninsula. Another day trip is to Paraggi, a lovely cove and beach, accessible by car--about three km from Portofino on the corniche. If you have more time, there are summer boat rides to the village of San Fruttoso, on the western peninsula. Your companions will probably be locals laden with supplies; the ride takes approximately 20 minutes.

San Remo

Only a few miles from the Cote d'Azur and Monte Carlo lies a scenic coastal strip, the Italian Riviera or Flower Riviera, whose capital is San Remo, a holiday resort with sun, sea and an ideal climate. Its modern facilities for leisure—golf courses, tennis courts, race tracks, a casino—complement a wide range of hotels, suitable to all tastes and all pockets. Restaurants also range from pizzerias to luxury establishments. The medieval borough, called Pigna (the Pinecone), the churches, the monuments, the museums, the stately homes and a fascinating hinterland, for a full immersion in nature, crown the varied offer of this town, with a rich program of events the whole year-round. Not to be missed are the Song Festival and the parade of flower-decorated carts in winter.

Where to Stay

Hotel Miramare

Moderate

Corso Matuzia 9 Just 600 yards from train station, 33 miles east of Nice, France, via A10.

☎ *(184) 667-601,* FAX *(184) 667-655.*

Credit Cards: *All Major.*

A first-class hotel commanding a palm-garden domain and a view of the sea. Some rooms here are even better than some deluxe accommodations. There are 64 rooms with bath, some with TV; five suites; restaurant is recommended; breakfast room; bar; lounges; terraces; heated indoor saltwater pool; solarium; marina; free parking. Open late Dec. through late Sept.

Royal Hotel San Remo

Expensive to Very Expensive
Corso Imperatrice 80Located 500 meters from train station, 33 miles east of Nice, France, via A10.

☎ *(184) 5391,* FAX *(184) 614-45.*

Credit Cards: *All Major.*

This century-old hotel continues to offer comfort and high-tone nostalgia in one of the last oases of peace and quiet and luxury on this part of the coast. There are a total of 145 rooms and 17 suites with handsome marble bath or shower, TV, some with whirlpool and terrace; three restaurants; two bars; room service is limited; Jacuzzi; solarium; baby-sitting available; supervised children's program during holidays and the high season; free parking. Nearby there is an 18-hole golf course and horseback riding. Expect the best in service here. Open Dec. through Sept.

What to Do
Nightlife

San Remo Casino   ★★

Corso Inglesi.

🕑 *11 a.m.–3 a.m.*

Special Hours: *Main Gaming rooms 2:30 p.m.–3 a.m.*

Like any fashionable casino, guests can either play elegant games of chance in the main rooms (in jacket and tie, only, please) dine and dance at the restaurant or watch musical entertainment (Fri. through Sat. 10 p.m.–12 p.m.). But you can also dress casually and skip an admission fee to play the slot machines (daily 11 a.m.–3 a.m.). Admission: varies.

Lombardy

Como

Como is the pivotal town of the Italian lake district. As it produces two-thirds of Italy's finished silk and one-third of the world's, fashion designers come to Como to plan the silk patterns for their next season's lines. It's a convenient base for day trips.

Where to Stay

Barchetta Excelsior ★★★★

http://www.hotelbarchetta.com/
Piazza Cavour 1 Located on main town square on the lake front.

☎ *(31) 3221,* FAX *(31) 302-622.*

Credit Cards: *All Major.*
This modern hotel is very inviting with a main piazza location facing the water. There are 85 rooms with bath, air conditioning, bathrobe, hair dryer, bidet, TV, some with Jacuzzi, a fax hookup and/or a balcony; three suites; wheelchair accessible; restaurant; room service; bar; sidewalk cafe; dry cleaning; baby sitting available; car rental; parking (fee). Very clean and a good buy.

Metropole e Suisse Hotel ★★★

Moderate to Expensive
Piazza Cavour 19 *Located 1/2 mile from the train station.*

☎ *(31) 269-444,* FAX *(31) 300-808.*

Credit Cards: *All Major.*
A traditional hotel dating back to 1892 set on a piazza facing the lake. There are 71 rooms with bath or shower, TV; three suites; wheelchair accessible; bar; sidewalk cafe in the summer; parking (fee). Most of the rooms have a view of the lake.

Bellagio

Situated on the tip of a peninsula in the center of a lake, this delightful town couldn't have a more scenic setting. Not only is it surrounded by Lake Como on three sides, giving it a feeling of a self- contained island, but it also has views of the hills and villas of the west shore as well as the wilder, more rugged cliffs of the eastern shore. The town itself is a medieval fishing village, and boats docked at the pier take visitors to all corners of the lake. A bus also departs from the pier for the Rockefeller Foundation's fabulous formal gardens at the **Villa Serbelloni.** Another villa you won't want to miss is the **Villa Melzi** (open to the public from April through October, as is the Villa Serbelloni). In addition to its fine garden and greenhouse, the Villa Melzi contains a collection of Egyptian sculpture. In the center of town, the 12th-century church of **San Giacomo** has interesting carvings as well. Visitors also enjoy shopping in the boutiques on Piazza Mazzina and resting in the lakeside cafés. Bellagio has several fine hotels—such as the **Hotel Du Lac,** the **Firenze** and the **Excelsior Splendide**—but the **Grand Hotel Villa Serbelloni** is in a class of its own. This magnificent, ornate villa is located on the town's main square, and its old-world decor is only overshadowed by its superb setting of terraced gardens overlooking the lake.

Grand Hotel Villa Serbelloni

http://www.villaserbelloni.it/ pag2.htm

Expensive

Via Roma 1 Located about 21 miles from Como train station.

☎ *(31) 950-216,* FAX *(31) 951-529.*

Credit Cards: *All Major.*

This is a national monument on the shores of Lake Como. It has operated as a hostelry since 1872, and today the land where it resides belongs to the Rockefeller Foundation. Venetian and Florentine bedchambers come with home-style comfort; about half of the 95 rooms and six suites boast waterfront reflections; only four feature balconies. All have bath, hair dryer, TV; some have air conditioning. The main salon has frescoed ceilings, parquet floors and a working fireplace; spectacular garden vista from the restaurant; outstanding kitchen with superb wines; room service; bar; lake-view terrace flanked by palm trees in its park; small sandy lido; beauty center; parking garage.

Cernobbio

Three miles northwest of Como, Cernobbio is a small, fashionable resort made famous by its deluxe hotel—**the Villa D'Este**. Set in an immense park, this 16th-century hotel is the most palatial on the lake. Although the Villa D'Este is undeniably the main attraction, visitors also enjoy the pleasant village on the western shore and the tranquil lake front—there are any number of good, less luxurious hotels and decent restaurants.

Regina Olga Hotel

http://www.hotelreginaolga.it/
Moderate

Via Regina 18 Located about 2 miles from the Como train station and Swiss border.

☎ *(31) 510-171*, FAX *(31) 340-604.*

Credit Cards: *All Major.*
Here is a pleasant hotel overlooking Lake Como and only a short walk from the boat dock. It is an alternate choice to the Villa d'Este and much less expensive. This villa hotel is comprised of 83 rooms with bath or shower, fridge, TV; three suites; wheelchair accessible; grill room; snack bar; bar; garden; free parking. Open all year.

Villa D'Este Grand Hotel

http://www.villadeste.it/cgi/index.asp
Very Expensive
Via Regina 40 Located 3 miles from Como train station.

☎ *(31) 3481*, FAX *(31) 348-844.*

Credit Cards: *All Major.*
Built in A.D. 1568 as a private residence for Cardinal Tolomeo Gallio, it was later occupied by the Dowager Empress of Russia, the Princess of Wales, the Princess Torlonia and other notables. It has been operated as a hotel since 1873. Alas, more than a century later,

a frightening number of bus tours have "discovered" this classic
estate set in 10 acres of parkland on Lake Como. There are 156 spacious rooms; 38 junior suites; eight suites. All with bath, bidet, hair
dryer, bathrobe, TV, view of the lake or the garden; some have a
Jacuzzi; some have a balcony; wheelchair accessible; a terrace restaurant; room service; outdoor restaurant for bathers; poolside bar; bar;
nightclub plus discotheque; woody grill in the Sporting Club for
informal meals; squash court; nearby 18-hole golf course; children's'
pool; sauna, gym, whirlpool are just a few of the many fitness amenities; private beach; horses available; business center. An absolutely
glorious setting. Open Mar. through Nov.

What to Do
Special Tours

Boat Tours   ★★

Piazza Cavour, ☎ *31-304-060.*

Special Hours: *Closed in winter.*

Most visitors pass through Como town, as it's affectionately called,
to immediately get on a hydrofoil or steamer out to Lake Como,
which has inspired poets, writers and others to write odes about it.
Bring pen and notebook or sketchpad in hand and scribble your own
tributes while skimming or zipping from point to point. Itineraries
may include Cernobbio and the startling Villa d'Este, where Queen
Caroline of England threw lavish parties, and now a world-class
resort, and the more sedate Villa Carlotta, former home of Princess
Carlotta of Prussia. Hither and yon are picturesque churches, villas
and little villages, surrounded by greenery and mountains in the distance. Boats are operated daily between lake towns by the Nav-
igazione Lago di Como. Admission: varies.

Bellagio
Parks and Gardens

Villa Melzi   ★★★

Lungolario Marconi, ☎ *31-950-318.*

🕐 *9 a.m.–6 p.m.*

Special Hours: *Open Apr. to Oct. 31*

This prosperous, silk-producing town near Lake Como is also known for some fine private villas, whose owners graciously allow commoners a glimpse of the good life behind the ivy-covered walls. Possibly the best known garden and museum is within the Villa Melzi, built in the 1800s for a former vice president of the republic. Besides the prime blooms, other treasures worthy of note here are a collection of sculptures in the Egyptian vein.

Cadenabbia

Villa Carlotta

On the western shore of Lake Como, ☎ *344- 404-05.*

South of Cadenabbia towards Tremezzo.

🕐 *9 a.m.–4:30 p.m.*

Special Hours: *Open until 6 p.m. Apr. 1 through Sept. 30.*

A whole fleet of gardeners are kept busy tending the magnificent grounds of the pleasure palace of Princess Carlotta of Prussia, who oversaw the layout of the park and grounds in the late 19th century. The spring months are the ideal time to come, when rhododendrons and azaleas, in particular, make a spectacular appearance. This is possibly the most visited spot on the lake. Admission: varies.

Val Venosta
Excursions

Stelvio National Park

☎ *(0342) 901582*

North and east of Lake Como is Italy's largest national park (135,000 hectares), which is a haven for every kind of activity: swimming, climbing, hiking and skiing. There are some 50 lakes, 100 glaciers and the second-highest pass in Europe, the Passo dello Stelvio (open June-Oct.). Visitors' centers along the way have information on trails and the varieties of flora (Norway spruce, Martagon lily) and fauna (chamois, ptarmigan, golden eagle). Call the main park offices for complete information and directions.

Milan

Primarily commercial, with a non-Latin aura of hustle and bustle, Milan is the financial and industrial center of the nation, boasting 37 percent of all Italian businesses; with less than one quarter of the country's population, it accounts for one fifth of all wages and pays 24 percent of the national tax bill. North American buyers flood the city by the plane loads to snap up next season's fashions. Because the hotels possess a classic "captive audience" of business clients who must come here, their prices tend to be exorbitant. In general, Milan is considered one of the most expensive cities in the world, with prices 20 percent higher than the national average. But it is a world-famous capital of Italian fashion and design. Not only are there marvelous shops, but you'll find some superb museums and galleries—as well as a number of exceptional churches.

Where to Stay

Cavour Hotel

http://www.hotelcavour.it/

Moderate to Expensive

Via Fatebenefratelli 21 Near Piazza del Duomo and La Scala; 1 mile from train station.

☎ *(2) 657-2051*, FAX *(2) 659-2263.*

Credit Cards: *All Major.*

Situated in the Brera, this hotel with a welcoming lobby and in a central location is a good overall accommodation. It has 115 elegantly yet simply furnished rooms with bath or shower, TV; two suites; wheelchair accessible; restaurant; some room service; bar; lounge. Choose your room location on the courtyard side away from the clattering street.

De la Ville Hotel

Moderate to Expensive

Via Hoepli 6 Between Piazza del Duomo and La Scala; 2 miles from train station.

☎ *(2) 867-651*, FAX *(2) 866-609.*

Credit Cards: *All Major.*

A popular modern hotel in an excellent location. The 104 sound-proof rooms have bath or shower, TV; two suites; wheelchair accessible; breakfast room; bar; antique furnishings; business center; free parking. The service is courteous.

Four Seasons Milan

http://www.fourseasons.com/milan/
Expensive
Via Gesu 8 Center of the designer district; 5 miles from Linate Airport.

☎ *332-3442,* ☎ *(2) 796-976,* FAX *(2) 798-85000.*

Credit Cards: *All Major.*

Blending the original architecture with its modern interiors, this hotel has been tastefully converted from a 15th-century convent. Located in the fashion district, it is where the sophisticated Milanese go for tea in the afternoons-although they more often actually sip coffee. There are 98 distinctly different rooms with marble bath, heated floors, bidet, hair dryer, bathrobe, TV, fridge; some have a microwave and Jacuzzi; most overlook the sunny and serene court-yard; 20 suites; two restaurants serving sumptuous cuisine; room service; lounge; active bar with operatic theme; spa; business center; parking (fee). The atmosphere is quiet elegance.

Grand Hotel Duomo

http://www.grandhotelduomo.com/
Moderate
Via San Raffaele 1 Beside Piazza del Duomo Cathedral; 1 block from La Scala; 1 mile from train station.

☎ *(2) 8833,* FAX *(2) 8646-2027.*

Credit Cards: *All Major.*

Situated on a traffic-free street in a landmark building, this hotel is an ideal base for your sightseeing expeditions. There are 156 rooms and 18 suites with contemporary decor, bath or shower, TV, fridge; restaurant serves Italian cuisine; some room service; bar; tea room; rooftop garden; baby-sitting available; parking (fee). The duplex suites would be the top choice, so ask for these first and then request to see other accommodations if desired.

Grand Hotel et de Milan

http://www.grandhoteletdemilan.it/ english/pagina.html

Moderate to Expensive

Via Manzoni 29 In center of town near La Scala and Piazza del Duomo; 1 mile from train station.

☎ *(2) 723-141,* FAX *(2) 864-60861.*

Credit Cards: *All Major.*

Close to the La Scala Opera House, this downtown hotel is where Verdi wrote *Falstaff* while residing here. The original decor of the hotel has been beautifully restored, and the rooms are decorated in simple, but tasteful furnishings. You will find 95 rooms and 10 suites with marble baths, glistening hardwood floors, antiques; wheelchair accessible; restaurant; bar; business center. There is no parking. The ambience created here is old-fashioned elegance.

Manin Hotel

Moderate to Expensive

Via Manin 7 Across from Giardini Pubblici; 5 minutes from train station.

☎ *(2) 659-6511,* FAX *(2) 655-2160.*

Credit Cards: *All Major.*

A charming hotel, situated in a wonderfully quiet location, whose owners try to greet every guest by name. There are 118 up-to-date rooms with bath, hair dryer, TV, some garden views; six suites; restaurant; some room service; garden dining; jogging track; parking.

Antica Locanda Solferino

Moderate

Via Castelfidardo 2In Brera near the Porta Nuova.

☎ *(2) 657-0129,* FAX *(2) 657-1361.*

Credit Cards: *All Major.*

You must reserve well in advance in order to stay in this simply superb little hotel. The decor is comfortably 19th century, with flowered curtains and wallpapers and original furnishings creating a soothing ambience. There are only 11 rooms with bath or shower, TV; restaurant downstairs serves Milanese cuisine. This charming accommodation is very popular, so planning ahead is a must and well worth the trouble.

Where to Eat

Aimo e Nadia ★★★★

Moderate to Expensive

Six Via Montecuccoli, ☎ *41.68.86.*

Closed: *Sun.*

Much praise has been bestowed on this Tuscan-style restaurant, featuring chef Aimo Moroni's highly personal cuisine. Essentially, only market-fresh ingredients are used, so what you get in your risotto or pasta today may never appear the same way again. Moroni has more or less kept one spectacular pasta dish on his menu: bow-tie pasta lightly kissed with watercress, tomatoes, ricotta, egg and basil. He always prepares a few homemade desserts that tingle on the tongue and manage to do very little damage to your waistline.

Alfio-Cavour ★★★★

Moderate

Via Senato 31, ☎ *76.000.633.*

San Babila.

Credit Cards: *All Major.*

The entrance stairs will give you a chance to spy the huge open freezer shelf, overhung with garlands of fruits and vegetables. This is only a colorful preview of what you'll be eating. The cuisine is excellent and so is the wine cellar; the specialties are antipasti and fish, but a huge menu boasts almost everything that grows; the prices are medium.

Boeucc Antico Ristorante

Moderate

Piazza Belgioioso, ☎ *(02) 760.20.224.*

Duomo.

Credit Cards: *A.*

Oddly named "hole in the wall," this elegant dowager of a restaurant is situated in a palazzo near the Duomo. One of the oldest eateries in town, the Boeucc has been serving fine wines and exemplary risotto to the smart set since the late 1600s. Undoubtedly honest too, near a chic shopping area, and reasonably priced for the surroundings.

Giannino

Moderate

Via Amatore Sciesa 8, ☎ *551-95-582.*

Credit Cards: *All Major.*

Closed: *Sun.*

This restaurant remains popular, and that disturbs many visitors—possibly because it seems to cater so heavily these days to tourist traffic. An excellent menu; including such characteristic Lombard dishes as tender breaded veal cutlet and risotto simmered in broth and coated with Parmesan cheese. Several modern dining rooms; glassed-in kitchen; winter garden; initial reception sometimes lax, but table service usually (not always) attentive and thoughtful.

Scaletta

Expensive

Piazzale Stazione Genova 3, ☎ *581.00.290.*

Located at 0.

Stazione Genova.

Closed: *Mon., Sun.*

There's a mood here of exclusivity and wealth that evokes faint stirrings of romance in dim places—just the spot where two Beautiful People might meet for a tete-a-tete. The cuisine, created by famed chef Pina Bellini, is a happy blend of Franco-Italian mastery, and the billings (there is no printed menu, so make sure you ask for prices) are high. Try a risotto with pumpkin as a novelty, or the persimmon mousse. Delightfully suave.

St. Andrews ★★

Moderate to Expensive

Via Sant' Andrea, ☎ *760.23.132.*

Public Transportation: *Bus 65, 96 or 97.*

Credit Cards: *All Major.*

Closed: *Sun.*

This trendy restaurant is beloved by locals, fashion designers (fashion groupies will be agog at the lineup) and businessfolk. The ambience is very "club prive": a central hearth dominates the room, there are bookcases on the walls, leather chairs and love seats around low tables, subtle lighting from overhanging hooded lamps, rust carpets, lime-green textiles, and profession- proud waiters in formal attire. The cookery is much better than average; it is much costlier than average, too. Different risottos daily, always creative and delicious.

Trattoria Aurora ★★★

Moderate

Via Savona 23, ☎ *835.4978.*

Credit Cards: *All Major.*

Closed: *Mon.*

This may be Piedmont cuisine at its best. Rolling carts offer boiled meats, cheeses and plates of wild mushrooms. Each of our several samplings was so delicious, so natural and so honest that I could happily dine here on a regular basis and never tire of the gastronomy. The prices are reasonable, too. Wonderful!

What to Do

Historical Sites

Basilica Sant' Eustorgio

 Piazza Sant' Eustorgio.

Public Transportation: *15.*

🕐 *8 a.m.–7 p.m.*

Special Hours: *Closed noon-3 p.m.*

The Basilica's bell tower was built in the 13th century, and construction continued for several hundred years. One of the extant chapels, however, dates from the 7th century, but it is embellished with 15th-century frescoes. According to legend, the large tomb inscribed "Sepulcrum Trium Magorum" contains the relics of the Magi. Admission: varies.

Basilica of Sant' Ambrogio

🖃 *Piazza di Sant'Ambrogio 15.*

Public Transportation: *50 or 54.* Metro Stop: *Sant' Ambrogio.*

🕐 *8 a.m.–7 p.m.*

Special Hours: *Closed in Aug.*

The original structure of this church was built in the late 4th century A.D. by St. Ambrose, the patron saint of Milan, while the enlarged basilica is a prototype of Lombard Romanesque architecture. The church museum, open daily except Thurs. (10 a.m.–5 p.m.), is noted for clerical vestments and textiles, some of which date back to the saint's day. Admission: inexpensive.

ITRAVELBOOK FREEBIE

Duomo   ★★★★

Piazza del Duomo.
Metro Stop: *Duomo.*

🕐 *9 a.m.–4:30 p.m.*

Special Hours: *June-Sept., open 7 a.m.–7 p.m.*

Some of the world's finest stained glass and 224 statues fill two acres in this famous landmark that is the artistic centerpiece of Milan. Construction on the Gothic cathedral began in 1386. Walk around the outside; you'll notice all the gargoyles (96 of them) peering out from the heights. The third-largest church in the world and Italy's largest Gothic building, this magnificent cathedral is crowned with 135 spires, the central one of which bears a gilded statue of the Madonna (known as La Madonnina). For a really good look at the details, take along binoculars.

Galleria Vittorio Emanuale

📧 *Piazza del Duomo.*

🕐 *9 a.m.–7:30 p.m.*

Special Hours: *Closed Sun.*

Designed by the same architect who put the finishing touches on the Piazza del Duomo, this restored 195-yard-long arcade is a huge glass-and-iron structure, dating from the Victorian era, when these were considered architectural marvels. Inside is an array of boutiques and shops where anyone with an appreciation of Italian design and craftsmanship will enjoy browsing, if not buying.

Palazzo Reale

📧 *Piazza del Duomo 14.*

Metro Stop: *Duomo.*

🕐 *9:30 a.m.–6 p.m.*

Special Hours: *Closed Mon.*

The 18th-century palazzo houses the Museo del Duomo, containing painting and sculpture from the 14th century. Highlights are the models and drawings of the duomo during its 427-year construction. Admission: inexpensive.

Santa Maria delle Grazie   ★★★★★

📧 *Piazza Santa Maria delle Grazie.*

Metro Stop: *Carioli.*

🕐 *8:15 a.m.–1:45 p.m.*

Special Hours: *Closed Mon.*

Here you'll find Leonardo da Vinci's *Last Supper* (1494–1497), although the church (6:50 a.m.–7 p.m. daily, Sun. opens at 3 p.m., admission free) is interesting for other reasons. Built in the last half of the 15th century, Bramante later added the large, triple-apsed tribune. On the left side of the church is the entrance to the former Dominican convent, where on the refectory wall, *The Last Supper*, perhaps the most famous mural in the world, draws thousands of pilgrims every year. Constantly barraged by the effects of moisture, deterioration of the refectory wall and just plain old age, it has undergone periodic restoration since the late 1970s. Admission: inexpensive.

Museums and Exhibits

ITRAVELBOOK FREEBIE

Archaeological Museum

Corso Magenta 15.

South of Castello Sforzesco.

Metro Stop: *Cairole.*

(Prob) *9:30 a.m.–5:30 p.m.*

Special Hours: *Closed Mon.*

Located within the former Monasterio Maggiore, a Benedictine convent, this museum is worth a stop for displays of neolithic and Bronze Age artifacts, Greek vases and Roman art.

Castello Sforzesco ★★

Piazza Castello. ☎ *620-83-943.*

Metro Stop: *Cairole.*

9:30 a.m.–5 p.m.

Special Hours: *Closed Sat.*

When the Sforzas, one of Milan's ruling families, fell from power in 1525, the castle became a fortress for 250 strife-torn years, until 1893 when its buildings were restored and transformed into not one but several museums. Civiche Raccolte d'Arte Antica, the museum of ancient art, houses substantial collections of paintings, sculpture, ceramics, glass, textiles, furniture and bronze. The most famous work in the museum is the Pieta Rondanini, Michelangelo's final sculpture. (He died before it was finished.) Also within this complex is Museo degli Strumenti Musicali Antichi, Museum of Ancient Musical Instruments. The museum contains hundreds of medieval and Renaissance instruments, including one of Mozart's spinets. Admission: varies.

Museo Poldi Pezzoli

http://www.museopoldipezzoli.it/ PP inglese/
Via Manzoni 12.
Metro Stop: *Montenapoleone.*

🕐 *9:30 a.m.–6 p.m.*

Special Hours: *Sat. open until 7:30 p.m.; closed Mon.; no afternoon hours Sun. from Apr. 1 through Sept. 30.*

Getting jaded? Not yet, *per favore.* Stop here to absorb Bellini's poignant Pieta, della Francesca's San Nicolo, Pollaiolo's *Portrait of a Woman,* or a processional cross by Raffaello. Not only is the collection wondrous, but the decorative scheme is richly rewarding. Admission: inexpensive.

Museo Teatrale alla Scala

Piazza della Scala.
Metro Stop: *Duomo.*

🕐 *9 a.m.–6 p.m.*

Special Hours: *Closed Sun. in winter.*

The theatrical museum of La Scala is a must for opera buffs. The documentation of the colorful history of La Scala includes posters and rare photographs as well as paintings and sculpture. There's an enormous library of music--some 800,000 volumes. Admission: inexpensive.

Pinacoteca Ambrosiana

http://www.ambrosiana.it/ita/ index.htm
Piazza Pio X.
Metro Stop: *Duomo-Cordusio.*
Special Hours: *Closed Mon.*

The second-floor art gallery is home to Botticelli's "Madonna and Angels," and other works by Titian, Raphael, and Michelangelo da Caravaggio, but most visitors are drawn to the pride of the museum and library: sketches attributed to Leonardo da Vinci, including his Atlantic Codes. The Library also holds 400,000 volumes and 30,000 original manuscripts. Admission: inexpensive.

Pinacoteca di Brera

 Via Brera 28, ☎ *864-63-501.*

Metro Stop: *Lanza.*

🕐 *9 a.m.–2 p.m.*

Special Hours: *Closed Mon.*

An excellent collection of paintings by Piero della Francesca, Raphael, Bramante, Correggio, Carpaccio, Titian, Tiepolo, Mantegna (*The Dead Christ*) and others. There's also a modern art gallery. Admission: inexpensive.

Nightlife

After dark, *the* place to go in the *summer* is **Rendez-Vous**. Garden ambience, with tables both inside and alfresco; good cabaret (for Milan!); dancing nightly; high-grade attention to cuisine and service; frankly expensive by national standards. Unrivaled during the warm months. For *winter* nightlife, **Astoria** *(piazza Santa Maria Beltrade 2)* is currently the most elegant. Rich, large and brightly illuminated; entertainment and lively orchestra; tiny "music fee" but robust booze bill; closed June through August. **Taverna dei Sette Peccati** *(via Imbonati 52)* presents an outstanding fixed-price dinner with its show; a quality meal is quite rare for this kind of establishment, but here's an exception. **Maxim** (Galleria Manzoni) offers coral-velvet banquettes, double-candle lamps on tables, dancing, a modest cabaret; closed on Sunday.

Cafe Cova ★★★

Inexpensive to Moderate
Via Montenapoleone.

🕐 *8 a.m.–8 p.m.*

Special Hours: *Closed Aug.*

Close to La Scala and fashionable boutiques, this grand, old-world cafe especially caters to people with a sweet tooth. Charming waiters serve a variety of chocolates, specialty breads, French pastry and luscious, dainty sandwiches to well-heeled or curious patrons. There's something for all budgets, especially if you don't sit at a table; have a coffee at the stand-up bar for only $.80. Confections available for take-out and clandestine munching later. For more cafe activity, try **Cafe Magenta**, which is trendy, crowded, and serves drinks until 2 a.m. *(13 Via Carducci, phone 805.3808)*.

Plastic Killer

📧 *Viale Umbria 120.*

🕐 *10 p.m.–3 a.m.*

Special Hours: *Closed Sun.*

Scary nightclub with a dark theme; music is on the cutting edge of something. Dress appropriately; if you have to ask, don't go. It must be doing something right--it's been open for more than two years. Admission: varies.

Shopping
Shopping Hours

Generally shopping hours are 9– 9:30 a.m. to noon or 12:30 p.m. and then 3:30 p.m. to 7:30 p.m. (winter); 4 to 7:30 or 8 p.m. (summer). However, some close for a shorter lunch break and reopen between 1:30 p.m. and 2:30 p.m. or don't close at all. Monday mornings most are closed, too. Department stores, such as Rinascente and Coin, stay open 9 a.m. to 7:30 p.m.

Best Areas

Via Montenapoleone is the local high point of chic. If you begin on its lower end and stroll through the short pedestrian mall of via della Spiga and then cut back down via Manzoni, this U-shaped trek will show you the choicest array of merchandise in this center; or draw a one-mile radius around the Duomo and start from here in any direction, and you'll discover some of the city's tip-top shops.

Although Milan spells fashion, prices are astronomical! Along the via S. Gregorio (between the piazza della Repubblica and the Central Station), you'll find store fronts that announce *"solo grossisti."* This is the wholesale district for the fashion trade. Many manufacturers are producing knockoffs of the hottest designers of the moment from Paris, Milan and Rome. If you have cash in hand and determination, look in the windows, take your pick, walk in and ask if you can buy. They might say "no," but it's likely, if they aren't terribly busy, that they'll say "yes." You'll probably try the garment on between packing cases, but it's worth it.

A Quick Wrap-Up

Some of the better boutiques to look for are **Giorgio Armani** (*via S. Andrea 9*), **Missoni** (*via Montenapoleone 1*), **Gianni Versace** (*via della Spiga 4*), **Trussardi** (*via S. Andrea 5*), **Fendi** (*via della Spiga 11* and *via S. Andrea 16*) and **Sharra Pagano** (*via della Spiga 7*). For **shoes** try **Raphael-Rossetti, Tanino Crisci** and **Santini** (all on the via Montenapoleone, the latter being very trendy). For **hats** there's only one—**Borsalino** (*Gallerie Vittorio Emanuele 92*). For handbags, suitcases and the like head straight for **Prada** (*via Dante 7*). Don't miss **Peck** (*via Victor Hugo*), the ultimate food shop. **Fraco Sabatelli** (*via Fiori Chiari 5*) has antique picture frames of museum quality. In addition there's **Jesurum** (*via Leopardi 25*), which has an enticing selection of lace and lingerie. Turn to "Venice" for more details.

Coin

▤ *Piazzale Cinque Giornate.*

Those of us intimidated by designer ateliers and snooty salespeople can buy the latest fashions off the rack in this democratic department store. There's another location at *Corso Garibaldi 72.*

Gianni Versace

▤ *Via della Spiga 4.*

Versace's vibrant colors, lustrous fabrics and witty designs are all here at this palazzo of haute couture (☎ *760-05451*). Another location is at 11 Via Montenapoleone (☎ *760-08528*).

Giorgio Armani

▤ *Via San Andrea 9,* ☎ *760-22957.*

🕐 *10 a.m.–5 p.m.*

Special Hours: *Open Mon. from 3:30 p.m. to 5 p.m.; closed Sun.*

This is the main outlet for the maestro of the unstructured look.

Armani's designs for men and women are all elegantly housed together in a vast, hangarlike building. There's also Armani's ready-to-wear line at **Emporio Armani** at *24 Via Durini* (☎ *760-13107*).

Missoni

⊡ *Via Montenapoleone 1.*

Dizzyingly patterned knits by the divine duo of Tai and Rosita Missoni are at this attractive shop.

Peck

⊡ *Via Victor Hugo,* ☎ *2-876-775.*

🕐 *Noon–10:30 p.m.*

The Italian answer to Fauchon, Peck is the food shop, packed with delicacies from all regions of Italy (balsamic vinegar from Modena, Parma ham, Parmesan cheese) and around the world.

Tanino Crisci

⊡ *Via Montenapoleone 3,* ☎ *760-212640.*

🕐 *10 a.m.–7 p.m.*

Special Hours: *Mon. 3 p.m.–7 p.m.; closed Sun.*

Handcrafted shoes and leather riding boots for men and women are the specialty here.

Theater

Teatro alla Scala

⊡ *Piazza della Scala.*

Metro Stop: *Duomo.*

🕐 *10 a.m.–5:30 p.m.*

Special Hours: *Box office is closed 1 p.m.– 3:30 p.m.*

The elegant interior of the auditorium attains acoustical perfection; music from the stage will reach you whether you have a hard-to-get orchestra seat or are perched high up in the balcony. The season runs from Dec. 7 through June 30, with intermittent performances in summer. Admission: varies.

Piedmont

Turin

Torino is a busy foothills metropolis in the Piedmont near the French border (readily discernible in the local dialect) that is close to the heart of Europe and has drawn its culture from the many peoples who have left their traces here—from the Celts to Hannibal, to Romans to Goths, to Charlemagne's Franks. Today there are close to a million citizens in this wide, verdant valley formed by the Po and the Dora Riparia. About 30,000 work in the Fiat auto works, largest plant in the world outside the Detroit area; the unique **Museum of The Automobile**, containing 370 vintage models, is fascinating. They are equally proud of their city's art treasures, **Museo Civico d'Arte Antica**, **Egyptology Museum** (second most important in the world), **Cinema Museum**, the overwhelmingly sumptuous former **Royal Palace** and **Palazzo del Lavoro**. Music and art are cultivated to a profound degree in Turin, obviously the products of lengthy prosperity and good taste among its leaders for many centuries. Based on a Francophile influence, here is a way of life which, like Milan's, differs from that of the rest of Italy.

Where to Stay

Hotel Victoria   ★★★

Budget to Moderate
Via Nino Costa 4 In town center.

☎ *(11) 561-1909,* FAX *(11) 561-806.*

Credit Cards: *All Major.*
Here is a small hotel located on a quiet cul- de-sac in the town center. Its decor enhances its comfort with antiques, lovely fabrics, tapestries, plush carpeting and well-chosen artwork. There are 85 rooms of individual design, all with bath or shower, TV, hair dryer, some with marble baths, some with air conditioning; lovely garden; bar; cheerful breakfast room. No restaurant.

Turin Palace Hotel

<u>http://www.thi.it/</u>

Expensive

Via Sacchi 8 Opposite Porta Nuova train station; near business center and shopping.

☎ *(11) 562-5511,* FAX *(11) 561-2187.*

Credit Cards: *All Major.*

With ample flair coupled with a graceful rich tradition, the Turin Palace is the leader among the luxury hotels in the area. You will find many businesspeople staying in this popular hotel. It has 125 sound-proof rooms with frigobar, climate control, TV; two suites; some room service available; restaurant serving international and regional Piedmont cuisine; busy, popular American bar; baby-sitting available; laundry; valet service; private parking garage.

Where to Eat

Al Gatto Nero

Moderate

Corso Unione Sovietica 14, ☎ *(011) 590414.*

Credit Cards: *All Major.*

The entrance is through a cozy bar and rather hard to find, but when you do the clublike atmosphere with red brick walls and hanging flora is intimate and inviting. The fish is the freshest in town, and the steaks are juicy too. It's a must to reserve in advance.

Cambio

Moderate to Expensive

Piazza Carignano 2, ☎ *(011) 546.690.*

Credit Cards: *All Major.*

Closed: *Sun.*

Here is our lead choice in town, the oldest restaurant in Italy (1757). You'll find grandiose decor featuring crystal chandeliers and velvet-swathed banquet rooms. Prime Minister Cavour had a special table here. The food is noteworthy, including Cavour's choice, *finanziera*, veal with porcini mushrooms. The friendly staff are decked out in tails and white gloves; only the top hat is missing. Patrons love to come here to be pampered.

Montecarlo

Via S. Francesco da Paola 37, ☎ *(011) 830815.*

Credit Cards: *All Major.*

Closed: *Sun.*

With the dining room under stone arches, the old-palace setting of this restaurant is divinely decadent and romantic. Notable specialties are duck prepared with fruit or an abundant antipasto tray.

Vecchia Lanterna

Moderate

Corso Re Umberto 21, ☎ *(011) 537047.*

Credit Cards: *All Major.*

Closed: *Sun.*

Turn-of-the century decor, all in a grand style, greets patrons at this tony salon that's popular with movers and doers. The superb foie gras makes up most beginnings, followed possibly by a homemade ravioli wrapping pieces of duck and lightly blanketed with truffle sauce. The lamb with alpine herb is also noteworthy. Reservations required.

What to Do
Historical Sites

Royal Palace

🖃 *Piazza Castello,* ☎ *11-436-1455.*

🕐 *9 a.m.–5 p.m.*

Special Hours: *Closed Mon.*

The regal residence of the pompous Vittorio Emmanuelle II; baroque interiors and hideous porcelain figures. Royal Armory of the Savoy kings (1600s–1800s). Its saving grace is the gardens designed by the fabled Le Notre. Admission: varies.

Museums and Exhibits

Cinema Museum

▣ *Palazzo Chiablese.*

Here you'll find exhibitions on the early days of cinema and the city's role in this celluloid art form; included are posters, memorabilia and technical innovations. An old-time theater used to show selected screenings, but it's closed for renovation.

Egyptian Museum

▣ *Via Accademia della Scienze 6,* ☎ *11-561- 7776.*

🕐 *9 a.m.–2 p.m.*

Special Hours: *Closed Mon.*

A visit here is almost as good as a trip to Cairo. Ramses II's funeral chamber and statues, the tomb of Kha and Merit (1400 B.C.), an architect and his wife, discovered almost intact in the 1900s, are highlights. The mummy art is intriguing and rare. Admission: varies.

Parco Valentino

Museo dell'Automobile

▣ *Corso Unita d'Italia 40,* ☎ *11-677-666.*

🕐 *10 a.m.–6:30 p.m.*

Special Hours: *Closed Mon.*

Heaven for car buffs, this megamuseum (4 acres) showcases the Italian flair for auto design through the ages. Gawk at current Ferraris, Alfas and Maseratis as well as their precursors. Celebrity sedans featured in movies like Sunset Boulevard and racing vehicles are big draws. Admission: varies.

Sicily

Palermo

Palermo, full of art treasures and beautiful historic buildings, is Italy's sixth-largest city and Sicily's largest center; the lion's share of commerce, however, is concentrated, around **Catania** on the East

Coast. Labeled by its promoters "The Golden Shell," it has some pleasant aspects including Moslem ruins, Norman heritage and baroque beginnings. There's a daily overnight ferry link with Naples, a Genoa connection three times a week and runs from Catania and Siracusa to Naples and Malta frequently; these ships are proud vessels of the Tirrenia Line.

Where to Stay

Grand Hotel Villa Igiea ★★★★

http://www.thi.it/english/hotel/ villa_igiea/

Expensive

Via Belmonte 43 *Take Via dei Cantieri Navali toward Acquasanta district.*

☎ *(91) 543-744,* FAX *(91) 547-654.*

Credit Cards: *All Major.*

Here is a secluded hotel nestled in its own hillside park by the sea. Its Art Nouveau style makes it a wonderful delight to behold, and you will find the original furnishings and decor exquisite. It accommodates 125 rooms with bath or shower, TV; six suites; wheelchair accessible; terrace restaurant; two bars—one by the pool; convention center is adjacent. Although showing its age somewhat, this hotel is well worth a stay.

Grand Hotel et des Palmes ★★

http://www.cormorano.net/sgas/ despalmes/home.htm

Moderate

Via Roma 398 *Located 1/2 mile from the harbor, 10 minutes from train station.*

☎ *(91) 583-933,* FAX *(91) 331-545.*

Credit Cards: *All Major.*

Originally built at the turn of the century as one of Sicily's great aristocratic estates, it is popular for its historical interest and central location. But its overall atmosphere is one of overweening institutionality, and it's showing its age virtually everywhere.

Accommodations include 187 spacious and clean but zestless rooms with bath or shower, TV; four suites; wheelchair accessibility is limited; restaurant; room service; terrace bar; parking (fee). If you do stop over, ask to see the modest little corner where Wagner composed Parsifal.

Where to Eat

Charleston ★★

Moderate

Piazzale Ungheria 30, ☎ *(091) 321.366.*

Credit Cards: *All Major.*
Closed: *Sun.*

Charleston has faded a bit from when it was Sicily's top choice for dining, but the friendly owners still have their faithful following. Nowadays, it's more comforting and less frenetic, although meals are still sky high. Nevertheless, if you want to taste traditional dishes among convivial folks (except for the fickle few who deserted it), there's no better place. Simple grilled fish is best.

Villa Igiea ★★★★

Expensive

Via Belmonte 43, 90142, ☎ *(091)543-744.*

Located at Villa Igiea.
Credit Cards: *All Major.*

Very well prepared and very high priced Sicilian and Italian specialties are served in a luxurious high-ceilinged room festooned with chandeliers. Excellent antipasti; the fresh-tasting *caponata* with juicy eggplant, capers and olives is highly recommended.

What to Do
Kid's Stuff

Puppet Shows ★

 Via Butera 1, ☎ *91-328-060.*

Puppet shows, or *teatro dei pupi*, are a Sicilian folk tradition that developed when Normans introduced the chivalric tales of the Roland and the knights of Charlemagne in the 12th century. These tales have been incorporated into the marionette shows performed weekly at this theater, which is also a showcase for valuable shadow puppets, costumes and scenery displays. The museum is open daily from 9 a.m.–1 p.m. and 4 p.m.–7 p.m.; shows are usually on Sat. or Sun.; call the museum for schedules. Admission: varies.

Museums and Exhibits

ITRAVELBOOK FREEBIE

Catacombe Cappucini ★★

🖼️ *Piazza Cappuccini,* ☎ *91-212-117.*

🕐 *9 a.m.–5 p.m.*

Special Hours: *Sun., holidays closes at noon*

Welcome to the orderly world of mummies. Some 8000 cadavers, once members of local families of varied rank, ages and stature, were embalmed by Capuchin monks from the 16th to the late 19th centuries. The mummies, with their features, for the most part, still intact, await your viewing pleasure. Although admission is free, a small donation is requested to help preserve this vanishing art form. Warning: This experience may frighten small children.

Museo Regionale Archeologico

Piazza Olivella, ☎ *91-587-825.*

🕐 *9 a.m.–1:30 p.m.*

Special Hours: *Tue. and Fri. 9 a.m.–1:30 p.m. and 3 p.m.–6 p.m.; Sun. 9 a.m.–1 p.m.*

Temple art *(metopes)* excavated from the Greek temples of Selinunte (5th and 6th century B.C.) are kept in their own room on the ground floor. These embellishments are rarely seen elsewhere. Upstairs, in the bronze room, two particular sculptures stand out: a Hercules and stag from Pompeii, and a ram (3rd century B.C.) from

Syracuse.

Palazzo dei Normanni

Corso Vittorio Emmanuele, at Piazza della Vittoria, ☎ *91-656-1879.*

🕘 *9 a.m.–5 p.m.*

Special Hours: *Sat., Sun. open only until noon.*

The Palazzo, the seat of the Sicilian Parliament, sitting on the crest of the city, is primarily famed for the Cappella Palatina, a chapel built by Roger II in the 12th century, when Sicily was the wealthiest court on the continent. The interior is remarkable for its Byzantine mosaics, Moorish ceiling and granite pillars.

Tuscany

Florence

Florence is the Athens of Italy. The metropolis is bursting with works of art bearing such signatures as Fra Angelico, Michelangelo, Botticelli, Donatello, Ghiberti, Cellini and Leonardo da Vinci. Unlike in Rome, you can easily walk to almost every major monument or attraction in this gracious center of culture. (A good thing, too, because cars of nonresidents are being banned from midcity.) Italian museum hours change more often than the temperature, so always inquire before setting out for the day. A telephone call by your hotel concierge can clarify such details when you arrive in Florence.

Where to Stay

Anglo American Hotel

Moderate

Via Garibaldi 9, P.O. Box 757 Near the Opera House; 700 meters from train station.

☎ *(55) 282-114,* FAX *(55) 268-513.*

Credit Cards: *All Major.*

An old-timer that still has flair set in a convenient and quiet location in the old town. The stately reception corridor and entry hall maintain their tone of dignity and warmth. Hospitable welcome. There are 107 rooms with bath, climate control, TV; 12 suites very handsomely furnished; wheelchair accessible; dining room; breakfast room; room service; bar; lounge and patio are enclosed; free parking.

Augustus Hotel

Budget to Moderate
Viccolo dell'Oro 5 Near Ponte Vecchio; 1-1/ 2 miles from train station.

☎ *(55) 283-054*, FAX *(55) 268-557.*

Credit Cards: *All Major.*
Tucked slightly off the main drag is this modern, quiet hotel in the center of old Florence. There are 62 rooms with bath or shower, TV, hair dryer, some with a balcony; six suites; wheelchair accessible; breakfast room; room service; modern, sunken, Nordic-style bar under a gently arched white ceiling. There is no restaurant here, but there are dining establishments nearby.

Berchielli Hotel

http://www.berchielli.it/
Moderate to Expensive
Lungarno Acciaioli 14, Piazza del Limbo 6 Downtown between Old Bridge and Holy Trinity Bridge; 1 km from train station.

☎ *(55) 264-061*, FAX *(55) 218-636.*

An Art Nouveau-style hotel with a welcoming black-and-white polished-marble lobby. A worthwhile investment; close to the major sights. There are 76 rooms with bath, TV, fridge, some have a balcony with views of Ponte Vecchio; three suites with colorful baths; wheelchair accessibility is limited; breakfast room; room service; bar; snack bar; parking (fee).

Grand Hotel

Expensive to Very Expensive
Piazza Ognissanti 1 🕮 *Located in historic area across the street from the Arno River.*

☎ *(55) 288-781*, FAX *(55) 217-400.*

Credit Cards: *All Major.*

Situated across the piazza from the Excelsior and owned by the same great hotel chain, this old-world hotel is one of the top luxury addresses in Italy. It offers 107 elegant rooms with bath, hair dryer, TV, fridge; six suites; 11 junior suites; wheelchair accessible; restaurant serves international cuisine; room service; winter garden; bar; parking (fee).

Grand Hotel Villa Cora   ★★★★

Expensive

Viale Machiavelli 18-20 ☞ *Just 3 miles from train station, 1-1/2 miles from Ponte Vecchio.*

☎ *(55) 229-8451,* FAX *(55) 229-086.*

Credit Cards: *All Major.*

Situated in a park above the town, this hotel resides in a wonderfully restored 19th-century villa of the neoclassical era. There are 48 very beautifully furnished rooms with bath or shower, TV, hair dryer, climate control, TV, fridge; 16 suites; two restaurants; bar; gym; business center; free parking. The frescoed ceilings and public sancta are marvels of their time and a joy to see. The large suite #333 is perfect for family use. The concierge is one of the city's finest.

Hotel Brunelleschi   ★★★

http://www.hotelbrunelleschi.it/

Moderate to Expensive

Piazza Santa Elisabetta 3 ☞ *Located midtown.*

☎ *(55) 562-068,* FAX *(55) 219-653.*

Credit Cards: *All Major.*

The conversion of a sixth-century Byzantine tower and a medieval church houses this interesting hotel with antique bricks and polished open beams. It is located in the very center of Florence; 96 rooms and seven suites make up the accommodations. All have very good baths with marble-top basins, bathrobe, hair dryer, TV; one room has a balcony; a dullish restaurant; a bar with piano.

Hotel Excelsior

Expensive to Very Expensive
Piazza Ognissanti 3 Located on banks of Arno River, 1 km from train station.

☎ *(55) 264-201*, FAX *(55) 210-278*.

Credit Cards: *All Major.*

Situated in the historic area of the town, this deluxe hotel boasts rooms and suites that are among the loveliest in Europe. The public areas are decorated with antiques, polished marble, intricately carved woodwork and many wonderful works of art; the marble on the floor of the lobby dates to the 16th century. There are 177 rooms with bath/shower, TV; 17 suites each with its own massive penthouse terrace overlooking the Arno or a townscape of gloriously untouched antiquity; wheelchair accessible; restaurant; room service; Donatello Bar with buffet service is very popular; rooftop patio is partially enclosed for year-round sipping and dining; enchanting barbecue area with view. This 5-star show is run with vigor and savvy by softspoken Paolo Guaneri.

Hotel Regency

Piazza M. D'Azeglio 3 Just 1 km from the train station, within walking distance to attractions.

☎ *(55) 245-247*, FAX *(55) 245-248*.

Credit Cards: *All Major.*

Poetic and elegant, this small, intimate hotel was originally a 19th-century Florentine villa, where Mussolini's sister once lived. It is located in what remains the finest residential district of Florence. All the accommodations are comfortably furnished with a homey atmosphere and very tastefully decorated. You will find only 35 rooms and five suites here, all with marble bath and shower, bidet, bathrobe, hair dryer, climate control, TV, and some rooms with a balcony or patio. Patrician main salon with crystal chandelier, stained-glass panels and textiled walls; courtly lounge; rich, dark wood-paneled dining room with fine china on casement shelves; delicate flower-dotted table settings. Services include a business center, baby-sitting, laundry/dry cleaning, concierge, parking (fee). The hotel itself is fronted by a park, which is close to the romantic Donatello Cemetery. While space is limited, the extensive use of mirrors effects an air of greater space both in the main house and gardenside annex. There is no elevator either, but the decor is so strikingly beautiful that few could carp at such trifles. A unique spot that may not be for everyone, but with qualities that are unmatched in large establishments.

Lungarno Hotel ★★★★

Expensive

Borgo San Jacopo 14, P.O. Box 55 *On the Arno River between the Santa Trinita and Vecchio bridges.*

☎ *(55) 264-211,* FAX *(55) 268-437.*

Credit Cards: *All Major.*

A prime location, with the quiet beauty beside the Arno River and only a few steps from the Ponte Vecchio. There are 66 rooms and 12 suites, including one atop the 13th-century stone tower; all with bath, TV, hair dryer; some with a terrace. You must be careful when booking, because the back rooms and many others are disgracefully small, so make sure you ask for one of the excellent balconied riverfront rooms; cozy bar; no restaurant, but there are many in the area. This small hotel is very colorful, tasteful and comfortable, providing you choose a suitably sized accommodation.

Plaza Hotel Lucchesi ★★★

http://www.plazalucchesi.it/inglese/ home.asp
Moderate to Expensive

Lungarno della Zecca Vecchia 38 On the Arno River near Santa Croce Church and Ponte Vecchio.

☎ *(55) 262-36,* FAX *(55) 248-0921.*

Credit Cards: *All Major.*

Built in the 1860s, this hotel is a very good choice for accommodations. The entrance is done in glass and brass; 97 rooms with bath, TV, climate control, some with a balcony; 10 suites; restaurant; room service; bar; garage.

Principe Hotel

http://www.hotelprincipe.com/

Moderate to Expensive

Lungarno Amerigo Vespucci 34 *Near Vespucci bridge; overlooks Arno River; 1 km from train station.*

☎ *(55) 284-848*, FAX *(55) 283-458*.

Credit Cards: *All Major.*

This intimate and tranquil hotel overlooking the Arno is located in a Florentine- style building. It contains only 21 rooms with bath or shower, hair dryer, TV; sitting room, some have a terrace with panoramic views; two suites; breakfast room; room service; bar; peaceful garden with fountain. There is no restaurant here, but there are many in the area. A wonderful choice for your retreat at the end of the day.

Grosseto

The most alluring target in this area is slightly to the northwest at **Punta Ala.**

Piccolo Hotel Alleluja   ★★★★★

Expensive to Very Expensive

Via del Porto Located 25 miles northwest of Grosseto along the coast via S327.

☎ *(564) 922-050*, FAX *(564) 920-734*.

Credit Cards: *All Major.*

Here is a contemporary hotel that is a tasteful and thoughtful conversion of an old farmstead. It sits peacefully on a lake in perfectly maintained lawns. Accommodations include 43 rooms with bath, TV; five apartments; wheelchair accessible; two restaurants; room service; bar; private beach; bridle paths for horseback riding.

Where to Eat

Acqua al Due

Moderate to Expensive

Via della Vigna Vecchia, ☎ *(055) 28.41.70.*

Credit Cards: V, MC.

Closed: *Mon.*

There are other items on the menu at this comfortable restaurant, but nobody orders anything but the assiagi, five varieties of pasta with five different, inventive sauces that cover the gamut of regional cookery. One must plan in advance (maybe a week) to eat here; there's a lot of people ahead of you waiting for a table.

Al Lume di Candela ★★★★

Expensive

Via delle Terme 23, ☎ *29.45.66.*

Credit Cards: *All Major.*

Closed: *Sun.*

In a medieval tower near the straw market, this restaurant is one of the more romantic settings for dining in the city. The room is long and inviting, with a bar at its entry. The Franco-Italian culinary efforts are commendable—especially the pasta mixed with shellfish; duck with orange sauce also is something to quack about.

Camillo

Moderate to Expensive

Borgo San Jacopo 57-59R, ☎ *21.24.27.*

Credit Cards: *All Major.*

Closed: *Tues., Wed., Thurs.*

Throngs of American businesspeople continue to pour in to one of the most talked-about and visited trattorias here; it's also popular with local boutique owners. Once a little hole-in-the-wall (founded back in 1946), there are now several dining rooms, decorated with paintings by local artists who used to trade canvas creations for culinary ones. While the prices knock it out of the trattoria league, the atmosphere is still that of a rough-and-tumble hash house. The food can be outstanding, especially if you arrive with somebody who is known to the young management.

Cantinetta Antinori

Moderate to Expensive

Piazza Antinori 3, ☎ *29.22.34.*

Credit Cards: *All Major.*

Closed: *Sat., Sun.*

Some Tuscan wine moguls have created this country-cozy nook in the Antinori Palace as a showcase for their excellent wines. There's a small ground floor restaurant with communal tables plus balcony in case there's a crowd. Lots of stylish people sip wines by the glass at the stand-up bar. Although emphasis is on regional wines, the moderately priced food is exciting and encompasses several regions of Italy—wild boar sausage, squid stewed with spinach and a spicy tomato sauce. Light eaters can also have a sandwich, a salad, or an espresso.

Harry's Bar

Expensive

Lungarno Amerigo Vespucci 22R, ☎ *(055) 239.6700.*

Credit Cards: *V, MC, A.*

Closed: *Sun.*

A Florentine landmark and only a long olive-pit throw from the Excelsior. Still small, still intimate, still cozy. Popular with American tourists, who can get a pretty good hamburger and meet other Americans. Service is smooth, by a staff that also happens to own the place. Animated, cosmopolitan, fun.

I' Cche C'e C'e

Inexpensive

Via de Magalotti, 11r, ☎ *21.65.80.*

Credit Cards: *V.*

Closed: *Mon.*

One of the most honest, forthright and altogether pleasing trattorias in Italy (the name means something like "what you see is what you get") I' Cche C'e C'e is the province of owner-chef Gino Noci, an experienced restaurateur known for a friendly welcome and a special way with fish. There's nothing spectacular about it (decor consists of wine bottles, paintings and a red-and-white color scheme), but Tuscans love it and its cuisine—as do I. Not expensive, but awfully good.

Il Latini

Inexpensive to Moderate

Via dei Palchetti 6r, ☎ *(055) 21.09.16.*

Closed: *Mon.*

Communal tables groan with Tuscan specialties, while diners ooh and aah over the succulent roast meats and delicious appetizers and soups. Fresh vegetables come with every dish, and they are really something to talk about. You can feast on a huge variety of appetizers, including crostini with liver.

La Rucola

Inexpensive to Moderate

Via del Leone 50, ☎ *(055) 224002.*

Credit Cards: *All Major.*

Fresh, trendy restaurant, with a choice of garden seating (much nicer than a dull dining room), that is named after the bitter arugula. Fans of this herb (and non-fans) should be aware that it appears in many of the dishes. Desserts are original and excellent.

Ottorino

Moderate

Via delle Oche 12-16R, near the Duomo, ☎ *21.87.47.*

Credit Cards: *All Major.*

Here you will find a linkage of interesting stone-lined rooms, being as it is on the lower level of a medieval tower, but otherwise the decor is not very distinctive. The "hay and straw" pasta, carpaccio and skewered mozarella garnished with toasted anchovy are splendid starters. Entrees are simply prepared, and usually consist of very tasty fish or pasta dishes. Excellent vintages accompany.

Pierrot

Moderate to Expensive

Piazza Taddeo Gaddi 25R, ☎ *70.21.00.*

Credit Cards: *All Major.*

Closed: *Sun.*

One of Florence's oldest restaurants, it occupies a 19th-century building that was formerly a grocery store. Magical things are still done with fish, especially the mixed grill or sole and a splendid octopus salad; grilled mushrooms also are delicious accompanied by a seafood risotto. If you have questions, ask amiable Enrico Bolognini, one of the brightest lights in Italian gastronomy and oenology. He's always on hand.

Sostanza

Moderate to Expensive

Via della Porcellana, ☎ *21.26.91.*

Closed: *Sat., Sun.*

A highly touted trattoria among Florentines, it has a rough, amusing atmosphere. Arrive early or late to avoid the peak of the throng; otherwise, it's a frenzy. Best bets are the breast of chicken, an enormous local beefsteak, and vegetable soup, served by Armani-clad (or inspired) waiters with lots of attitude. A popular stop located behind the Excelsior, but you gotta like sitting with strangers—all tables are communal. Lots of antique and crafts shops in the area.

Trattoria Casalinga

Inexpensive to Moderate

Via dei Michelozzi, ☎ *(055) 21.86.01.*

Credit Cards: *All Major.*

Closed: *Sun.*

Complete dinners, which typically include pasta or soup, entree and vegetable, are the best deal here, so come when you're hungry.

Otherwise, daily specials on the a la carte menu are probably the thing to order, especially penne pasta or ravioli and a moist chicken breast. Although often packed, the atmosphere remains mellow.

What to Do
Events

Gioco del Calcio

Piazzale Michelangelo.

This is football (actually soccer) like you've never seen--a hilarious and historic spectacle of athletes playing a traditional form of soccer, decked out in period costume from the 16th century. The event is centered around the feast day of St. John the Baptist (June 24), when there is also a fantastic fireworks show that engulfs the city. Dates are June 24-28.

Excursions

Flea Market

☎ *Piazza dei Ciompi.*

The Straw Market in the 16th-century Loggia del Mercato Nuovo (near the Palazzo di Parte Guelfa) offers straw and raffia items as well as leather. The big market is the Centrale on the Borgo San Lorenzo; morning is the time to go. An interesting fruit and vegetable patch at Piazza Santo Spirito functions until around noon every day but Sunday. Among the line of pushcarts along the via dell'Ariento (near the Medici Chapels), the bulky fishermen's pullovers and cardigans and other sweaters have mixtures of wool and synthetic yarns that enable them to stretch. This market is closed on Sunday. The Flea Market is at piazza dei Ciompi near the loggia del Pesce, which was the fish market of the 16th century; closed Sunday.

Historical Sites

Duomo (Santa Maria del Fiore)

Piazza del Duomo.

🕐 *10 a.m.–5 p.m.*

Special Hours: *Closed Sun.*

When you try to see Florence in your mind's eye, the towering dome of the Duomo di Santa Maria del Fiore is bound to dominate your picture, as it does this spectacular city. One of the largest cathedrals in the world, the building was begun in 1296 and is a composite of many contributing architects. There are 463 steps from the floor of the cathedral to the top of Brunelleschi's distinctive red-tiled 90- meter dome, the first one built in the Renaissance. Next door, Giotto's Tower or Campanile (open from 9 a.m.–4:30 p.m. daily, summer 9 a.m.–6:30 p.m.) was started by the artist in 1334 and finished by the sculptor Pisano. One must climb 414 steps to reach the top. The view from either point is much the same: glorious! Admission: inexpensive.

ITRAVELBOOK FREEBIE

The Baptistry ★★★★

Piazza San Giovanni, ☎ *55-213-229.*

🕐 *1 p.m.–6 p.m.*

Special Hours: *Sun. 9 a.m.–1 p.m.*

The oldest building in the city (sixth century), the Romanesque Battistero di San Giovanni beckons with its startling bronze doors, their panels depicting scenes from the New and Old Testaments. The eastern and northern doors were designed by a young Lorenzo Ghiberti (who finished them some 20 years later), the southern by Andrea Pisano. Dante was baptized inside under the 13th-century dome, watched over by figures of Christ being tempted by demons.

Museums and Exhibits

Galleria dell'Accademia ★★★★

60 Via Ricasoli, ☎ *23-88-609.*

🕐 *9 a.m.–2 p.m.*

Special Hours: *Sun. 9 a.m.–1 p.m.; closed Mon.*

Just a few blocks north of the Duomo, the Accademia gallery houses Florence's most sought-after attraction: Michelangelo's *David.*

The young Michelangelo fashioned a large block of Carrara marble into the definitive portrayal of the emerging Renaissance man of the period, although it is now surrounded by a Plexiglas screen. Michelangelo's unfinished *Prisoners*, commissioned for the tomb of Pope Julius II, can be seen here as well, and there are two floors representing Florentine painting and sculpture from the 13th through the 16th centuries. Admission: inexpensive.

Museo di San Marco (Fra Angelico Museum) ★★

Piazza San Marco, ☎ *55-210-741.*

☞ *One block north of the Accademia.*

🕘 *9 a.m.–2 p.m.*

Special Hours: *Sun. 9 a.m. to 1 p.m.; closed Mon.*

This small museum, situated inside the Renaissance convent of San Marco, was renovated and rebuilt by Michelozzo. It contains the most important paintings and frescoes of the early Renaissance master, Fra Angelico, who decorated its cells and cloister with deeply felt expressions of his simple faith, which to a cynic (or non believer) may seem maudlin in the extreme. Ghirlandaio's *Last Supper* is aptly placed in the refectory. Also of interest is the stark cell of Girolamo Savonarola, the monk who dominated the Florentine political scene in the 15th century. Admission: inexpensive.

Palazzo Pitti

Piazza Pitti, ☎ *55-213-440.*

🕘 *9 a.m.–2 p.m.*

Special Hours: *Sun. 9 a.m. to 1 p.m.; closed Mon.*

Brunelleschi designed this architectural boast for Luca Pitti, an adversary of the Medici family; in 1540 Cosimo Medici acquired the palace and the adjoining Boboli Gardens. Grafted to harmonize with the palazzo, the magnificent gardens are adorned with fountains and sculpture. Today, the Pitti houses three museums: the Galleria d'Arte Moderna (Gallery of Modern Art); the Galleria Palatina (Raphael, Titian, Lippi, Veronese and others); and the Museo degli Argenti (Silver Museum). In July and Aug., there are evening concerts in the palazzo courtyard. Incidentally, the Boboli is one of the best places for a picnic in the city. Admission: varies.

Palazzo Vecchio

=| *Piazza della Signoria,* ☎ *55-276-8465.*

🕘 *9 a.m.–7 p.m.*

Special Hours: *Sun. 8 a.m.–1 p.m.; closed Sat.*

Constructed between 1298 and 1314, the Palazzo Vecchio was once a Medici residence and is now Florence's city hall. The exterior, with its slender tower jutting above an overhanging battlemented gallery, is a monument to the secular life of medieval and Renaissance Florence. In contrast to the austere facade, the interior of the palazzo contains lavishly decorated rooms. The largest and most important is the Salone dei Cinqueccento (The Hall of the Five Hundred). Michelangelo's statue of Victory dominates the room. Ornate painted doors by Vasari open into what was once Francesco de' Medici's study. Admission: inexpensive.

Uffizi Gallery

http://www.uffizi.firenze.it/welcomeE.html

Piazzale degli Uffizi, ☎ *55-238-85.*

Public Transportation: *Bus 14 or 15.*

🕘 *9 a.m.–7 p.m.*

Special Hours: *Sun. and holidays 9 a.m.–1 p.m.; closed Mon.*
Admission: *varies.*

It is hard to spend less than two hours at this stunning museum; the sheer range of Italian painting, from the 13th to the 17th centuries, is staggering. Even seasoned art students need a good guidebook to map their way through such a comprehensive collection, although the building itself is not especially large. The premier period here is the Renaissance, and all the greats are represented, including Giotto, Da Vinci, Michelangelo, Carravagio, Rubens and Botticelli. Among its most famous holdings is Botticelli's *Birth of Venus,* Michelangelo's *Holy Family* and Raphael's *Madonna of the Goldfinch.*

Nightlife
Disco

The city's darkling hours are darkling even more lately; nightclubs are sparser and sparser in this city. **Jackie-O** remains the heartthrob for the bar-and-disco set. **La Cave**, in the Hotel Villa La Massa (Candeli), is sophisticated. **Full Up** currently is the fullest straight discotheque. Comfortable and highly agreeable for its type. **Space Electronic** is the leading edge when it comes to mod sounds. **Energia**, going the other direction, is agreeable as a piano bar. The **River Club** is well located, but no longer recommended. As nightclubs go, **La Caditale** is probably the better choice. **Arcadia** lifts spirits with its piano bar, cabaret and disco. Closed August 1 to September 15.

Shopping
Shopping Hours

General shopping hours are 9–9:30 a.m. to 1 p.m. and then 3:30 p.m. to 7:30 p.m., Monday closing; summertime 4–8 p.m., with closures on Saturday afternoons instead of Monday mornings.

Best Areas

Along the Arno (Lungarno Corsini, Lungarno Acciaioli); on the Ponte Vecchio; along streets running from the Ponte Vecchio toward the Duomo such as via Por S. Maria, Borgo S. Apostoli, via Porta Rossa, via Calimala and via Calzaiuoli; from Piazza S. Trinita along via Tornabuoni to Piazza Antinori; on the other side of the Arno, the Borgo S. Jacopo and via Guicciardini.

Markets

The **Straw Market** in the 16th-century Loggia del Mercato Nuovo (near the Palazzo di Parte Guelfa) offers straw and raffia items as well as leather. The big market is the **Centrale** on the Borgo San Lorenzo; morning is the time to go. An interesting fruit and vegetable patch at Piazza Santo Spirito functions until around noon every day but Sunday. Among the line of pushcarts along the **via dell'Ariento** (near the Medici Chapels), the bulky fishermen's pullovers and cardigans and other sweaters have mixtures of wool and synthetic yarns that enable them to stretch. This market is closed on Sunday. The **Flea Market** is at piazza dei Ciompi near the loggia del Pesce, which was the fish market of the 16th century; closed

Sunday.

Aurum

⊟ *Lungarno Corsini 16R,* ☎ *55-284-259.*

🕐 *9:30 a.m.–7:30 p.m.*

Special Hours: *Closed Sun.*

Aurum deals in 18-karat gold and silver jewelry, much of it in the distinctive Florentine style; bold Etruscan designs are a specialty. There's a wide variety of contemporary and classic pieces to suit the tastes of most customers. Director Domenico Palomba also can make up special designs for you personally.

BM Bookshop

⊟ *Borgo Ognissanti 4R,* ☎ *55-294-575.*

English-language books of all genres are available from this shop, which is the oldest of its kind in the city. Aside from current paperbacks, history and travel guides, you can pick up some very good Italian cookbooks to take home, a memorable memento of your trip.

Balatresi

⊟ *Lungarno Acciaioli 22R,* ☎ *55-287-851.*

🕐 *9:30 a.m.–7:30 p.m.*

Special Hours: *Closed Sun.*

So fascinatingly different that no one should fail to visit here, even if you're not buying. Lots of one-of-a-kind treasures, as this is a showcase for local artisans. Make a beeline for the impressive alabaster collection. There are magnificent pieces in semiprecious stones, such as malachite, lapis lazuli, rhodonite and other specimens. The most arresting of their vast array is the gorgeous original mosaics, created for the shop by the last pair of great Florentine mosaicists living, Maestro Marco Tacconi and Maestro Metello Montelatici. Proprietor Umberto Balatresi and his wife, Giovanna, are totally trustworthy. Safe shipment is made anywhere in the world.

Bottega San Felice

▭ *Via Maggio 39R,* ☎ *55-215-479.*

🕐 *9 a.m.–7:30 p.m.*

Special Hours: *Mon. 4 p.m.–7:30 p.m.; closed Sun.*

A specialist in rare 19th-and early 20th-century antiques, this store has some intriguing Art Deco pieces. Fans of the genre should have a fine time exploring.

Giulio Giannini & Figlio

▭ *Piazza Pitti 36-37R,* ☎ *55-212-621.*

🕐 *9 a.m.–7:30 p.m.*

The leading supplier of quality stationery in a city known for beautiful paper products. The proprietors have been in business for more than a hundred years. English spoken, heavy international clientele.

La Rinascente

▭ *Via San Raffaele 2 on piazza Duomo.*

This venerable department store, across from the Duomo, has all the essentials. Excellent clothing and cuisine sections; cafeteria with a view.

Lily of Florence

▭ *Via Guicciardini 2R,* ☎ *55-294-748.*

🕐 *9:30 a.m.–7:30 p.m.*

Special Hours: *Closed Sun.*

Lily's is one of the best bets, and bargains, within seven leagues of the Arno. These shops are the sole distributor of the world- famous Petra and the dressier Lily of Florence line along with many other fashionable labels. Styles are available in U.S. sizes and tariffs run 30 to 50 percent less than you'd pay back home.

Paperback Exchange

✉ *Via Fiesolana 31R,* ☎ *55-247-8154.*

🕐 *9 a.m.–7:30 p.m.*

This establishment specializes in recycling private and public collections of used fiction, nonfiction and textbooks. Popular with students and those on a budget, who like to read and not spend a lot of money.

Ponte Vecchio

The Ponte Vecchio is so old, one can only speculate as to how long it has spanned the Arno River. Current thinking tends to place the original structure to have been built in the 10th century or thereabouts; after countless floods and disasters, it was rebuilt in its present form in 1345. Since the 1500s, however, the bridge has been lined with shops that specialize in gold, silver and jewelry. Today, it's the most exclusive shopping area in Florence.

Straw Market

✉ *Near Piazza della Signoria.*

🕐 *9 a.m.–6 p.m.*

The 16th-century market, also called the Mercato del Porcellino (after a bronze boar nearby that is believed to bring good luck), specializes in Florentine crafts, leather, and souvenirs, as well as straw and raffia items. A good place to buy a little something for Aunt Millie back home.

Special Tours

Piazzale Michelangelo   ★★

✉ *At the end of the viale dei Colli.*

Take Bus No. 13 from the train station.

Public Transportation: *Bus No. 13.*

The Piazzale Michelangelo, a 19th-century lookout point on the opposite bank of the Arno, offers a fine panorama of the city. Its main square is adorned with a statue of David (a reproduction) as its centerpiece. Understandably a popular trysting point for locals, it's always crowded in the hot summer months with hawkers and vendors vying for attention.

Fiesole
Music

Estate Fiesolana festival ★★★★

📧 *Via Portigiani,* ☎ *55-597-277.*

☞ *Take Bus 7 from the train station.*

The Estate Fiesolana festival of music, dance and films is held annually in June-Aug., with many events in the spectacular Teatro Romano. Fiesole, a short ride from the train station, also is worth visiting for its Etruscan museum. And it's a peaceful getaway from the big city life.

San Lorenzo
Historical Sites

Cappelle dei Medicee ★★★★

📧 *Piazza Madonna degli Aldobrandini,* ☎ *55- 213-206.*

🕐 *9 a.m.–2 p.m.*

Special Hours: *Sun. 9 a.m.–1 p.m., closed Mon.*

Adjoining the presbytery of San Lorenzo, the Medici Chapels are elaborate Baroque mausoleums containing the tombs of six Medici grand dukes. The so-called "New Sacristy" ("Sagrestia Nuova"), was built by Michelangelo (1520-1557) to complement Brunelleschi's Old Sacristy in San Lorenzo. Begun in 1604, the domed Princes' Chapel is decorated with semiprecious stones, marble and gilt bronzes. The New Sacristy has Michelangelo's famous sculptured tombs: those of Lorenzo, Duke of Urbino and of Giuliano, Duke of Nemours. Atop each tomb are his reclining statues Dawn and Dusk and Night and Day. The artist also began a monument for Lorenzo the Magnificent but finished only the sculpture of Madonna and Child, which you'll see on display. Admission: inexpensive.

Lucca

Lucca is a beautiful and highly sophisticated walled city maintained in excellent preserve.

Where to Stay

Villa La Principessa Hotel   ★★★★

Expensive

Via Nuova per Pisa *Located 2 miles south of Lucca on SS12 bus toward Pisa, 10 miles from Pisa.*

☎ *(583) 370-037*, FAX *(583) 379-019.*

Credit Cards: *All Major.*

At this former 15th-century villa, you will find comfort and aesthetic rewards. There are 44 rooms with bath, TV; eight suites; wheelchair accessible; bar; lunch served al fresco; the main restaurant is located in the sister hotel, Villa La Principessa Elisa, across the road. Some may find the Boroque-style furnishings a bit heavy, but they are easily offset by the tranquility of the surrounding park and gardens.

Where to Eat

Solferino   ★★★

Moderate

Via delle Gavine 50, ☎ *(0583) 59118.*

Located three miles west of Lucca on the Viarreggio Road.

Credit Cards: *All Major.*

A fourth-century family runs this famous Tuscan restaurant noted for wild game. Somehow, the walls that surround the city provide the proper atmosphere for this kind of cuisine. In season, you can enjoy wild boar steaks. Otherwise, duck with truffles or seafood may have to do. It's quite expensive, but worth the experience.

What to Do
Special Tours

Bicycle Tours ★★

 Piazzale Verdi.

Join the Lucchese in their favorite activity—bicycling along the ramparts of the famous city walls, which were built in the 14th century as fortifications for protection during the Wars of Italy. They later served as models for other states and countries throughout Europe. Bicycles can be rented at the tourist office, located at the Vecchia Porta San Donato, in the summer months.

Pisa

Naturally, any first-time visitor must run to see its legendary **Leaning Tower**, venerable **Duomo**, **baptistery** and exquisite **Gothic church** by Nicola Pisano. You can take in a lot very quickly here, because the main sights are highly concentrated in one central area. Of course, scholars could pass a lifetime in the shadows of these timeless monuments; there's so much to study if you care. The 8th-century-old Leaning Tower leans 17 feet off the perpendicular and is tipping at a quicker and more perilous rate each season. Visits are restricted in the immediate surroundings, and, because of "cultural terrorism," closed-circuit television is on vigil at all times; the lovely district around the **Cathedral** is now closed to the public between 11 p.m. and 7 a.m. Don't stay in Pisa if you're in the area; Lucca, ten miles afield, is far more lovely.

Where to Stay

Grand Hotel Duomo ★★★

Moderate to Expensive

Via Santa Maria 94 *Near Leaning Tower in center of town; 1/2 mile from train station.*

☎ *(50) 561-894,* FAX *(50) 560-418.*

Credit Cards: *All Major.*

A contemporary hotel with a lovely rooftop terrace that overlooks the Piazza del Duomo. There are 94 rooms with bath or shower, air conditioning (fee), TV; two suites; wheelchair accessible; restaurant; some room service; bar; rooftop garden; business center; parking garage (fee).

Where to Eat

Al Ristoro Dei Vecchi Macelli   ★★

Moderate to Expensive

Via Volturno, ☎ *(050) 20424.*

Credit Cards: *All Major.*

Closed: *Sun.*

It's a toss-up between Vecchi Macelli and Sergio as to which is the "best" restaurant in the city. Residents divide their time almost equally between the two establishments, which, in any case, provide pampering service. Vecchi Maccelli's prodigious seafood antipasti is legendary; it's often difficult to go on from there. *Zuppa di pesce* and gnocchi with shrimp are continuing favorites.

Ristorante Sergio   ★★★

Moderate to Expensive

Lungarno Pacinotti 1, ☎ *(050) 580.580.*

Credit Cards: *All Major.*

Closed: *Sun.*

Sergio's is regarded as the city's temple of traditional Pisan cuisine, with a picture-postcard setting on the riverbank. The decor blends rusticity and splendor remarkably well, and service and attention by owner Sergio Loren and his family couldn't be more welcoming. The menu changes from time to time, but an enduring specialty is *tagliarini* with squid and vegetable sauces. The family grows its own greens and herbs for the restaurant, and there's an excellent wine list.

What to Do
Historical Sites

ITRAVELBOOK FREEBIE

Il Duomo

Piazza del Duomo 17, ☎ *50-560-547.*

🕐 *7:45 a.m.–6:45 p.m.*

Special Hours: *Nov.-Apr., closes 4 p.m.*

Facing the Leaning Tower, this 11th-century marble cathedral has treasures inside and out. The great bronze doors were designed by Bonnano (not Joseph) and portray events in the life of Jesus Christ. Within is Pisano's pulpit, a lamp by Galileo, and religious art by Andrea del Sarto.

Leaning Tower ★★★

📧 *Piazza del Duomo.*

Travelers used to enjoy huffing and puffing up 294 steps to this legendary tower, but visits into the interior were curtailed about five years ago. A restoration program of nearly $100 million is underway, involving steel cables, girth bands, concrete and lead counterbalances.

San Gimignano

Of the 72 medieval towers that once punctuated the heavens, only 14 still exist, but they are worth the half-hour drive from either Siena or Florence (Poggibonsi exit). Excellent frescoes and paintings in the cathedral and chapels.

Where to Stay

Hotel Bel Soggiorno ★★★

Moderate to Expensive

Via San Giovanni 91 ☞ *In town center; 23 miles northeast of Siena.*

☎ *(577) 940-375,* FAX *(577) 940-375.*

Credit Cards: *All Major.*

You will be warmly greeted upon arriving at this 13th-century house that has been in the same family for generations. The rooms are all lovely in their own way, as some face the street while others have breathtaking views over the countryside. There are 21 rooms and two suites with bath, TV, some with air conditioning, some with minibar; restaurant serves traditional cuisine and is well regarded for its fine food and service.

Hotel La Cisterna ★★★

http://www.sangimignano.com/lacisterna/indexe.htm

Moderate to Expensive

Piazza della Cisterna 24 *On main piazza; 7 miles from train station; 23 miles northeast of Siena.*

☎ *(577) 940-328,* FAX *(577) 942-080.*

Credit Cards: *All Major.*

Located in a walled palace, this former convent dates to the 14th century. Overlooking the lovely landscapes of Tuscany as well as the Val d'Elsa from a Florentine-furnished room can be heavenly. Accommodations include 50 traditionally decorated rooms and suites with bath or shower, TV; notable restaurant with panoramic views serving fine cuisine and wines. Open Mar. 10 through Nov. 10.

What to Do
Museums and Exhibits

Museo Civico ★★

 Piazza del Duomo, ☎ *0577-940340.*

🕐 *9:30 a.m.–6 p.m.*

Special Hours: *Closed Mon.*

Located in the Palazzo del Popolo, or town hall, is this museum notable for Taddeo di Bartolo's Bethroned San Gimignano and Memmo di Filipuccio's frescoes. Your ticket also gets you into the Cathedral, or Collegiata, the Torre della Rognosa, and the Museum of Sacred Art to the left of the Cathedral, containing medieval grave-stones and an Etruscan section. The tower, the highest of the city's 13 torres, is the only one you can climb.

Siena

Siena supplies a mesmerizing passageway to the Renaissance; it is probably the only city in Italy to retain so much ancient charm. As an illustration, filmmakers found that Verona had changed so radically over the years that they came here to shoot *Romeo and Juliet*. The **Duomo**, the **Pinacoteca**, the **Town Hall** and the **Music Academy** are musts; the capper is the spectacular **Palio** ("the world's craziest horse race"), a pageant climaxed by hell-for-leather riding in the huge piazza del Campo. But, for peace lovers, the prime attractions nestle in the surrounding hills.

Where to Stay

Park Hotel ★★★★

Expensive

Via Marciano 18 ☎ *One mile north of town center.*

☎ *(577) 448-03*, FAX *(577) 490-20*.

Credit Cards: *All Major.*

This landed estate built in the 15th century was originally designed as a villa by Peruzzi and later converted into a hotel. It sits in a private park a mile from town overlooking the Tuscan countryside and historic Siena. There are 69 rooms with bath, climate control, TV; four junior suites; one suite; annex surrounds a lovely flowered terrace and pool; enchanting dining patio but chilly dining room; elegant lounges. Tranquilizing and highly recommended.

Villa Scacciapensieri ★★★★

http://www.villascacciapensieri.it/

Expensive to Very Expensive

Via Scacciapensieri 10, Box 119 One mile from town center; 5 minutes from train station.

☎ *(577) 414-41*, FAX *(577) 270-854*.

Credit Cards: *All Major.*

"Scatter your cares" in this beautiful 18th-century estate transformed into a hostelry. It is located above the town on a hill, affording wonderful quiet and views. Accommodations include a total of 31 rooms: 20 rooms in the Villa, nine in the Villino and two in the poolside Villetta. Regaled with loving attention to detail, all rooms have bath or shower, TV; room service is limited; the dining room reflects devotion to cuisine and wines; bar in the chimney hall; gardenside pool; free parking; bus to the town. A truly international and discriminating clientele returns with regularity to this country estate. But not when winter winds blow. Open Mar. 20 through Jan. 7.

Certosa di Maggiano   ★★★

Moderate

Stada di Certosa 82 Just outside the town gates; 2 miles from train station.

☎ *(577) 288-180,* FAX *(577) 288-189.*

Credit Cards: *All Major.*

On the Certosa pike, you will find a very peaceful unusual throwback to old-world grace. This tiny hotel was built into the restored ruins of a 700-year-old Carthusian monastery—the oldest monastery in Tuscany. The 17 rooms and 10 suites are all choice and all have bath or shower, hair dryer; TV; intimate dining room; library; lounges; heated pool in park setting; business center; free parking. Very well recommended.

Pensione Palazzo Ravizza   ★★

Moderate

Pian dei Mantellini 34 In the town center; near the Duomo.

☎ *(577) 280-462,* FAX *(577) 271-370.*

This 17th-century palazzo is a lovely pensione. It has a wonderful location in the center of town and provides accommodations in an inviting atmosphere of antiques and frescoed ceilings. The 30 rooms and three suites are old-fashioned but spacious, most with a private bath and opening onto a delightful garden and terrace, all with phone. There is a restaurant, bar and a comfortable sitting room with piano. You must reserve in advance here, as it can be busy.

Where to Eat

Al Mangia ★★

Moderate

Piazza del Campo 42, ☎ *(0577) 281121.*

Credit Cards: *All Major.*

This eatery has an agreeable outdoor terrace facing the magnificent piazza del Campo, but it is oh-so-geared for masses of tourists. Despite all the comings and goings, the food is quite good. Game and beef stews are often on the menu, but the specialty here is desserts, particularly the Sienese panforte, known worldwide for its divine melding of honey, nuts and candied fruits, similar, but much better than fruitcake.

Al Marsili ★★★★

Expensive

Via del Castors 3, ☎ *(0577) 47154.*

Credit Cards: *All Major.*

Closed: *Mon.*

Found in the Old Town next to the Questura (Police) and the Duomo, it is an exceptional wine house with superb gastronomy of the region. Brick-arched room and high ceiling; careful service; game in season and delicious autumn mushrooms. Try the guinea fowl and the luscious tiramisu. One of the finest cellars in Tuscany, so here's the place to test your oenology.

Cafe Nannini ★★

Moderate

☎ *Banchi di Sopra 99.*

This stellar pastry-shop and ice-cream fantasy land is the place to go for satisfying your sweet tooth. After dark, you may find your sweetie in the evening *passagiata* (promenade) right in front of the cafe.

La Taverna di Nello

Moderate

Via del Porrione 28, ☎ (0577) 289043.

Credit Cards: *All Major.*
Closed: *Mon.*

With its open kitchen with hanging copper pots, rustic decor and corn hanging from the ceiling, you'd expect the Italian version of Robin Hood to walk in. Wines of the region are a specialty, to be swigged down happily with fresh salads and roasted meats or lasagne. Recommended and quite easy on the wallet.

Pizzicheria Morbidi

Moderate
Banchi di Sotto 27.

Fancy but affordable picnic fixings can be had at this deli, which is also a terrific stop for home-baked breads, pizza, fresh *ricciarelli* (egg-shaped cookie-cakes filled with almond paste), and the ubiquitous *panforte.*

Santa Caterina Da Bagoga ★★

Moderate

Via della Galluzza 26, ☎ (0577) 282208.

Public Transportation: *Pollicino C.*
Credit Cards: *V, A.*
Closed: *Mon.*

An old-fashioned neighborhood hangout, named after Palio jockey Bagoga, a local hero. Understandably, the place is swarming with folks during the horse race (see "Attractions" for description) and just plain crowded in August. The decor runs to rough-hewn wood, brick and greenery; it's all very amiable. Rabbit in a wine sauce, roast meats, and pasta with rabbit are menu favorites.

What to Do
City Celebrations

Palio della Contrade ★★★★

📧 *Piazza Il Campo.*

Siena's 17 neighborhoods come together to compete in a procession and bareback horse race; it's named after colorful banners that signify each district. Events twice a year: July 2 and Aug. 16. Much revelry and pageantry, food and fun. If you're at the square early, it won't cost a cent.

Historical Sites

Palazzo Communale

Piazza del Campo, ☎ *577-292-263.*

🕐 *9:30 a.m.–7:45 p.m.*

Special Hours: *Sun. and holidays open until 1:45 p.m.*

This Gothic structure housing the city offices has a museum with Sienese art of the pre-Renaissance era, including frescoes by Simone Martini (Maesta). Chapel with interesting choir seats.

Umbria
Assisi

Assisi is a wonderful little place with scenery that will bedazzle the most crusted traveler. If you haven't much time, plan at least a half day here. That should be sufficient to briefly admire the renowned **Basilica of St. Francis** and to drink in the view of the plains below. If possible, take a bit longer to be humbled by the **Basilica of Santa Chiara** and the **Cathedral of St. Rufino**. There's also a **Roman Forum**, the **Temple of Minerva** and a **Hermitage** (Eremo Carceri). At the **Basilica of St. Mary of the Angels**, you can actually enter the **Portiuncola**, a chapel where the Franciscan order was born. If you'd like a scholarly and pleasant tour, the brothers at the **Monastery of San Damiano** are beloved by many North Americans. Tourists have discovered Assisi, of course, so you can expect some souvenir shops in the ancient streets. The Christmas ceremonies in the various holy sites and in the streets constitute a stroll through a time warp to the Middle Ages.

You should keep in mind that some accommodations are chilly here in the cool months, due to their high altitude and low heating standards.

Where to Stay
Hotels and Resorts

Fontabella Hotel ★★

Moderate

Via Fontabella 25 *Near St. Francis Basilica.*

☎ *(75) 812-883*, FAX *(75) 812-941*.

Credit Cards: *All Major.*
A substantial choice if you decide to stay overnight in Assisi. The original building dates from the 16th century; 46 simply furnished rooms with bath, TV; some with minibar; its restaurant is one of the best among hotels; room service; bar; garden; parking. The views of the countryside from here are wonderful.

Hotel Giotto ★★★

Moderate

Via Fontabella 41 *Near St. Francis Basilica.*

☎ *(75) 812-209*, FAX *(75) 816-479*.

Credit Cards: *All Major.*
This hotel has fine views and gardens, and its restaurant is the culinary choice over the other hotel restaurants. There are 70 rooms with bath and shower, central heating; two suites; wheelchair accessible; open-air restaurant overlooks the Umbrian Valley; bar; free parking garage.

Where to Eat

Il Medio Evo ★★

Moderate

Via dell'Arco dei Priori 4B, *(075) 813.068.*

Credit Cards: *All Major.*

Closed: *Wed.*

A town favorite, partially because of the medieval decor; parts of it date back thousands of years. Owned by the Falsinotti family, the restaurant boasts authentically Umbrian cuisine, including duck with fennel, pasta with truffles and guinea fowl with grapes. Don't let the atmosphere fool you, elegant trappings don't necessarily mean high prices. You can eat well here for under $25.00.

Umbra ★★

Moderate

Via degli Archi 6, *(075) 812240.*

Located at *Umbra.*

Public Transportation: *Bus 2.*

Credit Cards: *All Major.*

Closed: *Tues.*

Excellent regional wines and toothsome truffles can be had at this charming hotel restaurant run by a local family for very reasonable prices (under $20!). Choice meats, pastas (try the homemade cappeletti) and vegetables are served with these delicacies in a pastoral setting—a protected garden shaded by foliage near the hotel's entrance. It's easy to get to as well, within walking distance of the central piazza.

What to Do
City Celebrations

Calendimaggio

 Citywide, *75-812-534.*

Admission: *free.*

As befitting its status as one of Italy's holiest cities and pilgrimage sites, Assisi has citywide Holy Week celebrations (mid-Apr., from Palm Sunday to Easter Sunday) according to rites dating back to medieval times. Expect a crush of crowds to overwhelm the city at this time with religious fervor.

Historical Sites

Basilica of Santa Chiara

▣ *Piazza Santa Chiara,* ☎ *75-812-282.*

🕐 *6:30 a.m.–6 p.m.*

Special Hours: *Closed noon to 2 p.m.*

Admission: *free.*

Santa Chiara, the patron saint of television (anointed by Pope Pius
XII in 1958) as well as the founder of the Poor Clares, is honored
in this pink-and-white striped church built in the late 13th century.
Her rather grotesquely preserved body lies in the crypt in a crystal
coffin. The basilica's principal chapel contains the Crucifix of San
Damiano, which was believed to have admonished St. Francis to
rebuild a church while he was kneeling in prayer. As in all churches
in this holy city, modern visitors are admonished to dress modestly;
no shorts or miniskirts, please.

Basilica of St. Francis   ★★★★

▣ *Piazza di San Francesco,* ☎ *75-812-238.*

🕐 *6 a.m.–7 p.m.*

Admission: *free.*

Built as a tribute to St. Francis, founder of the Franciscan order, the
Basilica of San Francesco consists of two Gothic churches, both
strikingly diverse in mood and feel. What both share, though, are
frescoes and priceless religious art by, among others, Giotto,
Cimabue, and Simone Martini. Pietro Lorenzetti's *Crucifixion* and
Cimabue's *Madonna, Child and Angels with St. Francis* overwhelm
the older, darker Lower Church, while the light- filled Upper
Church is devoted to frescoes depicting significant events in the life
of the saint; unfortunately, they are in dire need of restoration. St.
Francis' remains are entombed in the crypt in the Lower Church.

Monastery of San Damiano

Porta Nuova.

▣ *A short 1 km walk from Basilica di Santa Chiara.*

🕐 *7 a.m.–7 p.m.*

Special Hours: *Closed 12 noon to 2:30 p.m.*

For a quiet diversion from the throngs of tourists choking downtown Assisi, meander along to this serene monastery. The peaceful surroundings may have inspired St. Francis to write his masterwork, *Canticle of All Things Created*, here. Highlights include 14th-century frescoes in the monastery chapel. There is no charge for visiting this sanctuary, just alms to the church, which are voluntary.

Spoleto

Spoleto is known for its Festival of Two Worlds, comprising theater, opera, concerts, films, ballet and art exhibitions. This is a midsummer event usually from late June to late July. Science is also being spotlighted with relevant congresses. Experimental theatre occurs in August and September and another thespian festival follows Easter. For ticket information telephone **Teatro Nuovo** in Spoleto (0743- 40265 or **Festival Information** 0743- 44097); another choice is via **Teatro Olimpico** in Rome (06-3234890). The town is rich with antiquities and so are the shouldering Umbrian hills.

Where to Stay
Hotels and Resorts

Hotel Clarici   ★

Moderate
Piazza della Vittoria 32 Lower part of the town.

☎ *(743) 223-311*, FAX *(743) 222-010*.

Credit Cards: *All Major.*
Air conditioning in rooms, balcony or patio, in-room minibars.

Here is a modern hotel choice that is simply furnished but comfortable. It offers 24 rooms with bath or shower, TV; breakfast room; elevator; terrace; parking.

Hotel Gattapone

Budget to Moderate

Via del Ponte 6 🔖 *Five minutes from town center; 1 mile from train station.*

☎ *(743) 223-447*, FAX *(743) 223-448.*

Credit Cards: *All Major.*

One of the top hotel choices here and a favorite of visitors to the Spoleto Festival. It overlooks the Tessino Valley as well as the Ponte delle Torri from the winding road that leads up to it. The 13 rooms are modern but comfortable with bath, TV; seven suites; bar; spectacular panoramas of the countryside. Reserve in advance for this popular spot.

Where to Eat

Il Tartufo   ★★★

Moderate to Expensive

Piazza Garibaldi 24, ☎ *(0743) 40236.*

Credit Cards: *All Major.*

Closed: *Wed.*

The preparation of the prized black truffles of the region is highly regarded in this acclaimed restaurant in a prominent square in Spoleto. You can spend a fortune here, but it's also possible to be content with some humbler fare, including omelets, kid and lamb, either with or sans truffles.

What to Do

Two Worlds Festival   ★★★★

Piazza del Duomo 9, various locations.

Italy's premier performing arts festival is set in sparkling Spoleto, which shines even brighter every year in June and July. Major performances of dance, theater and music are performed by international stars and local talent. Tout Rome puts it high on the social calendar, with a round of parties and events. Most performances are classically oriented and highly traditional, but over the years, experimental works have begun to creep in. Performances are in various venues, including the Roman theatre, the Teatro Caio Melisso, and the Teatro Nuovo. Tickets should be ordered, as expected, way in advance. Dozens of fringe events go on at the same time, attracting lots of music lovers on a budget. In Rome, contact **Associazione Festival dei Due Mondi**, *Teatro Olimpico, Piazza Gentile da Fabbriano 15, Rome* (06) 393304 or *3962635.* In Spoleto, (0743) 40396.

Veneto

Venice

Venezia is an absurd and wonderful dream. To protect themselves from the approach of armies by land, a group of staid and somber citizens many centuries ago carved for themselves a slice of sea and proceeded to erect buildings on top of the waves. This fantastic conglomeration of houses, churches, gardens, factories, streets and squares rests on piles sunk deep into the mud. It has been called "a kind of poem in stone accidentally written by history on the waters." The main boulevard, most of the important arteries and many of the small streets are paved with *acqua* instead of asphalt—and sometimes this H_2O bears no resemblance whatsoever to *Quelques Fleurs or Chanel No. 5.*

Taxis, buggies, rickshaws, bicycles, roller skates and all types of transportation which can't dance on the water are forbidden. Visitors can count on the *Vaporetto* (Boat #1) as the Venetian equivalent of an around-the-town bus ride. (Boat #5, called the *circolare,* chugs out to the isle of Murano or to Giudecca (useful for those staying at the Youth Hostel). That, with the vessels of about 500 gondoliers (about a dozen now motorized) plus about 200 launch operators, is it; the fastest of the *motoscafi* is the *diretto* variety. A canal ride ticks off 45 minutes in travel time between the Marco Polo airport and the center of town. Ask about the *collegamento,* or Airport Connection. This terminus, built on reclaimed land, can accommodate only jets without full fuel loads at takeoff.

About 50 churches have been locked tight to prevent theft of the art treasures. Therefore, the only way to view these works is to attend services (hours usually posted on the portals). Most morning prayer is from 6–8 a.m. on weekdays or 7 a.m. to 1 p.m. on the Lord's Day. Check also for vespers, the evening mass, or devotions which often occur on Saturdays. *Deus Vult!*

It is from Venice that the super-posh antique train, *The Orient Express,* all polished, air conditioned and comfortized, departs for London on a sybaritic journey that recalls the glories of an earlier transportation era; an Alpine linkage also is available on a daylight schedule.

Ample funds are available to fight flooding, pollution and decay. In addition, Dutch hydraulics experts have teamed up with Italian engineers to seek a lasting solution to the city's permanent wave problem. These specialists have checked the tides by employing removable barriers at the three sea entrances plus industrial controls within the lagoon. Many wells have been permanently capped, providing a cushion upon which Venice can "float," the collapse of the city already has been markedly reduced and prospects are good that the Venetians will enjoy a new and long lease on life.

Where to Stay

If you arrive by car, many of the top hotels recommend the vaguely reliable **Mattiazzo garage** in *piazzale Roma*, where endless tips are expected and where you are bludgeoned by an 18 percent surcharge if you wish to pay for their cherished services by credit card.

Apartments and Condo

Palazzo del Giglio Apartments   ★★★★★

Very Expensive
Campo Santa Maria del Giglio 2462 Annex of the Hotel Gritti Palace; 5 minutes from Piazza San Marco.

☎ *221-2340,* ☎ *(41) 520-5166,* FAX *(41) 520- 0942.*

Credit Cards: *All Major.*

With their bright, joyful colors, modern comfort, and carefully selected antiques and works of art, these apartments, dating from the 18th century, have an enchanting, homey atmosphere. Just 19 suites in varying sizes with TV, radio, beautifully equipped kitchens; the works. Laundry, maid and other services are available. Guests also have full access to the restaurant and bar at the Gritti. The cheer, privacy, luxury and economics make these accommodations almost irresistible for travelers who plan to stay a week or more in Venice. Administration maintained by the Gritti staff, who are always at the beck or telephone call of their neighboring apartment clients.

Hotels and Resorts

Ala Hotel

Budget to Moderate

San Marco 2494/A Campo Santa Maria del Giglio *Five minutes from Piazza San Marco.*

☎ *(41) 520-8333*, FAX *(41) 520-6390.*

Credit Cards: *All Major.*

A moderately priced modern hotel in a 14th-century palace. The original ceilings are maintained here in their Venetian splendor. There are 85 simple rooms with bath or shower, hair dryer, TV; restaurant; some room service available.

Carpaccio Hotel

Moderate

San Polo 2765 *Just 1/2 mile from Santa Lucia train station facing the Grand Canal.*

☎ *(41) 523-5946*, FAX *(41) 524-2134.*

Credit Cards: *V, MC, E.*

Situated on the Grand Canal, this one stands out with a generous helping of flair for its bracket. The 20 rooms are large and simply furnished; 14 rooms have bath or shower; all rooms face the water; wheelchair accessible; breakfast bar. No restaurant, but plenty of choices in the area. The hotel is generally clean and its location is excellent.

Cavalletto e Doge Orseolo

Moderate

San Marco 1107 *Near Piazza San Marco overlooking Orseolo Canal.*

☎ *(41) 520-0955*, FAX *(41) 523-8184.*

Credit Cards: *All Major.*

In a building that dates back to the 1300s, this hotel overlooking the

Orseolo Canal, has improved a great deal, thanks in part to the takeover by the Best Western chain. The 96 charming rooms are furnished in traditional Venetian style and have bath or shower, TV; well-respected dining salon; breakfast room; bar.

Des Bains Hotel ★★★★

Expensive

Lungomare Marconi 17, Lido *In the Lido; 15 minutes from Piazza San Marco.*

☎ *(41) 526-5921,* FAX *(41) 526-0113.*

Credit Cards: *All Major.*

In its own park and on the sea, this early 1900s hotel is where the movie of Thomas Mann's novel *Death in Venice* was filmed. It is a relaxing hotel in a marvelous setting and offers 191 rooms with bath, climate control, TV, some with a balcony; one suite; 18 junior suites; wheelchair accessible; two restaurants; private beach across the road; warmed saltwater pool with bar; three tennis courts at its Sporting Club, a discotheque; courtesy launch to town. Open Apr. through Oct.

Europa & Regina Hotel ★★★

Moderate to Expensive

San Marco 2159, Canal Grande *Opposite Della Salute Church; near Piazza San Marco.*

☎ *(41) 520-0477,* FAX *(41) 523-1533.*

Credit Cards: *All Major.*

Linking two former independent neighbors, this is a first-class hotel that dates to the 18th century. It offers clientele an extra feature in its sprawling construction, as guests can view the Grand Canal from four sides. The main floor is distinctive in style, and the bedrooms are furnished in modern, Venetian or Baroque decor. There are 192 rooms with bath, climate control, TV, some with balcony; 13 suites. Beautiful garden restaurant and terraces that face the canal; bar; business center; parking (fee). Free transportation to golf, tennis, watersports at nearby Lido Beach.

Hotel Cipriani ★★★★★

Expensive to Outrageously Expensive

Giudecca 10 *Giudecca Island; 5 minutes from Piazza San Marco via hotel transport.*

☎ *(41) 520-7744*, FAX *(41) 520-3930*.

Credit Cards: *All Major.*

Located outside of mainstream Venice on the magical island of Giudecca, this magnificent hotel is only five minutes from Piazza San Marco by complimentary hotel launch. Aside from its extraordinary luxury, this establishment also features its own intimate harbor for independent yachtsmen, fully supplied with electricity, water and services. The heated, Olympic-size, filtered saltwater pool is a lovely centerpiece for the health club and surrounding garden suites, crowned by a tier of apartments. The cuisine is among the finest to be found in Italy and is known and praised by cognoscenti the world over. The spacious 104 beautiful modern units and 25 suites, with their own Jacuzzis, provide the ultimate in pampering. If greater exclusivity is desired, ask about the 14-suite annex called Palazzo Vendramin, in a nearby palace, with views of Venice across the lagoon. This tranquil deluxe enclave is masterminded by Natale Rusconu one of Europe's premier hosts. Travelers who have utilized this hotel's link to the nostalgic Orient Express will find a boutique with items from the train. Be sure to reserve in advance. Open all year.

Hotel Gritti Palace ★★★★★

Very Expensive

Campo Santa Maria del Giglio 2467 *On Grand Canal; 5 minutes from Piazza San Marco.*

☎ *221-2340*, ☎ *(41) 794-611*, FAX *(41) 520-0942*.

Credit Cards: *All Major.*

Of Ernest Hemingway fame, this hotel is just across the river from the gondola park and among the leading accommodations in the world. It is small, cheerful and almost clublike. In fact, the restaurant, with its canalside terrace, is called the Club del Doge and is one of the best in Venice. Nothing has been spared in decor, staff or the attributes of pure luxury. All 99 rooms and 10 suites come with stocked-bar-type refrigerators; all baths are marble. If expense is no object, try to reserve Suite #110. It's one of the finest hotel accommodations, in terms of taste and in ambience, to be found anywhere. In season, there are free boat shuttles to the Lido, Excelsior's pool or the Des Bains in the park. Open all year.

Hotel Metropole

Expensive

Riva Schiavoni 4149 ☞ *Opposite the lagoon; near Piazza San Marco.*

☎ *(41) 520-5044*, FAX *(41) 522-3679*.

Credit Cards: *All Major.*

An excellent address only a few steps away from the ferry landing, facing the lagoon and at the canal entrance for gondolas and water taxis. The downside to this convenient spot is that in the high tourist season it does get incredibly crowded. Accommodations include 72 generously outfitted rooms and three junior suites all with bath, TV; compact restaurant and American bar; business center. A sumptuous interior, a modern adaptation of the classic Venetian style. For situation and decor, this proud house is loaded with appeal, through its service standards are another story.

Hotel Villa Cipriani

Expensive

Via Canova 298 Located 40 miles northwest of Venice in town center, 15 minutes from train station.

☎ *(423) 952-166*, FAX *(423) 952-095*.

Credit Cards: *All Major.*

This hotel is situated about 50 minutes out on the main Venice-Verona highway and in the center of town and boasts being the celebrated former home of both Eleonora Duse and Robert Browning. All 31 comfortable and delightfully furnished rooms have private bath, TV; two have a balcony (try to reserve one of these, as they are very quiet); five deluxe suites; wheelchair accessible; huge garden; well-known and renowned restaurant; full pension with a la carte menu. This is a fine stop for lunch or for rest. Beautifully operated.

Luna Hotel Baglioni ★★

Expensive

Piazza San Marco 1243 *On Piazza San Marco near the boat landing.*

☎ *(41) 528-9840*, FAX *(41) 528-7160*.

Credit Cards: *All Major.*

This is the oldest hotel in Venice dating from 1474, but it was a religious retreat even prior to that. It claims not only a central but a quiet locale. Accommodations include 128 elegant yet comfortable rooms with bath or shower, TV; nine suites; seven junior suites; most baths replete with marble; public areas furnished in plush classical decor; waterside bar on tiny canal facing the Royal Garden; attractive rose-toned dining room and open terrace; currency exchange services. Ambitious billings and dining edicts sometimes cause irritation among visitors to this establishment.

Where to Eat

Antica Locanda Montin ★★★★

Expensive

Fondamenta di Borgo, ☎ *(041) 522.7151.*

Located at Locanda Montin.
Accademia.
Credit Cards: *All Major.*
Closed: *Tues.*

A traditional 17th-century inn and restaurant behind The Accademia, the Locanda has been a favorite of the famous from way back. Its picture-lined, rugged inner sanctum and adjoining bar are hot spots, but many prefer the vine-lined summer garden. The cookery is simple and substantial, and prices are decent. The place is still frequented by artists, the nobility and a grateful travel-writer or two.

Antico Martini ★★★

Very Expensive

San Marco 1983, Campo San Fantin, ☎ *(41) 522.4121.*

San Marco.

Credit Cards: *All Major.*

Closed: *Tues.*

Located in the piazza facing the famous Teatro La Fenice, this is both a nightclub (piano bar open until 2 a.m.) and a restaurant. The interior is luxurious with French curtains, gilt mirrors and crystal fixtures; professional service. Very costly, but there are both a fixed-price lunch and dinner that are good for trying as many specialties as possible.

Caffe Florian ★★

Moderate

Piazza San Marco 57, ☎ *(41) 528.5338.*

San Marco.

This spot sprung to life way back in 1720, and Casanova played here. It offers six little plush-velvet rooms, each with its own entrance, plus seven rows of outside tables. A seasonal band can be heard by anybody in the entire square from Apr. to Oct. The pick of the esplanade for wine, hors d'oeuvres and cheer.

Corte Sconta ★★★★

Moderate to Expensive

Calle del Pestrin 3886, ☎ *(41) 522.7024.*

Arsenale.

Credit Cards: *V, MC, A.*

Closed: *Mon., Sun.*

It's hard to find and not very attractive, having been a cow stall and not changed much since it was used for its original purpose. You sit in a spartan room or a lackluster courtyard with brown paper mats on bare tables. But Mamma Mia!!! Is the food delicious! Start with a lively, chilled white wine (Prosecco), then Spaghetti in Three Ways, shellfish or sepia in its own ink. A word of warning: Not too long ago, it was given an "A" award (for "Attitude," not a good grade) and a thumbs down for snarly service. Anyway, you'd better go before 9 p.m., or risk missing the best catch in all Venice. Reservations are essential.

Crepizza ★★

Inexpensive to Moderate

San Pantalon, 3757, ☎ *(041) 52.29.189.*

 Near the University

Credit Cards: *All Major.*

At this University hangout, you'll know what to expect: crepes, pizza, young people and good prices. One drawback is the small portions, you may have to order a few crepes to satisfy hunger pangs. Chicken or ham-filled pancakes are tasty, and there's a menu of dessert crepes, crowned with whipped cream and seasonal fruit. Fills up just before closing.

Da Fiore ★★★★

Expensive

Calle del Scaleter 2202, ☎ *(41) 721.308.*

Silvestro.

Credit Cards: *All Major.*

Closed: *Mon., Sun.*

This is a family spot where the fireworks are in the value, not in the atmosphere or the antics of the waiters. Hidden from view off the San Polo square, Da Fiore features one thing only: fresh, fresh fish and seafood. Specialties include spider crab and risotto with squid in its own ink. The restaurant bakes its own bread, and there's a small bar for serious imbibers.

Do Forni ★★

Moderate

Calle Specchieri 468, ☎ *(41) 523.7729.*

San Marco.

Credit Cards: *All Major.*

Folks break bread all year-round at this industrious eatery that used to be an ancient bakery. There's a choice of two places to dine: one a rather stuffy Art Nouveau style room near the entrance and the other a cozier pub. Either way, the food here is good and the service efficient. The cuisine is eclectic for Venice, catering to an international clientele.

Gelati Nico ★★★

Moderate

Zattere, 922, ☎ *(041) 52.25.293.*

 near the Giudecca Canal

Closed: *Thurs.*

Everyone has a favorite gelato spot, but the resounding winner seems to be this one near the vaporetto stop in Dorsoduro, fronting a popular promenade area. The place is open most of the year, and is also usually filled to capacity. Chocoholics crave the Gianduiotto, which is a hazelnut chocolate whipped-cream fantasy, a creation of this cafe.

Harry's Bar ★★★

Expensive

Calle Vallaresso 1323, ☎ *(041) 528.5777.*

Take the Vaporetto to San Marco.

San Marco.

Credit Cards: *All Major.*

Closed: *Mon.*

Harry's Bar remains faithful to the expectations of the Hemingway cult. It's intimate, friendly, sophisticated and cheerful, but with decor of no particular distinction. Great fun for people-watching; limited but excellent menu with many stateside delicacies (mainly sandwiches); everyone passes by for the world-famous Bellini— bubbly with peach nectar. Like the rest of Venice these days, it has shockingly high prices. Reservations required.

Harry's Restaurant ★★

Expensive

Calle Vallaresso 1323, ☎ *(41) 528.5777.*

San Marco.
Credit Cards: *All Major.*
Closed: *Mon.*

One floor above Harry's Bar, the Restaurant twinkles happily too and the view is terrific, with Piazza San Marco and the Vaporetto right in front of you. Service is so accommodating that a party of 60 can be nourished in style at one sitting. Try a batch of homemade ravioli and a plate of *scampi alla carlina.* This is the place where *carpaccio* was born. Always reserve in season.

Quadri ★★

Moderate

Piazza San Marco, *(41) 528.9299.*

S. Marco.
Credit Cards: *All Major.*
Closed: *Mon.*

A fixture on the Piazza San Marco, this 17th-century cafe-restaurant picks up the slack when the neighboring Florian is busy. The second-floor restaurant, with an all-encompassing view of Venice, is often loaded with celebrities and their watchers, especially at peak times. The decor is swank, but not as florid as the Florian. The cuisine encompasses a variety of seafood and beef dishes, and desserts are homemade and deluxe.

Trattoria Madonna ★★★

Moderate

San Polo 595, *(41) 522.3824.*

Rialto.
Credit Cards: *All Major.*
Closed: *Wed.*

If you want to savor local color and see how the Venetians really eat, try this trattoria, with some of the most reasonable prices in this veddy expensive city. Located near the Rialto at Calle della Madonna, it is handy, noisy and sprawling and a favorite for fish and risotto.

What to Do
City Celebrations

Biennale

 Giardini Pubblici, ☎ *41-522-6356.*

The modern art world invades Venice for two months between June and Oct. (in even years), with expositions throughout the city, but the bulk of the proceedings is centered in the Giardini Pubblici. Admission rates vary, so check with the tourist office.

Excursions

Burano

Burano is a charming island, with canals and narrow streets, where the inhabitants make their living as lacemakers and fishermen. The 16th-century church of San Mattino has an early painting by Tiepolo, *The Crucifixion.* Take along a picnic lunch and some extra lire if you expect to purchase some of the lace for which the island is famous. To reach Burano from Venice, take a #5 vaporetto from riva degli Schiavoni. Get off at fondamente Nuove; then take the boat called Line 12 marked "Burano."

Gondola Rides

 Grand Canal.

Once a "must-do" activity, the much touted, and still romantic gondola rides on the Grand Canal now cost about 50-80 Euros for 40 minutes; often travelers double or triple up to be able to afford the ride. I think it's worth it, just once, especially with someone special, along with a bottle of something and a hamper of goodies.

Murano

This island is primarily known for the products of its glass factory, which makes for an intriguing visit (when you arrive at Murano, disembark at Colonna, the first vaporetto stop). There's a Glass Museum on the main canal (Museo Vetrario, open 9 a.m.–7 p.m. daily except Wed. and Sun., winter 10 a.m.–4 p.m.). If you still have time, visit the 12th-century Basilica of SS Maria e Donato, across from the museum. To reach Murano, take vaporetto 5 from riva degli Schiavoni, near piazzetta San Marco.

Palladian Villas

Tour the summer homes of 16th-century Venetians on the Brenta Canal between Padua and Venice by boat, called the Burchiello loop, with stops at the more grandiose palazzos, including the Palazzo Pisano at Stra, with its legendary frescoes. Lunch is included on the tour, which lasts all day. The little vessel plies the Brenta Canal from Padova to Venice (and reverse) from Mar. 25-Oct. 27. Short tours are also available, if you prefer only glimpses; special cruises make short tours three times a week. For arrangements, contact CIT *(Piazza S. Marco 4850,* ☎ *5285480, open 8 a.m.–6 p.m. Mon. through Sat.).* For more leisurely sightseeing, the *vaporetti* depart from the Fondamenta Nuove (end of rio dei Gesuiti). These casual, point-to-point voyages should be among the most enchanting of your Venetian byway and seaway explorations.

Torcello

☞ *Take vaporetto 12 from Fondamenta Nuova on Murano.*

One of Venice's "out islands" and 40 minutes away by vaporetto, Torcello makes an interesting trip for its vast contrasts with Venice. On this sparsely populated island, whose importance was eclipsed by the rise of Venice, you'll see not only farmers' fields, cypress trees and palms, but also the Cattedrale di Torcello, originally founded in A.D. 639 and reconstructed in 1008. An arresting Byzantine mosaic of the Madonna and Child fills the apse, contrasting with another, entirely forbidding mosaic of the Last Judgment on the opposite wall. In front of the church is a museum and the Church of Santa Fosca, originally built in the 7th century and reconstructed around 1000. The Cathedral is open daily, 10 a.m.–12:30 p.m. and 2:30 p.m.–6:30 p.m. Admission: inexpensive. (041) 730.084.

Historical Sites

ITRAVELBOOK FREEBIE

Basilica di San Marco ★★★★★

Piazza San Marco, ☎ *41-522-5205.*

Metro Stop: *San Marco.*

🕐 *9:30 a.m.–5:30 p.m.*

Special Hours: *Sun. opens at 2 p.m.*

In A.D. 829 the remains of St. Mark the Apostle were shipped from Alexandria to Venice, and soon thereafter work began on the basilica. The current structure, with its domes and arches, has its beginnings in the latter part of the 11th century--Venetians wanted the cathedral of their patron saint to reflect the wealth and power of their state. The facade of St. Mark's is a synthesis of Byzantine, Romanesque and Gothic elements; a dividing gallery in the center displays four bronze horses of 4th-century Greek origin. Everywhere there are marble columns, sculptures of sacred personages and mosaics (400 square yards of them), all unified according to a complex iconographical plan. Spend some time, too, looking at the gem-encrusted Pala d'Oro, or Golden Altarpiece, which took centuries to complete and shows the Byzantine influence on a uniquely Venetian work. The Treasury *(open Mon. through Sat. 9:30 a.m.–5:30 p.m., Sun. 2 p.m.–5 p.m., admission $1.80)* has a sumptuous collection of vases, reliquaries and liturgical items, jewelry and other handcrafted objets d'art.

Ca' Rezzonico ★★★

 Fondamenta Rezzonico, ☎ *41-522-4543.*

Metro Stop: *Ca'Rezzonico.*

🕐 *10 a.m.–5 p.m.*

Special Hours: *Sun. 9:30 a.m.–12:30 p.m.*

Also on the Grand Canal, here you can see vestiges of the Golden Century of Venice (18th), in furnishings, artwork and elaborately painted ceilings, all in chambers of varying luxury. Pietro Longhi's

The Lady and the Hairdresser is installed on an upstairs entrance wall.
Admission: inexpensive.

Campanile di San Marco   ★★★

 Piazza San Marco, ☎ *41-522-4064.*

Metro Stop: *San Marco.*

🕐 *9:15 a.m.–8:30 p.m.*

Special Hours: *Nov. through Apr. 10 a.m.–4 p.m.; closed Jan. 15-31.*
The tall, majestic Campanile began as a lighthouse and was not built
up to its 300-foot height until the 16th century. That structure last-
ed about 300 years, collapsed and was reconstructed in 1912. An
elevator was installed to enable visitors to have a matchless view of
Venice from the tower heights. Admission: inexpensive.

Palazzo Ducale   ★★★★

Piazzetta San Marco, ☎ *41-522-4951.*

Metro Stop: *San Marco.*

🕐 *8:30 a.m.–7 p.m.*

Special Hours: *Nov. through Apr. 10 a.m.–4 p.m.*
The Palace of the Doges is one of the world's most beautiful public
buildings. The unusual exterior has two impressive loggias. The
columns of the lower arcade have 38 capitals carved with allegorical
figures and heads. Here is the famed "Staircase of the Giants"
(1567) by Sansovino. The opulent rooms are adorned with paintings, frescoes, sculptures and carvings by scores of Italian artists,
including greats like Tintoretto, Veronese, Titian and Tiepolo. After
you are dazzled by this monument to Venetian wealth and vitality,
visit the prisons that are reached via the Bridge of Sighs (not yet
built in the days when the Doges' jails were most active).

Piazza San Marco   ★★★★★

Metro Stop: *San Marco.*
When St. Mark's was first built, the square was a garden with a canal
running through it. In the year 1000, the canal was filled in and the

square enlarged, allowing the area to fulfill its inevitable function as the religious and political center of Venice.

San Giorgio Maggiore

✉ *Across from Piazzetta San Marco,* ☎ *41- 528-9900.*

Metro Stop: *Giudecca.*

🕐 *9 a.m.–6 p.m.*

On the island of San Giorgio Maggiore, this church was built by Palladio, the great 16th-century architect. Tintoretto's Last Supper and Descent of Manna are the prime treasures here. A stunning vista of the Doges' Palace across the water can be seen from the top of the church belfry. Admission: inexpensive.

ITRAVELBOOK FREEBIE

Santa Maria Gloriosa dei Friari

✉ *Campo dei Friari,* ☎ *41-522-2637.*

Metro Stop: *San Toma.*

🕐 *9 a.m.–6 p.m.*

Special Hours: *Sun. only open 3 p.m.–5:30 p.m.*

The centerpiece of this 14th-century church's main altar is Titian's major work, The Assumption; the artist's grandiose tomb is nearby. Other works are Bellini's Madonna triptych and Donatello's simple carving of St. John the Baptist.

Museums and Exhibits

Gallerie dell'Accademia

http://web.tiscali.it/wwwart/accademia/

Campo della Carita, ☎ *415-522-2247.*

Metro Stop: *Accademia.*

🕐 *9 a.m.–7 p.m.*

Special Hours: *Sun. open only until 1 p.m.*

Housed in the former Convent and Church of Santa Maria della Carita, the Accademia is a cornucopia of painterly riches (about 500 of them) from the 14th through the 17th centuries. You'll find works by Bellini, Giorgione, Titian, Tintoretto, Canova, Tiepolo and Vivarini, as well as of lesser Venetian artists and foreign artists who settled here. It is so popular that for security reasons only 180 visitors are allowed in at the same time. You might have to wait, but do come anyway. Admission: varies.

Museo Correr

📧 *Piazza San Marco,* ☎ *41-552-5625.*

Metro Stop: *San Marco.*

🕐 *9 a.m.–5 p.m.*

Special Hours: *Sun. 9:30 a.m.–12:30 p.m.*

This museum covers Venetian life and art from 1300 to 1700. There's a section devoted to the Bellini family, and the piece de resistance is Vittore Carpaccio's "Two Venetian Ladies" (The Courtesans).

Nightlife
Dance Clubs

Four suggestions: (1) the **Casino** at the Lido, (2) **Chez Vous** at the Excelsior-Lido, offering all-out competition, (3) a drink, a dance, or a pitch at the **Antico Martini** or (4) go to bed with a good book. Pleasant dinner dancing on the **Bauer-Grunwald** roof in season only. Venetians usually end their evenings (in summer) sitting outdoors in piazza San Marco—far more entertaining, in my view, than any nightclub could ever be.

Shopping

Buyers will find that this lodestone is teeming with guides, concierges, gondoliers and other fast operators hungry for commissions on their purchases. The usual bite is 20 percent to 25 percent on glass and 15 percent on lace. Don't tell anyone where you're going, inform the shopkeeper immediately that nobody directed you to his establishment (except a guidebook or other disinterested source), that you're paying cash and that you want the above scale of discounts for yourself.

To counter the fringe operators, the Chamber of Commerce and the legitimate old-line merchants, such as those mentioned below, set up the **Venetian Crafts Association** to attest to both product quality and business ethics among its members. Be sure to look for the Association's four-leaf-clover symbol displayed in all these companies.

Glass

We suggest that you avoid the island of **Murano** and the swindlers or seamier merchants throughout Venice itself and do 100 percent of your buying only in one of the oldest, largest and soundest houses— **Pauly & Co.** (*Ponte dei Consorzi, 3 branches in piazza San Marco*).This establishment is impeccably honest and reliable; glitters with beauty and is as much a part of the Venetian spectator's scene as the Square, the gondolas and the cathedral.

The venerable **Pauly & Co.** products have won 25 Gold Medals, 16 Notable Award Prizes, 33 Award Diplomas, the French Legion of Honor, the Crown of Leopold and the Crown of Italy. In their archives, you'll find more than 800-thousand one-of-a-kind sketches of antique, classical and modern patterns. A team of celebrated Glass Masters create exclusively for them. At their Ponte dei Consorzi headquarters there is a demonstration furnace and budget shop on the ground floor; upstairs you may wander through perhaps 20 glorious rooms full of treasures for the table, the home and the eye.

They guarantee safe arrival to your home of everything they ship—and you can absolutely trust them on this. But have limitless patience about shipment delays (months are par for the course, due to Italian export red tape and the monumental backlog snarls at U.S. docks)—and be sure to find out approximate delivery costs to your area, because port brokers' fees are sometimes wicked through no fault of these good artisans. Please remember that nobody is permitted to pay U.S. Customs duties and handling before our American officials can evaluate these foreign purchases upon entry, so it is impossible for this company to estimate the levy accurately.

Venetian Jewelry

In quality, in fame, in the distinction of its worldwide clientele who seek these treasures, the unchallenged King of this City of Palaces is **Nardi** (*piazza San Marco 68-71*). Since 1920 it has specialized in designing and creating exquisite bijous in gold and precious stones, all handmade and all signed as originals with the famed Nardi name. Full line of gems, including impressive antiques; the shop at No. 68 contains exceptionally fine rarities; at No. 71 there are hard semiprecious stones and watches (especially Piaget); no purchase tax ever. Ask for the knowledgeable Mr. Sergio Nardi, or for Messrs. Semenzato or Zambon.

Jesurum

✉ *Ponte Canonica 4310,* ☎ *45-520-6177.*

☞ *Behind St. Mark's Basilica*

Metro Stop: *San Zaccaria.*

🕐 *9:30 a.m.–7:30 p.m.*

Special Hours: *Sun. 10 a.m.–7 p.m.*

Famous for its lace, lingerie, delicate embroidery and boudoir fashions; this lovely old palace is brimming over with layettes, wedding veils, tablecloths and placemats. Don't miss the antique lace collection! There's a branch in Milan (via Verri) and one in Parma (via G. Tommasini 6). Although expensive in the main, the shop also sells special towels, napkins, pin cushions and such that are not so costly and make terrific gifts.

Nardi

✉ *Piazza San Marco 68-71,* ☎ *45-523-2150.*

Metro Stop: *San Marco.*

🕐 *9 a.m.–7 p.m.*

Special Hours: *Closes 12:30 p.m.–3 p.m. daily except Mon.; closed Sun.*

Here you'll find exquisite bijous in gold and precious stones, all handmade and signed as originals with the famed Nardi name. There is a full line of gems, including impressive antiques. The shop at No. 68 contains exceptionally fine rarities; at No. 71 there are hard semi precious stones and watches (especially Piaget).

Pauly & Co.

✉ *Ponte dei Consorzi, three branches in piazza Sa,* ☎ *45-520-9899.*

Metro Stop: *San Zaccaria.*

🕐 *9 a.m.–7 p.m.*

Special Hours: *Sun. open only until 1 p.m.*

For glass, there is no other place to go. This establishment glitters with beauty and is as much a part of the Venetian spectator scene as the Square, the gondolas and the cathedral. There are some 25-30 salons exhibiting varied designs for all tastes in a grand palazzo. Includes demonstration of glass firing.

Rialto Bridge

Metro Stop: *Rialto.*

The ancient Rialto district, which is still the busiest part of Venice, cannot be seen or experienced except by foot. Even if you are prepared to spend a small fortune to travel via gondola or vaporetto, take advantage of the filled-in streets and see the city by foot. Start at the 16th-century shop-lined Rialto Bridge spanning the Grand Canal, making sure you stop to survey all the activity below on the waterway. On either side of this landmark are numerous grand palazzos, many new municipal buildings and, always, crowds of Venetians buying and selling food, leather goods and other products. This is also where you'll find the colorful daily marketplace early in the morning. Besides its amazing display of fruit and vegetables, this district is also the Orchard Street of Venice, with clothing, souvenirs and accessories of varying quality. Some wonderful bargains await, but beware of knockoffs of trademark names. The Castello Market, on via Garibaldi, is also fine for produce and provisions.

Union of Venetian Artistic Artisans

✉ *Calle Larga San Marco 412/13.*

Metro Stop: *San Marco.*

Just behind the piazza San Marco, this is an exposition-sales outlet for some of the best local talent in all media, from glass and wood to the elegance of a local Countess' brilliant frames tipped in silver and brass. Vast variety and excellent prices. Look out for the four-leaf clover insignia displayed by participants.

Vogini

✉ *Four shops on four corners of San Marco-Ascension,*

☎ *45-522-2573.*

☞ *Near Harry's Bar.*

Metro Stop: *San Marco.*

🕐 *9 a.m.–7:30 p.m.*

Fine-quality shoes, boots, purses, attache cases, and a line of travel paraphernalia, in case yours have worn out. The prices are stunning values compared to those in the United States.

NETHERLANDS

The Netherlands is such a tiny country that South Carolina covers twice as much ground; multiply the population of Brooklyn roughly by five and you'll have every living being within its borders.

The **Dutch climate** is on a par with Ireland's. It's about as unattractive for year-round living as London or New York. There is a fair amount of sunshine—witness the phenomenal growth of a wide variety of plants—but when it's not raining, you can bet a guilder to a *dubbeltje* that it's foggy from the sea. The average humidity is high; February through May are the driest months.

Holland—as if you didn't know—is famous for its many flowers, which bloom until late fall. The best season is April to mid-May. The village of **Boskoop**, with 700 nurseries, is the largest horticultural center in the world. **Aalsmeer**, 10 mi / 16 km from Amsterdam, has weekday floral auctions that draw scores of fascinated tourists, plus a vast facility for experimental floristry. Within 20 mi / 32 km of **The Hague**, the court capital, is the tulip center. Don't miss the **Keukenhof Flower Exhibition** if you're in Holland around the end of March through mid-May (dates subject to weather). It's a comfortable afternoon expedition from Amsterdam.

The finest trip in Holland—one of the most stimulating holidays in Europe—is the **IJsselmeer circuit** with a stop off at the wild and beautiful island of **Texel** in the above-mentioned **Flevoland**.

If you're driving an automobile, you can make the circle in one day of hard pushing—omitting Texel, of course. The short, quick circle, however, is not recommended because the pace will knock you out. If you can spare two days, you must still skip Texel; in this case, the best places to spend the night are the **Hotel Wientjes** or the **Postiljon Motel**, both in **Zwolle** (or perhaps at the **Olde Brugge** in nearby **Kampen**). Though deep in the rural district, they have comfortable accommodations. If you can spare three or even four days, you are in for a junket you'll never forget, for here's the real heart of Holland.

Three points to remember: (1) The Texel ferry accepts automobiles only on a first-come, first-served basis; (2) sailings from Den Helder to Texel depart at least once an hour year-round; and (3) waiting times in midsummer and during public holidays can be irksome and long.

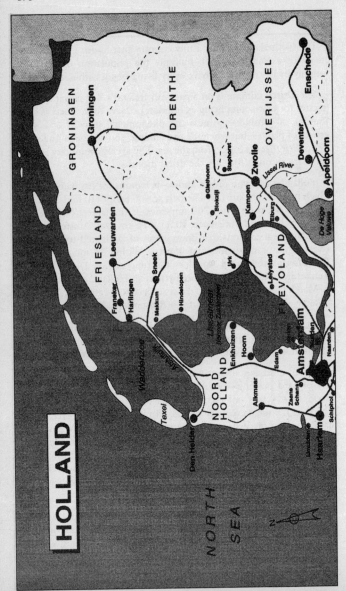

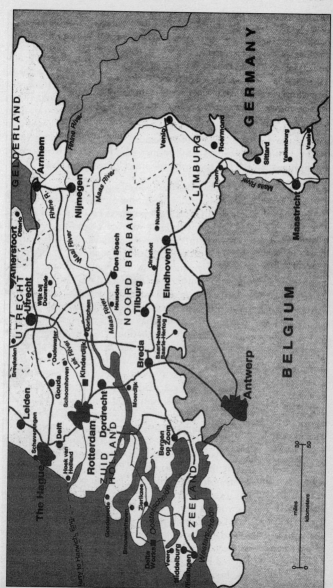

At the western flank of this crescent are the classic tourist meccas of **Marken** (closed to auto traffic but with parking lots at the fringe) and **Volendam**. At centers like these, try to arrive early or late before the buses herd in. The jumble of colorful houses, costumes and streets is worth attempting to see. If your timing is wrong, go to **Spakenburg** instead; it's in the middle of the crescent heading east out of Amsterdam. Here's a hamlet where the folk dress and charm are far more genuine. Customary hours for wearing these togs is on Sundays around church-meeting time. Or go on from **Zwolle** to **Giethoorn** (called "The Dutch Venice," but the residents seldom don costumes nowadays), the former island of **Urk**, **Rouveen** or **Staphorst**. In the last trio, folk still preen in historic finery.

Again, if you have a car, there are lots of sights to see in the more populated zones roughly within the Amsterdam-Rotterdam-Utrecht triangle. Whiz down to **Gouda** (pronounced HOW-da) to see **the plaza** surrounding the **Town Hall** with its contrasting red-and-white shutters and gold trim. You can sip coffee in the 400-year-old **Hotel de Zalm**, on the periphery of the main square, before pushing on to **Oudewater**. Here men and women can be weighed on the town scales. Those who register even one ounce more than the minimum for a true mortal are given a certificate declaring they are not warlocks or witches (who are presumed to weigh less than normal women). The tiny canalside path that ambles through Oudewater and stretches on to **Utrecht** is charming. Skim along east to **Soesterberg** for lunch before viewing the **Royal Palace** at nearby **Soestdijk**. Then a one-hour detour to **Muiden**, site of the beautifully preserved 13th-century fortress of the same name, is rewarding (but be sure to check on the exact closing time before leaving your hotel because it varies with the season). You could drive farther east to **Otterlo**, where there are 300 or so Van Gogh paintings or drawings plus those of other noted artists and a lovely sculpture garden at the **Kroller-Muller Museum**. A pause here should occupy the better part of a day. As for other rambles, **Zandvoort Beach** is passable. Except for the memorabilia of the **Pilgrim Fathers**, the **university** and the **ethnological museum**, **Leiden** is nothing special. **The Hague** has excellent museums. The lively beach resort of **Scheveningen** is worth a trip, as is the fairy-tale wonder for children and adults alike: **Madurodam**, the most amazing miniature city in existence. This modern-day Lilliput, condensed into approximately four acres / two hectares, employing 2-1/4 mi / 3.5 km of railway track and illuminated by **50,000 lights**, is a complete community of castles, churches, homes, shops, docks, airport—everything imaginable. And the thousands of details are a perfect 1/25 of their normal scale. More than 1 million visitors promenade its two-mi./three-km circuit annually. It's open from late March to December, the times varying slightly with the seasons. A restaurant is on the premises; don't miss this unique attraction, whether you're seven, 17 or 70. Rotterdam, slightly more than an hour from Amsterdam, has some glorious river views and some excellent harbor installations. Try the **VVV Historic Tram and Boat Tour**, operating daily from April through September, which costs about $10 per person. It fans out from the VVV Office. Or try one of the well-known **Spido** cruises of the fabulous docks—1-1/4 hours on the briny with frequent departures in both summer and winter from the Willemsplein Landing Stage. Day excursions to the awesome Delta works are also available. Amsterdam's **Holland International** fleet is excellent, too, for *rondvaart* canal tours; clean boats with fine visibility; and frequent departures. As another choice, spins by car to the Mill District have been inaugurated. The **Blijdorp Zoo** is perhaps the most modern in Europe.

Transportation

Airline

The **KLM** (http://www.klm.com/travel_en/splash.jsp) service is legendary, whether across the Atlantic, around Europe or globally. It remains one of my favorite carriers, and each new flight reconfirms my feelings. In addition its major gateway, Schiphol Airport at Amsterdam, is possibly the finest anywhere on earth (actually it is below sea level, and ships ride higher than the neighboring aircraft). KLM pays a lot of attention to children—from airborne minors (Junior Jet Lounge) to tots who need supervision in the VIB Lounge (Very Important Baby, of course). You can rest, shower, nap, pray, sip, dine or even book a tour and a minicruise with KLM. A train is available from the plane as Schiphol has a rail link to Amsterdam Centraal Station. Train runs from Schiphol operate to RAI and Amstel termini and to southeast Amsterdam. You can ride by rail from the airport into the city or link into the Euro-Express system to continue from Holland to any major hub on the Continent.

If you want to create your own personal travel package, ask KLM to send you its *Europe by Design* kit, which tailors your travel program and your budget to a do-it-yourself scheme of selections. It is a clever and interesting money-saver, but available only to you if you begin your journey from the United States—so be sure to request the information early. KLM offers a fine shuttle-bus service to a number of hotels in town. There are two lines (Orange and Yellow), so inquire locally as to which one may take you to your doorstep.

Taxis

You'll find it difficult to hail a cab; head for a taxi rank instead or for the nearest telephone.

Trains

Electric trains and intercity expresses run from Amsterdam to The Hague every quarter hour; some have coffee bars. "D" trains have adequate dining cars and charge an inexpensive supplement. It takes *Schiphollyn* only 30 minutes to link The Hague with Schiphol Airport. There are also night runs hourly linking major towns with Schiphol.

Watch out for the inland one-day excursion ticket because the return half expires as soon as the last train on the timetable of that night pulls out. The publication *Touring Holland by Rail*, available at the sales window of any station, has further information about this.

The best bet for serious riders (unless you have your Eurailpass) is the seven-day Rover ticket, which is valid all over the Netherlands Railways network.

Food

Dutch breakfasts—which generally are included in your hotel bill—offer a choice of various breads, butter, cheese (always), tea or coffee, a boiled egg and meat. The famous "Dutch Coffee Table" (sometimes a warm dish, then cold meats, cheese, fruits and beverage) is the national lunch.

Try minced beef *(rolpens)* with fried apples and, in winter, curly cabbage and sausage, hotchpotch *(hutspot)* and that famous, wonderful pea soup.

Some specialties of the Netherlands are herring (try *Hollandse*

Nieuwe—"new" herring; springtime gives it a special flavor that is not present other months), smoked eels (excellent) and other fish; cheese; Deventer gingerbread, currant bread, small sugared fritters *(poffertjes);* mouth-melting chocolate (Droste and Van Houten are the best); a special caramel candy *(Haagse Hopjes)* and an unusual egg-flip concoction *(Advocaat)*. Most of them are delicious.

As you travel, watch for the red-white-and-blue tureen symbol with the lettering **Neerlands Dis**, which means you are at a restaurant where Dutch specialties are featured at reasonable prices. Every province has several participants. Only Dutch ingredients are employed in the cooking, the selections alter with the seasons, and the fraternity carefully monitors quality and service. Over the years I have sampled about half of those listed nationwide (the VVV can provide a brochure on the entire group), and they indeed were agreeable for the medium price level.

Something no traveler should miss is the spice-blessed *rijsttafel* (pronounced "ryestaffel" and translated as "rice table"). This was the ceremonial feast of the Dutch colonists in Indonesia. It might contain as many as 25 small dishes for sampling. If you fear internal combustion, ask your waiter to indicate which are the super-hot sauces that are delivered with the platters.

If you're hungry at an odd hour of the day, try an *Uitsmijter* sandwich (translated as "Bouncer"). It's made with either roast beef, ham or veal, with lots of trimmings and a fried egg on top.

Drinks

Beer, of course, is the everyday beverage. Heineken and Amstel lead the parade. If you are looking for a tasty signature brand still made in the old steam process, try Gulpener.

Dutch gin *(jenever)* is for more refined taste buds. It's colorless, volatile, aromatic, slightly bitter—a flavor you'll find in no other bottle in no other land. The "Oude Klare" is stronger (80 proof) and has greater distinction than the more popular and lighter "Jonge" (70 proof), which compares vaguely to a vodka. A popular brand is "Bokma." Drink it from a shot glass; when you blow out your breath, be careful of that stranger's cigarette 20 feet away. (If proper form is followed, it will be served instead in a "tulip" glass— and your first sip must be slurped while the glass rests on the bar!) Bokma, incidentally, can be obtained anywhere. When you think you've graduated from that class, move on to the rarer "Corenwyn Bols," served ideally ice cold.

The liqueurs, more than 40 varieties, are interesting. Hansje in de Kelder is an herbal, rose-tinted delight. "Hansje" is a girl's name, and this means she is in the cellar, a story extending through 14 different drinks, each with its own yarn about the exploits of this little Dutch maid. Ask for this one—or for Bols or Hoppe products, which are dependable, while some imitations are not.

When the drinks are on you, say, "Let's have a borrel!" It's the universal Dutch invitation.

The historical national toast is Op uw gezondheid, which means "To your good health." Most Dutch settle for a simple *Proost* before the elbow bends, and a few use an affected *Sante*, derived from the French.

Since brewers usually are given exclusive contracts, most Dutch restaurants sell only one brand of beer.

CURRENCY: Euros.

Tipping

Hotels take 15 percent automatically, so there's no need to tip more unless you feel expansive. Waiters get 15 percent (also always included in your bill). Theater ushers and washroom attendants usually receive a guilder, but one might get away with 50 cents. A law bundles the gratuity into the hairdresser's chit. Taxi additives are 10 percent if you are feeling generous.

Telephone

Access code to USA: 09 (dial tone).

To telephone Netherlands: 31; time difference: Eastern Daylight plus six hours. Amsterdam telephone numbers went up to seven digits recently by adding a "6" to the beginning.

For More Information

The Netherlands Board of Tourism (NBT)
http://www.holland.com/

355 Lexington Ave., 21st Floor, New York, NY 10017, ☎ *(212) 370-7360;*

90 New Montgomery St., Suite 305, San Francisco, CA 94105, ☎ *(415) 543-6772;*

225 N. Michigan Ave., Suite 326, Chicago IL 60601, ☎ *(312) 819-0300.*

Working with the NBT are more than 400 local offices called VVV, one bureau for every Dutch hamlet. They are wonderful!

In Amsterdam VVV is located opposite the Central Station and at Leidsestraat 106. In Rotterdam it's at Coolsingel 67 and another booth at the Central Station. The Hague is served by an office out at neighboring Scheveningen, at Gevers Deynootweg 126 and, also, at the Central Station.

Central

Utrecht

Utrecht, fourth ranking in population, is the geographic center; it's one of the oldest cities in the land. As one typical example of its modern thinking, a huge construction program has modernized the rail center, developed a trade-fair site, filled in two major canals and incorporated a new hotel and business buildings into a melded metropolitan scheme. Its Hoog Catharijne shopping center shouldn't be missed by anyone with an interest in urban planning. The famous industrial fair is in March and September. Among museums: one called "From Music Clock to Barrel Organ"; the Central, with ancient and modern works; and the Railway are the best-known of its 15 candidates. In addition eight castle museums are within Utrecht Province. The cathedral is magnificent; the *Vismarkt* (fish market) is unusual.

Where to Stay

Auberge De Hoefslag ★★★
Budget to Moderate

8 Vossenlaan, Bosch en Duin.

☎ *(30) 25-10-51.*

Credit Cards: *All Major.*

Located in a wooded area a few minutes from downtown Utrecht, this country-house hotel offers a welcome alternative to the usual commercial establishments. In cold weather the homey lobby welcomes guests with the warmth of a fireplace. Each of the 38 rooms is different and furnished in English country style. The four suites each have a living room plus a private balcony or terrace. Amenities in all rooms include cable TV, minibar and private bath with hair dryer. Guests can stroll in the gardens or relax in comfortable chairs under the cedar trees. The restaurant enjoys an enviable reputation among locals and returning guests. Drinks are served in the cozy bar. There's also a small meeting/conference room that seats 24 people. Closed Dec.30–Jan. 1.

Malie Hotel ★★★

http://www.hampshirehotels.nl/maliehotel/

Budget

Maliestraat 2.

☎ *(30) 31-64-24.*

Credit Cards: *All Major.*

Located in two adjacent 19th-century buildings on a quiet street off the fashionable Maliebaan, the Malie offers personalized service and a change of pace for business travelers and visitors alike. The 62 rooms are spacious and modern but are devoid of any space-age gadgets save a color TV and telephone. All rooms have attractive private baths and lots of fluffy towels. A sunny breakfast room overlooks a secluded garden in the rear of the building. The Malie has a snug bar but no dining room. Worth exploring, the surrounding neighborhood has a pleasant combination of chic and hip.

Where to Eat

De Hoefslag ★★★★

Moderate

Vossenlaan 28, Bosch en Duin. ☎ *(030) 784-395.*

Credit Cards: *V, MC.*

A top-rated restaurant for cultivated continental cuisine, highlighting seafood and game. Located on wooded grounds, this old coaching inn attracts customers from miles around. The menu changes daily according to the freshest buys at the market. Dark wood and an open hearth create the opulence of an aristocratic hunting lodge.

Het Draeckie
Moderate

Oude Gracht 114-118. ☎ *(030) 321-999.*

A unique and memorable restaurant fashioned in a canalside vaulted cellar. The food, like the location, is authentically Dutch. Seasonal specialties tempt the palate, and you can't go wrong with the grills or the prized cheese fondue.

What to Do
Historical Sites

Neighboring castles

If castles are your passion, Utrecht is the place to be. Formerly the most important medieval city of the north, the remaining castles stand testimony to the wealth and power of the region. **De Haar—** *Kasteellaan 1, Haarzuilens,* ☎ *(030) 03407/1275,* is one of the impressive castles. The 15th- century stronghold has been restored to its original splendor. Now a private residence, it is also open to the public for viewing of the valued art and furnishings. **Kasteel Sypesteyn—***Nieuw Loosdrechtsedijk 150, Nieuw Loosdrecht,* ☎ *(030) 02158/3208.* This fine castle is now a museum with a wide collection of 16th-, 17th- and 18th- century paintings. Pottery, glassware, porcelain, silver, furniture and weapons of the period are also on display.

Museums and Exhibits

Dutch Railway Museum
Maliebaan station. ☎ *(030) 306206.*

🕙 *10 a.m.–5 p.m.*

Special Hours: *Sun. open at 1 p.m.; closed Mon.*

150 years of rail history are on parade at this former railway station. More than 60 steam engines, carriages and wagons, plus moving models, paintings and films that document the history and technological progression of the railway in Holland. Admission: inexpensive.

Het Catharijneconvent ★

Nieuwe Gracht 63. ☎ *(030) 313-835.*

🕐 *10 a.m.–5 p.m.*

Special Hours: *Sat., Sun., holidays open at 11 a.m.*

Tracing the development of Christianity in Holland from the eighth to the 20th century, this museum is appropriately located in Utrecht, the ecclesiastical center of Holland. The collection includes a wealth of medieval art, religious paintings, sculpture, breviaries, church vestments, manuscripts and relics. Admission: inexpensive.

North

Haarlem

Haarlem, with 155,000 population, has its points for some sightseers: the **Frans Hals Museum, a great cathedral** (St. Bavo with its famous organ), pure Dutch architecture, colorful gardens and the beach resort of **Zandvoort**.

Where to Stay

Golden Tulip Lion d'Or ★★

Moderate

34-36 Kruisweg. *Located 15 km from Schiphol Airport*

☎ *(23) 32-17-50,* FAX: *344.1212.*

Credit Cards: *All Major.*

With its neat gray-and-white paint, pristine white awnings and a mansard roof with dormer windows, the Lion d'Or exudes the air of a venerable institution. Concientiously maintained, it was recently renovated in 1993 without sacrificing the hotel's historic atmosphere. The 36 rooms are outfitted with color cable TV and private bath or shower. The hotel houses a restaurant and coffee shop.

Where to Eat

Cafe Restaurant Brinkman ★

Inexpensive

Grote Market.

A pleasant restaurant with a view of the Grote Market and a wide selection of affordable meals. Candlelight, greenery, stained glass and Delft tile soothe the ambience of this art nouveau continental cafe. Choose from sandwiches, *uitsmijters*, pasta, salad or quiche, relax and enjoy the expansive beauty of the square.

Restaurant Peter Cuyper ★★

Moderate

Kleine Houstraat 70.

A 16th-century town house and courtyard provide a sophisticated establishment for a leisurely affair. The chef has combined *nouvelle* and classic French cooking styles with the freshest local Dutch food such as salmon and lamb. The chocolate comes from Haarlem's own factory. Fresh cut flowers and romantic lighting from candles and copper lamps cast a lovely glow on the meal.

What to Do
Historical Sites

St. Bavo's/Grote Kerk ★★★

Oude Groenmarkt 23. ☎ *(023) 324399.*

🕐 *10 a.m.–4 p.m.*

Special Hours: *Closed Sun.*

The elegant, medieval square where the Grote Market resides has been called the "living room of Haarlem." Soaring above the square is Grote Kerk, the immense Gothic church built between 1390 and

1520. The entrance is lined with Delft tile, the pulpit is carved oak with brass handrails in the shape of snakes. The prized Mueller organ, built in 1978, utilizes more than 5000 pipes and has been graced by the hands of Handel and Mozart. Free organ concerts are offered Tues. at 8:15 p.m. May–Sept. and Thurs. at 3 p.m. July and Aug.

Museums and Exhibits

Frans Hals Museum
▢ *Groot Heigland 62.* ☎ *(023) 319180.*

🕐 *11 a.m.–5 p.m.*

Special Hours: *Sun. and holidays open at 1 p.m.; closed Christmas*

A magnificent collection of works, primarily from the 17th century, Holland's Golden Age. Originally a home for old men, where Hals spent his final years, the town house has been restored with gardens, a courtyard and an exquisite marble corridor lined with blue-and-white tiles. Such details enhance the viewing of Hals' paintings alongside other Dutch artists as well as period furniture, Haarlem silver and ceramics and an elaborate dollhouse.

Teylers Museum ★★
▢ *Sparne 16.* ☎ *(023) 319010.*

🕐 *10 a.m.–5 p.m.*

Special Hours: *Sun. open at 1 p.m.; closed Mon.*

This is the Netherlands' oldest museum, founded in 1788 by a silk merchant with an eclectic assortment of art and artifacts. Teylers pays homage to the Age of Enlightenment, displaying a wild collection of fossils, minerals, instruments of the scientist and alchemist, paintings and drawings. The works of Michelangelo, Raphael, Rembrandt, Correggio and Claude Lorraine are represented. The only lighting is natural light.

West

Amsterdam

The city is well over 700 years old, but it is younger than ever in spirit. A cleanup campaign is responsible for neater parks, but so many dropouts from foreign lands seem to live on the streets that the metropolis is finding it difficult to maintain the traditional levels of Dutch sparkle and gleam. There are plenty of fine restaurants and nightclubs; attractions such as the magnificent museums (see below); **Rembrandt's House; Royal Palace;** the **Concertgebouw** for symphonic music; the **Music Theatre,** which is home for opera and ballet; the **Anne Frank House**; historical maritime and aviation displays; diamond-cutting workshops; and the **House of the Sculptured Heads**—a wonderful panorama of color and beauty.

Where to Stay

American Hotel   ★★★★

Moderate to Expensive

Leidskade 97.

☎ *(20) 624-5322.*

Credit Cards: *All Major.*

Located in the heart of Leidseplein Square, the American, which is now run by the Crowne Plaza, has been a fixture on the Amsterdam scene for more than a century. The building, despite periodic renovations, retains the feel of a bygone era. The 188 rooms are relatively large and decorated with floral prints. Most rooms have comfortable chairs, perfect to relax in while reading a paper or watching TV. In summer the best rooms are the ones with balconies on the canal side. Amenities include minibars, cable TVs and private baths with hair dryers. The Cafe Americain is a holdover from the art nouveau era and is worth seeing for its vaulted ceilings and etched glass. For years it's been a gathering place for writers, journalists and other literati. The cafe offers a pleasant compromise between the formal dining room and the more mundane coffee shop. Even if you don't stay here, stroll through the lobby to admire the architecture—the building has been declared a national monument. Adjacent to the entertainment district, the hotel also offers the cozy Night Watch bar, which is a good choice for a pre- or post- theater drink.

Amstel Inter-Continental

Very Expensive

Professor Tulpplein 1.

☎ *(20) 622-6060*, FAX: *327.0200*.

Credit Cards: *All Major.*

Dubbed by faithful clientele as "the second queen of the Netherlands," the Amstel Intercontinental is located on the banks of the Amstel River. The 79 rooms and suites are furnished with Dutch and English antiques, and many of the fabrics and rugs have been custom-woven for the hotel. In- room VCRs and CD players are provided, and the hotel maintains a library of tapes and and discs for guests' use. Business travelers will appreciate the computer/fax hookups as well as the large desks and tables. Two butlers on every floor ensure that room service is practically instantaneous. Most rooms have exceptional river views, while the two penthouse apartments offer nearly 360-degree views of the city. Transportation for guests is provided for by a fleet of limousines, but those who prefer to travel the canals can enjoy a ride on a turn-of-the-century motor launch resplendent with polished teak and brass fixtures.

Garden Hotel ★★★

Expensive

Dijsselhofplantsoen 7.

☎ *(20) 664-2121.*

Credit Cards: *All Major.*

Located on a canal opposite the Amsterdam Hilton, the Garden Hotel offers the jet-lagged traveler an alternative to its larger and more commercial neighbor. The hotel bar offers live jazz and is a mecca for local aficionados. The 98 rooms are well proportioned and were renovated in 1991. Amenities include cable TV, minibar and, best of all, modern bath with private Jacuzzi. The hotel offers 24-hour room service. This small hotel has a loyal clientele, making reservations a must.

Hotel de L'Europe ★★★★★
Very Expensive

Nieuwe Doelenstraat 2-8.

☎ *(20) 623-4836.*

Credit Cards: *All Major.*

For many years this was THE hotel in Amsterdam, but now the L'Europe faces heavy competition from the newly renovated Amstel Inter-Continental. The hotel building dates from the late 1880s' and the exterior is a red-and-white version of Dutch gingerbread. The 100 luxurious guest rooms and 21 suites feature color TV, VCR, minibar, marble bath with phone, bathrobe and hair dryer. Some rooms have balconies, and a number of suites have private Jacuzzis. Dining and entertainment facilities include two restaurants. The acclaimed **Excelsior Restaurant** has a wine cellar that boasts 40,000 bottles.

Jan Luyken Hotel & Residence ★★★
Moderate

Jan Luyekenstraat 58.

☎ *(20) 573-0730.*

Credit Cards: *All Major.*

Owned and operated by the Van Schaik family, the Jan Luyken is popular with travelers who are tired of interchangeable commercial hotels. The hotel building is really three late-19th-century town houses that have been combined. The 63 guest rooms, renovated in 1993, are tastefully decorated in pastel shades. Several rooms have balconies. All rooms feature cable TV, minibars, safes, fax and computer hookups and baths with hair dryers. Breakfast is included in rate. Service here is especially attentive. The Jan Luyken is close to the Rijksmuseum and to good restaurants and boutiques. Meeting and banqueting facilities are provided in the Jan Luyken Residence opposite the hotel.

Where to Eat

Bols Tavern

Moderate

Rozengracht 106. ☎ (020) 624-5752.

Public Transportation: *tram 13, 14, 17.*

Credit Cards: *V, MC, A.*

Most famous as a tasting room where the Dutch gin and liqueurs
run freely, this tavern has now made a name for itself as an enviable
eating establishment as well. Seafood is the main draw, though not
the only choice on the menu. The building remains from the 17th
century, and the decor is a tribute to the sea.

Brown cafes

Inexpensive

Spui 18. ☎ (020) 623-7849.

Public Transportation: *1, 2, 4, 5, 9, 11, 14, 16.*

So named for the tobacco-stained walls and ceilings, these intimate
cafe/bars are on every street corner. These old establishments have
table tops covered with Oriental rugs and sawdust on the wooden
floors. The brown cafes serve beer, Dutch gin and snacks. *Hoppe* is
popular among the multitude of options.

Christophe

Moderate

Leliegracht 46. ☎ (020) 625-0807.

Public Transportation: *Tram 4, 9, 16, 24, 25.*

Credit Cards: *V, MC, DC, A.*

Named after chef Christophe Royer, who hails from Toulouse, this
restaurant counts France among its international influences.
Intriguing specialties include quail risotto with truffles, eggplant terrine with cumin, lobster with sweet garlic, and scallops with orange
and saffron. Crusty bread direct from Paris and a find Provencal-

inspired wine list round out this chic affair nicely.

D'Vijff Vlieghen
Moderate

Spuistraat 294-302. ☎ *(020) 624-8369.*

Public Transportation: *tram 1, 2, 5.*

Credit Cards: *V, MC, DC, A.*

A quintet of 17th-century houses, tilted with age, are the setting for this commendable restaurant. There are seven dining rooms draped in Renaissance flair, yet the tables are constantly full. Although large in size, the restaurant remains intimate, shadowed by candlelight and amiable, personalized service. The menu is a delightful melding of old favorites with *nouvelle* nuances. Some samplings include *watergooi*, roast wild boar stuffed with apples, and veal steak with prunes.

De Keyzer Bodega
Moderate to Expensive

Van Baerlestraat 96. ☎ *(020) 671-1441.*

Public Transportation: *tram 3, 5, 12, 16.*

Credit Cards: *V, MC, A.*

Its popularity is widespread, and its reputation is deserved. Next door to the Concertgebouw, this restaurant caters to the concert going crowd. The clocks are set slightly ahead so diners won't miss the overtures, and there are after-concert hours for late eaters. There is a cozy, traditional tavern in the front with brass lamps, carpeted tables and attentive service. Fish and seasonal game are tastefully prepared. In the back is a fancier dining room with candles, tablecloths and dishes such as *sole a la meuniere*, with an accent on French styles.

Oude Holland
Inexpensive

Nieuwe Zijds Voorburgwal 105. ☎ *(020) 624-6848.*

Public Transportation: *tram 1, 2, 5, 11.*

This landmark restaurant built in the 1600s was a meeting place for journalists in the 1920s. It is infused with their creative spirit as well as spirited, traditional Dutch cooking. Old favorites include hearty pea soup, smoked eel, herring, hotchpotsch, and omelets, all for an affordable price.

Pancake Bakery

Inexpensive

Prinsengract 191. ☎ *(020) 625-1333.*

Near the Anne Frank House is another historic building with a sweeter slant. The Pancake Bakery, one of the best known for this Dutch treat, serves pancakes that rival the size of the long, narrow warehouse. You can have your pancake plain, topped with powdered sugar, filled with ham and cheese, bacon and ginger or chestnuts and whipped cream; or try an *advokaat*, a Dutch egg nog.

Restaurant Adrian   ★

Inexpensive to Moderate

Reguliersdwarstraat 21. ☎ *(020) 623-9582.*

Public Transportation: *tram 16, 24, 25.*

Credit Cards: *V, MC, A.*

This restaurant is located one block from the floating flower market and possesses some of the same natural beauty and simplicity of the colorful flowers. Modest and elegant, this prize restaurant is wholeheartedly French. Candles and a well-laid table lend romance to the exquisite meals. Scallops with red wine and saffron sauce, filet of lamb with thyme, and the choicest fresh vegetables make the plates irresistible.

Sama Sebo

Moderate

P.C. Hoofstraat 27. ☎ *(020) 662-8146.*

Public Transportation: *tram 1, 2, 5, 6.*

Amsterdam is known for its international flavor, and Indonesian food holds out at the forefront. This authentic and spacious restaurant is considered one of the finest. Indonesian artifacts enhance the refreshing decor. Sama Sebo is famous for its *rijsttafel*, a traditional festive meal consisting of as many as 25 meat, seafood or vegetable dishes, served over a mound of steaming rice. Exotic and provocative dishes and a relaxed ambience are the reason for its popularity. Vegetarian meals are available.

What to Do
City Celebrations

Holland Festival ★★★
http://www.hollandfestival.nl/

Nederlands Reservings Centrum, Postbus 404. ☎ *(020) 621-1211.*

An acclaimed and diverse cultural event, the Holland Festival takes place each June. Presenting spectacles of music, dance and drama, the festival hosts a major event each night. Programs include modern dance, ensembles of the Dutch National Ballet, alternative music, the Dutch National Opera, comedic plays and avant- garde theater. There are guest performances by other European companies. Queen's Day on April 30 heralds a celebration in the streets with an all-day carnival. Floating Amsterdam occurs the last two weeks in May, when the length of the Amstel River is transformed into an outdoor stage for productions. The canals in August throb with the Prinsengracht concerts reigning from the boats. On Tuesday in Boekmanzaal and the Muziektheater, and Wednesday in the Concertgebouw, there are free lunch-time concerts from 12:15-1 p.m. The programs range from chamber music to symphonies to previews of full concerts. Admission: varies; inexpensive.

Historical Sites

Anne Frank House ★★★★
http://www.annefrank.nl/ned/ default2.html

Prinsengracht 263. ☎ *(020) 556-7100.*

Public Transportation: *Tram 13, 14, 17 to Westermarkt.*

🕐 *9 a.m.–5 p.m.*

Special Hours: *Sun. and holidays open at 10 a.m.; closed Dec. 25,*

For two years of the Nazi Occupation during World War II, this 17th-century canalside house was a refuge for Anne Frank, her family and four friends. They were sequestered in the annex from 1942 to 1945, during which time 13-year-old Anne Frank kept her diary of the endless days spent often in silence and fear. Eventually they were found and sent to concentration camps. The only survivor was her father, who later published the diary. Today the house is still barren, an echo of the Nazi destruction. Only the bookcase concealing the entrance to the annex remains. The museum is managed by the Anne Frank Foundation, which is dedicated to combating racism, discrimination and oppression. The house stands as witness to a sober moment in history and is a reminder of the injustices suffered.

Koninklijk Paleis (Royal Palace)   ★★★
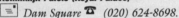 *Dam Square* ☎ *(020) 624-8698.*

Public Transportation: *All city-center trams.*

🕐 *12:30 p.m.–5 p.m.*

When this palace was built in 1648, Amsterdam was considered the richest city in the world. The scale and grandeur of the structure reflect the pride of the times. About 13,000 wooden pilings support the free-standing sandstone building in the soft, brackish soil. Designed by Jacob van Campen and originally built as the Town Hall, the palace took on its royal role in 1808 when Napoleon's brother Louis was made king of Holland. The palace is still officially the royal dwelling, although the queen and her family reside in The Hague. Admission: inexpensive.

Nieuwe Kerk   ★★★

http://www.nieuwekerk.nl/html/de_nieuwe_kerk_dhtml_uk.html

Dam Square, across from the Royal Palace. ☎ *(020) 626-8168.*

Public Transportation: *All city-center trams.*

🕐 *11 a.m.–4 p.m.*

Special Hours: *Sun. open noon-2 p.m.; closed Feb.*

Hardly new, despite its name, this Gothic church was begun in 1408 because Oude Kerk was not large enough to hold the entire congregation. This cruciform basilica has an ambulatory and radiating chapels, a vaulted nave and a polygonal choir gallery. The architecture is imposing and impressive, as is the carved pulpit and elaborately painted organ cases. The cathedral has been the site of the inauguration of Dutch monarchs since 1815—Queen Beatrix was crowned here in 1980. Nieuwe Kerk houses the sepulchers of many Dutch poets and naval heroes. Organ concerts are held in the cathedral.

Rembrandt's House   ★★★
http://www.rembrandthuis.nl/ index_eng.html

Jodenbreestraat 4-6. ☎ *(020) 624-9486.*

Public Transportation: *tram 9 to Mr. Visserplein.*

🕐 *10 a.m.–5 p.m.*

Special Hours: *Sun. and holidays open at 1 p.m.; closed Jan. 1*

The masterpieces may hang at the Rijksmuseum, but the substantial part of Rembrandt's legacy is on display in his former home. Low-level lighting and the allure of a three-story house gallery make this an intimate experience. Self-portraits and hundreds of etchings take the visitor on a pilgrimage through the daily routines and the sublime life of Rembrandt. His creative spirit envelops his home and studio. Also on display are paintings by Rembrandt's teacher and his students, which lend depth and add dialogue to Rembrandt's work. Admission: varies.

Museums and Exhibits

Rijksmuseum Amsterdam
http://www.rijksmuseum.nl/

Stadhouderskade 42, on Museumplein. ☎ *(020) 637-2121.*

Public Transportation: *tram 2, 5.*

🕐 *10 a.m.–5 p.m.*

Special Hours: *Sun. and holidays open at 1 p.m.*

Amsterdam's most prestigious museum houses the largest collection of Dutch paintings in the world. The neo-Renaissance building is vast and impressive, and one could spend days exploring treasure-filled halls. European masters are contained under one roof, including artworks by Frans Hals, Vermeer, Steen, Nicholas Maes, de Hooch, Jacob van Ruisdael, Gerard Dou, Paulus Potter, Goya, Rubens, Fra Angelico and Van Dyck. Rembrandt's "The Night Watch," the pride of the museum, has its own room. The painting was misnamed though, because after a restorative cleaning, a scene depicted in broad daylight was revealed under layers of grime. In addition to the magnificent paintings, there is a fine collection of prints, Delftware, glassware, furniture, Asiatic art, French and Flemish tapestries, Dutch and German sculpture and doll-houses. Admission: varies.

Stedelijk Museum   ★★★★★
http://www.stedelijk.nl/

Paulus Potterstraat 13, on Museumplein. ☎ *(020) 537-2911.*

Public Transportation: *tram 2, 5, 16.*

🕐 *11 a.m.–5 p.m.*

Ranked among the most prestigious modern art museums of the world, the Stedelijk presents all schools of the avant-garde. The displays highlight the stages of classicism, impressionism, cubism, abstract nonrepresentation and pop art. Artists featured include Monet, Manet, Cezanne, Van Gogh, Matisse, Chagall, Picasso, Mondrian, Appel, Calder, Pollock, Warhol, Anslem Keifer and Lichtenstein. Also of note is the sculpture garden and the photography collection. The museum also has a program of films, lectures and performances.

Van Gogh Museum
<http://www.vangoghmuseum.nl/>

Paulus Potterstraat 7-11 on Museumplein. ☎ *(020) 570-5200.*

Public Transportation: *tram 2, 5, 16.*

🕐 *10 a.m.–5 p.m.*

Special Hours: *Sun. and holidays open at 1 p.m.; closed Jan. 1*

A striking collection of 200 paintings, 500 drawings and 700 letters by Van Gogh are housed in this gem of a museum. Although famous worldwide today, the self-taught genius sold only one canvas before committing suicide in 1890. Most of his paintings were created during the five years prior to his death. The art is displayed chronologically so one can study the progression from his early primitive and disciplined works to his later works done in bold colors and violent strokes, signaling his slip deeper into insanity. The museum also houses works of Van Gough's contemporaries, including Gauguin and Toulouse-Lautrec, as well as a "self- expression room" replete with paintbrush, pencil and clay where visitors can exercise their own imaginations.

Music

Music

There are several music venues in Amsterdam. The music scene includes local and international bands. A fine mix of styles and cultures frequents the array of big clubs, intimate bars and concert halls. For world-class performances, spend an evening at **Concertgebouw**, *2–6 Concertgebouwplein,* ☎ *(020) 537-0573*, tickets Dfl 10-175, box office 10 a.m.–7 p.m., tram 2, 3, 5, 12, 16. This concert hall is famous for its superb acoustics. The facade is richly carved in a Greek Revival style. The orchestra gives performances almost every evening, and often programs include guest recitalists and chamber ensembles. Free lunchtime concerts are offered on Wednesday. **Bimhuis**, *73–77 Oude Schans,* ☎ *(020) 623-1361*, dfl 15-25, Mon.–Sat. 8 p.m.–3 a.m. The Dutch Jazz Orchestra plays on Wednesdays, workshops and musicians from all over Europe fill up the other nights. More music options abound at **Melkweg**, *234a Lijnbaangracht,* ☎ *(020) 624-1777*, dfl 5-20, Wed.-Sun. 2 p.m.-midnight. Brimming with popularity, this multifaceted club has a cafe, restaurant, bookshop and gallery. Bands, dance music, films and workshops are a few of the activities to relish.

Nightlife

Plentiful. Everything from Persian Rooms to gay bars, Times Square tourist traps to neighborhood taverns to honkytonks—the galaxy. With the tightening up of legal loopholes in England, France and Germany, Holland has become a haven for nonconformists. In this freewheeling society, narcotics are sold just in the shadow of a doorway and used openly by many. Because of such frequent changes in the after-dark scene, your best bet for up-to-the-minute information is the VVV office opposite the Central Railway Station.

Coffee shops

Since the amendment of the Opium Act in 1976, the use and sale of small amounts of soft drugs are not considered a criminal offense. Consequently, in Amsterdam, "coffee shop" can refer to a place where patrons can buy, sell and consume soft drugs such as marijuana and hashish. The liberal attitude permits the sale of homegrown varieties from around the world. Be warned; however, while coffee shops are designated as the acceptable location, drug consumption is not condoned in the city streets. Also beware of the "space cakes," which are unexpectedly potent for a sweet treat. Exercise good judgment with all purchases. The Grasshopper is one of the most popular coffee shops in town. Rolling papers are free at the bar, and there is plenty of fresh squeezed orange juice, backgammon, music and entertainment for all. The **Grasshopper**, *Nieuwezijds Voorburgwal 57*, Sun.-Thurs. 9 a.m.-midnight, Fri., Sat. 9 a.m.-1 a.m.

Red Light District

Nowhere is the renowned Dutch tolerance more visible than in Walletjes, the Red Light District of Amerersterdam. Prostitutes in their lace-and-leather splendor sit in neon-lit shop windows, creating their personal vignettes as they wait for customers. The world's oldest profession has a unique status in Amsterdam—prostitutes work rotations of six-hour shifts, pay taxes on their wages and undergo routine medical exams. The Red Thread Organization is dedicated to the protection and integrity of the women. Inevitably the district attracts its share of crime and drugs—so stick to the crowded main streets, avoid the street drug dealers and do not photograph the ladies of the night (or day) because you most likely will lose your camera by force. These simple rules should keep you out of trouble.

Parks and Gardens

ITRAVELBOOK FREEBIE

Begijnhof

Begijnhof, off Kalverstraat. *Accessible from the Spui or the Civic Guard Galler.*

Special Hours: *Open daily until sunset.*

This tranquil garden surrounded by almshouses is a sanctuary of charity and humanity. The Sisters of St. Begga, an order devoted to social justice and good works, established the pious community of Begijnhof in 1346. The history of the garden square has been affected by religious oppression. In the courtyard today are a secret Catholic chapel and an English Presbyterian church. House number 34 on the courtyard is Houden Huis. Built in 1475, the structure is Amsterdam's oldest remaining wooden house. Traditionally home to poor widows and Beguine nuns, the Begijnhof almshouses now lodge the city's impoverished senior citizens. Please respect their privacy and quiet after dark.

Shopping

Antiques ★★

Hundreds of antique shops make Amsterdam a shopper's paradise. **Nieuwe Spiegelstraat** offers many of the best and priciest. For cost-conscious browers, the **Jordaan** area has more affordable second-hand ware. Don't neglect the street markets—you never know when you'll find a gem among the junk.

Bloemenmarkt

Along Singel Canal at Muntplein.

On the south side of the Singel Canal is the world's only floating flower market. The spectacular flotilla spans four blocks with stall after stall of moored barges. Under the colorful awnings, bright blossoms, bulbs and potted plants are sold at very low prices. In Holland most occasions prompt the giving of flowers, and it is local practice to always take flowers when visiting a home for the first time. Open Mon.– Sat. 9 a.m.-5 p.m.

Books ★★

Amsterdam is home to numerous bookstores, including many that carry English language books. The **American Booke Center**, *Kalverstraat 185,* ☎ *(020) 625- 5573,* Mon.-Sat. 10 a.m.–9 p.m., Sun. 11 a.m.-7 p.m., has a fine selection of English language publications. **Athenaeum Booksellers**, *Spui 14-16,* ☎ *(020) 622-6248,* has an extensive stock of international magazines, newspapers and books for all interests. Endless paperbacks are for sale at **W.H. Smith**, *Kalverstraat 152,* ☎ *(020) 638- 3821,* daily 11 a.m.-5 p.m. **The Book Market** on *Oudemanhuispoort* between Oudezijds Voorburgwal and Kloveniersburgwal, Mon.-Sat. 10 a.m.-4 p.m., is another place to browse for titles, as is the market on the Spui that has some great secondhand bargains.

Delft ★★

Delftware, the blue-and-white earthenware that is a hallmark of Holland, comes in a million forms. But not every blue-and- white piece is true Delft. Look for works that are signed "Delftware" or "Delft Blue" with a capital "D" or "Makkumware" with a capital "M." These are the authentic crafts from the two most valued factories. Copies usually sport a lowercase "d" or "m." Check out **De Perceleyne Fles** for a fine selection of authentic pottery at *Prinsengracht 170,* ☎ *(020) 622-7509.*

Diamonds ★★★

The Amsterdam diamond "workshops" are world renowned. The high-caliber cutting skills that have kept Amsterdam in the trade since 1586 can be admired at several diamond factories. Tours include a brief history and advice on how to recognize quality stones, including the "Four C's": carat, color, clarity and cut. Visitors can watch craftspeople as they cut, polish or set stones. Stop at the **Amsterdam Diamond Center, Rokin 1**, open daily 9:30

a.m.-5:30 p.m., *(020) 634-5787*. Or visit **Van Moppes** and **Zoon**, *Albert Cuypstraat*, *(020) 676-1242*, 8:30 a.m.-5 p.m., daily.

Flea markets ★

The streets of Amsterdam are famous for their colorful open-air markets. Used clothing, books, sheet music, jewelry, old appliances, antiques, stamps, birds and cut flowers are just a hint of what is to be found in the stalls. The **Waterlooplein** market is one of the most popular, Mon.–Sat. 9 a.m.–5 p.m., as is the market on Albert Cuypstraat. At the **Spui Art Market**, local artists display their works in outdoor galleries along the Spui.

Special Tours

Boat tours ★★

Amsterdam is a city built on the shipping trade. Since its land mass is surrounded by water, boats are the most appropriate way to see the sights. The canals are constructed in a concentric pattern, fanning out from the city center, traversing every neighborhood. A waterside view from a glass-topped canal cruiser takes you right back into the Golden Age of the 17th century. The gabled houses, bridges and placid waterways have a timeless quality. At night the canals are magically illuminated. Narrators keep you informed of landmarks and relevant anecdotes along the way. Tours leave every 30 minutes from various *ronvaart* docks from 8:30 a.m. to 10 p.m.The cost varies, but is generally inexpensive. Operators and departure points: **Holland International**, *(020) 622-7788*, at *Central Station*; **Smits Koffiehuis B.V.** *(020) 623-3777*, at *Stationsplein 10*; **Rederij Lovers B.V.** *(020) 623-4208* from *Damark jetty No. 4–5*; **Rederij Plas C.V.** *(020) 624-5406* from *Damark jetty No. 1–3*. If you prefer to explore the canals on your own, there are sturdy pedal boats for rent. Rentals available at several moorings, and boats are configured as two- and four-seaters. Maps and route suggestions are available, too.

Cycling ★★

Almost everyone in this city rides a bicycle. For practicality's sake, bikes are cheap, environmentally sound, maneuverable in traffic, plus all you need is a single gear in this sea-level, flatland city. You see well-dressed businesspeople on the way to work, farmers, shoppers with groceries and even kids walking their dogs riding on bicycles. And for recreation and sightseeing, bikes are the best. Rentals and tours are offered throughout the city. **Holland Rent a Bike,** *Damrak 247,* ☎ *(020) 622-3207;* **Rent-a-Bike** at *Centraal Station, 33 Stationsplein,* ☎ *(020) 624-8391.* Guided group tours are offered by **Yellow Bike,** *66 Nieuwe zijds Voorburgwal,* ☎ *(020) 620-6940.*

Aalsmeer
Shopping

Flower Auction ★★★
Legmeerdijk 313. ☎ *(02977) 32185/34567.*

There was a time when the investment value of bulbs was on par with diamonds. Rembrandt is said to have traded several of his masterpieces for one tulip bulb. Many of Holland's flowers, which thrive in the below-sea-level soil, are grown in the region around Aalsmeer, which is the site of the largest flower auction. More than 4000 flower growers supply acres and acres of tulips, roses, carnations, freesias and others. Bidders sit in the grandstands above oceans of blossoms, buying from some 14 million flowers, many of which are sent same-day delivery to flower shops around the world. In a reverse auction, buyers bid on lots while the clocks ticks backward from 100-to-one. Open to the public 7:30–11 a.m. Monday–Friday. act of patriotism. As a result, the place can be overwhelmed by busloads of gawking tourists.

Where to Eat

Bali ★★★★
Expensive

Badhuisweg 1. ☎ *(070) 350-2434.*

Credit Cards: *V, MC, A.*

Touted as one of the finest Indonesian restaurants in the region, the name has a famous ring. Authentic *rijsttafel*, exquisitely prepared rice dishes, are served by Indonesian waiters in native dress. International cocktails in the Bali bar are a celebratory way to top off a day at the beach.

Ducdalf
Moderate

Dr. Lelykade 5. ☎ *(070) 355-7692.*

Credit Cards: *V, MC, A.*

Rest assured that the seafood in this nautical restaurant along the wharf is as fresh as it gets. Recently caught in local waters and retrieved from the fishing fleet the next harbor over, the selection of fish is quite sufficient. Herring, North Sea gray shrimp, Zeeland oysters and sole cooked 11 ways are among the choices, not to mention steak, chicken and a mixed grill for those who don't have their sea legs.

Kandinsky
Moderate to Expensive

Gevers Deynootplein 30. ☎ *(070) 416-2636.*

Credit Cards: *V, MC, DC, A.*

Signed lithographs by the abstract artist Wassily Kandinsky fill the dining room of this superb restaurant with grace and polish. Kandinsky, with windows overlooking the sea, was opened by Mme. Claude Pompidou, widow of the late French president. Classic French cuisine is served with an art deco flair. Vintage wines available by the glass.

What to Do
City Celebrations

North Sea Jazz Festival ★★★
http://www.northseajazz.nl/

Every summer in early July the seaside town comes alive with the strut, stomp and swing of the jazz masters. Four straight days of mercurial music and vitality. Founded in the '70s, this festival has seen the likes of Miles Davis, Dizzy Gillespie, George Benson and George Clinton. For information contact **Festival Organizers**, *P.O. Box 87840, 2508 DE Den Haag*. Admission: moderate, varies.

Nightlife

Casino Scheveningen

Gevers Deynootplein 30, Scheveningen 2586 CK. ☎ *(070) 416-2636.* ○ *1:30 p.m.–2 a.m.*

Try your luck at this sparkling casino located in the elegant Kurhaus Hotel. It's a main attraction among vacationers with 24 tables for roulette, blackjack and baccarat. This lavish gambling house is architecturally striking and worth a visit to admire the Kurzaal and its dazzling, frescoed, skylit dome ceiling. Admission: varies.

Special Tours

Promenade

This broad boulevard runs a mile or two along the beach in this popular seaside town. With the North Sea on one side and a wealth of shops and cafes on the other, it makes for a scenic and engaging stroll. Also on the promenade is a large, heated wave pool simulating the swells of the ocean. Fireworks are set off from the pier every Friday night in July and August.

The Hague

The Hague, with its narrow streets and compact town center, is a jewel of old Dutch architecture. Its museums are myriad and splendid; they cover not only art but subjects of specialized interest as well. Here is the seat of the government; Amsterdam is the capital, but national laws are made in The Hague. Have a look at the **Houses of Parliament**. The world- famous **Peace Palace** (meeting place for the Permanent Court of Arbitration and the International Court of Justice), the **International Institute of Social Studies**, the **Royal Palace** ("Huis ten Bosch") and a number of royal retreats are all at The Hague. Citizens are proud of the **concert and ballet center** on the *Spui*. Tots of all ages love a visit to the previously described **Madurodam**, a city created in miniature. If your tastes run to the exotic, visit the 11-day-and-night **Pasar Malam Besar**, the largest Eurasian festival in the world. Food, dance, music and aromas— all are part of the event, which draws more than 100,000 admirers each springtime, usually in late June.

Where to Stay

Des Indes Inter-Continental ★★★★★
Very Expensive

Lange Voorhout 54-56.

☎ *(70) 363-2932*, FAX: *327-0200*.

Credit Cards: *All Major*.

The Des Indes Inter-Continental began life as the residence of Baron van Brienen. Opened as a hotel in 1881, the Des Indes has become a mecca for socialities who visit the Dutch capital. The 76 guest rooms vary in size, but all reflect the atmosphere of the building. Most are elegantly appointed with brass beds, period engravings of life in the colonies, silk upholstery and extra-long, extra-deep bath tubs. However, some rooms have small bathrooms with no tubs at all. All rooms are outfitted with mini-bars, trouser press, in-room safes and color cable TVs. Some rooms have balconies and Jacuzzis. Dining and entertainment facilities include Le Restaurant for formal continental meals and the locally popular Le Bar. Not much in the way of leisure activities here save a jogging trail, but guests can use a nearby fitness club with a swimming pool.

Hotel Corona ★★★★
Moderate to Expensive

Buitenhof 39-42.

☎ *(70) 363-7930*.

Credit Cards: *All Major*.

The Corona has been around since the turn of the century. Management has gone to great pains to maintain the period atmosphere in the lobby and reception area. The 26 guest rooms are renovated on a regular basis, most recently in 1994, and are decorated in pastel colors with deep, rich carpeting. Amenities include color cable TV, minibars and private baths with hair dryers. There is also 24-hour room service. The sidewalk brasserie has a retractable roof, allows customers to dine alfresco if the weather permits. The renowned Michelin-starred dining room features French cuisine. Private meeting and banqueting facilities are available for up to 100 people.

Novotel Den Haag Centrum ★★★
Moderate

Hofweg 5-7.

☎ *(70) 364-8846,* FAX: *221-4542.*

Credit Cards: *All Major.*

Situated in the center of the fashionable Den Haagen Passage shopping area, the Novotel Den Haag has a bus and tram stop right out front making it a short two-stop hop from the main train station. KLM also maintains an in-house check-in facility. The 106 guest rooms tend to be rather impersonal, but they are well maintained and comfortable with good light for reading. Amenities include color cable TV and private bath or shower. The hotel has a decent restaurant open from 6 a.m. to midnight as well as a bar and lounge.

Where to Eat

Auberge de Kieviet ★★★★
Moderate to Expensive

Stoeplaan 27, Wassenaar. ☞ *Take A44 and follow the signs, a 10-minute drive.* ☎ *(070) 01751.*

Credit Cards: *V, MC, DC, A.*

The sumptuous cuisine at this select restaurant is enough of an incentive for the short trip out of town. Some say the drive is worth it all the way from Amsterdam. Gourmet food and a classical ambience make it a remarkable event. The dishes are anything but banal. Try the filet of hare with green pepper and mango or the salmon with strips of pumpkin and truffle; you won't be disappointed.

Garoeda

Moderate

Kneuterdijk 18A. ☎ *(070) 346-5319.*

Credit Cards: *V, MC, DC, A.*

Reservations required.

The ambience is welcoming and genuine at this Indonesian restaurant, which is the favorite choice of the natives themselves. The *rijsttafel* deserves high commendations, and the prices are reasonable. Expect good service and a crowd at lunchtime.

Le Bistroquet ★★★
Moderate to Expensive

Lange Voorhout 98. ☎ *(070) 360-1170.*

Credit Cards: *V, MC, DC, A.*

Reservations required.

A quietly refined restaurant in the city center. Quaint tables, cut flowers, patio dining and superb French cuisine featurinig lamb, fish and fresh vegetables account for this spot's popularity. Call ahead as most evenings are fully booked—or come for lunch.

Le Restaurant ★★★★
Expensive

Lange voorhout 54-56. ☎ *(070) 363-2932.*

Credit Cards: *V, MC, DC, A.*

Known as the most refined restaurant in The Hague, this fancy dining room is a jewel in the city center. The fine continental cuisine includes such luxury items as smoked breast of duck salad, filet of turbot in sauce, and a heavenly chocolate parfait. There's a lengthy list of vintage wines. Scrupulous service.

PORTUGAL

Portugal remains the least spoiled and one of the least expensive nations in the Western Alliance.

This historic republic, with fewer inhabitants than the city of Tokyo, measures only 350 miles in length and less than 150 miles in width. First spearheaded by Prince Henry the Navigator, Vasco da Gama and other epic explorers, during the 15th and 16th centuries it was one of the mightiest powers on the globe.

The visible east-west line between **Lisbon** and the Customs point beyond **Elvas** splits the country into two markedly diverse conformations, including a less pronounced cleavage in their California types of climate. The South, which possesses a massive chunk of the overall 500 miles of beaches, has as its matrix the coastal **Algarve** as its crowning playground. In the interior, you will find excellent roads with light traffic; tidy, serene, lovely landscapes; and sleepy, charming villages, where most of the dwellings have their own distinctive hue among a large range of soft pastels. The North is far more industrialized and far less colorful, although its inhabitants in general are equally hospitable. Because of their narrowness and the presence of caravans of heavy trucks, the main arteries are despairingly overcrowded. However, multitudes of splendid cultural attractions await voyagers here.

Portugal has a number of state-owned *pousadas* ("places to rest"), most of them country inns. They are located in restored castles, palaces, convents and monasteries in especially scenic parts of the country. For more information, see the "Special Remarks" at the end of this chapter.

Transportation

Airline

Air Portugal (HTTP://WWW.TAP-AIRPORTUGAL.PT/EPORTAL /V10/PT/JSP/ INDEX.JSP) works hard and is well into a program to rejuvenate its service aloft as well as on the ground. For a small-to-medium-size carrier, it delivers a lot of personality. The focus now is on quality and customer satisfaction. Aircraft are good; staff courtesy has improved and, we'd assume, will continue to. Lisbon Airport is a busy, but efficient terminus and handy to town.

PORTUGAL

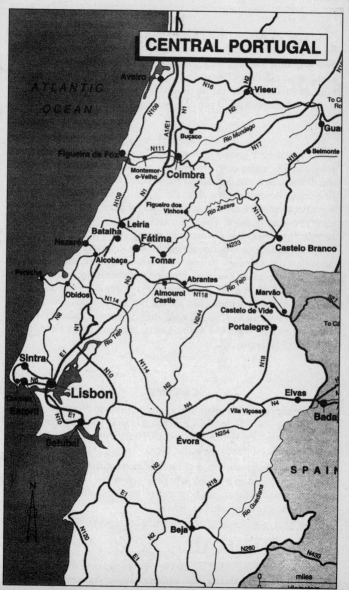

Taxis

All cabs are metered and rates are reasonable for the plethora of free thrills. *Set your price in advance on all out-of-town excursions;* here you must pay both ways, from cabstand all the way back to cabstand. Your cab driver cannot legally carry more passengers than the number stipulated over the meter. From 10 p.m. until 6 a.m. there's a night supplement of 20 percent on the meter.

Trains

The trains have greatly improved under a generous development program. The ticket costs are so low, the distances are so short and the differences in comfort are so pronounced that you should travel first-class wherever it's available. There are special deluxe runs both ways between three cities daily, which levy a peanut supplement for their first-class facilities. They offer club chairs, sofas, a hostess and service for drinks, plus a communal dining car. On the three-hour run from Lisbon to Oporto, for about $36 first-class and $20 second-class you can bask through the countryside on the nonstop ALFA Service train. In either direction between Lisbon and Faro, the capital of the Algarve, reservations may be made for about $36 first-class and $22 second-class aboard the *I C Rapido*. The fixed-price meal is about $15. As the road arteries between these hubs are the most heavily trafficked in the nation, the train offers a delightfully relaxed alternative.

Car Rentals

While car rentals are considerably steeper than in North America, the mileage you will normally cover is relatively so short that their tariffs shouldn't evoke too great a pain. Hertz, Avis and many other international companies are active here.

Hired cars with drivers are another alternative. However they work on the principle of the less time consumed, the higher the rates. To avoid what might be startling surprises, always check the price before climbing into the vehicle.

Seat belts are required for everyone occupying front seats in Portugal.

The Lisbon-Oporto highway was inaugurated in September of 1991 (3.5 to 4-hour ride), as was the new bridge over the Guadiana River that links the Algarve with southern Spain. Pedestrians are not allowed to use the bridge, but the ferry between Vila Real de Santo Antonio and Ayamonte (Spain) is still operative.

Food

The food in Portugal has greatly improved. With increasing prosperity, the Portuguese larder has expanded vastly; quality is tip-top nowadays.

In Portuguese cuisine, the French influence is pronounced. The creations are unique, delicate and flavorful. The wonderful fresh fish and seafood are preeminent, while the meat dishes are less special. Steaks and veal are staples. Cod is beloved; sole and all the crustaceans are still abundant; lobster (clawed or clawless) is snappingly expensive.

If you have a timid nature about certain flavors or styles of cooking, you'll have to remember three phrases: *sem azeite* ("without oil"), *com manteiga* ("with butter") and *sem alho* ("without garlic").

Since Brazil is a cultural offshoot of Portugal, coffee is the pillar of almost everyone's diet. The local version seems muddy to many neophytes. Actually, the quality is higher than can ordinarily be found in the United States; it's simply not blended, that's all. Some travelers find the "Carioca" style the most acceptable—equal parts of coffee and hot water; others like it *com leite*—coffee and milk, 50-50; after a heavy meal, most of us take it *bica* (plain)—but some follow the national custom of filling almost a third of the cup with sugar before consumption.

When it comes to cheeses, serpa is snappy, tangy and outstanding. Serra is a lighter, creamier version that is pure heaven as a complement to a glass of vintage port. *Queijo fresco*, a butter substitute with overtones of cottage cheese, is liked by many foreign visitors.

Agua de Luso is the best-known bottled water, though my favorite one is Pedras Salgadas.

Drinks

Port is the major national wine, of course. Economic conditions have forced the export of virtually all of the most superior class. Your best chance of securing fine vintage stock will be at some outlet that caters chiefly to foreigners. There are five kinds. Vintage, which takes 20 years to reach its prime, is the best; Crusted, never dated, is excellent; Ruby and Tawny (favorites of most travelers) are blends of up to 40 separate wines; White, light and pleasant, is the only type served before a meal. (The rest are consumed at the end, with the cheese.)

Madeira is the minor national wine—not as fashionable as it was when the clipper ships were sailing, but still as kind to the palate. It has the longest life of any. The three best types are Bual (our preference), Sercial (dry, characteristic flavor) and Malmsey (on the sweet side).

Portugal's stars for just about every second meal are the unique *Vinhos Verdes* from the old Minho region in the far north. Although they are called *verde* ("green") because their grapes are picked when young, most are white or straw-yellow and some are deep red. All of these light, dry, delicate, inexpensive bottlings, each with its official seal, which guarantees the contents as genuine, must be drunk cold. With virtually everything from meat to shellfish, the amber Gatao and Logosta are among the most popular brands. A traditional exception is the service of a red variety with freshly caught sardines. Literally dozens of vintners produce this different and delicious treat.

> **ITRAVELBOOK TIP:** VINHOS VERDES IS A GREAT WINE FOR SIPPING DURING THE WARM WEATHER; IT'S ALCOHOL CONTENT IS SUBSTANTIALLY LOWER THAN THAT OF OTHER WHITE WINES. SO IF YOU'RE IN IT FOR THE LONG HAUL, THIS IS THE WINE FOR YOU.

Among the standards, the leaders are Clarete, Ferreirinha (a very fine red), Quinta da Aguieira (excellent in red and white), Reserva Sogrape (another mellow red), Monopolio and Ermida (both exceptional whites), Bucaco (its supply rather severely restricted) and Grandjo, if you prefer a very sweet white. The reds from the Dao, the second largest area of growth, are full-bodied and strong, with a translucent ruby hue and a taste closer to burgundy than claret. It is especially useful to ascertain their age before ordering these; between seven and 10 years is normally their peak. Most of the rosés, including the famed Lancers and Mateus, are noticeably effervescent—a far cry from their confreres in the Provence or Côte de Rhone. All of the still versions seem undistinguished. As for the naturally sparkling choices, you might find Caves da Raposeira "Bruto" to be the most acceptable local substitute for champagne. Be warned, however, that most Portuguese bubbly is cloying and unpalatable. Last, there's always the wine of the country, in "open" servings; order this as *vinho da casa;* sometimes they furnish it with your table d'hôte (not à la carte) meal.

In terms of brandy, the best I've sampled (and I confess that my experience in this area is limited) is Antigua, in a lovely, tall, green, fluted bottle. Also in the prime category are Antiquissima, Velhissima, Fim do Seculo, Avo, Dom Teodosio and four or five others. In the more popular division, Marcieira Five Stars is a splendid black-label entry. A brand named Constantino is seen frequently, but I prefer the above choices.

All major Western spirits, except American whiskey, are available at very high prices due to heavy import duties.

Ginginha, the cherry liqueur first invented and distilled by local monks, is curious and worth a try.

Sagres, Super-Bock, Carlsberg and Tuborg have become the ranking beers. Imperial seems to vary in quality.

Telephone

Access code to USA: 001; same for Canada, Hawaii and Bermuda. To phone Portugal: 351; time difference (Eastern Daylight) plus 5 hours.

CURRENCY: Euros

Tipping

Give taxi drivers 15 percent on top of the meter reading; hairdressers, 10 percent; washroom attendants and theater ushers, 5 escudos; station porters should get their fixed charge only. For waiters, add only 5 percent inasmuch as service and a tourist tax are already included. In general, the Portuguese themselves tip minimally, but as many are so strained economically, you will win their hearts and gratitude if you tip normally—which will seem generous to them.

For More Information

Portuguese National Tourist Office
http://www.portugal.org/

590 Fifth Ave., New York, N.Y. 10036-4704, ☎ *(212) 354-4403.*

You may also obtain information from the Portuguese embassies or other government agencies.

Algarve

This glorious maritime province, Portugal's southernmost coastal region, is a prime vacation spot. It is a narrow ribbon 96 miles long, geographically separated by a barrier of hills.It is always ablaze with flowers, familiar and unfamiliar, for it basks in more sunshine than Mallorca, the French Riviera, or California. Spectacular rock formations of strangely eroded shapes enfold many of its golden-sand beaches. The scenery is hauntingly serene, when you escape from the occasional pockets of high-rise buildings. Over centuries its people have been known for their simplicity, their openness and their great capacity for making friends.

Albufeira

A major resort, Albufeira is widely known as "The St. Tropez of Portugal." Prices here copy those of St. Tropez, too; they're very high for the Algarve! While this is a colorful, hilly settlement with a good but crowded beach, its best quarters are in its environs.

Where to Stay
Hotels and Resorts

Alfa-Mar Hotel & Bungalows   ★

Budget to Moderate

Praia da Falesia. *Just 80 meters from beach; 6 miles from train station; 18 miles from Faro Airport.*

☎ *(89) 50-13-51,* FAX *(89) 50-14-04.*

Credit Cards: *Not Accepted.*

A contemporary hotel complex offering a total of 264 units. The bungalows have a small bath, telephone, sitting room, kitchenette and one, two or three bedrooms; the suites have bath, telephone; some less appealing units overlook a basement-level patio garden; interesting lobby stretches seven stories straight up; restaurants; pub; grill; nightclub; minimarket. Many recreational facilities offered, including surfing; massage is available for relaxation after a hard day of activities. The beach is wonderful but quite a good walk from the hotel.

Clube Mediterraneo da Balaia

Moderate

Praia Maria Luisa. ☞ *Five miles east of Albufeira.*

☎ *CLUB MED, (89) 58-66-81*, FAX *(89) 58-66-94.*

Credit Cards: *All Major.*

This cliff-top Club Med resort has employed striking and advanced architectural concepts in both its exterior and interior. Accommodations include 412 somewhat sterile rooms that face the ocean and customary block-style bungalows, all with private bath, telephone, balcony; sextagonal lobby ascends to 7th-story skylight; urbane but viewful Grill and restaurant; library; shopping arcade; all activities imaginable, including minigolf, volleyball, archery; splendid private strand of beach. Membership in Club Med and a minimum one-week stay is required.

Montechoro Hotel

Budget

Avenida Dr. Francisco Sa Carneiro. ☞ *Just 2-1/2 miles from Albufeira and Ferreiras train station; 21 miles from Faro Airport.*

☎ *(89) 58-94-23*, FAX *(89) 58-99-47.*

Credit Cards: *All Major.*

This multistory hotel is located in the Montechoro Vacation Complex, which is completely self-contained. The interior decor is of the Moorish influence, as evidenced in the white entrance hall and charming dining room. Accommodations include 362 spacious, well-furnished rooms with wall-to-wall windows, bath, balcony; 40 lovely suites; panoramic grill on 10th floor; blue lounge; two bars; two squash courts plus many other leisure activities available. An excellent choice, although it is not on the beach.

Sheraton Algarve Resort Hotel

Moderate to Expensive

Praia da Falesia Apartado 644. *6 miles east of Albufeira; 15 miles from Faro Airport.*

☎ *325-3535,* ☎ *(89) 50-19-99,* FAX *(89) 50-19-50.*

Credit Cards: *All Major.*

Set in a luxuriant forest atop sheer mountain drops, this resort overlooks Falesia beach 215 feet below. It is in a convenient location between Valamoura and Albufeira and only 15 miles from Faro Airport. Luxury is found here in the 215 rooms and 33 suites with attractive decor, bath, TV; two restaurants; bar; lounge; poolside bar; a lovely colonial garden; children's pool and every other amenity imaginable for leisure; laundry service; beauty salon and barber; baby-sitting available; currency exchange; concierge; car rental. The beach here is much less crowded than others closer to town which adds to the appeal of this spot.

Where to Eat

A Ruina   ★★

Inexpensive to Moderate

Cais Herculano. ☎ *(089) 51-20-94.*

This triple-level restaurant has vaulted ceilings, stone walls and wooden tables. The seafood is fresh from the market next door; you can pick your own.

O Montinho   ★★

Moderate

Estrada dos Calicos. *Just 2 miles northeast of Albufeira.* ☎ *(089) 51-39-59.*

Credit Cards: *V, MC.*

Closed: *Sun.*

A red-roofed restored farmhouse serving French cuisine, which some think is some of the best in the area. Featured are a changing selection of fish, poultry and meat dishes. The restaurant is closed Sun.—as well as from the first week of Jan. to the first week of Feb.

Alvor

Though becoming more and more inundated by tourists and encroached upon by recent hotel development, Alvor still manages to retain some of its charm. An ancient port town, it has narrow central streets, whitewashed houses and lovely views of the estuary—but what attracts travelers most is its huge beach.

Where to Stay

Alvor Praia   ★★★★★

Budget to Moderate

Praia dos Tres Irmaos. ☞ *Just 2 miles south of Portimao.*

☎ *(82) 45-89-00,* FAX *(82) 45-89-99.*

Credit Cards: *All Major.*

Commanding a heavenly, cliff-side, panoramic spot, above Tres Irmaos Beach, this opulent high rise offers just about every imaginable provision for travelers seeking seclusion, comfort and recreational activities. Accommodations include 201 small rooms and larger suites with fresh, bright furnishings, bath, shower, TV, balcony; split-level dining room with incredible sea views plus a candlelit Grill; cozy bar; wood-paneled lounge; its heated pool is the best on the coast; elevator to private strand; lovely gardens; minigolf; golf and horseback riding available for guests. Reserve a room on the ocean side to escape the busy road. A pacesetter in the Algarve.

Dom Joao II   ★

Budget

Praia de Alvor, Apartado 2. *Just 3 miles from Portimao.*

☎ *(82) 45-91-35/6,* FAX *(82) 45-93-63.*

Credit Cards: *V, A.*

Located directly on the beach, this hotel is somewhat commercial but does offer a wonderful location and good, basic accommodations. There are 220 comfortable rooms with bath, TV, balcony; 18 suites; restaurant; grill room; bars; lounges; water sports available nearby. The lovely wide sandy beach is the major attraction here.

Faro

Faro, the capital of the Algarve and site of its only commercial airport, is close to the center of the fine trunk road that runs from Sagres on the Atlantic tip to Vila Real de St. Antoni at the Spanish border. Its fortunate location almost cuts in half the travel distance to the resorts both to the east and west of this most popular gateway.

In Faro, you'll find swimming (because of fitful undertows, go only where there is a lifeguard), all water sports, tennis, horseback riding, *fado* singing, folk dancing, gambling, nightclubs, discos, hang-gliding, festivals, carnivals—name it and it's here. Today golfers fly in from all over the globe to enjoy its captivating courses, many of them edging the sea. With all of this, if you still have time to kill, there's the **Chapel of Bones**; it is in the Church of Our Lady of Monte do Carmo and composed of the bones from an adjoining monk's cemetery, including 1250 human skulls.

Where to Stay

Almansil

Apartments and Condo

Vale do Lobo　　　　　　　　★★★★★

http://www.substancia.com/valedolobo/

Moderate to Expensive

Vale do Lobo. ☞ *Eight miles west of Faro, between Faro and Albufeira.*

☎ *(89) 39-39-39*, FAX *(89) 39-47-13.*

Credit Cards: *All Major.*

Situated in 450 acres of pine forest along a rugged coastline, this completely self-sufficient villa complex is built around the Hotel Dona Filipa. The reception area at the main entrance has cobblestone floors and is operated 24 hours a day by a pleasant multilingual staff. Upon arrival, passports or identification cards must be presented. Special features are the villa-flanked 27-hole golf course designed by Henry Cotton and the excellent Roger Taylor Tennis Center with year-round coaching. There are a total of 1000 units with a wide range of interior dimensions and designs. Accommodations available include one-bedroom apartments up to a four-bedroom villa with three bathrooms, all with tile floors, stucco walls, pretty floral furnishings reflective of the region, marble baths, fully stocked kitchen, telephone, TV, minibar and air conditioning upon request; some have private pool. Other facilities include 12 restaurants, four nightclubs, coffee shops, bars, beauty shops, medical attention, drugstore, physiotherapy, beach and water activities and just about everything needed for resort living.

Hotels and Resorts

Hotel Quinta do Lago ★★★★★

http://www.orient-express.com/web/oalg/oalg_alb_flash.jsp?BV_SessionID=@@@@1021893953.1031854659@@@@&BV_EngineID=cccdadcgejigdjmcfngcfkmdffkdffg.0

Expensive to Very Expensive

Quinta do Lago. *Located 13 miles from center of city, 12 miles from airport.*

☎ *237-1236,* ☎ *(89) 39-66-66,* FAX *(89) 39-63-93.*

Credit Cards: *All Major.*

In Quinta do Lago, this modern Mediterranean-style hotel is one of the most luxurious resorts in Portugal. It resides on a 1600-acre estate of pine forest and sandy hills, overlooking the Ria Formosa estuary and the ocean. Accommodations include 141 bright but restful rooms with marble and tile bath, bathrobes, hair dryers, balcony with views, TV; nine suites; apartment complex overlooking its own seawater lake. Room service is available; excellent Shepherds Restaurant and Patio Club; intimate lounge with terrace; golf clinics available; one of the finest horseback riding facilities in southern Europe; water sports, deep-sea fishing and skeet shooting available nearby; car rental; concierge; baby-sitting available; laundry service. Truly world-class.

Penina

The plush **Alvor Casino** is only a five- minute walk from the resort and is open every day from 5 p.m.–3 a.m. Good restaurant with dancing and floor show; three bars; the normal games of chance. Don't forget your passport if you wish to play!

Penina Golf and Resort Hotel ★★★★★

Expensive

PO Box 146, Penina. *Located 3 miles from train station, 2 miles from the sea.*

☎ *225-5843,* ☎ *(82) 41-54-15,* FAX *(82) 41-50-00.*

Credit Cards: *All Major.*

This self-contained hotel complex owned by the Meridien group remains one of the most famous and illustrious golfing resorts in Europe. The great Penina estate, on which more than 400,000 trees have been planted since 1964, encompasses 300 acres on a hilltop and is only 2.5 miles from the sea. The magnificent championship 36-hole links were designed by Henry Cotton; fully outfitted clubhouse downstairs in main building a few steps from first tee; practice ground and putting greens; caddies, golf cars, caddy carts and golf clubs available for hire. Accommodations include 192 well-appointed and tastefully furnished rooms with bath and shower, bathrobes, TV, hair dryer, many with balcony; 17 suites; some units with French doors opening onto terrace; gardens. The attractive interior appointments are set amid modern Algarve architecture; clean-lined lobby with sumptuous adjoining lounges; spacious dining room; chic, intimate Monchique Grill with brass lanterns, touches of timber and glass-covered rotisserie; dancing nightly; complimentary transportation to the beach in the summertime; private landing strip; concierge; organized children's activities and play areas. Staff are welcoming and contribute greatly to the enjoyment here.

Where to Eat

Cidade Velha ★★★

Moderate

Rua Domingos Guieiro 19. *Near the Cathedral.*

☎ *(089) 271-45.*

Credit Cards: *V, MC.*

Closed: *Sun.*

This intimate eatery, situated in a renovated 18th-century house, is Faro's leading independent restaurant. Two handsome rooms are decorated in pastel tones and illuminated by candlelight; service is provided by a genteel staff.

Dois Irmaos

Moderate

Largo do Terreiro do Bispo. ☎ *(089) 82-33-37.*

Credit Cards: *All Major.*

This old-timer serves terrific fish dishes at prices we love. The atmosphere is nonexistent; concentration is all on the freshest seafood possible. You can get exotic with octopus or play it safe with sole.

La Reserve

Moderate to Expensive

Estrada de Esteval. *N125, 4 miles to Loule, 1 mile to Esteval, right to Santa Barbara de Nexe.*

Closed: *Tues.*

A pleasant excursion from Faro could culminate with dinner at this gorgeous property and seaside estate. The cuisine is French-styled, utilizing the best Portuguese ingredients. Prepare to be coddled.

What to Do
Historical Sites

ITRAVELBOOK FREEBIE

Capela d'Ossos (Chapel of Bones)

 Largo do Carmo, in the Igreja do Carmo.

🕓 *9:30 a.m.–5 p.m.*

Special Hours: *Closed between 12:30 p.m.–3 p.m.*

Whoever built this chapel really knew how to recycle. Its walls are entirely made of the bones from an adjoining monks' cemetery; included in the mix are some 1250 human skulls.

Parks and Gardens

Praia de Faro

🔲 *Faro Island.* 🕮 *Ferry from Arco da Porta Nova.*

Suddenly, you remember what you came here for: the beach! Faro's loveliest, the Praia do Faro, on Faro Island is reachable by ferryboat from the harbor; it runs from May to Sept. only. Otherwise, take bus #16, which stops in front of the tourist office; ☎ *(089) 803-604*, at Rua da Misericordia, check for hours.

Lagos

Lagos, toe to heel with Praia da Rocha, means "lakes"—but there's nary a one to be seen. Here is where the caravels were built that spearheaded the Age of Discovery; there are a 1000-year-old Moorish castle and the remains of Europe's first slave market. **St. Anthony's Church** features magnificent rococo gilt carvings, possibly the nation's finest, and the adjoining museum has some interesting and unusual exhibits.

While the shopping in general is routine here, **Porches**, on the main Faro-Portimao road, stocks a large, assortment of handmade, hand-painted pottery in the traditional regional style, most of which is made from the local red clay.

Where to Stay

Hotel Golfinho   ★

Budget

Praia de Dona Ana. *Near the town.*

☎ *(82) 76-99-00,* FAX *(82) 76-99-99.*

Credit Cards: *All Major.*

Here is a typical example of the hurriedly built hostelries in this area. This five-story hotel is located in a lovely coastal situation, which makes it popular with individuals and tour groups. There are 262 rooms with bath, TV, heating; room service; Penthouse Grill offers an appealing vista; ground-level restaurant crammed with too many tables; bar; disco; games room; children's program year-round.

de Lagos Hotel ★★★★

Budget to Moderate

Rua Nova da Aldeia. *Just 300 yards from train station.*

☎ *223-2862,* ☎ *(82) 76-99-67,* FAX *(82) 76-99-20.*

Credit Cards: *All Major.*

Centrally located and facing the harbor promenade, this hotel is situated in 3 acres on top of a hill. Its spacious arched lobby reflects the Moorish style as does its verdant interior courtyard. Accommodations include 317 rooms with marble bath, TV and terrace overlooking either the courtyard, town or pool; 11 suites; room service; dining room, Grill and Coffee Shop; comfortable, relaxing bar; six cozy lounges tucked away at different levels. All guests are extended free privileges at the Duna Beach Club, which is five minutes away at Meia Praia Beach. The courtesy hotel shuttle will take you to the clubhouse, tennis courts, beach, pool, solarium and daily buffets.

Where to Eat

Alpendre ★★★

Moderate

Rua Antonio Barbosa Viana 71. ☎ *(082) 76-27-05.*

Credit Cards: *All Major.*

This is one of the most sophisticated restaurants along the entire coast. Have a drink in the downstairs bar before emerging to dine in the handsome paneled and stuccoed dining area. There are about 20 tables in the L-shaped main section and rear nook. A strikingly lavish food display tempts in the center; you can watch a chef prepare your meal in a tiled and stainless-steel open kitchen. Both the presentation and preparation are excellent.

Dom Sebastiao ★★

Inexpensive to Moderate

Rua 25 de Abril 20. ☎ *(082) 76-27-95.*

Credit Cards: *MC, DC.*

Popular for fresh lobster, this bustling Portuguese restaurant offers reasonable tabs, comfortable decor, and an accomplished wine list.

What to Do

Historical Sites

ITRAVELBOOK FREEBIE

Antigo Mercado de Escravos ★

✉ *Praca Infante Dom Henriques.*

🕐 *24 hours.*

This unprepossessing arched structure was once the site of the first slave market in Europe, which was in full swing in the 15th century.

Igreja de Santo Antonio

✉ *Rua Silva Lopes.*

🕐 *9 a.m.–5 p.m.*

This church's rococo gilt carvings were laboriously recreated by dedicated craftsmen after many of the originals were damaged in the devastating 1755 earthquake. Adjoining the church is the rather curious Museu Municipal, housing a dubious hodgepodge of deformed animal fetuses (preserved of course), cork creations, 16th-century vestments, old embroidery, coins, building parts and other local artifacts.

Nightlife

Joe's Garage

✉ *Rua de Maio.*

🕐 *9 p.m.–4 a.m.*

You'll either love or hate this place, but it helps if you've had a few drinks somewhere else beforehand. Crowded, noisy dance floor.

Rumor has it that the staff likes to spray patrons with water to calm them down.

L.A. Woman/Club Route 66

⊟ *Rua Marreiros Neto 52.*

🕐 *Noon–5 a.m.*

This two-level cafe-bar-disco serves pizza and Mexican food from lunchtime till breakfast the next day. The dancing takes place downstairs, where drink specials are proffered from the bar from midnight until 2 a.m. If boredom sets in, you can go to Shots in the Dark *(Rua Primeiro de Mayo 16)* a backpacker's hangout not far from Joe's Garage; the hours vary, but it's probably open until way past 3 a.m., when the serious drinking has reached its peak.

Portimao

Portimao is the second-largest and second-busiest settlement in the province. Day and night, it is constantly bustling with residents and visitors. Despite its numerous high-rise buildings and its public market—which covers the central plaza with racks of clothing, textiles and other products, all sold to the strains of screeching rock music—much of its traditional color remains.

Shopping

Tourist junk abounds. Well above this in quality are **Vinda** (with a branch in Albufeira) for boutique items, celebrated **Vista Alegre** (see "Lisbon") for porcelains and **Galeria Portimao** for Portuguese paintings, tapestries and sculptures. All are on Rua Santa Isabel. Enchanting **Monchique**, 14 miles out, is famous for its spas, which date back to the Roman period. Its hot springs are reputed to cure rheumatism. Drive to the very top of Foia peak for a glorious panorama of the Algarve.

Where to Stay

Apartments and Condo
Hotels and Resorts

Globo Hotel ★

Budget

Rua 5 de Outubro 26. ☞ *In town center; 1/2 mile from train station; 30 miles from Faro Airport.*

☎ *(82) 41-63-50,* FAX *(82) 831-42.*

Credit Cards: *All Major.*

This hotel provides simple comforts and pleasant accommodations on the harborfront. It has 71 small but well-equipped rooms with bath, central heating, telephone; four suites with TV; panoramic rooftop restaurant and bar have wonderful views of the town and harbor; bar; comfortable lobby. There is complimentary transportation to the beach, which is about five minutes away.

Where to Eat

A Lanterna ★★

Inexpensive to Moderate

Parchal. ☎ *(082) 501-637.*

Credit Cards: *V, MC.*

Closed: *Sun.*

A popular, albeit viewless restaurant near the harbor bridge. Although the room is small, the 17 tables are split by an arched partition. Specialties include duck and seafood; an interesting treat is a dish of delicate small clams steeped with mild onions in a white sauce. The restaurant also has an intimate, plant-filled bar.

Praia da Luz

This delightful little fishing village boasts one of the best (and earliest) complexes in the region—the **Ocean Club**. Blending in well with the old-village surroundings, it still provides a high level of comfort for its guests and its apartments and cottages.

Where to Stay

Ocean Club ★★

Moderate

Rua Direita. 🖙 *In the town; 4 miles from Lagos.*

☎ *(82) 76-99-67,* FAX *(82) 76-99-20.*

Credit Cards: *All Major.*

Various accommodation choices can be found in this garden-filled complex, located on the beach. There are a total of 250 well-equipped and tasteful private apartments with bath, kitchenette, ocean view, some with balcony or terrace; two- and three-bedroom cottages are also available; small restaurant; coffee shop. The beach is virtually at your doorstep, as are many dining establishments.

Sagres

Sagres is a small harbor on the lee side of **Cape St. Vincent**, the magnificent harsh promontory that is the most southwesterly point of Europe and that for centuries has been called *O Fim do Mundo*—"the End of the World." Because the Continent first meets the onslaught of the Atlantic here, anglers will find the best fishing grounds in Portugal and scuba divers can glide through a virtually unrivaled aquarium. The drive to its famous fortress and lighthouse is a must for every visitor. Whenever this road takes you close to the edge of its all-embracing cliffs, there are thrilling views of the sea pounding away hundreds of feet below.

Where to Stay

Residencia Dom Henrique

Budget

Sitio da Mareta. 🖙 *Above Mareta Beach.*

☎ *(82) 641-33.*

Credit Cards: *Not Accepted.*

This tidy little hotel fulfills most traveler's fantasies of that little undiscovered charmer. Built in a garden, this pretty white stucco house is situated directly above Mareta Beach. It has 28 comfortable rooms, and the more expensive double rooms have ocean views; sunny restaurant serves lunch, dinner and even afternoon tea and cakes; garden bar; free parking. Kindly management.

da Baleeira Hotel

Budget

Sitio da Baleeira, Vila do Bispo. *Above the town overlooking the Bay of Sagres.*

☎ *(82) 642-12/3/4,* FAX *(82) 644-25.*

Credit Cards: *All Major.*

This modern hotel is situated directly above a good sandy beach and maintains wonderful views of the bay and beaches. Its 120 somewhat small rooms are very simply furnished but all have bath, telephone, terrace with views of the sea; its very good restaurant, where every table has a view over the water, specializes in seafood; bar; disco; garden; concierge; currency exchange; car rental; laundry service.

Inns

Pousada do Infante ★★★

Moderate

Ponta da Atalaia. *Located 20 miles from train station, between Mareta Beach and the harbor.*

☎ *(82) 642-22,* FAX *(82) 642-25.*

Credit Cards: *All Major.*

Perched on a rocky promontory, this inn affords a stunning panorama of the sea. It is so popular here that it is wise to try and reserve at least four months in advance. Within are 39 simply furnished, comfortable rooms with bath, heating, TV, telephone and incredible ocean views; one suite; outstanding restaurant serves regional cuisine; stone terrace where pre-dinner drinks or after-dinner coffee may be enjoyed while watching the surf roll in on the shore below; attractive, generously sized public areas in Moorish-style with tapestries and comfortable velvet couches. Open all year.

Where to Eat

Bossa Nova

Inexpensive

Rua Comandante Matoso. ☎ *(082) 645-66.*

One of the few budget choices in town, Bossa Nova offers pasta, pizza and vegetarian dishes, served on a nice patio. There's another restaurant in front, **O Dromedario** (☎ *(082) 76-42-19,* same owner), popular for American-style breakfasts and healthy short order meals.

What to Do
Excursions

ITRAVELBOOK FREEBIE

Cape of St. Vincent ★★★★★

Cabo São Vicente.

Any trip to the region should include a drive to Prince Henry the Navigator's fortress, the famous Fortaleza de Sagres, and lighthouse. If you are coming from Lagos, take N268 south from N125 at Vila do Bispo (one of Sagres' pretty beaches) to the fortress (follow the signs), on an imposing promontory above crashing waves. Although built in the 15th century, it was subsequently reconstructed two hundred years later. Another four miles west is the Cape of Saint Vincent, the possible site of Prince Henry's navigation school, attended by all the famous explorers. There's no bus service to the Cape, but you can rent a bicycle from Vila do Bispo at *Tourinfo, Praca de La Republica, Sagres* ☎ *(082) 645.20.*

Vilamoura

Vilamoura is perhaps Europe's largest privately owned vacation center. Its 1615 acres of beach and gently rolling hills make it bigger than Monaco.

Here you will find an array of hostelries, apartments and Holiday Villages. The Marinotel is one of the finest luxury hotels in the Algarve. There are also man-made lakes, excellent 18-hole golf courses designed by Frank Penninck, a casino, a private airport, a riding center, tennis courts, swimming pools, a 2-mile strand and much, much more. The Marina will eventually shelter 2800 boats. In the region are a number of private homes, rentable villas, a sizable shopping center, the moored floating **O Vapor** restaurant and a pub. The Tourist Villages (**Aldeia do Golf**, **Golferias**, **Aldela do Mar**, **Aldeia do Campo**, **Le Clube**, **Monte da Vinha**, **Prado do Golf**, etc.) consist of apartment blocks, "bungalows" in communal buildings and small groups of villas, all clustered around their central clubhouse with their restaurant, bar, pool and shared public precincts.

Where to Stay

Hotels and Resorts

Vilamoura Marinotel

Apartado 676, Quarteira. ☞ *Located 20 minutes from Faro airport, 10 minutes from Loule train station.*

☎ *423-6902, (89) 38-99-88,* FAX *(89) 38-98-69.*

Credit Cards: *All Major.*

Situated between the marina and the sea, this modern hotel affords wonderful views. Accommodations include 385 attractive, comfortable rooms with bath, TV, telephone; 18 junior suites; two Presidential suites with bulletproof doors; room service; restaurant overlooking the garden serves Spanish and Portuguese cuisine; popular grill, with views of the marina, serves fresh fish specialties; bars; live entertainment; putting green; children's pool; jogging track; free parking. An exciting location on the marina.

Coastal Beira

Coimbra

Coimbra is ancient, beautiful and serene. It spreads itself lazily over one big hill, rising from the banks of the Mondego River (the longest that has its source in Portugal) to a dominant clock tower at its cap. The nation's largest university, with more than 12,000 students, is here; its enormous library alone is worth a special trip for bibliophiles. The **Old Cathedral**, the **Santa Cruz Church** and the spellbinding **Machado de Castro Museum** with relics dating from the 14th through the 18th centuries, are sightseeing classics. The famous fado "April in Portugal" was composed as a tribute to this two-tiered town of the "miracle of the roses." When Queen Isabel was about to offer bread to the poor, legend has it that it was transformed into blossoms. Another attraction is the **Portugal dos Pequenitos** (Children's Portugal), a park where there are miniature reproductions of regional buildings.

Archaeology fans shouldn't miss the Roman remains of **Conimbriga** (9 miles south). Rediscovered in 1930, this formerly sumptuous settlement unearthed marvelous mosaic floors (some of which can still be seen), imposing temples and a forum.

Where to Stay

Astoria Hotel ★★★

http://www.jpmoser.com/hotelastoria.html
Budget to Moderate

Av Emidio Navarro 21. *Downtown opposite the Mondego.*

☎ *528-1234, (39) 220-55,* FAX *(39) 220-57.*

Credit Cards: *All Major.*
Overlooking the river in a central location, this old-world hotel has been a downtown landmark since 1927. There are 64 rooms with private bath, central heating, comfortable furnishings; renowned wood-paneled dining room; wine cellar; bar; lounges; laundry service; car rental; currency exchange available. The hotel maintains the ambience of its 1920s origins well. A room with a river view would be the ideal choice.

Hotel Dom Luis ★

Budget

Quinta da Varzea, Santa Clara. *Near the Santa Clara bridge; 2 miles from the town.*

☎ *(39) 44-25-10,* FAX *(39) 81-31-96.*

Credit Cards: *All Major.*
This attractive hotel is located on a hill and affords lovely views of the region. There are 106 clean, comfortable rooms with bath, TV, telephone; two suites; room service; restaurant; bar; lounge; free parking. Modern comfort is found in this basic accommodations choice.

Hotel Tivoli

Moderate

Rua Joao Machado 4. *In town center; 400 meters from train station.*

☎ *(39) 269-34,* FAX *(39) 268-27.*

Credit Cards: *All Major.*

Its 100 rooms, six suites, wonderful central location and multitude of modern amenities make this hotel a good choice, although you will not find much in the way of uniqueness or character. All rooms have bath, hair dryer, TV; restaurant serving excellent regional and international fare; bar; dry cleaning/laundry available; car rental; parking garage. Everything you would expect from an efficient, modern hotel can be found here.

Where to Eat

Churrasqueria do Mondego

Inexpensive

Rua Sargento Mor 25. ☎ *(351) 233-55.*

A pit stop for the grilled chicken that the Portuguese do so well. Takeout only. There's a regular menu, but almost everyone orders a half-chicken, barbecued over an open flame. Yum.

Democratica

Inexpensive

Travessa do Rua Nova. ☎ *(351) 237-84.*

Closed: *Sun.*

Although there's not much atmosphere here, you will find great people and stick-to-the ribs, generally healthy Portuguese food. Good soups and vegetables.

What to Do
Historical Sites

Conimbriga ★★★★★

Coindixa, 10 miles southwest of Coimbra.

🕐 *9 a.m.–8 p.m.*

Special Hours: *Closed 1- 2 p.m.*

One of the most important Roman excavations in Europe, Conimbriga was founded sometime in the 1st century. A defensive wall (4th century), remains of a public bath and striking mosaics reward the intrepid. The ruins of the House of Cantaber are especially interesting; it is known that one family lived here until the town was invaded in the fifth century. Visit the museum nearby (open Tues. through Sun. 10 a.m.–1 p.m., 2 p.m.–6 p.m.) for updates on what remains (no pun intended) to be unearthed. Admission: varies.

The Old Cathedral ★★

 Largo da Se Velha.

🕐 *9:30 a.m.–5:30 p.m.*

Special Hours: *Closed between 12:30 p.m.–2 p.m.*

One of the oldest churches in the country, this Romanesque cathedral dates back to the 12th century. Guided tours daily. Free admission, except cloisters.

University of Coimbra ★★★

Largo de Dom Dinis.

Not many universities can boast as alumni a revered saint, a reviled dictator and a celebrated poet. Well, this venerable institution (1537) has that honor; St. Anthony of Padua, Dr. Antonio Salazar (who also taught here) and Luis Vas de Camoes were all students at one time. Highlights of the university complex are its chapel and library, a baroque extravaganza dripping with endangered woods, marble and other froufrou. The massive bookshelves contain an extremely valuable collection of scholarly texts—close to a million volumes. Library hours are 9 a.m.–12:30 p.m. and 2 p.m.–5 p.m.;

free admission.

Kid's Stuff

Portugal dos Pequinitos

Jardin do Portugal dos Pequinitos. *Across the Ponte Santa Clara.*

🕘 *9 a.m.–7 p.m.*

Special Hours: *Open to 5 p.m. in winter*

This fascinating model village represents homes and structures from all the regions and the former colonies (Macau, Brazil, Goa) of the once-great empire. Admission: varies.

Museums and Exhibits

Machado de Castro Museum ★★★

📄 *Largo Dr. Jose Rodriguez.*

🕘 *10 a.m.–5 p.m.*

Special Hours: *Closed Mon.*

Built over Roman catacombs, this atmospheric museum is a stunning showcase of religious sculpture, dating from the 14th to the 18th centuries. Admission: varies.

Nightlife

Diligencia Bar

📄 *Rua Nova 30.*

🕘 *10 p.m.–2 a.m.*

The Diligencia is one of the better venues for fado singing, serving dinner as well, but it's best to go for the music and drinks. Sob along with the crowd into the wee hours; even if you don't understand the words, the emotions will get you.

Figueira
Da Foz

A major seaside resort, Figueira Da Foz is 123 miles north of Lisbon. It has a splendid beach and an imposing promenade; facilities include a gambling casino, a big open-air swimming pool and lots of hotels. The natives here are so proud of their mammoth strand that they claim this is the only place in Portugal where they could guarantee 10 or more square meters of beach per visitor. Every year toward the end of June, there's a fair celebrating the Feast of St. John, and crowds are "baptized" on the beach.

Where to Stay
Apartments and Condo

Aparthotel Atlantico

Budget

Avenida 25 de Abril. ☞ *On the beachfront Promenade.*

☎ *(33) 240-45*, FAX *(33) 224-20.*

Credit Cards: All Major.

This modern high-rise apartment-hotel is a good option at the beach, especially if you are staying in the area for a week or so. There are 70 fully equipped apartments that are functional and comfortably furnished; all have bath, bedroom, kitchenette, radio, living room, some with superb views of the sea. There is no restaurant, but there is a supermarket nearby for provisions; laundry service available; baby-sitting available. The views and the price are hard to beat.

Hotels and Resorts

Grande Hotel da Figueira

Budget

Avenida 25 de Abril. ☞ *On the beachfront promenade; 1/2 mile from train station.*

☎ *(33) 221-46/7/8*, FAX *(33) 224-20.*

Credit Cards: *All Major.*

Overlooking the beach, this 1950s six-story hotel is still the leader in town. There are 91 spacious rooms with private bath, TV, telephone; eight suites; the somewhat sterile restaurant, with wall-to-wall windows, serves international and regional cuisine; bar; lounge. A popular accommodations choice for travelers here, even though it's a little worn.

Where to Eat

Restaurante O Escondidinho   ★

Inexpensive

Rua Dr. Antonio Dinis 62. *(033) 224-94.*

Credit Cards: *All Major.*

Closed: *Mon.*

Hot! Hot!—the food, that is. Specialties include Indian curries as well as the inevitable Portuguese dishes.

Restaurante Tubarao   ★★

Budget to Moderate

Avenida 25 de Abril, on the Promenade. *(033) 234-45.*

Credit Cards: *All Major.*

It may look more like a glorified beach shack than a restaurant, but the Tubarao serves great fish dishes, fresh from the briny. Rushed service, rather harried atmosphere.

What to Do
City Celebrations

Festa de São Joao   ★★★

🗎 *Various Locations.*

You didn't really come here to relax, did you? The endless party is at its apex from June 19-24 during this fair celebrating the Feast of St. John. Join the crowds who are "baptized" at the town's two-mile-long golden-sand beach.

Estremadura

Alcobaca

In Alcobaca, about 87 miles from the capital, is one of the country's most visited sites—**St. Mary Monastery**. Begun in 1178, this classic Cistercian monastery consisted of the church, cloisters, chapter house and many other impressive sancta. Perhaps its most unusual feature is the brook that flows through its kitchens, where the monks presumably caught fresh fish and washed their dishes. Worth seeing here are the Tombs of Dom Pedro and Ines de Castro.

Where to Stay

Hotel Santa Maria   ★

Budget

Rua Dr. Francisco Zagalo. ☞ *In the town in front of the Monastery.*

☎ *(62) 59-73-95,* FAX *(62) 59-67-15.*

Credit Cards: *V, MC.*

Here is an attractive, modern hotel in a quiet but central location. Situated above the Monastery on a hilly street, it offers 31 impeccably clean rooms, some with a balcony overlooking the Monastery; the breakfast room is also the TV lounge and bar; free parking available. Good, simple accommodations.

Inns

Pensao Coracoes Unidos   ★

Budget

Rua Frei Antonio Brandao 39. ☞ *Opposite the entrance to the Monastery.*

☎ *(62) 421-42.*

Credit Cards: *V, MC.*

Located just off the town square in front of the Monastery, this hotel offers 16 large, clean rooms with windows that open onto a walkway; some have private bath; breakfast included; restaurant serves very good meals. Basic but cheerful accommodations.

Where to Eat

Celerios dos Frades

Inexpensive

Arco de Cister. ☎ *(062) 422-81.*

Closed: *Thurs.*

Another choice near the monastery, this one stays open late for its signature dish, roast chicken.

Trindade

 Praca Dom Afonso Henriques 22. ☎ *(062) 423-97.*

Specialties: *Acorda Mariscos.*

Lunch: *Noon–3:30 p.m., Esc1600–Esc1900.*

Dinner: *8–10 p.m., entrees Esc1600– Esc1900.*

Credit Cards: *V.*

Outside dining.

Ideal after visiting the monastery, this understandably popular eatery is situated just outside it, beckoning with outdoor tables in warm weather. Fortunately, it's no tourist trap; the food is substantial, reasonably priced and good. Takeout is available.

What to Do
Historical Sites

St. Mary Monastery (Mosteiro de Santa Maria)   ★★★★★

▤ *2460 Alcobaca.*

🕐 *9 a.m.–7 p.m.*

Special Hours: *Winter open to 5 p.m.*

One of the country's most impressive monuments, this 12th-century Cistercian monastery contains the tombs of star-crossed lovers Dom Pedro I, son of the first king of Portugal, and Ines de Castro, a Spanish noblewoman. Her sarcophagus, although slightly damaged, is beautifully carved. Inscribed on the tombs are the words *Ate ao Fim do Mundo* (Until the End of the World). The monastery has been restored and added to several times over the centuries, yet it still dazzles with the longest nave in Portugal (350 feet high). Before you forget that this was a working monastery, you can get an idea of how they lived (quite well, thank you), by visiting the Cloisters of Silence, and the kitchens, with a branch of the Rio Alcoa running through them. Admission: varies. Students, teachers, seniors are free.

Bucaco

Bucaco (pronounced Boo-SAH-Koh) is one of the most enchanting attractions on the Portuguese mainland, and the **Palace Hotel do Bucaco** is straight from the pages of a fairy tale. If time permits, you must make an excursion from Lisbon to this gem for at least one overnight stay. Start at about 10 a.m. on the heavily traveled inland main highway north, and stop for a leisurely lunch at the charming Pousada Do Mestre Afonso Domingues in Batalha. Before continuing, visit the fantastic 14th-century Gothic Cathedral next door. Then head for Coimbra, and turn off the road at Mealhada to conclude this 145-mile trip. The ultra-rococo Palace Hotel was originally the hunting lodge of a Portuguese king and is the last of its kind to be built. It has excellent cuisine and an amazing wine cellar and is set in a vast forest. Even if you don't stay overnight, you can have lunch or afternoon tea, but your departure from Lisbon would have to be earlier.

Where to Stay

Hotels and Resorts

Palace Hotel do Bucaco   ★★★★

http://www.almeidahotels.com/ bussaco_pt.htm
Moderate to Expensive

Mata do Bucaco. *Located 17 miles from Coimbra.*

☎ *972-3868,* ☎ *(31) 931-01/2,* FAX *(31) 936-09.*

Credit Cards: *V, MC, E.*

Here is a definite must-stay. This splendid palace is situated in a secluded 250-acre forest. It is adorned with a galaxy of works by notable artists and artisans, finely furnished and embraced by extraordinary gardens. Its public rooms are regal, and the grand, red-carpeted staircase with blue-and-white azulejo paneled walls depicting the history of Portugal is breathtaking. There are 68 rooms and suites with traditional high ceilings, bath, telephone, TV, hair dryer, some with four-poster bed. Excellent cuisine is served in a dining room with carved-wood ceilings and incredible inlaid hardwood floors. Its wine cellar reportedly maintains 200,000 bottles of wine from the hotel's own vineyard. Service here is amiable but very slow. If time permits, you must make an excursion from Lisbon to this gem for at least one overnight stay. Start at about 10 a.m. on the heavily traveled inland main highway north, and stop for a leisurely lunch at the charming Pousada Do Mestre Afonso Domingues in Batalha. Before continuing, visit the fantastic 14th-century Gothic Cathedral next-door. Then head for Coimbra, and turn off the road at Mealhada to conclude this 145-mile trip.

Caldas Da Rainha

Caldas Da Rainha, 50 miles north of Lisbon, is famous for its colored glazed tiles (*azulejos*) of Moorish influence, its pottery and its bustling fruit market. It also boasts one of Portugal's most beautiful parks, with trees that are hundreds of years old.

What to Do
Excursions

Bucaco National Park

▦ *Northeast of Coimbra.*

This 250-acre forest is a botanical wonderland, with more than 700 varieties of trees planted by Carmelite friars in the 17th century; since that time, due to papal intervention, none of the trees and plants have been destroyed. Natural springs abound as well. It was in this area that Arthur Wellington's forces, under Marshal Massena, defeated Napoleonic forces. The natural beauty here inspired Dom Manuel II to build a summer palace (now a hotel) that adds to the overall enchanted quality of the forest. The hotel has maps of the forest.

Cascais

This former fishing village, 12 miles from Lisbon, is now a major resort. Tourists are not only drawn to its harbor, with its fishing boats and yachts, but to its charming lace shops, cafés and restaurants. When it comes to hotels, the Hotel Albatroz is one of the finest along the coast.

Where to Stay

Hotel Albatroz ★★★★

http://www.albatrozhotel.pt/mus.htm
Moderate to Expensive

Rua Frederico Arouca 100-102. *Just 1 block south of train station; 18 miles from Lisbon Airport.*

☎ *(1) 483-28-21,* FAX *(1) 484-48-27.*

Credit Cards: *All Major.*

This tranquil retreat in a converted mansion dating from the late 1800s is situated on a craggy bluff, overlooking Cascais Bay and the beach. It has 40 elegantly furnished rooms and three suites with bath, TV, telephone; room service; the panoramic restaurant serving fish and international specialties is highly regarded and the spot to dine along this coast; bar; lounge; baby-sitting available; car rental; concierge; free parking. The refinement and sense of private luxury here attract the traveler wishing to avoid the larger, more modern and busier establishments nearby.

Hotel Cidadela ★★

Moderate

Avenida 25 de Abril. *Just 600 yards from beach; 20 miles from Lisbon Airport.*

☎ *528-1234,* ☎ *(1) 483-29-21,* FAX *(1) 486-72-26.*

Credit Cards: *All Major.*

Located outside the town in a busy residential area, this hotel is a very good choice for travelers. Not only are there 140 rooms and 10 suites with bath, TV and balcony, but also private apartments with a fully equipped kitchenette and the capacity to accommodate one to six people. Comfortable furnishings and tasteful decor in warm color combinations are found throughout the hotel; room service; well-known dining room serving a high standard of cuisine; glass-fronted and poolside bars; large terrace adjoining the main floor; beauty salon; two boutiques; small but well-stocked supermarket, where you will find provisions for the kitchenette; laundry service; concierge; free parking. For the traveler in search of peace and quiet, this haven will most likely be suitable.

Where to Eat

Beira Mar ★★

Moderate

Rua da Flores 6. ☎ *(351) 483-01-52.*

Credit Cards: *All Major.*
Small and friendly, this eatery, located across from the fish market, is noted for its excellent seafood.

O Batel ★★★

Moderate

Travessa das Flores 4. ☎ *(351) 483-02-15.*

Credit Cards: *All Major.*
Closed: *Wed.*

Situated in a tiny courtyard square opposite the fish market, this restaurant has two immaculate dining rooms divided by arches and colorful Portuguese draperies. A winning, friendly staff.

What to Do
Museums and Exhibits

Museo do Palacio de Conde Castro Guimaraes ★

▤ *Avenida Rei Umberto II De Italia.*

🕐 *10 a.m.–5 p.m.*

Special Hours: *Closed Mon.*

On the edge of the Marechal Carmona Park, this late 19th-century mansion houses the collections of Count de Castro Guimaraes.

There are some worthwhile furnishings, silverware, sculpture and pottery on view. The mansion is replete with a lake, zoo and cafe. Visitors are welcome to picnic on the grounds. General admission: varies, inexpensive.

Estoril

Gambling, swimming, yachting, golf, horseback riding, trap-shooting, tennis, fishing, thermal baths, dancing—the works. And it's less than 1/2-hour by car or 45 minutes by Toonerville-type train from the center of Lisbon. Big-time entertainment and gaming regularly are dealt out at the **casino**. At it's nightclub-restaurant, dinner is served from 9 p.m.–1 a.m., and a floor show is featured at 11:30 p.m. There are salons for baccarat, U.S.-style craps, boule and a slot machines. Other pastimes here include roulette, chemin de fer, blackjack and French Bank. The legendary **Palacio Hotel** in Estoril couldn't be more splendid, and its **Four Seasons** restaurant is the first choice in the region for patrician dining.

Where to Stay

Hotel Lido   ★ ★ ★

Moderate

Rua do Alentejo 12. ☞ *About 4 blocks to the beach; 20-minute walk to town center.*

☎ *(1) 468-41-23,* FAX *(1) 468-36-65.*

Credit Cards: *All Major.*

Located in a quiet residential zone on a fairly steep hill, this hotel sits above the town and offers panoramic views of the area. You'll find a relaxed family atmosphere at this simply but attractively furnished spot. There are 62 comfortable and quiet rooms with bath; seven 2-bedroom suites; cheerful rooftop restaurant and bar with breathtaking views of the sea; sundeck; pretty garden. There's a wonderfully informal ambience at this impeccably maintained hotel.

Lennox Country Club

Moderate

Rua Engenheiro A.P. de Sousa 5. ☞ *Located 500 meters from train station, 10 minutes from beach, 20 miles from Lisbon Airport.*

☎ *(1) 468-04-24,* FAX *(1) 467-08-59.*

Credit Cards: *All Major.*

Here is a perfect little gem for golfers and other travelers seeking tranquility. It is situated on a narrow, peaceful hill just a few minutes' walk from the center of town. Consisting of two buildings resembling a private-mansion complex, it has a total of 34 attractive rooms and five suites with private bath, most with a balcony with view of the sea; suites have a kitchenette; rooms on the top floor of the main building have the most space as well as a small lounge and large balcony. For meals, there is the glassed-in dining room opening onto a swimming pool with its own ranch-style bar; lounge with small honor bar. Only residents and their guests are permitted use of the public rooms, bars, pool or cinema; complimentary transportation to airport, golf course, riding stables and docks; free, unlimited supply of house wines, bottled water, fruit, midmorning coffee; afternoon tea served. The clientele consists mainly of contented repeat visitors, so make sure you reserve well in advance. The atmosphere here, enhanced by the friendly staff, is certainly worth the trip.

Palacio Hotel   ★★★★

Moderate to Expensive

Rua do Parque. ☞ *East of the park; 18 miles from Lisbon Airport.*

☎ *223-6800,* ☎ *(1) 468-04-00,* FAX *(1) 468-48-67.*

Credit Cards: *All Major.*

Fine antique furnishings glisten and old- world elegance abounds at this traditional hotel, located in its own gardens in the center of town. Accommodations include 162 tastefully furnished rooms with bath, climate control, TV, telephone, some with balcony; room service; sophisticated Four Seasons grill; popular terrace bar with views of the grounds; 19-hole free Golf Club within two minutes' walk plus an additional 9-hole course; car rental; concierge; free parking. This legendary house is immaculate.

Suitehotel & Club Estoril Eden ★★★★

Moderate to Expensive

Avenida de Saboia, Monte Estoril. *Located 300 meters from train station, 1/2 mile from Cascais town center, 18 miles from Lisbon Airport*

☎ *(1) 467-05-73*, FAX *(1) 467-08-48*.

Credit Cards: *All Major.*

Specializing in suites, this lovely resort is especially well suited to families. Not only does the hotel offer sweeping views of the bay and coastline, but its location is convenient to Monte Estoril beach, which can be reached via an underpass just behind the train station. There are 162 tastefully furnished suites with bath, soundproofing, TV, fully equipped kitchenette; restaurant serving regional and international cuisine; poolside bar; minimarket; currency exchange available; car rental; concierge. These self-contained accommodations give the feeling of a home away from home.

Where to Eat

A Choupana

Inexpensive

Estrada Marginal. ☎ *(01) 468-3099.*

Credit Cards: *All Major.*
Closed: *Mon.*

The cliff-dwelling A Choupana is located in São Joao do Estoril, about a mile or so away from Estoril. It has wide windows for coastline vistas, courteous service, lovely surroundings, and reasonably priced and well-presented seafood and other dishes. There's a supper club for dancing that comes to life around 10 p.m. and shuts down in the wee hours.

Restaurante Esplanada ★

Budget

Avenida Bombeiros Voluntarios. ☎ *(01) 468-18-54.*

At this restaurant, located near the train station, you can eat substantially for very little cash. Meat, fish and chicken dishes; fixed-price meals available.

Yate Restaurant and Bar

Budget

Parque do Estoril. ☎ *(01) 468-26-61.*

At this friendly place, you'll find nothing special in terms of cuisine, but the parkside setting is lovely and meals are available at all hours.

What to Do
Nightlife

Estoril Casino

📰 *Parque Estoril.*

🕐 *3 p.m.–3 a.m.*

Within this massive, modernistic, park- fronted structure, you'll find a Las Vegas-style nightclub-restaurant with a surprisingly inexpensive (albeit mediocre) dinner with a floor show. Acts perform on a prairie-size stage, backed by a sizzling orchestra. There are also a small nightclub, a cinema, two bars, and a snack bar. Separate salons abound for baccarat, craps, boule and slot machines, with individual admission fees. Don't forget your passport. General admission: varies.

Lisbon

Lisbon is the capital and heartbeat of the Republic and one of the most international and charming metropolises in the world. It's relatively small for its importance—only about 1 or so million people—and there's a small-town air about it, particularly in the winding little streets of its Old Quarters. The contrasts are striking: luxurious hotels, an overcrowded airport, epicurean food, shops overflowing with opulent goods from five continents—and centuries-old poverty between the cracks in the plush facade. Historic treasures and arts abound. The jewel in its crown is the 752-foot figure of *Christ the King*, with arms outstretched, which rises on the opposite bank of the Tagus facing the city.

Where to Stay

Lisbon's room tariffs are appreciably below those in North America—and dramatically below the scales in the hubs of Europe. Meals are also a great bargain if you dine on local products such as fish and fowl rather than on imported fancies.

Capitol Hotel

Budget

Rua Eca de Queiroz 24. *Beside Marques de Pombal Square; in center of city.*

☎ *(1) 53-68-11/5,* FAX *(1) 352-61-65.*

Credit Cards: *All Major.*

Situated on a quiet side street, this hotel provides a central location with relaxing accommodations. It opens onto a lovely little park with lots of trees, which enhances the private, peaceful atmosphere. There are 57 simply furnished, comfortable, spacious rooms with private bath, TV, telephone, most with a balcony; five suites; restaurant; bar; snack bar; lounge. Try to get one of the rooms that open onto a private balcony; these are the best.

Holiday Inn Crowne Plaza ★★★★

Moderate to Expensive

Avenida Marechal Craveiro Lopes 390. ☞ *Campo Grande district; 45 minutes from Lisbon Airport; 10 minutes from center of city.*

☎ *(1) 759-96-39,* FAX *(1) 758-66-05.*

Credit Cards: *All Major.*

A 10-minute drive from the airport in the Campo Grande district this gracefully contemporary hotel boasts plush furnishings and exquisite contemporary decor. It offers 221 luxurious rooms with private bath, bathrobes, soundproofing, TV, trouser press, hair dryer, fax /computer hookups, most with viewful balcony; 6th floor reserved for business executives. Excellent restaurant; large comfortable lounge; shuttle service from the airport. Supportive, welcoming staff.

Hotel Ritz Lisboa   ★★★★★

http://www.hotelritz.pt/

Expensive

Rua Rodrigo da Fonseca 88. *Downtown; opposite Parque Eduardo VII.*

Public Transportation: *1, 2, 9, 32.* Metro Stop: *Rotunda.*

☎ *327-0200,* ☎ *(1) 69-20-20,* FAX *(1) 69-17-83.*

Credit Cards: *All Major.*

This is the most imposing and famous hotel in the capital. In decor, it is a sumptuous contrast of old and new. There are 303 very spacious, well-appointed, tasteful rooms with marble bath and separate shower, bathrobes, hair dryer, TV, soundproofing; 20 suites; the elegant Grill Room serves savory cuisine; the Veranda and the Snack Ritz with piano and classical guitar; outdoor dining in summer; laundry service; concierge. Excellent service by a well-informed staff who have been here for many years.

Hotel da Lapa   ★★★★★

Moderate to Expensive

Rua do Pau da Bandeira 4. *Located 10 minutes from city center in Lapa district, 5 miles from airport.*

Public Transportation: *Bus # 13, 27.*

☎ *(1) 395-00-05,* FAX *(1) 395-06-65.*

Credit Cards: *All Major.*

Situated in one of Lisbon's most exclusive residential areas, this lovely hotel occupies the expanded and extensively restored palace of the Count of Valencas, originally built in 1870. It retains all of its original character and has quickly become one of the most highly regarded establishments in the city. Within the hotel, a magnificent ambience has been created using expensive woods, marble and unique stucco architectural features. The 94 luxurious rooms have marble bath, separate shower, hair dryer, bathrobes, most have a balcony; five suites are available, three with private Jacuzzi; renowned restaurant Embaixada; sunny lounge; relaxing bar; terrace. There are excellent views of Lisbon and beyond from the upper floors and of lush gardens from the lower areas. An attentive, unobtrusive staff will enhance your stay.

Meridien Lisbon

★★★★

Moderate

Rua Castilho 149. *In city center opposite Parque Eduardo VII.*

Public Transportation: *Bus #1, 2, 9, 32.* Metro Stop: *Rotunda.*

☎ *543-4300,* ☎ *(1) 69-09-00,* FAX *(1) 69-32-31.*

Credit Cards: *All Major.*

Located within a block of the Ritz, this is a distinctive hotel, boasting bold architecture and a white marble lobby with a tiered fountain. The 331 rooms are on the small side, but their furnishings are appealing; all have marble bath, hair dryer, TV, soundproofing; 17 suites; room service; glitzy mirrored Brasserie with clever illumination and numerous snack and lounge corners; car rental; parking. Ask for a room overlooking the Parque Eduardo VII.

Mundial Hotel

★

Budget

Rua Dom Duarte 4. *In center of city; 1 mile from train station; 2 miles from airport.*

Metro Stop: *Rossio.*

☎ *(1) 886-31-01,* FAX *(1) 87-91-29.*

Credit Cards: *All Major.*

In the center of everything there is to do and see in Lisbon, this popular hotel caters a great deal to tours and businesspeople. It offers 147 rooms that are simply furnished but comfortable and of adequate size; all have tiled baths, shower, bidet. The pleasant roof-garden restaurant, with views of St. George's Castle and the Alfama, is the major attraction here and serves regional cuisine as well as French and Portuguese; lounge; bar; laundry service; baby-sitting available; concierge; parking. Be aware that it can be noisy in this hotel, as it is located in a busy central area where the old town meets the new.

Inns

As Janelas Verdes Inn ★★★

Moderate

Rua das Janelas Verdes 47. Beside National Art Museum; 200 meters from train station.

☎ (1) 396-81-43, FAX (1) 396-81-44.

Credit Cards: *All Major.*

Built in the late 1700s, this intimate little inn was once the home of Portuguese novelist Eca de Queiros. It was formerly the annex wing of the York House but is now completely independent. The interior is exceptionally furnished and decorated to reflect its past. The 17 rooms are spacious and luxurious with bath, hair dryer, TV, some with balcony overlooking the terrace garden; room service; breakfast only served in the terrace garden; afternoon tea available in the lounge; travel desk; car rental; concierge; parking (fee). Although not entirely convenient in its location, this stately mansion still affords an enjoyable stay.

York House Pension ★★★★

Expensive

Rua das Janelas Verdes 32. Opposite National Art Gallery; outside city center; 2 miles from train station.
Public Transportation: *Bus # 27, 40, 49, 54,.*

☎ (1) 396-24-35, FAX (1) 396-73-98.

Credit Cards: *All Major.*

This converted 16th-century monastery is extremely special. Within its cloistered confines, you will be enwrapped in a homelike atmosphere. The 34 rooms are beautifully decorated and have private bath; intimate, traditional main dining room serves delicious French and Portuguese cuisine; cozy bar with fireplace for pre- and after-dinner relaxation. For an informal and friendly hideaway, this is one of the best choices you can find in the city. It's very popular, despite its somewhat inconvenient location, so make reservations well in advance.

Where to Eat

Aviz ★★★

Moderate

Rua Serpa Pinto 12B. *(351) 342-8391.*

Credit Cards: *All Major.*
Closed: *Sun.*
 Happening bar, own baking, reservations required.

A legend among independent restaurants, the Avis remains a beautiful spot and an impressive place for entertaining. The premises are one flight above street level. Upon entering, you can have a drink in the handsome oak and quilted-leather bar, with globe sconces, velvet-upholstered chairs, green brocade wall coverings and a small vitrine displaying a novel pocket-watch collection. You have your choice of three dining rooms, one in beryl and two in gold. For Portugal, it is very expensive.

Bonjardim ★★★

Moderate

Travessa de Santo Antao 12. *(351) 342-7424.*

Metro Stop: *Restauradores.*
Credit Cards: *All Major.*

The chicken's the thing here. Everyone raves about the delectable spit-roasted birds and tasty french fries at this establishment encompassing two floors. The restaurant serves Portuguese specialties too, but it's hard to break away from ordering the same thing over and over.

Cervejaria Da Trindade ★★

Moderate

Rua Nova de Trindade. ☎ *(351) 342-3508.*

Metro Stop: *Rossio.*
Credit Cards: *All Major.*

Snacking and grazing while quaffing lots of Sagres beer is the agenda at this venerable tavern owned by the Brewery. You can eat very well here for very little money; there's a tourist menu, but plenty of low-priced appetizers are available. Prawns, steaks (but don't expect huge ones) and clams are the specialties.

Conventual

Expensive

Praca das Flores 45. ☎ *(351) 60-91-96.*

Metro Stop: *Avenida.*
Credit Cards: *All Major.*
Closed: *Sun.*
Reservations required.

This highly personal antiques-filled restaurant is in an old convent building in a charming residential district. Sra. Dina Marques is the maestro here, and her guests have included the creme de la creme of Lisbon society. She does wonderful things with fish and herbs, albeit a tad heavy on the butter and garlic, but worth every calorie.

Do Leao

Inexpensive to Moderate

Castelo de São Jorge. ☎ *(351) 888-0154.*

Credit Cards: *All Major.*

The view is as delicious as the food, at this restaurant atop the Castle of St. George, old haunt of Dom Afonso Henriques, the first king of Portugal. Almost every diner is assured of a sweeping vista of Lisbon and the river. It's a great place for lingering. Excellent cuisine is served at surprisingly low prices; any seafood dish is good.

O Faz Figura

📧 *Rua do Paradiso 15B.* ☎ *(351) 886-8981.*

Metro Stop: *Santa Apolonia.*
Lunch: *12:30–3 p.m.*
Dinner: *8 p.m–midnight*
Credit Cards: *V, DC, A.*

Closed: *Sun.*

Happening bar, outside dining, reservations required.

This lovely restaurant resides up high in the Alfama district. Overlooking the harbor cranes and shipping channels of the Tagus, the two dining rooms have leather Chesterfield banquettes, large windows, air conditioning and a wonderfully posh, clublike atmosphere. The expansive 14-table open terrace shades diners with an awning in summer. Exceptionally kind reception and personal service. The shrimp cocktail and tiny gratinéed squids are delicious; Steak Portuguese is cooked in a casserole with boiled potatoes and smoked ham.

Pap'Acorda ★★★

Inexpensive to Moderate

Rua da Atalaia. ☎ *(351) 346-4811.*

Metro Stop: *Rossio.*

Credit Cards: *V, MC.*

Closed: *Sun.*

A gaudy, friendly and democratic eatery, specializing in the robust cuisine of the Alentejo region. You'll find plenty of shellfish: the house specialty is *acorda*, a stew of all kinds of seafood, eggs and other yummies in a bread crumb-based sauce flavored with coriander—a local favorite.

Sua Excelencia ★★

Moderate

Rua do Conde 40-42. ☎ *(351) 603-614.*

Credit Cards: *All Major.*

Closed: *Wed., Sat.*

Both Portuguese and Angolan dishes are featured at this discreet establishment. Not unlike a private home, there's no sign advertising the restaurant, and you have to ring a bell to get in. But it's very friendly, no menus are provided, and the owner will recite the day's dishes to you. The cuisine is slightly peppery and sultry; often one of the national dishes, *acorda*, a seafood stew, is served—don't miss it.

Tagide   ★★★★★

Expensive

Largo da Academia Nacional de Belas Artes 18-20. *Two blocks south of Rua Garett.* ☎ *(351) 342-0720.*

Metro Stop: *Rossio.*
Credit Cards: *All Major.*
Closed: *Sat., Sun.*

Perched on a hillside in the ancient Chiado district, this former town house probably provides the finest independent cooking in the city. Moreover, the mood is that of a distinguished old-world establishment. A spotless, polished brass banister leads to the entrance; the dining room has highly coveted window tables boasting dreamy views of the Tagus. Crystal chandeliers sparkle, and so does the polished, kind service. There's an interesting menu of international as well as national dishes. Very reasonable prices for such high quality.

What to Do

For a holiday in Portugal involving sun, swimming, dancing, sports, old-fashioned loafing and/or big-league gaiety, Lisbon isn't the spot. The experienced traveler, particularly during the hot months, splits his or her time between the capital and such neighboring resorts as **Estoril**, **Cascais**, **Guincho** and **Sintra**, which are described elsewhere.

From Lisbon you have ferry services to Cacilhas, Barreiro, Seixal, Montijo, Alcochete, Porto-Brandao and Trafaria. You may also enjoy a river tour on the Tagus from April to October daily; evening tours from May to September; departure from Praca do Comercio.

Historical Sites

ITRAVELBOOK FREEBIE

Castelo de S. Jorge ★★★

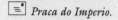 *Rua Costa do Castelo.*

🕐 *9 a.m.–9 p.m.*

Special Hours: *Oct. through Mar. open until 7 p.m.*

Although in ruins, the massive walls of this former Moorish fortification and Royal Palace (late 12th century) still stand, encircling gardens that are enjoyable for walking. On your route, you'll meet white peacocks, perhaps a flamingo, and other wildlife. The view of the river and the Alfama district is enthralling.

Jeronimos Monastery

 Praca do Imperio.

🕐 *10 a.m.–5 p.m.*

Special Hours: *Closed Mon.*

Very close to the Tower of Belem is this vast Gothic church, which serves as the burial place of Vasco da Gama, as well as various kings, poets and Portuguese heroes. Observe the building's distinctive Manueline style, noted for carvings of nautical symbols. Admission: varies.

Tower of Belem ★★

📧 *Praca do Imperio.*

🕐 *10 a.m.–5 p.m.*

Special Hours: *Closed Mon.*

The 16th-century Manueline-style tower stands poised by the Tagus River to welcome seagoing visitors, as it once did ancient explorers. The terrific view from the top is almost worth the price of admission. Admission: varies.

Museums and Exhibits

Coach Museum   ★★★

http://www.luso.u-net.com/ coches.htm
Praca Afonso de Albuquerque.

🕐 *10 a.m.–3:30 p.m.*

Special Hours: *Closed Mon.*

Before the automobile, these gilded beauties were the ideal transport of the rich and powerful. Appropriately housed in the former
Royal Riding Academy, on the grounds of the Belem Palace (now
the Presidential Residence), they come in all sizes, including a miniature one owned by the youthful Carlos I. General admission: inexpensive.

Gulbenkian Museum   ★★★★

http://www.gulbenkian.org/ index.asp
Avenida de Berna 45A.
Metro Stop: Sebastiao.

🕐 *10 a.m.–6 p.m.*

Special Hours: *Wed.-Sat. 2-7:30 p.m. summer; closed Mon.*

Portugal's greatest benefactor of the arts was the Armenian oilman
Calouste Gulbenkian, whose donation of a sizable private collection
led to the establishment of this world-class museum. Spread out over
two main buildings, the collection encompasses many major works
from ancient to modern eras; naturally, there is a significant array of
Near and Middle Eastern art and artifacts. Acquired from Russia's
Hermitage Museum in the 1920s are two famous Rembrandt paintings: Portrait of an Old Man and Alexander the Great. There are a
gift shop, an excellent cafeteria (with possibly the best salads in
town), a sculpture garden and an amphitheater on the grounds; call
the museum for schedules of concerts that are given here from time
to time. Admission: varies.

Maritime Museum   ★★★

 Praca do Imperio.

🕐 *10 a.m.–5 p.m.*

Special Hours: *Closed Mon.*

This is one of the most important maritime museums in Europe. The history of the Portuguese era of exploration is displayed with both models and the actual craft, representing over five centuries of marine exploits. Admission: varies.

Museu Nacional de Arte Antiga ★★★

Jardim 9 de Abril. *Take the Alcantara tram.*

🕐 *10 a.m.–5 p.m.*

Special Hours: *Closed Mon.*

Situated in the 17th-century palace of the Count of Alvor, this fine museum has a collection of 15th-century Portuguese paintings, as well as Nino Goncalves' beautiful wood-paneled altarpiece from the Monastery of St. Vincent. Other European paintings include religious art by Bosch (*The Temptations of St. Anthony*), Durer, Velazquez, Ribera and Holbein the Elder. There's also an impressive display of gold and silver pieces, decorative art, and furniture. Admission: varies. Free admission Sundays from 10 a.m.–1 p.m.

Music

San Carlos Theatre ★★★

✉ *Rua Serpa Pinto 9.*

🕐 *1 p.m.–7 p.m.*

Highbrow ballet and opera companies perform at this elegant 18th-century jewel box of a theater. Season is mid-Sept. through July. Ticket prices vary, 50 percent discount for students. Consult the local newspapers for schedules. Other venues include the **São Luis Municipal Theatre**, *Rua Antonio Maria Cardoso 40* *(351) 32-71-72*, for chamber music and symphony orchestras, and the Gulbenkian Foundation Museum, for a potpourri of dance and musical performances (for information, see Museums and Exhibits).

Nightlife

A Severa

📧 *Rua das Gaveas 15.*

🕐 *8 p.m.–3:30 a.m.*

An insistent choice of almost every concierge and taxi driver in town. They've got a point; the musical renditions are fine, and the local cuisine is tasty. Admission: varies.

Hot Club   ★★★

📧 *Praca de Alegria 39.*

🕐 *10 a.m.–2 p.m.*

Special Hours: *Closed Mon.*

Yes, there is a jazz scene in Lisbon. You'll probably find the best players here, at this appropriately snug and smoky joint. Admission: varies.

La Folie Discoteca   ★★

📧 *Rua Diario de Noticias 122.*

🕐 *10 p.m.–4 a.m.*

Special Hours: *Closed Sun.*

A winning bar-and-disco combo; the former has some "out there" drinks. Great dancing to a wide variety of music, both local and international. Admission: inexpensive.

Lisboa a Noite   ★★

📧 *Rua das Gaveas 69.*

🕐 *8 p.m.–3 a.m.*

Special Hours: *Closed Sun.*

This is the haunt of Fernanda Maria, a *fadista* with a soul-buffeting voice. A solid candidate—but the key is to go late; after midnight is best. Whitewashed den under arches; open tile-lined kitchen at one end; guitars and copperware on the walls. Substantial local fare; fado renditions every 30 minutes after 11 p.m. The only carp is that there's too long a pause between sessions. Admission: varies.

Memorial

▣ *Rua Gustavo de Matos Sequeira 42.*

🕐 *10 p.m.–4 a.m.*

Special Hours: *Closed Mon.*

The best gay disco and club in the city, at the moment. Reasonable bar tabs, interesting meeting spot. Admission: varies.

Senhor Vinho

▣ *Rua do Meio a Lapa 18.*

🕐 *8:30 p.m.–2 a.m.*

Owned by one of the great *fadistas* of recent times, Maria de Fe. The cooking here is better than at most clubs, and reasonably priced as well. Admission: varies.

The Port Wine Institute ★★

▣ *Rua Sao Pedro de Alcantara 45.*

🕐 *10 a.m.–11:30 p.m.*

Special Hours: *Sat. 11 a.m.–10:30 p.m.; closed Sun.*

Every day, except Sunday, you can come here and try more than 150 local wines by the glass. But do behave yourself, it's all very proper. Admission: varies.

Shopping
Shopping Hours

Shopping hours are generally Monday through Friday 9 a.m.–1 p.m. and 3 p.m.– 7 p.m. Saturday closings at 1 p.m. Shopping centers (see below) are open seven days a week until midnight.

Best Areas

The "Chiado" district encompassing Nova do Almada, Rua Garrett and Rua do Carmo; the "Baixa" section running roughly from the Rossio Square to the Tagus River; and the Rua da Escola Politecnica. Now the **Bairro Alto** zone and the **Praca das Flores**, once the flower market, are attracting attention.

Savings On Purchases

The 17 percent **IVA** is refundable from each store where you buy goods that cost a minimum of 11,000 escudos. The Portugal Tax-free Shopping Service oversees this rebate. Merchants working within the scheme display red-and-green stickers that say "Tax Free for Tourists." Ask them about how the Tax Free Cheques are reimbursed. The process is very easy. **IVA** on Madeira is somewhat less, ringing up at just 12 percent, but, of course, that's refundable too. You can get back 19 percent on any gold objects costing more than $98, which is irresistible.

Shopping Centers

There are numerous shopping centers that have sprung up. They stay open from 9 a.m.–12 p.m., seven days a week the year-round, including holidays. The **Imaviz Shopping Center** is across from the Hotel Sheraton. Of more recent vintage is the **Centro Comercial das Amoreiras** (Avenida Duarte Pacheco), about a 10-minute walk from the Ritz. This one boasts more than 300 establishments within its precincts, plus an exhibition hall. You can skip the one in the Rossio Railway Station, in our opinion.

Things NOT to buy: fabrics, perfumes and any imports.

Casa Quintao

▣ *Rua Ivens 30–34.*

🕘 *9 a.m.–7 p.m.*

Special Hours: *Closed Sun.*

Highly sought-after hand-stitched woolen rugs from Arraiolos are the specialty of this honest shop. Other centers are **Casa Regional da Ilha Verde** *(Rua Paiva de Andrada 4)* and **Centro de Artesanato** *(Rua Castilho 61)*. But this last one would also be my last choice.

Centro Comercial das Amoreiras

📧 *Avenida Duarte Pacheco.*

🕐 *10 a.m.–12 a.m.*

This high-rise mega-center is about a 10-minute walk from the Ritz (how convenient!). There are more than 300 establishments within its precincts, including an exhibition hall. If you don't mind the concept of small multi-screen movie theaters, there are several here, showing a number of films daily at very reasonable prices.

Feira da Ladra

📧 *Campo de Santa Clara.*

🕐 *7 a.m.–3 p.m.*

It's a combination garage and rummage sale Lisbon style. This hill-top (near the Castle) "thieves market" is an excellent place to absorb local color. As with any venue of this ilk, pick carefully among the trash; you may find a treasure here and there. Another interesting market is the **Mercado da Ribeira**, near the Cais do Sodre train station at *Avenida 24 de Julho*, open every morning, except Sundays, for luscious fruits and vegetables, clothing and crafts, and interesting people. Haggling is in order. Open early in the a.m., until 2 p.m.

Madeira Superbia

📧 *75A Av Duque de Loule.*

This shop has a fabulous array of stock, available directly from its studios and "factory" on the island capital of Funchal. Besides an extensive range of tableware, there are linen dresses, silk and linen blouses, fine handkerchiefs for both genders and daintily designed children's wearables. You can also buy needlepoint covers for your chairs, petit- and gros-point evening bags, colorful regional tapestries and wall hangings that are remarkably duplicated tapestry copies of classic and contemporary paintings. Splendid!

Sant' Anna

▤ *Rua do Alecrim 95-97.*

🕘 *9 a.m.–7 p.m.*

Special Hours: *Closed Sun.*

This 18th-century shop features, among other things, azulejo tiles that are faithfully reproduced from medieval designs. At your instruction, the borders on shades will be painted to match the design on any lamps that catch your fancy.

Solar

▤ *Rua D. Pedro V 68-70.*

🕘 *9 a.m.–7 p.m.*

Special Hours: *Closed Sat.*

A fruitful stop for the azulejo-tile aficionado; some of them are very rare indeed.

Vista Alegre

▤ *Largo do Chiado 18.*

🕘 *9 a.m.–7 p.m.*

Special Hours: *Closed Sat.*

The stock is lovely here and worth the attention of any collector. A wide range of designs, both contemporary and traditional. There's a discount outlet downstairs; check out the unbelievable prices on Baccarat crystal. Another store is at *52-54 Rua Ivens* ☎ *(351) 342-8581.*

Viuva Lamego

▤ *Largo do Intendente 25.*

Metro Stop: *Intendente.*

🕐 *9 a.m.–7 p.m.*

Special Hours: *1- 3 p.m.*

This ceramics shop is in its second century. You can reckon on quality, and continuity, too, obviously. Like the Sant'Anna, reproductions of antique tiles are its specialty.

W.A. Sarmento ★★★★

▤ *Rua do Ouro 251.*

🕐 *9 a.m.–7 p.m.*

Special Hours: *Closed Sun.*

Gold is the best bet in the country. According to the law, 19 carats is the minimum weight that can be sold over the counter. Of the many purveyors here, the nation's oldest and most respected specialist is W.A. Sarmento. The many small, delicate pieces among the store's wares are perfect for gifts.

Special Tours

Santa Justa Elevator ★★

▤ *Rua Aurea and Rua Santa Justa, near Rossio Square.*

Metro Stop: *Rossio.*

🕐 *7 a.m.–11 p.m.*

This "elevator" really goes to the top—of the city, that is. Actually a sort of tram that maneuvers the city's steep hillsides, this short, inexpensive, but thrilling ride takes you to the Carmo Church, a Gothic ruin on a picturesque square, Largo do Carmo. The views, needless to say, are stunning, especially on a starlit night.

Queluz
Historical Sties

Queluz Palace

▤ *Largo do Palacio, 9 miles nw of Lisbon.*

🕐 *10 a.m.–5 p.m.*

Special Hours: *Closed Tues.*

Sort of a mini-Versailles, this 18th-century rococo-style pink palace was commissioned by Pedro III. You can see the French influence in the furnishings and the manicured gardens, with their marble fountains and neatly trimmed hedges. State ceremonies are often held in the Throne Room, and foreign heads of state and royal personages (including several U.S. presidents and Prince Charles and Princess Diana) have been ensconced here. Admission: varies, free admission on Sunday mornings.

SPAIN

For the first-time visitor, the face of Spain can be compared to that of an ornate clock, with noteworthy points on the perimeter and Madrid, the heart of the movement, in the center. Starting at "XII," you have Santander, with a history going back to the Cantabrians and a might that reflected the power of ancient Rome. The hands sweep through the throbbing tourist sectors of the Costa Brava to burgeoning Barcelona, pride of Catalonia, which boasts the Cathedral and room where Queen Isabella celebrated Columbus' triumphant return from the americas. Then comes the gaiety of Valencia with its *Fallas* and the ever-present smell of citrus groves and roses. Granada and the fabulous Alhambra strike "VI," probably one of the most rewarding points in the passage of your time abroad. There's the slow and easy, sunlit Costa del Sol for lazing, golf and aquatic sports—not to mention the continuous nighttime activities for which the area is famous. If we had the space, we'd list every town, every nook, every cranny in this magnificent and reasonably-priced country: There are many important points in between the larger cities and fascinating fairy-tale towns in the interior but if time is pressing, this "clockwise route" probably includes the greatest variety on this vast and variable peninsula.

Transportation
Airlines

Iberia (http://www.iberia.com/iberia_es/home.jsp), schedules both domestic and global, are good, but ground services and labor strife can sometimes upset the smooth flow of traffic. Supervisors are understanding even if the system is burdened by forces beyond their control. It's a busy carrier and does a lot of air work very well, usually. **Aviaco**, a sister operation functioning on a highly localized basis, is more of the same.

Madrid's Barajas Airport, about 35 minutes from town in normal traffic, is one of the least inviting in Europe—in either the domestic or international terminal. Barcelona offers a train ride from town to tarmac, but on rainy days it is not always reliable; there's no bus connection.

Taxis

Fares are inching up to match fuel and other dollar-based infla-

SPAIN AND PORTUGAL

tion, but still a bargain compared to U.S. rates. Avarice seems to be the inevitable handmaiden of upward economic movement nation-wide. Many cars now have fancy digital meters on which there are four buttons the driver presses; #3 is used within the major city lim-its. As soon as these are passed, he presses #2, which ups the rate; #1 is for Sundays and holidays only; and #4 in the past has been a dummy. The result: Exactly the same distance could cost 25 percent more than it should on a purely distance basis.

Subways

In the capital, you can often avoid the hassle with hacks by opt-ing for this fast, clean and efficient public transport.

Trains

The trains are improving in comfort, but several accidents have put safety standards in question. Most lines are antiquated and sin-gle-track, leading to numerous traffic delays. Border-to-major-city and major-city-to-major-city schedules are convenient, but be sure to pick the fast trains only (strange as it sounds, the *expressos* are among the slower ones). AVE (an acronym meaning "bird" in Spanish) is the meteoric rapid service between Madrid and Seville, a $5.2-billion rail route that is darkly controversial in Iberia. It covers the 300-mile stretch in about three hours, but the tracks do not allow it to roll over the 8000 additional miles of the nation's net-work. The older but speedy *Talgo* links the capital with Irun, Barcelona, La Coruna, Malaga, Cordoba, Granada, Seville, Murcia, Santander, Bilbao and (across the border) with Lisbon, Paris and Geneva. Passenger fares are very modest by U.S. standards. For lux-ury lingering, you might like to sample the slower *El Andalus* or the *Transcantabrico*, updated antique trains that stop often for cultural browsing, even with entertainment aboard each evening.

You can save 15 percent buying a pass called *chequetren* that can be used by a maximum of six people with no time restrictions or val-idation period. The value of the coupons also applies to Talgo or sleeping surcharges. Passengers over 65 receive a 50 percent reduc-tion through the purchase of a *Tarjeta Dorada* (Golden Card); a passport is required for proof of age. The Eurailpass is a better bet—if you're traveling in other countries as well.

Food

Regional specialties are surprisingly good, and their varieties are enormous. Since the nation is chiefly agricultural, chefs have a hey-day in the marketplace. Through swift transport systems, fish gets to interior towns on the same day it is netted. Beef, once scorned for its toughness, is now tender and flavorful. Salads and fresh vegetables are safe wherever you go.

The *nouvelle cuisine* has its practitioners here, as well. The movement began among Basque chefs and is spreading throughout the nation. Catalans claim they taught the French how to cook—hyperbole, perhaps, but many swallow it.

The spellings and translations on the menus can be, well, startling. Women visiting the Catalonian fishing ports have been known to raise their brows over the "Rape (a fish) Sailor Style," while others wonder if "Amotic of Squalus" isn't some ancient hero of Iberia. Readers report squinting at "Pork Chok mit Peepers" or being put off by "Braised Spit" or "Gudgeons of Golden Bream George Sand."

Roast lamb *(cordero asado)* and roast suckling pig *(cochinillo)* are generally the finest meats. Spanish hams such as those from Jabugo, Trevelez and Teruel deserve their worldwide admiration. The poultry is usually delicious, especially when grilled on open fires. Spanish eggs, incidentally, are like those from dim memory in North america: real color in the yolk and genuine flavor, not the washed-out production-line products that we are fed by industrial poulterers.

There are all kinds of exquisite fruit, including the world's best oranges (winter only); the honey has the fragrance of rosemary, marjoram and orange blossoms; you'll find almond, nougat, marzipan and tons of confections. As for cheeses, the better types include the Tetilla (soft and greasy), Cabrales (fermented and piquant), Burgos (all cream), Asturias (smoked-cured) and Manchego. Try the last, which has been molded in matting and preserved in oil; it's a favorite. Your friends might avoid you for a couple of days afterward, but it's worth the gamble. If you have *real* courage, order a Teta, which literally means "breast" and comes in that shape and of varying dimensions. It's soft and creamy.

Spanish meal hours call for heroic belt-tightening and self-discipline on the part of the visitor. Breakfast is at your option, generally as early as or late as you choose. Lunch is from about 2–3:30 p.m.—so it might be 4:30 p.m. before you stagger away from the table to your siesta. Dinner usually starts at about 9:30 p.m. at the earliest—which often brings the dessert and demitasse swinging down the aisle after midnight.

Drinks

Sherry, the national wine, comes in seven major types, some with a number of subclassifications; like port (Portugal), it is always bottled blended rather than "straight." Call it Jerez (pronounced Haireth) if you want to please the bartender. Through the revolving *solera* system of mixing, the old and the new vintages are combined to produce a product that is always standard. Years ago, a small inner circle of British pukka sahibs made super-dry sherry a mark of social elegance in England; this foible, based on snobbism far more than on actual taste, quickly spread. Manzanillas and Finos are examples; now many are served chilled to soften the bite. San Patricio, when it's very cold, is very nice, but some Spaniards shudder at the thought of cooling sherries. Tio Pepe ("Uncle Joe" in Spanish) has the big reputation and international markets; Long Life (or any similar Oloroso blend) is old, soft and golden, with just enough dryness and richness of body to give pleasure to those who pucker up with the drier varieties.

Spanish red table wines are perhaps the most underrated of any in Europe. Countless gallons flow over the border each year to be sold as "French" types in France and elsewhere. Most of these reds resemble Burgundies rather than Bordeaux in their heaviness and fullness; the whites, not as fine, are most often too sweet. The other extreme is the type with no body, but they can be pleasantly refreshing. Some of the rosés (such as Marques de Riscal or Senorio de Sarria) are commendably dry and crisp.

If forced to pick out one of each kind for comparatively expensive daily consumption, take Vina Tondonia or Marquis de Riscal for red, Monopol for white, Cepa de Oro for Chablis and Codorniu N.P.U. for Spanish "champagne." *Cava*, incidentally, on labels of Spanish champagne means that it has rested in lodges (French style) and is of superior quality. Vina Pomal and Federico Paternina remain superior rubies in their "Reserva" class. Many "Reserva" and "Gran Reserva" types have deteriorated. Aside from N.P.U., the "champagnes" range from sweet to cloying to extremely cloying. You'll pay from $4 to $7 for all of these, save the N.P.U., which runs perhaps $10 per bottle.

All of the leading brands of beer on the Continent are now imported, and 40 breweries spread over 25 of Spain's provinces. Almost everyone agrees that San Miguel has taken over the leadership among domestic labels.

CURRENCY: EUROS.

Telephone

Access code to USA: 07. To telephone Spain: 34; time difference (Eastern Daylight) plus six hours.

For More Information

Spanish National Tourist Office
http://www.okspain.org/

665 Fifth Avenue, New York, N.Y. 10022, ☎ *(212) 759-8822;* FAX *(212) 759-8822.*

The well-known parador system consists of 86 usually government-operated inns and mountain lodges, ranging from remodeled ancient castles to modest shelters in remote areas. They used to be among Spain's hottest bargains, but now tariffs have crept up, and basic rates run from $70 to $175 per double, including breakfast. The food is usually typical of the region. Some of the nation's finest architects, archaeologists and scholars have cooperated to reproduce accommodations that are representative of the period in which they were built.

Andalucia

Costa Del Sol

The "Sunny Coast"—with Almeria, Marbella, Torremolinos, El Rodeo (an urban center) and other resort settlements strung along the 106-mile strip of seacoast on the Algeciras-Estepona-Malaga road—is geared to package tourism as well as independent travelers. Contrary to its neighbors, Marbella is much more select and sedate; the sea bathing is excellent, the golf courses are perfect, and the atmosphere is sportingly chic. For the independent travelers, apartment rentals (and there are many) can represent a sizable saving in the Euro department.

Where to Stay

El Moresco

This neo-Moorish, 145-room hotel hangs on a cliff higher up toward the whitewashed town. The octagonal rooftop pool is a marvel; the bedchambers, however, were somewhat disappointing.

Hotels and Resorts

Gran Hotel Almeria

Moderate

Avenida Reina Regente 8. *One block from the shore at the junction of two main streets.*

☎ *(951) 23-80-11,* FAX *(951) 27-06-91.*

This modern hotel is located near the yacht clubs and only a block from the water. It offers 117 simple, well-equipped rooms with bath, hair dryer, TV; three suites; lounge; bar; parking garage. A comfortable hotel in a great location.

Hotel Reina Victoria

★★★★★

http://www.infotu.com/roningle/Htreivic.htm
Moderate

Avenida Dr. Fleming 25. ☞ *On the east side of the town on the edge of Tajo Gorge; 500 yards from train station.*

☎ *(95) 287-12-40,* FAX *(95) 287-10-75.*

Credit Cards: *All Major.*

This marvelous English colonial-style hotel was built in 1906 and named the "Queen Victoria" in remembrance of the British monarch. The public rooms have large, comfortable sofas, mirrors with gilt frames and flowered Victorian-era carpeting as well as more modern Spanish decor, which creates a relaxing ambience. The 89 rooms are large and simply but attractively furnished, some with a terrace overlooking the Tajo Gorge, some with views of the lovely, lush hotel gardens. The dining room serves excellent cuisine; sitting rooms; free parking. The hotel is near the bullring and within walking distance of other sights in the town. Highly recommended.

Parador Reyes Catolicos ★

Budget to Moderate

Playa de Mojacar s/n. ☞ *Located 50 miles from Almeria train station.*

☎ *(951) 47-82-50,* FAX *(951) 47-81-83.*

Credit Cards: *All Major.*

This lovely white parador has all the modern amenities and is situated across from the beach. There are 98 attractive rooms with bath; room service; fine restaurant; bar; flower-filled gardens. A recommended choice.

What to Do
Excursions

Like many Christian houses of worship in Spain, Almeria's 16th-century Renaissance Cathedral was built on the foundations of a mosque. The ongoing threat of pirate attacks made it necessary to build the four thick towers, which give it a rather forbidding appearance. Behind the dour facade, though, is an airy interior, with a carved marble and jasper altar, and paintings by Murillo. Above the city, you will see the newly restored Alcazaba, or Moorish fortress. The royal palace and mosque that were sheltered behind its walls had been flattened in a 1522 earthquake.Until recently, nothing remained except a watchtower, the Torre de Homenaje. The gardens within are nice for strolling, and there's a small museum housing artifacts and sculpture from recent excavations of the palace. Open May-Sept. 10 a.m.–2 p.m. and 4:30–8 p.m.; winter, 9 a.m.–1 p.m. and 3–6:30 p.m. General admission: varies.

Granada

Granada is lovely. Allow plenty of time to browse through the world-famous **Alhambra** and the **Generalife**. They represent high moments in Muslim architecture, and the government is currently dedicating enormous funding for their preservation. The gardens alone command half a day to view properly. **Carlos V's Renaissance palace**, the **Cathedral** with the royal chapel and tombs of the "Catholic Monarchs" and the **Albaicin** also shouldn't be missed. As evening closes, look across the violet flat *vega* to the rise of the

Sierra Nevada, only 20 miles away. This sports center is a wonderful excursion point if you need a break from the artifacts of two great ancient civilizations. When it comes to accommodations, the **Parador Nacional San Francisco** is the first choice of most visitors to the Alhambra, and no wonder. It is beautifully situated, quiet, interesting, comfortable, magnificently decorated, within walking distance to all areas of the Alhambra, and the food is marvelous. If you can't spend the night, you must at least wander through or have a meal in the awesome dining room.

Where to Stay

Carmen Hotel Residencia   ★★★

Moderate

Acera de Darro 62. *Just 10 minutes from train station; 1/2 mile south of the Cathedral.*

☎ *(958) 25-83-00*, FAX *(958) 25-64-62*.

Credit Cards: *All Major.*
An attractive modern hotel with a central location in the main shopping district. Here you'll find clean accommodations and amiable service along with public areas that are furnished with comfortable couches that you will find difficult to leave. There are 283 delightful rooms with bath and six suites; restaurant serves pleasing cuisine; coffee shop for lighter meals; relaxing paneled bar with leather furniture; laundry service; concierge. A most convenient and welcome spot to rest after a day of touring.

Gran Hotel Brasilia Residencia   ★

Budget to Moderate

Recogidas 7. *In midcity area near shopping.*

☎ *(958) 25-84-50*, FAX *(958) 25-84-50*.

Credit Cards: *All Major.*
Here is a convenient, centrally located hotel with all the basic amenities. It has 68 comfortable rooms with bath and shower; six suites available; seventh-floor rooms at the front have views of the Sierra Nevada mountains. There are a snack bar and cafeteria for light

meals. This midcity hotel is a worthy accommodations choice.

Hotel Alhambra Palace ★★★★

Moderate to Expensive

Pena Partida 2-4. *Halfway up the hill in the Alhambra; 2 miles from train station.*

☎ *SPAIN-44,* ☎ *(958) 22-14-68,* FAX *(958) 22- 64-04.*

Credit Cards: *All Major.*

Built in 1910, this imposing hotel offers perhaps the best situation of any in the area for sightseeing as well as awesome views. With magnificent vistas extending over the Alhambra and the city, the hotel is a castlelike structure created in the Moorish style. The interior contains beautiful carved ceilings, arched doorways and windows, and colorful tilework. There are 144 spacious, comfortable rooms with bath/shower, bidet, some with bathrobes, some with balcony and view over the Sierra Nevada mountains or the city; 13 suites, of which the Andres Segovia is superb. The restaurant serves international cuisine; the bar and outdoor terrace offer breathtaking views. Certainly one of the superior hotel choices in Spain.

Where to Eat

Meson Andaluz ★★

Inexpensive to Moderate

Calle Elvira 10. ☎ *(958) 25-86-61.*

Credit Cards: *All Major.*

Closed: *Tues.*

Located near the Plaza Real and within walking distance of the Cathedral, this Andalusian eatery is comfortable and is willing and able to cater to travelers, although not too many have found it yet. Substantial fare, including soups, stews, seafood, chicken and meat dishes. Interesting desserts.

Restaurante Sevilla

Inexpensive

Calle Oficios 12. ☎ *(958) 22-88-62.*

Credit Cards: *All Major.*

Traditional and reliable, the Sevilla has had a famous clientele, including Granada-born poet and playwright Federico Garcia Lorca and composer Manuel de Falla. It's better as a tapas and vino spot (there's a bar), although the set meals are reasonably priced, and the quality is consistent, if not spectacular. Patio dining in good weather. Near the Cathedral is Granada's best seafood restaurant, **Cunini**, *Plaza de la Pescaderia, 14 (958) 25.05.77;* the variety is immense, from the selection of tapas to the soups and entrees. Upper-level bar, clubby dining room. Great tapas.

What to Do
Historical Sites

Alhambra   ★★★★★

▤ *Palacio de Carlos V.* *Enter via the Cuesta de Gomerez.* ☎ *(958) 22-75-27.*

🕘 *9 a.m.–8 p.m.*

Special Hours: *Nov. through Feb. to 6 p.m.*

Ever since Washington Irving wrote about this great Moorish palace-fortress of the Nasrid dynasty in his book *Tales of the Alhambra,* more than 20,000 people a day have climbed the steep hill (or taken the bus) to the complex, built by Muhammad I in the 13th century. As a means of crowd control, visits to the main palace (Palacios Nazaries), where all the goodies are, have been restricted to 30-minute slots—and you often have to wait three hours from your time of arrival. Entrance to the Alhambra is via the 14th-century gatetower, the Puerta de la Justicia; the square and the ticket booth are just beyond. Muhammad and his successors, particularly Yusuf I and Muhammad V, enclosed their respective families, government offices, royal concubines, mosques and schools within the red-tinted walls (Al Qal'a al Hambra means "red castle" in Arabic). Particularly notable is the Court of the Lions. Built as the private quarters of Muhammad V, it is dominated by its fountain, embellished with 12 water- spouting lions, a symbol of the 12 zodiac signs. The four channels that flow from the fountain are meant to denote the four corners of the Earth. It was in the Court of the

Lions that the sultan enjoyed his harem, the favorite of which he housed in the Hall of Two Sisters. Look up at the ceiling here—its dome, in the shape of a sunburst, looks like a million bees have set up shop; the honeycomb-shaped, sculpted stone stalactites are called *mukarnas*. Included with the admission price is Charles V of Castile's Renaissance palace, designed by a student of Michelangelo's. Charles flattened part of the Moorish section to build it. It contains a fine arts museum, ☎ *(958) 22-48-43* open Mon. through Fri. from 10 a.m.–2 p.m., and a museum of Moorish art ☎ *(958) 22-62-79*. And don't miss a climb to the top of the Torre de la Vela, an 11th-century watchtower, which is all that is left of the Alcazaba fortress, where 40,000 men were once stationed; it's located on the west side of the complex. General admission: varies, inexpensive.

Nightlife

The gypsy dancing remains a racket. The sucker is levied the fixed price for a package deal, and the tour operator then selects the cave that will yield the most profit for the least effort. The average performance is less than 30 minutes, with "artists" so untalented no top operation would hire them (the best migrate to Madrid, Barcelona or Seville). However, away from the city, there are the nightly two-hour performances at the poolside **Jardines Neptuno**, where the entrance fee of around $15 includes one quaff and the show. The flamenco sessions at **La Cueva de la Golondrina** (advance notice necessary) have been sterilized, dehumanized and left bereft of any cultural significance. As a curiosity, however, they still may be worth a jaunt. If you can stand a so-so dinner and want to dance till dawn, go to **El Corral de Principe**, Campo del Principe. Otherwise, **Zócalo**, *Granada 7*, four km out of town at Ogijares, provides a soothing ambience in its lovely garden while you enjoy classical music.

Parks and Gardens

Generalife   ★★★★★

🖃 *Cerro del Sol, above the Alhambra.* ☎ *(958) 22-75-27.*

🕐 *9 a.m.–8 p.m.*

Special Hours: *Nov. through Feb. to 6 p.m.*

This terraced garden of earthly delights is where the Nasrid sultans went to get away from it all. Several minutes' walk from the Alhambra, the Generalife (no, nothing to do with Franco, its name comes from "Jennat al-Arif," Arabic for "Garden of the Architect") is built above the palace on a slope of the Cerro del Sol. There are more than 100,000 varieties of roses, all manner of trees and plants, including succulents and cacti. One feature no other garden in the world has is the Camino de las Cascadas, a unique staircase with water running down the rails. From several patios (some quite secluded), you are afforded incredible views of the city, the Alhambra and the surrounding countryside. Don't miss it. Admission is included with the Alhambra.

Special Tours

Albaicin

📧 *Carrera del Darro, off Plaza Nueva.*

Take time to explore the ancient Moorish section of Granada, on the right bank of the Darro River, with streets that wind and turn like serpents. It's a little down at the heels, but some of the whitewashed old houses still have walled gardens, called carmenes (derived from the Arabic word for "orchard"). Walking along Carrera del Darro, you'll come onto the well-preserved Moorish baths, or El Banuelo, at #31, built before the Alhambra in the 11th century. Open daily from 9 a.m.–6 p.m. Admission, free. Up the Cuesta del Chapiz is St. Nicholas' terrace, with excellent views of the Alhambra and Generalife. There are also some atmospheric bars and restaurants north of St. Nicholas' terrace—but the area is a little sleazy after hours.

Seville

Seville is glorious, with its wealth of archaeology and art. Be sure to give yourself time to see the **Cathedral**, the 12th-century **Giralda** and the centuries-spanning **Alcazar** of King Don Pedro. There are churches, spacious parks, convents (La Merced is exceptional), tombs, museums and galleries on practically every block; palm and orange trees line the winding streets. Either walk to the sites or ride in the gradually vanishing horse-drawn carriages with their bright yellow wheels (an air-conditioned coach is too sterile). The **Feria**, held soon after Holy Week, is the biggest, most frenzied, most colorful traditional celebration in Spain. Everyone in town dons regional attire, and for nearly a week all work is forgotten. This event alone is worth a special trip to Spain—but reserve your space months in advance, because every pallet in the district is sought after by the hordes of outside visitors.

Where to Stay
Hotels and Resorts

Casa de Carmona

Moderate to Expensive

Plaza de Lasso 1. ☞ *Located 30 minutes east of Seville; in center of Carmona.*

☎ *(95) 414-33-00*, FAX *(95) 414-37-52.*

Credit Cards: *All Major.*

Converted from a 16th-century Renaissance palace, this unique and intimate Andalusian-style hotel is found in the medieval town of Carmona. The outstanding original marble columns have been retained, and the inner courtyard reflects the Moorish influence. The interior is decorated with period pieces, and the furnishings are plush and comfortable. There are 32 individually styled rooms, including three suites, 15 junior suites, a six-room Grand Suite and two apartments; some have shower; some have kitchenette; all are elegantly appointed and luxuriously furnished. The restaurant serves regional as well as international cuisine; library bar/ lounge; laundry service; supervised children's program; travel services; car rental; concierge; free parking. A real gem indeed.

Hotel Alfonso XIII

Moderate to Expensive

San Fernando 2. ☞ *In historic town center; 500 yards from train station; 8 miles from airport.*

☎ *(95) 422-28-50*, FAX *(95) 421-60-33.*

Credit Cards: *All Major.*

For nostalgic visitors to Andalucia, this deluxe Moorish-style hotel is a virtual shrine. The overall air of historic grace is so pervasive that merely walking through the magnificent lobby and atrium is a rewarding experience in itself. Lavish and detailed workmanship is in evidence throughout the interior, with its baked and hand-painted tiles, graceful archways, abundant use of beautiful marble and mahogany and intricately carved ceilings, all enhanced by tapestries, paintings and priceless antique furnishings. The rooms surround a captivating Andalusian inner courtyard with colorful flowers and a bubbling fountain. There are 149 rooms with bath, all luxuriously furnished and decorated; 19 suites, including the Royal Suite. The restaurant specializes in Italian as well as continental cuisine; bright lobby bar; terrace bar; gardens; parking garage. The hotel was originally built as a home away from home for the wealthy during the 1929 Exposition and remains a fine example of Spanish and Moorish styles that shouldn't be missed.

Hotel Dona Maria   ★★

http://www.sol.com/hotel/d-maria/

Don Remondo 19. ☞ *On the square opposite the Giralda and Cathedral; in center of city near train station.*

☎ *(95) 422-49-90,* FAX *(95) 421-95-46.*

Credit Cards: *All Major.*

This intimate little hotel with its attractive wrought-iron balconies possesses a perfect midtown situation almost touching the Cathedral from the narrow Calle don Remondo. You will be enchanted at once upon entering the brick-pillared lobby with its stone floors and lovely domed ceiling. There is a tasteful selection of Iberian antiques throughout. The rooftop pool is a rare find in the middle of the city. It is surrounded by trellises overflowing with flowering plants and offers a view over the city to the Cathedral. Accommodations include 61 rooms and two suites that are comfortable and pleasantly furnished, each unique in style, all with private bath, some with French doors leading to a balcony, some with a four-poster bed; corner room #110 overlooks the Giralda and Cathedral. The restaurant in Moorish decor serves only breakfast; rooftop bar; lounge; parking (fee). Very tasteful, very comfortable, very highly recommended.

Hotel Hispalis

Budget

Avenida Andalucia. *two miles from train station; 1 mile from the harbor.*

☎ *(95) 452-94-33*, FAX *(95) 467-53-13*.

Credit Cards: *All Major.*

This conveniently located hotel is modern and comfortable. It offers 68 clean, well-equipped rooms with private bath; one suite available. The restaurant serves regional and international fare; relaxing bar; parking (fee). A sound choice with an efficient staff.

Where to Eat

Egana Oriza ★★★

Moderate to Expensive

San Fernando 41. ☎ *(95) 422-72-11*.

Credit Cards: *All Major.*

Seville's most expensive restaurant specializes in wild game, much of which is shot by the owner himself, and beef dishes. The plush, two-story establishment was once the greenhouse of an exclusive home. It has a bar at the entrance where you can stop for elegant tapas (with caviar and asparagus tips). The light-filled main dining room on the second floor has a glass wall, and seating is on plush, cream-colored barrel chairs. The linens and tableware are of the best quality, and the staff is exceedingly well trained. Cocktails come with complimentary appetizers, but after that expect to shell out the big bucks.

El Burladero ★★

Moderate to Expensive

Canalejas 1. ☎ *(95) 422-29-00*.

Credit Cards: *All Major.*

The food, although expensive, is secondary to the ambience at this cave-like, warmly lit hotel restaurant with clever, arched ceilings decorated with tiles depicting bullfighting scenes. It's frequented by matadors and aficionados of the sport, who have their favorite dishes and are well known to the management. The portions are hefty, but prepared with a minimum of finesse.

La Albahaca

Moderate to Expensive

Plaza de Santa Cruz 12. ☎ *(95) 422-07-14.*

Credit Cards: *All Major.*
Closed: *Sun.*

Not only is this restaurant lovely, with a tree-covered patio overlooking the much photographed Plaza de Santa Cruz, the food is exceptionally well prepared and flavorful. Specialties are somewhat lighter than what is usually offered on Andalusian tables. Good gazpacho, veal and fish. There are also three indoor dining areas decorated with tile and polished woods.

La Alicantina

Inexpensive to Moderate

Plaza del Salvador. ☎ *(95) 422-61-22.*

A wild and swinging kind of place, this tapas taberna is a happy-hour spot for office workers who crowd the bar and sidewalk tables every day after work. They probably drawn by the central location near the Cathedral and the ultrafresh shellfish served raw, grilled or broiled. Beer is the drink of choice. If you travel across the river to the Triana district, you'll find a string of stylish bars, especially along the Calle Betis, between the Isabel II and San Telmo bridges. A notable stop is **La Albariza**, *Betis 6,* ☎ *(95) 433-20-16,* where tapas and drinks are served on sherry casks in the bar. There's also a private dining room. Ham from Jabugo is a specialty. Open daily.

Rincon de Curro

Moderate to Expensive

Virgen de Lujan, 45. ☎ *(95) 445-02-38.*

Credit Cards: *All Major.*

Closed: *Sun*.

Not far from the Alfonso XII hotel, this clubby restaurant is a favorite with well- heeled business types, who attack the prime steaks and chops served here with gusto. Management claims they obtain the best beef in Spain, and they may be right. The light, delicate dessert souffles provide a suitable finish to this prodigious fare.

What to Do
City Celebrations

Semana Santa/Feria de Abril

▤ *Various locations.*

If you're in Seville for Semana Santa (Holy Week, beginning on Palm Sunday and ending on Easter Sunday), you might think the Inquisition is still alive and well. But the hooded, gloved, mysterious figures walking the evening processions are members of La Confradia, a brotherhood dedicated to the Virgin Mary. Each of the 50 churches in the city have individual statues (La Macarena is the most well known), which require a new float (*paso*) and costume every year. As the heavy floats pass through town, women fervently sing *saetas* (arrows of faith) that have deep roots in flamenco. For something a lot less somber, don't leave town, for in two weeks, Feria de Abril begins. Once an agricultural fair, the Feria is a nonstop, weeklong party that signals the beginning of the bullfighting season (Maestranza). Along with *corridas* are the daily equestrian parades, dancing of the Sevillana (an 18th-century court dance) and plenty of food and drink. People stay up all night, eating churros and downing hot chocolate.

Historical Sites
ITRAVELBOOK FREEBIE

Alcazar ★★★★

📧 *Plaza de Triunfo.* ☎ *(95) 422.71.63.*

🕐 *10:30 a.m.–5 p.m.*

Special Hours: *Sunday 10 a.m.–1 p.m.; closed Mon.*

Moorish craftsmen built this little Alhambra for King Pedro the Cruel (he supposedly murdered his own brother, Don Fadrique, here) in the 14th century. Since that time, it has been used as a royal palace, and contains the former apartments of Ferdinand and Isabella and Philip II. Carlos V, apparently discontented with the living quarters left behind by his predecessors, built his own palace within the walls, hung with 16th-century Flemish tapestries. You can also tour his gardens and a labyrinth. A series of arched courtyards, embellished with lacy stone- and decorative tilework, lead into the Casa de Contratacion, where plans to exploit the New World were hatched. The Alcazar gardens, with fountains, pools and terraces, are a refreshing oasis from Seville's desert-like summer heat. General admission; 600 ptas.; students, children, free. Across from the Alcazar is the Casa Lonja, a 16th-century building designed by Juan de Herrera, housing the Archivo General de Indias, a rare collection of letters, maps and other documents relating to the discovery of the americas by Magellan, Columbus and others. Unfortunately, most of this priceless data is off-limits to the public.

Barrio Santa Cruz ★★★

📧 *Barrio Santa Cruz.* *East of the Cathedral.*

When you first set foot into this former 14th-century Jewish quarter (east of the Cathedral), everything seems a little manufactured—the iron gates to the picturesque white-painted houses are wide open so you can admire (or envy) the patios and gardens within. At night people actually burst into spontaneous song or dance the flamenco in the tiny squares. But everyone soon gets into the spirit of the thing, and so will you, so don't forget to bring extra film for your camera.

Catedral

▤ *Avenida de la Constitucion.* ☎ *(95) 421-28-00.*

Although it had been used by Christians as a church since the 13th century, the precursor to Seville's present-day Cathedral still bore the traces of its origins as an Almohad mosque, when, more than 100 years later, builders had a vision to flatten what was left and build the biggest house of worship in the world. They almost succeeded—the Cathedral is officially the third-largest (and bulkiest) of its kind in Europe, but not necessarily the loveliest. Within the dim interior (sometimes you need a flashlight) of the Gothic-Renaissance structure there are almost 80 stained-glass windows and 40 columns. Near the main entrance is the Chapter House, seat of the bishop of Seville, containing a large Murillo canvas; just inside is the sacristy and treasury with priceless art and religious relics, including the skulls and bones of saints and the teeth of Alfonso the Wise. The rest of Alfonso is buried behind the domed Royal Chapel. Relegated to a spot below stairs are the tombs of Pedro the Cruel (who built the Alcazar) and his mistress. At the southern entrance is Columbus' ornate tomb, but there's some question as to whether he is really buried there. On the northern side of the Cathedral is the fragrant Patio de las Naranjas, planted with orange trees, where you can still see the outline of the old mosque courtyard. General admission: inexpensive.

Museums and Exhibits

Plaza de Toros

▤ *Paseo de Cristobal Colon.* ☎ *(95) 422-3152.*

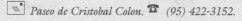 🕐 *10 a.m.–1:30 p.m.*

The Seville bullring, Plaza de Toros, is a graceful, 18th-century building that hosts the finest bullfighters in all Spain during the season, which begins after the Feria de Abril (see City Celebrations) and lasts until the end of October. You can also tour the oval building, constructed so that everyone has a good view of the action (the best seats are those with the least exposure to the sun).

Nightlife

Los Gallos

📧 *11 Plaza de Santa Cruz.* ☎ *(95) 422-85-22.*

You'll find authentic, highly professional flamenco performances in this intimate *tablao* (the local name for flamenco clubs) right in the heart of the Barrio de Santa Cruz. Admission: moderate.; two shows nightly, at 9 and 11 p.m. Also reliable is **El Arenal**, near the Cathedral, at *7 Rodo,* ☎ *(95) 421-64-92.* Admission: 3500 ptas. Another good bet is **El Patio Sevillano,** in the town center, at *11 Paseo de Cristobal Colon,* ☎ *(95) 421-41-20.* Admission: moderate. Three shows nightly from 7:30, 10, and 11:45 p.m., Mar. through Oct. Other months, the last show is omitted.

Shopping

Convento de Santa Paula

📧 *11 Calle Santa Paula.* ☎ *(95) 442-13-07.*

We'll let you in on a secret: Convent nuns make the best jams and confections in Spain. The nuns at Santa Paula will sell you handsomely gift-packaged or individual jars of marmalade made from the famous Seville oranges. If you don't have time to visit the good sisters, a specialty shop, **El Torno**, *Plaza del Cabildo,* ☎ *(95) 421-91-90,* sells delicacies from several area convents, including rich bonbons made from egg yolks as well as handmade children's outfits.

San Pedro de Alcantara
Historical Sites

San Pedro de Alcantara

📧 *43 miles west of Malaga on N-340.*

Once a thriving old fishermen's village, San Pedro is now a pretty resort town that's fancier than Estepona and more subdued than Marbella. It's also much less developed than either place. There are a great beach and Roman and Paleo-Christian ruins that have been designated a National Monument.

Catalunya

Barcelona

Barcelona was the starting point for the Age of Discovery, and five centuries later this Old-World port witnessed new surprises. After having experienced the feverish and joyful challenge of hosting the 1992 Olympic Games, vast changes have turned global spotlights on a brighter, fresher and more prosperous Catalonia. Already one of the most densely populated cities in the world, Barcelona (after Madrid) is considered second in importance—a point that any good Catalan will heatedly refute. It's on the Mediterranean coast, northeast of Madrid, about 100 miles from the Pyrenees, sitting on a rich plain between two rivers and two towering mountains. Catalans feel a very special identity with their metropolis, which proudly produces so much of the nation's wealth; since 1980, it has had its own provincial government called "La Generalitat." Artistic activities abound; cultural attractions are numerous; it conducts business in an energetic style; and is a huge commercial port. Its glass-sheathed airport terminal, while attractive to the eye, is one of the least efficient buildings to ever absorb such quantities of public funding. One detriment within the city itself is the occasional throat-rasping smog from its booming industries. Although restaurants are superb, the hotels have gone price happy while remaining below continental standards for a city of such significance.

Where to Stay

Hotels and Resorts

Avenida Palace Hotel ★★

http://www.avenidapalace.com/

Moderate

Gran Via de les Corts Catalanes 605-607. *In city center; 2 miles from train station.*

Metro Stop Gran Via.

☎ *(93) 301-96-00,* FAX *(93) 318-12-34.*

Credit Cards: *All Major.*

Although this hotel was built in the mid-1950s, it maintains an old-world atmosphere throughout with its antiques, comfortable furnishings, beautiful marble stairway leading from the busy lobby, flower-filled rooms and attentive staff. It has a wonderful location close to many attractions and shopping. The 159 traditionally furnished rooms have bath, TV, soundproofing. There are a dining room, with a glassed-in fountain, appealing cuisine; charming lounge/bar for relaxing; concierge. Immaculately maintained and a very peaceful place to rest after a day of sightseeing.

Derby Hotel Residencia   ★★

http://www.barcelona-spain- hotels.net/derby/hotel.htm
Moderate

Calle Loreto 21-25. *One mile from Sants Central train station;*
two blocks from Avenida Diagonal and Avenida Sarria.
Metro Stop Hospital Clinic.

☎ *(93) 322-32-15,* FAX *(93) 410-08-62.*

Credit Cards: *All Major.*

Located in a tranquil area of the city, this hotel is across the street from the all-suite Gran Derby Hotel. It is less inspired aesthetically, but the facilities here are agreeable and pleasant. Accommodations include 117 rooms with simple but comfortable furnishings, private bath; eight suites. Basic, quiet accommodations.

Hotel Condes de Barcelona   ★★★

Moderate to Expensive

Paseo de Gracia 75. *In city center.*

Metro Stop Paseo de Gracia.

☎ *(93) 484-86-00,* FAX *(93) 216-08-35.*

Credit Cards: *All Major.*

This opulent hotel is patronized by a discreet and loyal international clientele. It is located in the ancient Casa Batllo, a registered art nouveau building that dates from 1876 and is known for its special beauty and Gaudi-influenced facade. There are 184 luxurious soundproof rooms with subtle decor and marble bath; six suites. Cafe Condal restaurant serves regional cuisine; attractive curved bar in lobby; laundry service; parking (fee). Try to reserve a room overlooking the pretty garden. Young but cordial and efficient staff.

NH Calderon

Moderate

Rambla de Cataluna 26. *Just 10 minutes from Sants Central train station.*

Metro Stop Placa de Catalunya.

☎ *(93) 301-00-00,* FAX *(93) 317-44-53.*

Credit Cards: *All Major.*

An attractive contemporary hotel is in a convenient location. All 264 rooms with bath are pleasingly furnished in subtle colors and vary in size and arrangements; 16 large suites. There are an extremely handsome, spacious mirrored lounge; cocktail bar with comfortable upholstered chairs; well-regarded, tasteful dining room; rooftop pool with a small bar and separate solarium affording magnificent views of the city; parking (fee). The attentive service as well as the conveniences found here make this a popular hotel with business and pleasure travelers.

Regente Hotel ★

Budget to Moderate

Rambla de Cataluna 76. *Just 1 mile from Sants train station.*

Metro Stop Placa de Catalunya.

☎ *(93) 487-59-89,* FAX *(93) 487-32-27.*

Credit Cards: *All Major.*

Conveniently located, this modern and functional hotel has a lovely art nouveau facade and a traditional, comfortably furnished lobby. Its panoramic rooftop solarium and open terrace provide guests with a retreat overlooking the city to the harbor. There are 78 delightfully furnished, well-equipped rooms with bath, wall-to-wall carpeting, cleverly designed bed lamps, door chimes, night bins for shoe shining; eight rooms have a private terrace; one suite. There are a restaurant at salon level; bar; parking (fee). All attractions are within easy access to this good hotel choice.

Where to Eat

Azulete   ★★★★

Moderate to Expensive

Via Augusta 281. ☎ *(93) 203-59-43.*

Credit Cards: *All Major.*

Closed: *Sun.*

This is a romantic oasis in a northern outpost of the city. Owner-chef Toia Roque renovated a luxurious town house by commissioning designer Oscar Tusquets to fashion a glass "cage" in the back garden, set around a gurgling pool. Before dining there, however, you and your party can relax over drinks, as the regulars do, in the mansion's front room, which has been converted into a bar. A well-trained and polished staff. It's easier to get a reservation at lunch.

Cafe de la Ribera   ★★

Moderate

6 Placa de les Olles. ☎ *(93) 319-50-72.*

Closed: *Sun.*

You may want to bring earplugs to this cacophonous hangout, where the youthful and the restless fill up on bowls of garlicky soup and seafood for under 900 ptas. (a bit more with wine). There's not an inch left of wall space here to hang one more painting or photograph. Next door, at #7, is a more sedate establishment, a venerable old sweets shop, **Patisseria Guell La Mallorquina,** ☎ *(93) 319-39-83.* Here traditional pastries and cookies are made before your eyes. Open daily, except Tues., from 8–2 p.m. and 5–8:30 p.m.; Sat. to 3 p.m.

Cafe-Bar Pinocho   ★★

Inexpensive to Moderate

La Boqueria Market. ☎ *(93) 317-17-31.*

Metro Stop Liceu.

Closed: *Sun.*

Juan Bayan and his sister Maria own this popular 10-stool counter that's situated near the entrance to the Central Market. Some regulars (including ladies of the night getting off of work) wouldn't think of starting the day without breakfast here accompanied by gossip and a cup of strong espresso. It's open for lunch as well, and what you get depends on whatever's available. Cheap, earthy and good, and a very authentic experience. There are two excellent choices located behind the market in the Barri Xines. One is **Garduna**, *Morera 17-19,* ☎ *(93) 302-43-23,* featuring excellent paella, seafood and steaks served on two levels. Then there's **Egipte**, *Jerusalem 3,* ☎ *(93) 317-74-80,* where the tables are fashioned out of old sewing machines. Two dining rooms and a patio; crowded and noisy. The area is chancy at night. No credit cards. Open daily, except Sun., from 1–4 p.m. and 8:30 p.m.–12:30 a.m. Also worthy in the Las Rambles district is the art nouveau-ish **Cafe de l'Opera**, at #74 ☎ *(93) 317-75-85,* for wonderful coffee (Spain's is probably the best in Europe), pastries (good almond tart) and sandwiches. The atmosphere is often blue with cigarette smoke, but there are tables outside. Open from 9 a.m.–2 a.m. daily. Across the street from the cafe is a pastry shop, **Patisseria Escriba,** *at #83 Las Ramblas,* ☎ *(93) 301-60-27;* it's a favorite with chocoholics.

Eldorado Petit ★★★

Moderate

Dolores Monsorda, 51. ☎ *(93) 204-51-53.*

Metro Stop Via Augusta-Sarria.

Credit Cards: *All Major.*

This award-winning restaurant, converted from a Mediterranean-style 19th-century residence, sits on top of a hill in a wealthy northern suburb. Its interior decor is rustic-chic, a combination of wicker and antiques, with polished wooden floors. Although the old house is quite large, the dining areas are small, with less than 12 tables; there's extra seating in summer when a patio is open. The menu is limited to a few items, but the Catalan-style cuisine is robust, with plenty of garlic, olive oil and top-of-the-market produce and seafood. The appetizers and desserts are sometimes better than the entrees. There's a tasting menu of seven courses. One drawback is the moody service, which can alternate from welcoming to offensive, depending on who you are and how the staff is feeling that day.

La Odisea ★★★

Moderate to Expensive

7 Copons. ☎ *(93) 302-36-92.*

Credit Cards: *All Major.*

Closed: *Sat.*

A couple of rooms (a bar and a parlor) lead into this sensuous, romantic restaurant, painted in rouge tones. The walls are hung with paintings of voluptuous nudes and modern canvases collected by owner-chef Antonio Ferrer, who also happens to be a poet. The voluminous, handwritten menu is adorned with doodles by the art-loving Ferrer. His creative bent also translates well in the kitchen, where inventive dishes such as fresh fish steamed in seaweed coexist nicely with perfectly cooked renditions of broiled lamb or *merluza* (hake). His desserts are fabulous.

Reno ★★★

Moderate

Tuset 27. ☎ *(93) 200-91-29.*

Metro Stop Diagonal.

Credit Cards: *All Major.*

Closed: *Sat.*

For more than 40 years, Reno has been serving classic French cuisine and excellent Catalan seafood dishes to a silk-stocking crowd. The air-conditioned room, with wood-paneled walls and oversize windows, overlooks a lively square. Seating is on comfortable black banquettes or at tables on a glassed-in sidewalk terrace. Service is deft and discreet.

Siete Portes (Seven Portes) ★★★

Moderate to Expensive

Passeig d'Isabel II, 14. ☎ *(93) 319-30-33.*

Metro Stop Barceloneta.

Credit Cards: *All Major.*

At this venerable spot (more than 150 years old), you can sit in Picasso's favorite seat: It's marked by a brass plaque. And, yes, there are seven doors; the place is that big. Spiffed up awhile back, it is painted in cheerful yellow tones, with a black-and-white harlequin-tiled floor. There are upstairs and downstairs sections, divided into several small, cozy dining areas. The restaurant is always packed and bustling, with a mixture of businesspeople and curious tourists, but the seasoned waiters usually manage to be attentive and cheerful to everyone. There are many old favorites you've heard about and tried elsewhere but nowhere near as good as here: gazpacho, paella and *suquet*, a Catalan version of bouillabaisse. A somewhat less familiar local specialty worth trying is spinach prepared with raisins and pine nuts.

What to Do

Museums and Exhibits

ITRAVELBOOK FREEBIE

La Sagrada Familia ★★★★

http://www.sagradafamilia.org/

Mallorca 401. ☎ *(93) 455.02.47.*

Metro Stop Sagrada Familia.

🕐 *9 a.m.–9 p.m.*

Special Hours: *May-Sept. and Mar.-Apr. to 7 p.m.*

Appalled (or jealous) fellow artists including Salvador Dali, reviled this unfinished cathedral by Modernisme (art deco with a Moorish touch) architect-sculptor Antonio Gaudi. Begun in the neo-Gothic style by Villar in 1882, the project was taken over by Gaudi, who added on to it for the better part of 40 years, even living in a shed on the premises. He passed away suddenly after being hit by a tram, and his plans died with him. He did finish the four hollow towers that make up the Nativity facade; the structure looks like an intergalactic sand castle. Gaudi also left behind a slew of apartment buildings, private homes, street lamps (on the Placa Reial, near the

Ramblas), even a housing project, left unfinished as well. Commissioned by wealthy businessman Eusebio Guell Bacigalupi, the **Parc Guell** (on Carrer de Larrad, 40 minutes northwest by car from the center of town; Metro: Alfonso X) was to consist of 60 homes; only two (Gaudi bought one) were completed, but the gardens surrounding the development are now a city park. You can see the sinuous, futuristic walkways, benches made with multicolored tiles and other fantasia. ☎ *(93) 424.38.09.* Open daily 10–9 p.m. May through Sept., to 6 p.m. Oct. through Apr.

Parc de Montjuic ★★★★

📧 *Montjuic.* *Bus 61 from Placa Espanya every 10 minutes.*

Once an ancient Jewish cemetery and 12th-century hilltop fortress, Montjuic ("Mountain of the Jews" in Catalan) is now a public park. Located on Barcelona's south side, it overlooks the city and boasts loads of attractions, including a museum of Catalan art (currently closed for renovations) in the Palau Real, a Joan Miro museum and two leftovers from the 1929 International Exposition, an encapsulated Spain (Poble Espanyol) and the Mies Van der Rohe Pavilion (open 9 a.m.–8 p.m.). The **Poble Espanyol**, *Marques de Comilias* ☎ *(93) 325-78-66,* allows you to visit Spain through its varied architecture. You'll see reproductions (facades only) of typical houses and churches, Galician cottages and gay re-created streets of all the regions of Spain. There are handicrafts exhibitions, shops, restaurants, even bars and clubs, which locals actually patronize. Open Sun. through Mon. 9 a.m.-8 p.m., Tues. through Thurs. to 3 p.m., Fri. through Sat. to 4 p.m.; shops from 10 a.m.–8 p.m. The **Fundacio Joan Miro**, *Placa de Neptu,* ☎ *(91) 329-19-08,* housed in an award-winning modern structure designed by Josep Lluis Sert, is located near the stadium built for the '92 Summer Olympics. Within are sculpture, graphics and paintings by the Catalan surrealist painter. Open daily, except Mon. from 11 a.m.–7 p.m.; Sun. from 10:30 a.m.– 2:30 p.m. Admission: varies.

Music

Palau de la Musica Catalan ★★★

 Sant Francest de Paula 2. ☎ *(93) 268-10-00.*

🕐 *10 a.m.–9 p.m.*

A triumph of *Modernisme*, this concert hall for symphonic and choral music was designed by Domenech i Montaner in 1908. The ceiling is a mass of carved wooden rosettes, dominated by a stunning, upside-down cupola. The collection of flamboyant sculpture includes a winged Pegasus. Admission: varies.

Nightlife
Flamenco

Los Tarantos (Plaza Real 17) has shows at 10 p.m. and midnight. Every performer is a serious artist in this ethnic specialty. Gypsy-camp ambience; lantern illuminations. Other candidates are **El Cordobes** (Rambla Capuchinos 35) and **El Patio Andaluz** (Aribau 242).

Bodega del Toro (Conde del Asalto 103) has terrific musicians and performers. But watch out for this smoothly executed swindle here. After 10 or 12 gypsies have come to your table to show their stuff, they'll coolly invite themselves to one or two rounds of drinks at your expense—and suddenly you'll find you have a $100 tab. To avoid this slick charade, your best protection is to glue yourself to the bar from the time you enter; you can see and hear all the performers from there.

Gambling

There are three centers in the region: **Gran Casino de Barcelona**, **Casino Castillo de Perelada** and **Casino Lloret de Mar**. Opening times, meals and shows vary, so inquire through your concierge before going.

La Pira ★★

 C. Provenca, 171. ☎ *(93) 323-72-71.*

Metro Stop Diagonal.

🕐 *7 p.m.–3 a.m.*

Special Hours: *Fri. through Sat. to 4 a.m., Sun. 6 p.m.–midnight.*

An amusing bar in a converted amusement park, with music (no dancing). Entertainment is provided by looking at sophisticates quaffing drinks while sitting in old bumper cars (they don't go anywhere). A laser-video bar and disco that has been up and down in popularity is **Nick Havanna** (it's currently up). Postmodern decor, bars galore, and a fashionable crowd, *C. Rosello, 208*, Metro: Diagonal ☎ *(93) 215-65-91*. Open 8 p.m.–4 a.m., Fri. through Sat. to 5 a.m., Sun. from 7 p.m.–3 a.m. But don't think of coming before midnight. Other places to hit include **TickTackToe**, a pool hall-bar-restaurant with whimsical decor, and the *Otto Zutz Club*, which looks and feels like "Sprockets" nightclub on "Saturday Night Live"; it's high-tech, trendy and expensive.

Xampu Xampany

📃 *Gran Via de los Corts Catalanes.* ☎ *(93) 265.04.83.*

Metro Stop Girona.

🕐 *6:30 p.m.–3:30 a.m.*

Features sparkling wines from Catalan and Spanish caves, by the bottle or glass, and tapas. Postmodern decor juxtaposed with swing music from the '40s and '80s techno-pop.

Parks and Gardens

Shopping

Parc de la Ciutadella   ★★★

📃 *Barri de la Ribera.*

Metro Stop Ciutadella.

🕐 *8 a.m.–9 p.m.*

Special Hours: *Oct. through Mar., to 8 p.m.*

This seaside park, site of the 1888 World's Fair, was established as a public recreational area in 1873. There was a fortress here constructed by Philip V in the 18th century; the old Arsenal remains and is now the headquarters for the Catalonian Parliament and the Museum of Modern Art. The **Museum of Modern Art** ☎ *(93) 319.57.28*, is largely dedicated to 19th- and 20th-century Catalan artists, with paintings, sculpture and furniture by Fortuny, Dali, Miro and Puig i Cadalfach. Open daily, except Tues., from 10 a.m.–9 p.m. Probably the best zoo in Spain is in the park, just south of the Museum, ☎ *(93) 221.25.06.* Its biggest draw is Snowflake, a rare albino gorilla; this is the only zoo in the world to have one. Most of the larger animals can be seen in simulated natural habitats, and there's an Aquarama with a marine mammal show. Open 10 a.m.–5 p.m.; summer from 9:30 a.m.–7:30 p.m.

Groc ★★

▤ *Ramble de Catalunya.* ☎ *(93) 215-74-74.*
Metro Stop Placa de Catalunya.

🕐 *10 a.m.–2 p.m.*
Special Hours: *and 4:30 p.m.–8 p.m.; closed Sun.*

Modish, original clothing for men and women can be found at this high-fashion boutique owned by Tony Miro, a leading Barcelona designer. Expensive. Also in the Placa, at #14, is a branch of the national chain **El Corte Ingles**, for all your shopping needs, from porcelain to CDs. Decently priced places to eat on the premises as well. Open daily, except Sun, from *10 a.m.–8 p.m.*, Sat. to 9 *p.m.* Not far away in the Passeig de Gracia is **Loewe**, ☎ *(93) 216-04-00*, one of Spain's finest purveyors of leather goods. A class act, and a pricey one, but the shoes, handbags, luggage, coats, jackets and accessories are trendsetting. Open daily, except Sun., from 9:30 a.m.–2 p.m. and 4:30–8 p.m.

Special Tours

ITRAVELBOOK FREEBIE

Cathedral and Gothic Quarter Tour ★★★★★

✉ *Placa de la Seu.* ☎ *(93) 315.15.54.*

Metro Stop Jaume 1.

🕐 *8 a.m.–1:30 p.m.*

Special Hours: *and 4–7:30 p.m.*

Barcelona's Cathedral is in the heart of the Barri Gotic, or Gothic Quarter, which is the oldest section of the city. This pedestrian-only zone, which is less than a mile long, has an intense concentration of 13th– 14th-, and 15th-century buildings. The church was completed in the 15th century, yet the main facade (it has three entrances) was restored in the 19th century following original plans drawn by a medieval master mason. It sits upon the foundations of early Christian chapels (4th–6th centuries) and an 11th-century Romanesque temple. Visitors are drawn to its cloister, with four vaulted galleries and a pleasant garden. In the choir, you can see stalls carved especially for European royalty, including England's Henry VIII and Emperor Maximilian; they were created for a meeting of the chapter of the Order of the Golden Fleece in 1519, summoned by Spain's King Carlos I. On the Placa Nova, in front of the Cathedral, an antique market is held Thurs. from 9 a.m.–8 p.m. On Sat. and Sun., everyone can join in a Catalan folk dance called the Sardana, accompanied by a brass band. Expressing Catalan unity, it was banned for many years by Generalissimo Franco.

You can round up your tour of the Barri Gotic back in the 20th century: the Museo Picasso, at *Carrer Montcada 15-17*, is a repository of the artist's work from his early years (1890-1904). Here you'll find 200 paintings, pastels and watercolors housed in two adjoining 14th-century palaces. Open Tues. through Sat. from 10 a.m.–8 p.m., Sun. until 3 p.m. General admission: varies.

Madrid

Madrid

This capital of more than 3 million people is right smack in the middle of the country. In size, it ranks just under Philadelphia; in temperature, hotels, food and gracious living, it's hard to find an equal in Europe. While it used to be inexpensive, it is even more costly than New York today for the visitor who wishes to live and dine well. May and October are the best months; midwinter is sometimes surprisingly cold due to the city's situation and altitude. It's uncomfortably hot for only about two weeks each summer—and many hotels are now fully or at least partially air-conditioned.

Where to Stay
Hotels and Resorts

Alameda Hotel   ★

Budget

Avenida de Logrono 100. ☞ *One mile from Madrid airport and Exhibition Center.*

☎ *(91) 747-48-00,* FAX *(91) 747-89-28.*

Credit Cards: *All Major.*

Here is a worthy alternative for airport accommodations. It offers modern surroundings and generous amenities. Accommodations include 145 comfortable and well-equipped rooms with bath; nine suites available. There are two restaurants plus a cafeteria for quick meals; bar; shops; concierge; parking (fee). A good choice for recharging between travels.

Barajas Hotel   ★

Budget to Moderate

Avenida de Logrono 305. ☞ *Just 1/2 mile from the airport; 5 miles from center of Madrid; near Exhibition and Convention Center.*

☎ *(91) 747-77-00,* FAX *(91) 747-87-17.*

Credit Cards: *All Major.*

Situated on a hill overlooking Madrid's busy airport, this attractive, modern three- story hotel is ideal for travelers in need of some rest before or after their trip. Accommodations include 230 spacious rooms with bath, soundproofing, some with private balcony; executive floor available; 18 suites. For dining there are four restaurants to

choose from, including an elegant one on the terrace and a 24-hour
coffee shop; bar; disco; beauty salon; laundry service. A good hotel
choice for pre and apres travel.

Gran Hotel Reina Victoria   ★★★★

Expensive

Plaza de Santa Ana 14. *Opposite Santa Ana Plaza in the Old
Town.*
Metro Stop Puerta del Sol; Tirso de Molin.

☎ *(91) 315-32-46,* FAX *(91) 314-31-56.*

Credit Cards: *All Major.*

Conveniently located right in the center of old Madrid, this hotel
was once the favorite of the famous bullfighter, Manolete, and the
writer Ernest Hemingway. It's the best choice for location, convenience and reasonable rates. The hotel was built in the early 1920s,
and, while offering all the modern amenities required of travelers
today, it retains its glorious past, evident in its impressive facade with
its ornate steeple, which continues as a city landmark. The welcoming lobby adjoins a popular lounge, where you will find traditional
comfort in upholstered furnishings as well as displays of interesting
bullfighting memorabilia. Accommodations include 200 rooms and
suites that are simply but delightfully furnished, all with soundproof
windows, some with a balcony that overlooks the park. There are a
good restaurant within the hotel; room service; concierge. Spend
some time in the lovely plaza that opens from the hotel before
exploring this very interesting area.

Gran Hotel Velazquez   ★

http://www.hotelvelazquez.com/
Budget to Moderate

Velazquez 62. *In city center; 1 mile from Atocha train station.*

☎ *(91) 75-28-00,* FAX *(91) 75-28-09.*

Credit Cards: *All Major.*

This classically styled hotel, built in the late 1940s, is in an excellent
location in the Salamanca residential district. Within you'll find sim-

ple traditional comfort provided by the decor and furnishings. The 145 rooms are pleasingly furnished; all have bath, bidet; some have a balcony; Las Lanzas restaurant serves good international fare; English-style bar that's popular with locals; health club nearby for guests; laundry service; car rental; concierge; parking (fee). A recommended hotel in a very convenient location.

Hotel Carlos V ★

Budget

Maestro Vitoria 5. ☞ *Near Puerta de Sol in pedestrian area.*

Metro Stop Callao; Puerta del Sol.

☎ *(1) 531-41-00,* FAX *(1) 531-37-61.*

Credit Cards: *All Major.*

Although the exterior may be deceiving upon first glance, this early 1900s art nouveau hotel has retained its original elegance. Accommodations include 67 updated and tasteful rooms with bath, some with a balcony or terrace. There are a pretty breakfast room; lovely sitting room enhanced with crystal chandeliers and moulded ceilings; bar. Although this popular spot can be somewhat noisy, its superb location can't be beat.

Where to Eat

Botin

Expensive

Calle de Cuchilleros. ☎ *(91) 366-42-17.*

Metro Stop La Latina.

Credit Cards: *All Major.*

Always crawling with tourists, Botin is a tried-and-true standby, famous all over the world for its matador guests and roast suckling pig and baby lamb *(cordero asado)*. This is the restaurant where Jake Barnes, hero of *The Sun Also Rises,* plays his last scene; Hemingway gave the place considerable attention in *Death in the Afternoon* as well. The cooking is still done in the original oven, dating from 1725.

Cafe Gijon

Inexpensive

Paseo de Recoletos. ☎ *(91) 521-54-25.*

Metro Stop Banco de Espana.

Closed: *Sun.*

More than 100 years old, this multipurpose coffeehouse bar, restaurant and sidewalk cafe was a Hemingway hangout. Summertime is a scene, especially at the sidewalk tables. Coffee, served black with a scoop of ice cream, is a favorite cooler. The food here isn't particularly memorable, although a fixed-price menu is offered for a good price, including wine.

Casa Paco   ★★

Moderate

Plaza Puerta Cerrada 11. ☎ *(91) 366-31-66.*

Metro Stop Puerta del Sol.

Credit Cards: *DC.*

Closed: *Sun.*

This busy bullfighter's hangout is best for beef—steaks to be specific, ordered by weight. Terrific fried potatoes and rice pudding. Soups, stews and seafood platters are also worth ordering. There are three small dining rooms on two levels; hectic atmosphere.

El Cabo Mayor

Expensive

Juan Ramon Jimenez, 37. ☎ *(91) 350-87-76.*

Metro Stop Cuzco.

Credit Cards: *All Major.*

Closed: *Sun.*

This restaurant specializes in seafood but has an enviable larder of meat, fowl and game. Resembling a private yacht, the woodsy interior has nautical panels, copper lamps and brass portholes. The *besugo* (sea bream) with green peppercorns and a salmon steamed with saffron were delicious. One of the most interesting maritime menus

in Europe, with a focus on northern-water rather than
Mediterranean fish.

El Mentidero de la Villa

Moderate

Santo Tome 6. ☎ *(91) 308-12-85.*

Metro Stop Gran Via.
Credit Cards: *All Major.*
Closed: *Sun.*

This is one of the more adventurous restaurants in town, serving
Asian-French-Spanish food in a carnival setting. The owners raided
midways and bought up old carousel horses, with which they've
decorated the tiny space. In Spanish, the name means "Talk of the
Town," and that's just what happened about 10 years ago, when a
Japanese chef (since departed) created the menu, combining local
fish with oyster sauce or lemongrass, but it has survived and is now
a distinguished part of the local culinary scene. Wild game (pheas-
ant, hare, pigeon) is featured in the fall.

El Pescador

Moderate

Calle Jose Ortega y Gasset, 75. ☎ *(91) 402-12-90.*

Metro Stop Lista.
Credit Cards: *V, MC.*
Closed: *Sun.*

The seafood of Galicia is prepared here in a nautically themed
restaurant. Most of the offerings are served *au naturel*, boiled,
broiled or grilled with barely a hint of sauce. Prawns are big (literally) among regular clients, as are oysters.

Horcher ★★

Moderate

Alfonso XIII, 6. ☎ *532-35-96.*

Metro Stop Retiro.
Credit Cards: *V, DC, A.*

Closed: *Sun*.

Well-known and intimate, this restaurant was moved from its original Berlin location toward the end of World War II. Sometimes the food seems not to have changed much from that time, either, but that's just fine by the loyal regulars. This is the kind of establishment where jackets and ties are *de rigueur*, and flaming desserts are prepared tableside by highly professional waiters.

La Trucha   ★

Inexpensive

Manuel Fernandez Gonzales 3. ☎ *(91) 492-58-33.*

Metro Stop Sevilla.

Closed: *Sun*.

One of the best tapas bars in the tapas- choked Plaza Santa Ana area is this bustling hive, featuring its namesake specialty, trout—the whole fish fried with Serrano ham and garlic. You can eat from an a la carte menu or stand up and order at the bar. Walk down the street to **La Chuleta**, *Echegaray 20,* ☎ *(91) 429-37-29,* for *tortillas de patata* and little lamb chops; open from noon to 1 a.m. and until 3 a.m. on weekends; closed Wed. and Sun.; they take american Express. Keep walking until you reach **R. Lacon**, at *Manuel Fernandez 8,* ☎ *(91) 429-60-42*; the specialty is juicy Jabugo ham; closed Wed. The aforementioned La Trucha has another restaurant, which many prefer as it's less crowded and the service is especially attentive. Located at *Nunez de Arce, 6* ☎ *(91) 532-08-82*, **La Trucha II** is somewhat dowdy and plain, but the fish is just as crisp; especially good are the mini-toasts topped with smoked trout, anchovies and roe, called *verbena*, "a festival" of fish. Wine is best with these dishes, which are served to you at the bar. But don't eat too many here because the night is still young, and just across the street is **Vina P.**, *Pl. Santa Ana, 3* ☎ *(91) 231-81-11.*

Zalacain

Expensive

Alvarez de Baena 4. ☎ *(91) 561-48-40.*

Metro Stop Ruben Dario.

Credit Cards: *All Major.*

Closed: *Sun.*

This is Madrid's (and possibly Spain's) most prestigious restaurant, praised by all, and possessing a three-star Michelin rating. Dining is in a saffron-and-black quartet of rooms with tasteful, subdued art on the walls. The modern cuisine, with an emphasis on seafood, reflects the tastes of the Basque owners. Make your reservations way ahead of time.

What to Do

Old Town/La Ciudad Antigua

✉ *Starts at Plaza Mayor.*

Metro Stop Puerta del Sol.

This tour of medieval (14th and 15th centuries) and Hapsburg-era Madrid (16th and 17th centuries) begins from the heart of the old city, the Plaza Mayor. (From the Puerta del Sol subway exit, you head west on Calle Mayor for about two blocks, taking the third right into the Plaza Mayor.) With nine arched gateways leading into it, this grand square was built by Philip III in 1619. In the center is the equestrian statue of the monarch by Giovanni de Bologna. Each evening, particularly in the warm summer months, the square is enlivened by chatter from notoriously night-owlish Madrilenos, who fill the cafe tables until the wee hours. On Sun. (9 a.m.–2 p.m.), there's a coin and stamp market, and in May (usually the 8th-15th), the Festival of San Isidro is held here to honor Madrid's patron saint, with varied activities, including free concerts, dramas and pageants and a parade. Extending from the plaza are two lively streets, Calle Cuchilleros and Cava Baja, with plenty of old-fashioned taverns, called *mesones*, and tapas (savory Spanish appetizers) bars. Close by is the Plaza de la Villa, with two important buildings constructed in the Middle Ages: the Casa y Torre de los Lujanes and the Hemeroteca Municipal. The tower of Los Lujanes was the prison of Francis I of France in 1325 (he and Carlos I of Spain were bitter enemies) after he was captured in the Battle of Pavia. To the right of Los Lujanes is the Hemeroteca Municipal, with more than 70,000 bound volumes of 18th- and 19th-century newspapers (open daily from 9 a.m.–1 p.m.). Also within the plaza is the City Hall, or Casas Consistoriales, designed in 1648 by Gomez de Mora; the civic goings-on are closed to the public, but you can view a collection of tapestries and furniture on Mon. from 5–7 p.m. ☎ (542-55-12).

Free tours in Spanish. Adjoining the City Hall is the Casa de Cisneros, built in 1537 for Jimenez de Cisneros, a famous cardinal, who was Queen Isabella's finance minister; she later made him regent of Spain. Tour hours the same as City Hall.

Historical Sites

El Escorial

🖹 *Calle San Lorenzo de El Escorial.* ☎ *91-890-59-02.*

🕐 *10 a.m.–7 p.m.*

Special Hours: *Oct. through Mar. until 6 p.m.*

El Escorial is the 16th-century royal palace, monastery and mausoleum of the Hapsburg and Bourbon kings of Spain. Built on the site of a mine, it was begun by architect Juan de Toledo, who worked on the Basilica of St. Peter in Rome (although he died before it was finished). Perhaps Philip II, whose project this was, intended to remind the Protestants of Northern Europe that he was as powerful as the Pope, and that he could keep their Reformist ideas well away from his doorstep. The massive complex, built over 21 years, still stands as boldly today as it did 400 years ago, with thousands of doors and windows, seven handsome towers and 15 gateways. The Royal Palace consists of Philip's subdued quarters and the more grandiose salons of Charles III and successive monarchs. In the Pantheon lie the gray marble tombs of 26 kings and queens and 60 royal children. The bookish Philip's wood-paneled library, with a frescoed ceiling by Tibaldi, contains almost 3000 priceless manuscripts, including a 5th-century text of St. Augustine and some 50,000 volumes on scholarly subjects from philosophy to mathematics. The Nuevos Museos (New Museums) are packed with Flemish, Italian and Spanish art, including works by Goya and Velasquez. It's about an hour away from Madrid by Herranz Bus from the Moncloa metro station; ☎ 543-36-45 for further information. From the Plaza Virgen de Gracia in El Escorial, it's a short walk to the entrance of the monastery. Admission: varies.

Palacio Real

📧 *Calle de Bailen, Plaza de Oriente.* ☎ *542-00-59.*

Metro Stop Opera.

🕐 *9 a.m.–6:15 p.m.*

Special Hours: *Sun., holidays to 3:15 p.m.*

The last king to live here was Juan Carlos' grandfather, Alfonso XIII, just before the Spanish Civil War in 1936. Now the Royal Palace is used for state functions and to house foreign dignitaries. At this site once stood the old Moorish stronghold, the Alcazar, which was renovated by the Hapsburg Emperor Charles V in the 15th century; it later burned down in 1734. The present neoclassical structure was begun several years later by the first Bourbon monarch, Philip V, who inherited the throne from a Hapsburg cousin. Philip took so long to build the palace, he died before it was completed; his son Carlos III was the first real occupant. There are almost 3000 rooms in the palace, most of them off-limits to the public, but an all-inclusive ticket will get you a guided tour (usually in Spanish) of the former royal apartments, the Throne Room with a Tiepolo ceiling, the State Dining Room, Library, Royal Pharmacy, the Armory, containing Carlos V's suit of armor, and the Royal Carriage Museum. Admission: varies.

Museums and Exhibits

El Prado

http://museoprado.mcu.es/

Paseo del Prado. ☎ *420-28-36.*

Metro Stop Atocha/Banco de Espana.

🕐 *9 a.m.–7 p.m.*

Special Hours: *Sun. open to 2 p.m.; closed Mon.*

The Prado houses the art treasures of the Spanish crown from the 15th through the 19th centuries. The museum reflects the impeccable taste of various monarchs, including Charles V, who favored the Italians, particularly Titian, and Philip IV, who was responsible for putting Diego Velasquez's on the artistic map. You'll have to fight your way around tourists surrounding Velasquez' famous *Las*

Meninas, the artist himself appears in the huge canvas, interrupted in the act of painting Philip IV and his queen (who are reflected in a mirror) by the arrival of the couple's daughter, the Infanta Margarita. Besides its sheer size, the uncommon perspective brings out the voyeur in all of us. Paintings by Francisco Goya, another court painter, occupy a whole wing of the museum and include the oft-copied *La Maja Vestida* (The Clothed Maja) and his "Black Paintings," which he worked on toward the end of his life. The Prado also has a definitive collection of paintings by Domenikos Theotokopoulos (aka El Greco), including the sublime *Adoration of the Shepherds.* Besides the Spanish painters, there is also an impressive array of Dutch, Flemish (Hieronymus Bosch's allegorical *Garden of Earthly Delights* was acquired by Philip II), Italian and German masters. Admission: varies.

Museo Arqueologico Nacional ★★★

http://www.man.es/noticia.htm

C. Serrano, 13. ☎ *403-65-59.*

Metro Stop Colon/Serrano.

🕐 *9:30 a.m.–8:30 p.m.*

Special Hours: *Sun. until 2:30 p.m.*

This excellent museum of the past contains artifacts, sculpture, jewelry and art from ancient Greek, Phoenician, Carthaginian, Visigothic and Moorish as well as Iberian civilizations. Most visitors are drawn to the mysterious women on the first floor, the Dama de Elche and the Dama de Baza, two exquisite examples of Iberian sculpture from the fourth century B.C. Another interesting attraction is the subterranean reconstruction of the Altamira Caves at the entrance of the museum; the 100,000-year-old cave paintings are painstakingly reproduced. Your admission ticket also gets you into the National Library in the same building; it houses a first-edition copy of Cervantes' *Don Quixote.* Admission: varies.

Museo Nacional Centro de Arte Reina Sofia ★★★

http://museoreinasofia.mcu.es/

C. Santa Isabel. ☎ *467-50-62.*

Metro Stop Atocha.

🕐 *10 a.m.–9 p.m.*

Special Hours: *Closed Tues.*

This acclaimed museum, housed in the former Hospital General de Madrid, is dedicated to the Spanish art censored by Generalissimo Franco's administration. A few years ago, the Centro acquired its prize possession, Picasso's *Guernica*, which had previously hung in the Prado. Painted in shades of gray, somber black and chalky whites, it depicts a screaming, tortured mass of assorted humans and animals who perished in the bombing of the Basque capital of Guernica by the Germans during the Spanish Civil War. Also worth seeing are early works by Dali, major canvases by Juan Gris and Miro, and sculpture and drawings by Julio Gonzalez. The museum, still somewhat cold and stark, even after a $60 million renovation, also has an excellent gift shop, library and research center. Admission: varies.

Music

Cafe de Chinitas

✉ *Torija, 7.* ☎ *559-5135.*

Metro Stop Santo Domingo.

🕐 *9 p.m.–2 a.m.*

Special Hours: *Dinner to 11 p.m.; closed Sun.*

Once just a little modest cafe, this is now considered the classiest and the best nightspot for authentic gypsy flamenco music and dance in all of Madrid. The decor consists of red-framed portraits of renowned matadors and a gazpacho-colored bar. Excellent costumes, top guitarists and singers and good drinks. Also hot is **Corral de la Moreria**, *Moreria 17*, Metro: La Latina, ☎ *365-84-46*, open daily for dinner at 9 p.m., shows starting at 11 p.m.; one drink minimum. Spanish-style operettas, called *zarzuelas*, go way back to the 15th century; literary giant Lope de Vega even wrote music for them. Today you can see this unique art form at **Teatro Lirico Nacional de la Zarzuela**, near Plaza de la Cibeles at *Jovellanos 4*, Metro: Sevilla, ☎ *429-82-25*. Because of the fast pace and catchy melodies, you don't have to understand Spanish to enjoy them. Call for show times.

Nightlife

Los Gabrieles

⌷ *Echegaray 17.* ☎ *(91) 429-62-61.*

Metro Stop Tirso de Molina.

🕐 *1 p.m.–2:30 a.m.*

This typical Madrileno hangout has been popular for more than 100 years. Its Andalusian tiles on the walls and around the bar are a real conversation piece, good when you run out of small talk. Students and other like-minded types have nosed out the **Parador de la Moncloa** for tapas and a liter of beer (which is about as cheap as Los Gabrieles). It's located northwest of the center of town at *Calle Isaac Peral 2*, Metro: Moncloa, ☎ *(91) 544-1135.* Open daily from 11 a.m. to 1:30 a.m. on weekends, until midnight during the week. From here you can continue to **Viva Madrid**, *Manuel Fernandez y Gonzalez*, Metro: Sol ☎ *(91) 410.5535*, which looks like an arts-and-crafts emporium, with decorative tile and wooden animals. It fills with party animals after 11 p.m., but it's open at noon and closes at 2 a.m. on Sat., other days at 1 a.m. The clubby **Balmoral**, *Hermosilla 10*, Metro: Serrano ☎ *(91) 431-4133*, has a distinguished clientele from the combined business, arts and diplomatic communities; surprisingly, drinks are very reasonable. Tapas are served. Open 7:30 p.m.–2 a.m. daily.

Parks and Gardens
ITRAVELBOOK FREEBIE

Casa de Campo

⌷ *Casa de Campo, across the Manzanares River.*

Metro Stop Lago/Batan.

🕐 *8 a.m.–9 p.m.*

It's fun to reach this huge park (almost 5000 acres, surrounded by forests) by the *teleferico*, or cable car, which affords the visitor with one of Madrid's loftiest views. Although it was once a royal hunting ground, the only animals seen today are in the zoo, ☎ *711.99.50*, which is popular with families; open daily from 10 a.m. to 6 p.m. The kids will probably enjoy the cutesy Parque de Attracciones, with decent rides, including two roller-coasters. Admission: varies.

Shopping
Shopping Hours

Most shops selling anything but food: from 9:30 or 10 a.m.–1 or 1:30 p.m. and 4:30 or 5–7:30 or 8 p.m. (even 8:30 p.m. in summer) weekdays, with Sat. afternoon closings (usually in summer, but this isn't standard, either). Department stores stay open till 9 p.m. Public markets: from 7:30 a.m.–2 p.m. These are merely a rule of thumb, because now that Spain is part of the E.E.C., the nation's shopkeepers have been told they may keep *any* hours they wish.

Savings on Purchases

I.V.A. is Spain's designation for a "value-added tax," and it's set at 15 percent. If your shopkeeper participates in the program and is cooperative, you could receive a significant rebate. There are several provisions: (1) The item must cost more than 15,000 pesetas, including the tax; (2) you must receive a form from the shop; and (3) upon departure from Spain, Customs must stamp this form. Be sure your sales receipts show the price of each item and that its I.V.A. has been noted as well. If there is only one grand total, the authorities will not reimburse you. You must then mail the document back to the store where you made your purchase, and finally the rebate will be sent directly to you. If your hometown bank has a Spanish correspondent, then it is possible for your refund to go through this channel; still, it's risky because this method is new. Other countries with greater experience and a longer history of tax refunding are able to offer more efficient and less time-consuming systems. It will take Spain awhile to latch on to these techniques.

NOTE: Wherever you wander in today's Iberia, be extremely leery of any of the stores or so-called factories where tour guides might lead you. The commissions they collect on *your* purchases with *your* money normally average 25 percent. You'd be wise to comparison-shop and then to patronize *only* reliable independent merchants.

Don't buy Spanish shawls. The only real ones are antiques from China. This has become a tourist racket.

Antiques   ★★

🖃 *Calle del Prado, near the museum.*

Metro Stop Serrano/Velazquez.

🕐 *10 a.m.–8 p.m.*

Special Hours: *Closed Sun.*

Madrid's antique haven is the Calle del Prado, with many of the shops clustered together in covered arcades. These include the **Centro de Anticularios Lagasca,** *Lagasca 36,* for crystal, furniture and housewares, and the **Central de Arte Antiguedades**, a five-story mall with 50 shops, at *Serrano 5*, Metro: Retiro, ☎ *(91) 576.96.82*. The city's smelly old fish market, the **Mercado Puerta de Toledo**, was gutted and gentrified into a fragrant, five- story, fashionable shopping center with antiques, *haute couture*, jewelry and more; there's a lively outdoor scene as well. Metro: Puerta de Toledo; see above for hours. In the Old Town (Plaza Cascorro and Ribera de Curtidores), you'll find the famous flea market, **El Rastro**, with an interesting jumble of junk—some good, some dreadful. Haggle hard, wear a money belt. Open daily, except Mon., from 9:30 a.m.–1:30 p.m. and 5–8 p.m.

Artespana   ★★

🖃 *Various locations.* ☎ *(91) 413.62.62.*

🕐 *9:30 a.m.–8 p.m.*

Special Hours: *Closed Sun.*

A variety of the finest crafts from regions all over Spain are for sale in these shops sponsored by the government. You'll find pottery, furniture, woodwork and decorative items for the home, office and garden. Locations: *3 Plaza de las Cortes, 14 Calle Hermosilla, 33 Calle Don Ramon de la Cruz and Centro Comercial Madrid 2, La Vaguada*. Call ☎ *(91) 413.62.62* for further information.

Galerias Preciados

📧 *Plaza del Callao 1.* ☎ *(91) 522.47.71.*

Metro Stop Callao.

🕐 *10 a.m.–8 p.m.*

Special Hours: *Closed Sun.*

Stuffed with merchandise at people prices, this vast department store is right next to another monster, **El Corte Ingles**, at *Calle Preciados 3,* ☎ (91) 532.81.00. You'll find branches all over the country.

Both are located off the Gran Via, Madrid's main shopping district. Two major malls are the Mercado Puerta de Toledo (see Antiques) and the **Galeria del Prado**, *Plaza de las Cortes, 7,* Metro: Banco de Espana, below the Hotel Palace. The Galeria is on two stories, and many of Spain's top designers have boutiques here.

Sports & Recreation

Plaza de Toros Monumental de las Ventas

📧 *Alcala, 237.* ☎ *(91) 356.22.00.*

Metro Stop Ventas.

Many people swear they hate bullfights, even if they've never been to one. Like it or not, the teasing dance to the death of bulls by matadors is ingrained in Spanish life, and it's worth going just to experience the reactions of the crowds. The season begins during the Feast of San Isidro, May 15–Oct. 31. The Plaza Monumental seats more than 22,000 spectators. You can buy them from your hotel concierge or at the box office, which is open on weekends (fights are held on Sun.) from 10 a.m.–8 p.m., with a break for siesta from 2–5 p.m.

SWITZERLAND

Switzerland is like a beautifully illustrated book—everywhere you turn you are surrounded by history, adventure, glamour and glorious vistas. There are medieval guild houses clustered around ancient squares, ice-capped mountains that attract world- class climbers, sophisticated resorts and, of course, spectacular scenery. The Alps and their valleys are postcard-perfect. Nowhere else, it seems, are the skies such a perfect blue, the lakes so clear and the flower-spattered meadows so lush.

Geographically considered the "rooftop" of Europe, Switzerland is dominated by glaciers and massive mountains. The most famous peak is the Matterhorn, but the highest is actually a neighboring crag, the Dufourspitze, which rakes the sky at 14,200 feet. Rocky mountain slopes are home to curve-horned ibex and nimble chamois, while alpine meadows provide habitat for deer, birds and a host of small creatures. Glaciers feed the rivers that lace the landscape, including the mighty Rhine and the Rhone. The forces of glaciers have led to the creation of Switzerland's lakes, from the smallest gemlike sea to immense Lake Constance. Throughout Switzerland, thermal springs bubble up, releasing therapeutic mineral waters that have been valued since Roman times.

Switzerland has more than 6.6 million inhabitants and four recognized national languages—French, German, Italian and Romansh (a Romance dialect)—though many Swiss speak English. The population centers are found in the Swiss Plateau, a slab of relatively flat land that lies between the Jura Mountains and the Alps. The major cities—**Geneva**, **Lausanne**, **Basel**, **Bern** and **Zurich**—are found in this region.

Geneva hugs the southern border, drawing on its neighbor France for flavor and dazzling visitors with its lakeside views. Lausanne reigns on the northern shore of Lac Leman, as the Swiss call Lake Geneva, and offers both its medieval *Altstadt* (Old Town) and a new, expansive International Olympics Museum. Basel straddles the Rhine River and contains dozens of architectural treasures and 28 museums. The Swiss capital, Bern, has the brown bear as its mascot, and the Bernese still gladly maintain the medieval-era Bear Pits. Zurich, the banking center and the largest city in Switzerland, is an international airport hub and a worthy destination in its own right, full of art museums, gardens and historic lakeside quays.

Interlaken, **Grindelwald** and **Zermatt** deserve special consider-

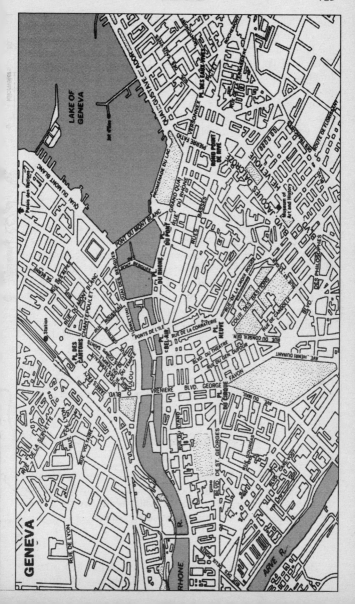

ation. While excellent as ski resorts, each offers other diversions, any one of which can be the highlight of a Switzerland visit. Situated in the heart of the Bernese Oberland, Interlaken sits between Lake Thun and Lake Brienz. From Interlaken, you can board the famous Jungfrau railway, which heads to the highest rack railway station in Europe—the summit of the Jungfrau. Also near Interlaken is the Schilthorn cableway, where you can take a four-stage cable-car route to reach a revolving restaurant that crowns the Schilthorn at 9744 feet. Grindelwald also connects with the Jungfrau railway and is a favorite launching point for hikes to explore the Grindelwald glacier. Zermatt, in the southern Valais, crouches at the base of the imposing Matterhorn and provides a base for hikes and cable rides up the Matterhorn's slopes.

At the higher northern elevations, the glittering ski towns draw an endless stream of visitors—royalty and celebrities mingle with student hikers and hard-core skiers. The resort names are well known: **Davos**, **Gstadd**, **Klosters** and **St. Moritz**. In the past 20 years, the resorts have experienced phenomenal growth and modernization, but many still have their charm, even if it takes a full wallet to experience their delights. Without a doubt, Gstaad and St. Moritz vie for the title of "most chic." In the Grisons, Davos is known for the devotion its skiers bring to the sport, while next door, Klosters still appeals to celebrity visitors, including Prince Charles and his entourage. Gstaad sparkles as well, reigning as the most sophisticated resort in the Bernese Oberland.

Another treasure is **Lucerne**, on the shores of Lac Luzern, a town that typifies everything that is Swiss. Then there is **Montreux**, on the southern end of Lake Geneva. Montreux is the site of the Chateaux Chillon, celebrated by Lord Byron in his poetry.

Transportation

Airlines

As of March 2002, Swissair, the national airline, ceased operations. Most major international carriers, including Lufthansa, British Airways, and American (the latter of which is affilated with Swiss), fly to all larger Swiss destinations including Geneva.

Trains

The **Swiss Federal Railway** (http://www.sbb.ch/) is known for its punctuality—schedules are met to the split-second, and departures to major destinations leave once or twice an hour. Trains are 100 percent electrified and they run at fast speeds, especially the commuter links between Geneva and Zurich. Passenger cars are generally clean, and stations are well marked, with signs in various languages.

Ticket prices are reasonable but most visitors take advantage of one or more passes. The Swiss Pass/Swiss Flexipass entitles the bearer to transportation by rail as well as by lake steamer and postal bus. The pass also is good for reduced-price tickets for cableway transportation. Regional passes are available for the Bernese Oberland and other geographically contained areas. Inquire about regional passes as you book your trip. The Swiss Card is valid for one month and allows the holder to free transfer from any Swiss border point to any destination in Switzerland as long as the transfer is completed in one day. The Swiss Card also procures unlimited half-price trips on the entire Swiss transportation system.

If you are touring beyond Switzerland, the Eurailpass may be your best bet (**http:// www.eurail.com/**). Valid for 15 days to three months, depending on what you purchase, the Eurailpass permits travel over 100,000 miles of European railroads. The pass is convenient because it eliminates the need to buy individual tickets, although some destinations require advance reservations. Students and groups can take advantage of even more economical Eurailpass discounts. Children under four ride free if they don't occupy a seat (otherwise the cost is half-fare), and children under 12 pay half fare. *The most important thing to remember is that the Eurailpass cannot be purchased in Europe. Buy your pass before you leave home.*

Bus

If mountain curves give you white knuckles, relax and let a seasoned bus driver steer you safely from railroad stations to most Alpine destinations. The Swiss postal route network is made up of a fleet of eye-catching yellow buses, and the bus network offers thorough, efficient service, especially for ski resort-hopping. Once at your destination, you'll find that even the smaller resorts offer a bus to shuttle passengers around within their own city limits. In car-less towns, electric trams or taxis provide mechanized transport. Within the larger cities, fleets of buses and trams make urban transit a snap.

Car Travel

Roads and highways in Switzerland are modern, well-built and efficient. Except for the toll through the Great St. Bernard Tunnel, there are no other tolls levied on roads. Switzerland finances its road projects by collecting an annual fee. When the fee is paid, a sticker is affixed to the vehicle. Rental cars in Switzerland have the sticker, but if you drive a rental car from another country into Switzerland, be prepared to pay for a permit sticker. Stickers can be purchased in advance at the Swiss National Tourist Office in Italy, Austria and Germany. Stickers are not sold in France. The permit is required on superhighways, and the fine for noncompliance is stiff.

Car rental in Switzerland can be handled through various firms. In the U.S., Budget Rent-a-Car has a good record of reliability. Contact **Budget** at ☎ *(800) 472-3325.* **Hertz,** ☎ *(800) 654-3001,* and **Avis** ☎ *(800) 331-212,* also offer rental cars.

Taxis

Geneva has a Taxi Telephone Center. Simply dial 141 and one of a fleet of 150 cars will be at your disposal. In Bern, the number is ☎ *24-24-24;* in Zurich, ☎ *44-44-41.* There's no need to tip, as your bill already includes a 15 percent service tax.

Food

Swiss cuisine is not all chocolate and cheese as many foreigners suppose. Switzerland's crossroads status means that influences from France, Germany, Austria and Italy enter into the kitchen. In addition, Switzerland offers its own traditional dishes.

Sausage is a national specialty and each region has its own type. The big, fat Zurich version, a bologna with a Napoleonic complex, is one of the most succulent. Even more famous is the St. Gallen Bratwurst. Sausage is generally served with the hearty hash-brown potatoes called *Rosti*. Organ meats and veal are common center-pieces in Swiss entrées. Throughout Switzerland, you'll find *Geschnetzeltes nach Zurcher Art* (thin-sliced veal with a cream sauce), *Zurcher Leberspiessli* (liver strips with sage seasoning, spit-roasted and served with beans) and *Ratsherrentopf* (mixed grilled meats on a bed of rice or noodles). If you're truly hungry, order *Tellerservice*, which is the opposite of à la carte. The food arrives on a large platter, and, after you've finished one serving, you are invited to polish off the rest if you can.

Fondue is a common dish, and it comes in many varieties. Blends of melted cheese are flavored with garlic, herbs, meats and sometimes champagne. Bread chunks are dipped into the warm pot, and the result is delightful. From Valais comes *raclette*, another melted-cheese dish, which is prepared by roasting a block of cheese over a flame until the outside melts. The melted cheese is scraped off and served warm with bread and pickles.

While dinner at some of Switzerland's stellar restaurants is considered world-class, you'll pay for the privilege. Final tabs can top $400 for two, and most good, substantial meals will average about $100. But economical choices do exist—fixed-price menus at lunch or dinner range from $20 to $30 per person. Even the most chic restaurants may offer a scaled-down price for lunch. Of course, you can sate your appetite at cafés or tearooms, or dine with the locals at the Movenpick restaurant chain—an interesting combination of drugstore and diner, with branches in major cities. Grocery stores stock breads, fruit, sausage and cheeses that you can buy for your own picnics. A memorable feast can result from a wedge of cheese, some grapes and a tub of Swiss yogurt, all enjoyed by the banks of an Alpine stream.

Some of the best Italian food in Europe is to be found in Switzerland. The ingredients are what count, and Swiss standards are almost flawless in this regard (not always the case, alas, in the home country of peninsular cuisine).

Desserts and sweets, including Lindt or Toblerone chocolate, are available at pastry shops in almost every town. Some regions feature signature desserts, such as the cherry cake served in Zug. Called *Zuger Kirschtorte*, it is a waist-expanding concoction of pastry, biscuit, almond paste, butter and cream blended with cherry brandy. Generally, the tiniest *stublis* to the grandest restaurants offer an array of sinfully delicious strudels, tortes and soufflés.

Drinks

If you want to expand your palate, ask for a glass of Swiss white wine—it has a slight effervescence and leaves a distinct tang on the tongue. It takes learning before true enjoyment can come. Most vintages should be ordered young.

The majority of visiting North Americans seem to prefer

Johannisberg as their white and *Dole* as their red. More particular drinkers pick *Dole Fin Bec*. Other choices are *Altstatter* and *Churer-Schiller* (St. Gallen and Graubunden), *Crepy* and *St. Saphorin* (Lavaux). Or consider *Torrente-Chateau la Tour* (Valais) and *Cru de Champreveyres* or the sparkling whites of Bienne or Neuchatel. If you can find it, *Heida-Gletscherwein* from near Visp's glacier zones comes from Europe's highest-altitude vines.

Swiss beer varies in quality. *Helles* refers to light beer, *Dunkles* is dark beer. All major European beers are available.

Kirsch, made from the juice of compressed cherry pits, is one of the national hard drinks. Don't miss a sample of this fiery, rather bitter spirit, especially good with cheese or fruit. Pear liqueur and brandies provide a powerful kick with a heart-melting aroma. Sip pear brandy freezer-chilled after fondue or raclette—ask for a Williams (the W is pronounced as a V, i.e., Villiams).

The most astonishing Swiss liqueur is *Appenzeller Alpenbitter*. Appenzell is the town famous for its Alpenbitter, or "Alpine Bitters," a brew composed of the essences of 67 different flowers and roots. In taste, it is vaguely reminiscent of a gin-and-tonic, but don't let this stop you from sampling a genuine curiosity.

The nonalcoholic, noncarbonated, natural white or red grape juice called *Grapillon* is wonderfully uplifting if you like a sweet drink. A glass runs about $2, but be sure it's served icy-cold. *Apfelsaft* (apple juice) is a pleasant and soft apple cider. Domestic sodas are preferred by locals to U.S. brands, which tend to be more expensive.

CURRENCY: THE SWISS FRANC.

Tipping

An automatic service charge of 15 percent across the board in all cafés, restaurants and hotels is standard. This means you can greatly reduce or eliminate your individual gratuities. Even taxis now include a 15 percent supplement automatically, so the tab alone is what you should pay.

Telephone

Access code to U.S.: 001. To telephone Switzerland: 41; time difference (Eastern Daylight) plus six hours.

For More Information

Swiss National Tourist Office
http://usa.myswitzerland.com/en/welcome.cfm
608 Fifth Ave.
New York, NY 10020
☎ *(212) 757-5944*
FAX *(212) 262-6116*

Bernese Oberland

Grindewald

At Grindelwald, in the heart of the Bernese Oberland, you can get a close look at the most active glacier in Europe. Surrounded by the towering north face of the Eiger and the massive Wetterhorn, the village is a skier's and hiker's dream come true. With its sunny terraces, alpine meadows and the **Blue Ice Getto** nearby, Grindelwald is filled with visitors for the day all-year-round. The **Parkhotel Schoenegg** is especially popular with skiers, as the local ski runs and the lift to the ski school are right beyond its door. The **Grand Hotel Regina** is luxurious, while also refreshingly informal.

Where to Stay

Apartments and Condos

Grand Hotel Regina ★★★★★

Exppensive to Very Expensive

CH 3818. ☞ *Across from train station.*

☎ *036/54-54-44*, Fax: *223-6800*.

Credit Cards: *V, A*.

Turrets and red-tile roofs attest to this deluxe six-story hotel's 19th-century beginnings, though it was only converted to a hotel in 1953. Located in a prime spot on the village's main street, it affords dazzling mountain vistas. Inside, the lobby and other public areas are decorated with antiques, artworks and Oriental carpets. The 102 rooms have a good mix of antique and contemporary furnishings and feature a tiled bath, hair dryer and guest robes. An annex connected to the main building by a tunnel houses nine luxury apartments. A pool, sauna and tennis courts are located in a glass-and-steel extension. Considered a chic, popular gathering spot, the hotel offers a nightclub, cocktail lounge, poolside bar, inside bar, and restaurants. Closed Oct. through Dec. 18.

Hotels and Resorts

Belvedere ★★★★

http://www.jungfrauregion.com/grindelw/ad/belved/belvedere.htm

Expensive

CH 3818. *A five-minute walk from center of the resort.*

☎ 036/54-54-34.

Credit Cards: *V, MC, DC, A.*

With dramatic Eiger views, this four-star hotel has been run by the Hauser family for three generations and is known for its personalized service, It offers six suites and 45 rooms, 22 of which are rated as "luxury twins" or "junior suites." All have private bath, robes and radios. Guests can take advantage of "bio-sauna" spa facilities and Finnish massages. For families, there is a children's game room.

Hotel Kruez & Post ★★★

Moderate to Expensive

CH 3818. 🖝 *Main square of town.*

☎ 036/54-54-92.

Credit Cards: *V, MC, DC, A.*

Across from the Sports Center, this family-run hotel offers a good value and magnificent views from its rooftop sun terrace. Each of the 50 rooms has a bath or a shower as well as phone, TV and radio. Many rooms have a balcony affording an additional opportunity to enjoy the scenery. Two suites are available. Also featured are a sidewalk cafe out front for light meals and a relaxing whirlpool bath. Closed Apr. and May.

Parkhotel Schoenegg ★★★★★

http://www.parkhotelschoenegg.ch/
Moderate to Expensive

CH 3818. *Near ski lift and ski school.*

☎ *036/53-18-53.*

The local ski runs and the lift to the ski school are minutes away from this balcony-fronted hotel, built in 1890 by the Stettler family. The basement bar, Gydis-Bar, has been warming patrons both inside and out since 1940. Snug and comfortable, all 50 rooms have private baths; the south-facing rooms have unparalleled mountain views. Closed Nov.

Inns

Hotel Fiescherblick ★★★★

http://www.fiescherblick.ch/
Moderate to Expensive

CH 3818. *Far end of village from train station, car parking available.*

☎ *036/53-44-53.*

Credit Cards: *V, MC, DC, A.*

This wood-framed chalet is especially popular with skiers and backpackers. The staff caters to the outdoor needs of its guests by packing sack lunches and providing hot thermoses of tea, and half-board guests can eat their fill at the restaurant. The 25 rooms are simply furnished in brown and beige color schemes, and all have private bath or shower. Each of the 12 rooms in the new wing have TV, phone, and hair dryer. Closed: Mid-Nov.–mid-Dec., and Easter–mid-May.

Where to Eat

La Pendule d'Or/Jagerstube ★★★★★

Expensive

CH 3818. ☎ *036/54-54-55.*

Credit Cards: *V, A.*

For elegant food beautifully served, La Pendule d'Or inside the Regina is a superb choice. This extremely dressy restaurant serves Swiss and French cuisine in formal style and offers both a la carte and fixed- price meals. Classic choices include French snails, Russian caviar and steak tartare. For a slightly less formal but equally delicious dinner, the richly rustic Jagerstube offers a selection of appetizers, soups, grilled meats and desserts.

Restaurant Alte Post   ★★★

Moderate

CH 3818. ☎ *036/53-11-43.*

Credit Cards: *V, MC, A.*

This is where the locals come for traditional Swiss dining. To get a table, you need to reserve a couple of days in advance. The dining room is pine paneled and rustic; the dishes include air-dried ham, lamb and pork cutlets, and smoked trout.

Restaurant Francais   ★★★★★

Expensive

CH 3818. *In the Hotel Belvedere.* ☎ *036/ 54-54-34.*

Credit Cards: *V, MC, DC, A.*

Overseen by owner Urs Hauser, this establishment is acknowledged as among the best in Grindelwald. Guests can choose from specialties for two or from entrees such as beef stroganoff made from an original recipe created by Alexj Elkhoff, at one time the head chef of Moscow's Carlton Restaurant. Many dishes are flavored with herbs from the hotel's own garden. Special buffets highlight regional cuisine.

Restaurant Sportzentrum   ★★★

Inexpensive to Moderate

CH 3818. *Inside the Sports Center near the hockey rink.* ☎ *036/53-32-77.*

Located in the heart of the Sports Center, this rustic, wood-paneled dining room has large windows that look out onto an indoor pool and an ice hockey rink. Enjoy a light meal while watching the athletics. It's also a good spot for a morning coffee or for lingering over a late-night drink and a pot of fondue.

What to Do
Sports and Recreation

First Mountain Gondola

Special Hours: *Runs all year.*

Carrying hikers and skiers up First Mountain, the Firstbahn gondola cableway is one of Europe's longest. The 30-minute ride takes you to 7100 feet, while providing magnificent views of the snow-clad Alps. At the top, you can stroll through a nearby Alpine Garden (open summer months) splashed with edelweiss, anemones, gentian and Alpine asters. From the First Mountain terrace there are numerous hikes, including a three-hour round-trip hike to Lake Balchap. Admission: inexpensive.

Grindelwald Hikes

 Sportzentrum, Hauptstrasse. ☎ *036/53-12- 12.*

Special Hours: *June to Oct.*

Situated under the north face of the Eiger, Grindelwald has more than 55 miles of signed trails designed for both beginners and experts. For guided excursions or information on specific trails, contact the tourist office. A popular half-day hike is from Grindelwald to Milchbach. The hike from Grindelwald to the Upper Glacier and the Blue Ice Grotto takes about one and a half hours. Or you can take the postal bus from the village to the Hôtel Restaurant Wetterhorn where it's a 15-minutes hike to the Blue Ice Grotto. The Grotto is a cave formed by a slowly moving glacier; its 150-foot-thick ice walls have a bluish tinge, especially at midday. A series of steep trails and wooden ladders (separate fee) allow you to climb alongside the ice flow, providing splendid views of the Eismeer or "Sea of Ice." Allow two hours for this hike. Afterwards, hike back to the village or take the bus down. Before setting out, confirm weather conditions and make sure you have appropriate footwear and clothing. Admission: inexpensive.

Gstaad

Nestled in the beautiful Saane region of the Bernese Oberland, Gstaad offers some of Switzerland's most magnificent alpine vistas. Although it lures a steady stream of celebrities, royalty and the well-heeled to its glamorous hotels and weathered-wood chalets, Gstaad has managed to retain its village charm, with the sound of cowbells in the morning and a pot of hot fondue at night. Here, storybook endings are possible, whether at the **Palace Hotel**, a kingly paradise crowned with turrets, or at the **Olden Chalet**, where the amiable owner treats each guest, famous or not, with gracious hospitality.

Where to Stay
Hotels and Resorts

Les Hauts de Gstaad   ★★★★

Moderate to Expensive

CH 3777 Saanenmoser-Gstaad. ☞ *Above Saanenmoser, near railroad station.*

☎ *030/83-23-32.*

Credit Cards: *DC, A.*

Combining modern comforts with antique touches, this chalet-style complex is situated outside Gstaad near a working farm. A 26-passenger 1949 yellow postal bus shuttles guests between Gstaad and the hotel. The 30 rooms are comfortably modern with painted wooden beds and large tiled bathrooms with double wash basins. Hair dryer, TV and telephone are all standard. Close to a golf course and mountain- biking and hiking trails, Les Hauts is an ideal headquarters for an active vacation. Closed: Mid-Apr.–mid-June, and mid-Oct.–mid-Dec.

Palace Hotel Gstaad   ★★★★★

http://www.palace.ch/
Very Expensive

CH 3780.

☎ *030/8-31-31,* Fax: *223-6800.*

Credit Cards: *V.*

The Taj Mahal of Gstaad, the Palace radiates a royal atmosphere from the moment you set your eyes on its towers and neo- medieval facade. Built in 1912, this landmark has been a magnet for a glittering parade of celebrities, corporate CEOs and European aristocrats. They come to savor the luxurious amenities such as the indoor pool with underwater music, the on-site ice rink, water-jet massages and chauffeured Rolls-Royces. The rooms are palatial, and prices soar like a king's ransom as you consider upgrades; 120 bedrooms (each with huge private bath), 17 junior suites, 12 standard suites and six luxury suites. Guests can dine in a variety of restaurants, from black-tie formal to sunny terraces and even a poolside barbecue. The bars and disco are all places to see and be seen. Closed late Mar.–May, and late Sept.–mid-Dec.

Inns

Hotel Alpenrose ★★★★★

Expensive

CH 3778 Gstaad-Schonried. *Just 4.4 miles north of Gstaad.*

☎ *036/46-767.*

SFr235–SFr265. SFr390–SFr510.

Credit Cards: *V, MC, DC. n.*

A charming family-run chalet-inn situated on a high plateau above the village. Monika Von Siebenthal is the manager and her personal touches can be seen in the country-style furnishings that fill the rooms. Each of the 21 rooms has private bath, phone and TV. The chalet's restaurants are acclaimed, and described separately. The Alpenrose is a member of Relais & Chateaux. A great choice for its excellent cuisine and air of warmth and comfort. Closed Easter–May, and Nov.–Dec. 15.

Where to Eat

Grill Room ★★★★★

Very Expensive

CH 3778. ☎ *030/8-31-31.*

Showcasing the talents of some of the best chefs in the region, the Grill serves guests in three elegantly appointed, paneled dining rooms. Prices are kingly and attire is definitely formal, men without ties will be asked to dine at the Sans-Cravatte, which serves the same menu (and has the same prices) as the Grill. The cuisine is classic and impeccably prepared. Caviar, foie gras and beef tartare are among the appetizers. Focusing on innovative twists on formal dishes, the extensive menu is divided into fish or shellfish, beef, veal, poultry and lamb. Desserts are marvelous, whether you choose an artistic torte or a dish of freshly made sorbet.

Hostellerie Alpenrose   ★★★★★

Expensive

Hauptstrasse, Schonried-Gstaad. ☞ *In the Hotel Alpenrose.* ☎ *030/4-12-38.*
Credit Cards: *V, MC, DC.*

Housed in the Hotel Alpenrose and lovingly overseen by Monika von Siebenthal, this restaurant draws savvy locals and guests from other hotels. Open daily for lunch and dinner during the Dec. through Mar. high season, the Alpenrose offers entrees and a full-course fixed-price dinner. Seated at tables with country-fresh linens in paneled rooms, guests can sample superbly prepared Swiss favorites. Closed: Easter–May, and Nov.–Dec. 15.

Restaurant Chesery   ★★★★★

Expensive

Lauenenstrasse. ☎ *030/4-24-51.*

Closed: *Tues., Thurs.*

Make your reservations as early as possible at this establishment, considered one of the top 10 restaurants in Switzerland. Always busy, it offers late-night dining, featuring a changing menu based on market-fresh ingredients. Chef Robert Speth puts a twist on region-al dishes by combining exotic spices and fruits with duck, veal or fish. The dining rooms are as lively as the menu with pink marble flooring and light pine paneling; Piano music nightly from 9 p.m to 3 a.m.; Jacket advised.

What to Do
Nightlife

Sammy's Bar/Bistro ★★★★★

Moderate to Expensive

Hauptstrasse Schonried. ☞ *Located in Hotel Alpenrose* ☎ *030/ 4-12-38.*

🕐 *7 p.m.–3 a.m.*

Special Hours: *Off-season, 10 p.m.–3 a.m.*

Named after the owner's dog, this lively bar/bistro is hidden in the basement of the Hotel Alpenrose in the satellite resort of Schonried. The paneled walls are hung with an ever-changing array of paintings and other artwork. The menu offers grilled meats, raclettes and regional platters. In winter, pizzas are enormously popular. Live music adds to the charm. Closed: Easter–May, and Nov.–Dec.15.

Sports and Recreation

Outdoor Activities ★★★

🖃 *Tourist Office.* ☎ *030/4-71-41.*

Gstaad has many outdoor delights. During winter, the skiing region surrounding Gstaad offers 155 miles of runs and 69 lifts. In summer, hiking trails lace the area, with many easy excursions. Tennis and horseback riding are also available. White-water rafting tours on the Saane River provide a unique way to see the area.

Interlaken

Situated between Lake Thun and Lake Brienz, Interlaken is the hub of the Bernese Oberland. Rail connections from Bern are numerous, and a network of railways, lake steamers, cable cars and hiking paths extends out from the city. The Grand Hotel Victoria-Jungfrau is more than a century old and considered one of the great classic resorts in not only Switzerland but in all of Europe. You'll want to stroll through the Hoheweg, a 35-acre park with a famous flower clock, or take a ride in a horse-drawn cab. The best excursion is the rack railway route from Interlaken to Jungfrau. Other attractions include a cable-car ride to a mountaintop revolving restaurant on the Schilthorn, year-round outdoor sports, afternoon concerts and the summer festival that celebrates Schiller's version of the William Tell story.

Where to Stay

Hotels and Resorts

Grand Hotel Beau-Rivage   ★★★★★

http://www.beaurivage-interlaken.ch/

Expensive

Hoheweg 211. ☞ *Situated between Hoheweg and the Aare rivers.*

☎ *036/21-62-72,* Fax: *528-1234.*

This venerable art nouveau hotel offers guests gorgeous mountain or river views and luxurious accommodations. All 99 rooms have private bath, phone, TV; three deluxe suites are available. The hotel has a central tower of covered loggias that connects two gabled wings. Rooms on the wings have wrought-iron balconies. Guests can relax on a "sunning lawn" and dine in the La Bonne Fourchette restaurant by candlelight. Piano music is offered nightly in the Le Vieux Rivage, one of its three bars.

Hotel Grand Victoria-Jungfrau   ★★★★★

http://www.victoria-jungfrau.ch/ flash.asp

Expensive to Very Expensive

Hoheweg 41. ☞ *Overlooking the Hohematte*

☎ *036/21-21-71.*

Credit Cards: *V, MC, DC, A.*

Grand and gracious, this is Interlaken's most famous, and one of Switzerland's most prestigious, hotel resorts. The Victoria was built in 1865, then combined with the Jungfrau creating the complex that reigns over the town center. Mark Twain slept here, and so did the

King of Siam. Meticulously restored, the elaborate Victorian buildings house 228 rooms, each with private bath, phone, TV. There are two restaurants, three bars, a disco, an indoor golf center, a beauty parlor and a medical center that provides physiotherapy.

Hotel Interlaken ★★★

http://www.interlakenhotel.ch/
Moderate to Expensive

Hoheweg 74. *East of the casino.*

☎ *036/21-22-11.*

First a hospital, then a cloister, the Interlaken is the city's oldest hotel, having served guests since the 1400s. Byron stayed here, as did Mendelssohn. The building has been renovated into a fairly modern facility but you can see the original walls in the dining room. The 60 rooms are well-furnished, some with antiques, and all contain private bath, phone. In addition to the dining room, where regional and international cuisine is served, there are a Swiss tavern, a sidewalk cafe and a Chinese restaurant. Conference facilities; sheltered garden.

Hotel du Lac ★★★

Moderate

Hoheweg 225. *Near train station and boat dock.*

☎ *036/22-29-22.*

Credit Cards: *V, MC, DC, A.*

Right on the banks of the Aare River, this hotel has a French-style mansard roof, a pink facade and wrought-iron balconies. Owned and managed for more than a century by the Hofmann family, the hotel is situated near the train station and the boat docks, making it an ideal headquarters for Jungfrau excursions or trips out on Lake Brienz. The 40 rooms each feature a private bath, and many have waterfront views. During high season, the managers prefer to avoid large groups, focusing instead on pleasing individual guests. Closed: Mid-Jan.–mid-Feb.

Inns

Gasthof Hirschen

http://www.kappl.at/hirschen/
Moderate to Expensive

CH 3800 Interlaken-Matten. ☞ *North side of Interlaken, a 10-minute walk from town center.*

☎ *036/22-15-45.*

Credit Cards: *V, MC, DC, A.*

The dark timbers and hip roof testify to this family-run inn's farmhouse heritage, which dates back to the 1500s. The public areas are decorated with antique spinning wheels, cowbells and numerous old clocks. Accommodations include 22 rooms, with comfortable light-pine furnishings, bath or shower; guests can have their breakfast on the balcony with view of the Jungfrau. The restaurant serves produce from the owner's gardens. The eggs, butter, cheese, poultry and beef come from the family's farming enterprises. A recommended hotel just outside the bustle of Interlaken.

Where to Eat

Schuh

Moderate

Hoheweg 56. ☞ *Near the Hotel Metropole.* ☎ *036/22-94-41.*

Credit Cards: *V, MC, DC, A.* Closed: *Mon.*

Renowned for its artistic and delicious pastries, this restaurant-tearoom has a sweets shop adjoining its dining room. In the Vienna-style cafe, you can listen to piano music and enjoy anything from a cup of tea and a croissant to a complete hot meal. Outside, during summer, guests can dine on a shady terrace that faces the Hohematte gardens.

What to Do
Excursions

Jungraubahn

📧 *Jungrau Railways, Hoheweg 37.* ☞ *East station in Interlaken.*

☎ *036/26-41-11.*

🕐 *8 a.m.–4 p.m.*

Towering 11,333 feet high, Jungfraujoch is the site of Europe's highway rack railway station. The day-trip excursion from Interlaken to the summit is the highlight of a Switzerland trip, especially if the weather cooperates. On clear days, the route provides magnificent vistas of Switzerland's "Big Three" mountains, Jungfrau, Monch and Eiger. Trains ascend steep grades and snake through long tunnels. Departing Interlaken in the morning, passengers ride the Wengernalp train on a rack railway that opened in 1893, ascending to Lauterbrunnen at 2612 feet. From there, they board a train to Kleine Scheidegg station at 6762 feet. At Kleine Scheidegg, they change trains again. The final leg ascends six miles up the Jungfrau, four of those miles are through a tunnel carved into the mountain. At Eigewand (9400 feet) and Eismeer (10,368 feet), the train stops so that passengers can view the "sea of ice" from windows cut from the tunnel. Emerging from the tunnel at the Jungfraujoch terminus, the air is thin and the sun has a glaring brightness. On the summit of the "Queen of Mountains" are a post office, several restaurants and the Eisaplast (Ice Palace). Begun in 1934, the Ice Palace is a man-made gallery where the walls and various sculptures are hewn out of solid ice. Perched like an aerie on the mountain's gray face, the Top of Europe restaurant, opened in 1987, offers dizzying views of the Aletsch Glacier, a 14-mile river of ice. The Sphinx elevator carries visitors to the mountain's topmost heights where there is a weather station and viewing terrace. Cap this truly peak experience with a dog-sled ride, then retrace your route to Interlaken, or continue the loop to Grindelwald. In order to enjoy your trip in comfort, check ahead for weather conditions and wear sunglasses and sturdy walking shoes. Be sure to bring lots of film.

Historical Sites

Lake Thun and Schloss Zahringen ★★★★

🗐 *City of Thun.* ☞ *From Interlaken, take the N6 and go 6 miles west.* ☎ *033/23-20-01.*

🕐 *9 a.m.–5 p.m.*

Special Hours: *Open daily, Apr.–Oct.*

East of Interlaken in an ancient glacier basin is Lake Thun, a beautiful region that has earned it the title, "Riviera of the Oberland." Boating tours leave from Interlaken (☎ *033/26-02-58* for schedules and fees). Other outdoor activities include water-skiing, windsurfing, swimming, golf, tennis, horseback riding and hiking. Stroll across wooden bridges, wander down narrow arcades and visit the Old Town where rooftop-terraced sidewalks have stairs leading to the first floor of shops below. Follow the covered stairway to Schloss Zahringen, a 12th-century castle with four turrets. Built by the Duke of Zahringen, the stronghold now houses a museum. On view is a collection of medieval weapons, tapestries, locally made ceramics, 19th-century Swiss household objects and Victorian-era toys. The views from the ramparts are breathtaking.

Special Tours

Aare Gorge

▣ *East of Interlaken, one mile southeast of Meiringen.*

☎ *036/71-43-22.*

🕐 *8 a.m.–6 p.m.*

Special Hours: *Open May–Oct.*

The Aare River has carved a sinuous gorge through the Kirchet, a rocky barrier near Meiringen. The 1500 yard-long gorge is equipped with walkways and galleries to allow explorations of the narrow passages. The towering walls pinch together so closely at the top that daylight penetrates to the floor only a few minutes a day at about 12 p.m. This natural wonder can be reached by car from Meiringen, or by bus tour. Near the gorge is access to the Upper Reichenbachfall where the rivers of the Rosenlaui Valley converge. Made famous by Sir Arthur Conan Doyle in his Sherlock Holmes book, *The Final Solution*, the falls can be visited mid-May–mid-Sep. Access is by funicular which is a 10-minute walk from Meiringen. Admission: inexpensive.

Murren-Allmendhubel Cableway   ★★★★★

In Murren. *Nineteen miles south of Interlaken.*

☎ *036/23-14-44.*

🕐 *8 a.m.–6 p.m.*

Don't miss the chance to ride the Murren-Allmendhubel Cableway to the top of the Schilthorn (9742 feet), where the Piz Gloria revolving restaurant provides 360-degree panoramas of the Bernese Oberland. The four-stage cableway ride begins near Murren, 19 miles south of Interlaken. Murren is not open to passenger cars so visitors leave their vehicles at Stechelberg and take a two-stage cable car to Murren. During summer, you'll see flower-spattered alpine meadows and, on the gray cliffs, sure-footed chamois sheep. At Murren, cable cars leave every 30 minutes . Each red cabin holds up to 100 people. Half way up, passengers disembark and change to another cabin. At the icy summit is the Piz Gloria restaurant, offering stunning views of the Big Three, Eiger, Monch, and Jungfrau, and vistas of Lauterbrann Valley and the Jura. On clear days, views extend all the way to Germany's Black Forest. The **Piz Gloria** is famous as the location for the James Bond movie, *On Her Majesty's Secret Service.* The summit is also the start of the world's longest downhill ski race. Admission: varies.

St. Beatusholen   ★★★★

 West of Interlaken, above Lake Thun. ☎ *036/41-16-63.*

🕐 *9:30 a.m.–5:30 p.m.*

Special Hours: *Open daily, Apr. to Oct.*

Legend says a dragon inhabited these caverns above Lake Thun, and that the beast was slain by a 6th-century Irish missionary named Beatus. Today the caverns can be reached by boat on Lake Thun, by bus or car along a cliff-bottom road or by hiking on foot along the historic pilgrim's path. Walking tours along electrically lit pathways winding through the caverns depart every half hour. Visitors can explore a 3000-foot network of grottoes and huge galleries filled with stalactites and stalagmites. There's a restaurant that serves light meals and snacks inside the cave or outside on a terrace. Admission: inexpensive.

Central

Bern

With roots stretching back to the 12th century, Bern has a long and glorious history. The third-largest city and the capital of Switzerland, it is home to the Parliament, the Bear Pits and a whimsical clock tower. Nestled in the gooseneck of the River Aare on a thumb-shaped peninsula, the city is famous for its colorful Onion Market, held the fourth Monday of November. Bern is a central base for excursions into the recreational areas of the Bernese Oberland. The elegant Hotel Schweizerhof has earned its stripes with the diplomatic corps. Outside Bern, the Innere Enge offers intimate lodging in a parklike setting. Nearby is Murten (Morat), a small mountain town, where you can stay in an old Normandy-style manor, Le Vieux Manoir au Lac.

Where to Stay

Hotels and Resorts

Belle Epoque ★★★★★

Moderate to Expensive

Gerechtigkeitsgasse. ☞ *West of Nydeggbrucke (bridge).*

Public Transportation: *Bus 12.*

☎ *031/311-43-36.*

A stay at this medieval-era house provides a unique experience for lovers of art. In 1989, the family owners renovated the house into an intimate hotel and decorated it throughout with art nouveau (belle epoque) paintings and Jugenstil (Teutonic art nouveau) period furnishings. on the walls are paintings by Toulouse-Lautrec, Sandier, Gaudi and others. The 16 snug rooms and one spacious suite are decorated in airy pastel color schemes and feature many amenities such as modern baths, phone and FAX outlet.

Bellevue Palace ★★★★★

http://www.bellevue-palace.ch/

Expensive to Very Expensive

Kochergasse 3-5. *Next to the Bundeshaus (Swiss governmental seat).*

Public Transportation: *Tram 3, 9, 12.*

☎ *031/320-45-45.*

Credit Cards: *V, MC, DC, A.*

Known for its opulent luxury, this five-star hotel often is heavily booked when Parliament is in session. There are 141 spacious rooms and 14 suites. Featuring light blue, cream or pale orchid color schemes, all rooms have bath, TV, phone. The back rooms have a view of the Bernese Alps. The dining room has a sun terrace with table umbrellas to provide shade.

Le Vieux Manoir au Lac ★★★★★

http://www.relaischateaux.ch/ pages/relais/objets individuels/ le vieux manoir au lac 040/ RCI Accueil.cfm

Expensive

3280 Murten-Meyriez (Morat). *Located 12.4 miles east of Bern.*

☎ *037/71-12-83.*

Credit Cards: *V, MC, DC, A.*

Designed and built by a homesick French general, this Normandy-style mansion is close to the medieval-walled city of Murten and within easy driving distance of Bern. Set in a landscaped park near the eastern shore of Lake Murten, the inn has steeply pitched roof lines, half-timbers, white chimneys and turrets. Inside, the public areas are decorated with fresh-cut flowers, and Biedermeier antiques. The 20 rooms have parquet floors or Oriental carpets, bath or shower, TV, phone, hair dryer. Two hexagonal suites in one of the turrets have windows that look out on the lake and park. The restaurant is known for its Franco-International cuisine. A highly recommended 19th-century retreat. Closed: Mid-Dec.–mid-Feb.

Weisses Kreuz ★★★

Moderate

CH 3280 Murten (Morat). *Located 12.4 miles from Bern by car.*

☎ *037/71-26-41.*

Credit Cards: *V, MC, DC.*

The "White Cross," with marvelous views of Lake Murten, has been meticulously run by the same family for 70 years. A 10- minute walk from the train station, the "La Croix Blanche" (in French) has two buildings, one having once been a stable. Guests can choose from 27 rooms, all with bath or shower and view of the lake or the Altstadt. Most rooms have decor and furnishings in either Beidermeier, art nouveau, Empire or Louis XVI style. Simpler rooms in Scandinavian pine or contemporary decor are less expensive. The hotel restaurant features tiny perch fillets caught from the lake.

Hospiz Zur Heimat   ★★★

http://hospiz-zur-heimat.ch/
Budget
Gerechtigkeitsgasse 50. 📖 *Near the clock tower and cathedral.*

Public Transportation: *Tram 12.*

☎ *031/311-04-36.*

Credit Cards: *V, MC, DC, A.*

Without frills but ideally situated, this hospice-style establishment is located in the Altstadt, opposite a gilded fountain—five-star Old World surroundings at an economical price. The 40 rooms are clean and simple, with sinks and flower boxes at the windows. Seventeen rooms have showers, while the others share hallway facilities. The quietest rooms are in the back. Breakfast is included in the price and is served in a neighboring building.

Hotel Goldener Schlussel   ★★★

Budget to Moderate
Rathausgasse 72. 📖 *Overlooking Rathausgasse, near Kronhausplatz.*

Public Transportation: *Tram 9.*

☎ *031/311-02-16.*

Once a 13th-century stable, this hotel's building has been rebuilt over the years until it looks like the home of a wealthy patrician.

Wood-paneling and carpeting warm the 20 rooms. Rooms with showers have tiled baths. Nine rooms share hallway bath facilities. The ground floor houses a popular *stubli*, which serves Swiss home-style lamb or sausages and Rosti in a wood-planked, stone-trimmed dining room.

Where to Eat

Bellevue-Grill ★★★★★

Expensive

Kochergasse 3-5. ☎ *031/311-45-45.*

Public Transportation: *Tram 3, 9, 12.*
Credit Cards: *V, MC, DC, A.*

After a day in Parliament, officials retire to this establishment known throughout the city as a top restaurant. Extremely formal, but not stuffy, the restaurant serves French cuisine with cosmopolitan style. Reserve your table well in advance, and expect the dining room to be full. Enjoy American-bred beef grilled and served with a fruited butter sauce, game dishes or veal liver.

Brasserie zum Barengraben ★★★

Moderate

Muristalden 1. ☞ *Directly across from the Bear Pits.* ☎ *031/331-42-18.*

Public Transportation: *Tram 9.*

Here's where the locals come for hearty meals and a demi-liter of wine. Arched windows and intimate seating set a relaxing tone for Swiss basics and brasserie meats, followed up by freshly baked pastries. The daily specials and one-plate dinners are the best, both for taste and a lower bill.

Klotzlikeller ★★★★

Moderate

62 Gerechtigkeitsgasse. ☞ *Near Fountain of Justice and Clock Tower.*
☎ *031/22-74-56.*

Public Transportation: *Tram 9.*

Credit Cards: *V, MC, A.* Closed: *Mon., Sun.*

If you have time for only one wine-tasting stop while in Bern, take it here at the oldest wine tavern in the city. Dating from 1635, and marked at the entrance with a lantern outside its angled cellar door, the keller is decorated with wall murals inside and offers more than 20 different wines by the glass. There's an array of appetizers and snacks, and Bernese specials are featured on a rotating menu that changes every six weeks.

Piazza Lorenzini   ★★★★

Moderate

Marktplatz Passage 3. ☎ *031/22-78-50.*

Public Transportation: *Tram 3, 5, 9.*

Credit Cards: *V, MC.* Closed: *Sun.*

Whether for lunch or late night dinners, this popular restaurant attracts a cheerful crowd that comes to enjoy a changing menu of Italian dishes prepared with homemade pastas. Tuscan rabbit and beefsteak are standards but the menu might include truffles (in season) or trifle. The decor is bright and the ambience high-energy. Singles and young professionals dally at the tables or head to the downstairs level to the cafe-bar.

Ratskeller   ★★★★

Moderate

Gerechtigkeitsgasse 81. ☞ *Near the Fountain of Justice and Nydeggbrucke.*

Public Transportation: *Tram 9.*

Credit Cards: *V, MC, DC, A.*

At this historic Keller, the portions are ample and the service is brisk and friendly. Try the meat platters for two, the light meals served from noon, or Bernese favorites from the fixed-price menu.

Schultheissenstube   ★★★★★

Moderate to Expensive

Bahnhofplatz 11. ☎ *031/311-45-01.*

Public Transportation: *Tram 3, 9, 12.*
Credit Cards: *V, MC, DC, A.*

Inarguably one of the top three restaurants in the city, this culinary mecca seats guests in a dining room that was transported, board by board, from an old mansion and then reassembled. The famous horseshoe-shaped bar, the paneled walls and elegant place settings all contribute to an air of high-class sophistication. The chefs prepare refreshing combinations of classic ingredients—lobster soup flavored with tarragon, oyster-and-champagne risotto, seafood lasagna laced with saffron. Ask about daily specials from the fixed-price menu. Next to the more formal dining room is the popular, heartily rustic Simmentalstube.

What to Do
Historical Sites

Albert Einstein's House   ★★★

✉ *Kramgasse.* 🖙 *In Altstadt.* ☎ *031/311-76- 76.*

Public Transportation: *Tram 9.*

🕐 *10 a.m.–5 p.m.*

Special Hours: *Sat 10 a.m.–4 p.m., Closed Dec.–Jan.*

Switzerland is famous for its timepieces, but since time is relative, you shouldn't miss Albert Einstein's house where the physicist labored over his famous theory in 1905. Letters and mementos are on display, and the stop provides a counterpoint to the musical whimsy of the Clock Tower. Admission: inexpensive.

Barengraben   ★★★★★

✉ *Near Nydegg Bridge, on right bank of River Aare.*

☎ *031/311-76-76.*

Public Transportation: *Tram 9.*
Special Hours: *Daily, dawn to dusk*

According to legend, the founder of Bern vowed to name the city after the first animal slain during a royal hunt, and the dubious honor went to a bear. Today, the bears that live in the "bear pits" on the right bank of the River Aare are the pride of the city. Stout brown bears entertain by performing tricks and munching on carrots and other tidbits; you can buy the treats from vendors at the bear pits. Incidentally, anywhere in Bern, you'll find lots of "bear" souvenirs and toys to help you remember your visit. A walk across the Nydegg Bridge to see the bears is well worth it. From the 180-foot stone bridge, you have a splendid view of the Old City. Below the bear pits, you can visit a rose garden, featuring as many as 200 varieties.

ITRAVELBOOK FREEBIE

Cathedral of St. Vincent   ★★★★★

🖹 *Munsterplatz.* ☞ *At the top of Junkerngasse.*

☎ *031/311-05-72.*

Public Transportation: *Tram 9.*

🕐 *10 a.m.–4 p.m.*

Special Hours: *Cathedral closed daily 12–2 p.m.*

Begun in 1421 but completed only in 1893, the Cathedral has a 300-foot-tall belfry with a viewing platform (separate fee) that can be reached by climbing more than 270 stairs. This late Gothic edifice is most famous for its tympanum over the main portal, which details The Last Supper with 234 carved figures, a work that was spared destruction during the Reformation. The Matter Chapel feaures a huge stained-glass window illustrating the Dance of Death, installed in the last year of World War I. The ornately carved pews and wood choir stalls are other highlights.

Zytgloggerturm   ★★★★★

🖹 *Kramgasse.* ☞ *Stand at Kramgasse and Hotelgasse.*

☎ *031/311-76-76.*

Special Hours: *Open daily, tours of clockworks vary.*

Bern's clock tower is the most popular subject on souvenir picture postcards. Built in 1911, this city landmark has been embellished over the centuries, and now it features bells and automated dancing figures that perform at four minutes to every hour. Arrive before the hour to get a good view of the mechanical show, set into motion by a court jester who rings two bells. Following the jester is a parade of horsemen and bears (the city symbol), including soldier bears and a king bear. The procession ends with a metal rooster that crows and flaps its wings while a gold-armored knight hammers out the hour. Father Time watches over the spectacle, keeping time with his scepter and hourglass.

Museums and Exhibits

Musee Historique ★★★★★

▣ *CH 3280 Murten (Morat).* ☞ *Located 12.4 miles east of Bern by car.* ☎ *037/71-31-00.*

◷ *2 p.m.–5 p.m.*

Special Hours: *Closed Nov.–Jan.*

While staying in Murten (Morat) or on a day tour from Bern, visit this museum to learn the history behind the thick walls and 13th-century medieval gates that still surround this small mountain town. Situated in a renovated mill, complete with two water-powered mill wheels, the museum contains exhibits ranging from prehistoric finds to relics from the 1476 Battle of Morat. According to legend, after the Swiss Confederacy won a victory over the Burgundians, a runner carrying a linden branch was sent from Murten to Fribourg. The runner expired when he reached the Fribourg Town Hall, and today, the first Sunday of October, a 17-kilometer race that draws 15,000 runners is held to commemorate the event. Admission: inexpensive.

Special Tours

Mount Gurten ★★★

▣ *Monbijoustrasse (road to Thun).* ☞ *Tram 9 to Funicular, or by car.* ☎ *031/311- 76-76.*

◷ *8 a.m.–dusk*

Splendid views await from the lookout point at Bern's summit, Mount Gurten. Go by car or tram to the funicular, which takes you to the top, where you can stroll in a children's fairyland or wander on a network of walking paths. The views of the city, nestled in the gooseneck of the Aare are unforgettable. On clear days, you can see the high Alps. Admission: inexpensive.

Lucerne

Situated on Lake Lucerne's northern end, Lucerne is considered the "most Swiss" of cities and known for its historic wooden bridges and cobblestone streets. An ideal base for touring central Switzerland, Lucerne is linked to Lugano by the William Tell Express, a rail-and-boat network. It hosts the International Festival of Music each August and September, and also offers a dazzling summer night festival with fireworks by the lake. Whether you stay at the glamorous **Palace Hotel** or at the home-style **Hofgarten** in the shadow of Hofkirche, there is much to enjoy.

Where to Stay

Hotels and Resorts

Carlton Hotel-Tivoli   ★ ★ ★

http://www.carlton-tivoli.ch/

Moderate to Expensive

Haldenstrasse 57. *North side of lake, just over 1/2 mile from town center.*

Public Transportation: *Bus 24.*

☎ *041/51-30-51.*

Credit Cards: *V, MC, DC, A.*

Located on the quieter end of a street lined with lakefront hotels, this 19th-century building is surrounded by a landscaped garden and features its own private marina. The rooftop deck and garden restaurant affords splendid views. The 100 rooms have large windows, private bath with hair dryer, TV and phone. Three suites are available. Some rooms have balcony and lake views. For families, rooms can be combined to form triples. The hotel offers dining for groups only, two bars featuring live music, a playroom and equipment rentals for water sports.

Chateau Gutsch

Expensive to Very Expensive

Kanonenstrasse. *On hillside above Lucerne.*

☎ *041/22-02-72.*

Perched on a hill above Lucerne, this extravagant chateau-style hotel is like a storybook castle. There are turrets, stone stairways, suits of armor, game trophies and canopy beds, not to mention a private tram to carry guests to the entrance. Here, historical accuracy is secondary to romantic appeal, but the views are postcard-perfect, and amenities include an outdoor pool, a private forest, wine tastings each evening in the wine cellar, plus dancing after dinner. The 35 rooms are lavishly decorated, with large private bath, phone, TV. The banquet rooms often fill with special groups on weekends.

Grand Hotel National

http://www.national-luzern.ch/
Expensive to Very Expensive
Haldenstrasse 4.
Public Transportation: *Bus 24.*

☎ *041/50-11-11,* Fax: *882-4777.*

Credit Cards: *V, MC, DC, A.*

Built in 1870, this kingly establishment was the first major hotel constructed in Lucerne. Grand in scale, the complex occupies two city blocks, and commanding prime lake views, the hotel is trimmed with French balconies and cheerful awnings. The 79 rooms, all renovated recently, have private bath, hair dryer, phone, TV. The streetside rooms have double-glazed windows, and some units are reserved for nonsmokers. The lakeside rooms are best, many with private balcony. Luxurious room touches include chocolate on pillows, turndowns, fresh fruit and flowers. There are five dining areas, a grill, a garden terrace, a tearoom, a formal French dining room and a Viennese-style cafe, in addition to a piano bar.

Hotel Krone

Moderate

Weinmarkt 12. ☞ *Two blocks from the river.*

☎ *041/51-62-51.*

Credit Cards: *V, MC, DC, A.*

In a city full of expensive luxury resorts, this reasonably priced hotel in the Weinmarkt district offers a great location in the heart of the city. The rooms are simply but comfortably furnished, and all 24 units have private bath or shower. The rooms in front overlook the plaza, while those in back face out toward a quiet street. The restaurant serves buffet breakfast and light meals. If you're feeling energetic, take the spiral staircase to reach your room, otherwise there is an elevator.

Where to Eat

Old Swiss House ★★★★

Moderate to Expensive

Lowenplatz 4. ☞ *Near the Lion Monument.* ☎ *041/51-61-71.*

Public Transportation: *Bus 1.* Metro Stop: *Lowenplatz Stop.*
Credit Cards: *V, MC, DC, A.*

Don't be surprised if this half-timbered house near the Lion Monument seems familiar, it's one of the most photographed sights in Lucerne, and so well-known that a replica was built in 1964 at Busch Gardens in Florida. Here at Lowenplatz, the crowd runs to flocks of tourists, but the food is excellent and even the overdone Swiss kitsch is worth seeing at least once. Decorated with 17th-century furnishings, porcelain tiles, hand-carved wood doors, leaded glass and lots of silver and pewter, the Old Swiss House is a antique-lover's heaven. The dining areas include inside rooms decorated with oil paintings, upstairs private banquet rooms and an outdoor terrace. The restaurant has been delighting patrons for 130 years with its homemade cheese croquettes, lake fish (try the perch fillets), veal and Rosti (hash-brown potatoes), and Wiener Schnitzel.

Rebstock/Hofstube ★★★

Moderate

St.Leodegarstrasse. ☞ *Next door to Hofkirche. Located at Rebstock.*

☎ *041/51-35-81.*

Credit Cards: *V, MC, DC, A.*

Reservations recommended.

This pair of restaurants offers a menu of international, East Asian and vegetarian dishes, all lovingly prepared with fresh ingredients. Served in a homey but classic ambience, the formal dining room is filled with fresh-cut flowers, polished wood and brass, while the brasserie has an inviting bentwood bar, the dishes include original specialities and continental favorites. Outside is a flower-filled terrace with great views of Hofkirche. Popular with locals, this is a place to try something different.

Schiffrestaurant Wilhelm Tell ★★★

Moderate

Langungsbruck9. ☎ *041/51-23-30.*

Public Transportation: *Bus 2.*

Credit Cards: *V, MC, A.*

Schiff is German for boat, an apt name for this 1908 Lake Lucerne steamer that has been converted into a permanently moored floating restaurant. Guests linger at tables scattered on the outside decks over coffee, snacks or a beer, or retire inside to the aft section where formal cuisine is served in elegant style. The best choices are fillet of perch or sole, or grilled veal and beef. Fish selections vary with the season. You can view the highly polished ship's engine, visible behind glass as a mechanical "work of art," or feed the battalions of swans that gather at the waterline to nibble on scraps.

Wilden Mann ★★★★

Moderate

Bahnhofstrasse 30. ☞ *Near the Kapellbrucke. Located at Wilden Mann.* ☎ *041/23-16-66.*

Credit Cards: *V, MC, DC, A.*

Founded as a rest stop in 1517 for weary travelers, this complex of dining rooms serves an array of Swiss favorites enlivened with a French accent. The original dining room was the Burgerstube, which today is an ornate room filled with heavy beams and family crests. The Liedertafel is a vaulted room brightened by the glow of candles on the tables. Chef Andreas Stubli oversees both rooms, treating guests to lamb, duck break or smoked salmon served wrapped in Rosti. Lighter dishes include roast chicken with risotto or *Wursli* (sausage). There's also dining on a covered patio, the Geranium Terrace, where you can choose from an alfresco menu. This establishment is especially popular with groups, which are generally served in a separate area.

What to Do
Museums and Exhibits

Am-Rhyn-Haus ★★★★

Furrengasse 21. ☎ *041/41-17-73.*

Public Transportation: *Bus 1.*

🕐 *10 a.m.–6 p.m.*

Special Hours: *Nov. through Mar., Fri.–Sun., 11 a.m.–noon.*

A small but impressive collection of works by Picasso is housed in this 17th-century townhouse. On display are works such as Woman and Dog Playing (1953), Woman Dressing Her Hair (1954) and the sculpture Woman with a Hat (1961). Also extremely interesting is the exhibit of photographs by David Douglas Duncan. Famous for his photographs of World War II battles for *Life* magazine, Duncan also shot pictures of Picasso at work. More than 200 of Duncan's photographs are on display.

Verkehrshaus Der Schweiz ★★★★★

http://www.verkehrshaus.ch/ intro.htm

Lidostrasse 5. *Just beyond the Haldenstrasse cable-car station.* ☎ *041/31-44-44.*

Public Transportation: *Bus 2.*

🕐 *9 a.m.–6 a.m.*

Special Hours: *Nov.–Feb. 10 a.m.–4 p.m.; Sun., 10 a.m.–4 p.m.*

More than half a million people a year visit this large, popular museum. The network of halls houses displays of all modes of transportation, including train engines, railcars, airplanes, automobiles, ships and spacecraft. Among the highlights is the scale model of a Swiss railway crossing, the Gottard, where a dozen trains move simultaneously. The Swissorama is a 20-minute film of a whirlwind tour of Switzerland. The film gives viewers a "you- are-there" feeling of touring on foot and by road, sea and air. Hands-on exhibits delight children. Admission: inexpensive.

Special Tours

Mount Pilatus Tour   ★★★★★

Nine miles south of Lucerne, Mount Pilatus (6964 feet) was rumored to be haunted by the ghost of Pontius Pilate. Medieval Lucerners feared that if travelers ascended the peak, the angry ghost would unleash violent storms. However, today the mountain is one of the best (and most popular) excursions in Switzerland. During summer, the cog railway carries visitors to the summit from Alpnachstad at the edge of Lake Lucerne. To get to Alpnachstad, you can take the 90-minute lake steamer ride from Lucerne. The cog railway operates at a 48 percent gradient, one of the steepest in the world. At the top, paths lead to vista points for panoramas of Lake Lucerne, Lake Zug and the Alps. You can descend by cable car in a two-stage route that will deposit you at Kriens, a suburb of Lucerne, where Tram 1 connects back to the heart of the city. The cog railway does not run during winter months.

Sports and Recreation

Boat Tours and Water Sports   ★★★★

 Lake Lucerne Navigation Company. ☞ *Landing station is opposite the Hauptbahnhof.* ☎ *041/40-45-40.*

🕐 *8 a.m.–5 p.m.*

The Lake Lucerne Navigation Company operates 19 boats, including five paddle- steamers. Tours and schedules vary. The most popular tour is the full-lake route from Lucerne to Fleulen, the farthest point from Lucerne. First-class tickets cost SFr53. Be sure to check departure times as the last boats returning to Lucerne leave Fleulen before 5 or 6 p.m. Other ways to get out on the water abound. SNG at Seebrucke (north bank) rents rowing boats, motorboats and even two-person pedal-boats by the hour, half-day or day. Contact SNG for rates at ☎ *041/44-45-44*. You can take a dip in the lake for free by heading to Seepark off Alpenquai.

Engadine

St. Moritz

Celebrated as the most glamorous resort town in Switzerland, St. Moritz has been the destination of choice for savvy world travelers since 1864 when hotelier Johannes Bardrutt hosted his first guests. St. Moritz is situated at 6000 feet in the Southern Engadine Alps. Today, the snow, the thermal waters and the grand mountain views draw an endless parade of skiers, spa guests and hikers to its hotels and inns. A night at the magnificent Palace Hotel during the winter high season is a royal fantasy come to life. In summer, when prices melt, the Meirei country inn provides a peaceful spot from which to view the lake and mountains.

Where to Stay

Hotels and Resorts

Badrutt's Palace Hotel ★★★★★

http://www.badruttspalace.com/
Expensive to Off-the-Scale
Via Serlas 27.
Public Transportation: *Bus 1.*

☎ *082/2-11-01.*

Credit Cards: *V, MC, DC, A.*

Built by Caspar Badrutt in the early 1900s, the Palace has a stone facade and fortified towers that emphasize its opulence and grandeur. Celebrity guests, both the famous and the infamous, have visited here, including the former shah of Iran, Aristotle Onassis and Greta Garbo. Reservations for Christmas and New Year's are booked a year in advance. Inside, the Great Hall is decorated with two black-marble fireplaces, antique furnishings and enough fresh flowers to cover a Rose Parade float. Guests are required to dress to match the opulence, after 7 p.m., a formal dress code specifies ties and dark suits. Each of the 270 rooms is lavishly appointed and elegantly furnished and has a private bath, phone, TV. There are 18 luxury suites and 21 privately owned one- and two-bedroom condominiums on the grounds. The hotel has nine restaurants, two bars, two nightclubs, a private cinema, a ski school, complete business services and on-site child care. The outdoor pool features a huge waterfall. The Palace is the place to be seen, attracting genteel old money as well as the flashy rich, not to mention those with more aspirations than means. Closed: Apr.–June, and Sept.–Dec.

Carlton Hotel ★★★★★

http://www.carlton-stmoritz.ch/
Very Expensive
Via Badrutt Dorf.

☎ *082/2-11-14.*

Credit Cards: *V, MC, DC, A.*

Restrained luxury is the hallmark of this nine-story chateau hotel, once the home of Nicholas II, the last tsar of Russia. Not as flashy as the Palace but comparable in quality service, this hotel is located on the edge of the village near the lake. The hotel offers 99 spacious rooms, each with a new private marble-tiled bath, hair dryer, phone, TV. The six suites are elegantly appointed. There's a glassed-in pool; staff- run playroom for children; hairdresser. A complimentary shuttle ferries guests to the town center or the ski lifts. Closed: May and Nov.

Hotel Schweizerhof ★★★★

Expensive

Via dal Bagn 54. *Center of town.*

☎ *082/2-21-71.*

Credit Cards: *V, MC, DC, A.*

Built by the Von Gugelberg family in 1896 and managed by the same family today, this six-story Victorian hotel offers luxury at a reasonable price, especially for St. Moritz. Emphasizing personal service in the classic Swiss tradition, this year-round hotel is known for its restaurants, which include an Alpine hut in the nearby mountains that serves meals by a cheery corner fireplace. The 85 rooms, in pastel color schemes, have modern private bath, phone, TV. Thirty rooms are considered deluxe, and these face south with lake views. Ten suites are also available. Dinner dancing, child care and winter-sports programs are offered.

Meierei Langasthof   ★★★★

Moderate

CH 7500. *Across the lake from St. Moritz reached by car or postal bus.*

☎ 082/3-20-60.

Credit Cards: *Not accepted.*

This small country inn is a renovated farmhouse whose origins date back to the 17th century when it belonged to a bishop. It is situated in a meadow at the end of a rural road just outside St. Moritz. Although known best for its restaurant, the terrace is especially popular at lunch with hikers. The inn has 10 simply furnished, airy rooms, each with its own private tiled bath. Families with children will appreciate the playground area and the corrals filled with ponies, horses and even a donkey or two. Paths along the lake provide relaxing strolls. It's a 20-minute walk to the town or to the spa at St. Moritz-Bad.

Hotel Waldhaus Am See   ★★★

Moderate
Via Dimiej 6.

☎ 082/3-76-76.

Credit Cards: *Not accepted.*

Removed from the glitter by its location on a peninsula overlooking the lake, this family-run lodge was once a tavern, then a private home. Now it offers a relaxing retreat in simple, sunny surroundings, catering primarily to weeklong guests. Twenty-eight of the 38 rooms have private bath; those without share facilities. Furnishings are basic but comfortable, and all rooms have phone and TV. Guests can dine inside or on the sun terrace beside the lake where featured on the menu is delicious fresh fish right from the lake. The hotel offers planned excursions and theme buffets to tempt guests. Rates by the week are less. Closed Nov.

Where to Eat

Chesa Veglia ★★★★

Expensive

Via Veglia 2. ☎ *082/3-35-96.*

Public Transportation: *Bus 1.*
Credit Cards: *V, MC, DC, A.*

Situated in a restored 17th-century *bauernhof,* or farmhouse, the restaurant draws its name from the Romansh word chesa, for "house." With its heavy timbers, stone-and-stuccowork, the building is the only authentic Engadine-style house in the resort. Comprised of three separate restaurants, each with its own distinct ambience, the Chesa draws crowds from lunch until 12 a.m. The upscale and most expensive is the Chadafo Grill where guests dine on haute cuisine, featuring meats roasted over a wood fire. The Patrizier-Stube serves regional dishes, including a hearty farmer's platter of various cheeses. In the Hayloft, the pizzeria turns out pizza dishes and salads. Teatime features fruit tarts and dancing, while evening meals in the Grill Room are enhanced by piano music. Owned by the Palace Hotel, the restaurant delivers a pricey but memorable experience.

Hanselmann ★★★

Inexpensive to Moderate

Via Maistra 8. ☎ *082/3-38-64.*

Public Transportation: *Bus 1.*

Breakfast, lunch, tea and light meals are featured at this historic tavern inside a building embellished with sgraffito plaster designs. Popular and relatively inexpensive, the family-owned restaurant has been serving patrons since the mid-1800s. For breakfast, a number of omelettes and country platters, big servings of Black Forest ham and Valais-style rye rolls are offered.The upstairs restaurant opens at 11:30 a.m for lunch.

La Marmite   ★★★★★

Expensive

Corviglia Bergstation. *By Corviglia funicular from St. Moritz.*

☎ *082/3-63-55.*

Credit Cards: *V, MC, DC, A.*

This woodsy top-of-the-world restaurant run by the Mathis family is "top of the line." You need to take the funicular to reach this spot, and to make reservations early during high season. Dishes include exquisite soups, game served with truffles and a seafood omelette. A six-course caviar menu (the ultimate extravagance!) is also offered. You can choose from two dozen or more sumptuous desserts. Attached to the main dining room is a cafeteria; it's somewhat less expensive and popular with skiers.

Landgasthof Meirei   ★★★

Moderate to Expensive

Via Dimiej 52. *No cars. By foot (20 minutes), taxi or horse-drawn sleigh.* ☎ *082/3- 2060.*

Situated at the end of a lakeside promenade, this century-old restaurant was once used as a relay station for the Swiss Postal Service. The four rustic dining rooms have served a renowned clientele, including Picasso, the former shah of Iran and King Farouk of Egypt. Today guests must walk up the lakeside path or hire a taxi or horse-drawn sleigh to reach the restaurant. Before heading out, call ahead to make sure the restaurant is open. Though somewhat expensive, the cuisine is traditional and simple.

Restaurant Engadina   ★★★

Moderate

Piazza da Scoula 2. *Across from Town Hall.* ☎ *082/3-32-65.*

Public Transportation: *Bus 1.*

Credit Cards: *V, MC, DC, A.* Closed: *Sun.*

In a resort where the tab can clean out your wallet, this pair of family-style dining rooms serves reasonably priced hearty dishes in comfortable, woodsy surroundings. There's dining inside at pine tables or outside, weather permitting, on a wooden deck. Fondues are the most popular dishes, but selections generally include grilled steaks and *frites* (french fries), goulash, escargot and Spatzli. Apres ski or after a hike, you could hardly do better.

What to Do
Excursions

Parc Naziunal Svizzer ★★★★★

⊟ *Nationalpark-Haus CH 7530.* *Northeast of St. Moritz on Route 27.* ☎ *082/8-13-78.*

🕒 *8:30 a.m.–6 p.m.*

Special Hours: *Open June to Oct.*

Covering 64 square miles of nearly virgin wilderness, the Swiss National Park is a Swiss federal preserve located in the Engadine Alps north of St. Moritz. Here visitors might catch a glimpse of ibex, wild sheep with long curving horns, or short-horned chamois. Other native animals seen include red deer, tiny roe deer and marmots. Trails lead to magnificent viewpoints or wander through coniferous forests. Unlike most U.S. national parks, this preserve has not been developed, there are no campgrounds or picnic sites. Even the rangers live outside the park boundaries. Admittance is strictly regulated, and visitors must stay on marked trails. All trash must be packed out, and nothing can be removed from the park. The main entrance is at Zernez, approximately 18 miles northeast of St. Moritz. Allow at least half a day for your visit. Admission: varies.

Special Tours
Julier Pass ★★★

⊟ *Approximately 20 miles southeast of St. Moritz.*

☎ *082/3-31-47.*

Switzerland's mountain passes are renowned for their dizzying heights and the challenges they have presented to travelers over the centuries. As you drive along Route 3 over Julier Pass, linking St.

Moritz with Chur, imagine what it was like for the Roman legion-
naires who trooped through here around the 4th century. Traces of
paving and two stone columns at the summit remain as testimony to
Roman endurance. Today a modern road winds up the scenic pass,
providing views of the Bernina range and the Engadine lakes.
Usually kept open year-round, the road passes the Julier Mountain
Refuge Hut, then crests Julier Pass at 7494 feet. The steep zigzag
descent continues through a barren alpine valley to the hamlet of
Bivio, once a staging post, then on to Tiefencastel, a hub for routes
leading north to Chur or southwest to Lugano.

Sports and Recreation

Winter Sports   ★★★★★

📧 *Kur-and Verkehrsverein, Via Maistra 12.* ☎ *082/3-31-47.*

Special Hours: *Winter months.*

Synonymous with skiing, St. Moritz is home to the world's oldest
ski school founded in 1927 at Moritz-Dorf. The surrounding slopes
support five ski complexes, with 58 lifts leading to 250 miles of
downhill ski slopes and more than 100 miles of cross-country ski
trails. St. Moritz hosted the Winter Olympics in 1928 and 1948, and
has an Olympic-class ski-jumping hill. Various ski passes are available. For more information on prices, ☎ *082/3-62-33.* Curling
rinks abound, and lessons in the sport are available. The frozen lake
is used for winter golf and tobogganing. Contact the tourist office
for more details.

Davos

   This ancient town dates back to 1160, and its crisp mountain air
made it popular as a health resort for consumptive patients. Thomas
Mann used Davos as the setting for his novel *The Magic Mountain*,
but today the city is most famous as a hard-core ski resort and sports
center. In the summer, hikers, walkers and cyclists fill the valley.
Originally built as a sanitarium, the secluded **Berghotel Schatzalp**
still offers an array of massage therapies and other health services.
Hubli's Landhaus is a charming country inn, especially known for
its outstanding restaurant, located in a former relay station for the
Swiss post office.

Where to Stay

Berghotel Schatzalp   ★★★★★

http://www.schatzalp.ch/ index2.html

Very Expensive

Davos-Platz. *By funicular, from Davos center (last car 11 p.m. summer, 2 a.m. winter).*

☎ *081/44-13-31.*

Credit Cards: *V, MC, DC, A.*

Once a sanatorium for those seeking "the cure" at Davos, this art nouveau hotel is perched above the city and is accessed by funicular. There are 93 rooms, all with bath, TV, phone. Many rooms have antique furniture; the quietest rooms are at the far end, away from the cog railway noise. Harkening back to its roots, the hotel offers massage therapies and other health services. Half-board is required in both summer and winter, served either in the formal dining room or in the wood- detailed Schatzalp pavilion. The Strela ski lifts are 165 feet from the hotel. Closed: May, and Oct.–Nov.

Hubli's Landhaus   ★★★

Moderate

Kantonsstrasse. *By car, two miles north of Davos-Dorf, along Route 28 toward Klosters.*

☎ *081/46-21-21.*

Credit Cards: *V, MC, DC, A.*

This family-owned country inn is set in its own private garden enhances the intimacy. The 28 comfortable rooms are decorated in earth-toned shades; 15 rooms have private bath. Your stay is complemented by great dining, the hotel restaurant (connected to the inn by a tunnel) is available on an a la carte basis or to guests who pay half-board. Closed: Mar. and Nov.

Where to Eat

Davoserstubl/Jenatschtubl   ★★★★★

Expensive

Bahnhofstrasse. ☎ *081/43-68-17.*

Metro Stop: *Stop 11.*
Credit Cards: *V, MC, DC, A.*

Two restaurants inside the hotel offer seasonal specialities, freshly
made, with an emphasis on modern accents. During the low season,
residents fill the tables at the Davoserstubl or on the terrace of the
larger, lighter-toned Jenatschstubl. The decor is understated Old
World in both rooms, with paneled walls and ceilings and antique
sideboards. But guests come for the food, prepared by owner-chef
Paul Petzold, and to sample the extensive wine list. Dishes include
elegant roast lamb with herbs and fillet of beef with shallots. Half-
board guests can enjoy the cuisine as part of their room costs.

Hubli's Landhaus Restaurant   ★★★★

Moderate

Kantonsstrasse. 🕼 *Two miles north of Davos-Dorf. Located at Hubli's*

Landhaus. ☎ *081/46-21-21.*

Credit Cards: *V, MC, DC, A.* Closed: *Mon.*

Operated by Felix and Anne-Marie Hubli, also owners of Landhaus
inn, this restaurant seats diners in what was once a relay station for
the Swiss post office. Well- known and respected, the Landhaus is a
must for those who appreciate good cuisine made with fresh ingredients. The atmosphere is simple, but the food is sophisticated and
lovingly prepared. The menu changes by season and might feature
quail or lobster, pigeon or duck. Guests at the hotel can enjoy meals
through half-board in a private dining room reached via a tunnel.

What to Do
Nightlife

Cava Grischa-Kellerbar   ★★★★★

 Promenade 63. 🕼 *In the Hotel Europe.* ☎ *081/43-59-21.*

🕐 *9 p.m.–3 a.m.*

Special Hours: *Nightly-all-year round.*

Active people head here after a day on the slopes or tennis courts. Authentic Swiss folk tunes are played on traditional instruments—the flugelhorn, Alpine guitars and accordions. The melodies beg you to dance, and most people do. Admission: inexpensive.

Sports and Recreation

Winter Sports   ★★★★★

Special Hours: *Prices and hours vary.*

Davos and active winter sports are synonymous; the region has attracted skiers since 1888. In 1889, Davos inaugurated a huge ice-skating rink to host the European ice- and speed-skating championships. The number of ski lifts here has soared, and today there are hundreds of miles of downhill and cross-country trails. The ski crowd at Davos tends to be young and very dedicated to the sport. (Unlike other resorts, they're more interested in skiing than posing in fashionable clothing apres ski.) **The Swiss Ski School** offers lessons, ☎ *081/43-71-71.* Or you can take up curling; the **Davos-Village Curling Club** has more information, at ☎ *081/43-73-54.* Sledding and ice skating are also available.

Klosters

Near Davos, but less tourist-oriented, Klosters was founded as a cloister in 1222. The village has managed to retain a quaint atmosphere in spite of the celebrities and royal visitors who flock here during ski season. Situated in the Prattigau Valley near the River Landquart, the town has only chalet-style buildings and is surrounded by lush meadows, forests and majestic mountains. Among its famous past visitors is Robert Louis Stevenson who is said to have finished writing *Treasure Island* here.

Where to Stay

Hotels and Resorts

Hotel Ratia   ★★★★

Budget to Moderate

CH 7252 Klosters-Dorf. ☞ *West of Klosters center.*

☎ *081/69-47-47.*

Credit Cards: *Not accepted.*

Only a farmhouse, this popular inn added a wing to accommodate guests. A large fireplace and a log-beamed ceiling in the dining hall create a rustic air. During summer, guests sit outside on a broad porch under the eaves. All 26 rooms have bath or shower, and, while some rooms are plain, many have glorious views of broad meadows. Rooms are booked by the week, and loyal guests return year after year. Closed: Easter to mid-June, and mid-Oct. to mid-Dec.

Hotel Chesa Grischuna   ★★★★★

Moderate to Expensive

Bahnhofstrasse 12. ☞ *Near the train station.*

☎ *081/69-22-22.*

Credit Cards: *V, MC, A.*

Stucco and dark wood enhance this former farmhouse that has served as an inn for more than a century. Attracting royal and upscale travelers, the inn is famous as an apres-ski gathering place. You can have a warm drink by the open hearth or head to the cozy bar. The lobby areas and cafe are paneled with carved wood and filled with antiques. The 26 rooms are snug and radiate a country feel; some have a balcony. Seventeen rooms have private bath; rooms without cost slightly less. All rooms have phone and TV. The dining room is acclaimed for its cuisine. Closed: Six weeks after Easter and in Nov.

Where to Eat

Alte Post   ★★★★★

Moderate to Expensive

Doggilochstrasse. ☞ *Outside town, in roadside chalet.*

Metro Stop: *018/69-17-16.*

Credit Cards: *V, MC, DC.* Closed: *Mon., Tues.*

The dining rooms are woodsy, with paneling and hunting trophies, a visual tip-off about this restaurant's speciality: wild game. A native of Kloster, chef John Ehrat-Flury creates superb dishes with game and fish, especially salmon and trout. Meats are grilled over an open fire in front of guests. Based on fresh ingredients, the menu may offer rabbit, lamb or smoked trout. The Lachsmenu is a fixed-price full-course meal with salmon as a principal ingredient in every dish, except for the sorbet. Well worth a visit, this is a favorite place for locals and celebrity guests alike.

Walserstube ★★★★★

Expensive

CH 7250. *On main road, at edge of village. Located at Hotel Walserhof.*

Closed: *Mon.*

Plank panels and heavy wooden beams rescued from a 300-year-old farmhouse decorate this hotel dining room. A country-formal tone is set by the heart-shaped wooden chairs, tapered candles, flowers and crisp linens. In addition to the ambience, guests come here to enjoy chef Beat Bolliger's talents. Specializing in regional Prattigau dishes, the menu may include game terrines, fresh asparagus, trout, cabbage dumplings or lamb stew. The veal and Rosti is simple but highly recommended. The restaurant bakes its own breads (four different kinds) and offers 40 different cheeses to accent your meal.

What to Do

Hiking Trails ★★★★

 Take the Gotschnagrat cableway at Kloster-Platz.

☎ *081/69018-77.*

Special Hours: *Summer months only.*

During summer, the Gotschnagrat cableway carries hikers to the Gotschna-Pasenn region, site of many scenic trails designed for a variety of hiking abilities. Each gondola car carries more than 50 passengers and ascends to 7545 feet. At the top, you can take a 30-minute hike along the footpath to reach the Parsenn Hut, affording views of the Upper Prattigau and Silvretta mountain ranges. From the Parsenn Hut it's a two-hour hike to the Hoheweg station, site of the Davos-Weissfluhjoch funicular. You can also take the cableway to the Weissfluhjoch from Parsenn. Contact the tourist office for more hiking routes in the area.

Winter Sports

Special Hours: *Season varies.*

Near Davos, Klosters offers some of Switzerland's best skiing. The village sits at 4000 feet and is surrounded by 200 miles of ski trails serviced by 55 lifts, many of which are connected to the Davos region, adding even more miles to the routes. The season peaks in February but snow conditions can last much longer. The runs are equally divided between beginner, intermediate and advanced. Known for its celebrity skiers, Klosters is frequented by Prince Charles (an accident involving the prince's entourage highlighted the dangers of skiing off trails). Tobogganing, which is said to have begun at Klosters is popular, as are ice skating and curling. Horse-drawn sleigh rides are also available.

Lake Geneva

Lausanne

Rising in hillside tiers above the shores of the Grand Lac of Lake Geneva, Lausanne has attracted famous people such as historian Edward Gibbon, writer Honore de Balzac, aviator Charles Lindbergh and actors like Charlie Chaplin, who is buried in nearby Corsier. Lausanne has Roman ruins, a splendid Gothic cathedral and several outstanding museums. The ornate and sophisticated **Lausanne Palace** reigns as one of the city's best hotels. Nearby in Morges, the **Fleur du Lac** overlooks the lake. You can reach Lausanne by lake steamer from Geneva or drive through the vineyards of the Lavaux Corniche east of the city.

Where to Stay
Hotels and Resorts

Beau-Rivage Palace

http://www.beau-rivage-palace.ch/
Expensive

Chemin de Beau-Rivage 17–19.

Metro Stop: *Ouchy.*

☎ *021/617-21-21.*

Credit Cards: *V, MC, DC, A.*

Sophisticated and formal, the Beau- Rivage offers the ultimate in European luxury. Set amid 10 acres of splendidly landscaped gardens, this 1861 building was enlarged in 1901. Recently renovated, with careful attention to its period detail, the hotel features a massive rotunda linking its two wings. Inside, the lobby has a stunning stained-glass skylight and glittering chandeliers. The 181 rooms are exquisitely furnished, all with private marble-tiled bath, phone, TV. Many have in-room FAX machines and balcony. There are six junior suites and nine deluxe suites, most with balcony and lake view. Eight suites have in-room Jacuzzis. A playground, jogging trails, garden paths decorated with sculptures and a giant chess board are available to guests. Three restaurants, three bars, a piano bar and a disco are also offered.

Fleur du Lac ★★★★

Moderate to Expensive

Quai Igor-Stravinsky 70, Route de Lausanne. ☞ *Seven miles west of Lausanne, by bus, train, or boat.*

Public Transportation: *Bus 57.*

☎ *021/802-43-11.*

The lakeside town of Morges is a pleasant hub for Lake Geneva touring, and this year-round hotel makes a perfect headquarters. The building is not distinctive, but the surrounding gardens add color and cheer, and all 27 rooms face south and have lake views. Each room has a private bath or shower, hair dryer, phone, TV, trouser press. Three suites are available. Half-board pension is offered and children are welcome. The acclaimed restaurant serves Lake Geneva perch and other fish dishes. The wine list includes 250 vintages. Guests can dine inside or on a garden terrace.

Royal Savoy ★★★★

Expensive

Avenue d'Ouchy 40. *Between the lake and town.*

☎ *021/614-88-88.*

Credit Cards: *V, MC, DC, A.*

Once the residence of the exiled Spanish royal family, this six-story Victorian castlelike villa transports guests to a world of intimate luxury. It is set back from the street in a large park with ancient trees and landscaped flower beds. Recently renovated, the 168 spacious rooms have reproductions of period furnishings, tiled bath or shower, phone, TV. Most have French doors that open onto a balcony with lake or city view. Three suites are available. The park contains a pool and a terrace restaurant where guests can dine to melodies played by strolling musicians.

Pre Fleuri   ★★★

Moderate

Rue de Centre 1. *Six miles from Lausanne on Lausanne-Geneva Lake Road.*

☎ *021/69-12-02-1.*

Credit Cards: *V, MC, DC, A.*

This country house with its shingled roof and dormer windows is lovingly run by the Von Buren family. Situated not far from the lake, the inn has simple but special features; umbrella-shaded tables are scattered across its landscaped lawn, and an intimate dining room serves beautifully prepared French and Swiss cuisine. The 15 rooms all have private bath or shower, although some bath quarters are small. All rooms have phone, TV, radio. Closed: Christmas to Feb.

Where to Eat

Cafe Beau-Rivage   ★★★★★

Expensive

Place du General Guisan 18. *In the Beau-Rivage Palace.*

☎ *021/26-96-57.*

Metro Stop: *Ouchy.*

Credit Cards: *V, MC, DC, A.*

Whether for lunch on the flower-filled lake-view terrace or for dinner inside the mirrored dining room with bay windows, guests at this lively bistro-brasserie are surrounded by chic luxury. And the menu is filled with fresh-market choices at reasonable prices, especially considering the cafe's upscale location within the hotel. You can dine on classic dishes such as steak tartare or duck with wild mushrooms, and select a sinfully delicious dessert from the rolling trolley. Later in the evening, the dining room transforms into a piano bar. It's a place to see and be seen.

Cafe du Jorat ★★★

Moderate

Place d L'Ours 1. ☎ *021/20-22-61.*

Public Transportation: *Bus 7.*

Closed: *Sun.*

Off the beaten tourist track, this is where the locals go for a hearty pot of warm fondue. Six different cheese and three different meat fondues are available, along with pastries, fixed-price meals and a continental breakfast combination. The ambience is businesslike, the service attentive and efficient.

Pinte Besson ★★★★

Moderate to Expensive

Rue de L'Ale 4. *Where Rue St-Laurent becomes Rue de l'Ale.*

☎ *021/312-72-27.*

Public Transportation: *Bus 7, 16.*

Closed: *Sun.*

Truly a hole-in-the-wall, this tiny restaurant has been serving fondues to locals since 1780. The 20-by-40-foot cafe is housed in a room with hand-chiseled masonry. Patrons also fill the Lilliputian terrace. In addition to different fondues, specialties include crouetes and dried Alpine beef. It's sometimes smoky, always busy.

What to Do

Historical Sites

ITRAVELBOOK FREEBIE

Cathedral of Notre-Dame   ★★★★★

Place de la Cathedrale. ☎ *021/44-71-85.*

Public Transportation: *Bus 7, 16.*

🕐 *7 a.m.–7 p.m.*

Special Hours: *Sun., 2.–7 p.m.; Oct.–Mar. 7 a.m.–5:30 p.m.*

Acknowledged as Switzerland's finest Gothic-style cathedral, the Cathedral of Notre-Dame stands 500 feet above Lake Geneva and is a skyline landmark. Construction began in 1175, and in 1275, the Church was consecrated by Pope Gregory X in the presence of King Rudolf of Hapsburg. By the 15th century, the Cathedral was reformed, and today its austere interior reflects its Protestant heritage. Restoration began in the 19th century by Viollet-le-Duc. Its notable artwork includes the Apostles Doorway and a magnificent stained-glass window in the south transept. Composed of 105 individual windows (78 of them still the original 13th-century glass), it illustrates a mystic, geometric arrangement of the signs of the zodiac, the elements, the four winds and other symbols.

Museums and Exhibits

Musee Militaire Vaudois   ★★★★

CH 1110 Morges. *Seven miles west of Lausanne, on N1.* ☎ *021/9-1-26-16.*

Public Transportation: *Bus 57.*

🕐 *10 a.m.–5 p.m.*

Special Hours: *Closed 12–1:30 p.m.*

Built in 1286 by the duke of Savoy as a defensive against the bishop-princes of Lausanne, the Castle of Morges has a long history as a military stronghold. Today it houses the Vaud Military Museum with displays of weapons, uniforms and military models, inducting a collection of lead soldiers. Highlights include a hall dedicated to

General Henri Guisan, the Swiss officer who was instrumental in maintaining Switzerland's neutrality during World War II. Admission: inexpensive.

Musee Olympique ★★★★★

http://www.olympic.org/uk/passion/museum/home_uk.asp

Quai d'Ouchy 1. ☎ *021/621-65-11.*

🕓 *10 a.m.–7 p.m.*

Special Hours: *Oct.–Apr. open 10 a.m.–6 p.m.*

Lausanne is the headquarters of the International Olympic Committee, and the museum showcases the history of the Olympics in a multimedia format that combines interactive videos, film clips, soundtracks and photo archives with displays of coins, stamps, medals and famous mementos such as the shoes worn by Gold Medal winner Carl Lewis. Other highlights include Rodin's *The American Athlete* and a sixth-century Etruscan torch. Surrounded by a beautifully landscaped park filled with sculptures, the museum has a bookstore that sells posters, pins and other Olympic souvenirs as well as a cafe that overlooks the lake.

Musee Romain ★★★★

 Chemin du Bois-de-Vaux 24. ☞ *Vidy/ Lausanne-Maladiere exit from E25/N1.* ☎ *021/ 265-10-84.*

Public Transportation: *Lausanne.*

🕓 *11 a.m.–6 p.m.*

Special Hours: *Thurs. open to 8 p.m.*

A Roman community called Lousonna from 15 B.C. to the fourth century A.D., Lausanne traces its Roman history in this museum on the site of a reconstructed private home. A working well and painted murals add to the reality. The displays feature an impressive collection of coins, votive figurines and ordinary objects, such as carved combs, toga pins and jewelry. Guided tours of the museum (separate fee) are on the first Sunday of the month. Tours of archaeological sites also are available. Admission: varies.

Musee de l'Art Brut

Avenue des Bergieres. ☎ *021/37-54-35.*

Public Transportation: *Bus 3.*

🕐 *10 a.m.–6 p.m.*

Special Hours: *Closed noon to 2 p.m., open Sat.-Sun. 2–6 p.m.*

This unusual museum was founded by the postwar primitivist painter Jean Dubuffet as a response to what he perceived as pretentiousness in art. The museum highlights the works of nonartists, works by the criminally insane, the institutionalized, prisoners and other untrained painters and sculptors. More visceral than painterly commercial work, and often chillingly disturbing, many pieces have an experimental feel that is brutally authentic. Housed in the west wing of the chateau that dates from 1756, the museum will widen your perspective about art. Admission: inexpensive.

Shopping

Store Hours

Hours vary but most stores are open Mon.–Fri., 8 a.m.–6:30

ITRAVELBOOK TIPS:

• As canton capital, Lausanne offers good buys on watches, clothes, chocolates and Swiss souvenirs.

• The main shopping area is located in the heart of the city around Place St-Francois, Rue St. Francois, Ru du Grand-Pont and Rue de Bourg. Other places to try are along Rue St-Laurent and Rue de l'Ale. Watch shops are especially common in Place St-Francois.

• Department stores worth noting in Lausanne include Bon Genei at *Place St-Francois,* ☎ *021/320-48-11,* or Placette, a chain known for its lower prices, located at *Rue St-Laurent,* ☎ *021/320-67-11.*

• Fruits and vegetables are offered at markets along Rue de l'Ale, Rue de Bourg and Place de la Riponne each Wednesday and Saturday morning. A flea market comes to life at Place de la Palud on Wednesdays and Saturdays.

p.m., and on Sat. from 8 a.m.–5 p.m. Most major stores are closed Sun.

Special Tours

Lavaux Corniche

✉ *A 15-mile drive between Lausanne and Montreux.* ☞ *West of Lausanne, including Cully and Chexres.* ☎ *0217/617-14-27.*

Enjoy a leisurely driving excursion through the Lavaux Corniche east of Lausanne. Composed of hillside vineyards surrounded by hand-built rock walls, forests, picturesque Savoy-style villages and baronial castles rising above the fields, the Lavaux attracts the wealthy who come to build second homes. At Corsier, stop at the 12th-century church where Charlie Chaplin, who loved this region, was buried in 1977. At Cully, five miles east of Lausanne, the small bay offers swimming, fishing and boating. Also while in Lavaux, sample wines at various chateaux-vignobles or stop at Chexbres, a summer resort popular with the Swiss. Here the Corniche Road runs alongside Lake Geneva, offering delightful views. Chexbres also can be reached by taking the CFF-Puidoux train from Lausanne.

Montreux

Exuding an Edwardian-French air, Montreux is the principal city on the "Swiss Riviera" of Lake Geneva. The site of Switzerland's most famous castle, the **Chateau de Chillon**, Montreux is also known for its Jazz Festival in July and a classical music festival held in conjunction with nearby Vevey in September. The town's ancient buildings and narrow streets add to its romantic feeling, and, throughout history, it has attracted a number of poets and writers including Lord Byron, Victor Hugo, Flaubert and Nabokov. Grand hotels like the block-long opulent **Palace**, in the center of town, just aren't built anymore. On the mountain above Montreux is the **Hostellerie de Caux**, an intimate chalet, affording glorious vistas. A visit to Montreux wouldn't be complete without sampling the Lauvaux wines produced in the surrounding vineyards.

Where to Stay
Hotels and Resorts

Eden au Lac   ★★★★★

Expensive

Rue du Theatre 11. *At Quai du Casino, on the lakeside point by the casino.*

Public Transportation: *Bus 1.*

☎ *021/963-55-51.*

Credit Cards: *V, MC, DC, A.*

This is a classic European hotel, and more reasonably priced (for the region) than the palace-style establishments. The 19th-century-style building is alluring and romantic; inside, the Victorian look is augmented by an updated Gay Nineties style and bright colors. The 105 rooms are spacious and well-appointed, with private bath, phone, TV. Many offer a splendid view of the water. The six suites are luxurious with balcony and lake view. Closed: Mid-Dec.–mid-Feb.

Grand Hotel Excelsior   ★★★★★

http://www.montreux.ch/excelsior/index.html

Expensive

Rue bon-Port 21.

Public Transportation: *Bus 1.*

☎ *021/963-32-31.*

Credit Cards: *V, MC, DC, A.*

Hospitable and warm, this lakeside villa is known for its low-key luxury and quality service. Set in a quiet area, the hotel has a foyer decorated with Queen Anne antiques, Baroque sculptures and oil paintings. The 76 rooms vary in size but most have a wonderful lake view. The room decor is more modern with bold colors, French doors and tiled private bath. Three suites are available. All units have phone, TV, hair dryer, robes. Amenities include a solarium, an extra-large heated pool, hairdresser and beauty services.

Hostellerie de Caux   ★★★★

Moderate to Expensive

Caux-sur-Montreux. *Above Montreux, by cog-railway to stop*

Hauts-de-Caux, or 20 minutes by car from Montreux.

☎ *021/963-76-08.*

Credit Cards: *V, MC, DC, A.*

If 20 hairpin turns up a mountain road sound too daunting, take the funicular up to the mountain above Montreux to discover this family-run inn. The cheerful dark wood and white stucco chalet offers half a dozen rooms as well as an acclaimed restaurant. With windows framing glorious views of the Alps, the four doubles each have small private bath or shower while the two singles share facilities. The furnishings in the rooms are simple but comfortable. Hiking and skiing are nearby diversions, and Lake Geneva sparkles below.

Where to Eat

Cafe/Restaurant du Raisin ★★★

Moderate

Place du Marche. 🖙 *Facing the marketplace.* ☎ *021/921-10-28.*

Credit Cards: *V, DC, A.* Closed: *Mon.*

This cafe/restaurant overlooks the marketplace in Vevey, and is a great place to stop while touring the Lake Geneva region or before sampling the wine merchants offerings (Vevey is the hub of the Lavaux region vineyards). You can settle on the cafe terrace or sit inside the cafe for a salad or *pomme pannee*, a breaded cheese dish that is lightly fried. Or you can head upstairs to the intimate, more expensive restaurant where sophisticated fresh-market entrees are complemented by a bottle of locally produced wine.

L'Ermitage ★★★★★

Expensive

CH 1815 Vufflens-le-Chateau. 🖙 *Near Chateau Chillon at Vufflens-le-Chateau.* ☎ *021/964-44-11.*

Credit Cards: *V, MC, DC, A.* Closed: *Sun.*

Inside this two-story house with its gray mansard roof and dormer windows is a restaurant known throughout the region for its exquisitely prepared food. The dining room walls are painted with trompe-l'oeil frescoes and the tables are beautifully appointed, but it's the food that attracts loyal patrons to return again and again. Local fish and game are the highlights of many dishes, including terrines and grilled entrees accented with delicate sauces. Wines from the regions enhance the cuisine. The desserts are sumptuous, including the restaurant's signature dish, almond and chocolate "cigarettes" with chestnut cream.

What to Do
Historical Sites

Chateau de Chillon   ★★★★★

▭ *CH 1820.* ☞ *Two miles from Montreux center.* ☎ *021/963-39-12.*

🕐 *10 a.m.–4:30 p.m.*

Special Hours: *Apr.–June, and Sep. 9 a.m–5:45 a.m.*

Famous as the castle that inspired Lord Byron's poem "The Prisoner of Chillon," the Chateau de Chillon is one of Switzerland's top attractions. Although the guided tours through the restored rooms and turrets are crowded and involve tedious waits, this is a don't-miss experience. Built on Roman foundations, the somber medieval castle overlooks the lake. The castle's construction was overseen by Peter II of Savoy during the 12th century. Serving as a state prison, the castle is known for its most famous prisoner, Francois Bonivard, a supporter of the Reformation who spent six years here chained to a pillar in the dungeon. Today the rooms have been restored with furnishings, tapestries, period ceramics and pewter. If you stand on the shore beside the ramparts, you will understand why Byron's imagination was so fired by the sight. Admission: inexpensive.

Museums and Exhibits

Swiss Museum of Cameras   ★★★

http://www.cameramuseum.ch/ museum-e.htm

Ruelle des Anciens Fosses. ☞ *Near Grand Place.*

☎ *021/921-48-25.*

🕐 *10:30 a.m.–5:30 p.m.*

Special Hours: *Closed 12–2 p.m. daily, open Mar.–Oct.*

Filled with 150 years of camera equipment, this museum outlines the history of cameras and photographic equipment, including a "camera obscura," which led to the invention of the modern camera. Exhibits include a display of an early dark room and a Chevalier lens used by Daguerre. Also on display is an 1888 "photosphere" and an 1895 "physiograph." Hands-on displays let visitors touch early models, and a computerized quiz lets them test their "photographic IQ." Admission: inexpensive.

Northern

Basel

Cosmopolitan and intriguing, Basel is Switzerland's third-largest city. Located astride the Rhine River, and once a Roman fort, Basel has superb rail and bus connections as well as cultural ties with France and Germany. With 28 museums and romantic river sojourns, Basel is also a year-round commercial hub known throughout Europe for its trade shows. During January and the week after Ash Wednesday, it turns into a carnival town, celebrating festivals with ancient beginnings. Overlooking the Rhine and near the train station is Switzerland's oldest hotel—the grand **Hotel Drei Konige**. At the avant-garde **Kultur Gasthaus der Teufelhof**, every room is an artwork. The **Restaurant Stuckl Bruderholz**, just outside Basel, features French cuisine and is renowned throughout the country.

Where to Stay
Hotels and Resorts

Euler Manz Privacy   ★★★★

http://www.hoteleuler.ch/
Moderate to Expensive

Centralbahnplatz 4. *Near the train station.*

Public Transportation: *Tram 6, 10, 16, 17.*

☎ *061/272-45-00.*

Credit Cards: *V, MC, DC, A.*

Close to the train station, this hotel is popular with local and international businesspeople. Built of white and gray stone with half-columns, the hotel exudes a prosperous Old World feeling. The 65 paneled rooms have comfortable furnishings and a modern bath. The triple-glass windows reduce noise from the trains, and the rooms over the back-alley court are even quieter. The landmark leather-and-red-velvet bar is always crowded while the Weiner Salon is worth seeing just to admire the lush landscapes that decorate its walls.

Hotel Drei Konige   ★★★★★

Expensive to Very Expensive

Blumenrain 8. *On the waterfront*

Public Transportation: *Tram 1,6, 8, 14, 15.*

☎ *061/26-15-522.*

Credit Cards: *V, MC, DC, A.*

Dating back to 1026 as a coach stop under the name *Zur Blume*, meaning "At the Flower," this is the oldest hotel in Switzerland. The modern name, "The Three Kings," reflects the hotel's role as host to a treaty signing that resulted in the division of western Switzerland and Southern France. Once the place where Voltaire, Napoleon, Queen Victoria and Kaiser Wilhelm II stayed, the white building overlooks the Rhine. Today the hotel still retains a grand air, with 19th-century antiques and paintings and a sweeping stair-case built in 1835. All 83 rooms have bath, TV, radio, phone. Three suites are available, and some of the riverfront rooms have balconies. Close to the train station and the famous Middle Rhine Bridge.

Hotel Schweizerhof   ★★★

Moderate to Expensive

Centralbahnplatz 1. *By the train station, facing a park.*

Public Transportation: *Tram 6, 10, 16, 17.*

☎ *061/271-28-33.*

Credit Cards: *V, MC, DC, A.*

Operated by the same family since 1896, this hotel has hosted famous guests, including Toscanini, Casals and Menuhin. The six-story building has marble floors and a mix of Biedermeier and modern furnishings. Pine, beech and rosewood paneling add warmth. All 75 rooms have modern bath, but the rooms can be noisy, and only half the rooms are air-conditioned so you must specify your preference. The terrace restaurant serves French cuisine. Popular with businesspeople.

Where to Eat

Brauerei Fischerstube   ★★★★

Moderate

Rheingasse 45. *Second right from Mitteire Bridge.*

☎ *061/692-66-35.*

Specialties: *Privately brewed beer.* Credit Cards: *V, MC.* Closed: *Sun.* Brewing four labels of its own beer in copper tanks inside the bar, the Fischerstube is Basel's smallest brewery. Near the sights, but not well-known by tourists, the restaurant also features hearty local favorites such as sausage loaf with eggs and frites (french fries). Join the locals and munch on the thick, fresh-baked pretzels that hang on racks on each of the wooden tables or settle into the beer garden in back.

Chez Donati   ★★★

Moderate

St. Johanns-Vorstadt 48. ☎ *061/322-09-19.*

Public Transportation: *Tram 15.*
Credit Cards: *V, MC, DC, A.* Closed: *Mon., Tues.*
Long a favorite with Baslers, this restaurant is famous for its homemade lasagna, ravioli and scaloppine. Always busy, the restaurant seats guests in rooms painted with vivid murals and lots of gilt. Some feel the decor borders on kitsch, but the food is the big draw. White truffles are offered in the late fall, complementing the various dishes. The fixed-price menu offers good value.

Restaurant Stucki Bruderholz   ★★★★★

Expensive

Bruderholzalle 42. *Just outside the city limits in a residential area.*

☎ *061/35-82-22.*

Public Transportation: *Bus 15.*
Credit Cards: *V, MC, DC, A.* Closed: *Mon., Sun.*

This outstanding restaurant draws connoisseurs who come to enjoy chef Hans Stucki's talents. Housed in what was once a private mansion, the restaurant offers dining on the backyard terrace or in one of three salons. The salons are elegantly decorated with Empire chairs, Oriental carpets, paintings, brass chandeliers and polished crystal. A range of options is offered on the menu, from a la carte entrees to a sumptuous 10-course "surprise." The cuisine is French, with innovative touches that turn ragouts, terrines and compotes into memorable meals.

Zum Goldenen Sternen

Moderate
St. Albanrheinweg 70.
Public Transportation: *Tram 6, 12.*
Credit Cards: *V, MC, DC, A.*

Perhaps Switzerland's oldest restaurant, this establishment has been authentically restored to reflect its 15th-century roots. Moved to its current site in the early 1990s, the restaurant is situated near the Rhine and has antique beams, stenciled ceilings and unvarnished wood-plank paneling. The tables are beautifully set with flowers and fine linens, adding to the romantic atmosphere. The cuisine is classic French with dishes such as smoked trout, rack of lamb and game in season.

What to Do
Excursions

Spalentor

 West of the University. ☎ *061/261-50-50.*

Like most medieval cities, Basel was once fortified, and today three of its gates still remain. The most impressive is the Spalen Gate on the west side of town. The town walls were destroyed in the 18th century, but you still can view the huge gate, which features two castlelike turrets and a steepled tower with a clockface and patterned shingles.

Historical Sites

Munster ★★★★★

✉ *Munsterplatz.* *In Old Town.* ☎ *061/271- 21-82.*

Public Transportation: *Tram 2, 8.*

🕐 *10 a.m.–5 p.m.*

Special Hours: *Sat. 10 a.m.–12 p.m., and 2–5 p.m.*

Consecrated in 1019, this red sandstone Gothic/Romanesque structure dominates the Old Town. Destroyed by an earthquake in 1356, it was rebuilt and is distinguished by a green-and-yellow-tile roof and two towers. The recessed arches of the primary doorway are decorated with statues and ornate carvings. Inside, the 1486 pulpit was carved from a single block of stone. Also worth seeing in Grossbasel is the Rathaus (near Markplatz), restored and enlarged in the late 1800s. Elaborate frescoes and shields of the city guilds adorn the building. Admission: inexpensive.

Museums and Exhibits

Kuntsmuseum ★★★★★

St. Alban-Graben 16. *By the theater.* ☎ *061/271-08-28.*

Public Transportation: *Tram 2, 12.*

🕐 *10 a.m.–5 p.m.*

Established in the 16th century, this is the oldest museum in Switzerland, and it houses one of the finest collections of works by both old masters and modern artists. The large courtyard contains sculptures by Rodin, Calder and Hans Arp. Inside, you'll see work by Swiss artists from the 14th through the 17th centuries. A highlight is the portrait of the philosopher Erasmus by Holbein. The rest of the collection is dedicated to 20th-century art and includes Impressionists, Expressionists and Surrealists. Among the artists featured are Gaugin, Van Gogh, Cezanne, Kandinsky, Paul Klee, Juan Gris, Dali, Max Ernst and Picasso (who generously donated four paintings to the museum). Free admission on Sunday. Admission: inexpensive.

Zoologischer Garten ★★★★★

✉ *Binningerstrasse 40.* *Adjoining the Hauptbahnhof.*

☎ *061/281-00-00.*

Public Transportation: *Trams 1, 2, 6, 8, 10, 17.*

🕐 *8 a.m.–6:30 p.m.*

Special Hours: *Nov.–Mar. open 8 a.m.–5:30 p.m.*

Founded in 1874, and today known as one of the finest zoos in the world, this zoological garden is home to more than 5600 animals representing 600 species. Specializing in the breeding and rearing of threatened or endangered species, the zoo cares for rhinoceroses, gorillas and spectacled bears. Many rate this large zoo as better than the one in Zurich. Exhibits of trained elephants and a vivarium are other highlights. Admission: inexpensive.

Special Tours

Colonia Austasta Raurica ★★★★★

✉ *Augst.* *By boat tour (also by car or train).*

☎ *061/261-24-00.*

🕐 *9 a.m.–4 p.m.*

Combine a boat tour of the Rhine with an excursion to the ancient Roman ruins at Augst, just east of the city. Boats leave Basel from a dock near the Three Kings Hotel, passing the old city and the Cathedral on the way to Augst, where passengers disembark and tour the ruins on foot (separate fee). The 2000-year-old settlement has been rebuilt; it's not hard to imagine seeing a Roman citizen by the grassy paths near the theater where today are staged a number of open-air productions. A reconstructed Roman house contains objects unearthed during excavations. Dating back to the 4th century, the collection includes coins, silver plates and small statues. Other ruins can be seen on foot but be prepared to do a considerable amount of walking. You can return to Basel by boat (the last one leaves at about 5 p.m.) or by train. Other boat tours are available, including some with hot meals. Admission: varies.

Zurich

Switzerland's largest city, Zurich contains the world's fourth-largest stock exchange, the world's largest gold exchange and is also the headquarters for dozens of banks. While all this financial muscle helps Zurich pump out one-fifth of Switzerland's national income, Zurich is more than a bastion of bankers and number-crunchers. Zurich is an international hub and an attractive tourist destination, offering elegant shopping along its historic quays, more than a half dozen excellent museums, plus the beauty of Lake Zurich. Accommodations are world-class, and often heavily booked, but it's well worth it to spring for a night at the **Hotel Dolder Grand**, located on a wooded hilltop overlooking the city and the lake. With more than 1200 restaurants, Zurich offers an array of options when it comes to cuisine. But no visit to the city would be complete without sampling the hearty sausages, *Rasti* and fondues served with steins of local beer at the popular **Zeughauskeller**.

Where to Stay

Baur au Lac ★★★★★

http://www.bauraulac.ch/htmlsBAL/homebal.html
Expensive

Talstrasse 1. *At the end of Bahnhofstrasse by the Schanzengraben Canal.*

Public Transportation: *Tram 4.*

☎ *01/221-16-50.*

Credit Cards: *V, MC, DC, A.*

Long a favorite with guests who want to avoid the crush of group bookings or slick, commercial accommodations, this three- story grand-dame hotel is situated within a private park near the canal. The 139 rooms and 16 suites have been recently renovated (freshening will continue into 1996) and come in a variety of layouts. The deluxe doubles are a superb value and offer a corner view. All units have private bath, phone, TV, double-glazed windows and slide-out luggage racks. The hotel has several acclaimed restaurants, although not all are open year-round.

Dolder Grand   ★★★★★

http://www.doldergrand.ch/

Expensive to Very Expensive

Kurhausstrasse 65. *By cogwheel funicular from the center of Zurich.*

Public Transportation: *Tram 3, 8, 15.*

☎ *01/251-62-31.*

Credit Cards: *V, MC, DC, A.*

Undeniably one of the top hotels in Switzerland, and among the best in Europe, the Dolder Grand earns a high reputation for its service, quality and style. Past guests have included Albert Einstein, Winston Churchill and Henry Kissinger, and today the hotel is the prime pick for well-heeled travelers. Built on the top of a 50-acre forested promontory overlooking Zurich, and accessible by private funicular, the 1889 building combines palatial architecture with Victorian details. All 187 rooms are elegantly furnished and have private bath, phone, TV. Most in the modern addition have air conditioning. The older rooms retain their period opulence, with alcoves and patterned tiles in the bathroom. Both singles and doubles feature sitting areas. Views include mountain or lake vistas. Eighteen palatial suites are available. Guests can enjoy a number of resort activities; there is a nine-hole golf course, a pool with a wave-making machine and ice rink in winter. The hotel staff is extensive and well-trained, although the European style of service may seem somewhat cold to North Americans. The hotel has a bar, a French restaurant with a garden terrace and private limousine to carry guests to and from the airport or train station.

Ermitage   ★★★

Moderate

Seestrasse 80. *Seven minutes from town center by car in the suburb of Kusnacht.*

☎ *01/910-52-22.*

Credit Cards: *V, MC, DC, A.*

Surrounded by a landscaped garden and leafy trees, this 360-year-old country inn, with its steeply pitched red-shingled roofs and dormer gables, looks like an upscale private home. Inside, the grand piano, fresh flowers and plushly upholstered furnishings radiate quiet luxury. With the lake only steps away, the inn offers its own private "beach club" and a shoreline terrace where guests can relax and watch the boats. The 20 spacious rooms are uniquely decorated, and each has a large white-marble bath, phone, TV. The most expensive rooms have a view of the lake. Also offered are a French restaurant and appealing bar area.

Hotel Schweizerhof ★★★★

Expensive

Bahnhofplatz. *Across the square from the train station.*

Public Transportation: *Tram 4.*

☎ *01/211-86-40.*

Credit Cards: *V, MC, DC, A.*

Across from the train station, this landmark stone building has gables, turrets and columns, giving it a regal air. The central location makes the hotel a favorite, and renovations that include triple-glazed glass help to mute noise. Decorated in pastel color schemes, the 114 rooms have modern bath or shower, phone, TV. The 5th floor is smoke-free, while the 4th floor is given over to executive suites. Guests flying out of Zurich can check their luggage at the train station.

Neuss Schloss ★★★★

Expensive

Stockerstrasse 17. *South of Paradeplat between Bahnhofstrasse and Lake Zurich, near Tohlle and Kongresshaus.*

Public Transportation: *Tram 7, 8, 10, 13.* Metro Stop: *Stockerstrasse.*

☎ *01/201-65-50.*

Credit Cards: *V, MC, DC, A.*

Owned by the Seiler family, the highly regarded hotel dynasty in Zermatt, this establishment offers a more intimate city-hotel experience than the other grander properties. The 59 freshly renovated rooms have bath, phone, TV, desks. Soundproof windows temper noise; friendly, discreet service. The hotel restaurant, featuring French and international cuisine, attracts business types for lunch.

Where to Eat

Bierhalle Kropf ★★★★

Moderate to Expensive
In Gassen 16.
Credit Cards: *V, MC, DC, A*. Closed: *Sun.*

Situated in a historic burger house, this restaurant is decorated with boars' heads and deer antlers, hunting paintings, stained glass and chandeliers. But locals gather here for the food: generous portions served at shared tables where diners feast elbow to elbow. Dishes include veal or pork shank served with Rosti (the Swiss version of hash browns), sausages and liver dumplings. The desserts are delicious, especially the apple strudel. The service is friendly, the atmosphere livelier than you'd expect.

Confiserie Sprungli ★★★★★

Moderate

Am Paradeplatz. *Near Bahnhofstrasse and Blieicherweg.*

☎ *01/221-07-95.*

Public Transportation: *Tram 2, 9, 11.*

Founded in 1836, this Zurich institution is similar to a Viennese pastry shop. Here pastries are given the star treatment, the artful array brought to tables by crisply attired servers. The ground floor sells all kinds of pastries and chocolates. The house specialty is the famous Lindt chocolate—indulge here if you don't have time to tour the factory.

Fischstube Zurichhorn ★★★★

Moderate

Belleriverstrasse 160. ☎ *01/422-25-20.*

Public Transportation: *Tram 2, 4.*

Credit Cards: *V, MC, A*.

A great way to top off a day touring Lake Zurich would be a sunset dinner at this restaurant on the left bank. Dining is at tables set on a pier that extends over the lake. Here you can enjoy a moderately priced meal of fresh fish (naturally!) and a memorable view. Specialties include lake trout and grilled lobster. Many dishes are enlivened with saffron and curry, adding an international accent to your meal. Closed in winter.

Hitl Vegi ★★★★

Moderate

Sihlstrasse 28. ☞ *One street toward the Sihl from Bahnhofstrasse.*

☎ *01/221-38-70.*

Not everything is sausage and *Rosti* in Switzerland as this famous and long- standing vegetarian restaurant attests. Founded in 1887, the two-story restaurant is a mecca for vegans who come to sample salad bars and buffets, enjoying pasta and curry dishes as well as veggie-burgers. The atmosphere is contemporary, with lots of bright colors and chic accents. Hearty soups, lavish desserts and more than two dozen types of tea are offered. Takeout is also available.

La Rotonde ★★★★★

Expensive

Kurhausstrasse 65. ☞ *By tram, car or private funicular. Located at Dolder Grand Hotel.* ☎ *01/251-62-31.*

Public Transportation: *Tram 3, 8, 15.*

Credit Cards: *V, MC, DC, A*.

Whether inside the vast and sumptuous dining room or outside on the elegant garden terrace, this romantic hotel restaurant provides an unforgettable experience. Softened by candlelight and graced with beautiful linens, the large, arched dining room offers stunning views of Zurich. Service is above reproach. Menu choices are contemporary-style French. Grilled salmon, lobster and scallops are offered as are game and Swiss-French sweetbreads. On Sundays, a brunch buffet of hors d'oeuvres tempts even the choosiest guests.

The fixed-price dinner is an excellent value and a superb way to sample the chef's talents.

Zeughauskeller ★★★★

Moderate

Am Paradeplatz. *Near Bahnhofstrasse and Bleichrweg.*

☎ *01/211-26-90.*

Public Transportation: *Tram 2, 6, 7, 8, 9.*

In a building dating back to 1487 and that once was used as an arsenal, the Zeughauskeller is a huge establishment, seating up to 200 people. It wears its history proudly: the enormous stone-and- beam hall is decorated with heraldic plaques and rustic wooden chandeliers hanging from heavy cast-iron chains. Always crowded, this boisterous establishment offers marvelous traditional Swiss dishes and a variety of local brews, including Hurlimann draft, which is poured from 1000-liter barrels. Feast and drink, try the yard-long sausage, enough to fill up four very hungry people, and enjoy the atmosphere. Tourist-friendly but also a local favorite.

What to Do
Historical Sites

Fraumunster ★★★★★

📄 *Fraumunsterstrasse.* *On left bank, overlooking Munsterhof Square.* ☎ *01/202-59- 21.*

🕘 *9 a.m.–6 p.m.*

Special Hours: *Sun., 12–6 p.m. Oct.–Apr., closes at dusk.*

Built on the site of an 9th-century Benedictine abbey, this church, with its tall, slender blue spire, is a Zurich landmark. The abbey was founded by Charlemagne's grandson, Emperor Ludwig, and it was Ludwig's daughter, Hidegard, who became the first abbess. What visitors view today was constructed beginning in the 13th century but the undercroft contains the crypt of the old abbey. In 1970, a series of five stained-glass windows designed by Marc Chagall was installed in the Romanesque-style choir. The church is famous for its

pipe organ and its Gothic-style cloister painted with scenes illustrating the legends of old Zurich.

ITRAVELBOOK FREEBIE

Grossmunster   ★★★★★

Grossmunsterplatz. *On right bank, beyond Munsterbrucke.*

☎ *01/252-59-49.*

🕐 *9 a.m.–6 p.m.*

Special Hours: *Oct. through Mar. open 10 a.m.–4 p.m.*

According to legend, this church stands on the spot where
Charlemagne's horse knelt, bowing down to honor the deaths of
three early Christian martyrs. Today this twin-towered Protestant
cathedral, built on a natural terrace above the Limmatquai, dominates the skyline. Construction began in 1039 but the building was-
n't completed until the 14th century. Styled with Romanesque and
Gothic details, the church is dedicated to the three martyrs. Inside,
the choir contains stained-glass windows completed in 1933 by
Giacometti. A statue of Charlemagne is housed in the crypt. The
famous Reformer Zwingli preached here, challenging his parishio-
ners to avoid the "worship of images." Consequently, Grossmunster,
originally a Catholic edifice, has been stripped of its imagery and
ornamentation, resulting in a sparse, somewhat severe interior. A
climb to the top of one of the towers (separate fee, open May to
Oct. during good weather) rewards visitors with impressive city
views.

Rapperswil Castle   ★★★★

🖃 *CH 8640 Rapperswil.* *Nineteen miles south by boat or car
from Zurich.* ☎ *055/27-44- 95.*

🕐 *1 p.m.–5 p.m.*

Special Hours: *Closed Jan.-Feb.*

Known as the "City of Roses," the Old World town of Rapperswil is
located on a peninsula on the north side of Lake Zurich. For visitors
who can't spend much time in Switzerland, the town is a good day

trip from Zurich. The Rathaus is picturesque, and the Friary rose garden is famous for its blooms. Rapperswil Castle, constructed on a hillock, was built around 1200. The triangular layout includes two towers (recently restored) and a castle keep. In 1834, the castle became the home of Graf Plater, the exiled leader of a resistance movement against the occupation of Poland by Russian Tsars. Today the castle houses the Polish Museum, with displays depicting events in 19th-and 20th-century Polish politics. Also in Rapperswil is the Knie's Kinderzoo (Children's Zoo), run by the Knie National Circus. Admission: varies.

ITRAVELBOOK FREEBIE

Landesmuseum ★★★★★

📧 *Museumstrasse 2.* *In Platz-Promenade, across from the Hauptbahnhof.* ☎ *01/ 218-65-65.*

Public Transportation: *Tram 3, 4, 11, 13, 14.*

🕐 *10 a.m.–5 p.m.*

A castlelike Victorian-era building houses the Swiss National Museum, the most important museum in the country. Exhibits include prehistoric artifacts from 4th-century Switzerland, when the region was part of the Roman empire, as well as displays of medieval silverware, 13th-century Gothic art, 14th-century gilded drinking bowls, 16th-century wool embroidery and Swiss clocks from the 16th to 17th centuries. Many exhibits recreate the surroundings typical of the artifacts. For example, rural ways of life are depicted in reproductions of a spinning room from Eastern Switzerland. Also on display are 18th-and 19th-century Swiss regional costumes. Military displays include arms and weapons as well as a diorama of the battle of Murten that features 6000 tin figures. Religious art is shown in exhibits of stained-glass windows, altarpieces and bas-relief carvings.

Museums and Exhibits

The Lindt and Sprungli Chocolate Factory ★★★

📧 *Kilchberg.* *From Hauptbahnhof by tram, then a three-minute walk.* ☎ *01/716-22-33.*

Public Transportation: *Tram S1, S8.* Metro Stop: *Kilchberg.*

🕐 *9 a.m.–4 p.m.*

Special Hours: *Closed 12–1:30 p.m.*

What would a trip to Switzerland be without a visit to a chocolate factory? The Lindt and Sprungli Chocolate Factory, in a suburb of Zurich, allows visitors a behind-the-scenes look at the production process. Visitors can also see exhibits (the captions are in German, but the subject is universal!) and view a film on the history of chocolate making. Perhaps the best part is the chance to sample the factory's sweet products.

Shopping
Store Hours

Hours vary but most stores are open Mon.–Friday, 8 a.m.–6:30 p.m., and on Sat. from 8 a.m.–4 p.m. Some larger stores stay open until 9 p.m. on Thurs. Some shops open late on Mon., around 1:30 p.m. Most major stores are closed Sun.

What to Buy

Watches, jewelry, artwork, embroidery, epicurean chocolates, flatware and silver, copperware, ceramics, wood carvings, ironworks, handmade toys, leather goods and Bally shoes.

Where to Shop

The quays form the heart of the shopping promenade, with the most prestigious names occupying addresses near the Paradeplatz end of Bahnhofstrasse. Near Bahnhofplatz is a cluster of shops and boutiques known as Shop Ville. In Old Town, along Storchengasse near Munsterhof, you can peruse upscale and pricey designer fashions. Around Niederdorf, you'll find less expensive but still high-quality clothing options. Interesting shops are located at Lowenstrasse, southwest of Hauptbahnhof.

High-end department stores include *Globus, Bahnhofstrasse at Lowenplatz,* ☎ *01/221-33-11,* and *Jelmoli, Bahnhofstrasse at Seidengasse,* ☎ *01/220-44-11.*

While in the Zurich area, take a peek inside one of its illustrious banks—there's no charge for looking. A splendid choice would be the *Bank LEU at Bahnhofstrasse 34*. As you tread on the elegant marble flooring and gaze at the gold leaf, you can dream of unlimited wealth.

For the frugal shopper there are flea markets in Zurich. At Burkliplatz at the lake end of Bahnhofstrasse, a market is held every Sat. from dawn to mid-afternoon May–Oct. A "curio market" operates on the Rosenhof each Thurs. and Sat. from Apr. to the end of Dec.

Special Tours

Lake Zurich Boat Tours ★★★★★

 Tickets/departures from end of Bahnhofstrasse.

☎ *01/482-10-33.*

🕐 *8 a.m.–6 p.m.*

Special Hours: *Apr.–Oct., Winter hours vary.*

Lake steamer tours of Lake Zurich are a relaxing way to experience the city. Tours range from 90 minutes to two days. One popular excursion takes visitors from Zurich to Rapperswil (described separately under "Rapperswil Castle"), with a round- trip first-class ticket priced at SFr42. Another option is a boat trip along the River Limmat, which provides camera- perfect views of the historic buildings that line the banks. This trip departs from the Landesmuseum and ends at the Zurichhorn, a large lakeside park with a restaurant. The cost is SFr10 per person. Departure times vary, with several tours available each day from Apr.–Oct.

Regensberg Tour ★★★★

 CH 8158 Regensberg. 📖 *By car or bus, 10 miles northwest from Zurich.* ☎ *01/211-40- 00.*

Surrounded by vineyard-covered hillsides and encircled by an ancient wall, the village of Regensberg lets visitors step back in time. Founded by Baron Lutold V in 1245, the village is filled with half-timbered houses set around a typical Old World square. The Rote Rose House dates from 1540 and contains a collection of paintings featuring roses painted by Lotte Gunthart. The garden that inspired the paintings is nearby and contains more than 1000 varieties of roses. The 16th-century village church and a 16th-century castle once owned by the Hapsburgs dominate the village skyline. Regensberg is well worth a day trip from Zurich.

The Quays ★★★★★

The promenades along the historic and scenic quays offer something for everyone, from sidewalk cafes and elegant and exclusive shops to landscaped gardens and views of the lake. Limmatquai is the most famous, beginning at the Bahnhof Bridge and heading east to the red facade of the *Rathaus* (Town Hall). Uto Quai follows the shore of Lake Zurich, and running from Badeantadt Uto Quai (a public swimming pool open daily from 8 a.m. to 7 p.m.) to Belleveuplatz and Quai Brucke. General-Guisan Quai edges the western shoreline and leads out of town into the rural suburbs.

Southern

Geneva

Switzerland's second-largest city, Geneva sits in the Rhone Valley at the southwestern corner of Lake Geneva (Lac Leman in French). Cosmopolitan without gritty urban edges, Geneva is a truly international city, influenced not only by France, but by Switzerland's policy of neutrality. Once the base for the League of Nations, Geneva is now the headquarters for the European United Nations as well as the World Council of Churches and the World Health Organization. Geneva offers the best of Europe: world-class restaurants, legendary hotels, famous auction houses, outstanding museums, lakeside promenades and a medieval-era Old Town.

Where to Stay

Hotel Beau-Rivage ★★★★★

http://www.beau-rivage.ch/

Expensive

Quai du Mont-Blanc 13. *Across from Brunswick Gardens.*

Public Transportation: *Bus 6, 33.*

☎ *022/731-02-21.*

Credit Cards: *V, MC, DC, A.*

Dating back to 1865, this historic hotel, facing the lake, creates a world of luxury. The hotel had the dubious honor of providing lodging for the Empress of Austria who was assassinated in the street just yards from the hotel; later the hotel was the site of WWI treaty signings. Built by Jean-Jacques Mayer and today operated by his great-grandson, the hotel has an open, five-story lobby with an elegant marble fountain. There are 104 rooms and six suites, each offering private bath, TV, phone. Some rooms have air conditioning. The front bedrooms have right bank views. Its La Chalet-Botte is one of the best restaurants in Geneva and described separately; the hotel's plush terrace restaurant is popular and a good spot for people-watching.

Hotel Bristol   ★★

Moderate to Expensive

Rue du Mont-Blanc. ☞ *Near Mont-Blanc and Rue des Paquis.*

Public Transportation: *Bus 1, 6, 8, 9, 23.*

☎ *022/732-38-00.*

Credit Cards: *V, MC, DC, A.*

Melding tradition and modern amenities, this 130-year-old hotel has earned a solid reputation. Built in a park near the Mont-Blanc bridge, the hotel has a central position and attractive accommodations. The 94 rooms and five suites have soundproof windows, modern bath, and antique accents. The rooms away from the elevator are the quietest. Rates without breakfast are lower.

Hotel La Reserve   ★★★

Moderate to Expensive

Route de Lausanne 301. ☞ *Just 12 minutes by car from airport and center of town.*

☎ *022/774-17-41.*

Credit Cards: *V, MC, DC, A.*

Its eight acres of spruce-dotted gardens, private pier with boat rental on the lake and country location just a few miles from the heart of Geneva all contribute to this plush hotel's ability to attract a loyal following. Serving guests with taste and flair, the hotel offers sports and relaxation along with scenic views. There are 115 rooms and nine suites, each with bath, phone, TV. Most rooms have a terrace or balcony. Guests can dine at four restaurants, choosing from French, Italian, Chinese or Japanese cuisine. (The Chinese restaurant is recommended separately.) A buffet lunch is served at the outdoor pool in the summer.

Le Richemond ★★★★★

http://www.richemond.ch/fr/ index.html

Expensive to Very Expensive

Jardin Brunswick. *Across from Brunswick Garden, close to train station.*

Public Transportation: *Bus 1, 9.*

☎ *022/731-14-00.*

Credit Cards: *V, MC, DC, A.*

Near the lake and across from a small park, Le Richemond is probably the finest hotel in Geneva. Built in 1875 and managed by the Armleder family for three generations, the hotel combines the ultimate in luxury with personalized service. Decorated with museum-quality antiques, the lobby and other public rooms are spacious and refined. The 67 rooms and 31 suites vary widely, but all have phone, TV, marble bath, hair dryer, robes, luxury toiletries. The hotel's **Gentilhomme** restaurant may be the best in the city; its stylish cafe, **Le Jardin**, has a flower-filled terrace; tasteful Old World bar; conference facilities; business services; excursions by private luxury car. A stream of famous people have stayed here, from Collette and Miro to Michael Jackson.

Auberge de Confignon ★★★

Budget to Moderate

1232 Confignon, Place de l'Eglise. *Outside Geneva, near airport.*

Public Transportation: *Tram 2.*

☎ *022/757-19-44.n.*

This small, no-frills inn is situated in the hills above Geneva in Confignon, near the village church. The eight rooms are snug, with green plants, Scandinavian colors and either a bath or shower. Guests often congregate with locals in the ground-floor dining room or bar. The restaurant is closed on Sundays and Mondays. A perfect place to escape all the tourist glitz.

Hotel Les Amures   ★★

Moderate

Rue des Puits-St-Pierre 1. ☞ *In the center of the Old Town, 2.8 miles from the train station. Call for directions.*

Public Transportation: *Bus 3, 33.*

☎ *022/311-42-42.*

Credit Cards: *V, MC, DC, A.*

Hidden away in a maze of streets in Vieille Ville (Old Town), this inn offers an intimate atmosphere to rejuvenate your spirits. Once a printing factory, the 17th-century stone building was converted to a hotel in 1981. The restored public areas have original painted ceiling beams and blue-gray frescoed walls. Antiques, including a suit of armor, lend an Old World air, and the 28 snug rooms continue the theme with antiques, high-backed armchairs, round tables and wood-paned windows, though all have marble-tiled bath, hair dryer. The best rooms overlook the square. Guests can dine in the inn's reasonably priced multilevel restaurant.

Where to Eat

Brasserie Lipp   ★★★

Moderate to Expensive

Rue de la Confederation 8, Confederation-Centre. *Near Place Bel-Air, top floor of the Confederation-Centre shopping complex.*

☎ *022/331-10-11.*

Public Transportation: *Bus 12.*

Named after a well-known Parisian bistro, the Geneva Lipp seats guests inside and outside on a rooftop terrace. Always bustling, the restaurant has a definite French flair; the waiters wear black jackets and long white aprons, and the charcuterie dishes would be right at home in France. If you can't make it to Paris, sample the dishes here.

Cafe du Centre ★★

Moderate

Place du Molard 5. *Near Place du Rhone, in the square with the clock tower.* ☎ *022/311-85-86.*

Public Transportation: *Bus 12.*
Credit Cards: *V, MC, DC, A.*

Genevoises stop on their way to work at this cafe-brasserie for coffee and croissants. Situated in a busy square that fills with vendor stalls during the summer, the Cafe du Centre has lots of outdoor tables for the lunch crowd. The hefty English- language menu features more than 120 items including fish (fera, the local white lake fish is recommended), beef and other meats. Upstairs, the cafe has indoor dining and slightly more expensive prices. Late- night dinner hours, until 2 a.m. on Fri. and Sat., make this a popular evening spot.

Le Chat-Botte ★★★★★

Expensive

Quai du Mont-Blanc 13. *Inside the Hotel Beau-Rivage.* ☎ *022/731-65-32.*

Public Transportation: *Bus 6, 33.*
Credit Cards: *V, MC, DC, A. Closed: Sat., Sun.*

Housed in the elite Beau Rivage Hotel, "Puss in Boots" ranks consistently as one of the top restaurants in Geneva. Reflecting the classic menu, the establishment's decor is elegant and luxurious with tapestries, wood paneling and sculptures. The extensive menu features ocean and freshwater fish as well as beautifully prepared chicken and game bird dishes. Fixed-price menus are available for both lunch and dinner.

Le Pied-de-Cochon ★★★

Moderate

Place du Bourg-de-Four 4. *Facing Palais de Justice.*

☎ *022/310-47-97.*

Public Transportation: *Bus 2, 22, Tram 12.*
Credit Cards: *V, MC, DC, A.*

Across from the Palais de Justice, this active bistro is especially frequented by lawyers and barristers. Of course, pig's feet (the bistro's namesake) are on the menu along with other sweetmeats, but if you aren't up to tackling tripe, the ham or other cuts of pork are delicious. Beef and poultry also are available. Always busy, often smoky, but definitely worth it after a day afoot exploring Old Town.

What to Do
Excursions

Excursion to Cologny ★★★★

 Bodmeriana Library, Chemin du Guignard. *Nine miles northeast of Geneva.* ☎ *022/736-23-70.*

Public Transportation: *Bus 9.*

🕐 *2–5 p.m.*

Special Hours: *Library open Thurs. only.*

On this excursion, you can explore a library housing a private book and art collection, then take a step back in literary history and trace the exploits of Lord Byron and Percy Bysshe Shelley, both of whom lived in the suburban village of Cologny in 1816. Plan your Cologny tour for a Thurs. when the Bodmeriana Library on Chemin du Guignard is open. While in Cologny, you can see the Villa Diodati where Byron stayed. The three-story building overlooks the lake. During the evenings, Byron and Shelley, along with Mary Wollstonecraft Shelley and her sister Claire Clairmont, passed the hours at the villa by telling ghost stories. Those long summer nights and at the Villa Diodati provided much of the inspiration for Mary Shelley's novel, *Frankenstein.* Admission: varies.

Historical Sites

Cathedrale de Saint-Pierre ★★★★★

⊟ *Cour St-Pierre.* *In Old Town.* ☎ *022/ 738-56-50.*

🕐 *10 a.m.–6 p.m.*

Special Hours: *Closed 1–2 p.m.*

Built on what recent excavations have shown to be the site of a 4th-century Roman-era Christian sanctuary, this Gothic-style cathedral was largely constructed between the 12th and 13th centuries. On a tour of the excavation site (separate fee), you can see 5th-century floor mosaics, an early baptistry and the foundations of a Romanesque cathedral that date to the year 1000. St. Pierre's did not remain Catholic, however. In 1536, the same year that John Calvin fled Paris for Geneva, the citizens voted for a Protestant church. Calvin preached from the pulpit, and today the cathedral retains the same austerity in its ornamentation that the Reformer advocated. Outside, the north tower features a metal steeple that was constructed in the late 1800s. The steeple has a viewing platform, and, if you climb 145 stairs, you'll be rewarded with views of Lake Geneva and the Alps.

Palais des Nations ★★★★

⊟ *Parc de l'Ariana 14, Ave. de la Paix.* *Bus 8 to Appia on weekdays.* ☎ *022/743- 63-50.*

Metro Stop: *Place des Nations.*

🕐 *10 a.m.–4 p.m.*

Special Hours: *Closed daily 12–2 p.m. Apr.- June, Sep.–Oct.*

Nowhere in Switzerland is the stance of Swiss neutrality more apparent than in Geneva. The base for worldwide humanitarian organizations, Geneva is also home to the Palais des Nations, a complex that served as the League of Nations headquarters until 1936 and is now the headquarters of the European United Nations. Inside, the corridors and assembly areas are decorated with bronze *torchieres* and marble tiling and the Council Chambers feature murals by Jose Maria Sert. The Palais des Nations sits solidly in the middle of landscaped lawns and is surrounded by trees and monuments. The complex can be toured daily during high season and on weekdays from Jan.–Mar. and Nov.–Dec. Hour-long tours are conducted in English, but you may have to wait until enough English-speakers arrive to fill a group. A bookstore is on the premises, and visitors can view an introductory video program. Admission: inexpensive.

Museums and Exhibits

Musee Arianna

✉ *Avenue de la Paix 10.* ☞ *West of the Palais des Nations.*

☎ *022/734-29-50.*

Public Transportation: *Bus 7, 8 or F.* Metro Stop: *Appia.*

🕐 *10 a.m.–5 p.m.*

Housed in an Italian Renaissance-style building, the Musee Arianna is one of the best museums of porcelain and pottery arts in Europe. Pieces on display include Sevres, Delft faience and Meissen porcelain as well as outstanding examples of Japanese and Chinese ceramics. The museum is also the headquarters of the International Academy of Ceramics. Admission: inexpensive.

Musee International De La Croix-Rouge

✉ *Avenue de la Paix 17.* ☞ *Across from European United Nations headquarters.* ☎ *022/734-52-48.*

Public Transportation: *Bus 8 or F.*

🕐 *10 a.m.–5 p.m.*

The Red Cross was founded in 1863 in Geneva by Henry Dunant, and the famous Red Cross symbol was created by reversing the design of the Swiss flag. This is just part of what you'll learn during a tour of the International Red Cross Museum. Both sobering and inspirational, the museum offers multimedia exhibits that detail the organization's efforts to ease suffering in the face of disaster, whether war, riot, fire or flood. Many displays are graphic and disturbing such as one showing a 10-by-6-1/2-foot prison cell that held 17 political prisoners. The Mur de Temps is a grimly fascinating human timeline that records year by year all disasters (human or natural) that have killed more than 100,000 people. In spite of the statistics, hope survives—the museum also highlights the people, including Henry Dunant, who have brought aid to so many. If you have time for only one museum, spend your time here. Admission: inexpensive.

ITRAVELBOOK FREEBIE

Musee de L'Horlogerie et de l'Emaillerie ★★★★

⊞ *Route de Malagnou 15.* ☎ *022/736-74-12.*

Public Transportation: *Bus 6.* Metro Stop: *Museum.*

🕙 *10 p.m.–5 p.m. .*

Situated in a huge renovated townhouse, this museum pays tribute to the history of watches and the art of watchmaking. The collection includes timepieces dating back to the 16th century, with an emphasis on enameled watchcases, each visual and mechanical masterpieces. Many of the timepieces were produced in Geneva, acknowledged as the Swiss capital of watchmaking. One clock features an elephant that moves its ears. There are also displays of elaborate music boxes and art nouveau jewelry. At the top of every hour, the museum fills your ears with the sound of hundreds of chiming clocks.

Parks and Gardens

Walking Tour ★★★★★

⊞ *Begin at Quai Gustave-Ador by the fountain.* *Directly off Quai General-Guisan.* ☎ *022/738-52-00.*

Public Transportation: *Bus 9.*
Perfect for strolling, Geneva is easily explored on foot. Beginning at the Jet d'Eau fountain just off Quai Gustave-Ador, you can enjoy a walk along the historic quays. The city's best-known landmark, the Jet d'Eau shoots, a frothy column of water 460 feet into the air above the lake. Visible for miles, the fountain was built in 1891 and renovated in 1951. Pumping 132 feet of water per second, it operates continuously from Apr.–Sept. Next, proceed south along the Quay to the Jardin Anglais (English Garden) where you can see the Flower Clock, the symbol of Geneva's role as a clock producer.

Located directly off Quai General-Guisan, the Flower Clock is a real working timepiece, except its clockface is created entirely out of intricately landscaped flowerbeds. From Jardin Anglais, cross the Mont-Blanc Bridge over the Rhone then turn left along Quai des Bergues. Continue to the des Bergues bridge and cross it to enter Ile Rousseau, once a favorite spot of Jean-Jacques Rousseau who was born in Geneva and later spent many years here. Today a statue on the island commemorates the philosopher. From Ile Rousseau, you can return to Quay des Bergues, heading left along the quay to Place St. Gervais. Cross Quai Moulins to see the remains of a chateau built in 1219. Today the island of Tour-de-I'lle is where the Geneva tourist office is located and the site of a number of art galleries and bistros.

Shopping

A shopper's heaven, Geneva is filled with department stores and boutiques offering everything from watches and jewelry to chocolate and Swiss army knives. Embroidered blouses and linens, music boxes and Swiss cuckoo clocks also are good bets. Timepieces, of course, are what have made Geneva famous, but be careful when purchasing a Swiss watch. Legitimate jewelers display the symbol of the Geneva Association of Watchmakers and Jewelers; don't be misled by souvenir-stand "bargains."

Main Shopping Areas

For boutique and luxury shopping, the main districts are the Rue du Rhone and the adjacent street, Rue de la Confederation. La Confederation changes names, becoming Rue du March, Rue de la Croix d'Or and Ru de Rive. Both Rue du Rhone and Rue de la Confederation run parallel along the Left Bank.

The Centre-Confederation is a chic three-story shopping center accessible from the ground floor at Place Bel-Air. The center also has a rooftop restaurant if you need a place to take a break. Les Cygnes, north of the train station, is the Geneva version of a high-end shopping mall.

In the Old Town, Grand-Rue and other streets that angle off from Place du Bourg- de-Four offer a variety of boutiques. Rue du Mont-Blanc on the Right Bank tends to feature lower-priced jewelry and souvenir shops.

Upscale department stores worth visiting include **Au Grand**

Passage at *Rue du Rhone 50,* ☎ *022/310-66-11,* and **Bon Genie** at *Rue du Marche 34,* ☎ *022/31-82-22.*

Geneva is famous for its auction houses, and you can visit **Christie's** at *Place de la Taconneirie 8,* ☎ *022/310-25-44,* and **Sotheby's** at *Quai du Mont-Blanc 13 (below the Hotel Beau Rivage),* ☎ *022/832- 85-85.* If you care to bid on antique watches, the **Antiquorum** at *Ru du Mont- Blanc 1,* ☎ *022/738-02-22,* is the place to go.

A flea market is held in the Place de Plainpalais every Wednesday and Saturday. Arts and crafts are offered at a market on Place de la Fusteire each Thursday during the summer. You can browse through books and clothing daily at Place de la Madeleine.

Special Tours

Lake Geneva Boat Tours ★★★★★

📧 *Quai du Mont-Blanc.* ☎ *022/738-52-00.*

Lac Leman, as Lake Geneva is known to the Swiss, is best appreciated by boat. From the deck, you can see the mountains and vineyards and the skyline of Geneva. Appealing to many tastes, various companies offer boat tours between May and Sept. The tourist office can provide you with current schedules, but tempting itineraries include: Le Tour du Petit Lac, a half-day tour with morning and afternoon departures that cruises only the lower portion of the lake, including the lakeside towns of Nyon and Yvoire. Half-day tours are offered by **Key Tours S.A.,** ☎ *022/731- 41-40,* and by **Mouettes Genevoises,** ☎ *022/ 732-29-44.* Full-day cruises are also available. Castle lovers should catch the Castle Cruise offered May–Sept. For this tour, you board a boat from the Mont-Blanc quay to Chillon, where you visit the Chateau de Chillon. Then you board a bus to Montreux where you can stay (separate fee) or return to Geneva by train. For more information about the Castle Cruise, contact ☎ *022/311-25-21.* You can also take a river trip on the Rhone; 2.5-hour tours are offered daily aboard the Bateau du Rhone, which has English commentary. Contact Mouettes Genevoises for more information.

Zermatt

The jewel of Switzerland, Zermatt is tucked at the base of the famous Matterhorn. Towering at more than 12,500 feet, the Matterhorn's summit was first conquered by the English climber

Edward Whymper in 1865 at a cost of the lives of four men in Whymper's climbing team. Climbers come to pay homage to the peak, but most visitors take advantage of the cog railway and cable cars that ascend the Matterhorn's slopes. Snow abounds at Zermatt, with skiing even during the summer. The hotels range from the chic and luxurious Grand Hotel Zermatterhof to the homey atmosphere of the Romantik Hotel Julen, where the owner's sheepdog might greet you at the door.

Where to Stay

Hotels and Resorts

Alex Schlosshotel Tenne   ★★★★

http://www.reconline.ch/tenne/

Moderate to Expensive

CH 3920. ☞ *Across from the train station.*

☎ *028/67-18-01.*

Credit Cards: *V, MC.*
Recently renovated, this family-run modern alpine inn is located in the center of town. The original building is a weathered- wood chalet while the stucco addition rises behind with arched balconies and wood railings. The 35 rooms are decorated in an eclectic manner with contemporary wicker blending with Flemish prints and alpine accents. All rooms have private bath, phone, TV. The 10 junior suites have a private Jacuzzi and a sitting room with a fireplace. The hotel features an acclaimed restaurant (listed separately), open for dinner. The public areas are enlivened with murals, and the intimate bar has a rustic stone fireplace. Guests can take advantage of two squash courts or relax on the terrace. Closed: Apr., and Oct.–Nov.

Grand Hotel Zermatterhof   ★★★★

Moderate to Expensive

Bahnhofstrasse. ☞ *At the end of the main street.*

☎ *028/66-11-00.*

Credit Cards: *V, MC, DC, A.*

Given a five-star rating by the Swiss government, this hotel is the choice of celebrity visitors. The hotel's Regency-style facade is suave compared to the chalet architecture that dominates the village. Inside, polished marble floors and gleaming chandeliers set a classy mood. The lobby has an embellished ceiling, antiques and upholstered chairs. There are 61 rooms with contemporary furnishings, roomy tile-and-marble bath, hair dryer, phone, TV. The front rooms have double-glazed windows to soften noise. Most of the 32 suites face south and are air-conditioned. Two restaurants and a popular nightclub are also offered. Closed: Oct.–Nov.

Hotel Romantica ★★★

Moderate

Bahnhofstrasse. ☞ *A 10-minute walk from rail station. Complementary taxi available.*

☎ *028/67-15-05.*

Hidden away at the end of a side street, this small flagstone-roofed hotel has a comfortable atmosphere. Its rustic interior is decorated with game trophies and an old-style stove. There are 14 rooms with private bath or shower. Though snug and plainly decorated, the rooms have big windows and balconies with mountain views. Two small log cabins near the entrance have been converted to guest houses. During the summer, guests can relax in a small flower garden. Closed: Nov.

Hotel Touring ★★★

Moderate

CH 3920.

☎ *028/67-11-17.*

Credit Cards: *V, MC.*

If you want to avoid the formalities and fussiness at the more glamorous resorts, this warm, family-run chalet-style hotel may be just what you're looking for. Built in 1958, it is reasonably priced, and ski racks are set up by the front door. The 28 rooms are plain but comfortable, and 15 rooms have private bath or shower (those without cost less, of course). The rooms with a Matterhorn view for only a few SFr extra. A restaurant and a stubli provide meals and drinks. Closed: May and Nov.

Hotel Alphubel

Budget

CH 3920. *Near the train station.*

☎ *028/67-30-30.*

Credit Cards: *V, MC, A.*

Skiing, sauna.
Named after a local peak, this reasonably priced chalet-style pension is perfect if you plan to spend your time hiking or skiing.The 50 rooms all have private bath or shower, phone, TV. The south-side rooms have a mountain view. The furnishings are simple, but guests have the use of a basement sauna. Closed: Nov. 20–Dec. 20.

Where to Eat

Alex Schlosshotel Tenne ★★★★★

Moderate to Expensive

CH 3920. ☎ *028/67-18-01.*

Credit Cards: *V, MC.*
Open for dinner only, this hotel restaurant is reputed to serve the best grilled meats in Zermatt. The decor is unique with a wrap-around gallery and ceiling frescoes of celestial figures. The menu changes and might feature a seafood soup followed by rack of lamb, beef or fish. The desserts are sumptuous, and the specialty is cherries flambe. It is more crowded during the winter months, making reservations then a must.

Elsie's Bar ★★★

Moderate

CH 3920. *Directly across from the church, near Hotel Zermatterhof.* ☎ *028/67-24.*

Housed in a snug log cabin, this place is always packed with skiers who crowd around a handful of tables at the bar. Knotty pine and casement windows lend the place a country air. Here you can get American-style cocktails, light meals and snacks though Elsie's is best known for Irish coffee, guaranteed to warm up chilly bones.

Sports & Recreation

Summer Activities

Special Hours: *Schedules vary.*

Scaling the Matterhorn is so challenging that each year approximately 10 people die in the attempt. If you wish to tackle the peak, be aware of the prerequisites. Previous climbing experience is a must, and a week's time is needed to adequately prepare for the trip. Plus, the guide's fee is SFr610. For a less demanding excursion, both physically and financially, Zermatt offers 240 miles of posted trails suited to a variety of hiking capabilities. Weather conditions change rapidly at such high elevations, and, even for day hikes, visitors should wear proper footwear and carry additional warm clothing, extra food, rain gear, sunglasses and sunscreen. The tourist office (see "winter sports" for phone number) can provide hiking information, while would-be mountain climbers can contact the **Mountain Guides Office** in Zermatt at ☎ *028/67-34-56.*

Winter Sports

▣ *Tourist Office, by train station.* ☎ *028/66- 11-88.*

Special Hours: *Hours vary.*

The Matterhorn rises above the town of Zermatt like an ice-white hook, an image that's as familiar as the Grand Canyon or Mt. Fuji. Although people come year- round to view the Matterhorn or climb its slopes, the snow conditions make Zermatt a downhill skier's paradise. With trail conditions geared primarily to intermediate to advanced skiers, the Zermatt region offers 73 lifts and 145 miles of downhill ski trails. Glacier skiing, heli-skiing and ski excursions into Italy also are available. Other winter sports include cross-country skiing, ice skating and paragliding. The high season is from mid-Dec. to the end of Feb., but at higher elevations, snow cover lasts through the warm months. In fact, Zermatt is the only Swiss resort besides Sass-Fee where skiing is available all-year-round.